Energy Policy

SECOND EDITION

CONGRESSIONAL QUARTERLY INC.
1414 22ND STREET, N.W.
WASHINGTON, D.C. 20037

March 1981

Congressional Quarterly Inc.

Congressional Quarterly Inc., an editorial research service and publishing company, serves clients in the fields of news, education, business and government. It combines specific coverage of Congress, government and politics by Congressional Quarterly with the more general subject range of an affiliated service, Editorial Research Reports.

Congressional Quarterly was founded in 1945 by Henrietta and Nelson Poynter. Its basic periodical publication was and still is the CQ *Weekly Report*, mailed to clients every Saturday. A cumulative index is published quarterly.

CQ also publishes a variety of books. The CQ *Almanac*, a compendium of legislation for one session of Congress, is published every spring. *Congress and the Nation* is published every four years as a record of government for one presidential term. Other books include paperback books on public affairs and textbooks for college political science classes. The public affairs books are designed as timely reports to keep journalists, scholars and the public abreast of developing issues, events and trends. They include such recent titles as *Congressional Ethics, Health Policy* and *Defense Policy*. College textbooks, prepared by outside scholars and published under the CQ Press imprint, include such recent titles as *The Supreme Court, Congress Reconsidered, 2nd Edition* and *Energy, Politics and Public Policy*.

CQ Direct Research is a consulting service which performs contract research and maintains a reference library and query desk for clients.

Editorial Research Reports covers subjects beyond the specialized scope of Congressional Quarterly. It publishes reference material on foreign affairs, business, education, cultural affairs, national security, science and other topics of news interest. Service to clients includes a 6,000-word report four times a month bound and indexed semi-annually. Editorial Research Reports publishes paperback books in its fields of coverage. Founded in 1923, the service merged with Congressional Quarterly in 1956.

Library of Congress Cataloging in Publication Data

Main entry under title:

Energy Policy.

Bibliography: p.
Includes index.
1. Energy Policy — United States. 2. Power resources — Law and legislation — United States. I. Congressional Quarterly inc.

KF2120.E54 1981	333.79′0973	81-1225
ISBN 0-87187-167-X		AACR2

TABLE OF CONTENTS

CHARTS, TABLES AND GRAPHS

Author: Ann Pelham
Contributors: Irwin B. Arieff, Alan Berlow, Kathy Koch, Martha V. Gottron, John L. Moore, Patricia Ann O'Connor, Andy Plattner, Laura B. Weiss, Elder Witt, Michael D. Wormser
Design: Mary McNeil
Cover, Graphics: Richard Pottern, Bob Redding
Production Manager: I.D. Fuller
Assistant Production Manager: Maceo Mayo

Editor's Note. *Energy Policy, 2nd Edition,* discusses problems of energy supply and cost that the United States and other nations will face for the remainder of the 20th century. The book focuses on the efforts of the federal government to deal with the fundamentally changed conditions of energy supply in the years since the 1973 Arab oil embargo. The book examines the use of energy that left the nation dangerously dependent on supplies of oil from other nations, particularly those in the politically unstable Middle East. It then examines the response to this problem by describing alternatives to foreign oil including conservation, more use of coal which the United States has in abundance, nuclear power and new technologies such as solar energy and snythetic fuels. Other chapters describe the conflict between energy supplies and environmental protection, emergency preparedness and energy policymakers in Washington. The latter part of the book contains a chronology of energy legislation from 1973 through 1980 and the major energy speeches of Presidents Nixon, Ford and Carter. There also is a glossary of terms and a selected bibliography.

Search for Consensus: 1973-80

The United States headed into the last two decades of the 20th century with a fundamentally different attitude about energy than had prevailed in all the years since the nation began to industrialize more than 100 years earlier.

For the first time, Americans — and their elected representatives — had to face some unpleasant realities:

● Far too much of the oil used by Americans came from foreign nations, of which the most important were located in the politically unstable Middle East.

● Energy was vastly more expensive than it had ever been in the past.

● The lifestyle of much of America — from big cars to big homes to urban sprawl — that was suitable to an era of cheap energy all of a sudden was outmoded.

● The political attitudes that supported inexpensive energy were no longer suitable to the changed world conditions that drove fuel costs to heights virtually no one believed possible at the beginning of the 1970s.

It was an unpleasant shock to average citizen and politician alike. Moreover, it all happened in less than a decade, rendering obsolete attitudes, business and personal practices and financial arrangements that had taken decades to construct.

In a sense, then, it was remarkable that by the end of 1980, after seven years of intense and often bitter debate over energy policy, Congress had put in place an outline of steps that would help bring America more safely into the new energy reality. The most important part of this policy was to reduce America's dangerous dependence on the oil of foreign nations; that dependence, almost everyone agreed, mortgaged the nation's well-being, prosperity and even its future to the vagaries of foreign events and foreign leaders whose interests might well be inimical to those of the United States.

The task was by no means completed by 1980; indeed, it had just begun. At the heart of the matter was a decision to let the price of energy rise to whatever level individuals thought it was worth to them, on the theory that at some point energy that cost too much would force users to consume less. Even as early as 1980, there was good evidence that this would occur. In addition, higher prices were thought likely to encourage development of new energy supplies.

Beyond prices, commitments were made to development of new energy sources such as synthetic fuels made from coal and other basic resources that America had in ample supply. Better conservation of energy also was given a key role in the future. Nuclear power remained highly controversial, but its advocates said the nation had no choice but to make further use of this source of energy for the nation.

But energy pricing — what it costs Americans to heat their homes and drive their cars and carry on their businesses — was at the center of the policy decisions made by Congress in the late 1970s. It was a dramatic change from past thinking.

Use Much, Pay Little

In the years after World War II, as oil and natural gas became the nation's primary fuels, U.S. energy policy was guided by a central theme: "Use as much as you want; pay as little as possible."

Declining domestic production of oil and gas began to erode that policy in the early 1970s; the 1973-74 Arab oil embargo and subsequent quadrupling of world oil prices forced its demise. Suddenly aware of its dependence on foreign countries for more than a third of its oil, the United States began the long search for a new energy policy.

For the rest of the 1970s, presidents and Congresses fought over energy, struggling to reach a consensus. One common goal united them: Reduce oil imports. The problem was deciding how.

Wrapped up in the energy debate were some of society's most basic questions. "How will the burden of uncertain supplies and skyrocketing energy prices be shared?" summed up Senate Majority Leader Robert C. Byrd, D-W.Va.

There didn't appear to be an easy answer. Regional conflicts, wide differences in the philosophies of the two political parties, mistrust of the energy industry, lack of knowledge about the Middle East, uncertainty about emerging energy technologies — these factors made for slow progress. Although its dependence on imports was a continuing threat to U.S. security, the danger was insidious. Only long waits in line to buy gasoline seemed convincing evidence to most Americans that the country had energy problems; when the lines were gone, they thought the problem was, too.

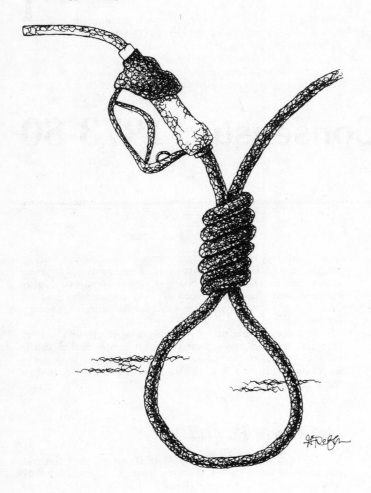

Americans could begin to adjust their cars, houses and factories to the more expensive energy. The controls might also prevent oil producers from getting a windfall of billions of dollars for sales of oil once available at one quarter the price.

Congress' power was not confined to pricing, although that was the most important authority in existence. Confronted with a new energy era, the legislators had to decide how far the government should go in forcing new energy habits on Americans. Gas-guzzling cars were wasteful, but the consumer had traditionally been relatively independent from government rules. Windows could be caulked to save energy, but the bureaucracy had no easy way of dictating that it be done.

Also to be considered was how to encourage domestic production and use of both conventional fuels, such as uranium and coal, and new alternative sources, such as liquids from coal, energy from the sun and oil from shale. Utilities could be ordered to burn coal, but there had to be exceptions and, in the political arena, the list of exceptions grew and grew. Nuclear power was a possible salve, but the problems of radioactive waste disposal kept coming up. Solar energy sounded wonderful, but as a practical matter seemed limited. Congress also had to prepare for the possibility of another energy emergency, such as an oil embargo or war in the Middle East.

Confusion, Frustrations

The public was confused about energy in the 1970s, skeptical about shortages and ready to blame the oil companies for the nation's woes. Few people realized how dependent the country had become on an unstable region on the other side of the globe. A poll by George Gallup in June 1977 led him to conclude that "approximately half of the public can be said to be relatively unconcerned about our energy problems."

The public's confusion about the energy situation was reflected in Congress, where the lack of a consensus about existence of the problem made it even harder to agree on a solution. The frustrations of dealing with energy often prompted the legislators to lament their task. "It is extremely difficult to write an energy bill," said House Speaker Thomas P. O'Neill Jr., D-Mass., in late 1975. "This, perhaps, has been the most parochial issue that could ever hit the floor."

A leading Republican on energy matters, Rep. Clarence J. Brown, R-Ohio, agreed. "I have come to feel like the mythological Greek, Sisyphus, who was condemned to rolling the great rock up the hill in Hades, only to have it slip when he got it close to the top and roll to the bottom again where he had to start over," said Brown. Sisyphus was mentioned frequently by legislators during the years of energy debate.

Another critic of congressional progress was Jim Wright, D-Texas, who later became House majority leader. "In total candor, I must say . . . that what began as a thrilling and dramatic enterprise has degenerated at times into a farcical comedy of frustrations," said Wright in 1975. "Too often the Congress has been simply unwilling to make the hard decisions and take the difficult steps necessary to achieve energy sufficiency for the United States."

Congress Has Key Role

Congress, rather than the president, had the major role in the search for energy policy because of laws already on the books at the time of the embargo. Government controls had been holding down the price of domestically produced oil since 1971, when price controls were imposed as part of an overall anti-inflation effort. Natural gas prices had been regulated at the wellhead since 1954, except when gas was sold within the producing state.

The question of oil and gas pricing became the vehicle for putting the nation's energy problem squarely on the legislative agenda. Through the controls, Congress had power over 60 percent of total U.S. energy supplies, as domestically produced oil and gas each provided about 30 percent of U.S. needs. The dilemma for Congress was whether to continue the controls or to allow prices to rise to the new, much higher world levels.

The situation was nightmarish; it seemed all possible solutions had drawbacks.

Should the legislators allow the price of domestic energy to rise sharply to the new world level, set by a cartel? That might encourage production and force a cutback in consumption, thus reducing U.S. dependence on unreliable foreign suppliers. Or should Congress keep domestic production priced at its existing level? That might give the economy a shield from the enormous price increases until

Avoiding Tough Decisions

That Congress shied away from making decisions about energy was not surprising, as that was usually the case on difficult questions until a general consensus had developed. Congress first had to learn about energy and the ramifications of various alternative policies. The public also had to become better acquainted with the new energy situation, a process that took years.

Presidents Nixon, Ford and Carter tried to help with this education by making speeches in which they urged the public to emulate the traditional American approach of acting strong in the face of adversity. Each aimed his energy message at this self-reliant aspect of the American character. *(Texts, p. 239)*

"We have an energy crisis, but there is no crisis of the American spirit," said Richard Nixon in November 1973. "Let us go forward, then, doing what needs to be done, proud of what we have accomplished together in the past, and confident of what we can accomplish together in the future."

Gerald Ford used no less sweeping phrases. "In every crisis, the American people have closed ranks, rolled up their sleeves and rallied to do whatever had to be done," said Ford in a January 1975 television address. "I ask you and those who represent you in the Congress to work to turn our economy around, declare our energy independence, and resolve to make our free society again the wonder of the world."

Jimmy Carter continued the appeal along the same lines. "Our decision about energy will test the character of the American people and the ability of the president and Congress to govern this nation," Carter said in April 1977. "This difficult effort will be the 'moral equivalent of war' — except that we will be uniting in our efforts to build and not to destroy."

However, Carter expressed less optimism than his predecessors had. In the four years since the embargo, the U.S. energy situation had grown worse, not better. Carter in that April speech warned of the danger. "The energy crisis has not yet overwhelmed us," he said, "but it will if we do not act quickly."

In July 1979 Carter revealed even more doubts and worries when he talked of a national "crisis of confidence." He temporarily abandoned his role as a source of support and reassurance for the public. By the end of that speech, though, Carter was back in the traditional presidential mold of boosting public confidence, though with a twist. "We simply must have faith in each other, faith in our ability to govern ourselves and faith in the future of this nation," Carter said. Later he added, "On the battlefield of energy, we can win for our nation a new confidence, and we can seize control again of our common destiny."

Rhetoric and Reality

The rhetoric made it appear there was a simple solution to the nation's energy problems. Spirit, cooperation and faith could clear up the mess, the presidents seemed to be saying. They also wanted action from Congress. If Congress would just pass this or that energy bill, the presidents argued, then the energy crisis would be lessened.

Congress also felt pressure from constituents to do something about energy. The legislators kept hoping for

a miracle solution. At first, they sought energy independence, but for most that dream slowly faded with a better understanding of the hard facts about available domestic supplies. Still, though, the hope lingered that one special bill could make a major difference. The subsidy for synthetic fuels, for example, was held up as such a bill, and it developed bipartisan, feverish support in Congress in 1979. The public wanted "bold action; they do not want timid action," Wright said. That it would be years before the measures had even a small impact on oil imports was seldom mentioned.

Just the act of getting major energy bills through Congress sometimes seemed more important than the substance of the legislation as the desire for action became the overriding concern. For example, the 1978 natural gas bill was criticized even by those who wrote the compromise language in conference. "It's the best we can hope for," was the frequent remark by Sen. Henry M. Jackson, D-Wash. The lack of enthusiasm, though, was no reason not to pass the bill, and Jackson and others urged a favorable vote. The Carter administration also focused on the symbolic aspects of the legislation, rather than the substance.

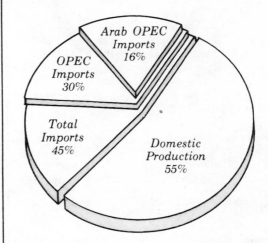

U.S. Oil Supply

Arab OPEC Imports 16%

OPEC Imports 30%

Total Imports 45%

Domestic Production 55%

	Thousands of Barrels per Day	Percent of Total
U.S. Production	10,258	55%
Imports:	8,411	45%
OPEC Nations[1]	5,612	30%
Non-OPEC Nations	2,799	15%
Total[2]	18,669	

[1] Arab OPEC: 3,037,000, 16%.
[2] Total approximate U.S. supply in 1979. Consumption, after exports and losses, was 18,434,000 barrels per day.

Source: Department of Energy

Major Oil Suppliers to the United States, 1979

(thousands of barrels)

Country	Crude Oil	Petroleum Products	Total
*Saudi Arabia	488,278	3,308	491,586
*Nigeria	389,115	4,211	393,326
*Venezuela	106,554	145,680	252,234
*Libya	232,704	6,020	238,724
*Algeria	220,074	10,062	230,136
Canada	97,526	96,848	194,374
Mexico	157,795	637	158,432
Virgin Islands	—	157,486	157,486
*Indonesia	137,362	14,793	152,155
*Iran	107,811	2,839	110,650
*United Arab Emirates	102,108	—	102,108
Netherlands Antilles	—	84,428	84,428
United Kingdom	71,923	1,501	73,424
Trinidad	43,861	24,143	68,004
Bahamas	—	53,907	53,907
Puerto Rico	—	33,509	33,509
*Iraq	32,052	—	32,052
Norway	27,523	17	27,540
Malaysia	18,786	4,981	23,767
Egypt	20,205	103	20,308
Peru	14,746	1,689	16,435
Oman	13,466	2,662	16,128
*Ecuador	11,363	4,545	15,908
Angola	14,088	1,499	15,587
*Gabon	15,328	134	15,462
*Qatar	11,450	—	11,450
Total imports by U.S.	2,364,499	705,576	3,070,075

U.S. Imports from OPEC in 1979

	Crude Oil	Petroleum Products	Total
Thousands of barrels	1,855,713	192,677	2,048,390
Percent of Total Imports	78.5	27.3	66.7

U.S. Imports by Region in 1979

	Crude Oil	Petroleum Products	Total
North America	255,321	97,485	352,806
South America	176,852	183,731	360,583
Europe	101,995	28,520	130,515
Middle East	759,944	10,168	770,112
Asia	163,473	30,878	194,351
Africa	906,914	22,659	929,573
Central America and Caribbean	—	329,664	329,664

*Denotes member of the Organization of Petroleum Exporting Countries. The 13th member is Kuwait, which in 1979 exported 2,599,000 barrels to the United States, or 7,121 barrels a day.

Source: Department of Energy

"Unless Congress acts soon on a natural gas bill," Carter wrote to senators in August 1978, "the world will remain convinced of our unwillingness to face the energy problem with continuing uncertainties and pressures on the dollar in foreign exchange markets." Energy Secretary James R. Schlesinger also stressed the need for U.S. action on the gas bill. "It is a very important symbol, internationally, of America's ability to face up to its energy problem," he said.

This tactic led to grumbling among the legislators. "They don't talk about the merits of the bill," said one senator. "They tell you that the president needs a bill to save face politically and that the country needs it for international prestige."

A similar mood prevailed during 1980 debate on another major energy bill to set up a special board to force speedy decisions by the bureaucracy on permits and other approvals needed for priority energy projects. "This is a bill not to be loved, but to be passed," said Rep. Philip R. Sharp, D-Ind. "It is the best we could achieve, and it does make substantial progress," said Rep. John D. Dingell, D-Mich. This time the pleas fell on deaf ears; the House killed the bill by rejecting the conference report.

The New Policy

By the end of 1980, after seven years of debate, Congress had agreed on steps that would help the United States meet the goal of reducing oil imports. The principal decision was to end controls on the prices of domestically produced oil and natural gas, with a tax placed on the "windfall" profits the oil industry would reap as controls were lifted. During the 1970s, a majority in Congress had come to realize that a decontrolled price was the best way to encourage new production and to tell consumers that new energy habits were in order. Democrats who favored continued controls had tried to use taxes or mandatory conservation rules to force a cut in consumption, but this approach proved politically unacceptable.

Despite the decision to end price controls, Congress was not willing to let the marketplace be the sole guide to U.S. energy use and production. During the 1970s, the legislators devised an array of incentives and penalties to push and pull energy choices in the marketplace. These "carrots" and "sticks" were designed to cut oil imports by encouraging conservation and the development, production and use of domestic energy sources, including coal, solar energy and synthetic fuels. Among other moves, Congress set mandatory fuel efficiency standards for automobiles, prohibited construction of new oil- or gas-fired power plants, offered tax credits to homeowners who installed insulation or other conservation equipment and promoted electric rate reform.

Congress also tried to prepare for another disruption in oil supplies, such as an embargo or war in the Middle East. Storage of oil in a strategic petroleum reserve, development of a standby scheme for gasoline rationing and contingency plans for strict conservation steps were part of emergency preparedness efforts.

Many energy questions still remained unresolved, however, as of 1981. Congress was still debating how to allocate subsidies among the various energy sources and how to reconcile the frequent conflicts between energy and environmental protection.

Share of U.S. Oil Consumption
Supplied by Imports, 1949-1979

Millions of Barrels per Day

Year	Total Consumption	Percent Provided by Imports	Total Imports
1949	5.76	11.3	0.65
1950	6.46	13.2	0.85
1951	7.02	12.0	0.84
1952	7.27	13.1	0.95
1953	7.60	13.6	1.03
1954	7.76	13.5	1.05
1955	8.46	14.8	1.25
1956	8.78	16.4	1.44
1957	8.81	17.8	1.57
1958	9.12	18.6	1.70
1959	9.53	18.7	1.78
1960	9.80	18.5	1.81
1961	9.98	19.2	1.92
1962	10.40	20.0	2.08
1963	10.74	19.7	2.12
1964	11.02	20.5	2.26
1965	11.51	21.4	2.47
1966	12.08	21.3	2.57
1967	12.56	20.2	2.54
1968	13.39	21.2	2.84
1969	14.14	22.4	3.17
1970	14.70	23.3	3.42
1971	15.21	25.8	3.93
1972	16.37	29.0	4.74
1973	17.31	36.2	6.26
1974	16.65	36.7	6.11
1975	16.32	37.1	6.06
1976	17.46	41.9	7.31
1977	18.43	47.8	8.81
1978	18.85	44.4	8.36
1979	18.43	45.6	8.41

Millions of Barrels per Day

U.S. Consumption

Imports

Source: Department of Energy/Energy Information Administration

Congress had agreed to support a variety of energy sources, but advocates of solar energy or nuclear power or synthetic fuels all continued to scramble to make sure their favorite energy source got a major share of the federal budget and top billing in government programs. To the former top energy adviser to President Carter, the fight among different energy sources is a mistake. "We hear conservation *vs.* nuclear, or solar *vs.* synfuels," said Elliot Cutler in 1980, when he was practicing law in Washington, D.C. "There isn't any room for *'vs'* in this business." He added, "The biggest threat is that we will delude ourselves into abandoning one of these paths at a very premature stage." Instead, Cutler said, government policy should "lead us down all of these paths at once so we get the maximum from each."

The clash between energy and environment is one of the most complex questions facing Congress in the 1980s.

How to dispose safely of radioactive waste from nuclear power plants, whether to allow pollution from increased burning of coal, what energy development to permit on federal lands — these were some of the dilemmas.

The issue of energy *vs.* environment was frequently part of energy debates, but the choice was seldom clear cut. Most developers argued that any environmental consequences of their activity could be mitigated, but most environmentalists had a different idea of what would be proper mitigation.

To some persons, though, the questions were straightforward. "The question is, are you willing to have dirtier air for a short period in order to achieve national priorities such as coal gasification?" asked Brown, the Ohio Republican. "Are you willing to tear up a little wilderness scenery to have oil shale? Until we confront those problems, we're not going to get anything done."

Another pending question for Congress was which federal controls to retain over the oil and gas industry after price controls expired. Some members wanted the government to be able to restore both price controls and fuel allocation authority in an emergency. Even ardent advocates of a free market agreed that some authority should be retained. The fight was likely to be over how "emergency" was defined.

"People will feel better if there is something there [in the law]," said Rep. Dave Stockman, R-Mich., in 1980 But he added, "We should reserve allocation authorities only for the most extreme shortfall."

Working for a more liberal definition of when an emergency exists were expected to be many of the same members who earlier fought decontrol.

Consumption Down, Production Up

The continuing debate in Congress over these questions would be influenced by the future course of energy consumption and production in the United States. Predicting that course became even more difficult than usual in 1979 and 1980, as analysts scrapped forecasts made before oil prices doubled from $18 to $36 a barrel. The price hikes also prompted more rapid and extensive conservation than had been anticipated, thus throwing doubts on the basic premises of analysts about how much conservation was possible without curbing economic growth.

Although oil imports were expected to continue as a major contributor to U.S. energy supplies, the developments in 1979 and 1980 produced optimism that imports would play a lesser role, instead of a larger role as once thought, as a result of conservation and increased use of domestic coal. The Energy Department's statistical arm, the Energy Information Administration, predicted in July 1980 that imports would decline to 5.9 million barrels a day by 1985.

The improved U.S. energy picture of 1980 showed up in preliminary estimates of 1980 oil consumption, which was down to 17.14 million barrels a day, according to the American Petroleum Institute. That was a decline of 7 percent from the 1979 level of 18.434 million barrels a day. Imports dropped more dramatically — by 18 percent compared with 1979 levels — but the size of that shift was attributed to decisions by oil companies to draw down their stocks, which had been at an all-time high because the Iranian revolution and the Soviet invasion of Afghanistan had prompted heavy buying.

Also improved was U.S. crude oil production, which had dropped in 1979 after increases in 1977 and 1978 because of new production from Alaska. The American Petroleum Institute said U.S. production increased by one and a half percent in 1980 compared with 1979 levels. Most encouraging was that production in the continental United States, which had dropped in both 1978 and 1979 by 350,000 barrels a day, was down by only 100,000 barrels a day in 1980 compared with 1979 production.

In terms of overall energy use, the Energy Information Administration predicted in 1980 that the annual growth rate through 1990 would be 1 percent; its forecast for that period had been a rate of 2 percent just a couple of years earlier.

These figures were early straws-in-the-wind. Moreover, because they were encouraging — and energy officials and politicians had had very little encouraging energy news for a long time — they were seized on quickly as harbingers of better times to come in the 1980s. That remained to be seen. But the policies that had emerged from the seven years of debate after the oil embargo in 1973 did at least suggest that the favorable trends in the figures might continue.

In the chapter that follows, the patterns of energy use that led the United States into such a vulnerable position are described.

The chapters that come after describe the response of U.S. leaders to that vulnerability.

2

America Becomes Vulnerable

Anyone planning to disrupt the United States' economy by cutting off its foreign oil supplies could hardly have picked a better year than 1973.

In the months before the Arab oil embargo began in October 1973, U.S. oil prices were actually lower than they had been during the 1950s and 1960s, once inflation was considered. This low cost encouraged use, and U.S. oil consumption that year climbed to a record 17.3 million barrels a day. But the increased demand could not be met by domestic crude oil production, which had been dropping since 1970. Instead, oil imports had to be increased and, in 1973, reached 6.26 million barrels a day — the highest level to that date.

The country was the most vulnerable it had ever been to an interruption in foreign oil supplies. *(Chart, oil consumption and imports, p. 5)*

EFFECTS OF CHEAP AND ABUNDANT ENERGY

It took several years for the United States to reach this level of vulnerability, just as it was several years before the public and government grasped the new energy situation and reacted to it. In thousands of ways, Americans had applied the prevailing belief: Oil is convenient, cheap and in abundant and reliable supply. Even if everyone had realized at once that this was no longer the case, the adjustment would have taken years. Houses, cars, factories, even cities had all been built based on cheap energy. Workers in suburbia had become accustomed to commuting miles to jobs in cities. Trucks powered by cheap diesel fuel had taken over transportation duties once handled by trains. Everyday habits had developed in response to inexpensive fuel. Frosty air conditioning had become commonplace, and homes in winter were kept so warm that a sweater seldom was needed. Household appliances had increased in popularity with little thought to whether they would consume more energy. *(Graph, p. 11)*

The cost of energy was simply not a concern of the newly affluent Americans. Per capita real income had doubled between 1950 and 1970, while at the same time energy prices declined in real terms by 28 percent. Americans had more money, and the new income went even further in the energy marketplace.

Oil was not the only inexpensive fuel prompting these developments. New pipelines had linked natural gas fields in Texas to Eastern markets. Two of the pipelines, known as "Big Inch" and "Little Inch," had been built by the government during World War II to carry oil, and were later sold and converted to carry natural gas.

The postwar economic boom — and the more affluent lifestyle it spawned — depended on oil and gas, with coal for the first time relegated to a less important role.

Coal Out, Imports In

Although coal had served the nation well during several decades of industrialization, it couldn't compete with the convenience of low-priced oil and gas. Coal was dirty and bulky and had to be transported by train or barge. Piles of coal had to be stored on site, ready to be fed into generators or furnaces. In comparison, oil and gas moved by pipeline, without the loading, unloading and other handling required by coal. The fuels were held in storage tanks, often out of sight underground or even miles away. In addition, a boiler using oil or gas was mechanically less complicated than one fired by coal, and thus less expensive.

In 1949 coal had been the nation's primary fuel, meeting 40.5 percent of energy needs. The next year petroleum displaced coal from the top spot. In 1958 coal fell to third place, behind natural gas, and provided only 24 percent of U.S. energy. Coal's relative importance continued to decline in the 1960s and 1970s. Not until 1979 was there a significant increase in the share of U.S. energy provided by coal. That year, coal met 19 percent of energy needs, compared with 47 percent from oil, 26 percent from natural gas, 4 percent from hydropower and 3.5 percent from nuclear plants. *(Chart, overall energy use by source, p. 8)*

The new popularity of oil and gas was accompanied by a dramatic overall increase in U.S. energy consumption. Between 1950 and 1980, energy use increased at an average annual rate of about 3 percent. Over the 30-year period total consumption increased by 132 percent, from 33.6 quadrillion Btus to 78 quadrillion Btus.

At the same time, domestic energy production was also increasing, but not at so fast a pace as consumption.

Between 1950 and 1960, production went from 34.5 to 62.8 quadrillion Btus, an increase of about 82 percent. *(Chart, overall energy production by type, p. 104)*

The shifts in consumption patterns also affected the share of overall production from each energy source. Coal production lagged behind oil after 1952, and dropped behind natural gas in 1959. Domestic oil and gas production was increasing, but it simply couldn't keep up with the voracious U.S. appetite for those fuels. Demand for oil already was outpacing production — and requiring imports — when U.S. oil output began to decline after 1970. The year before, natural gas had become the primary domestic energy source, but then in 1973 its production also started to decline. Only coal production, constrained for so long by lack of demand, had the potential to increase significantly.

But, as energy policymakers later came to realize, coal couldn't be easily substituted for oil or natural gas. The habits developed in response to inexpensive, plentiful oil would not be easy to break. Chunks of coal couldn't run automobiles. Homeowners and store operators certainly wouldn't return to coal shoveling to have heat. Industry would be reluctant to return to wholesale use of inconvenient coal, even though boilers and some processes could be fueled by coal. Only one sector of the economy still depended heavily on coal, and that was the electric utility industry. When Congress started trying to write an energy policy, it's not surprising that one of its first decisions was to try to force utilities to use even more coal. There were few other obvious outlets for the fuel that had once been king.

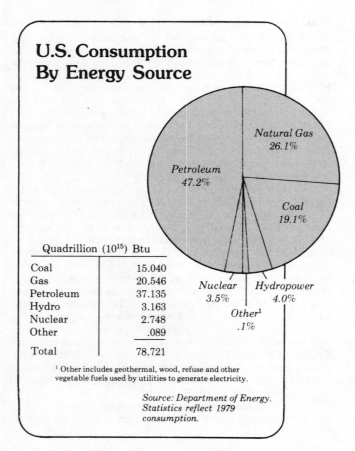

U.S. Consumption By Energy Source

Petroleum 47.2%

Natural Gas 26.1%

Coal 19.1%

Nuclear 3.5%

Hydropower 4.0%

Other[1] .1%

Quadrillion (10^{15}) Btu

Coal	15.040
Gas	20.546
Petroleum	37.135
Hydro	3.163
Nuclear	2.748
Other	.089
Total	78.721

[1] Other includes geothermal, wood, refuse and other vegetable fuels used by utilities to generate electricity.

Source: Department of Energy. Statistics reflect 1979 consumption.

The Import Surge

As a result, instead of turning back to coal, the U.S. economy in the 1960s and 1970s satisfied its growing energy needs in the easiest, most readily available way: imports. As oil demand steadily increased, so did imports — and at a faster pace. Between 1950 and 1980 daily oil consumption more than tripled, but oil was imported in 1980 at a daily rate almost 13 times that of 1950. Thus, the foreign oil provided an increasingly larger share of U.S. oil consumption. In 1950 imports supplied only 13.2 percent. By 1960 the share had increased to 18.5 percent, and by 1970 to 23.3 percent.

In 1973, the time of the embargo, almost half of U.S. energy was provided by petroleum, with about 36 percent of that provided by imports. Six years later, oil still supplied almost half of U.S. energy, and the share from imports had risen to 45 percent.

The worst year was 1977. Alaskan production had barely begun, and prices were relatively low, once adjusted for inflation. The United States used a record 8.8 million barrels a day of imported oil, which equaled 47.8 percent of consumption.

Between 1950 and 1980, every sector of the U.S. economy had grown more and more dependent on oil — and thus on imports. By far the biggest share of petroleum went for transportation. Cars, trucks, buses, airplanes and other forms of transportation annually used 52 percent of oil. Industry's share was 20 percent, and the residential and commercial sector consumed 19 percent. Those latter two sectors also shared the electricity generated by utilities from the remaining 9 percent of the U.S. oil supply.

In terms of total energy consumption of all fuels, the share used by each sector breaks down like this: residential and commercial, 37.8 percent; industrial, 37.1 percent; and transportation 25.1 percent. *(Chart, energy use by sector, overall, p. 10)*

Transportation

Just the increasing number of vehicles on the road between 1950 and 1980 would have contributed to the rising consumption of gasoline and diesel fuel. But those vehicles also were driven more and more miles each year. In addition, fuel efficiency got worse.

In 1960 there were 74.4 million cars, trucks and buses in operation on the nation's highways. By 1979 that number had more than doubled to about 160 million. The ratio of people to cars had dropped to less than two to one, from three to one.

Vehicles were driven an average of 9,650 miles in 1960, but by 1978 the annual average had increased to 10,060 miles. A temporary break in the steady increase had come during the 1973-74 Arab oil embargo, when shortages of gasoline and skyrocketing prices curtailed motoring trips and other non-essential driving. Average mileage that year dropped to a low of 9,530 miles. That sensitivity to price also was expected to show up in 1979 and 1980 figures, and perhaps permanently lower the average mileage per car.

Because vehicles were driven more miles, fuel consumption also increased, from an average of 4.11 million barrels a day in 1960 to 8.26 million barrels a day in 1979. *(Chart, motor vehicle mileage and fuel consumption, p. 59)*

But another factor in this doubling of oil consumption was the astounding decline in the number of miles each car traveled on a gallon of gasoline. In 1960 the rate was 14.3 miles per gallon — a high mark not approached again until after 1978. The low point for fuel efficiency was 1973 — ironically, the year the embargo began. Cars on the road then got an average of only 13.1 miles per gallon.

The decline in fuel economy was the result of a number of factors, including a penchant on the part of consumers and car makers for bigger, heavier cars with automatic transmissions, power brakes, air conditioning and other extras. Automobile manufacturers also blamed federal clean air laws that restricted the emission of pollutants.

The major role played by motor vehicles in U.S. oil consumption has made fuel efficiency an obvious target for energy policymakers trying to reduce oil use. In 1975 Congress ordered improvements in automobile gas mileage over the objections of automakers, who complained of damaging government interference. But by 1980 these same officials were battling rising imports of fuel-efficient cars, and saying they would exceed the 1985 average of 27.5 miles per gallon, a standard they had earlier said was far too stiff.

The payoff for improved fuel efficiency could be very high. The anticipated level of oil consumption could be cut by more than 600,000 barrels a day if cars got an average of 20, instead of 14, miles per gallon. (That calculation assumes that 120 million cars were driven an average of 10,000 miles a year.)

But the demand for fuel economy is expected to conflict eventually with some consumers' need for a four- to six-passenger family car. The solution, according to experts in the field, could be to have two or three cars: a two-seater mini-car or a motorcycle for commuters and a larger car for family outings. Some analysts have speculated that rental companies could provide the larger car for those who needed it only rarely.

Mass transportation has been another route to energy savings in the transportation sector. Unfortunately, though, the popularity of the automobile doomed the nation's privately operated mass transit systems. By the 1970s all major bus, trolley and subway systems were government-operated and usually required subsidies to stay in operation. Mass transit ridership had dropped from a high of 23.7 billion trips in 1947 to a low of 6.6 billion trips in 1972. Since then, however, transit use has increased, with 8.13 billion trips taken in 1979. But that was estimated still to be only 5 percent of urban passenger travel.

Many older cities, such as New York, Philadelphia and Boston, were blessed with mass transit networks built before the automobile's rise to prominence. However, many of those systems were deteriorating and would require extensive renovation in the 1980s. Other cities have had to expand their systems since the embargo to handle new riders. The rapidly growing newer cities of the Sun Belt, such as Los Angeles, Houston and Dallas, depend almost totally on a maze of freeways and privately owned cars. For them, building a successful bus system or subway would be incredibly expensive. Two cities trying to do just that — Atlanta and Washington, D.C. — required billions in aid from the federal government.

For most communities, such a large-scale solution to the new energy crunch has not been practical either logistically or financially. Instead, city planners began to learn in the 1970s that cities can take a dozen less-dramatic steps to encourage more energy efficiency in local trans-

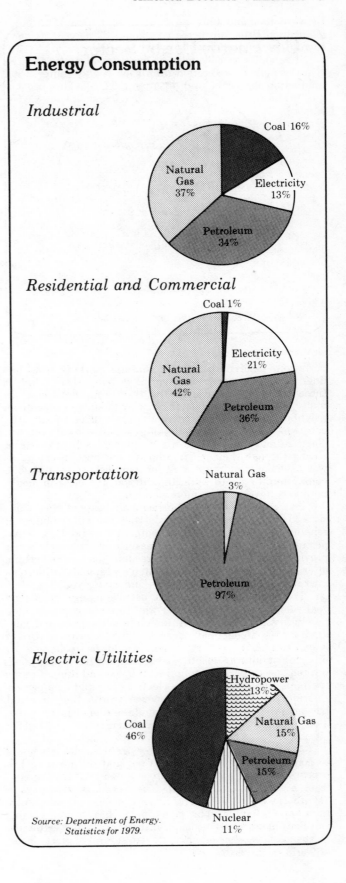

Energy Consumption

Industrial

Coal 16%
Electricity 13%
Petroleum 34%
Natural Gas 37%

Residential and Commercial

Coal 1%
Electricity 21%
Petroleum 36%
Natural Gas 42%

Transportation

Natural Gas 3%
Petroleum 97%

Electric Utilities

Hydropower 13%
Natural Gas 15%
Petroleum 15%
Nuclear 11%
Coal 46%

Source: Department of Energy. Statistics for 1979.

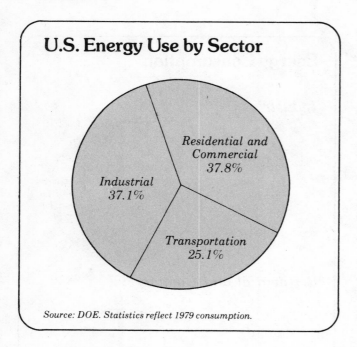

U.S. Energy Use by Sector

Residential and Commercial
37.8%

Industrial
37.1%

Transportation
25.1%

Source: DOE. Statistics reflect 1979 consumption.

An oil substitute already on the market is gasohol, a blend of 10 percent ethanol and 90 percent gasoline. Ethanol is alcohol made from grain, sugar beets or other agricultural products and waste. Gasohol supporters, who won an exemption for the product from the 4-cent-a-gallon federal excise tax, hope that eventually all motor fuel sold in the country will contain some ethanol.

These substitute fuels are targeted at cars, trucks and buses, which use more than three-quarters of the fuel consumed by the transportation sector. Another 10 percent powers airplanes and jets, which demand a high quality fuel. The rest of the sector's energy use is divided among boats, with 6 percent; rail, with about 3 percent; pipelines, with 2.6 percent; and other, with 2.4 percent. Pipelines account for the only natural gas used by the transportation sector; they consume some of the gas in the process of transporting it over long distances.

Homes and Businesses

Since 1975 the residential and commercial sector, not industry, has been the nation's major energy user. Homes, offices and stores consume about 38 percent of total energy. The most dramatic change in energy use by this sector came in the 1950s and 1960s, when millions of homes and offices switched from coal to natural gas and heating oil. Between 1950 and 1960, the percentage of homes heated with coal dropped from 34.6 percent to 12.2 percent.

By 1970 natural gas heated more than 55 percent of the homes and apartments in the United States, and gas retained that share throughout the 1970s. When gas supplies have been short, federal regulators have given priority to these residential consumers over industrial users. The residential consumer also has paid more for gas than industry, but nevertheless has still gotten a better deal than his neighbors buying tanks of fuel oil.

Another shift in this sector began in the 1970s: from oil to electricity. The percentage of homes heated by electricity increased from 7.7 in 1970 to 14.8 in 1977. In new homes, the change is far more pronounced. A 1977 government survey found that 40 percent of new homes were heated with electricity.

At the beginning of the decade, electric heat was touted by utilities as part of the "all-electric" home, which won a customer lower, preferential rates. The goal was to boost consumption of electricity. But that approach was made obsolete by the price hikes and supply squeeze that followed the 1973-74 embargo.

Still, electricity has continued to be attractive as a fuel for heating. In addition to a reluctance to use expensive and perhaps scarce heating oil, there are three major factors: restrictions in many areas on new hookups for natural gas, which is usually cheaper; the availability of — and improvement in — the electric heat pump, which vastly increased efficiency; and the lower initial investment required for baseboard electric heat in comparison with oil and gas furnaces. This last factor is especially important to home builders, who when selecting the type of heating that goes into a house tend to be more sensitive to capital costs than to long-term operating costs.

The electric heat pump deserves special attention. An air circulation system, the pump in winter taps the warmth in outside air, bringing it indoors, while in summer it removes the hot air from the interior and takes it outside.

portation. Bike paths, free commuter parking near bus lines, more downtown residential development — all of these affect energy use in the transportation sector. In many cities, such as Raleigh, N.C., residents of downtown neighborhoods banded together in the 1970s to stop the construction of freeways linking suburbs to downtown. Their primary motivation was to prevent a highway from slicing through their neighborhoods, but an indirect result was to make it more difficult for long-distance automobile commuters to get to work. In addition, the close-in neighborhoods have become more popular.

But even the most enthusiastic advocate of mass transit and bike paths will concede that the automobile will remain for some time the key component of the U.S. transportation system. Among the reasons are the mobility it provides, including a sense of freedom; lack of a feasible alternative in less densely populated areas; and the nation's massive investment in highways and motor vehicles.

For someone trying to cut petroleum use, then, one goal would be finding another way to make cars run. One possibility is electricity. Automobile companies and government researchers have been working for years to perfect a car run on a battery, which would be recharged by plugging it into an electrical socket. The car would have limited speed (perhaps 40 miles an hour) and limited range (perhaps 100 miles). But the electric car could be a perfect solution for commuters. The power to run the car could be generated by coal, that abundant domestic resource. This prospect appeals to policymakers trying to reduce oil use.

Another way to tap coal for transportation uses is to convert it into liquid form. Coal and oil are both hydrocarbons, and a chemical process can convert the coal from a solid to liquid form. The liquid is known as a "synthetic fuel," a type of energy discussed more fully in a later chapter. The government has begun a multibillion-dollar investment in synthetic fuels, but estimates of the cost per barrel have stayed several dollars ahead of world oil prices.

The efficiency of the heat pump means operating costs are comparable to natural gas, even though electricity is four times as expensive as natural gas. A heat pump costs as much as a conventional gas furnace, while electric base-board heat is inexpensive to install but usually very expensive to operate. Heightened consumer awareness of operating costs has increased the use of heat pumps, but builders still install baseboard heat in about half of the new housing units heated with electricity.

In 1978 only 1.3 million of the nation's 77.2 million occupied housing units had heat pumps; that was under 1.5 percent of the total. But the increase in heat pump sales was dramatic during the 1970s, suggesting that this form of heating would capture a significantly larger portion of the home heating market in the future. In 1970, heat pump sales were 97,687 units, according to the Air Conditioning and Refrigeration Institute, a trade group. By 1979, that figure had risen to 559,844, an increase of 473 percent. The 1979 figure, in fact, was down slightly from the all-time high of 572,167 units sold the previous year. The decline was attributed to the slowdown in home building in 1979 as a result of recession, inflation and sky-high interest rates.

Natural gas is the chief energy source for the residential and commercial sector, providing about 42 percent of consumption. Petroleum, usually in the form of heating oil, provides about 36 percent. Electricity's share is 21 percent. Only about 1 percent of the sector's energy is still provided by coal.

Most of the energy used in the residential and commercial sector heats buildings. Almost 60 percent of energy used in homes and about 50 percent of energy used in stores and offices provides space heating. Hot water heaters rank second on the list of energy users.

The other major use of energy in this sector is cooling. In the 1950s air conditioning was still enough of a rarity that stores advertised their cool air with pictures of polar bears. By the 1970s all new offices and stores were air conditioned. Many had elaborate, energy-intensive air circulation systems that removed humidity and cooled or heated air. In homes, also, air conditioning was becoming commonplace. Only about 15.1 percent of homes in 1960 had any type of air conditioning. By 1979 the percentage had increased to 55.5 percent. More than two-thirds of new housing is air conditioned, usually with a central system.

Air conditioners are only one of many new ways homeowners have used energy since World War II. Appliances have been extremely popular and now consume about a third of the energy used in homes. While only 19.6 percent of homes had a clothes dryer in 1960, more than 61 percent did in 1979. Though only 7.1 percent

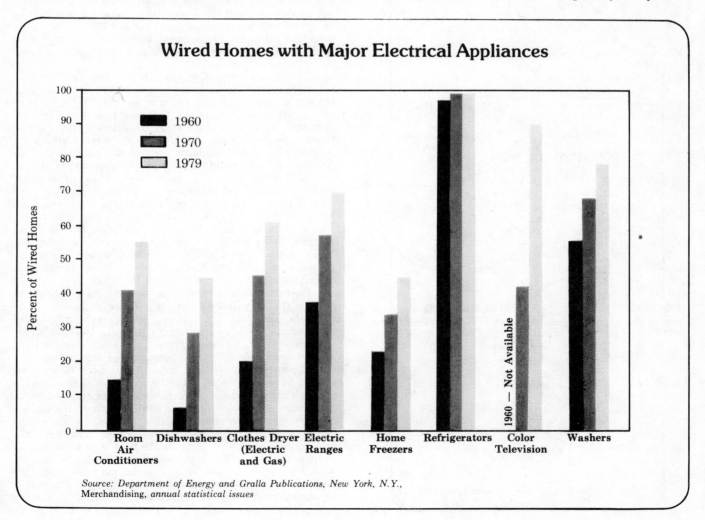

Wired Homes with Major Electrical Appliances

Source: Department of Energy and Gralla Publications, New York, N.Y., Merchandising, annual statistical issues

of homes had a dishwasher in 1960, the percentage had increased to 43 by 1979. One of the most widely used appliances, after refrigerators, is the color television set, which could be found in almost 90 percent of U.S. homes in 1979. *(Chart, use of major electrical appliances, p. 11)*

With such a variety of new appliances and a supply of inexpensive electricity, Americans had every reason to use more kilowatts, and they did. Between 1960 and 1979 average residential consumption of electricity more than doubled, from 3,843 kilowatt hours in 1960 to 8,828 kilowatt hours in 1979.

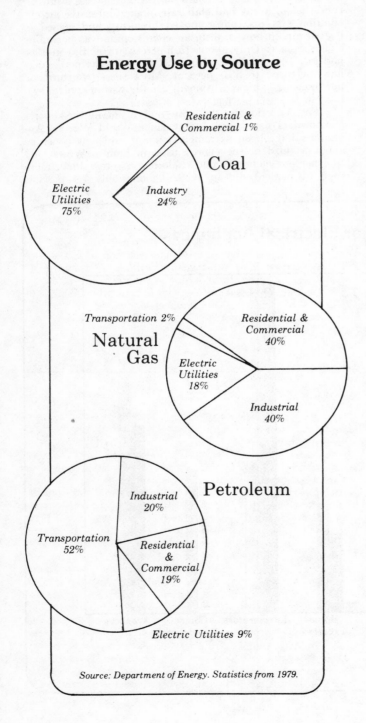

Energy Use by Source

Coal

Residential & Commercial 1%

Electric Utilities 75%

Industry 24%

Natural Gas

Transportation 2%

Residential & Commercial 40%

Electric Utilities 18%

Industrial 40%

Petroleum

Industrial 20%

Transportation 52%

Residential & Commercial 19%

Electric Utilities 9%

Source: Department of Energy. Statistics from 1979.

The government has targeted appliances for improvements in energy efficiency. Congress first simply required a label estimating annual operating costs. Then the legislators passed a law in 1978 requiring manufacturers of appliances to meet standards limiting energy use. But writing the specific standards has proven to be a time-consuming and difficult task.

Because this sector uses the bulk of its energy for heating and cooling, most conservation efforts have been directed at those areas. Tax credits have been offered to homeowners who install insulation, add storm windows, put weatherstripping around doors and take other steps to make their homes airtight. On 1979 federal tax returns, more than 4.8 million taxpayers took advantage of the residential energy credits (including those for solar energy equipment). The year before, 5.9 million taxpayers had claimed $600 million in credits. Grants for conservation improvements have been given to hospitals, schools and low-income families. With less leakage, the same levels of warmth or coolness can be achieved with a smaller amount of energy.

The next energy-saving step for this sector has been for the occupants of houses, offices and stores to get accustomed to less air conditioning and less heat. The government in 1979 issued thermostat restrictions for stores and offices, with 78 degrees the minimum setting for cooling in summer and 65 degrees the maximum for heating in winter. Although almost nothing has been done to enforce the rules, the Department of Energy says that most building operators have complied and in the process saved money on energy bills.

The government also has tried to prevent the construction of new buildings that waste energy. But the building energy performance standards, or "BEPS," have been very controversial. Although Congress first asked in 1976 that they be written, the Energy Department did not plan to have the final rules ready for congressional review until August 1981. The standards restrict the number of Btus per square foot a building can use, but they do not specify how this Btu "budget" is to be divided among heating, cooling, lighting and other areas. Just the concept of such federal rules has drawn complaints at the state and local level, where building codes traditionally have been set. The construction industry never has liked the idea and stepped up its criticism when the standards were drafted. Major supporters of BEPS include advocates of energy conservation and architects, who will be in demand to design buildings that comply with the rules.

Energy-conscious designers already have begun to change the way houses and offices are engineered. For example, the heat from lights, people, typewriters and other equipment is often adequate to warm an office building comfortably, making a furnace unnecessary or at least seldom used. Many simple steps, given up in the days of cheap energy, are back in favor. A house can be oriented toward the south, with most windows on that exposure to catch the sun's heat. Adjustable awnings and deciduous trees can shade a building from sun in summer, but expose it in winter. Solar energy, either passively with south-facing windows or actively with rooftop collectors, has great potential as an energy source for the residential and commercial sector. The high capital cost of solar equipment is still a major barrier, though, even with low-cost government-backed loans and tax credits. The 1979 increases in energy prices and the scheduled decontrol of domestically produced oil and gas were expected to make solar energy more competitive economically. Higher prices too spur conservation.

But the government also has tried in a limited fashion to publicize various energy-saving steps that cost little or nothing, yet are remarkably effective. Among these are shower attachments that restrict the flow of hot water, window caulking, regular cleaning of furnaces to improve efficiency and closing curtains at night in winter to insulate against the cold and during the day in summer against the hot sun.

Industry

Industry reacted more quickly to the new energy era than any other sector of the economy. While other sectors were increasing consumption by about 7 percent between 1973 and 1979, manufacturers held about even on their energy use. Their change during that period was just 0.5 percent, from 28.67 to 28.82 quadrillion Btus.

At the same time, production of manufactured goods increased by about 17 percent. That means the same amount of energy yielded more goods. An industry group, the National Association of Manufacturers, has estimated that industry improved its energy efficiency by about 14 percent. Without that advance, the association says, industrial energy use in 1979 would have been higher by the equivalent of 850 million barrels of oil.

According to industry officials, a surprising amount of energy has been saved by simple housekeeping steps, such as cleaning furnaces more frequently or fixing leaky steam pipes. Recycling and burning once-discarded waste products also have reduced total demand. Industry also is redesigning processes and developing new technologies that reflect the new, higher value of energy. These new approaches are particularly important in the energy-intensive segments of industry, which consume two-thirds of the energy used by the sector. The top energy users among manufacturing industries are paper, chemicals, petroleum and coal, stone and clay, and primary metals.

Heat generated in manufacturing that once was wasted is now often recaptured and returned to the process, or tapped to heat the building. Because more than a third of industrial energy use is in the form of steam, for manufacturing processes, even waste heat of varying or low temperatures can be readily tapped. The demand for steam makes industry particularly suitable for cogeneration, which is the production of both electricity and steam heat at the same time.

When electricity is generated, only about one-third of the energy value of the coal, oil or other fuel is retained. The rest of the Btus are lost, usually in the form of waste heat at low temperatures. Industry also wastes energy when fossil fuels are burned at temperatures as high as 3,600 degrees Fahrenheit to produce heat, when only steam at much lower temperatures — less than 400 degrees F. — is needed. With cogeneration, the waste, or reject, heat from electrical production is tapped to produce steam for industrial processes. By combining the two systems, less energy is required to produce the same amount of electricity and steam.

Although industrial generation of electricity in 1950 provided 15 percent of U.S. electricity supply, the availability of reliable, inexpensive power from utilities has reduced that share to 4 percent. But analysts believe the

Btus and Quads

Oil is counted by the barrel. Coal is sold in tons. Gas is measured in terms of cubic feet. Trying to compare these fuels or add them together is like dealing with apples and oranges.

To get around this problem, energy statisticians have figured out the amount of energy each type of fuel actually generates. They measure this energy in terms of British thermal units, or "Btus," an ages-old universal measurement. One Btu is the amount of energy required to raise the temperature of one pound of water by one Fahrenheit degree.

By this measure, a 42-gallon barrel of crude oil contains about 5.8 million Btus of energy. A thousand cubic feet (Mcf) of natural gas is equivalent to about 1 million Btus. That means it takes about 5.8 Mcf of natural gas to equal a barrel of crude oil.

The major drawback to using Btus as a measurement is that 1 Btu is a very small amount of energy. If a single barrel of oil contains 5.8 million Btus, then just one day's consumption of 18 million barrels would be equivalent to roughly 104,400,000,000,000 (or 104.4 trillion) Btus. Dealing with an entire year's energy consumption — or the whole world's — in terms of Btus would get messy. The solution has been to convert most Btu measurements into "quads," short for quadrillion, which is the next step after trillion. Oil consumption in a year when daily use averaged 18 million barrels would be the equivalent of about 38.1 quads (365 days x 104.4 trillion Btus).

new energy situation has made industrial cogeneration economically attractive and important to the national energy conservation effort.

However, a number of barriers exist, not the least of which is the sizable capital investment required in cogeneration equipment. One possible approach is to have utilities share the investment at the industrial site in return for excess electricity — or the chance to avoid constructing a new power plant because of reduced demand. Some problems of cogeneration were addressed in the 1978 national energy legislation. Utilities were required by the new laws to sell electricity to cogenerators at non-discriminatory rates, as well as to buy electricity from those with excess power. A plant installing a cogeneration facility was allowed an exemption from federal prohibitions on the use of oil or gas to run large industrial boilers. Industry selling electricity from cogeneration was assured of not being classified — and thus regulated — as a utility.

Industry depends on a variety of sources for its energy. Natural gas is its primary fuel, providing 37 percent of energy consumption. Petroleum is next, with 34 percent, followed by coal, with 16 percent, and electricity with 13 percent.

In many industrial processes, oil and natural gas will continue to be the preferred fuels. For example, the textile industry uses gas in the manufacture of synthetic fibers, and the chemical industry requires petroleum to make plastics. In small industrial boilers, the extra costs of handling and storing coal usually make it uneconomical to switch fuels. But coal could be used in many areas where industry now uses oil and gas, and companies are turning back to coal as the prices of other fuels continue to increase more rapidly.

To spur the shift, Congress agreed in 1978 to prohibit the installation of large, new oil- or gas-fired boilers — those with a firing rate of at least 100 million Btus an hour. However, the law allows exemptions.

Controlling pollution from coal by conventional methods can be expensive, and the conflict between using more coal and controlling pollution is unresolved. But industry is expected to be attracted to the new, cleaner methods of using coal that are now being developed. Particularly promising is fluidized-bed combustion, in which particles of coal are mixed in a bed of gravel-like ash, limestone and other solids held in suspension by a stream of air. Sulfur released as the coal is burned reacts chemically with the limestone, so the sulfur is contained as a solid in the ash instead of being released through the air as sulfur dioxide. Emissions of nitrogen oxide also are reduced because the fluidized bed burns coal at lower temperatures than conventional combustion equipment.

Utilities

Although electrical power plants are not actually a separate sector of the economy such as industry or transportation, these utilities deserve special attention because they consume almost a third of the energy used by the United States. The generation of electricity requires 75 percent of the coal, 18 percent of the natural gas, 10 percent of the petroleum, all of the nuclear power and almost all of the hydropower.

About 40 percent of electricity is tapped by industry, about 35 percent by residential users and the remaining 25 percent by offices, stores and other commercial users.

Electricity is the easiest to use and most versatile type of energy. As a result, U.S. electricity consumption in 1980 was more than seven times what it had been in 1950, while total energy used increased by a factor of 2.3 in the same period.

The annual growth rate in electricity use was about 7 percent until the 1973-74 price increases and the recession that followed. For the 1970s, the rate ended up being 4.8 percent a year, but the trend at the end of the decade was toward an annual rate of 3 percent or less. This major shift — from a 7 percent rate to 3 percent — has forced utilities to re-evaluate their long-range planning, leading to cancellations of new power plants — particularly nuclear reactors — that were once thought crucial to meeting future demand.

Average residential use of electricity was about 3,854 kilowatt hours in 1960. For 1979 the figure was 8,828 kilowatt hours, an increase of 129 percent. But conservation efforts have begun to show up in the annual figures. The total for 1979 was slightly less than for 1978, the first decrease except during recessions.

Industry used 815.6 billion kilowatt hours in 1979, while the commercial sector consumed 493.5 billion kilowatt hours. Because electricity generation retains only about 35 percent of the energy content of the feedstock (oil, gas or other fuels), the utilities require two-thirds more in Btus than they return to the economy. Total energy consumption by utilities in 1979 was 20.21 quadrillion Btus; electricity sales for the year were 7.03 quadrillion Btus.

Although most energy users abandoned coal in the 1950s and 1960s, utilities continued to use coal in large quantities. Oil and natural gas did take a share of utility business from coal, but the strong demand for electricity meant that utilities still regularly increased the amount of coal they used.

Petroleum use by utilities jumped in the early 1970s, so that in 1973 about 18 percent of electricity was generated by oil. Coal's share was down to only 43 percent. The low sulfur content of oil, compared with most coal, made switching to oil an easy way for utilities to comply with the 1970 Clean Air Act and with local rules prompted by that federal law. Since 1977, however, the price of oil and federal prohibitions on new oil- and gas-fired power plants have helped lower actual oil use by utilities. Oil's share of the utility market in 1979 was down to 15 percent. That same year, coal provided 46 percent of the energy for electricity; natural gas, 15 percent; hydropower, 13 percent; and nuclear, 11 percent.

The federal government has tried to encourage utilities to quit using petroleum and natural gas in existing power plants. Unlike the transportation sector, utilities have substitutes for oil readily available. But attempts to force switches from oil and gas to coal have failed for a number of reasons. Many of the targeted plants are so old that an investment in coal-burning and handling equipment is just not economical. In 1980 Congress even considered paying utilities to switch, but the legislation died in a House committee after passing the Senate.

EMBARGO, REVOLUTION: TWO SHOCKS TO THE WORLD

On Oct. 8, 1973, representatives of the major oil exporting countries were scheduled to meet in Vienna with officials from the world's top oil companies. The topic was oil prices, which the participants had discussed at many earlier negotiating sessions in the late 1960s and early 1970s. During that time, the oil producing nations had consolidated their bargaining efforts under the auspices of the 13-member Organization of Petroleum Exporting Countries (OPEC). Venezuela, Saudi Arabia, Iran, Iraq and Kuwait had been the original members of the group formed in September 1960.

The oil companies still set the prices in 1973, but the countries had grown increasingly influential in the preceding few years. They recently had won price increases to make up for the devaluation of the dollar. In addition, nationalization, part ownership, higher royalty and tax payments and other moves by the individual countries in the early 1970s had given them control over production by the corporations operating in their oil fields, a situation that greatly enhanced their bargaining power.

The OPEC negotiators apparently were going to the October 1973 session with the idea of winning a substantial price increase. In mid-1973 they had seen the market price of oil for the first time exceed the posted price, which was an artificial figure on which companies based the royalties and taxes they paid the producing countries. The countries wanted the posted price not just equal to the market price, but higher — to increase their take.

Many of those gathering in Vienna already were on their way to the meeting on Oct. 6, when news came from the Middle East. An Egyptian foray into Israeli territory had reopened the Arab-Israeli conflict, starting what was to become the Yom Kippur War. For the OPEC representatives the war served to strengthen their resolve for higher prices. They asked for $6 a barrel, up from the existing $3. The companies countered with $3.50. When the OPEC officials finally offered $5.12 as their minimum acceptable price, the oil company officials tried to stall, asking for a two-week recess. OPEC representatives, led by Sheikh Ahmed Zaki al-Yamani of Saudi Arabia, rejected any delay and stood by their demand. The oil companies refused, and the meeting broke up.

The next step for OPEC was a meeting Oct. 16 in Kuwait. Already the Arab oil producers had scheduled a session there for Oct. 17, and the rest of the producers expected some retaliation from them against oil consumers who supported Israel in the war — notably the United States.

At their historic Oct. 16 session, the OPEC representatives agreed to set the posted oil price at $5.12 a barrel. They informed the oil companies.

For the first time, the countries themselves had unilaterally set the price. In doing so they were carrying through on a philosophy adopted in 1968, at a Vienna OPEC meeting. At the session, they had endorsed the rights of producing countries to own and control production from their fields and to set prices.

The success of their grab for power was assured the next day, Oct. 17, when the Organization of Arab Petroleum Exporting Countries (OAPEC) agreed to cut production by 5 percent each month until Israel had withdrawn from Arab territories occupied since the 1967 war and had agreed to respect the rights of Palestinian refugees.

Saudi Arabia the next day stiffened the punishment, announcing it would cut oil production by 10 percent and end all shipments to the United States if the United States continued to supply Israel with arms and didn't modify its pro-Israel policy. The United States did just the opposite. On Oct. 19 President Richard Nixon asked Congress for a $2.2 billion appropriation for emergency military aid for Israel.

Libya imposed an embargo the same day. On Oct. 20 Saudi Arabia reduced production by 25 percent and completely cut off the United States. By Oct. 22 most other Arab producers had joined in the additional production cutback and the embargo.

The world oil market reacted frantically to these developments. Fears of inadequate supplies pushed prices upward, making even the once-shocking OPEC price of $5.12 seem reasonable. Premium oil was sold at auction for $20 a barrel. With renewed confidence, OPEC met again in Tehran on Dec. 22. On Dec. 23 the oil ministers announced a new posted price of $11.65 a barrel.

Suddenly and painfully aware of its dependence on a dozen once-obscure countries, the Western world paid the price that OPEC asked. The result of the quadrupling of world oil prices was a worldwide recession in 1974-75 that most economists labeled the worst since the Great Depression.

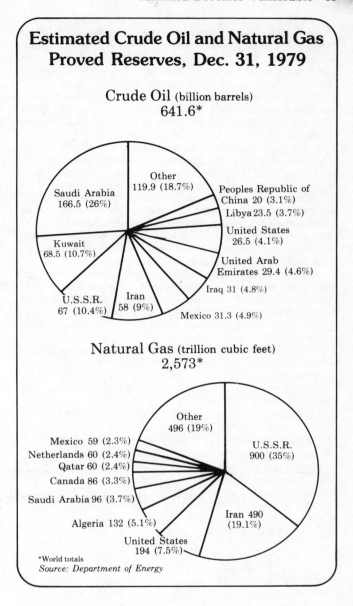

Estimated Crude Oil and Natural Gas Proved Reserves, Dec. 31, 1979

Crude Oil (billion barrels)
641.6*

Saudi Arabia 166.5 (26%)
Other 119.9 (18.7%)
Peoples Republic of China 20 (3.1%)
Libya 23.5 (3.7%)
United States 26.5 (4.1%)
United Arab Emirates 29.4 (4.6%)
Iraq 31 (4.8%)
Mexico 31.3 (4.9%)
Iran 58 (9%)
U.S.S.R. 67 (10.4%)
Kuwait 68.5 (10.7%)

Natural Gas (trillion cubic feet)
2,573*

Other 496 (19%)
Mexico 59 (2.3%)
Netherlands 60 (2.4%)
Qatar 60 (2.4%)
Canada 86 (3.3%)
Saudi Arabia 96 (3.7%)
Algeria 132 (5.1%)
United States 194 (7.5%)
Iran 490 (19.1%)
U.S.S.R. 900 (35%)

*World totals
Source: Department of Energy

Power in the Ground

Although OPEC's power to act as a cartel wasn't evident until 1973, the organization had long had another type of power: geological. The OPEC countries owned most of the world's oil.

At the time of the embargo, OPEC produced about 86 percent of the world's oil exports and 55 percent of total production. They were likely to retain that position because they controlled two-thirds of the world's proved oil reserves, which is an estimate of the amount of oil that experts think can be produced in the future on the basis of today's methods and prices. In comparison, the

United States, having depleted much of its domestic supply, now owns just 4.1 percent of the estimated 641.6 billion barrels of world proved crude oil reserves. OPEC's share is now about 68 percent. Other estimates of the size of world reserves are less conservative, but OPEC's prominence is not disputed. *(Chart, world reserves, p. 15)*

The enormous oil reserves of the OPEC countries mean something because they are in great demand by the world. Like the United States, Western Europe and Japan went on oil binges in the 1950s, 1960s and early 1970s. Prices were low, oil was plentiful and their economies for the most part were rapidly growing. Western Europe in 1973 used more than 14 times the amount of oil it had consumed in 1950. Japan's oil appetite in 1973 was an astonishing 167 times what it had been in 1950, when recovery from the war was just beginning. Developing countries also increased their oil consumption, quadrupling oil use between 1950 and 1973. The United States, already the world's leading oil consumer in 1950, held that title by increasing consumption 2.6 times between 1950 and 1973.

But increasing consumption during that period had not been matched by increasing production from traditional sources. Instead, the non-communist world had become increasingly dependent on oil imports for its energy supply, and those imports came primarily from OPEC countries.

By 1978 the developed countries were using almost two-thirds of the world's oil, and producing less than a quarter of it. OPEC was providing almost half of the world's supplies. *(Chart, world oil production and consumption, pp. 17, 18)*

However, the world's top oil-producing country, the Soviet Union, is not a member of OPEC, though it reportedly once requested membership and was turned down.

The U.S.S.R. produced 11.47 million barrels of oil a day in 1979, compared with Saudi Arabia's second-place 9.53 million barrels. Third place belonged to the United States, with 8.53 million barrels a day. *(Chart, leading world oil producers, this page)*

Although U.S. oil production began to decline in 1970, it retained its longtime place as the world's leading producer until 1974, when the U.S.S.R. took over. The Soviets had been increasing production steadily and continued to do so. The United States fell further behind in 1975, when Saudi Arabia's production exceeded U.S. levels. For just one year, in 1978, the United States regained the second position because of new production from Alaska and a temporary drop in Saudi output. The next year the United States dropped back to third place.

Iran was the fourth leading producer until its revolution cut production to less than 1 million barrels a day in early 1979, a sharp drop from the usual rate of 5.5 million barrels a day. Production increased later in 1979, putting the year-end average at about 3 million barrels a day. However, that was not enough to keep Iraq, with production of 3.4 million barrels a day, from assuming fourth place. Iranian production had declined further by mid-1980, and then stopped almost completely when it plunged into war with Iraq.

Iran had been providing about 500,000 barrels a day to the United States when President Carter on Nov. 12, 1979, banned such imports as part of sanctions against Iran for taking 52 Americans hostage earlier that month. For the year, Iran ended up ranking 10th among U.S. suppliers of crude oil and petroleum products. The top five U.S. suppliers in 1979 were all members of OPEC — Saudi Arabia, Nigeria, Venezuela, Libya and Algeria. *(Chart, leading U.S. oil suppliers, p. 4)*

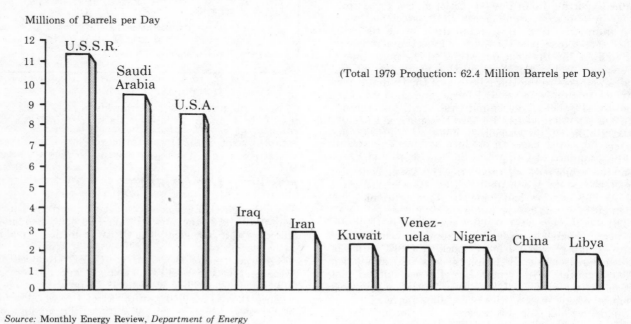

Major Petroleum Producing Countries of the World

Millions of Barrels per Day

(Total 1979 Production: 62.4 Million Barrels per Day)

Source: Monthly Energy Review, *Department of Energy*

World Oil Consumption

(thousand barrels per day)

Year	United States	Canada	Japan	Europe	Developing Countries	OPEC	Total Free World
1950	6,451	324	31	1,048	1,992	196	10,042
1955	8,458	548	152	1,960	3,116	342	14,576
1960	9,577	837	644	4,535	2,796	666	19,055
1965	11,294	1,143	1,803	8,257	3,840	840	27,177
1970	14,457	1,472	4,183	13,580	5,856	1,162	40,710
1971	14,857	1,538	4,411	14,066	6,662	1,291	42,825
1972	15,703	1,689	4,805	14,713	6,469	1,430	44,809
1973	16,971	1,867	5,207	15,153	7,784	1,925	48,907
1974	16,354	1,892	5,499	14,294	9,292	1,985	49,316
1975	15,854	1,782	5,123	12,726	7,265	2,296	45,046
1976	16,825	1,762	5,370	14,034	8,505	2,398	48,894
1977	18,428	1,928	5,731	14,013	7,918	2,637	50,655
1978	18,276	1,850	5,115	13,924	8,588	2,522	50,275

Source: Department of Energy. Amounts prior to 1973 estimated by DOE.

Industrialized nations went on an oil consumption binge beginning about 1950 when prices were low, supplies plentiful and their economies growing rapidly. The United States, already the leading oil consumer in 1950, increased consumption 2.6 times between then and 1973 when the oil embargo fundamentally changed energy relationships in the world.

Origins of OPEC

The oil-producing countries traditionally had played a rather subservient role toward the major international oil companies that began developing their oil fields in earnest in the 1920s and 1930s. One of the first breaks with this pattern came in Venezuela, where in 1945 the democratic government demanded a 50-50 split of profits with the companies. Author of the new rules and taxes was the oil minister, Juan Pablo Perez Alfonzo, later a founding father of OPEC.

Oil-producing countries in the Middle East, which had been getting royalties of 12.5 percent, adopted the new sharing agreement. By the early 1950s, it was the norm.

As the relationship between the countries and the companies evolved, another important factor was the entry into the oil production business in the 1950s of many new, independent firms. The seven major companies that had controlled the world oil market found the smaller, aggressive companies eager to produce at high levels. Gulf, Texaco, Standard of California (Socal), Mobil and Exxon were the five major American corporations, with the Royal/Dutch Shell Group and the British Petroleum Co. rounding out the "Seven Sisters." In the past they had reduced overseas production when the world oil market was saturated, thus preventing a drop in price. But the independents, such as Occidental, Amoco and Getty, were more difficult to control, and their inexpensive oil upset the ordered market. By the end of 1957 prices were dropping. As a result, in February 1959 the major companies cut the posted oil price to reflect the lowered market prices, thus reducing the royalty and tax income of the producing countries.

The turmoil in the pricing structure was felt also in the United States, where producers found sales of oil from domestic wells being undercut by cheaper foreign oil. The federal government studied the situation, worried in public about dependence on foreign oil and more privately about protecting the U.S. companies. The Eisenhower administration asked the suppliers of foreign oil to limit their imports voluntarily to about 12 percent. But that didn't work, and Eisenhower decided in 1959 to impose mandatory quotas. Venezuela and the Arab producers suddenly found themselves cut out of the market of the world's biggest oil consumer.

Further adding to the anger of the producing countries was a second price cut in August 1960 by Exxon, a move soon copied by the other companies.

When Iraq called a meeting in Baghdad in September 1960, a favorable response came quickly from Saudi Arabia, Iran, Kuwait and Venezuela. Leaders of the gathering were Perez Alfonzo of Venezuela, whose country was then the top world producer, and Sheikh Abdullah Tariki, the oil minister of Saudi Arabia. The result of their session was establishment of the Organization of Petroleum Exporting Countries, which 13 years later would be known throughout the world simply as OPEC. Their initial goal was to get prices back to earlier levels and to win the right to prior consultation on future pricing. They pledged to work together as a group.

No further cuts in posted prices were made by the oil companies.

During the 1960s OPEC membership expanded. Qatar, Libya and Indonesia were the first to join, followed by Algeria, Nigeria, Ecuador, Gabon and the United Arab Emirates (Abu Dhabi, Dubai and Sharjah).

Individual countries continued to make progress in negotiations with the oil companies, who tried to ignore the existence of OPEC. A high point for OPEC was a Vienna session in June 1968, when the organization issued a declaration of principles asserting member nations' right to control world oil production and prices. At the time they seemed far from achieving that goal.

That same year, the Organization of Arab Petroleum Exporting Countries was established.

It was a revolution in Libya that tilted the balance of power toward the producing countries, making it possible for OPEC to press for further authority. In September 1969 Muammar al-Qadaffi seized control of the Libyan government. One of his first moves was to force production cuts and to demand, and eventually get, higher oil prices and a greater percentage of profits in the form of taxes. It didn't hurt Qadaffi's cause when, in May 1970, a bull-

dozer accident severed the Trans-Arabian Pipeline, known as Tapline. Tapline had carried Saudi oil to the Mediterranean Sea, and from there it went to Europe. With the pipeline out of operation, Libya's output was suddenly in even greater demand, particularly by the Occidental Petroleum Co., the focus of Qadaffi's efforts. Armand Hammer, owner of Occidental, needed petroleum for his refineries in Europe, and Libya was a key source of his supplies. After Hammer gave in to higher prices and taxes, Qadaffi moved on — successfully — to the major companies.

The lesson was not lost on the rest of OPEC. In February 1971 the Persian Gulf countries of Abu Dhabi, Iran,

Petroleum Supply and Disposition, 1978

Crude Oil Production

OPEC Nations

	Billion Barrels	% of Total
United States	3.18	14.5
U.S.S.R. and Eastern Europe	4.25	19.4
China	.73	3.3
Other non-OPEC nations	2.89	13.2
Saudi Arabia*	3.03	13.9
Iran*	1.90	8.7
Iraq*	.92	4.2
Venezuela*	.79	3.6
Nigeria*	.70	3.2
United Arab Emirates*	.67	3.1
Libya*	.72	3.3
Kuwait*	.76	3.5
Indonesia*	.60	2.7
Other OPEC nations	.73	3.3
World Total	21.87	

*Organization of Petroleum Exporting Countries

Refined Petroleum Consumption

OECD Nations

	Billion Barrels	% of Total
United States*	6.88	30.0
Japan*	1.88	8.2
West Germany*	1.11	4.8
France*	.79	3.4
Italy*	.79	3.4
United Kingdom*	.70	3.0
Canada*	.63	2.7
Other OECD nations	2.02	8.8
Other non-OECD nations	3.78	16.5
U.S.S.R. and Eastern Europe	3.72	16.2
China	.66	2.9
World Total	22.96	

*Organization for Economic Cooperation and Development

Source: *Department of Energy*

Iraq, Kuwait, Qatar and Saudi Arabia met in Tehran with oil company officials. Following the precedent set by Libya, they demanded and won what was considered a major price increase of 30 to 50 cents a barrel. Their Tehran agreement also raised the minimum tax rate from 50 to 55 percent. Another agreement was reached in April at Tripoli with the Mediterranean countries, led by Libya. Iraq negotiated an East Mediterranean agreement in June. But the price agreements reached in 1971 were short-lived. In December the United States devalued the dollar. By January the OPEC countries were demanding adjustments to reflect their loss of buying power. The companies gave in — and did so again June 1973, when another adjustment was made for the devalued dollar.

On another front, also, the countries were building their power at the expense of the oil companies. Algeria, long frustrated with the leftover colonial tinges of the French oil company, in 1971 nationalized the French holdings. Libya took over British Petroleum's interests in its country the same year, later adding other foreign companies. Iraq joined the group in 1972, nationalizing the consortium operating there. Iran, which had taken over its fields in 1951, assumed full control of the companies in 1973.

Other less radical countries, such as Saudi Arabia, wanted to have a more orderly transfer of control. In December 1972 a participation agreement was reached by oil companies and Saudi Arabia, Kuwait, the United Arab Emirates and Qatar. They would get an immediate 25 percent interest in the companies, increasing to 51 percent by 1982. As it turned out, though, the countries had control of the companies by the mid-1970s, though management for the most part remained in the hands of Westerners.

Oil as a Political Weapon

In 1956 the Egyptian-Israeli conflict closed the Suez Canal, blocking the shipment of Middle Eastern oil to Western Europe. But the United States was able to draw on its excess production capacity and sent extra oil to Europe, thus moderating the crisis.

In 1967, during the Six-Day War, the Arab producing countries shut down their wells to protest support of Israel by oil-consuming countries. But the consumers turned to the United States, Venezuela and Indonesia, which raised production levels to keep the balance between supply and demand. Eventually, the Arab countries broke ranks, as shipments leaked out and eroded the effectiveness of the shutdown. The political move hadn't been helped by the fact that Saudi Arabia, the top Middle East oil producers, never had been enthusiastic about the boycott.

In 1973 the Arab producers again turned to oil as a political weapon after the Yom Kippur War began. Already the 13 OPEC countries had moved to raise oil prices, asserting a new role in the world market. The Arab countries were powerful, by this time producing 37 percent of the oil consumed by the non-communist world. In contrast, U.S. production had been falling since 1970. The excess capacity that had been called on before was gone. In addition, Saudi Arabia was firmly behind the decision by OAPEC to reduce production and to embargo the United States and other countries. That support — in fact leadership — was extremely important, as the Saudis then produced 7.6 million barrels of oil a day. That was

42 percent of the Arab countries' production and ranked the country third in the world in oil production. With aid from Saudi Arabia, the production cutbacks had a chance of success.

An Effective Embargo

The Arabs were systematic in their embargo, with countries being divided into categories. On the boycott list were nations considered to be friends of Israel. The United States was at the top. The Netherlands followed, because the Arabs were angered by what they saw as a pro-Israel stance and reports that the Dutch had offered to aid in the transit of Soviet Jewish emigrants to Israel. In late November, Portugal, Rhodesia and South Africa were officially placed on the embargo list. Shipments of

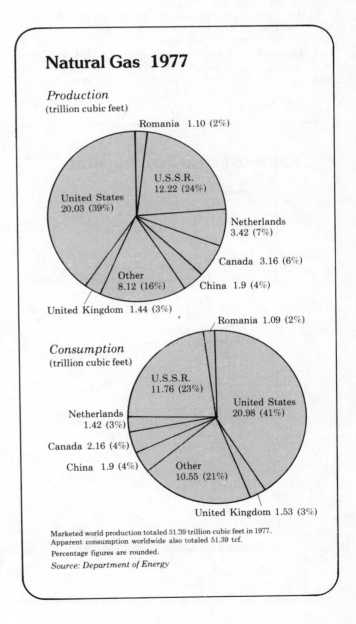

Natural Gas 1977

Production
(trillion cubic feet)

Romania 1.10 (2%)
U.S.S.R. 12.22 (24%)
Netherlands 3.42 (7%)
Canada 3.16 (6%)
China 1.9 (4%)
United Kingdom 1.44 (3%)
Other 8.12 (16%)
United States 20.03 (39%)

Consumption
(trillion cubic feet)

Romania 1.09 (2%)
U.S.S.R. 11.76 (23%)
United States 20.98 (41%)
Netherlands 1.42 (3%)
Canada 2.16 (4%)
China 1.9 (4%)
Other 10.55 (21%)
United Kingdom 1.53 (3%)

Marketed world production totaled 51.39 trillion cubic feet in 1977.
Apparent consumption worldwide also totaled 51.39 tcf.

Percentage figures are rounded.

Source: Department of Energy

oil to Canada were cut off because the Arabs feared the oil might be reshipped to the United States.

Exempted nations included France, Spain, Arab and Moslem states and — on a conditional basis — Britain. These nations were permitted to purchase the same volume of oil as they had purchased in the first nine months of 1973, but, since the fourth quarter of a year is normally a heavy buying period, these nations were also expected to feel the pinch.

All the remaining countries fell into the non-exempt category, which meant that they would divide what was left after the needs of the exempted nations had been met.

In addition to the embargo, the Arab states made monthly reductions in production. The effects of the oil squeeze were soon felt in the consuming nations. Measures taken to cope with the oil shortage included gas rationing, bans on Sunday driving, reduced speed limits, increased prices, restrictions on energy usage, cutbacks in auto production and reductions in heating fuels.

Although estimates varied, the embargo was said to have resulted in the loss to the United States of about two million barrels of oil a day. However, Arab oil did leak through the embargo, reportedly from Iraq and Libya. In October, the United States began classifying data on its oil imports to prevent these leaks from being plugged.

Hardest hit were Japan and Western Europe, areas most dependent on oil imports. Most of Northern Europe suffered from the total embargo against the Netherlands, because the Dutch port of Rotterdam was Europe's largest oil-refining and transshipment center.

The embargo also was effective in a political sense. On Nov. 6, 1973, representatives of the European Economic Community (EEC), meeting in Brussels, adopted a statement calling on Israel and Egypt to return to the Oct. 22 cease-fire lines that had been drawn before Israeli troops completed the encirclement of Egypt's III Corps. They called on Israel to "end the territorial occupation which it has maintained since the conflict of 1967" and declared that peace in the Middle East was incompatible with "the acquisition of territory by force." Moreover, they declared that any settlement must take into account "the legitimate rights" of the Palestinian refugees.

Later in the month Japan followed suit. On Nov. 22 the Japanese Cabinet announced that it might have to reconsider its policy toward Israel. The Arabs rewarded Western Europe and Japan by exempting them from the 5 percent cut in December.

On Dec. 13 Japan switched from a neutral position and appealed to Israel to withdraw to the Oct. 22 cease-fire lines as a first step toward total withdrawal from occupied Arab territory. On Dec. 25 the January cutback

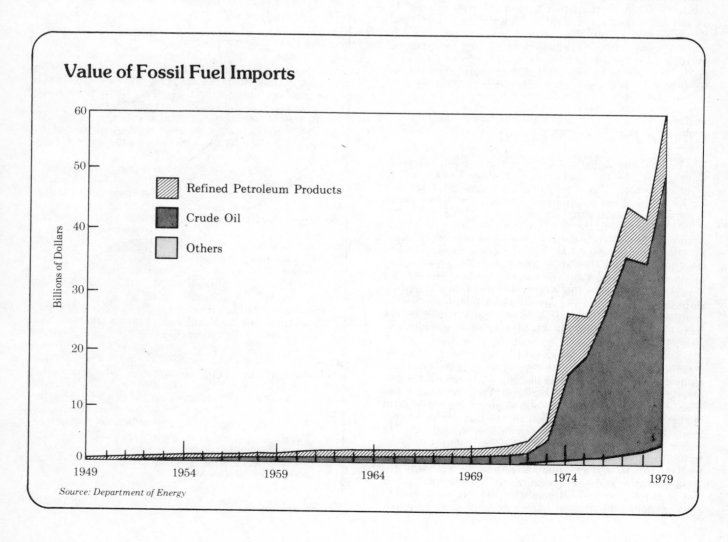

Value of Fossil Fuel Imports

Refined Petroleum Products

Crude Oil

Others

Billions of Dollars

60

50

40

30

20

10

0

1949   1954   1959   1964   1969   1974   1979

Source: Department of Energy

was canceled, and OAPEC anounced that oil production would be increased by 10 percent.

These statements by the EEC and Japan, while one-sided in favor of the Arabs, were in keeping with United Nations Resolution 242. That resolution, approved by the Security Council in 1967, had called for a return to pre-1967 boundaries in the Middle East and a respect for the sovereignty and territorial integrity of all states in the Middle East.

The United States, too, was influenced by the embargo. Although Washington officials repeatedly denounced the Arab tactics and declared that the country would not submit to such coercion, the oil squeeze undoubtedly was the driving force behind U.S. peace-seeking efforts.

Secretary of State Henry A. Kissinger shuttled relentlessly throughout the Middle East in attempts to mediate a settlement. A series of peace missions produced the Nov. 11, 1973, cease-fire agreement between Israel and Egypt, resumption of diplomatic relations between the United States and Egypt, the Dec. 21-22 first round of Geneva peace talks, the Jan. 18, 1974, Egyptian-Israeli disengagement accord and the May 31 disengagement agreement between Israel and Syria.

As this progress was made toward a peace settlement, the United States became increasingly insistent on an end to the embargo. Kissinger told a Jan. 22, 1974, press conference that he had been given assurances by Arab leaders that when an Israeli-Egyptian accord was reached, the embargo would be lifted.

Egyptian President Sadat led the way to ending the boycott. On Jan. 22, Sadat said Arab oil states should take note of the "evolution" in U.S. policy toward the Middle East. Although he did not mention the embargo, he said that "now that the Americans have made a gesture, the Arabs should make one too." And at a Feb. 24 press conference, Sadat said that the United States would now probably pursue a more evenhanded approach toward the Middle East.

OAPEC's formal announcement of an end to the embargo against the United States came at a Vienna meeting March 18. Libya and Syria, however, refused to end the boycott until later in the year.

Post-Embargo Pricing

After the embargo, there was hope among the consuming countries that OPEC would fall apart. But the producers showed their acumen by moving cautiously in 1975, when the worldwide recession depressed demand for oil. Saudi Arabia cut production sharply, from 8.5 million barrels a day in 1974 to 7.1 million barrels in 1975. Iran, Venezuela, Kuwait and Nigeria also reduced production. The average OPEC price in 1975 actually dropped, to $11.02 a barrel.

In October 1976, at an OPEC meeting in Bali, the Saudis argued that the world economy was still too fragile to risk further price increases in 1977. Although other countries were eager to add to their earnings, Saudi Arabia's rank as OPEC's leading producer meant it spoke from a position of strength — and it prevailed.

However, the Saudis were less successful at the December 1976 OPEC session in Qatar. Unable to agree on a single price, OPEC ended up with a two-tier pricing system. Iran and 10 other countries agreed to raise prices by 10 percent in January and another 5 percent in July. Saudi Arabia and the United Arab Emirates limited their total increase to 5 percent.

But the countries at the higher price level soon found they were losing business. At a July 1977 meeting they agreed to forgo the scheduled 5 percent hike. In return, Saudi Arabia, with prices 5 percent below the others', would raise its price by 5 percent, putting all of the OPEC countries again at the same level.

The next OPEC session was in Caracas, in December 1977. This time Saudi Arabia was joined by Iran as it argued against any price increase. The two leading producers were successful, and the meeting adjourned without any action on prices.

Demand for OPEC oil slackened in 1978, and one factor was new production from Alaska and the North Sea. Together they added 1 million more barrels a day to world supply than the previous year's average.

It was another brief period of optimism for the consuming countries. Consumers had returned to pre-embargo habits, and the lack of any recent price increases only added to the feeling among some that the crisis had passed.

But the OPEC countries were arguing among themselves about the need for more revenues, with the loudest complaints coming from Algeria, Libya and Iraq. Inflation was shrinking their real income, they argued, and prices should be increased to reflect the reduced value of currency. Their position was enhanced in the second half of 1978, when oil field work stoppages and other political disruptions began to affect Iran's production, tightening the world market. The lull was over.

Market Takes Over in 1979

In December 1978 OPEC met in Abu Dahabi and agreed to end the 18-month freeze on its prices. The oil ministers decided to make the 1979 increase effective in four stages, beginning Jan. 1. By Oct. 1, the price would be up to $14.54 a barrel, for a total increase of 14.49 percent. OPEC called it a 10 percent increase, noting that the volume of oil bought in 1978 would cost 10 percent more in 1979 because the full increase would not be in place until October.

But the market quickly outdated the OPEC plans.

Iran's output dropped in early 1979 to only 1.1 million barrels a day, down from the 1978 average of 5.2 million barrels. Even though Saudi Arabia and others increased production, there was still not enough oil to meet the strong world demand. The pressure prompted OPEC to decide in March to move at once to a price of $14.54 a barrel, the level originally scheduled for October. The organization also agreed to allow countries to add surcharges to the official price, the first time it had authorized members to set prices individually.

Importers bid hungrily for oil. Spot prices, the term for oil sold "on the spot" instead of under contract, were the first to reflect the competition for supplies. Reports of oil sold at spot prices of $25 and $30 a barrel simply spurred the scramble. Evidence of the tight world oil market, and the vulnerability of importers, was particularly visible in the United States. For the first time since the embargo, Americans were lining up for gasoline. The lines began in California in spring and by May had spread to the East Coast. Stations closed at mid-day, purchases were limited and daily lives were thrown into disarray by the apparent lack of fuel.

The mood reflected a renewed concern about the stability of the Middle East. Shah Mohammed Reza Pahlavi had left Iran on Jan. 16, calling his exile a "vacation." On Feb. 1, the Ayatollah Khomeini returned triumphantly to Iran after 15 years, greeting the followers who had successfully carried out the instructions for revolution he sent from Paris on cassette tapes. By Feb. 11, the government of Premier Shahpur Bakhtiar, set up by the shah, had been overthrown. Khomeini moved ahead with his plans to establish an Islamic Republic in Iran.

The Iranian revolution had turned on the long-simmering conflict between ancient, conservative religious mores and a modern society created with oil money. The situation was not unique to Iran. Other Moslem oil producers include Saudi Arabia, Iraq, Libya, Kuwait, Qatar and the United Arab Emirates.

OPEC was in effect ratifying the market price when the oil ministers met again in June. Saudi Arabia, along with the United Arab Emirates and Qatar, increased prices to $18 a barrel. But the others raised prices to $20, and surcharges were authorized by OPEC so long as the contract price didn't exceed $23.50.

Although Iran's production was back up to about 3.6 million barrels a day by summer, the market was still extremely tight. Nothing had happened to alleviate the fears of importers that political unrest might lead to further disruption in world supplies. The oil companies continued to buy at high levels, building stocks. Leaders of the United States, Japan, Canada, Italy, Britain, West Germany and France met in Tokyo in June, and for the first time agreed to cut imports by specific amounts and to work together to increase coal use and develop alternative energy sup-

plies. In the past, the consuming countries had spent most of their time competing with one another for oil, not working together. President Jimmy Carter said the United States would limit future oil imports to less than 8.5 million barrels a day. The Europeans agreed to a ceiling of 10 million barrels a day. The new cooperation came in part because Carter in April had agreed to lift price controls on domestic oil by October 1981. The Europeans had complained since the embargo that the U.S. controls were encouraging — even subsidizing — imports, thus taking oil from the rest of the world.

Hostages, Invasion

Any possible reassurance about the future from the new accord among consuming companies was negated by two other events: Iran's taking of hostages and the Soviet invasion of Afghanistan.

The former shah of Iran had ended up living in Mexico, but, on Oct. 22 he went to New York City for six weeks of medical treatment. His presence in the United States was electrifying news in Iran, where the ayatollah already was having trouble with militant "students." The students had long resented the United States because the Central Intelligence Agency was involved during the early 1950s in the overthrow of Mohammed Mossadegh and in the restoration to power of Reza Pahlavi as shah. On Nov. 4 hundreds of young militants stormed the U.S. Embassy

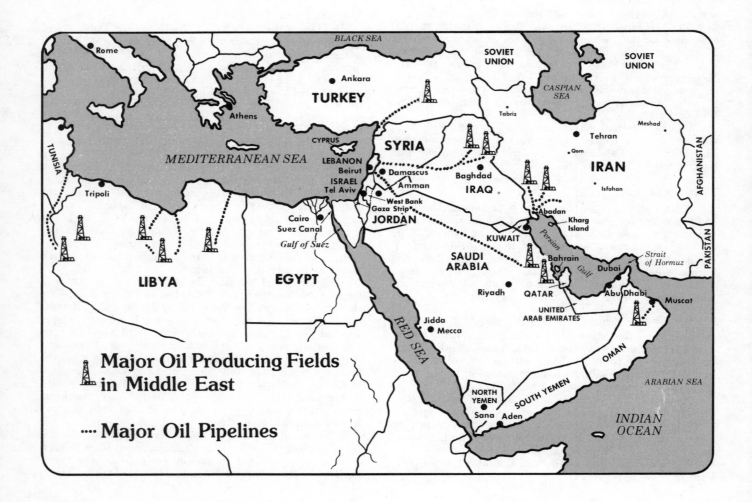

Major Oil Producing Fields in Middle East

···· Major Oil Pipelines

in Tehran, seizing as hostages 63 Americans. (Some were later released.) Their demand was that the United States return the shah to Iran.

The second event took place in Iran's neighbor, Afghanistan. To oust a Marxist ruler who had become too independent from the Kremlin, the Soviet Union in mid-December 1978 began pouring troops across its border into Afghanistan. On Dec. 27 the Soviets had the president in power assassinated, replacing him with a former deputy prime minister who had been living in exile. But the troops had to stay in Afghanistan to contain Moslem rebels, who controlled much of the countryside.

'Carter Doctrine'

The immediate concern among oil consumers was that the Soviets would continue their march into the oil-producing countries of the Persian Gulf. Carter warned the Soviets: "An attempt by any outside force to gain control of the Persian Gulf region will be regarded as an assault on the vital interests of the United States, and such an assault will be repelled by any means necessary, including military force."

Iran and Afghanistan were stark reminders of the world's dependence on the OPEC countries, and the dangerous results of spreading hostilities in the Middle East. Oil buyers worked under the assumption that they were purchasing from a supply of oil that would probably only get tighter in the future. Carter's pledge to protect American access to its share of that oil quickly became known as "the Carter Doctrine."

$30 a Barrel

In this mood of uncertainty, OPEC was set to meet again in Caracas in December 1979. Aware there would be demands for major price increases by the Africans and others, Saudi Arabia and three other countries tried to head off the "price hawks" by raising prices in advance of the scheduled session. The Saudi price went from $18 to $24 a barrel, an increase of 30 percent. This "moderate" hike was still lower, though, than the price of about $26 a barrel that Nigeria, Algeria and Libya already were asking, and getting, for their premium oil in the tight market.

In response to the Saudis, the other countries raised their prices still higher just as the formal session began. Libya, Indonesia and Iran announced increases, followed by Nigeria and Algeria. The highest price was $30 a barrel.

The Caracas session ended without agreement on either a price ceiling or a price floor. For the first time, OPEC had been unable to achieve even a semblance of accord. But the members considered it a temporary situation.

By the time OPEC met again in Algiers in June 1980, the Saudis had raised their price to $28 a barrel. This time the countries were more successful in reaching general agreement. Although Saudi Arabia continued to refuse to increase its price, the other countries worked around them to stake out a position. The base price, they announced, would be $32 a barrel, and the ceiling would be $37 a barrel for top quality crude oil. OPEC was still split and Saudi Arabia had not regained control, but some order had been restored. In December 1980 the range of allowable prices was increased, with the base price going to $36 a barrel and the ceiling on premium oil at $41 a barrel. Saudi Arabia continued to lag behind, charging $32 a barrel.

The doubling of prices between January 1979 and January 1980, combined with even further increases in 1980, had added to inflation, slowing economic growth in the consuming countries. For example, the U.S. bill for imported oil was expected to be about $80 billion in 1980, up from $60 billion in 1979. In the developing world, staggering debts for oil purchases threatened the stability of several countries. However, the higher prices also had led to conservation; U.S. gasoline sales through November were down by 7 percent from the previous year. Total U.S. oil consumption dropped by about 8 percent in 1980; imports were down 18 percent. Panic buying had ended. Oil stocks were at an all-time high. *(Chart, value of U.S. imports, p. 20)*

But the balance in the world oil situation was extremely fragile. At the end of 1980, most of the hostages still were being held in Iran. The Soviets still were struggling to contain rebels in Afghanistan. War between Iran and Iraq continued, and oil fields were a key military target for both sides. To meet world oil demand Saudi Arabian production stayed at more than 9.5 million barrels a day, even though its leaders preferred a level of 8.5 million or less. The royal Saud family wanted to minimize the strains and stresses that had finally snapped in Iran, and, as part of that effort, tried to protect their country from having to absorb too much wealth too quickly. Although the United States had urged the Saudis to keep production at the high level, its wish could turn out to have been short-sighted should the ruling family lose control. Without Saudi oil, the world would be desperate.

3

Pricing: Key Issue for Congress

Conflict over oil and natural gas pricing dominated congressional energy debate in the 1970s. The energy problem had been creeping up on the United States for several years as domestic production fell, consumption increased and imports rose. When the Arab oil embargo helped quadruple world oil prices in the winter of 1973-74, the energy situation suddenly was in the headlines — and on Congress' legislative agenda.

Most such major crises draw attention on Capitol Hill. But energy became a particular concern of Congress because of existing price controls on oil and natural gas. Overall federal wage and price controls since 1971 had held down the price of most oil.

A bill already moving through Congress at the time of the embargo provided a special extension of oil price controls. Natural gas pricing authority had been provided in a 1938 law, and a 1954 Supreme Court decision had clarified and broadened the federal government's regulatory powers.

Issue Forced on Congress

The dramatic gap between domestic prices and the higher world prices served as a stark reminder that Congress had to do something about energy. For the Republican presidents then in office and for the GOP in Congress, that something meant getting rid of those existing price controls. To them, pricing was the crux of the matter. Most Democrats agreed, but they had a different solution: Extend and retain the controls.

Congress was the arena for their bitter and divisive fight, which took several years to resolve. There was no easy answer; each solution seemed flawed. The memory of 30-cent-a-gallon gasoline faded very slowly. The long struggle was in many ways a reflection of the slow, painful realization on the part of the American public that the era of cheap, plentiful oil and gas was truly over; the Organization of Petroleum Exporting Countries would not fall apart; greedy oil companies had not pulled a hoax; the 55-mile-an-hour speed limit was not temporary; insulation and storm windows were not a passing fad.

Finally, in 1978, Congress began gradually lifting controls on natural gas, and in 1980 voted a windfall profits tax to accompany oil decontrol. Decontrol became the key element in U.S. energy policy.

In the intervening years, though, many of the initial objections to decontrol had been satisfied in some fashion.

The philosophy embraced by decontrol advocates was straightforward. They believed higher prices would encourage domestic production and discourage consumption. This "free market" approach was championed most forcefully by Republicans. "The free enterprise system spurred to action by unregulated oil and gas prices is the quickest, most efficient and fairest way of accomplishing . . . reasonable energy sufficiency," said Sen. Dewey Bartlett, R-Okla., in May 1975. Also supporting decontrol were many Democrats from energy-producing states and those who usually endorsed the Republican philosophy. Only in the late 1970s did this group pick up support from moderate and liberal Democrats from energy-consuming states.

Proponents of price controls had a more complex philosophy. A primary concern was that rising domestic oil prices would worsen inflation and further burden consumers. They also saw the pricing regulations as an important element in an overall scheme designed to change U.S. energy habits. They wanted to use new taxes to signal consumers that energy had gotten more valuable, and to offer new tax credits to reward conservation. In addition, the legislators sought to enact rules to discourage consumption — such as bans on fuel-inefficient cars and appliances, limits on national gasoline consumption, mandates for industrial use of coal. As for encouraging production, most considered prices high enough already to spur industry. Besides, they considered it patently unfair to allow prices three to four times higher for oil already flowing and willingly produced for $5 a barrel. Skeptical of the existence of competition within the energy industry, advocates of regulated prices scoffed at those who contended that lifting controls would end the energy problem. Many argued that the controls were a shield against OPEC. "This debate will show whether we are going to let the OPEC nations dictate to this land what we are going to have in the way of oil and what price we are going to pay for it," said House Commerce Chairman Harley O. Staggers, D-W.Va., in July 1975. For many, the controls were also a useful handle on the powerful oil and gas industry.

These were the guiding philosophies in 1975 as Congress and President Gerald Ford wrestled with pricing and conservation. They ended up with the Energy Policy and Conservation Act of 1975, which extended oil price controls through September 1981 and contained several conservation provisions.

Experience Yields New Ideas

In the process of that debate, though, and in the ensuing few years, the assumptions of many who favored controls were proven wrong or impractical. Getting energy taxes approved — especially on gasoline — just wasn't politically feasible, or so they learned as a 1975 Ways and Means plan was first butchered by the House and then ignored by the Senate. Not only did legislators not want to be responsible for raising their constituents' prices; the taxes were also strongly opposed by the oil industry and others seeking decontrol. President Jimmy Carter made another attempt at winning approval for new energy taxes in 1977-78, but his gasoline tax and crude oil equalization tax failed badly.

Democrats also learned that conservation requirements were unpopular among their colleagues, though there were exceptions, such as the automobile efficiency rules. No one wanted to be forced to change his habits, especially by the federal government. If a rule did get through Congress, it had often been so watered down as to be ineffective. Others proved too complex to carry out. "There's a recognition that we have a terrible time designing at the federal level how to do things, and that generated great political resistance," said Philip R. Sharp, D-Ind., as he reflected in 1980 about his earlier activity on the House Commerce energy panel. Energy efficiency standards for buildings were one example he cited. "Ours is a very complex economy," Sharp said. "If we built all houses alike it would be very simple. But we don't. And Americans are not willing to give up that freedom and others." Sharp said he and others began to realize in the late 1970s that, rather than try to dictate new energy habits with legislation, it might be preferable to "let the silent hand, the marketplace do it." He added with a smile, "Let the silent hand take hell."

Faced with the failure of taxes and federal rules as a way to change energy habits, proponents of price controls slowly came around to the idea that higher prices spurred conservation. By the late 1970s articulate defenses of that position were coming from academicians with liberal credentials and from interest groups, such as environmentalists. They contended that conservation and alternative energy sources, such as solar, would be more economically competitive if oil prices were decontrolled. So long as people could get relatively inexpensive oil and natural gas, they had no incentive to adapt to the new energy era, they argued. The oil companies and Republicans who had been arguing for years against controls suddenly had company.

Even some in Congress who traditionally supported controls adopted this view. The Northeast had provided many of the staunchest advocates of price controls because of the area's cold climate and heavy dependence on oil as a fuel. But two new senators elected in 1978 were examples of the new breed: Paul E. Tsongas, D-Mass., and Bill Bradley, D-N.J., were resigned to having the market play a primary role in energy policy. Personally, Tsongas said, he felt that controls were needed to protect consumers. But as a policy maker he had found "a strong argument in favor of decontrol," he admitted. "The price of energy has to reflect its real value."

Veteran legislators who had been longtime supporters of controls also changed their positions. Among them was John D. Dingell, D-Mich., who as chairman of the House Commerce Subcommittee on Energy and Power had been a key defender of price controls. "It was my view that

we ought to hold prices down," he said in a 1980 interview. "Then all of a sudden I realized that a lot of the conservation was coming from cost increases. Now I don't like that [price increases], but it has provided a far stronger stimulus than anything I have been able to do through the passage of legislation." Asked if anything in particular had changed his mind, Dingell admitted that personal experience had been a factor. "I moved into a little townhouse and it cost me $70 a month to heat it," he said. "Then I insulated and caulked to beat hell and double glazed the windows, and all of a sudden it's costing me $40."

As for the argument that controls provided a shield from OPEC, the controls failed the test. Prices went up anyway as rising import costs and higher prices allowed for new domestic discoveries combined to water down the benefits of having a share of domestic oil priced at $5 a barrel. Tough talk about U.S. supplies and U.S. controlled prices didn't faze OPEC, which continued to set world oil prices.

Controls also failed to have much impact on inflation, which raged on in the 1970s. Increasingly, economists argued that growing dependence on imports was damaging the economy even more than higher oil prices. By holding down consumer energy prices, price controls were in effect subsidizing and thus encouraging imports, they contended. Therefore, decontrol was seen as a damper to inflation, instead of primarily as a spur to it, which was how decontrol had been viewed in the past.

National security continued to be a concern, with U.S. dependence on oil from the unstable Middle East considered a major weak spot in the national defense. Events in late 1978 and 1979 in Iran and Afghanistan only reinforced those worries and provided ample evidence to the public of reasons to curb imports. "Our national strength is dangerously dependent on a thin line of oil tankers stretching halfway around the earth, originating in the Middle East and around the Persian Gulf — one of the most unstable regions in the world," Carter said in an April 1979 television address.

The Iranian revolution also had sparked another round of oil price increases that in absolute terms — the extra dollars charged — was greater than the 1973-74 price hikes. The gap between oil under domestic price controls and world prices grew even wider. The dream of continuing the era of cheap oil was even more unrealistic.

Gradual Decontrol, Windfall Tax

The long list of arguments against decontrol that had guided the Democrats in the mid-1970s thus had been eroded during the late 1970s. Protecting consumers, and especially the poor, from high prices was still a concern, but more and more legislators recognized that special aid programs probably did a better job than overall price controls. Less easy to rectify was the sense of inequity associated with suddenly increasing the price of oil found and tapped when prices were less than $5 a barrel, thus giving the producers a "windfall" profit. Many legislators also were uncomfortable with the idea of giving the oil and gas industry full control of the nation's energy supplies.

A windfall profits tax on oil was proposed by Carter in 1979 as he announced plans to carry out the decontrol scheme set out in the 1975 pricing law. Decontrol was to be complete at the end of September 1981. The tax, passed in 1980, satisfied most remaining concerns for a majority of Congress. Besides providing revenues to aid low-income families, the tax prevented the oil industry from getting an undeserved windfall, and it kept a government handle on the industry.

For natural gas, the decontrol scheme was agreed on in 1978 after a protracted fight. The new law continued controls indefinitely on most gas contracted for prior to 1977, thus avoiding a sudden windfall for producers. The ceiling price of new discoveries was raised and set to be lifted entirely in 1985.

However, the accommodations made to opponents of decontrol didn't satisfy everyone. "I still feel very strongly that decontrol was a mistake," Rep. Toby Moffett, D-Conn., a leader on the issue, said in 1980. In a last-ditch effort to block decontrol, Moffett had sponsored an amendment to an energy authorization bill. The House vote in October 1979 was 2-1 against continuing controls, with all but seven Republicans teaming up with half of the Democrats to oppose price limits.

Another stalwart advocate of controls, Senate Energy Chairman Henry M. Jackson, D-Wash., also continued in 1980 to lament their removal. He had realized that any move to stop decontrol in 1979-80 was doomed in the Senate. "It's the new academia," Jackson complained, trying to explain the widespread support of decontrol. "There's an ethic among the conservationists, among the economists, that everything has to be disciplined in the marketplace. These young people have lost interest in the poor."

But Moffett and Jackson were in the minority in 1980. In the years since the 1973-74 price hikes, the inefficient and often-flawed democratic process had given Congress and the public time to learn, time to adjust to the radically different energy situation, time to try out different solutions, time to develop means of rectifying inequities. The majority had prevailed.

OIL PRICING: CONTROLS EASED

Midnight, Sept. 30, 1981. Across the United States, oil company executives are pouring champagne, toasting the event they had awaited for a decade: decontrol of domestic oil prices. At last, they tell one another over the clinking of glasses, the complex system that cost us billions in income is dead.

But, as sophisticated oilmen know, decontrol isn't really decontrol.

First, there's the oil windfall profits tax — the price industry paid for an end to the rules that since 1971 had governed the cost of domestically produced petroleum. The tax takes a share of the difference between controlled and decontrolled prices. Then there are other controls that could be triggered in emergencies, such as war or severe supply shortages. During such a time, the government would have the power to allocate oil supplies, taking that responsibility from the private sector.

These ties with the government are things the oil industry could do without. But the long history of government entanglement in the oil marketplace provides a clue

to another side of the picture: government controls that the industry likes. Years ago, this meant restrictions on domestic production and, later, limits on oil imports — both designed to control supplies and keep prices high. Two things have happened to change that. The world oil balance shifted around 1970, when the problem became excess demand instead of excess supply. In addition, another force — a cartel of producing countries — is now ordering the market that government once helped manage for industry.

Industry Benefits

Even before full decontrol, the push was on to keep friendly government hands on the oil industry. Refiners who don't produce oil, known as independents, were scrambling for guarantees that the major companies would continue to provide them with supplies. Eventually, the entire refinery industry could ask for government protection from foreign refineries, such as those in the Caribbean, that can process oil more cheaply. Without price controls, U.S. refiners will have lost the supply of inexpensive domestic oil that helped them compete.

In other ways, too, the relationship between industry and government benefits the oil companies. Though the windfall profits tax is punitive, other sections of the U.S. tax code reward the oil industry. Independent producers, which are non-integrated companies, still get a special depletion allowance. All producers can count as expenses the intangible costs of drilling. Another major tax advantage enjoyed since the 1950s is the foreign tax credit, which allows oil companies to charge taxes paid to foreign countries against all of their income, not just that from overseas.

In addition to these indirect subsidies, the government also hands out aid directly to the industry. Much of government-financed research on enhanced recovery techniques and other new methods is carried out by oil companies. The oil industry is also heavily involved in synthetic fuels development, and thus gets a major share of the billions of government dollars channeled to research, demonstration projects and commercialization.

In short, decontrol does not take the government out of the oil market. But the move by a Democratic president to end the controls originally imposed by a Republican president was hailed by the oil industry — and also by advocates of energy conservation, solar and other renewable resources, and increased use of coal. They saw price decontrol as a step in the right direction.

That all of these groups ended up on the same side of the question, after years of debate, is a major reason President Carter was able in 1979 to begin ending the controls that his predecessors had failed to abolish. The windfall profits tax was another reason, since it appeared to take care of the inequity involved in suddenly tripling the price consumers paid for oil, once gladly produced for less than $10 a barrel. A third reason came from outside the United States. The Iranian revolution in late 1978 had strained world oil supplies, doubling prices, causing waiting lines for gasoline — and reminding Americans of their dependence on the Middle East. The energy problem, which had seemed a lot of rhetoric in 1977 and 1978, suddenly was real again.

States Had First Rules

The state governments were the first involved in regulation of the fledgling oil industry in the first three dec-

Prices of Domestically Produced Fossil Fuels

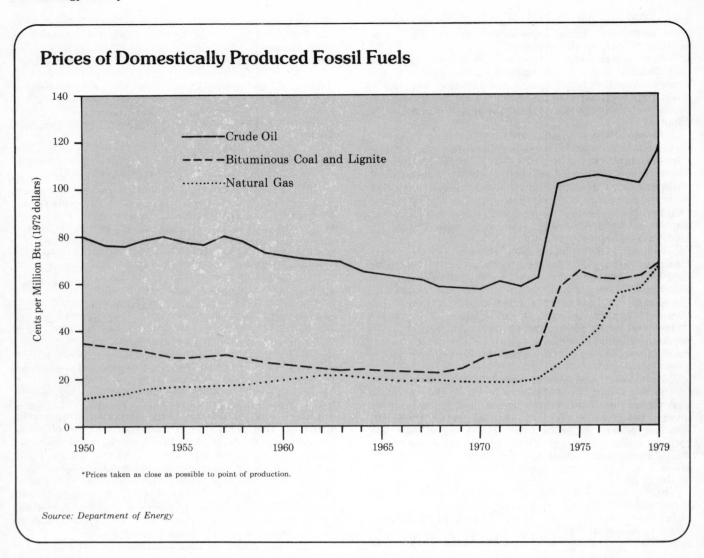

*Prices taken as close as possible to point of production.

Source: Department of Energy

ades of the 20th century. The states called the rules "conservation" because they were designed to prevent the waste of oil. But another effect — when the rules worked — was to keep overly abundant supplies from depressing prices.

The oil industry always had operated under the "rule of capture," which in law meant that whoever got the oil from the ground owned it. If two wells on separately owned tracts of land happened to tap the same underground pool of oil, then the race was on to see who "captured" the most oil. This scramble usually meant waste in oil production because rapid pumping quickly depleted the natural pressure in the deposit that normally pushed oil to the surface. A lot of oil — more than the usual one-third to one-half — ended up being left in the ground. To prevent such waste, the states eventually required wells to be a certain distance apart, set out drilling practices and monitored production. They also determined what would be the most effective rate of production to ensure maximum recovery from a field and then gave each well or producer a share of that. Giving credence to the states' efforts to save oil were the periodic predictions during

this time by government geologists and others that the United States was running out of oil.

Among the most effective regulators were the states of Oklahoma and Texas, which eventually expanded conservation efforts into an overall system for controlling oil prices and production. Starting in 1917, the Oklahoma Corporation Commission and the Texas Railroad Commission were given clear authority over oil production. By 1930 both had issued mandatory statewide prorationing orders, which limited overall state production to a certain amount, based not only on geological considerations but also on anticipated sales at the desired price per barrel. But the moves by the two states quickly were upset by booming production from two new fields in Oklahoma City and East Texas. By one theory, established producers had welcomed the state rules because the Great Depression had reduced demand, and less oil meant prices wouldn't drop so much. But the new operators in the just-found fields, wanting to take as much oil as they could, simply ignored the rules. Another theory fingers the major companies as the ones exceeding production limits in an effort to drive down prices — and thus drive out the new operators. Whoever the culprit, production levels soared, and prices plummeted to just 10 cents a barrel.

The chaotic situation further unraveled when fights broke out in the fields. In both states, the governors in 1931 declared martial law and sent in state troops to enforce a temporary shutdown of wells in the new fields. When production resumed, the militia stayed for several weeks to make sure the state production limits were not violated.

During this period, the governors of nine top oil-producing states got together to share information and discuss a mutual problem — how to control the sales of illegal, excess production that had been shipped outside of the producing state. They decided the federal government was in the best position to regulate interstate sale of this "hot oil," which threatened to undermine the state regulations. Legislation was drafted and, after lobbying by the states, eventually incorporated in 1933 into the National Industrial Recovery Act, the foundation of President Franklin Roosevelt's plan for ending the Depression. The act also sanctioned the formulation of an oil industry code to govern prices and allocation of supplies.

The mood of cooperation was a sharp contrast to the trust-busting years in the early 1900s when the desire for competition led to the government's 1911 decision to break up the Standard Oil Co.

A group of oil industry representatives drafted the code, which was then administered by the government and an industry advisory council. A key role in these decisions was played by the American Petroleum Institute, an industry association established in 1919 just as wartime government controls over the industry were dismantled. The first priority for the administrators of the code was limiting production, and the direct power over prices wasn't used. Lowered production levels, however, indirectly kept prices higher than they would have been with more oil on the market.

Enforcement of the "hot oil" provisions, while difficult, apparently was having some effect when the courts intervened. In January 1935 the Supreme Court declared unconstitutional the section of the National Industry Recovery Act that authorized federal regulation of oil produced in excess of a state's quota and shipped across the state line. Then, in June, the court said the entire act was unconstitutional, thus invalidating federal authority over oil production and prices.

Spurred by a Democratic senator from Texas, Tom Connally, Congress responded quickly to the January ruling. Federal authority over excess production was restored in 1935 by the Interstate Transport of Petroleum Products Act — better known as the Connally Hot Oil Act. The act was made permanent in 1942, and was enforced by the Interior Department.

Congress was slower in replacing the authority over production and prices. Bills had been introduced, with some legislators willing even to expand federal power over oil so that the industry would be treated as a utility. Perhaps influenced by oilmen worried about too much central control, the governors of the oil-producing states decided to try another approach to controlling production. They realized that individual states working alone had been unsuccessful, so they agreed to work together. Led by Texas and Oklahoma, the governors of six states formed an interstate compact to coordinate production with demand. As in all interstate agreements, this one had to be approved by Congress, which went along in August

1935. Eventually, 20 states joined the compact. They continued to hold oil production below capacity, thus keeping prices stable. A 1949 report by the Senate Small Business Committee said that the state prorationing laws and the interstate compact were "a perfect pattern of monopolistic control over oil production . . . distribution . . . and price." Describing the situation, the report continued, "There is a mechanism controlling the production of crude oil to market demand (or below) that operates as smoothly and effectively as the finest watch."

The system eventually was made obsolete in the late 1960s by rising demand for oil and declining production capacity. The quotas were formally ended in 1972.

Quotas on Imports

Between the 1930s and 1970s the oil industry had another problem that threatened to mess up the carefully ordered, government-regulated market, and that was inexpensive imports from foreign countries.

Exploration overseas had been encouraged in the early 1920s by the naysayers of U.S. oil reserves. The stunning successes assured most people there was a lot of oil left in the world, particularly in the Middle East and Venezuela. American companies helped develop these fields, but their sales were for the most part to countries other than the United States, which had its own supplies.

Presumably, the supplies from the new fields might have found their way into the U.S. market, thus undercutting U.S. prices and upsetting the prorationing system. But there was yet another market-ordering arrangement to prevent that. This time it wasn't government officials, but representatives of the world's seven major oil companies who sat down together as oil from the profluent new fields sent prices downward. At a castle in Scotland, in 1928, the American, Dutch and British companies essentially split up the world oil market. Instead of pushing up production from the new fields, flooding the market

Cost to Refiners Of Acquiring Crude Oil

(Dollars per Barrel)

Year	Domestic	Imported	Composite
1974	7.18	12.52	9.07
1975	8.39	13.93	10.38
1976	8.84	13.48	10.89
1977	9.55	14.53	11.96
1978	10.61	14.57	12.46
1979	14.27	21.67	17.72
1980*	22.60	33.26	27.05

*Average through July.

Source: Department of Energy

and dropping prices to beat out competition and make a sale, each company agreed to keep production in balance with anticipated demand. Increases would be allowed only to keep up with expected growth. Each also let the others keep their shares of the market — and a similar share in the future — in return for a secure market of its own. International prices also were set — the price of oil in the Gulf of Mexico plus whatever it would have cost to ship oil from the Gulf to the point where it was sold. The castle gave the agreement its name — Achnacarry.

According to a 1952 Federal Trade Commission report, "The International Petroleum Cartel," the Achnacarry agreement achieved its purpose — restoring order to the world market. Though its specifics were soon outdated, the practice had been established of respectfully leaving alone another company's market. What competition existed was subtle, and the tactic of bringing in barrels of low-priced fuel to beat out a competitor was not common.

The grip of the major companies on the world oil market was not iron tight in the 1930s and 1940s, but its first major cracks came as economic recovery from World War II began. Oil had fueled the war, and oil was fueling the recovery. The market expanded rapidly, making it easier for new companies to come in. Though concessions on the key fields in the developing world had been held since the 1920s by the major companies, the smallest enterprises began to win concessions of their own as North Africa and other new areas opened up. Their often-higher bids were especially appealing to the new governments in former European colonial holdings who needed revenue. To sell their supplies, the aggressive companies cut prices, violating any remaining remnant of the majors' old pricing system. At the time, oil from the Middle East and other areas was much less expensive than oil from U.S. production.

Eisenhower Limits Imports

The U.S. appetite for oil, already the world's biggest, continued to grow in the 1950s as the economy expanded and other fuels, such as coal, were abandoned. The foreign oil had a ready market, particularly on the East Coast. In 1953, when Dwight D. Eisenhower took over the presidency, imported oil provided more than 12 percent of U.S. supplies. The concern among government officials about this dependence on foreign supplies was reinforced in 1956 when Egypt closed the Suez Canal, thus cutting off key European oil supplies.

But the loudest arguments against rising imports were made by domestic producers. They didn't want the foreign oil depressing domestic prices or production. By 1954 the state oil regulators had begun to curb domestic production in an effort to keep the foreign oil prices from lowering U.S. price levels. In Texas, for example, producers in 1948 had been able to operate wells about 100 percent of the time under state rules. In 1954 they were down to only 53 percent. Production also was limited in other states.

The non-integrated companies, known as independent producers, pressed Congress in 1955 to impose import quotas. They were led by the Independent Petroleum Association of America. On their side also was the Foreign Oil Policy Committee, an organization of coal companies and railroads that saw cheap foreign oil as a further threat to their already-ailing industries. Working against import quotas were the major oil companies, who brought in the foreign oil, and oil jobbers, who profited from distributing the inexpensive, abundant supplies of imports.

Though Congress refused to impose quotas, the legislators did give the president new authority in a provision of the Reciprocal Trade Agreements Extension of 1955. If the volume of an imported product were large enough to "threaten to impair the national security," the act said, then the president could restrict imports of that product.

Eisenhower had two presidential commissions study the problem of oil imports, and twice — in 1955 and 1957 — he asked companies to limit their imports voluntarily. But even the more formal 1957 program didn't work, and the domestic independent producers continued their pressure on the government for quotas. Also of continuing concern were the national security considerations. Officials worried that the imports were damaging the U.S. oil industry, and they thought that would in turn hamper national defense efforts.

In March 1959, using the national security clause in the trade bill, Eisenhower imposed mandatory quotas. Each refiner was given a certain allotment of imports — a license — and those who didn't have access to foreign oil or chose not to use their license could sell their allotment to other refiners.

From 1959 to 1973 the import quota was the key element in the nation's oil policy. During most of that time imports were held to about one-eighth of total supply. But the program was controversial. By 1969 the criticism had grown loud enough that President Richard Nixon appointed a group to study the quota system. Chief opponents were New England politicians, who argued that their region's energy bills were much higher because of the quotas. National consumer groups also complained because domestic oil averaged about $3.30 a barrel, while foreign oil sold for $2. They wanted consumers to benefit from lower prices.

Nixon's advisory panel recommended an end to the quotas, but Nixon decided instead to loosen the import restrictions. In the early 1970s exemptions were provided to Canadian and Venezuelan oil, and to heating oil.

However, demand continued to grow, and domestic prices increased by 15 to 25 cents a gallon, reflecting the gap between available supply and demand. Nixon on June 4, 1971, sent the first presidential energy message to Congress, warning of an energy problem and urging several steps to increase domestic production.

But one unmentioned spur to more production — higher prices — was eliminated by the overall freeze on wages and prices that Nixon imposed Aug. 16, 1971. The second phase of the controls limited profit margins, and ran from Nov. 15, 1971, to Jan. 10, 1973. The third phase was voluntary, but ended on June 13, 1973, with another price freeze.

Particularly affected by the first Nixon price freeze were supplies of heating oil. In late summer, gasoline prices usually are high because of the peak driving season, while heating oil prices usually are depressed. Fuel oil was especially low-priced in August 1971, because a mild winter the year before had left heating oil stocks at high levels. As a Senate Government Operations study of the situation noted in 1973, "It was not surprising to find industry more anxious to convert its crude oil into gasoline than into fuel oil. The profits were in gasoline." The next winter, in 1972-73, was a cold one and heating oil supplies were very tight. Extra imports weren't coming in, even though heating oil was by then exempt from the quotas. Foreign oil prices had been catching up with those in the United States, but under the price controls importers couldn't easily pass on the most recent price increases. As a result, they didn't increase imports to meet the demand. There was no extra domestic production capacity, either, as there had been in the past.

Nixon Abandons Quotas

After winters with fuel oil shortages and predictions of tight gasoline supplies in summer, Nixon finally abandoned the quotas on April 18, 1973. Instead, he set an additional fee on imports that would be levied in stages over the next two years. At first, though, importers had to pay the fee only on imports in excess of the levels allowed them for 1973 by the quota system. By May 1, 1975, under Nixon's plan, the extra fee on crude oil would total 15.75 cents a barrel and, on gasoline and other products, 10.5 cents a barrel. Once combined with the fees existing prior to Nixon's 1973 action, the totals were to be 21 cents a barrel for crude and 63 cents a barrel for gasoline and other products. (The fees were still at that level in 1980.)

The first import fees had been imposed by the Internal Revenue Act of 1932 in an effort to protect the domestic oil industry. A fee of 21 cents a barrel was levied on crude oil, but the fee for gasoline and some other refined products was much stiffer because Congress wanted to encourage domestic refining. The fee for gasoline was $1.05 a barrel, or 2.5 cents a gallon. By 1948 the rate on crude oil had been dropped to 10.5 cents a barrel, and in 1963, all of the import fees were reduced by half. That meant the fee for crude oil was 5.25 cents a barrel, and the fee for gasoline was 52.5 cents a barrel. Those were the levels when Nixon imposed the additional fees in 1973.

President Jimmy Carter in 1980 tried to impose an import fee on oil as a preliminary step toward asking Congress for a tax at the pump. But the legislators in June voted to block him and then easily overrode his veto of their resolution.

Price Controls on Oil

The peculiar problems of controlling oil prices under wage and price guidelines led the Cost of Living Council to develop a special system for the oil industry in May and August of 1973. To encourage production, the council took controls off new supplies — from wells tapped since 1973 or from existing wells when production exceeded the level for the same month in 1972. For existing production,

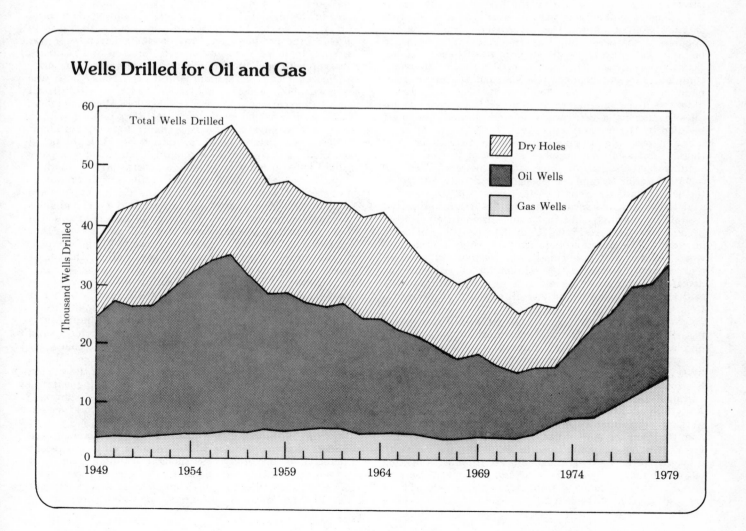

Wells Drilled for Oil and Gas

Total Wells Drilled

Dry Holes
Oil Wells
Gas Wells

Thousand Wells Drilled

60
50
40
30
20
10
0

1949   1954   1959   1964   1969   1974   1979

the controls were retained. This "old" oil was priced at about $4.25 a barrel (increased to $5.25 in December). Though information about the price of the uncontrolled "new" oil was sketchy, government estimates later showed the price was about $5.12 in September. The gap between the two tiers of oil didn't really begin to widen beyond $1.00 until the Arab oil embargo in October. By December, new oil was priced at $10.35 a barrel, while old oil sold for $5.25. That put the average domestic price at about $6.75, since at the time about 70 percent of the oil was classified as old oil. The share provided by old oil declined as production from the wells dropped off. The price of imports, of course, couldn't be controlled by the U.S. government.

Price Freeze

When Nixon realized his voluntary "phase three" controls weren't working, he again froze prices on June 13. The freeze lasted through Aug. 13, when less restrictive controls were imposed. Nixon's pricing authority came from the Economic Stabilization Act of 1970, and an extension — through April 30, 1974 — that Congress passed in April 1973.

The new pricing system for oil devised by the Cost of Living Council managed to satisfy the Nixon administration and Congress during the first three quarters of 1973. Their conflict was instead over federal allocation of oil. Congress wanted the government to allocate the apparently scarce supplies of crude oil and gasoline to be sure that priority needs, such as health care and agriculture, were met. The legislators also sought to answer complaints by independent retailers that the major companies were cutting back their supplies. Nixon, however, didn't want the federal government deciding where oil supplies should go, a task he considered complex and best handled by the marketplace.

Congress voted to give the president discretionary authority to allocate oil supplies as part of legislation extending Nixon's general price control powers. Then the Senate Interior Committee pushed the Senate into going further. In June the Senate easily passed a law mandating that the president allocate supplies. He was also directed to stabilize oil prices, but that clause drew little attention because the Cost of Living Council was still overseeing oil prices. The question of pricing did come up, though, when Oklahoma Republican Dewey Bartlett proposed an amendment requiring a free market for oil. But he was defeated, 21-71, when Senate Interior Chairman Jackson said the amendment would end all existing oil price controls.

When the House dragged its feet on the bill, the Senate passed it again in August, attaching it to a minor, unrelated measure. Another impetus to the House was a September protest demonstration in Washington, D.C., by several thousand independent retailers of gasoline and heating oil. Their complaint: that their supplies were being curtailed unfairly by the major companies.

On Sept. 29 the House Commerce Committee finished work on a mandatory allocation bill. On Oct. 2 Nixon admitted that the marketplace allocation he earlier favored wasn't working. He announced he would use the authority provided earlier by Congress to allocate supplies of heating oil, diesel fuel and jet fuel — but not gasoline. "The philosophy here is to manage a projected shortage," said Rogers C. B. Morton, Nixon's top energy adviser. "The severity of the shortage will depend on Old Man Winter and where he strikes, how long he strikes and what the temperatures are." Thus, worries about shortages that winter were common even before the oil embargo.

The House already had started debate on the allocation bill when the Arab oil producers announced their decision to cut production and embargo the United States. The legislators easily passed the measure Oct. 17. Included were more specific instructions on pricing than in the Senate bill. They were similar to the Cost of Living Council rules.

When conferees met to resolve House and Senate differences, they retained the stricter pricing rules. They later explained in a report that it did "no good to require the allocation of products if sellers are then permitted to demand unfair and unrealistic prices. . . . Congress intends to force the administration to rationalize and harmonize the objectives of equitable allocation of fuels with the objective" of price controls.

Price Control Law

The Emergency Petroleum Allocation Act (EPAA), cleared Nov. 14, was still considered just a temporary law. It was to expire Feb. 28, 1975. However, the EPAA was eventually to become the primary legal force behind the nation's controls on oil prices.

In the meantime, though, Congress and Nixon focused on a bill — the Energy Emergency Act — that was to provide the president an array of emergency powers over energy. Included were authority to force oil and gas users to switch to coal, power to ration gasoline and authority to loosen clean air standards. But the House also was worried about another problem: excess profits by the oil industry because of the OPEC price hikes. House members convinced a conference committee to go along with a scheme that gave consumers a chance to complain about unfair prices before the Renegotiation Board. If the board found there had been price gouging, then the oil company would have to repay or provide a general price reduction.

This concern about windfall profits wasn't unique to Congress. Nixon too sensed that the public might have a point as it grew angrier and angrier at the oil companies because of higher prices. On Dec. 19 Nixon proposed a tax on windfall profits, which were defined as those that exceeded a level to be set by the Cost of Living Council. If the income were reinvested in exploration, though, it would be exempt from the tax.

However, the Senate's leading oil-state senators thought limiting profits was a terrible idea, whether it came from Nixon or the House. Finance Chairman Russell B. Long, D-La., argued persistently that the windfall profits restriction in the conference report was a tax and should go through his committee. He and his oil-state colleagues kept talking, delaying action on the allocation bill and frustrating those who wanted to pass it before the session ended. Eventually, the Senate gave in, leaving out the windfall profits section. But the House stood its ground. The result was to put the conferees back to work in February 1974.

Senate Interior Chairman Jackson was among the leaders of the conference who were outraged at the recent increases in oil prices. He thought it unfair that U.S. producers suddenly were doubling the price of their "new" oil, when the earlier pre-OPEC price levels had given what he called an "adequate incentive" to explore and produce.

Production and Prices Closely Tied In Debate Over Maintaining Oil Reserves

For several decades, the United States had been squeezing oil and gas from underground. Though blessed with vast petroleum deposits, the country also had — and has — a voracious appetite for oil and gas. More and more energy had to be found and pumped to the surface to satisfy demand. New discoveries just couldn't keep up with consumption. In the late 1960s, additions to proved reserves of both oil and gas fell behind the rate of production. By the early 1970s, production had peaked.

A major argument on behalf of ending price controls was that decontrol would mean more production. Oil company officials are usually among the first to admit that their goal is not to step up production but to keep it from going further down. Reversing the decline is unlikely. One oil company official even said that "if crude oil went to $100 a barrel, we couldn't arrest the decline rate."

The reason is that most major, easily tapped oil and gas reservoirs have been found. The Alaskan fields that began producing in 1977 and 1978 were an exception. Alaska holds additional promise, though the cold, frozen North is often a hostile environment for drilling. Hopes for quick, major finds on the outer continental shelf dimmed in the late 1970s as dry holes far outnumbered successful ones in areas such as the Baltimore Canyon. The industry has little optimism about major breakthroughs in the lower 48 states, where depleted fields are pockmarked with wells. Deposits yet to be found tend to be smaller, deeper and more costly to recover. According to the American Petroleum Institute, it can cost about $1 million to drill the first 12,000 feet of a well; another $1 million to reach 15,000 feet; and then $2 million more to drill just 3,000 feet farther to a depth of 18,000 feet.

Drilling traditionally has increased in response to price. The number of wells drilled declined for several years after a peak in 1956. That was also a period when the real price of petroleum was decreasing. When prices began to climb after 1973-74, even under government price controls, drilling increased. The industry was expected in 1980 to exceed the record level set in 1956 of 57,170 wells. Improved techniques have meant that the industry is more likely to find oil or gas once the decision has been made to drill. The success rate was 66 percent in 1949, dropping to 57 percent in 1969, and then climbing to about 73 percent in 1979 — the best ever. *(Chart, total wells drilled for oil and gas, p. 31)*

Federal Lands

Much of the land eyed for exploration in the 1980s — offshore, in Alaska and in Western areas such as the Overthrust Belt in the Rocky Mountains — is owned or controlled by the federal government. Now that Congress has settled most oil and gas pricing questions, the oil and gas industry is focusing on what it considers to be excessive restraints on its access to the federal land and on slow timetables for what leasing is permitted. Some of the restrictions are designed to protect the environment, while others are in response to local concerns about rapid, uncontrolled economic growth that could result from large-scale energy development.

Enhanced Recovery

The potential source of oil considered most responsive to higher prices is the petroleum left behind by those who first tapped a reservoir. Usually two-thirds — but sometimes just one quarter — of oil remains after the two initial types of recovery, known as primary and secondary recovery. Tertiary, or enhanced, recovery can tap that leftover oil, but it's an expensive process.

Primary recovery is the natural flow of oil from the high pressure area underground, through the well and to the surface. Secondary recovery is the reinjection of either associated gas or water to maintain the pressure. Though once used only after primary recovery, the two methods are now used simultaneously. Enhanced recovery is the injection into the reservoir of heat or chemicals, such as carbon dioxide, that help the oil begin to flow again.

For gas, costly-to-produce sources made more attractive by high prices include tight sands and Devonian shale.

Higher prices probably won't mean a jump in U.S. oil and gas production, but they could make economical the more expensive recovery techniques, such as enhanced recovery, and the more costly exploration, such as deep offshore wells. These new supplies could avoid a precipitous drop in domestic production in the next couple of decades.

Jackson found a majority of other conferees sympathetic, and they agreed to replace the windfall profits section with new restrictions on oil prices. Not only was "old" oil to stay at the level of $5.25, but the price of "new" oil would be rolled back, from about $10.35 to $5.25. Only certain types of hard-to-get oil would be priced at $7.09.

This sweeping provision was added to the omnibus emergency bill and it passed the Senate, 67-32, and the House, 258-151, with the legislators generally voting along party lines. The margins on the late February votes were surprisingly wide considering the severity of the pricing restrictions, but they reflected the mood of the moment:

anti-oil industry. However, the margin of victory was not enough in either house to give the price control proponents a two-thirds majority, which they would need to override Nixon's threatened veto.

Nixon did veto the bill, on March 6. The Senate, aided by the vote switches of some oil-state Democrats and others, sustained the veto.

The setback led the Senate Interior Committee to strip the pricing section from the emergency bill, which the panel still wanted to get through Congress. In the House, the Commerce Committee also tried to save part of the emergency bill, splitting off certain provisions into separate legislation. (This measure eventually became the Energy Supply and Environmental Coordination Act of 1974.) But the members still wanted the pricing provisions enacted, too. Michigan's John Dingell, a leader on the panel, had tried the day of Nixon's veto to attach a pricing amendment to an energy reorganization bill already on the House floor. He won, 218-175. However, the next day, March 7, the House reversed its vote, defeating the amendment on a 163-216 vote. Both Nixon and the oil industry helped bring about the reversal.

Dingell and his colleagues decided to continue their efforts. The bill they reported, with price controls, rationing authority and other presidential powers, finally got to the House floor May 21. It was defeated, 191-207.

The Mood Changes

Though the House eagerly had embraced price controls in February, there had been a sharp swing in mood. The Arab embargo had ended in March, waiting lines at gasoline stations were gone and the price spiral had halted temporarily, as it turned out. Winter, with the spectre of chilly homes without heating oil, was over. Rep. James T. Broyhill, R-N.C., was among those who had changed his vote to oppose price controls and emergency powers. The earlier pricing provisions, he said, had been written "in a different year and a different time and under different circumstances than exist today."

In the oil market, though, prices still were being controlled. The pricing provisions of the Emergency Petroleum Allocation Act (EPAA) were regulating the price of old oil, so the expiration of wage and price control authority in April meant little to oil prices. An energy reorganization bill had set up the Federal Energy Administration (FEA) and had given the new agency responsibility for overseeing oil price controls. EPAA also had been extended for six months, putting its expiration date at Aug. 31, 1975, instead of in February.

Congress in 1973 and 1974 had 1) passed both the EPAA and the Energy Supply and Environmental Coordination Act, which tried to force more coal burning by utilities, 2) delayed some air pollution standards and 3) broadened the powers of the new FEA. But the failure to enact conservation rules or to tighten price controls had left many Democratic members with "energy" as the leading topic on their legislative agenda for 1975. On the other side of the aisle, the Republicans wanted to pass legislation to encourage more energy exploration and production — and to let EPAA and price controls die quietly in 1975.

In Gerald Ford's few months in office in 1974, after Watergate forced Nixon's resignation in August, the president had little time to make legislative proposals to Congress. But by January energy policy, along with the economy, had become the heart of his legislative program.

However, things didn't work out quite as Ford had planned. For much of his first full year as president, Ford and Congress played a complex, seemingly endless tug-of-war over national energy policy — and particularly over oil pricing.

Ford vs. a Democratic Congress

Though Richard Nixon endorsed oil decontrol, he let the public know it was a limited endorsement. The windfall profits tax proposal was one bow to public opinion. Another was this Nixon statement: "We will not have consumers paying a dollar a gallon for gasoline."

At first, Gerald Ford seemed more forceful in his conviction that higher prices were the best way to encourage production and conservation. Not only did Ford call for decontrol of domestic oil and gas production; he also wanted to levy new excise taxes that would make energy prices even higher. The only sweetener in the tax proposal was that revenues would be returned to individuals and corporations through income tax cuts. Like Nixon, Ford also called for a windfall profits tax on income above a base level per barrel that was not reinvested by industry in exploration and development.

Yet another element of Ford's 1975 energy package was a $3 import fee. But Ford apparently didn't intend to leave the fee on permanently. Instead, it was to be a bargaining chip — or rather a club — to use in his negotiations with Congress.

When Ford announced Jan. 23 he would impose the first $1 of the fee on Feb. 1, he told Congress he wanted his tax proposals passed within three months. In the meantime, another $1 fee would be added March 1, and then another on April 1. The president wanted quick action on the taxes because he intended to decontrol oil prices April 1, unless Congress vetoed him as provided under EPAA authority. By acting within five days, either house could veto a presidential oil pricing action. Decontrol of natural gas required separate, new legislation from Congress.

Democratic Plans

But Ford's bullying — and his proposals — angered the Democratic majority in Congress. The Democrats wrote their own energy plan, calling for continued price controls, rationing, a stiffer gasoline tax to discourage wasteful consumption, reform of utility rates to encourage conservation and other changes. A remark by Robert C. Byrd, D-W.Va., in early February was typical; Byrd called Ford's plan a "sock-it-to-the-consumer" approach. The Democrats argued that Ford's plan would only worsen the recession. They also argued that, without domestic controls, OPEC would be setting energy prices in the United States. They preferred, they said, to have the federal government do it.

In response to Ford's $1 import fee and his threats to raise the fee, Congress voted to rescind for 90 days his authority to levy import fees. But Ford March 4 vetoed the bill. There had been discussions, though, between Ford and congressional leaders. As a result, he announced he would delay his plans to increase the fee by another $2. He also agreed to delay decontrol. The new deadline for Congress to pass the tax measure was May 1, Ford said, because that was when he would decontrol.

Ford made another concession April 30. Instead of immediate decontrol, he agreed to end controls gradually, with the price of "old" oil going up about 4 percent a month over a period of 24 months. "New" oil would remain free of controls. The formal proposal for gradual decontrol wouldn't be made until June, Ford said, so Congress could have more time to work.

By then, the Senate already had passed a major energy bill, but the April 10 action was not what Ford had in mind. Along with emergency powers for the president, the senators had extended EPAA through March 1, 1976. They also had voted to require the president to put a price ceiling on "new" as well as "old" oil. The ceiling of $5.25 would require a price rollback for "new" oil, which was selling for $12 to $14 a barrel. Four attempts on the Senate floor to remove price controls, rather than tighten them, had ended in failure — and by margins of almost 3-1.

In the House, the Ways and Means Committee was working diligently on energy taxes, but its legislation was more similar to the Democratic energy plan than to Ford's. A new chairman, Al Ullman, D-Ore., had found the larger, 37-member panel difficult to control, even with help from the Democratic leadership. But, after weeks of work, the badly divided committee finally finished its bill on May 12. The vote was 19-16 — not the sort of ringing endorsement that supporters of a controversial bill like to take to the floor. Ways and Means called for an extra tax on gasoline of 3 cents a gallon, which would rise gradually to 20 cents if imports went above the 1973 level of 6.67 million barrels a day. They agreed to tax gas-guzzling cars, and to charge excise taxes on industrial use of oil and gas when coal could be used instead. They provided individuals and businesses with tax breaks for insulation, solar equipment and other energy-saving steps. And the committee set import quotas. Ford's windfall profits tax and excise tax on crude oil apparently were dead. No constituency had developed behind the Ford proposals. The Republicans were interested in decontrol, not in increasing taxes. Democrats for the most part worked to continue controls, which in their opinion would avoid the need for a windfall profits tax. Only if the Democrats were unable to stop decontrol could they have reasonably been expected to go along with the tax.

Impending Defeat

The shaky support for the Ways and Means bill prompted Democratic leaders to delay floor action until June, when Congress would return from its Memorial Day recess. Ford's other energy proposals were still in committee.

The president was losing patience. Ford went on national television May 27 to announce an additional $1 fee on imports as of June 1. He also complained about Congress, as he had during his traveling campaign for his energy plan. "February, March, April, May," Ford said, tearing off the pages of a calendar at his side, marking the months since his energy package had been sent to Capitol Hill. "The Congress cannot drift, dawdle and debate forever with the American future." But Ford did not make any moves to end price controls.

When the House returned in June, the members took up the Ways and Means energy tax bill. It was a disaster. The 20-cent gasoline tax was defeated almost 5-1. Even the 3-cent tax lost, 209-187. The tax on "gas guzzlers" was rejected in favor of fines on manufacturers of fuel-inefficient cars. The import quotas were retained, but

Top 12 States Producing Crude Oil

	Thousands of barrels in 1979	Percent of U.S. Production
Texas	980,839	32.5
Alaska	511,327	16.4
Louisiana	413,230	15.9
California	351,926	11.3
Oklahoma	128,441	4.6
Wyoming	124,062	4.0
New Mexico	74,420	2.5
Kansas	53,253	1.8
Florida	47,967	1.5
Michigan	34,589	1.1
Mississippi	34,582	1.1
Colorado	31,652	1.0

Source: Department of Energy

weakened when the House raised the limits. The user taxes were dropped. The House, and thus Congress because tax measures have to originate in the House, rejected the idea of using taxes to discourage energy consumption. Only the "carrots," such as tax credits for insulation, remained.

The demise of the tax plan focused attention on the omnibus legislation drafted by the Senate Interior and House Commerce committees. Oil price controls were an element in that debate, but both panels also reported separate legislation just on oil prices to be sure that EPAA didn't expire Aug. 31, before the omnibus bill had been passed. The EPAA extension that passed July 17 gave Congress more time to modify EPAA controls. Instead of just five days the legislators gave either house 20 days to veto a presidential oil pricing plan. In addition, they added a major new element to the EPAA pricing provisions. A ceiling of $11.28 was placed on the price of a barrel of "new" oil, which was then not under price controls.

However, Ford vetoed the EPAA extension on July 21, saying it allowed "a drift into greater energy dependence."

Jockeying on Decontrol

After months of delay, the president in July finally made a formal proposal to end price controls. His plan called for the price of "old" oil to be lifted gradually over a 30-month period. In an attempt to win support from congressional Democrats, Ford called for a ceiling of $13.50 on the price of "new" oil.

Ford apparently believed that outright decontrol, without a phaseout or price ceilings, would not get through Congress. Though the president could have accomplished decontrol simply by waiting until the Aug. 31 expiration date of EPAA, that would have meant that Ford would have taken the heat for decontrol and rising prices alone. The congressional Democrats would have had a heyday blaming Ford for higher prices and for causing more of the inflation he was trying to whip. Rather than act alone, Ford wanted Congress for his accomplice and was willing to delay decontrol if that was necessary.

The House, however, returned the favor to Ford on July 23, by rejecting his decontrol plan. The resolution of disapproval passed on a 262-167 vote.

After meeting with congressional leaders, Ford July 25 announced a compromise decontrol plan. This time the phaseout was spread over a period of 39 months, not just 30. In addition, Ford lowered to $11.50 the price ceiling on "new" oil and on "old" oil released from the tighter, existing controls during the phaseout.

The House still didn't like Ford's plan. It passed the July 30 veto resolution less handily, though, by a 228-189 vote. The Republicans had picked up more Democratic support for Ford.

The Aug. 31 deadline for EPAA was fast approaching. Congress July 31 passed another EPAA extension, this time through March 1, 1976, and without new price ceilings. It delayed sending the bill to Ford until Aug. 28, to avoid a pocket veto during their August recess.

House Omnibus Bill

In the meantime, the House had been at work on a complex omnibus energy bill that eventually would become the Energy Policy and Conservation Act. Along with a variety of conservation provisions, the legislation, a companion to one passed by the Senate in April, also dealt with price controls.

The newly formed Energy and Power Subcommittee of the House Commerce Committee had drafted the first pricing provisions. Prodded by Robert (Bob) Krueger, D-Texas, the panel in May agreed to end price controls if a windfall profits tax were passed. But the full Commerce Committee on July 9 voted to continue price controls. By just a one-vote margin, a radical proposal was approved that extended existing price controls to "new" oil and set the ceiling price on such oil at $7.50 a barrel. The committee plan was radical because it required a substantial rollback in the price of new oil, then selling for $12 to $14 a barrel.

The omnibus bill was on the House floor for several days in mid-July, during which time the legislators also were approving the EPAA extension with the more widely accepted $11.28 ceiling on "new" oil. They were also rejecting Ford's two proposals for gradual decontrol, which had still higher price ceilings.

The confusion in the House voting was typical of its action on major energy legislation. The two sides — proponents and opponents of decontrol — were so closely divided that the outcome often was in doubt until the last minute.

Krueger, arguing that decontrol would increase production, had tried to restore the subcommittee's decontrol language on July 23, but he lost by 18 votes.

Charles A. Vanik, D-Ohio, had been among those fighting the amendment. "Anybody who supports this amendment is applying for an exit visa from the Congress," he said. To Krueger's claim of more production, fellow Texas Democrat Bob Eckhardt had a rebuttal. "A person can pay me to jump two and a half feet for $5, but he cannot get me to jump six feet for $15. I just cannot do it," said Eckhardt. "Such is analogous to the theory that you can bring in new oil quickly by merely raising the price."

However, later that same afternoon, the House voted to strike all of the pricing provisions from the omnibus bill. The price rollback was just too severe. The vote was 215-199.

But the House wasn't finished. Floor action on the omnibus bill dragged on and on. Two major votes took place before the August recess temporarily stopped action. First, supporters of Ford's second, compromise decontrol plan tried unsuccessfully to add it to the omnibus energy bill. Then Eckhardt and other advocates of continued controls offered their own compromise proposal. They added a third category of hard-to-produce oil that would get the higher price of $10. "Old" oil would still be priced at $5.25, and "new" oil at $7.50. Though the House had rejected a similar plan July 23, when Commerce provisions were struck from the bill, this time the House agreed, voting 218-207 for the amendment. Later it added a fourth category of oil. The first 3,000 barrels of production each day by an independent producer was allowed a price of $11.50 a barrel.

The August recess meant the unfinished bill had to be set aside. The key piece of legislation became the simple EPAA extension, which Ford received Aug. 28. Before vetoing the bill, Ford told Congress that if it went along with the veto, he would then sign a measure extending EPAA for 45 days — instead of the extension of several months that Congress had approved. After heavy lobbying by the White House, the Senate Sept. 10 sustained the veto. Then Congress Sept. 26 sent Ford a temporary extension of EPAA, beginning retroactively as of Sept. 1, and continuing through Nov. 15. After fussing at the legislators and calling their attempt to hold down prices "nonsense," Ford signed the bill.

The House had gone back to work on the omnibus energy bill in September. The members reaffirmed their August decision to require a price rollback for "new" oil and to continue controls on "old" oil. On Sept. 23 the House finally passed the massive bill.

Conferees began work Oct. 1. By mid-November they had agreed to scrap the approach by both houses of mandating "old" and "new" oil prices. Instead they set a single average price for oil of $7.66, which was less than the current average of $8.75. In the conference agreement, the president and his regulators were given flexibility to decide how to price various categories of oil to encourage production. But the average price could not exceed $7.66. This average could be increased annually by the president to reflect inflation or to encourage production — but the combined increase could not exceed 10 percent a year. The president was required to maintain the controls for 39 months after the regulations were in place. The date turned out to be June 1, 1979. After that, the president's pricing power would be discretionary, through Sept. 30, 1981, when EPAA and price control authority would expire.

Though the conferees had reached their agreement in mid-November, putting it into legislative language was expected to take several weeks — beyond the Nov. 15 expiration date of EPAA. So Congress on Nov. 14 passed another extension, through Dec. 15. Ford signed the bill.

The conferees finally filed their report Dec. 9. Not a single Republican conferee signed it.

Compromise Bill Enacted

House Republicans and other opponents of the price controls provisions tried to knock them out of the conference report during floor action. House Minority Leader

Oil and Gas Industry Enjoyed Important Federal Tax Breaks

From 1926 to the mid-1970s, the oil and gas industry enjoyed a generous tax break: the percentage depletion allowance. Two other tax incentives were still in effect in 1981: foreign tax credits and a deduction for intangible drilling costs.

Percentage Depletion

Congress in 1926 enacted percentage depletion to establish a rule-of-thumb measure for depletion (depreciation) in the value of a well as its oil or gas is pumped out. Investment in the resource was considered to be a capital investment. The depletion allowance was set at 27-1/2 percent as a compromise between the Senate's 25 percent and the House's 30 percent. Because the deduction was set at an arbitrary percentage of production, the allowance bore no relation to actual costs and permitted tax-free recovery that in some cases vastly exceeded the amount invested in the property. Producers were allowed to deduct 27-1/2 percent of gross income from taxable income, with a limit on the deduction equal to 50 percent of taxable income.

Among the leading critics of the allowance was President Harry S Truman, who in 1950 said it was the most inequitable of all the tax loopholes. He cited the "shocking example" of one beneficiary who had built up a tax-free income of almost $5 million.

But Truman's efforts were ignored in Congress, which refused throughout the 1950s to modify the allowance despite the efforts of Sens. Paul H. Douglas, D-Ill., John J. Williams, R-Del., and William Proxmire, D-Wis.

Not until 1969 was any dent made in the special privilege accorded the oil and gas industry. The 1969 Tax Reform Act cut the oil and gas depletion allowance to 22 percent.

Skyrocketing oil prices and widespread animosity toward the industry in 1973-74 renewed attacks on the depletion allowance. Voting for the first time on the question since 1926, the House in 1975 went on record against the allowance, 248-163. Though the Senate Finance Committee had deferred action, a floor amendment offered by Edward M. Kennedy, D-Mass., and Ernest F. Hollings, D-S.C., was successful. They won enough votes by continuing the allowance for independent producers. The final agreement phased in a lowered allowance for independents, leaving it at a permanent level of 15 percent by 1984 for the first 1,000 barrels of oil production and the first 6 million cubic feet of gas production. Other producers lost the allowance as of Jan. 1, 1975.

Intangible Costs

The deduction for intangible costs related to oil and gas production was introduced to the tax code through a series of administrative rulings by the Treasury Department. Congress gave its approval to the practice of rapid write-offs of drilling costs when it passed the Revenue Act of 1954.

The deduction allowed the owner to take an immediate tax deduction for "intangible" expenses expenditures — on labor, fuel, power, materials, supplies and tools — associated with drilling and preparing an oil or gas well for pumping. The deduction was not available for "tangible" costs such as expenditures for pipe, tanks and pumps used in an oil or gas rig.

For most construction projects, intangible costs could be deducted, but they had to be spread over the number of years that the building would be used. For intangible drilling costs, in contrast, a full deduction could be taken in the year the expenditures were made.

Foreign Tax Credits

Under existing law, corporations can take a tax credit against their U.S. corporation income taxes for taxes paid to foreign governments in nations where their overseas operations are located. In other words, a U.S.-based corporation could cut the taxes it owed the U.S. government by subtracting the amount of taxes it paid to foreign governments on income from overseas operations.

The practice was sanctioned by the government in the 1950s as an indirect means of providing U.S. aid to the oil-producing countries, particularly Saudi Arabia. By labeling as "taxes" most of the charges assessed foreign companies operating on their land, the producing states cooperated with the U.S. government to increase their total take — but at the expense of the U.S. Treasury instead of the oil companies.

President Jimmy Carter in April 1979 asked Congress to tighten the foreign tax credit, but the proposal never moved beyond the hearings stage.

John J. Rhodes, R-Ariz., told his colleagues that the "name of the game as far as energy is concerned is supply. We do not set a price on petroleum by law if we expect to get an adequate supply." But the move to vote on decontrol was blocked, 215-179. The conference report finally was adopted Dec. 15 on a 236-170 vote that broke down along party lines.

Opponents in the Senate tried to delay the final vote, but lost out when the Senate Dec. 17 adopted the conference report on a 58-40 vote. A leading Republican opponent, Oklahoma's Bartlett, provided an example of the rhetoric common during the final debate when he called the legislation "a hackneyed nostrum, conjured up by the nation's congress of energy alchemists hoping to turn hot air into black gold. It will not work."

Ford, who had opened 1975 with a call for immediate decontrol of oil prices, still had a chance to accomplish his goal. EPAA had expired Dec. 15. If he vetoed the omnibus energy bill, then oil would be free of price controls. If Congress passed another bill, he could also veto that. But Ford, as suggested by his actions throughout the long year, didn't want to decontrol without a majority of Congress on his side — and his Republican ex-colleagues couldn't provide that majority. Ford didn't want to be the sole object of the public's wrath at higher prices. Had he chosen to decontrol, the president would not even have been able to point in defense to a windfall profits tax, because his plan had not even gotten out of congressional committee. Frank Zarb, Ford's chief energy adviser and head of the Federal Energy Administration, was urging the president to sign the legislation. Along with the pricing provisions, it contained an array of emergency powers for the president, including authority to order rationing and to mandate conservation. Ford had been complaining all year that the nation did not have an energy policy and that it was Congress' fault. If the president vetoed the bill at the end of the session then Ford, not Congress, could be blamed for the lack of an energy policy.

Ford signed the bill Dec. 22. Instead of decontrol, he was endorsing a price rollback and at least three and a half more years of control. "This legislation . . . puts into place the first elements of a comprehensive national energy policy," said the president.

Implementing Controls

In 1976 Ford implemented the modified and extended EPAA, as provided in the omnibus bill. To reach the mandated average price of $7.66, Ford and his regulators decided to keep "old" oil priced at about $5.25 a barrel. "New" oil would be priced as high as possible under the rules. Their estimate of the allowable price — about $11.75 a barrel — turned out to be too high. By the year's end, the average exceeded the allowable price, and so the price in 1977 had to be dropped temporarily, to $11.22, to make up for the 1976 overcharge.

Also under EPAA provisions, the Ford administration in 1976 ended price and allocation controls on several refined petroleum products. If either house passed a resolution against a presidential plan within 15 days, then the president was blocked from implementing it. Residual fuel oil, home heating oil, diesel and jet fuel were decontrolled during the year. Decontrol of heating oil stirred up the most controversy. However, a House attempt to bring a disapproval resolution to a vote was blocked, 194-208. The Senate tabled a similar motion, 52-32. The proponents of price controls appeared already to be losing some of their earlier support. Controls remained on gasoline and on crude oil.

Congress, hoping to encourage production, also in 1976 modified the pricing provisions. Oil from stripper wells — those producing less than 10 barrels a day — was exempted from price controls. The provision was included in the Energy Policy and Conservation Act, which extended the life of the Federal Energy Administration until Dec. 31, 1977. The FEA had been created as a temporary agency to cope with 1974-75 fuel shortages.

Carter Takes Over

When Jimmy Carter took office in 1977, the Organization of Petroleum Countries was still setting the world price of oil. But the economies of the developed countries had rebounded from the 1974-75 recession, and the higher prices no longer were hindering consumption. In the United States, a two-year decline in average consumption — prompted by the embargo and price hikes — had ended in 1976, and oil use was expected to go even higher in 1977. Imports of petroleum, it turned out, reached an all-time high that year. Officials were worried about the squeeze on world oil supplies. A Central Intelligence Agency report released in April warned that further competition for oil might develop by 1985, when the agency said the Soviet Union could become an importer, instead of an exporter, of oil. Faced with this situation, Carter made energy a top priority for his administration.

On April 18 Carter went on national television to tell the country about his energy plan. Implementing it, he said, would be the "moral equivalent of war." A major principle endorsed by Carter was that "prices should generally reflect the true replacement cost of energy."

"We are only cheating ourselves if we make energy artificially cheap and use more than we can really afford," Carter said.

Two days later, Carter addressed a joint session of Congress and provided more details about his overall energy plan. The oil pricing proposals were a new combination of old ideas.

Even though he didn't want energy to be "artificially cheap," Carter didn't call for an end to oil price controls. He said he wanted the price of "new" oil to be raised gradually, so that by 1980 the price would equal the 1977 world price plus inflation. "Old" oil would stay under controls.

Another Try at Taxes

Though continuing controls, Carter wanted consumers to be made aware that oil had become more valuable in the 1970s. To do so, he asked Congress for an excise tax, at the wellhead, equal to the difference between domestic and world — or decontrolled — prices. At the time, domestic oil averaged about $8.60 a barrel, while imports cost $13 to $15 a barrel. Revenues from the tax would be returned to the public through the income tax system. Ford also had wanted taxes to discourage consumption. Another signal to consumers Carter sought was a higher gasoline tax that would be imposed gradually, five cents at a time starting in 1979, if gasoline consumption continued to increase. It was similar to the ill-fated proposal made by the Ways and Means Committee in 1975. Still another tax sought by Carter was a user tax on large industrial consumers of oil and gas to encourage them to convert to coal.

The first stop for Carter's various tax proposals was the House Ways and Means Committee. Displaying a longer memory than Carter, the panel killed the extra gasoline tax, retaining the existing four-cent-a-gallon federal tax. But the committee did agree to the industrial user tax, with exemptions, and to the wellhead tax, which became known as the "crude oil equalization tax," or COET, for short. Carter also had asked for a tax on gas-guzzling cars, which the committee approved, along with a variety of energy tax credits. The legislation was reported July 13.

Independents vs. Majors: The Fight Over Taxes

As House and Senate conferees discussed the windfall profits tax in early 1980 — a time when oil companies logically should have been making their final pitch against the tax — the industry instead found itself deeply divided over how the tax should be written.

On one side were the major companies. On the other were most independent producers, who don't refine or retail oil. Each side wanted the other to pay more of the tax. The contest ended in a draw, but the fight preceding it was fierce.

The major companies attacked as "a special deal" the valuable tax exemption voted by the Senate for the first 1,000 barrels a day of oil production. Small independent producers would benefit most from that exemption.

"Neither the integrated companies [majors] nor the independents are disadvantaged. Thus neither needs a special deal," Shell Oil Co. said in a letter to its stockholders and royalty owners.

But the independents contended they deserved the exemption because they drill most wells and, unlike the major companies, can't depend on other enterprises to generate capital.

Legislators who voted against the exemption would be "voting the independents out of existence in favor of the majors," charged C. John Miller, president of the Independent Petroleum Association of America (IPAA). "A vote against the exemption will be seen as a vote for the major international oil companies and against greater domestic production."

'Most Serious Rupture'

The two groups of oil producers had differed in the past, but not so seriously — or so publicly.

"This is the most serious rupture I'm aware of," said Miller at a press conference he called Jan. 16 to denounce lobbying by the major companies against the exemption.

The Carter administration also was involved, siding, for once, with the majors. Officials said the exemption would not lead to additional oil production. A Treasury Department position paper called the exemption "unneeded relief for a politically influential group of persons."

The split within the industry loomed over the windfall tax conferees. "This is the guts of the conference," said Rep. Sam Gibbons, D-Fla.

In a way, the conferees put themselves in the position of having to choose between the two groups when they set $227 billion as the revenue goal for the bill. The conferees had two principal ways they could tighten the Senate tax to reach their revenue goal: increasing the tax on the major companies or watering down the $57 billion Senate exemption for independents.

"Once that circle is drawn, then the push and shove starts about how you slice the pie and who gets the exemptions," said Miller, calling the situation "deplorable."

Traditionally, the independents have been more successful than the major companies in dealing with Congress. They have been effective in handing out campaign contributions, and the national trade associations of independents call on local oil producers to lobby individual congressmen.

But their best advertisement is that they are not "big oil."

"The major companies have a bad image, which has in large part prompted this tax," said Finance Chairman Russell B. Long, D-La.

'Mom and Pop' Millionaires

While the major companies are known for their huge profits, the independents are thought of as "Mom and Pop" operations — despite the fact that anyone selling 1,000 barrels of oil a day is usually a multimillionaire. They have been called "the sentimental favorites of the oil industry."

Part of the political appeal of the Senate provision aiding independents was that it also would give a tax exemption to royalty holders who leased land to independents for drilling. Long noted that the numerous royalty owners would be upset if they lost that advantage.

"That's the sort of thing that makes a guy want to go and take his shotgun down off the wall, load it with buckshot and come at politicians," Long said.

Even legislators who seldom vote with the industry voted for the independents. When the Senate voted 53-41 for the independents' tax exemption, the winning side included Dale Bumpers, D-Ark., George McGovern, D-S.D., and others who rarely sided with the industry.

The House never voted on the independents' exemption. But in the early weeks of 1980, two freshmen from Texas, Democrat Kent Hance and Republican Tom Loeffler, signed 170 cosponsors on a bill embracing the Senate exemption.

The major companies appreciated the independent's political strength. Even after the sharp attacks by IPAA's Miller, the major firms refused to directly criticize the independents.

"We're not picking a fight," said John Grasser of Sun Oil Co. "We just think if you exempt them, you should give the majors the same treatment."

The major companies contended privately that the independents started the fight by asking for special treatment. Miller had his own opinion about who was to blame. "If the major oil companies had fought as hard against the tax as they did against the independent exemption, we would not have as bad a bill as we do," he said.

Ad-Hoc Committee in House

However, the Ways and Means bill was not headed for the House floor. The Democratic leadership had set up a special ad-hoc energy committee because the Carter plan had fallen within the jurisdiction of five House committees. Once each had passed the section of the bill that was its responsibility, the legislation was to go to the ad-hoc panel, which could develop amendments to be offered on the floor. That way, reasoned Speaker Thomas P. O'Neill Jr., D-Mass., the package had a better chance of passing. O'Neill set strict, tight deadlines for action by the five committees and the ad-hoc committee.

The gasoline tax was revived by the Ad-Hoc Energy Committee. Dan Rostenkowski, D-Ill., a senior member of Ways and Means, made the proposal, which won on a 22-18 vote. None of the committee's Republicans voted for the tax. Different from Carter's proposal, the committee's plan imposed a two-cent-a-gallon tax in 1978 and added another two cents in 1979. The new tax revenues would be used in the following way: two cents for energy research and a strategic oil reserve; one and a half cents for car-pooling and mass transit programs, and one-half cent to go to state transportation programs, such as highways. The four-cent tax would be in addition to the four-cent tax already flowing into the Highway Trust Fund, which helps build and maintain the nation's highways.

The ad-hoc committee endorsed the other Carter tax proposals that had been recommended by Ways and Means. The Commerce Committee, which oversaw oil price controls, made no recommendations on oil controls, concentrating instead on natural gas pricing.

The package of energy legislation went to the House floor in early August. The rule governing debate limited floor amendments, but the gasoline tax proposal by the ad-hoc committee was among the authorized amendments. The rule also required that the package of bills be kept together, with a final up-or-down House vote on the package.

The gasoline tax proposal reached the floor Aug. 4 when the ad-hoc committee submitted its controversial proposal for a tax increase. But James J. Howard, D-N.J., chairman of the Public Works Subcommittee on Surface Transportation, made an alternative gasoline tax proposal.

Howard and his panel had spoken out earlier about the need to shore up the Highway Trust Fund. Inflation had boosted construction and maintenance costs, and many of the nation's highways were deteriorating. Howard said there were 105,000 unsafe bridges that needed to be repaired. His substitute proposal was to increase the gasoline tax by another five cents, on top of the existing four-cent tax. However, instead of spreading the revenues among several energy programs as the ad-hoc committee proposed, Howard wanted half the money to be channeled into the Highway Trust Fund and the other half to mass transit programs. Unlike the ad-hoc panel and Carter, who stressed the energy conservation that would result from the extra gasoline tax, Howard emphasized the need for the revenues to fix highways and, secondarily it seemed, to aid mass transit.

Surprisingly, the Carter administration supported Howard's amendment. The Democratic leadership and Democrats on the ad-hoc committee had stuck their necks out for the unpopular tax that Carter had requested. But instead of fighting for their proposal, and benefiting from the support of the leaders, Carter backed the five-cent tax amendment made by a subcommittee chairman not even involved in the drafting of the energy legislation.

Liberal Democrats opposed to raising prices with a tax, members from rural areas skeptical of benefits for them from mass transit, Republicans long critical of additional taxes — all of these groups joined to reject overwhelmingly the Howard amendment. The vote was 82-339.

With their strength thus affirmed, opponents of the ad-hoc committee's proposal for an additional four-cent tax insisted on a record vote. As it had in the summer of 1975, the higher gasoline tax went down by the widest of margins. The vote was 52-370.

Though Republicans led an effort to knock out the crude oil equalization tax, they didn't have quite enough votes. A procedural move designed to delete the tax was rejected, 203-219. The final vote on the energy package, on Aug. 5, was 244-177 in favor.

Carter's approach to oil pricing — through continued controls and new taxes — had done remarkably well in the House. Rejection of the gasoline tax was a major defeat, but the survival of the crude oil equalization tax and the industrial user tax was a major accomplishment. Carter's success depended on full support from the Democratic leadership. Of particular help were the decisions to establish a special committee, to set strict deadlines for action and to treat the package as one bill.

Senate Approach

The Senate, however, was a different body. Unlike the House, which traditionally follows rules and directions from its leadership, the Senate is more free-wheeling in its operation. With only 100 members, instead of 435, the Senate can usually afford not to restrict debate or amendments. The leadership also wasn't accustomed to setting deadlines for committees.

In addition to these institutional differences, the Senate also had an independent-minded tax-writing committee. Its chairman, Democrat Russell B. Long from the oil state of Louisiana, was naturally inclined toward the views of the industry. He wanted oil companies to have enough income to encourage additional exploration and production. Long's views were shared by the Republicans and many of the Democrats on his Finance Committee.

Though Long had endorsed the crude oil equalization tax, he insisted that the revenues be channeled toward the production of more energy, instead of back to consumers. "Send your money to Washington, and we'll send it back having deducted postage and handling expenses," Long said, scoffing at the rebate plan. But Long's committee didn't like even a tax tilted toward the oil industry. They killed the tax. The panel also rejected the tax on industrial users of oil and gas and the tax on gas-guzzling cars. Though the senators on the committee weren't inclined toward additional taxes on industry to begin with, their attitude toward Carter's proposals was reinforced by the administration's failure to check with the committee before writing the energy legislation — which depended so heavily on taxes.

On the floor, Sen. Howard M. Metzenbaum, D-Ohio, managed to win approval of a limited industrial user tax. Only companies using boilers originally designed to burn coal would be taxed for using oil or gas instead. The tax wouldn't affect 89 percent of existing boilers not capable of using coal.

The Senate finally passed the energy tax bill Oct. 31. The next step was a conference.

Separate conferences were held of each of the five parts of the energy package. Bills dealing with energy conservation, coal conversion and utility rates were the first dealt with by conference committees, and the differences between the two houses were quickly resolved in October and November. The fourth part, natural gas pricing, proved to be the hang-up. The conference committee on gas met Dec. 2, but made no progress. On Dec. 7 the tax conferees finally got together, but Long insisted that the natural gas pricing dispute would have to be resolved first — before the tax conferees met again. Long prevailed.

Not until July 13, 1978, did the tax conferees meet again. Their gathering was merely symbolic, though, as Carter headed for an economic summit in Bonn where energy was expected to be the major topic. The tax conferees wanted to provide some evidence that the United States was working on its oil problem, but the session accomplished little else. At the summit, Carter pledged that U.S. oil prices would equal world levels by the end of 1980. But it appeared that his plan for reaching that goal — the crude oil equalization tax — was dead.

In March, Long had said, "The White House is beating a dead horse when they talk about that [crude oil equalization] tax." He said it would not pass the Senate in 1978 "under any imaginable set of circumstances."

Two days after the Sept. 27 Senate vote on natural gas pricing, the tax conferees met again — as Long had wanted. But they made most of their progress on Oct. 3 and 4. Most of the attention was focused on the various energy tax credits for industry and individuals. The industrial user tax was deleted when the House conferees accepted a package of provisions. The package did retain the gas-guzzler tax, which would begin with 1980 model cars that used excessive amounts of fuel.

Tax Program Fails

The Carter oil pricing program of taxes and continued controls was officially dead. The controls, however, stayed in place under the 1975 amendments to and extension of EPAA.

The tax bill reached the Senate floor Oct. 12, but a filibuster by James Abourezk, D-S.D., delayed action. Even after cloture was invoked Oct. 14, thus limiting debate, Abourezk continued to use delaying tactics, such as quorum calls. The House, in the meantime, was waiting for the Senate to pass this last conference report so the five bills could go before the House as a package. About 12:15 a.m., Oct. 15, Abourezk finally wound down. The tax conference report passed, 60-17. Later that morning, at 7:15, the House voted on the overall energy package, approving it 231-168. (Box, filibuster-by-amendment, p. 50)

Carter Faces Dilemma

The crude oil equalization tax had failed. OPEC in December 1978 announced that oil prices would rise by 14.5 percent over the next several months — thus widening the gap between domestic and world prices. Inflation was a continuing problem. As 1979 began Carter was no closer than before to reaching his goal of raising domestic prices to world levels.

Particularly troublesome was balancing the conflicting goals of raising oil prices and controlling inflation. "We are on the horns of a terrible dilemma," said Alfred E. Kahn, Carter's chief inflation fighter. Reconciling the two aims was "tearing us apart," Kahn said.

Domestic prices had been rising, even under controls. The EPAA rules allowed increases of up to 10 percent a year, and some domestic oil wasn't covered by controls. But the biggest change in domestic pricing rules could come June 1, 1979, when the mandatory controls became discretionary. If the president wanted to, he could begin decontrol then. But even the discretionary controls would end Sept. 30, 1981, when EPAA expired.

However, Carter was reluctant to use those new powers to decontrol because of what his administration called the "massive transfer of wealth" from consumers to the oil industry.

But administration officials also saw advantages to ending controls. They expected a slowdown in growth in oil demand, an increase in domestic production of hard-to-get oil, improvement in the competitiveness of alternative energy sources, such as solar, and speedier adaptation of the nation's houses, cars and factories to expensive energy.

Carter's most logical choice appeared to be gradual price increases, coupled with some sort of tax on the oil industry's extra income from domestic production. However, Carter had not done at all well on his most recent oil tax proposal, in 1977-78.

As Carter and his aides searched for a solution in the first few months of 1979, the administration was more attentive to Congress than it had been two years earlier. The president met several times with congressional leaders. A key question was whether any price increases should be allowed prior to passage of the tax — or saved for afterwards, as a reward. "If we had decontrol first, I think Congress would be reluctant to pass a tax," said Sen. Edward M. Kennedy, D-Mass. Senate Finance Chairman Long said he thought the tax would have a better chance of passing if controls were lifted first.

The Choice: Decontrol and Tax

On April 5 Carter announced his decision. Domestic oil prices would be decontrolled gradually, starting June 1, a move Carter called a "painful step." To accompany decontrol, the president asked Congress for a tax that would take a share of the oil industry's extra income as domestic prices rose to world levels. Carter labeled it a "windfall profits" tax.

At the time, U.S. oil sold for an average of $9.50 a barrel, while the world price was about $16 a barrel. Carter wanted the tax to take 50 percent of that $6.50 price increase. However, by the time Carter's tax plan could have gotten through Congress, the world price would have more than doubled.

"As surely as the sun will rise," Carter said, the oil industry will "fight to keep the profits which they have not earned. Unless you speak out, they will have more influence on the Congress than you do."

Kahn, the inflation adviser, urged consumers to "get out there and fight like hell for that tax."

Carter wanted to use the tax revenues to help low-income families with high energy costs, to aid mass transit and to establish an "energy security fund" that would finance development of new energy sources, such as synthetic fuels from coal, solar and new hydroelectric power facilities. Later, in July, after rising prices had boosted potential tax revenues, Carter beefed up his proposals for synthetic fuels development.

Carter's plan was quickly criticized by consumer groups because it ended controls, and by the oil industry, because it called for an oil tax.

Congress Involved

Though Carter appeared to be making a bold move by decontrolling prices, he later moved to share that responsibility with Congress. "This is not a decision I made," Carter told reporters April 30. "I am complying with an existing law." He was referring to the 1975 extension of EPAA.

Carter's new attitude apparently was in response to the clamor on Capitol Hill to extend controls. However, one longtime supporter of controls, Senate Energy Chairman Jackson, had admitted even before Carter's April decision that his side couldn't stop decontrol in the Senate. "We don't have the votes," Jackson said.

Prospects were slightly better in the House, although Speaker O'Neill, who favored controls, said, "I can't conceive of it [an extension of oil price controls] being enacted into law." That didn't stop Connecticut Democrat Toby Moffett and others from trying, though. In Commerce Committee action, they came within one vote of attaching an oil price control amendment to the annual authorization for the Energy Department. The 21-21 vote on May 2 was a surprising show of strength for the proponents of price controls.

As waiting lines for gasoline became more common across the nation, those favoring controls won another victory. The House Democratic Caucus, whose decisions don't bind Democrats, voted 2-1 on May 24 in favor of continued price controls.

But the threat of a potentially messy fight over oil pricing prompted the Democratic leadership to keep the authorization bill — and Moffett's amendment — off the House floor until October. By then any momentum the control advocates had in the spring had disappeared, along with the waiting lines for gasoline. The amendment lost, 2-1.

Windfall Profits Tax

Those unhappy with Carter's plan in late spring had another arena in which to fight — the tax-writing committees. Liberal Democrats vowed to stiffen the proposed windfall profits tax. They were countered, as could be expected, by Republicans who favored no tax — or at least a weaker tax and a return of revenues to the industry for exploration and production, a scheme known as a "plowback."

The Ways and Means Committee drafted its tax proposal in early June. Instead of a 50 percent rate, as proposed by Carter, they set a rate of 70 percent, which would be applied to the difference between the controlled price of oil, known as the base price, and the selling price after decontrol. Moderate Democrats on the panel had helped liberals increase the tax rate. Then they teamed up with Republicans to ease the tax on new discoveries by lowering the rate to 50 percent. The Republicans had no success winning a "plowback."

On the floor, however, the Ways and Means proposal ran into a substitute cleverly crafted by two Ways and Means members from oil-producing states.

James R. Jones, D-Okla., and W. Henson Moore, R-La., wanted to ease the tax on new discoveries and hard-to-get oil. But they recognized the sentiment in the House against the oil industry. So the two legislators came up with a tax rate of 60 percent, instead of Carter's proposal for 50 percent and that allowed them to argue that their plan would bring in more revenues than Carter's original proposal in the short run. In the long run, though, the Jones-Moore proposal saved the oil industry billions because the tax on newly discovered oil ended in 1990. Both Carter and Ways and Means would have continued the tax indefinitely. Jones and Moore also raised the base prices on oil that was expensive to extract, thus reducing the tax bite.

Jones and Moore were victorious on a 236-183 vote. Final passage June 28 was by voice vote.

The House still hadn't considered how to spend revenues from the tax. Ways and Means Chairman Ullman had chosen to separate the tax from the expected fight over spending as interest groups sought their share and congressional committees protected their jurisdiction. But his panel was a long way from deciding what to do with the income. Hearings hadn't been held and, in fact, the panel was never to vote on the question.

Friendly 'Briar Patch'

In the meantime, though, the windfall tax would be considered by the Senate Finance Committee. Back in March, Rep. Bob Eckhardt, D-Texas, had called that panel "a briar patch the oil companies might well want to be thrown into." The prospect of the Senate's weakening the tax also had been a major concern for the House. "We've got to make it tougher in order to have something to deal with, with Russell Long," said Sam Gibbons, D-Fla., before he and his Ways and Means colleagues marked up the tax. Senators were also wary of the tax's fate in Finance. "When they get through plowing it back, they will have plowed it under," said Jackson of the panel.

Carter was also worried that the Senate would substantially weaken the tax. At a news conference in late July, he warned of a "massive struggle to gut" the tax bill. "I cannot prevail along here in Washington with an oil lobby working quietly, unless the American people let their voice be heard," Carter said.

Long, whose name usually is preceded by the word "powerful," was resigned to having a windfall profits tax. "I have no doubt if we don't pass a tax, the president is going to withdraw his decontrol plan," Long told the Finance Committee in September, when markup began in earnest after the August congressional recess. "It's like getting old. When you think about the alternative, you don't feel so bad about it." Later, Long added, "By the time we come out of conference with the House, we're going to have a substantial tax."

The Finance Committee spent much of its time arguing over what tax credits to provide for energy production. They considered that to be "spending" the new tax revenues. When the tax itself was considered, Long found much sympathy for weakening the levy. In the bill completed Oct. 25, several types of oil were exempted from the tax, including oil discovered after 1978 and most hard-to-get oil. Oil from wells producing as of mid-1973, known as "old" oil under the pricing system, would be taxed at a rate of 75 percent. For oil from wells that began producing between 1973 and 1978, the tax rate would be 60 percent. Independent producers were given special treatment for their "stripper" wells, which were exempted from the tax. The Finance Committee also agreed to phase out the tax once the government had collected 90 percent of anticipated revenues.

Revenue Estimates

Tax bills usually are compared in terms of the revenue they will raise. The rising world oil prices meant that the oil industry's income was expected to swell by about $1 trillion by 1990, according to estimates by the Joint Tax Committee and the Treasury Department. Once state and local taxes and royalty payments were subtracted, the additional income was reduced to $893 billion. Once federal income taxes were paid — about $388 billion — the industry would be left with about $506 billion. Of that, $138 billion would go to the government under the Senate Finance Committee's version of the windfall profits tax. That's an overall tax rate of about 27 percent.

In comparison, the House-passed bill would bring in about $273 billion, for a tax rate of about 54 percent. The overall rate from the administration proposal was calculated at about 58 percent, and revenues estimated at $296 billion.

However, the analysts who made the revenue estimates emphasized they were very rough and would vary widely depending on assumptions about future oil prices and economic growth.

"Each estimate appears to capture some aspect of reality," said James Wetzler, chief economist for the Joint Tax Committee, describing a range of revenue projections made by his staff. "We have trouble coming up with anything more exact. . . . The real world is probably somewhere between the extremes."

When the Finance bill reached the Senate floor in mid-November, a group of Republicans and oil-state Democrats tried to reduce the tax rate on "old" oil from 75 percent to 60 percent. They lost on a 32-58 vote. After Thanksgiving, another move that had the effect of reducing revenues was more successful. On a 53-41 vote, the Senate gave independent producers an exemption from the windfall profits tax for the first 1,000 barrels they produced each day. Independent producers do not refine or transport oil, but engage solely in exploration and production. The amendment, sponsored by Lloyd Bentsen, D-Texas, reduced anticipated revenues by $10 billion, but supporters said it would lead to increased production.

Tax on 'New' Oil

Two Finance members, Bill Bradley, D-N.J., and John H. Chafee, R-R.I., proposed stiffening the tax rate on oil from wells tapped between 1973 and 1978. Long called the proposal "confiscatory." When Long's motion to table the amendment failed, 39-58, he and other oil-state senators threatened to filibuster. They ended up meeting for four days with Senate leaders and sponsors of the amendment. Eventually, a vote on the Bradley-Chafee amendment was permitted as part of an agreement that allowed votes on several weakening amendments. The "new" oil amendment was approved, 58-35. It increased anticipated revenues to a total of $150.5 billion by 1990.

The Senate prolonged the life of the tax when it adopted an amendment by Daniel Patrick Moynihan, D-N.Y., that postponed the phaseout of the tax. Under the amendment, the phaseout would begin when 90 percent of $210 billion — $189 billion — had been collected.

Retail Gasoline Prices In United States and Abroad

	Regular		Premium		Diesel Fuel	
	Price[1]	Tax	Price[1]	Tax	Price[1]	Tax
United States						
1973	40	12	44	12	35	13
1976	59	12	64	12	51	13
1977	63	12	69	12	53	13
1978	63	13	70	13	54	14
1979	86	13	93	13	79	14
1980	122	14	130	14	112	15
France[2]						
1973	114	77	123	82	79	47
1976	165	91	178	96	115	56
1977	199	121	215	129	130	65
1978	225	149	244	159	147	84
1979	249	162	268	172	174	95
1980	294	168	314	179	221	103
Italy[2]						
1973	80	61	85	62	44	28
1976	138	91	145	94	75	31
1977	221	159	230	165	71	20
1978	221	159	230	165	76	21
1979	221	159	230	165	79	21
1980	338	216	345	217	152	31
United Kingdom						
1973	67	42	70	42	67	42
1976	140	70	144	71	116	51
1977	156	84	160	84	158	78
1978	141	72	145	73	158	78
1979	203	87	207	89	226	98
1980	247	119	251	119	260	121
West Germany						
1973	150	109	167	110	151	103
1976	194	113	207	114	189	106
1977	189	113	201	115	188	106
1978	195	115	204	115	192	109
1979	209	115	219	117	209	126
1980	253	123	264	123	253	117

1. Prices in U.S. cents per U.S. gallons. Price column includes taxes. Converted at Feb. 29, 1980 exchange rates. 1973 prices for October; all others for July.
2. Government price ceilings in effect.

Source: Central Intelligence Agency

The most controversial amendment proposed extending the tax to newly discovered oil, oil produced by tertiary recovery methods, such as chemical injection, and heavy oil. These types of oil and oil production had been exempted by the Finance Committee. The tax rate proposed by the amendment was 20 percent, with anticipated additional revenues at $25.7 billion by 1990.

The amendment was offered by Bradley, Majority Leader Robert Byrd and Abraham Ribicoff, D-Conn. Long tried to table the amendment Dec. 12, as Energy Secretary Charles W. Duncan Jr. and Treasury Secretary G. William Miller watched from the Senate gallery. Carter had urged Senate Democrats to stiffen the tax bite of the committee bill. Long's motion was rejected, 44-53, indicating support for the amendment.

Long and others began to filibuster against the amendment. Their opponents sought cloture, but fell seven votes short of the 60 needed to limit debate. Leaders of the two sides moved to Byrd's office to negotiate.

The discussions focused on the proposed tax on newly discovered oil. "You cannot have a windfall profit on something you have not found," Robert Dole, R-Kan., explained later on the Senate floor. But supporters of the tax said rapidly escalating oil prices would give the oil industry more than enough for exploration and production even after a tax. Aiding their cause was Saudi Arabia's announcement Dec. 13 that it was raising prices by 33 percent, a move seen as paving the way for further OPEC price hikes at a scheduled Dec. 17 meeting.

A second cloture vote failed, this time by four votes.

A third cloture vote, in as many days, was held on Dec. 14. Again, the Democratic leadership was four votes short. Byrd warned that by Monday, Dec. 17, he would have the necessary votes in hand.

The negotiations reached a new stage after the third cloture vote. Both sides were tired, and the prospect of a successful cloture move on Dec. 17 tempered the tenacity of Dole and his allies. A new compromise emerged. The tax on new discoveries would be 10 percent, instead of 20 percent as proposed, and the base price would be $20, instead of $17. The amendment would add $23.4 billion to revenues anticipated in the next decade, making $178 billion the total expected from the Senate bill.

The amendment was adopted 52-38. The Senate passed the bill on Dec. 17, by a 74-24 vote.

Search for Compromise

House and Senate conferees got to work two days after the Senate vote, hoping to make some progress before Congress left for the holidays. The House went to conference even though its members never had voted on how to spend the tax revenues. Unhappy with the Carter administration's proposed energy tax credits, the Ways and Means panel had not completed action. In contrast, the Senate bill contained a raft of energy credits expected to cost the government $61.8 billion by 1990.

In terms of revenues raised, the conferees faced two vastly different bills. The House measure was expected to bring in $227 billion in revenue in the next decade, while the Senate bill would raise $178 billion. Two other major differences were the treatment of new discoveries and independent producers. The Senate taxed newly discovered oil at a rate of only 10 percent, while the House rate was about 50 percent. The Senate exempted the first 1,000 barrels of production a day by independents, but the House gave independents no special treatment. Still

a third area of disagreement was when the tax would end. The House bill ended the tax on new discoveries in 1990, but continued the tax on oil found before 1979 until those wells ran dry. The Senate, instead of setting a date to end the tax, used a maximum revenue total of $214 billion. Congressional economists estimated that figure would be reached in 1994, if oil prices increased by 2 percent a year plus inflation. But a more rapid increase in prices would mean that the windfall tax would stop being levied long before 1994.

Following a long tradition of congressional conferences, the conferees handled the problem of differing revenue totals by splitting the difference down the middle. The same method had been used by conferees in 1926 to set the oil depletion allowance. The conferees saved until January the trickier problem of how to raise that amount. Dole likened the order of decision making to "getting your dinner before you read the menu." But Long said he agreed to the quick decision because he assumed the figure would end up there anyway.

When they resumed meeting in mid-January, the conferees had to decide how they would reach the $227 billion figure. The choice appeared to be between deleting the Senate's exemption for independents, a move that would increase revenues by $57 billion, or stiffening the tax rate on new production, which was 10 percent in the Senate bill.

Even though the House had voted a 60 percent tax rate on newly discovered oil, the conferees opted to fight for a lower tax rate on new discoveries instead of an exemption for independents. "Thirty percent is as high as we ought to go" on new discoveries, Ullman urged his colleagues on Ways and Means.

The reversal was not missed by Long. "How can the House be arguing for 30 percent when they voted in committee and on the floor for a rate of 60 to 70 percent?" he asked. The Carter administration also had changed its position, though the president had fought against having the rate on new discoveries reduced even from 70 to 60 percent when the bill was on the House floor. When asked by senators about the switch, Assistant Treasury Secretary Donald C. Lubick replied, "We've gotten true religion. We want to promote development of new sources of energy. We've simply adopted your view that the best place for incentives is on new discoveries."

Agreement

The conferees finally reached agreement on the tax structure on Jan. 22 and 23, after several hours of negotiations. For most of that time, the conferees were holed up privately, with the House and Senate members meeting in separate rooms. Staff members shuttled between the two groups, carrying compromise proposals. In all, about 30 different possible solutions were put before the conferees.

In the end, both sides could claim victory. On new discoveries by all producers, the tax rate was kept at 30 percent, as the House preferred. But the independents won a special tax rate on part of their production, as the Senate preferred. Instead of a tax rate of 70 percent on oil from wells in production before 1979, which was the rate for major companies, the rate for independents would be 50 percent on their first 1,000 barrels a day of production. Instead of a rate of 60 percent on production from stripper wells, the rate for independents would be 50 percent.

Depending on the type of oil, the conferees set a range of base prices from which to compute the tax. The base

— from $12.81 to $16.55 a barrel — would be adjusted annually to reflect inflation.

Of the extra $50 billion needed to bring total revenues from the Senate bill up to the $227 billion compromise, less than half — $22.5 billion — was to come from the independents. That meant the tax fell heaviest on oil currently under production by the major companies.

For most of February, the conferees dickered over how to end the tax and what tax credits to approve. They finished work Feb. 27 and filed the conference report March 7.

The conferees decided to phase out the tax over a three-year period, either at the end of 1990 or, if it took longer to reach the $227 billion figure, at the end of 1993. If oil prices went up more than 2 percent a year plus inflation, the tax could raise billions more than $227 billion by 1990. In addition, future Congresses could vote to extend the tax beyond the scheduled phaseout.

Tax credits were voted for homeowners installing equipment powered by the sun, wind or heat from the earth, and for companies using or producing exotic types of energy or tapping waste heat.

Instead of earmarking the windfall tax revenues for energy programs as Carter wanted, the conferees decided to put most of the money into the general revenue fund, to be spent by the 96th and future Congresses. They did offer suggestions for spending the money, but their outline didn't bind future legislators. They asked that 60 percent of the revenues be used for income tax cuts for individuals and corporations, 25 percent for aid to the poor and 15 percent for government grants, loans and programs to save or produce energy.

The conferees inserted in the bill a fiscal 1981 authorization for $3.1 billion in fuel assistance for low-income families. To qualify, an average family of four would have to have an annual income below about $11,600.

When the conference report reached the House floor March 13, opponents tried to return it to conference. But they failed, 185-227. Then the House endorsed the report on a 302-107 vote.

Opponents in the Senate also tried to derail the legislation by asking for additional committee hearings. But the Senate rejected their motion, 35-61. The landmark legislation was cleared on a 66-31 vote.

Finance Chairman Long called the tax "the price we have to pay in order to have decontrol." He continued, "Those who have to pay the tax can afford it. You're not going to see anybody applying for welfare because he had to pay this tax."

But another oil-state senator, David L. Boren, D-Okla., called the act a "tragic mistake." He told the Senate, "We will have more taxes and more government instead of more oil."

Shared Accomplishment

For Carter, the victory came at an opportune time, just after he lost two presidential primaries in New York and Connecticut. "It's good news for the whole country, and I think also good news for the whole world," Carter told Senate leaders in a telephone call, with reporters looking on.

There were two ways to look at the outcome of the second major fight over oil pricing in 1977-80 — the first fight being the 1975 struggle between Ford and Congress.

Decontrol and the windfall profits tax could be seen as a major accomplishment for Carter. The president had

seized the initiative. He, not Congress, had taken the political risk of decontrolling oil and raising prices. Otherwise, the traumas of 1979-80 — waiting lines for gasoline, the doubling of oil prices, record oil company profits, double-digit inflation — could have revitalized the efforts to continue controls. Carter also had recognized the need to rectify the inequity of the transfer of billions of dollars from consumers to the oil industry and had won passage of the windfall profits tax to meet that need.

But decontrol and the tax also could be viewed as the culmination of several years of debate in Congress. As early as 1973, the House had been concerned about windfall profits. As for decontrol, it was Congress that had voted in 1975 to end mandatory controls as of June 1979, and discretionary controls in October 1981. Carter had at first sought new taxes and continued price controls. According to this second view then, Congress was the dominant force in 1977-80, with the president following the legislators' lead.

NATURAL GAS PRICING: THE FIGHT FOR DECONTROL

The courts, as much as Congress, were responsible for the natural gas pricing system in effect for most of the 1970s. The 1938 Natural Gas Act had been the first major gas regulation law, setting out broad principles for the Federal Power Commission to follow. But the commission's interpretation of congressional intent was challenged almost every step of the way, and many of the cases went all the way to the Supreme Court.

The most important court decision ranked with the 1938 act in setting gas pricing policy. By siding with the state of Wisconsin against the Phillips Petroleum Co., the Supreme Court in 1954 clarified the right and responsibility of the FPC to regulate the price of all gas sold outside of the producing state. The controls kept gas inexpensively priced in the 1960s and most of the 1970s. The result was rapidly rising demand for the clean-burning, convenient fuel.

But the two different markets for gas — one regulated (interstate) and one free of controls (intrastate) — exacerbated a situation that probably would have developed anyway in the 1970s: demand exceeding available supply. U.S. consumption of natural gas began to outpace discoveries of new supplies in the late 1960s and early 1970s. By 1973 annual gas production had begun to decline. Those who paid the highest price got the scarce supplies. In the case of natural gas, only those in the intrastate market were able to offer higher prices — prices often triple or more those allowed in the controlled interstate market. Rising oil prices in 1974 only heightened the demand for the lower priced gas, but adequate supplies just weren't available in the interstate market. Even FPC moves to allow higher prices didn't help. A cold winter in 1976-77 forced job layoffs and school closings in the Midwest and on the East Coast.

The legislators who favored price controls had been arguing for years that government intervention was necessary to protect consumers and to curb the monopolistic nature of the gas industry. Among their numbers in the 1960s and 1970s were key committee chairmen and Democratic leaders in the House and Senate. When deregulation advocates had had the upper hand in the 1950s, proponents of controls had benefited from a key veto and the taint of scandal on the deregulators.

The old arguments, though, weren't enough by the mid-1970s, as shortages and price differentials pointed up the flaws in the controls and the dual market system. Only with the help of a Democratic president and tenacious fighting by veteran legislators, such as Rep. Dingell and Sen. Jackson, did the advocates of price controls avoid immediate deregulation. Instead, they ended up with a gradual phaseout of controls, with decontrol of most gas set for 1985. Gas already flowing as of 1977 would stay under regulations. The 40 previous years of court challenges and controversy over regulations had influenced those writing the Natural Gas Policy Act of 1978, for they drafted a detailed, complex statute that spelled out almost every move for the regulators.

Growth of Regulation

Regulation of natural gas began at the consumer end of the distribution system. Even when the fuel being distributed was gas manufactured locally from coal, instead of natural gas from miles away, the cities stepped in to oversee the vast network of pipes that had to be built under city streets. The need for such an elaborate physical structure encouraged a natural monopoly. In place of competition, the cities provided regulation.

States

When states began to regulate oil production more closely in the first three decades of the 20th century, their

rules included gas because the two fuels usually were found together. Though at first gas prices were very low because only a few pipelines were available to transport it, to the states natural gas was very valuable because it aided oil production. Pressure from the gas still underground kept the oil flowing naturally to the surface. To "conserve" oil the states regulated gas production, giving each well a "ratable take" of gas. The method was similar to "prorationing" of oil.

In the 1920s improvements in pipeline welding made it possible to transport gas for long distances to the urban markets. By the 1930s many cities outside the producing areas, such as Detroit and St. Paul, were using natural gas.

But the cities soon found a gap in the government oversight of natural gas. In between the state regulation of production and city regulation of distribution were the companies that owned the long-distance pipelines. Usually each city was linked to the gas fields by just one pipeline. When gas supplies were inadequate or overpriced, the cities could not turn to a competitor. Because the pipelines moved across state lines, the local governments couldn't ask the state governments for relief. As had the oil producers — to reach markedly different goals — the consumers of gas turned to the federal government.

Federal Regulation

In 1938 Congress responded to lobbying by the cities and others and passed the Natural Gas Act. The Federal Power Commission was given responsibility for regulating interstate transmission of natural gas. The FPC reviewed plans for new pipelines and sales contracts. The FPC also regulated the rates the pipelines charged local distributors. With the help of the Supreme Court, after challenges by pipeline companies, the FPC devised a formula for determining prices.

But the commissioners soon found their powers were limited. Because their authority covered only the transportation of gas, their hands were tied when a producer charged a pipeline what the FPC considered excessive rates for supplies. That "overcharge" was then passed on down the line, with consumers forced to pay more for gas. A majority of commissioners decided this situation was particularly unfair when the producing company was a subsidiary of the pipeline company. As a result, the FPC extended its jurisdiction to cover transactions between integrated pipeline companies and producers. When the producers challenged their decision, the Supreme Court clarified FPC authority in several rulings in the 1940s.

Still unclear, though, was whether the FPC could regulate sales by independent producers not involved in transporting gas. At the time most of the commissioners were reluctant to do so, but a 1947 Supreme Court ruling indicated the FPC had such authority. The decision involved the Interstate Natural Gas Co. of Louisiana.

The FPC issued an order later that year designed to reassure the independent producers that they wouldn't be regulated. The producers had reacted angrily to the court ruling and had begun lobbying Congress to pass legislation curbing FPC authority. The FPC order said that transactions by independents "at arm's length" would not be subject to FPC jurisdiction under the Natural Gas Act.

The producers, though, still wanted legislation making that same point. Their champions in the Senate were Democrats Robert Kerr of Oklahoma and Lyndon B. John-

---

Top 12 States Producing Natural Gas

	Million cubic feet in 1979
Louisiana	7,223,674
Texas	6,812,795
Oklahoma	1,659,568
New Mexico	1,113,446
Kansas	791,351
Wyoming	392,304
California	330,378
Alaska	225,281
Colorado	190,863
Michigan	163,116
Mississippi	159,591
West Virginia	153,096

Source: American Gas Association

son of Texas. Kerr in 1949 drafted a bill exempting independent producers from FPC jurisdiction. The proposal was similar to one endorsed in 1947 by the FPC.

But this time three of the five commissioners came out against the legislative curbs on FPC power. Their decision upset those from producing states. The senators managed to delay for several months the confirmation of a new term for Thomas C. Buchanan, one of the three commissioners opposing the Kerr bill. For another, Leland Olds, the wrath of the gas-state senators and the suspicion prevalent in the McCarthy era would mean the end of his decade-long career on the FPC.

President Harry S Truman requested a third term for Olds in June 1949. By the time Johnson's Senate Commerce subcommittee voted against confirmation in September, Johnson and his colleagues had found Olds to be not only harmful to the gas industry but also to have pro-communist leanings. In October, Johnson led the fight against Olds on the Senate floor, and the nomination was soundly rejected.

Work on the Kerr bill continued. In March 1950 the Senate voted 44-38 for the legislation. Opposition was stronger in the House, where Speaker Sam Rayburn of Texas made a personal plea on the floor for the natural gas measure. It passed by only two votes, 176-174. However, Truman, who was concerned about rising prices and lack of competition in the industry, vetoed the legislation.

Court Decision and Aftermath

The next major decision on natural gas regulation was made by the Supreme Court in a landmark 1954 ruling. The Wisconsin Public Service Commission had called for FPC regulation of the Phillips Petroleum Co., which was a large integrated corporation. But Phillips argued that it produced gas only within the state of Louisiana, and thus was not covered by the 1938 law. The Supreme Court ruled that the FPC did have authority and responsibility over Phillips and over thousands of other gas producers earlier considered outside its jurisdiction. Justice Sherman Minton wrote the opinion: "Regulation of the sales in interstate commerce for resale made by a so-called independent natural gas producer is not essentially different from the regulation of such sales when made by an affiliate of an interstate pipeline company."

The decision prompted increased lobbying of Congress by the producers. In July 1955 the House narrowly passed a bill cutting back FPC authority. The vote was 209-203. By February 1956 the legislation was on the Senate floor, and the gas producers appeared close to victory. Even the Republican president, Eisenhower, was on their side. But those seeking to ease federal controls on natural gas producers were thwarted again.

Just before the vote, Sen. Francis H. Case, R-S.D., announced he would vote against the bill because he had been offered a $2,500 campaign contribution by an oil company lawyer "interested in passage." At no time was there any suggestion that Case had acted improperly. Despite the taint of scandal, a majority of the Senate voted for the legislation, passing it 53-38.

However, on Feb. 17 Eisenhower vetoed the bill because of the Case incident. The president, who was seeking re-election in November, called lobbying on the bill "so arrogant" as "to risk creating doubt among the American people concerning the integrity of governmental processes."

During later investigations and court trials, the Superior Oil Co. officials involved in the incident denied

Regulating Gas Prices

The Federal Energy Regulatory Commission, set up in 1977 to replace the Federal Power Commission, is responsible for administering the Natural Gas Policy Act of 1978.

The law, the second major gas pricing act passed by Congress, extended federal jurisdiction for the first time to sales of gas within the producing state. Such intrastate sales account for 40 to 45 percent of total nationwide gas sales.

Also set out by the 1978 law was a scheme for gradually ending price controls on new discoveries and on certain intrastate gas. For wells in production before 1977, controls were to continue indefinitely, until the wells had been depleted. More than 20 different categories of gas were defined by the complex pricing law.

The first categories of gas to be deregulated were high-cost gas produced from below 15,000 feet from wells drilled after Feb. 19, 1977; from geopressurized brine; from coal seams; and from Devonian shale. The deregulation date was November 1, 1979.

Gas sold under intrastate contracts existing as of April 1977 was to be decontrolled on Jan. 1, 1985, if the price exceeded $1 per million Btus (per thousand cubic feet) as of Dec. 31, 1984. If the price were lower, then the gas was not to be deregulated.

New natural gas was defined as that tapped after April 20, 1977. The price of gas from new reservoirs, from new onshore wells either 2.5 miles from or 1,000 feet deeper than the nearest pre-1977 well and from new outer continental shelf leases, was to be decontrolled on Jan. 1, 1985. Also to be decontrolled then was gas from wells closer to producing wells, but still from below 5,000 feet. On July 1, 1987, gas from new onshore wells above 5,000 feet was to be decontrolled.

Gas already under production in 1977 was to continue under FERC regulation, and prices could not exceed price ceilings set by the commission. The ceilings were to be adjusted to reflect inflation.

At the end of 1980, the price ceilings per million Btus of gas were roughly as follows: new reservoirs, $2.60; new wells, $2.35; stripper wells, $2.80; wells tapped after 1974, $1.95; wells tapped in 1973-74, $1.25-$1.65; pre-1973 wells and other low-cost gas, $.25-.90.

it was an attempt at bribery. They eventually pleaded guilty to not registering as lobbyists — and the bribery charges were dropped.

Among the arguments opponents of FPC authority over producers had made was that the utility type of pipeline regulation usually practiced by the FPC was not suited to gas producers. Measuring a logical return on investment was impossible, they contended, when some expensive-to-drill wells turned out to be dry, while others tapped at low cost proved to be rich finds. In the wake of the 1954 Supreme Court ruling, the FPC had struggled to apply its traditional method to producers. But in 1960 the FPC decided the arguments against utility-type regulation of producers were valid. Their attempt to treat thousands of producers as utilities and to work out a fair rate of return for each had been more than the FPC could handle. The backlog of paperwork was out of control. The commission instead set out a new procedure for determining prices known as "area rates." For each geographic region, the FPC set two prices — one for oil already in production and a higher rate for new discoveries. Then the commissioners began the long process of examining each region separately to determine permanent pricing rules.

Two Markets for Gas

The gas producers, which were in many cases also oil companies, continued to chafe under FPC control and to complain that prices were too low. However, they did have an outlet that brought them higher prices. Sales of gas within the producing state — intrastate sales — were not regulated by the FPC, which was responsible only for interstate commerce.

In the 1960s and 1970s demand for natural gas continued to grow. But reserves of gas began to shrink, decreasing by 20 percent between 1966 and 1973. In 1972 the FPC adopted a new pricing system designed to encourage production. Certain gas could be sold at more than the regulated price, and in response drilling increased. But production began dropping in 1973 despite the slightly higher prices. The interstate market was most affected by the decline.

A 1974 Library of Congress study found that the share of gas going to the interstate market was declining as the intrastate market and its higher prices attracted those with gas to sell. The contrast was especially evident for new production. Though the interstate market gained 52 percent of all new gas dedicated in 1971, the share was down to 22 percent in 1973, according to the study.

In response to the problems in the marketplace, the FPC in June 1974 abolished area-wide rates and replaced them with a nationwide rate for new discoveries of 42 cents per thousand cubic feet, with an annual price increase of 1 percent.

New Push for Deregulation

As part of his response to the Arab oil embargo, President Richard Nixon in November 1973 called for an end to most price controls on natural gas. Nixon sought to end FPC control over the price of natural gas from new wells, gas newly dedicated to interstate sales and gas from old wells, once the existing contract for its sale expired. The Interior Department was to retain the power to set price ceilings if prices rose too sharply.

In Congress, though, attention was focused on oil pricing. In addition, legislators in key positions favored controls on gas. The Senate Commerce Committee, chaired by controls advocate Warren G. Magnuson, D-Wash., held hearings in 1973 and 1974, but no legislation was reported.

President Gerald Ford in January 1975 also asked Congress to end most price controls — and to add a wellhead tax of 37 cents per thousand cubic feet to further discourage use. The tax proposal died quickly in the House Ways and Means Committee. The Senate, as it had been in the 1950s, was sympathetic to price decontrol. Aiding the arguments of the producers was new evidence that the existing system was not working well. The price of gas in unregulated intrastate markets was three to four times the top regulated interstate price, then at 51 cents per thousand cubic feet, and that situation made it easier to argue that the controlled price was artificially low. In addition there were predictions of gas shortages in the coming winter of 1975-76 that threatened to shut factories and force job layoffs.

The Senate Commerce Committee in June 1975 scrapped the Ford plan and reported a complex bill that continued price controls while allowing higher prices for new discoveries. Though this measure never was brought up on the floor, a decontrol amendment was offered in October during action on an emergency natural gas bill. The emergency bill permitted interstate pipelines that had inadequate supplies to buy natural gas wherever they could find it and at whatever price.

The amendment, offered by James B. Pearson, R-Kan., and Lloyd Bentsen, D-Texas, was adopted, 50-41. For the first time since 1956, the Senate had voted on and endorsed gas deregulation. Prior to approval of the amendment, though, advocates of price controls had attached several changes designed to shield residential consumers from higher prices and to tighten the definition of new discoveries. The result was legislation deregulating new discoveries, but retaining control over sales of already-flowing gas, even after existing contracts expired.

As in the Senate, leaders of the House committee with jurisdiction over gas pricing favored continued controls. The emergency gas bill was sent to the floor without long-term changes in the pricing system. However, the House Rules Committee voted to allow a floor vote on a substitute proposal similar to the Senate-passed deregulation bill. The House in early 1976 went along with the Rules decision, voting 230-184 to allow a vote on the substitute, which was sponsored by Texas Democrat Robert (Bob) Krueger, the same freshman congressman who had been active in seeking oil deregulation.

Commerce Chairman Staggers, Energy and Power Subcommittee Chairman Dingell, Texas Democrat Eckhardt and other strong supporters of price controls managed to delay the vote on the Krueger substitute, which seemed likely to prevail because of the vote on the rule. In the meantime, they drafted a substitute designed to attract votes from moderate Democrats. As was often the case in energy pricing legislation, the beneficiary of compromise was the independent producer. Neil Smith, D-Iowa, offered the compromise Feb. 4. For independent producers, defined as those with sales of less than 100 billion cubic feet a year, controls would be lifted on new discoveries. Major producers would remain under controls in interstate markets, and, in addition, their intrastate sales were placed under federal controls for the first time. The FPC was to set a national average price for gas, but under rules expected to give producers higher prices than existing regulations. The House Feb. 5 approved the Smith compromise 205-201, then passed the bill, 205-194.

However, senators favoring decontrol chose not to go to conference with the House. The House-passed bill did not do enough to end controls, the Senate decided. A conference on the two vastly different bills didn't seem promising to them.

Also easing pressure on Congress was a July 1976 FPC decision that almost tripled the ceiling price on new gas discoveries. For gas produced or contracted for after Jan. 1, 1975, the rate was increased from 52 cents to $1.42 per thousand cubic feet. For gas put on the interstate market in 1973 and 1974, the ceiling was 93 cents per thousand cubic feet. Allowable prices for "older" gas continued at previously set levels.

Carter Proposals

Unlike Nixon and Ford, Jimmy Carter was less sure of how to resolve the dispute over natural gas pricing. He wanted higher prices as an incentive to producers, but Carter did not think decontrol was the best means of achieving those higher prices.

An especially cold winter in 1976-77 reminded Carter of the serious, urgent problems that plagued the existing pricing system. The gas shortages that the FPC had predicted for the past couple of years finally materialized — in non-producing states. By Feb. 1, 11 states were in emergency status, with industries and schools closed because of gas cutoffs. Carter won congressional approval in only six days of a bill allowing interstate pipelines to purchase gas at prices much higher than the regulated rate. The temporary legislation was similar to bills considered, but not completed, in the winter of 1975-76.

Carter tackled the problem of natural gas pricing as part of his 1977 national energy plan, announced in April. After debating the issue for more than 30 years, Congress was ripe to resolve it. The winter shortages had made natural gas supplies a very visible issue once again. In addition, sympathy for producers' demands for higher prices had been increasing because of the gap between interstate and intrastate prices. For years the cheapest of the fossil fuels, gas seemed even less expensive after the 1973-74 oil price increases reordered old ideas about energy prices. Economists called gas "underpriced."

Carter proposed ending the dual marketing system for gas by extending federal controls to intrastate sales. In this new nationwide system, Carter's plan called for linking the price of new gas discoveries to the price of oil. But the president wasn't talking about the price of decontrolled oil — he meant the average controlled price of domestic oil, which was expected to be the equivalent of $1.75 per thousand cubic feet of gas by early 1978. Gas from wells already in production could get higher prices under the proposed legislation, but the ceiling price for such gas would be $1.42 per thousand cubic feet, plus inflation. That was close to the maximum price ever allowed previously on interstate sales.

House Support

Carter's plan won support from House Democrats favoring continued regulation of natural gas. Advocates of decontrol thought it was a terrible idea. Not only did controls continue, and at relatively low price, but they were extended to the intrastate market, where gas always had sold free of federal control.

The House Commerce Subcommittee on Energy and Power in June narrowly endorsed a Krueger proposal that would deregulate the price of new discoveries. But the full Commerce Committee in early July reversed their decision, voting 23-20 for a Dingell amendment embracing the Carter proposal. The special Ad-Hoc Energy Committee set up to handle the energy plan retained the Commerce approach. However, they did endorse an amendment by Eckhardt broadening the definition of "new" gas that would be eligible for the highest allowable price. Eckhardt was trying to head off those seeking deregulation.

As floor action began in early August, Eckhardt continued his compromise efforts. The gas industry had been lobbying earnestly against the Carter proposal, eroding the already-fragile House support for continued regulation. To ensure success for the amendment endorsed by the ad-hoc panel, Eckhardt teamed up with fellow Texas Democrat Charles Wilson. Eckhardt favored government controls, while Wilson usually opposed them. Their amendment was adopted by voice vote.

When advocates of deregulation got their turn on the floor, they found their ranks thinned of Democrats who had been on their side in earlier fights. An important defector was Majority Leader Jim Wright, D-Texas, who had joined Wilson in endorsing the amended administrative proposal.

Clarence E. Brown, R-Ohio, offered the deregulation amendment, with support from Krueger and Timothy E. Wirth, D-Colo. Like earlier deregulation proposals, the amendment removed controls on new discoveries and phased out controls on existing production. Its list of backers was long enough to bring Speaker O'Neill onto the House floor, just as gas pricing had prompted a rare appearance by Sam Rayburn in 1950. O'Neill, however, was on the other side. The white-haired Speaker, slapping his hands together for emphasis, urged his colleagues to vote against the amendment and against "big oil." The Speaker shouted, "Never have I seen such an influx of lobbyists in this town."

"America is watching this legislation more than it has watched any legislation in years," O'Neill said. "Will the House fail? Can the House act? Can the House pull together an energy policy?

"Believe me, the future of this nation . . . is at stake," he concluded, sparking a round of applause.

The amendment was rejected, 199-227. The House went on to pass the package of energy legislation.

Senate Impasse

The Senate already was on recent record in favor of deregulation because of the 1975 adoption of the Pearson-Bentsen amendment. The major difference in 1977 was that a different committee, the new Senate Energy Committee, had jurisdiction over energy regulation, including natural gas pricing. Essentially a revamped Interior Committee, the panel was chaired by Henry Jackson, a longtime proponent of price controls. But the 18-member committee was split. The members voted 9-9 against an amendment that would phase out regulation of new gas within five years. Immediate decontrol had lost earlier, 6-12. To allow a Senate vote, the committee reported the Carter proposal without recommendation.

When Pearson and Bentsen offered another gradual deregulation proposal on the floor, it appeared the Senate was simply going to repeat its 1975 votes. A move to table their substitute was rejected, 46-52. But then two new players seized control of Senate action on natural gas pricing. Ardent opponents of deregulation, Democrats James Abourezk of South Dakota and Howard M. Metzenbaum of Ohio, launched a nine-day, new-styled

The Two Who Led a Filibuster-by-Amendment

On the surface they made an unlikely pair.

One half of the filibuster team was the urbane, reserved Howard M. Metzenbaum, D-Ohio — a symphony-goer.

The second author of the filibuster-by-amendment was a guitar-picking, cigar-chomping extrovert who insisted on first-name informality with staff and strangers — James "Jim" Abourezk, D-S.D.

What they shared was a deep conviction that, as Abourezk put it, "the natural gas deregulation issue is the most important economic issue in several decades."

For nine days in the fall of 1977 this "odd couple" managed to delay Senate action on a bill to deregulate natural gas prices. Because debate was limited, choking off conventional filibustering, the pair tried unsuccessfully to amend the bill to death.

Abourezk: Nothing to Lose

James Abourezk was what lawyers call "judgment-proof" — in terms of political capital he had nothing to lose. He was planning to retire anyway.

By reputation a maverick and by status a lame duck in the Senate, Abourezk seemed relatively immune to the pressures that developed during the tedious "filibuster-by-amendment" he crafted with Metzenbaum.

In January 1977 the 46-year-old Abourezk had announced he would not seek a second term in 1978. He concluded that "the only way to get legislation passed is to do something that favors corporations." He was tired, he said, of "marginal victories."

Abourezk reportedly faced a tough, though not impossible, re-election fight — a distinct shift from 1970 when he was handily elected to his first and only term in the House from South Dakota's 2nd District. He was the first Democrat to represent the district since the New Deal era. Abourezk in 1972 captured the Senate seat of Republican Karl E. Mundt (1948-73) by 43,000 votes.

Never comfortable with the often clubby atmosphere of Congress, Abourezk resisted compromise to the point where some observers questioned his effectiveness. His mastery of parliamentary intricacies during the natural gas filibuster showed colleagues a new side.

Abourezk had set himself conspicuously apart from the mainstream on some touchy issues. Almost alone he had worked to raise the congressional level of consciousness of Indian problems, despite post-Wounded Knee reaction against Indian rights in South Dakota. The son of a Lebanese peddler, Abourezk grew up on a Sioux Indian reservation in South Dakota.

As the Senate's only Arab-American, Abourezk urged creation of a Palestinian homeland and bluntly criticized what he called the "Israel lobby" in Washington. He parried the heavy criticism this stance provoked with the observation that a Jewish doctor was instrumental in developing his interest in politics.

Abourezk, a former bartender, rancher and used-car salesman among other things, had worked his way through mining engineering and law schools.

The natural gas filibuster dramatized Abourezk's longstanding efforts to restructure the energy market. During the natural gas deregulation battle of 1975, Abourezk carried the floor fight on a vertical deregulation measure he sponsored with the late Philip Hart, D-Mich. (1959-76). He also was deeply involved in a 1976 congressional lawsuit to cut natural gas price boosts allowed by the Federal Power Commission.

Metzenbaum: Long, Tough Fights

Metzenbaum had a penchant for tough and protracted fights. With five-plus years of his first Senate term stretching ahead of him he had risked the rancor of filibuster-weary colleagues to fight deregulation on behalf of labor and consumer constituents. The scenario was not new to the tenacious Cleveland senator.

A self-made millionaire and former labor lawyer, the 60-year-old Metzenbaum had to run three times before conservative Ohioans elected him to the Senate in 1976. In the process he took on the Internal Revenue Service and a well-known figure — astronaut John Glenn, now a senator from Ohio himself.

Metzenbaum surprised all observers by beating Glenn in the 1970 primary. Though he later lost the general election, he showed himself to be a workhorse campaigner who was not shy about deploying his considerable resources. His lavish television campaign drew criticism, as did his endorsement by a chain of Cleveland newspapers he owned at the time. Hefty campaign contributions by family members, including his 12-year-old daughter, also raised eyebrows.

In 1976 Metzenbaum finally won, unseating Republican Robert Taft Jr. (1971-76). It was a notable victory in a state that had been sending Tafts to Washington for decades.

Once in the Senate, Metzenbaum identified himself with some highly visible liberal causes, such as school busing and corporate accountability. During his abbreviated first term he also compiled a perfect AFL-CIO voting record.

In 1977 his energies were focused on what he viewed as a monopolistic and unresponsive energy market. With Abourezk, he cosponsored an oil company divestiture bill and introduced related measures himself.

filibuster against the amendment. Because cloture was invoked, limiting debate, the two senators had to try another approach: amending the natural gas bill to death. They called up amendment after amendment and requested time-consuming roll-call votes on each.

While Abourezk and Metzenbaum tied up action on the Senate floor, Jackson and others tried to work out compromises. In response, Pearson and Bentsen agreed to shift the brunt of higher gas prices to industrial customers, saving the lower priced, "old" gas for residential and other high priority users. They also put a ceiling of $2.84 per thousand cubic feet, valid for 24 months, on the price of deregulated gas.

But Abourezk and Metzenbaum continued their delaying tactics, frustrating the Senate and particularly Majority Leader Byrd. Finally, on Oct. 3, with the help of Vice President Walter F. Mondale, who sat in the chair, Byrd managed to derail the two senators. The rapid-fire parliamentary maneuverings and controversial rulings by the chair angered many senators, who charged Byrd with abusing the privileges of the leadership post. The floor statements prompted an unusual, impassioned speech from Byrd, who defended his efforts to stop the "abuse of the Senate itself." Energy legislation once again had propelled the legislators into an emotional, tense debate. Two hours after Byrd's speech, Metzenbaum and Abourezk, citing lack of support from the Carter administration, gave up their filibuster. The next day, Oct. 4, the Senate voted on the deregulation amendment, adopting it 50-46. *(Abourezk-Metzenbaum, box, p. 50)*

The conference committee faced a Senate bill that deregulated gas prices and a House bill that continued controls, though with higher ceilings, and that covered the intrastate market for the first time. Any compromise was bound to be complicated — if an acceptable compromise could be found. The long negotiations, which carried over into 1978, prompted Energy Secretary James R. Schlesinger to remark at one point, "I understand now what hell is. Hell is endless and eternal sessions of the natural gas conference."

1978: Gradual Decontrol Voted

In late February 1978 members of the Senate Energy Committee, all of whom were conferees, began meeting behind closed doors. On March 7 nine of the 17 conferees announced they had reached a compromise. (Lee Metcalf, D-Mont., had died Jan. 11, leaving a vacant seat on the Energy Committee and giving those favoring deregulation a 9-8 edge. His spot on the conference was never filled.) The senators agreed to gradual deregulation of new discoveries over the next five years, instead of immediately as in the Senate bill. Controls would be extended during that time to the intrastate market. The date for decontrol was Dec. 31, 1984. Already-flowing gas would remain under controls.

When the plan was presented March 22 to the full conference, in a Rayburn Building room jammed with spectators, House members of the conference committee responded by voting 13-12 to present their own proposal. The close vote revealed a deep split among the House conferees, just as there was among the senators. But, even though each side refused the other's offer, the House and Senate compromise proposals were surprisingly similar. For the first time, a majority of House conferees had agreed

to gradual deregulation of new gas discoveries, with controls set to end only six months later than the Senate had proposed. The House left more gas under controls by having a stricter definition of new discoveries and also required incremental pricing, the scheme to shield residential consumers from the highest prices. The Senate simply required that such a pricing plan be submitted to Congress for consideration.

Shaky Compromise

The leading House and Senate conferees — a group of a dozen or so — began meeting in closed sessions. They were urged along by Carter and Schlesinger. On April 21 they emerged to announce a compromise. "New" gas would be decontrolled on Jan. 1, 1985; a modified version of incremental pricing was required; the Senate definition of "new" gas was tightened; and the president was given a chance in 1985 to postpone decontrol for 18 months. The compromise, though, needed support from a majority of the 43 conferees.

The House conferees proved particularly stubborn. Those who favored immediate deregulation sided with members who wanted continued controls. Each group thought it could do better than the compromise. Eventually, though, on May 23 and 24, a majority of the conferees formally approved the agreement.

Another hang-up developed in early August, after the complex compromise had been put into legislative language. Some of those who had earlier voted for the agreement balked when they saw the written provisions. By Aug. 17, though, a majority had signed. Again, Carter had had to intervene personally to keep the legislation alive.

But the conference report still was not popular. Opponents as well as proponents of deregulation continued to criticize the compromise. The strange assortment of groups speaking out against the legislation included the U.S. Chamber of Commerce, the Independent Petroleum Association of America, the AFL-CIO, the Consumer Federation of America and Americans for Democratic Action. Attempting to counter their lobbying was the Carter administration, which in addition to seeking a resolution of gas pricing also believed the fate of the entire energy package hinged on the gas bill. Without it, the other bills might never be passed.

Passage

On the Senate floor, Metzenbaum tried to send the compromise back to conference. He lost, 39-59. A few days later, a Republican try, by Robert Dole of Kansas, also failed, 36-55. The final tally Sept. 27 was 57-42.

The House took up the natural gas conference report as part of the package of five energy bills. By only a one-vote margin, the legislators on Oct. 13 had agreed to keep the package intact, as O'Neill originally had decreed. The 207-206 vote meant the gas pricing provisions were protected, in a way, by the desire of many members to have the energy package passed — both because of the symbolic political value of taking action and because of support for specific provisions, such as energy tax credits, contained in other parts of the package. The House Oct. 15 voted 231-168 for the conference report, completing action on the second major gas pricing act ever passed by Congress.

4

Beyond Price: Carrots and Sticks

Oil and gas price controls — although the most powerful — are only one of many ways the federal government has intervened in the energy marketplace. Also shaping the way energy is produced and used are a variety of "carrots" and "sticks."

In the initial stages of the pricing debate in the 1970s, many congressional Democrats hoped that such rewards and penalties would lead to changes in U.S. energy habits. Price controls, they reasoned, could then stay in place to protect consumers. Among the early proposals were higher gasoline taxes, taxes on industrial oil and gas use, limits on gasoline consumption and even gasoline rationing. But the unpopularity of this approach eventually helped convince a majority of Congress that price decontrol, and subsequent higher prices, would probably be the most effective way to reorder old patterns of energy use.

Still, though, Congress was not satisfied to let the marketplace alone guide energy policy for the nation. That was too slow, many argued, and adjustments should begin immediately in order to curb dependence on oil imports. The marketplace was also flawed, others contended, because it did not differentiate between insecure imports and domestic supplies. For Congress, the idea of influencing the energy market wasn't new, as evidenced by laws on the books long before the 1970s.

As a result, the legislators since the oil embargo have assembled an array of laws to push and pull the way energy choices are made. Most of the rules have been designed to discourage oil and gas consumption and to encourage development of other energy sources.

Not surprisingly, Congress has found it much easier politically to vote for "carrots." Tax credits and low-cost loans for homeowners and businessmen who save energy or tap new sources, subsidies for development of new fuels, such as synthetic fuels or solar energy, and aid to mass transportation are examples of the rewards Congress has agreed to hand out. A steady stream of aid has bubbled from the government to the nuclear industry since private development was authorized in the 1950s. Even those who made support of the "free market" their guiding philosophy have been pleased to go along with most subsidies, particularly when they benefit business.

More difficult to get through Congress have been "sticks." Many conservative legislators object to government interference in what they consider private decisions about what type of car to drive or what sort of building

to construct. Few politicians want to require constituents to make unpleasant changes in lifestyle. In fact, such moves haven't traditionally been in the purview of the federal government.

Reluctance to Force Change

The history of unsuccessful attempts to increase gasoline taxes is a prime example of the reluctance to enact penalties for energy use. The 1980 defeat of President Carter's oil import fee is another example.

Congress has approved measures designed to force utilities and industry to switch existing plants to coal, but the laws have been riddled with exemptions. (Prohibitions against new plants using oil and gas have been more effective.) Gasoline rationing authority and plans, even when reserved for emergencies, have made Congress extremely skittish. Energy efficiency standards for buildings were passed, but attempts to implement them have raised an outcry.

The idea of federal mandates for conservation aroused such concern about the potential political damage that Congress quickly shifted that responsibility to the states. Rules on energy use that have been relatively easy to pass usually have little bite, such as requirements for energy labels on appliances. A rare exception to this pattern were requirements for automobile fuel efficiency.

The trend as the 1980s began was toward more "carrots," with "sticks" even less popular than in the 1970s. Paying for the rewards became less of a problem when the windfall profits tax was passed in 1980, and new credits were attached to the bill. (Even tax credits "cost" the Treasury in the form of lost revenues.) But future efforts to expand or extend existing subsidies and credits are likely to run into stiff competition from other interests as Congress struggles to balance the budget.

Arguments Against Subsidies

Not everyone agrees that intervening in the marketplace is a good idea.

"If you need a subsidy, it means you're paying more than the value of the oil saved," said Morris Adelman, an energy specialist who is a professor of economics at the Massachusetts Institute of Technology.

Another critic is Edward J. Mitchell, an economist at the University of Michigan who is associated with the

Real GNP and Energy Consumption

	Real GNP			Energy Consumption			Ratio= Gross Energy/GNP
Year	Billions 1972 Dollars	Annual Percent Change	Total Net	Electric Utility Loss	Total Gross	Annual Percentage Change	Thousand Btu/GNP 1972 Dollars
1973	$1,235	+5.5	60.7	13.9	74.6	+4.2	60.4
1974	1,218	−1.4	58.7	14.1	72.8	−2.4	59.8
1975	1,202	−1.3	56.3	14.4	70.7	−2.9	58.8
1976	1,273	+5.9	59.3	15.2	74.5	+5.4	58.5
1977	1,340	+5.3	60.4	16.1	76.5	+2.7	57.1
1978	1,399	+4.4	62.1	16.7	78.8	+3.0	56.3
1979	1,432	+2.4	61.7	17.1	78.8	0.0	55.0

Source: Department of Energy

American Enterprise Institute. "If you select alternatives that are 'blessed,' then you create an artificial inducement to do certain things," Mitchell said. "That must result in waste."

Both men think price controls were a major mistake. Adelman contends that congressional energy rules and subsidies were enacted in hopes of "overcoming with the right hand what they are doing with the left hand," which was controlling prices.

Although most Republicans espouse the benefits of the free market, many GOP legislators voted for the 1980 bill aiding synthetic fuels. Asked to explain this apparent inconsistency, Mitchell replied that he had found two types of Republicans: free enterprise advocates and "pro-business types who will vote for anything that gives money to business."

Another camp also tolerates inconsistency. Support for decontrol from advocates of solar energy and conservation was an important factor in ending price restrictions on oil and natural gas. They see a free marketplace as one of the best ways to boost conservation and use of renewable energy sources. But supporters of this approach have also made tax credits and federally subsidized loans their top legislative priorities. Asked about this apparent inconsistency, legislators and lobbyists point to years of subsidies for nuclear power and conventional fuels, such as oil and gas, as well as to the more recent rush to bestow federal monies on the synthetic fuels industry.

A 1979 Library of Congress study of federal incentives to coal and nuclear power put it bluntly, "If solar energy must compete in the marketplace on its own merits, that is without government-provided subsidies or benefits, then it will likely be at a disadvantage in comparison with other forms of energy which have been receiving government incentives for quite some time."

Subsidies Easy to Approve

Politicians typically find it difficult to vote against energy subsidies. Approving a "carrot" gives them a chance to do something visible about energy, to take credit for effecting change even if the dollars end up making little difference in the long run. When the House in June 1979 was ramming through multi-billion dollar legislation aiding synthetic fuels, complaints about waiting lines for gasoline were still ringing in members' ears. "They want action," Rep. Millicent Fenwick, R-N.J., told her colleagues. "They don't really care how much it costs."

Only rarely do energy subsidies prompt effective criticism about the amount of money involved. Ironically, synthetic fuels had been an example of such a situation just a few years earlier. In 1975 and 1976, the House had refused to provide such massive subsidies. Rep. Ken Hechler, D-W.Va., called the proposed program "sort of like attaching a big platinum-plated caboose to the end of the [research funding] train. . . . It is very heavy. It is very well-appointed. It is very difficult for the rest of the taxpayers of this nation to pull it along."

Even some persons who endorse subsidies, such as tax credits, apparently have a limit on what they will accept. Although the House Ways and Means Committee had been voting for tax credits since 1974, most of the members opposed plans for new energy credits that the Carter administration presented in September 1979. A raft of credits ended up as part of the windfall profits tax bill anyway because Senate Finance Committee members decided credits were a good way of retaining control over the money brought in by the tax they were writing.

Whether Rewards and Penalties Work

Measuring the effectiveness of rewards and penalties related to energy is often difficult. It is seldom possible to isolate specific results from investment in research and development, and energy investments are no different.

Homeowners are using tax credits for energy conservation, but they might have bought insulation anyway, without the credits. Coal use is increasing, but utilities eyeing the bottom line could have turned to the cheaper fuel without a federal push. Thermostats in offices and factories may be in compliance with federal rules, officials say, but it is also in the economic interest of building owners to reduce energy bills.

The Price-Anderson Act, the federal law limiting liability of the nuclear industry in case of accident, is one indirect subsidy that apparently has had results. Without it, most experts say, private use of nuclear power would not have progressed as far as it has.

Fuel efficiency standards for automobiles also appear to have been effective. "The auto industry would be in much worse shape now than if we hadn't passed those 1975 standards," said Sen. Dale Bumpers, D-Ark., in 1980. But Adelman, the MIT professor, has another view. The standards were a mistake, he said; the industry "sweated to get fuel efficiency in big and powerful cars" because those were the cars consumers wanted in the 1970s. Car buyers then weren't attuned to energy efficiency because they still could buy oil at artificially low prices resulting from U.S. price controls, Adelman said. The small car demand comes from the marketplace, he said.

Congress even tried to write into law a requirement for good results from federal aid to synthetic fuels. The legislators set goals for future "synfuels" production. But, in the past, the cost of liquids from coal and other such fuels has stayed just ahead of the world price, even with subsidies. The goals in the law will be difficult to reach if history is any guide, despite a multi-billion dollar federal investment.

In theory, the Energy Department is monitoring the effectiveness of many of the rewards and penalties. But, at least for its oversight of those related to conservation, the agency has drawn sharp criticism. A General Accounting Office Report in July 1980 said, "The department has not explained how its ever increasing collection of separate programs and activities will reinforce and complement each other to achieve overall national energy conservation goals."

Another watchdog agency took a look at the Energy Department's conservation efforts, as well as those on behalf of solar energy. "DOE has no consistent method for evaluating program performance," an Office of Technology Assessment report stated in June 1980. "There is a pervasive belief within and outside of DOE that senior DOE management does not really care about conservation and solar energy programs, and that quality of management has been inadequate as well as transient."

The federal government's various energy "carrots" and "sticks" fall into four major categories: conservation, increased use of coal, support of alternative fuels and, finally, nuclear power, which is a special case because of the long government involvement in development of this energy source.

CONSERVATION: PAINFUL BUT POSSIBLE

When Americans first heard about energy policy from President Jimmy Carter in April 1977, they were told, "Ours is the most wasteful nation on earth." The administration's energy plan was going to "demand that we make sacrifices and changes in every life," Carter continued. "To some degree the sacrifices will be painful — but so is any meaningful sacrifice." The cornerstone of this plan would be conservation, he said.

It was not the sort of introduction that stirred up great enthusiasm for conservation.

By mid-1979, Carter, along with the public, was more sophisticated about what energy conservation meant. "We often think of conservation only in terms of sacrifice," Carter said. "In fact, it is the most painless and immediate way of rebuilding out nation's strength."

"Painful" had been replaced with "painless."

The shift, though, wasn't just a reflection of better public relations. Some of Carter's first proposals, such as the higher gasoline tax, might well have been painful, but they didn't make it through Congress. Carter had found out Congress would rather not endorse the biggest energy "sticks." In the meantime, too, Americans had been doing that dread thing: conserving. And it wasn't so bad.

Users Cutting Costs

Industry had been cutting energy use by increasing efficiency, without affecting profits. Homeowners had begun to realize that caulking a window could keep expensive heat from leaking outdoors. Fuel efficient cars turned out to be just as convenient to use, drivers decided, as the old gas guzzlers.

The concept of conservation had suffered during the years of debate over oil and gas pricing because it had been a major rallying point for advocates of continued price controls. Those seeking decontrol had in contrast adopted supply as their chief goal. Because the two sides were so polarized over pricing, there was little hope of reconciling their competing notions of conservation and supply as the keys to the U.S. energy future.

Slowly, though, Congress learned that the government needed to encourage both conservation and supply — that the goals were compatible. Democrats and Republicans still fought over how to achieve these goals, with Democrats tending to opt for moves such as mandatory energy efficiency standards while Republicans sought voluntary change. But the shrill rhetoric against conservation had died down. Few people talked any more as Richard Nixon had in a speech Nov. 26, 1973, cited by Robert Engler in *The Brotherhood of Oil.* "We use 30 percent of all the energy" in the world, Nixon said. "That isn't bad; that is good. That means that we are the richest, strongest people in the world and that we have the highest standard of living in the world. That is why we need so much energy, and may it always be that way."

Gloomy Forecasts Disputed

The initial impression of conservation had been as Carter first painted it: painful sacrifice and an end of the traditional U.S. lifestyle. Many legislators and others argued that economic growth required ever increasing amounts of energy and that without it the United States would falter. Advocates of conservation were labeled "no-growthers."

One way energy analysts demonstrated the inaccuracy of that idea was by studying the relationship between increases in energy consumption and growth in the gross national product (GNP). They found that slower energy growth did not result in reduced economic growth. In fact, a massive National Academy of Sciences study completed in January 1980, which said conservation should be the nation's top priority, offered a new twist to that concept. The study noted that "as energy prices rise, the nation will face important losses in economic growth if we do not significantly increase the economy's energy efficiency." Unless energy growth slowed, they were saying, economic growth would be reduced.

The ratio of GNP to energy consumption has been declining since 1970, and the trend of improved energy productivity is expected to continue. That means the same amount of economic growth can be achieved with less energy. For 1979, the ratio was 55 thousand Btus for every dollar of GNP (in 1972 dollars). *(Chart, Real GNP and Energy Consumption, facing page)*

A 1979 report by the White House Council on Environmental Quality used its title, "The Good News About Energy," to describe the potential of conservation. Only a few years ago, "and occasionally still today," the report said, "simple extrapolations of historic energy growth 'showed' that the United States would need to more than

Congress Passed Seven Major Laws . . .

Seven major laws enacted in the 1970s and 1980 dealt with energy conservation, including two tax bills. The laws are the Energy Policy and Conservation Act of 1975 (EPCA); the Energy Conservation and Production Act of 1976 (ECPA); the National Energy Conservation Policy Act of 1978 (NECPA); the Public Utility Regulatory Policies Act of 1978 (PURPA); the Energy Security Act of 1980, and the two tax laws, the Energy Tax Act of 1978 and the Windfall Profits Tax Act of 1980. In addition, Congress made regular appropriations to states to aid in weatherization of schools, hospitals and dwellings occupied by low-income families. Highlights from the legislation include:

Conservation Provisions

● Requirements for state conservation plans, with federal aid to states whose plans included each of the following: mandatory thermal efficiency standards and insulation requirements for new and renovated non-federal buildings; mandatory lighting efficiency standards; programs promoting carpools and public transportation; mandatory energy efficiency standards to govern state procurement practices; and traffic laws permitting a right turn on red lights where safe. (EPCA, 1975)

● Federal standards for the energy efficiency of new automobiles. Automakers had to meet a fleetwide average of 18 miles per gallon in 1978, increasing to 27.5 miles per gallon in 1985. Penalties for noncompliance were increased in 1978. (EPCA, 1975)

● Federal standards for the energy efficiency of new buildings, due to be written by August 1980. The building energy performance standards would give each building a Btu allowance, to be allocated among different energy uses. However, the Energy Department postponed issuing final standards until August 10, 1981, because of public complaints that the rules as drafted would be costly and ineffective. Under the law, Congress has to review the standards and vote on whether to impose sanctions against those not in compliance. Both houses would have to agree to impose the sanction proposed in the legislation: denying federal assistance — including mortgage loans from federally regulated institutions — for construction of any building in a state which did not certify its adoption of and the building's compliance with the federal performance standards. (ECPA, 1976)

● Federal standards for energy efficiency of major home appliances. The rules were to be in place by the mid-1980s. Congress in 1975 had required labeling of appliances to indicate estimated annual energy consumption. (NECPA, 1978)

● Establishment of a conservation bank in the Department of Housing and Urban Development that could subsidize loans made by commercial lending institutions to persons who installed energy-saving equipment. The bank was authorized to spend $2.5 billion in fiscal 1981 through 1984. The subsidy for conservation improvement loans would be limited to owners or tenants of existing residences with one to four units whose household income did not exceed 150 percent of their area's median income level.

The maximum subsidy for a borrower whose income was 80 percent or less of the median would be 50 percent of the cost of the improvements, up to $1,250 for a single family dwelling and up to $3,500 for a four-unit building. A borrower whose income was 120 percent to 150 percent of the median could be subsidized for only 20 percent of his costs, up to $500 for a single family house or up to $1,440 for a four-family building.

double its current energy consumption by the year 2000. Revised and more realistic estimates now indicate that with moderate effort to improve energy productivity, our energy consumption in the year 2000 need not exceed current use by more than about 25 percent, and that with a determined effort it need not increase by more than about 10-15 percent."

The oil industry's association, the American Petroleum Institute, gave a nod to conservation in its August 1980 report, "Two Energy Futures." "A few years ago most people thought of conservation as simply 'doing without,' and many experts believed that there was little opportunity to reduce energy consumption without economic hardship," the report said. "The experience of the past few years, as consumers have adjusted to rising prices, has dramatically altered this belief." However, the report, which set out routes to increased domestic energy production, was careful to note: "The potential for saving energy is not unlimited . . . it is not the total answer."

Savings Without Lifestyle Penalties

A 1979 study by the Harvard Business School's Energy Project put it simply. "The United States can use 30 to 40 percent less energy than it does, with virtually no penalty for the way Americans live," the directors of the project said in a book on their work, "Energy Future."

By the end of 1980, forecasters had made major revisions in their projections for future energy consumption. The response to the 1979-80 price increases had been a quick drop in consumption levels, providing new evidence that energy use was far more "elastic" — demand in-

. . . To Promote Conservation of Energy

Owners of larger multi-family or commercial buildings could receive up to 20 percent of their conservation improvement costs, with a cap on the subsidy of $400 per unit of multi-family dwellings and $5,000 for a commercial building.

The bill specified at least 15 percent of the funds authorized for conservation ($375 million) be used to assist owners or tenants in existing buildings whose income did not exceed 80 percent of the area median income. In addition to qualifying for loans, those persons would be eligible for direct grants. However, no grant would be available unless the total conservation expenditure exceeded $250. (Energy Security, 1980)

● Requirements that electric and gas utilities get involved in conservation by: informing customers of energy-saving measures; offering to inspect homes to suggest specific improvements; offering to arrange financing and installation of insulation and other conservation equipment; offering to provide financing or to provide equipment and installation as long as the work was subcontracted to qualified independent firms; allowing the costs of such measures to be repaid by consumers through utility bills, regardless of who provided or installed the equipment. The 1978 National Energy Conservation Policy Act had prohibited utilities from providing more than $300 in financing or installing conservation equipment as a protection for small businesses in the field. But Congress repealed the prohibition in the 1980 synthetic fuels bill after hearing from many sources that utilities were the best equipped to provide the conservation service. (NECPA, 1978; Synthetic Fuels, 1980)

● Directions to state utility commissions to consider rate structures that encourage conservation by methods such as charging more for power produced at higher cost during peak hours of the day or seasons of the year, or ending the practice of giving lower prices to large volume users, called "declining block rates." (PURPA, 1978)

● Requirements that utilities sell electricity at nondiscriminatory rates to companies generating their own power from excess industrial heat, a process known as "cogeneration." Utilities were also directed to buy extra electricity from cogenerators. Companies cogenerating electricity were given assurances that they would not be classified — and thus regulated — as utilities.

Tax Provisions

● Residential tax credits for installation of insulation and other energy conserving improvements. The credit could equal 15 percent of the first $2,000 of expenditures, for a maximum credit of $300, and was to be available through 1985. (1978)

● Business investment credits, available through 1982, of 10 percent for property that conserved energy using certain specified methods. (1978)

● A tax credit of 10 percent, available through 1985, for vans used at least 80 percent of the time for commuting. (1978, 1980)

● A "gas guzzler" tax on the manufacturer of fuel inefficient cars. The tax increased between model years 1980 and 1986, with a tax of $550 on 1980 cars getting less than 13 miles per gallon and a tax of $3,850, the maximum penalty, on 1986 cars that got less than 12.5 miles per gallon. A lower tax would apply to all 1986 cars getting less than 22.5 miles per gallon. (1978)

● A cogeneration tax credit equal to 10 percent of the cost of cogeneration equipment, as long as the system were not more than 20 percent dependent on oil or natural gas for all fuel used annually. (1980)

---

fluenced by price — than expected, and that efficiency improvements could sharply curb use without major economic upheaval. Instead of annual growth in energy consumption of 2.5 percent through 1990, which was the 1978 outlook, the Department of Energy was predicting by the end of 1980 that growth could average 1 percent a year through 1990, or possibly even less.

Congressional Conservation Efforts

In major conservation legislation between the 1973 Arab oil embargo and the end of 1980, Congress had:

● Provided aid to states for weatherization of schools, hospitals and dwellings occupied by low-income families.

● Directed states to develop conservation plans.

● Required minimum energy efficiency standards for automobiles, major home appliances and new buildings.

● Suggested to state utility commissions revised rate structures designed to encourage conservation.

● Required utilities to promote residential conservation.

● Provided subsidies for loans to persons installing conservation equipment.

● Provided business and residential tax credits for conservation. *(Highlights, list of laws, above)*

Key Proposals

Two programs existing in 1980 and one proposed program deserve special attention: automobile fuel efficiency standards, utility reforms and new taxes or fees on oil.

The automobile standards were the first tough, mandatory conservation rules approved by Congress and successfully carried out. Legislators in the 97th Congress, in

1981-82, were expected to consider extending the rules beyond 1985, the date in existing law. Arguments over that question reveal how the U.S. energy situation and the policy it requires have changed since 1975, as well as how many of the same issues were still being debated after five years.

The federal government traditionally had not been involved in regulating utilities, leaving that primarily to the state. However, a 1977 proposal by Jimmy Carter called for a major expansion of federal responsibility. He wanted federal standards for ratemaking to be adopted across the country. The congressional reaction to this plan and general background on rate reform provide some insight into expected future debate on the same question.

New taxes on oil and natural gas were rejected by Congress as ways to raise prices during the long debate over price controls. However, after decontrol was underway, the Carter administration and others argued that the conservation effect of price should be amplified with gasoline taxes or oil import fees. A majority of Congress responded "no" in 1980, but the debate was likely to continue in future Congresses.

Automobile Efficiency Standards

When Congress set standards for auto fuel efficiency in 1975, the automobile industry reacted angrily. Officials warned of dire consequences if they were forced to make small cars to meet the gas mileage requirements. One industry representative predicted the layoff of more than 100,000 workers. Another foresaw development of a "quasi-black market for larger cars during the latter months of the production year," because big cars would then be in short supply.

By mid-1980, more than 250,000 auto workers had been laid off. The premium was not on larger cars, which were piling up unsold on dealers' lots. The demand was instead for cars that got top mileage.

A major reason for the woes of the industry in 1980 was that its fleet of cars had not satisfied the fuel-conscious American consumer, who turned to imports. Almost 30 percent of the cars sold in the United States in 1980 were foreign-made.

Had it not been for the fuel economy mandate by Congress in 1975, the U.S. automobile industry would probably have been in worse shape than it was in 1980. Several senators made that point as they argued for extension of the standards beyond 1985, the last year covered by the 1975 Energy Policy and Conservation Act. The bill they supported in 1980 would have required U.S. cars to get an average of 40 miles per gallon by 1995, a jump from the 1985 requirement for 27.5 mpg. Further efforts to enact new standards were expected in the 97th Congress which opened in January 1981.

Debate over Standards Extension

The auto industry, however, has been strongly opposed to any extension of the standards beyond 1985. Officials have said they are working furiously for continued improvement in fuel efficiency and hope to exceed the 40 mpg standard. But they don't want to have to follow government rules.

"Our argument, and we believe this with a passion, is that we'll be doing everything on our own that any standards would have us do," said Chris M. Kennedy, director of government affairs for Chrysler Corp. "All standards can do is cause us awkwardness and difficulties along the way."

There is sympathy for the industry position, even from those who helped write the standards in 1975.

"I want to wait for the studies expected from the Department of Transportation at the end of the year," was the comment in 1980 from Rep. Philip R. Sharp, D-Ind., a prime mover behind the standards in 1975.

At that time, the legislators were clearly exasperated with Detroit's refusal to respond quickly to the world oil crisis. But, by 1980, despite some lingering frustration with the automakers, the representatives had grown more sensitive to their problems, particularly the high cost of retooling plants to make fuel efficient cars.

Many worried that the already struggling industry would not have the financial resources to make continued improvements in fuel economy mandated by the government.

Such concern prompted White House officials to quash Energy Department testimony — to be delivered in April 1980 before the Senate Energy Committee — that would have endorsed the 40 mpg standard.

The United Auto Workers (UAW), who supported the 1975 law, also cautioned against hasty action by Congress when the automobile industry "is in tremendous jeopardy," in the words of Howard G. Paster, UAW's chief lobbyist.

"There simply isn't sufficient data in hand to know what gains in fuel economy are possible," Paster said in 1980. "It's time to stop, wait and study. It's simply the wrong time to legislate on the basis of what you would like to happen."

The Foreign Competition

But there's another side to that argument.

Without a strong commitment to more efficient cars, the U.S. auto industry could continue to lose out to foreign manufacturers. The question is whether the industry will recognize and respond to that threat without the pressure of new government rules, and without the help of special government financing.

"What I fear is that Detroit will be building a fleet of cars averaging 28 or 29 miles per gallon when Americans are buying imports that achieve 40 or 50 miles per gallon," said Sen. Henry M. Jackson, D-Wash., chairman of the Senate Energy Committee in the 96th Congress and sponsor of the bill setting post-1985 standards.

Jackson has admitted the auto industry might need financial help from the government to meet the standards he proposed. But to him it's worth it. U.S. cars and light trucks use almost 40 percent of the oil consumed in the United States, or one of every nine barrels of oil used in the world each day.

The shift to more fuel efficient vehicles contributed to the drop in gasoline consumption from an average of 7.03 million barrels a day in 1979 to 6.57 million barrels a day in 1980, a decline of about 7 percent. Higher gas prices also were a major factor.

When Congress wrote the 1975 law, it never considered federal subsidies to help the industry retool.

The question by 1980, however, was whether additional fuel efficiency standards would overburden the industry. The legislators also had to consider the effect that federal subsidies could have on traditional government-industry relationships.

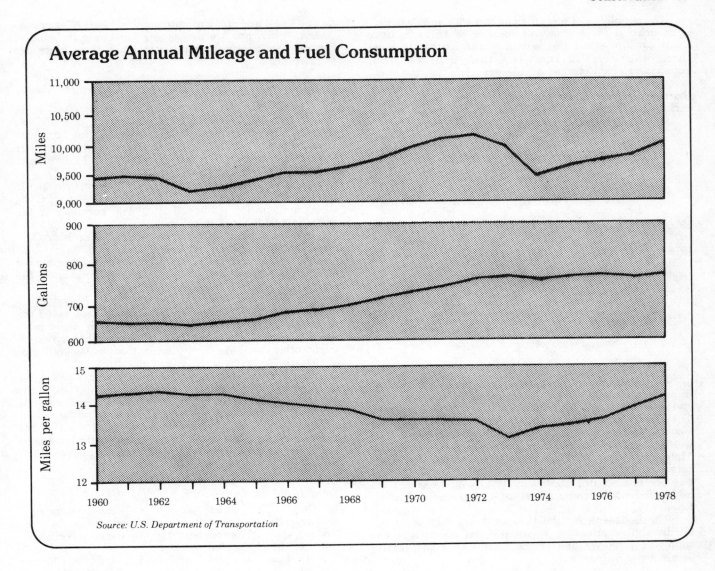

Average Annual Mileage and Fuel Consumption

Source: U.S. Department of Transportation

"We are committing billions [of government dollars] to synfuels, and we will probably commit billions more to the utility industry to reduce consumption of fuel oil," Jackson said. "Given that one out of every five American workers is associated with highway transportation or related fields, surely the auto industry deserves similar attention."

But most industry officials, except Chrysler, firmly opposed heavy government investment in the auto industry. Congress authorized $1.5 billion in loan guarantees for Chrysler in an effort to help the company avoid bankruptcy.

Consumer Demands

Auto industry officials contend that they want to respond to the demands of the U.S. consumer, not to government rules.

They argued in 1975 that Americans did not want small, fuel-efficient cars. And, after an initial surge of popularity for smaller vehicles, it appeared their thinking was not completely off track. The popularity of subcompacts actually declined in 1977 compared to the previous year. *(Car sales table, below)*

At the end of 1978, buyers were continuing to drift back to larger vehicles. The price of gasoline, while increasing with inflation, was fairly stable. Shortages and waiting lines at the pumps were just a memory. Fuel efficiency was not the top priority for many buyers.

Even more telling was the situation on dealer lots in late 1978. Ford dealers, for example, were asking the company for more gas-guzzling Lincolns, while the more miserly models, such as Bobcats and Pintos, were falling short of expected sales. Foreign-made imports were waiting, unwanted, on the docks.

But then came the Iranian revolution, price hikes by the Organization of Petroleum Exporting Countries and, finally, gasoline lines in California that spread eastward.

At first, car sales plummeted as consumers held back, worried about not being able to buy fuel. When buyers did return to the car market, autos that used little gas were at the top of their shopping list.

The popularity of fuel efficient cars shot up in a matter of months in the spring and summer of 1979. In 1980, small cars increased their share of the market to more than two-thirds, up from less than half. For U.S. automakers, 1980 marked a milestone. For the first time, U.S.-made compact and sub-compact cars comprised more than 50 percent of their domestic car sales. In 1977, small cars had accounted for less than 36 percent of all the U.S.-made cars sold nationwide.

Retail Sales of American Cars

(Percentage of domestic sales)

	Subcompact	Compact	Intermediate	Full-size*
1976	12.1%	26.9%	33.1%	27.9%
1977	10.9	24.6	33.0	31.5
1978	13.0	23.9	32.3	30.8
1979	21.2	23.3	28.0	27.5
1980	25.4	25.5	27.9	21.2

Vans make up about 1.5% of the full-size class until 1980, when they are counted as light trucks.

Source: Ward's Automotive Reports

By the summer of 1980, industry officials were haggling in public over who had the better record for fuel efficiency and who would get top efficiency in the next few years. They had learned how to get consumers' attention. After General Motors Corp. said its cars would average 31 mpg in 1985, ahead of the 27.5 mpg mandated in law, American Motors President W. Paul Tippett Jr. retorted that AMC cars would do as well, and one better. "We'll hit that number, too, not in 1985, but in 1983," Tippett said. Then he blasted GM's computations for overestimating fuel efficiency.

The bad news for the U.S. auto industry, as it belatedly shifted attention to gasoline use, was that it was supplying just over half of the small cars being eagerly sought by U.S. buyers.

Politicians Listen

The automakers' problems did not go unnoticed by politicians on Capitol Hill.

Rep. Charles Vanik, D-Ohio, charged that the industry "likes to complain of federal regulations and their cost." He was chairman of a Ways and Means subcommittee that was considering trade barriers to foreign cars. "If it had not been for regulations, Detroit would still be lagging in making a high mileage auto," Vanik said.

Even those who prefer voluntary to mandatory standards blasted the industry. Sen. Pete V. Domenici, R-N.M., an active member of the Energy Committee, asked industry officials at an April 1980 hearing, "How can we believe you will be more competitive [with imports] in 1987 or 1988, when it seems obvious you would have been less competitive today if you hadn't been pushed to increase fuel efficiency?"

President Carter added his criticism at an April 1980 press conference. He recalled his 1977 request to Congress for heavy taxes on gas-guzzling cars, which had prompted automakers to complain that "the market was not there for the small and efficient automobiles." Now, Carter continued, Americans are demanding "precisely the kind of car we were encouraging them to make three years ago or more."

Industry Responds

The response of the auto industry to these assessments has varied. For example, Ford Motor Co. officials will concede the government miles-per-gallon standard may have helped the shift by consumers and manufacturers to fuel efficient cars. But officials of General Motors Corp. insist the government rules had no effect.

"The cars that are on the street are not in response to congressional action at all," said David S. Potter, GM's vice president for public affairs. "The customer is the one who has dictated those products."

Instead of blaming the auto industry or praising Congress, energy expert Daniel Yeargin takes a different view. Yeargin is a lecturer at Harvard University and co-author of *Energy Future: Report of the Energy Project at the Harvard Business School.*

"In retrospect," Yeargin told the Senate Energy Committee April 1980, "these regulations may have saved the American auto industry — pushing [it] to move more speedily toward producing more efficient vehicles than it might otherwise have done during the phoney [oil] glut of 1974-78."

But Yeargin also notes that price controls on oil, set by Congress, were sending "misleading signals" about the availability and value of oil. Consumers found gasoline relatively inexpensive and so bought cars without considering fuel economy. "It is possible that a lot of the autoworkers who are not working today would have been had it not been for price controls during the phoney glut," he said.

Solid Industry Opposition

Despite the varied views of the current standards, industry officials are united in their opposition to post-1985 standards. They contend that the market has changed and that they have changed.

"Fuel economy sells," explained Kennedy of Chrysler in a 1980 interview. "It didn't a year ago. We think the market for fuel economy will take us every bit as far as technologically possible. At the time we griped and groaned [in 1975], gasoline was still at 40 cents a gallon. We said you have to decontrol. If gasoline had not been decontrolled, the standards would have been an outright disaster," Kennedy said.

GM's Potter agreed: "The problem was induced by insisting on cheap energy and then beating the consumer over the head because he chose to take advantage of the cheap energy" and drive larger cars.

But the tendency of automobile executives to blame controlled gasoline prices for the now outdated marketing strategy prompted a heated response from Sen. Domenici.

"I believe that executives in your industry until very recently were not major spokesmen for taxing gasoline and raising prices," Domenici told auto officials. "The fact is to the contrary. Whenever that was occurring, they were concerned it was going to cut the sales of automobiles."

Some arguments by industry against imposition of new standards are similar to those heard in 1975.

"If the customer, the American public, is still convinced that fuel is scarce and they want fuel economical cars, they'll ask for them and we'll provide them," Potter said in a 1980 interview. "And if they don't want them, Congress can't legislate them into buying them. It's a simple free market argument that says there's no point in Congress trying to force the American public into buying things they don't choose to buy."

The Technical Aspects

Most studies project that U.S. automakers should be able to meet or exceed the 40-mile-per-gallon standard for 1995 suggested by Jackson and other senators in their legislation.

Preliminary analysis by the Energy Department found that domestic companies by 1990 could probably be making a fleet of cars that got an average of 35 to 40 miles per gallon. By 1995, the agency projected, the average could be 43 to 50 miles per gallon.

Numerous factors influence the projections. For example, use of diesel engines is important to continued improvement in fuel economy. Energy Department figures show that without diesels, the projected average for 1995 would drop to 35 to 41 miles per gallon. On the other hand, a surge in the use of electric vehicles could improve the fuel economy average. So could a dramatic increase in the use of lighter weight materials, such as aluminum or Fiberglas, but that would also mean higher prices for automobiles.

A 1980 Congressional Budget Office (CBO) study was based on the very conservative assumption that no new technologies for fuel efficiency would be developed in the next 15 years. Even so, CBO said, a 37-mile-per-gallon average was possible by 1995.

Still greater efficiency appears technologically achievable, according to the study. "But such improvements may not be economically achievable by the industry," cautioned Alice Rivlin, CBO director.

A more radical method of projecting future fuel economy was used in a study requested by Deputy Secretary of Energy John Sawhill, a supporter of efficiency standards.

Lovins: Pied Piper of New Energy School

There were many preachers of the new alternative energy theology in early 1978 but one stood out above the others, viewed by followers as something of a messiah.

His name was Amory B. Lovins. At 29, he was slightly built, bespectacled, and looked like comedian Woody Allen.

He might have been created by central casting to dramatize the philosophical debate over energy. He studied two years at Harvard and two at Oxford in England, but the only degree he held was a masters from Oxford given him by special resolution because he did not meet the formal academic requirements.

Yet even his critics conceded his brilliance. Llewellyn King, a respected energy analyst, wrote in November 1977 that "as it was difficult to see what Mahatma Gandhi meant to the future of British imperialism, so it is difficult to see what the effect of leaders such as Amory Lovins and Ralph Nader will have on the future of industrialized society and the capitalist system itself."

An American, Lovins worked in London as British representative of Friends of the Earth, a San Francisco-based environmental group. He had served as an energy consultant to the federal government, outline his theories before Congress and met with Energy Secretary James R. Schlesinger's staff.

Lovins' theories were first propounded in his article "Energy Strategy: The Road Not Taken?", published in the fall 1976 issue of *Foreign Affairs*. He later expanded his ideas into a full-length book, "Soft Energy Paths: Toward a Durable Peace."

His arguments rested on four broad bases.

First, he maintained that with rigorous conservation, society could double its mileage from energy expenditures. That meant economic growth need not require parallel expansion of energy supplies.

Second, he made an important theoretical distinction between what he termed "soft" and "hard" technologies. Soft technologies were those such as solar or wind power that tap energy sources that cannot be depleted. Hard technologies were those such as nuclear power or fossil fuel electric plants that rely on depletable resources and require massive capital investments.

Third, he espoused conversion to decentralized sources of energy. By his theory an individual building, for example, might get its own heat and power from a rooftop solar collector. Decentralization in Lovins' scheme was more efficient, cheaper and philosophically superior to the current system.

Fourth, Lovins said that as science made improvements in "soft" technologies, their cost would drop. "Hard" energy prices would rise and at some point, the economic curves would cross, he said.

Lovins recognized that modern society was in an era of energy transition. By around the year 2025, he said, the "soft" technologies could be firmly in place if society's managers began to implement them now. In the meantime, he insisted, nuclear power could be avoided altogether.

The Edison Electric Institute, the trade association for the nation's privately owned utilities, devoted an entire issue of its bimonthly magazine to refutations of Lovins' analyses. Ten critical essays attacking Lovins' views were published in June 1977, as a book: "Soft vs. Hard Energy Paths," by Charles Ulish, a consultant to the nuclear industry.

Charles L. Gray Jr., director of the emission control technology division of the Environmental Protection Agency, headed the study task force coordinated by the government's Solar Energy Research Institute.

Gray told the Senate Energy Committee in April 1980 that the government standards should be 50 miles per gallon in 1990 and 80 miles per gallon in 1995.

For those not meeting the standard, he suggested a $100 tax on each vehicle for each mile-per-gallon under the target. And Gray suggested loan guarantees for the auto industry.

The study considered the ways most Americans use their cars and how that affects fuel economy. For example, Gray suggested that Americans could use cars more suited to their uses — such as fuel efficient 2-passenger "urban vehicles" for commuting or in-town trips. His projections showed that a fleet that included 20 percent two-passenger cars could, using today's technology, achieve an average of 75 miles per gallon by 1995.

Gray said the family of the future might have one or two urban vehicles and a four or six passenger car for long trips. Considering that almost half of U.S. households own two vehicles, Gray's projections did not seem that farfetched.

Utility Rate Reform

When President Carter in 1977 asked Congress for reforms in electricity ratemaking, he was endorsing concepts first developed by consumer advocates angry at rising power bills. For Carter and others, the value of the new ideas was their contribution to energy conservation.

The thrust of Carter's plans was to require that electricity rates reflect the actual cost of providing electricity, which varies depending on when the power is used. In the past, electricity had often become cheaper as more was used, even though the cost of providing it might be increasing along with the volume. Carter expected the new approach to reduce this type of wasteful consumption, leading to conservation.

Promoting Conservation

At the same time he proposed rate reforms, the president also asked that utilities be required to get into the business of promoting residential conservation.

This second request, giving utilities a new role, was well received by Congress and incorporated into the National Energy Conservation Policy Act of 1978. The law did not directly order utilities to offer to do energy audits or to arrange installation of storm windows. Instead, the states were told to write conservation plans requiring such action by utilities. If the state did not act, then the federal government would step in.

This distance between the federal government and the utilities satisfied the concern of many legislators that the states, not the federal government, should retain their traditional role of regulating utilities. This idea of state responsibility was one reason Congress rejected Carter's plans for utility rate reform. The administration's approach was also opposed by the major industry associations and most utilities.

The bill Congress ended up passing, the Public Utility Regulatory Policies Act of 1978, only suggested to state utility commissions that they consider a list of rate reforms. The role of the federal government was reduced to that of an intervenor, arguing before the state regulators for reforms. Carter had wanted to require compliance with minimum federal standards for ratemaking.

The House had gone along with Carter's approach, considering the nation's need for energy conservation as adequate justification for expanding federal responsibility. But the Senate refused. Sen. J. Bennett Johnston, D-La., floor manager of the bill and chairman of the Energy subcommittee that dropped Carter's initiatives, explained why. The administration bill, he said, "contemplated a radical extension of federal authority into the highly complex matter of the design of retail rates for electricity." Johnston said the Senate continued to support the traditional role of the states in handling ratemaking, a role which was based on geographic, climatic and economic differences among the regions.

Many States Change Rules

Many state regulators and utilities, such as those in California, made sweeping reforms in the 1970s as prices rose and they recognized the economic benefits of rate structures that encouraged conservation. However, the question of federal standards for ratemaking could come before Congress again in the future should some states prove unwilling to ask utilities to adjust to the changing energy situation with new rate structures and aggressive conservation programs.

Another issue that could stir congressional interest in federal rate reforms is solar energy. Many advocates of solar energy have said that cooperation, even support, from utilities is crucial to widespread use of solar systems, which are usually dependent on electricity as a back-up source of energy. Some seek favorable rates for solar users, arguing that they reduce overall demand and thus lower costs. But utilities argue that increasing use of solar could create a new time for "peak" demand: cloudy days. That would be expensive to meet, they say, and charges should reflect that cost. Utility officials deny that they see solar as unwelcome competition.

Traditional Approach to Pricing

In setting rates for electricity, regulators analyze a utility's costs and then set billing formulas that will guarantee the utility will get back enough cash to cover its expenses. For the 80 percent of utilities that are investor-owned, the ratemakers allow rates high enough to generate enough profit to give the utility's stockholders a fair return on their investment.

The state ratemakers have to determine what costs are eligible to be included in a utility's rate base, which is the total value of assets and costs on which a rate of return is allowed. The regulatory authority also determines the costs borne in serving customers, and these are reflected in monthly bills.

Each of the three customer classes — residential, commercial and industrial — imposes different costs on the utility. Residential and commercial class customers require an extensive and expensive distribution system to convert high voltage power to low voltage and carry it to each final user. Industrial users, on the other hand, often can handle power straight from transmission lines at full strength high voltage. Industrial users also consume power in steadier, more dependable time patterns, imposing a

Going, Going, Gone

At a conference on the 1978 energy conservation bill, Senate conferees sought a stiffer penalty on makers of fuel inefficient cars. Existing law, passed in 1975, charged an automaker $5 for each tenth of a mile by which his fleet's average fuel economy exceeded the federal standard. The senators wanted to double the fine, to $10, but the House resisted. They ended up authorizing a range of penalties, from $5 to $10, depending on certain findings by the transportation secretary. The lively debate was a fair representation of energy conference action.

As the Senate conferees made their pitch for tougher penalties, they ran into opposition from Rep. John D. Dingell, a Democrat from Detroit who was worried that higher fines might lead to layoffs of automobile workers in his district. At one point, Senate Energy Chairman Henry M. Jackson, D-Wash., whispered to a colleague, "John's like a stone wall."

Dingell insisted that the increased penalties be contingent on findings by the secretary of transportation that they definitely would lead to energy savings and would not harm the economy.

"The moral equivalent of war, and we just lost it," Sen. Howard M. Metzenbaum, D-Ohio, said quietly after one of Dingell's aides recited a long list of procedures necessary to meet the requirement.

The difficulty of showing absolutely that the penalties would result in energy savings and wouldn't harm the economy would "drag out the hearings, literally for years, and that's not achieving the objective, which is energy savings," Metzenbaum said.

Metzenbaum then tried to define more loosely what the secretary would have to prove. He suggested the secretary need show only that the penalties would "be likely to lead to" energy savings. Others offered other phrases.

The dickering over a few words caused Rep. Paul D. Rogers, D-Fla., to lose patience.

"What about $7.50?" Rogers asked, suggesting that conferees simply raise the $5 penalty without requiring formal findings by the secretary.

"I'll take that," Metzenbaum replied from the other end of the table.

"$7.50," announced Rogers.

"This is not an auction," grumbled Dingell.

"$7.50 is not bad," Rogers implored Dingell. "Why not, John?"

Conference Chairman Harley O. Staggers, D-W.Va., offered, "Let's talk it out here, John."

"I'll make the same offer I did with the $7.50," said Dingell, insisting on the requirement that the secretary make a substantial finding.

Just then there was a vote on the House floor. But agreement seemed imminent, and Rep. Bob Eckhardt, D-Texas, missing the vote, tried another phrase. "What about 'will result in or tend to compel' substantial energy conservation?" he asked.

"Let's take 'tend to compel,' " said Rogers, looking at Dingell. "That's all right."

"That's your judgment, not mine," said Dingell.

"Ill take 'tend to compel,' " offered Metzenbaum.

"Let me just put a little paragraph on the end," said Dingell, still not willing to give in.

The impatience in the room seemed to swell. Dingell made his last stand: "My signature is not only needed on this report, but my support is needed on the gas bill."

The thinly veiled threat rankled Jackson. "In my 38 years here, I have never said my vote on one thing would affect my vote on another unrelated issue," he told Dingell.

Dingell didn't apologize.

House members returned from voting. The talk returned to words.

"Significantly encourage?" suggested Rogers.

Rep. Joe D. Waggonner Jr., D-La., strolled back in from voting, called out like an auctioneer, "Going up to $7.50, $8, give me $8 and a half, $9." The conferees laughed, still able to see humor in their situation.

"How about 'affect'?" someone asked.

"Will result in or affect," said Dingell, agreeing.

"Howard?" asked Jackson.

"That's not bad," Metzenbaum replied.

A little more haggling and a phrase seemed finally to fly: "Result in or substantially further."

"Sold," said Staggers, banging his gavel.

---

more stable — if larger — drain on the power generation system over a 24-hour period.

More Is Cheaper

In part because of these factors, the traditional approach to electricity pricing has been based on the principle of "declining block rates." Under that structure, in general use throughout the nation in the 1970s, the price charged a customer per unit of electricity dropped as his consumption increased. This structure was based on the premise that the utility company's costs of serving each customer declined with increased consumption because the utility's fixed costs were spread further.

The declining block rate structure applied to all classes of customers. What it meant in practice was that if the first block of electricity used — say 100 kilowatt hours — were priced at 4 cents per kilowatt hour, the next 100 would be priced at 3 cents, and succeeding blocks at successively lower prices.

The end result under that system was that large volume users ended up paying less per unit of electricity than did small volume users.

Stimulating Consumption

In the industry's early days, the utilities sought to promote electricity consumption through such pricing practices. Their aim was to stimulate enough consumption to create a need for plant expansion, which would lead to economies of scale and lower average costs for all.

But the cost of constructing new facilities began to rise rapidly in the late 1960s and 1970s, far exceeding the often galloping rate of inflation. Any savings from economies of scale were dwarfed by higher building costs. Because adding new plants no longer lowered overall utility costs, reformers in the 1970s began to argue that the rationale behind declining block rates — with their discounts for industry — was no longer valid and, in fact, penalized residential users. The outcry grew louder as electricity bills increased.

For utilities in the 1970s, the most expensive electricity to provide was that required to meet new demand or demand at "peak" times of the day or year.

Growth: 3 Percent a Year

Traditionally, growth in electricity consumption had averaged 7 percent a year, and utilities built new capacity in order to have sufficient power available to meet anticipated demand. Annual growth dropped off to about 3 percent after the mid-1970s, but most utilities continued to plan for the new, expensive generating facilities that they thought this still-growing demand would require.

Utilities had also traditionally provided enough electricity to satisfy all anticipated demand, even during "peak" consumption periods, such as a hot summer day or the morning hours before work. In fact, most regulators required utilities to be prepared for such demand as a matter of course to avoid brownouts or blackouts. Often the generators used for peak production, such as gas turbines or intenal combustion engines, were less expensive and quicker to produce power, but not fuel efficient when compared to the plants providing the utility's base load of power. As fuel costs escalated, providing peak power thus became increasingly expensive.

Alternative Approaches

Those seeking rate reforms argued that the costs of new and peak capacity should be reflected in utility rates. By avoiding the need for new plants or operation of peaking facilities, rates to all users would be lowered, they contended. From the standpoint of national energy policy, the changes could help lower overall energy consumption. Less use of the frequently oil- or gas-fired peaking power was particularly desirable.

This approach is known as marginal cost pricing, which means the price of an extra unit of a commodity equals the cost of producing that extra unit. Under conventional electric rates, peak period power was priced below its marginal cost and thus tended to be oversold. Electricity consumed during off-peak periods was priced above its marginal cost and consequently often undersold, according to the classic economic argument. Rates that accurately reflected the varying costs of providing electricity could be expected to lead consumers to change their consumption patterns, reasoned the reformers, thus cutting overall costs.

Off-Peak Electricity Use

Money could be saved by using a clothes dryer at off-peak hours, for example. On the other hand, running an air conditioner at noon on a sweltering summer day — when units were humming for miles around — could end up being a cooling, but very expensive experience.

The concern that people would probably turn on their air conditioners at such a time despite the cost, thus creating a costly "needle peak" in electricity demand, led many reformers and government officials to suggest two other "load management" concepts to accompany "time-of-use," or marginal pricing: (1) interruptible rates, which would give large industrial consumers reduced rates in exchange for agreement that their service could be shut off on short notice, and (2) mechanical load control systems, which would allow selective reduction of electricity flow for short periods of time.

The prospect of lower rates for interruptible service did not quiet industry complaints about the reform plans. Industry officials argued they deserved lower rates, as in declining block rates, because distribution costs were actually lower for large users. Industry representatives also argued that they had less flexibility than residential users in adjusting to peak pricing and would thus be unable to avoid rising electricity bills.

Devices to Limit Use

As for the load management devices, designed to manage power flow for the utility, these could include:
- Circuit breakers, which would automatically cut power off to certain circuits when switched on.
- Time switches, which are clocklike devices that cut power to certain circuits at pre-set times.
- Cycling regulators, which cycle power to certain circuits, such as air conditioners, on and off in regulated spurts, such as each 15 minutes.
- Instruments that would regulate which of several competing loads would get power when several were turned on simultaneously, perhaps allowing power to flow to an electric range while cutting power to an electric water heater.
- "Ripple" or radio control systems which allow the utility to send short bursts of high voltage current, or radio signals, to automatically cut power to selected appliances.
- Utility storage systems, with which electricity generated during off-peak hours could be converted into another energy form, such as heat, and stored for later reconversion and use during peak hours.

Taxes and Fees

Attempts by Democrats in Congress and later by President Carter to increase energy taxes as part of efforts to retain price controls failed in the 1970s. The taxes were unpopular with the increasing number of legislators who favored an end to price controls. To them, taxes were an attempt to postpone decontrol, and they opposed that. Even advocates of controls opposed new taxes, not agreeing with the strategy that taxes could avoid decontrol. To them, higher prices, whether from decontrol or taxes, were to be avoided.

With decontrol underway, though, the Carter administration again proposed new energy taxes and fees. The intent of its March 1980 proposal was to increase conservation even beyond that induced by decontrolled prices. Because he wanted to curb non-essential uses of energy, Carter said the oil import fee he requested would be shifted onto the cost of gasoline, thus avoiding increases in heating oil prices. That meant the $4.62-per-barrel fee translated into a 10-cent-a-gallon price hike for gasoline. The president said he would eventually send Congress a formal proposal for a permanent 10-cent increase in the federal excise tax on gasoline to replace the fee.

One problem for Carter's plan was that it was announced as part of an anti-inflation package. Legislators were quick to label the fee as a revenue-raising step designed to help Carter balance the budget or finance a tax cut later in the year, closer to the November election. Energy Secretary Charles W. Duncan told Congress that conservation was the primary goal, but his critics said the projected saving of 100,000 barrels a day was not worth the higher cost of $10.3 billion a year.

The sharpest criticism came from legislators who had also opposed decontrol. They still did not want higher prices. Among them was Rep. Edward J. Markey, D-Mass. "You are generating revenues and justifying it under the shibboleth of conservation — it is nothing more than a fig leaf. . . . You ought to be called the secretary of taxation," Markey charged in April.

Duncan continued to emphasize conservation. "The unpleasant fact is that the gasoline tax, as much as we might like to deny it, is the best available means to get on with this important national priority — the conservation of gasoline," he said.

Others argued that the low tax on gasoline might have been justified during the years when U.S. domestic oil supplies could meet most demand. With imports providing close to half of supplies, the tax should be higher to encourage conservation, they argued, as it was in European countries long dependent on imports. *(Chart, p. 43)*

But the argument for conservation was not as potent as politicians' reluctance to raise prices at the pump, especially when prices had already almost doubled in the past years and especially when an election was just months away.

Import Fee Blocked

Congress had more ammunition against Carter's import fee than it had had against Ford's in 1975. After

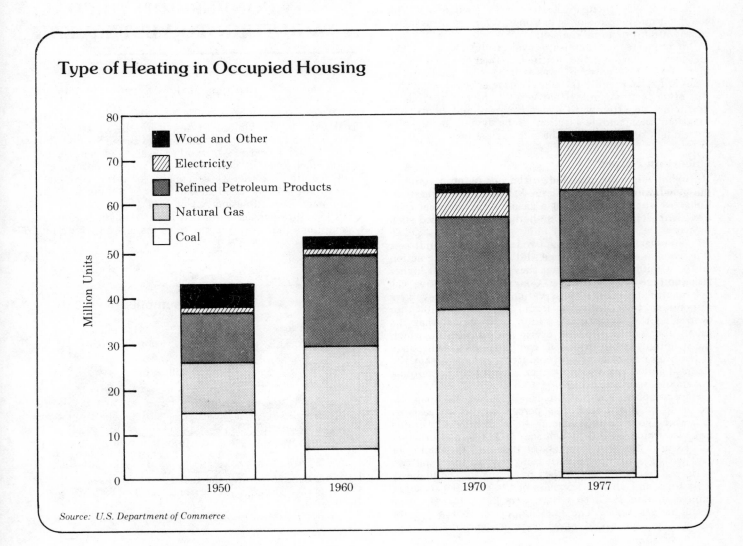

Type of Heating in Occupied Housing

- Wood and Other
- Electricity
- Refined Petroleum Products
- Natural Gas
- Coal

Million Units

1950 1960 1970 1977

Source: U.S. Department of Commerce

Carter in July 1979 announced ceilings on future oil imports, some legislators grew concerned he would use fees to enforce the quotas. They wanted a role for Congress in the decision. The law allowing the president to impose quotas and fees, which was first approved in 1955, gave the president authority to act unilaterally.

An amendment giving Congress a say on quota setting was attached by the Senate to the oil windfall profits bill, and survived conference. Long before the scheduled May 15 date for imposing the fee, the new tax law had given Congress authority to block it by passing a joint resolution of disapproval. The president could veto the action by both houses, but then Congress, by a two-thirds vote in both houses, could override the president.

Congress Overrides Veto

In early June, the House and Senate voted overwhelmingly to kill the fee. Carter vetoed their action, but then they overrode his veto. It was the first time since 1952 a Democratic president had been overridden by Congress. The fee was dead.

The fee had picked up support both from those who had favored continued controls and those for decontrol. Rep. James R. Jones, R-Okla., was among the decontrol proponents who thought the fee was a good idea. "You could not muster a majority in Congress for any meaningful conservation program," he said.

If the votes on the disapproval resolution were a fair measure of congressional sentiment, then the new alignment — post-decontrol — was still heavily against using taxes or fees to amplify the conservation effect of decontrol. But other factors guiding that vote — the link to budget-balancing, an attempt to assert congressional rights over taxation, the pending election probably put more votes than might be expected on the side against fees and taxes.

Uncertain Future

What might be expected in the future, on a vote not burdened with these other issues? It's an open question. Congress was unlikely to get a gasoline tax proposal from President Ronald Reagan, who had strongly opposed such measures.

However, members of the two tax-writing committees, Ways and Means and Finance, did promise during action on the windfall profits tax that they would consider higher gasoline taxes during the 97th Congress. Their motive was not related to energy conservation, though. They were responding to complaints from those responsible for overseeing the highway trust fund, who argued that the exemption from the federal excise tax for gasohol, which the windfall tax bill extended, combined with rising costs of highway construction and maintenance meant that the 4-cent-a-gallon tax was no longer adequate. The gasoline tax should be higher, they urged.

In response, Finance Chairman Russell B. Long, D-La., said he might support a percentage tax on gasoline that would go up as prices increased. That drew a favorable response from Sen. Lloyd Bentsen, D-Texas, and others.

Even if the 97th Congress in 1981 and 1982 does not deal with gas taxes, the 98th Congress the following two years will be forced to. The law providing for the highway trust fund and all but 1.5 cents of the current excise tax expires in late 1983, so Congress is likely to vote once again on gas taxes. The question is whether a bid for better highways would make a higher gasoline tax any

more popular than when it was linked to energy conservation.

Another issue that might prompt renewed consideration of gasoline taxes is emergency preparedness. Opponents of rationing, such as Rep. David Stockman, R-Mich., have argued that an emergency gasoline tax would be the most effective way to ration scarce supplies. Such an approach was prohibited in the 1975 law providing the president authority to impose rationing. At the time, the Democratic Congress was rejecting Ford's "conservation-by-price" approach, and did not want to give him a chance to implement that philosophy. Although Congress revised the rationing law in 1979, the prohibition on use of taxes or fees stayed in effect. Stockman, selected by Reagan to head the Office of Management and Budget, could be in a position in the administration to advocate making a request to Congress for standby authority for emergency taxes. Based on past congressional action on gasoline taxes, though, Reagan's political advisers might be wary of starting another round of an old fight on what would likely be the losing side.

CONVERSION TO COAL: A RETURN TO YESTERYEAR

Congress started trying in 1974 to get utilities to use more coal.

Utilities, consumers of almost three-fourths of the coal used in the United States, were the best hope for making use of the nation's ample coal resources and thus reducing oil imports. Most other users had long before abandoned coal for more convenient oil and natural gas. The requirement that those capable of using coal make the switch was included in the Energy Supply and Environmental Coordination Act of 1974.

The 1974 act accomplished little, though, because of exemptions that critics of the rules managed to write into law.

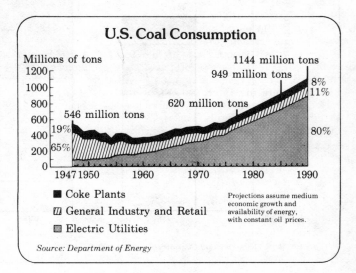

U.S. Coal Consumption

Millions of tons

1200 · 1000 · 800 · 600 · 400 · 200 · 0

1144 million tons
949 million tons
620 million tons
546 million tons

19%
65%
8%
11%
80%

1947 1950   1960   1970   1980   1990

■ Coke Plants
▨ General Industry and Retail
▧ Electric Utilities

Projections assume medium economic growth and availability of energy, with constant oil prices.

Source: Department of Energy

In response to a proposal in Carter's 1977 national energy plan, Congress tried again in 1978 to spur coal conversion by utilities and industry. This time strict prohibitions were laid down against construction of new oil- and gas-fired power plants and large industrial boilers. The Powerplant and Industrial Fuel Use Act of 1978 told utilities using gas and oil to switch their existing facilities to coal, although exceptions were allowed, and flatly banned gas burning by utilities starting in 1990. Carter had also wanted to tax utilities and industries for their use of oil and gas, but that plan was killed by the Senate Finance Committee.

Federal Money for Conversion

The rules on new construction appeared to be working, but utilities with existing oil- and gas-burning plants were clamouring for exemptions from the 1978 law. By 1980, President Carter had decided to try again. Under his plan, the federal government actually would pay financially stricken utilities to convert to coal. Carter had traded in the stick for a carrot.

With the help of powerful senators from coal-producing states, notably Majority Leader Robert Byrd, D-W.Va., the bill was passed by the Senate. Along the way, though, in order to win a majority of votes, legislation picked up an amendment repealing the prohibition in the 1978 act against gas use by utilities after 1989. The amendment gained support for the bill from senators representing gas-producing states, where utilities didn't want to make the conversion.

In the House, however, the competing demands of 435 members drowned out the wishes of those from coal producing districts and the Northeast, the location of most utilities expected to benefit from the funds. Critics labeled the proposal a giveaway to utilities. Their complaints were louder than in the Senate, where the powers of the majority leader made it risky to attack his favorite piece of legislation. Some House members also didn't want to chance losing the 1990 prohibition and so wanted to avoid opening up existing law to amendment. The measure never emerged from the House Commerce Committee.

Increasing Use a Difficult Task

The potential of coal was widely recognized in the 1970s, but the government seemed unable to spur a rapid upturn in consumption.

Many of the problems of coal were far beyond the reach of government programs. A long coal miners strike in 1978, which stopped production for 110 days, merely reminded potential users of past labor problems in the industry. (The agreement eventually negotiated was scheduled to expire in March 1981.) The need to mitigate pollution from the dirty fuel required expensive equipment. In addition, coal simply was less convenient to use than oil or natural gas, requiring more direct handling, on-site storage space and, eventually, disposal of often toxic residues. These factors curbed coal use, even though coal was two to three times cheaper than oil and gas. *(Chart, utility fuel costs, pp. 70, 28, 29)*

The future looks brighter for coal, as utilities and many industries turn to coal to fuel new powerplants and factories. New demand for exports to Europe and Japan sparked optimism in 1980 about that outlet. A new spirit of cooperation colored the relationship between the United Mine Workers and coal operators, as evidenced by their

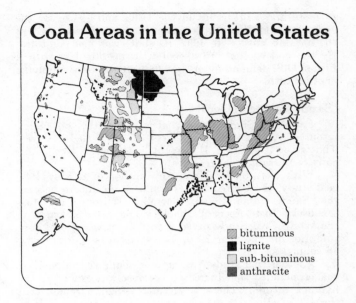

Coal Areas in the United States

bituminous
lignite
sub-bituminous
anthracite

cosponsorship of a radio and newspaper ad campaign using the slogan, "Let US do it."

Background

In its early days, coal was a simple oddity, a rock that burned. But in the burning, the black rocks released noxious odors and foul gases. Coal was such a smelly source of heat that England's King Edward I (1239-1307) ordered the death penalty for those found guilty of burning it. But within a few centuries the regal objection was overridden by economics.

Coal began its rise to dominance in the 16th century. English brick manufacturers found that coal was a useful fuel for their ovens. A serendipitous benefit was that bricks fired in coal-burning ovens were more fire resistant. This allowed people to burn coal on their hearths without jeopardizing their houses, leading to greater use of coal in home heating. Ralph Waldo Emerson, in his 1860 essay "Conduct of Life," described coal as "a portable climate."

Slower Development in U.S.

The development of the iron market in England in the 17th and 18th centuries opened vast markets for coal, but development in the United States was slower. Coal did not come into widespread industrial use in the United States until the middle of the 19th century. The American iron industry developed slowly, using wood instead of coal to fuel the process that turns ore into metal.

The coal industry expanded enormously in the late 1800s. The first commercial shipments from "the Pittsburgh seam," the richest coal bed in the nation, came in 1853, just six years before the discovery of oil in Western Pennsylvania.

The invention of the steam locomotive gave further impetus to coal-production, both as a consumer of coal to fire its boilers and as a means of transportation that opened vast new markets. By the 1920s, coal was king in the United States. In 1925, 80 percent of all energy in the country came from what English folk songs called "those dusty diamonds."

But coal soon began to lose out to cheap, convenient oil and to the inexpensive natural gas that was piped to more and more cities in the 1930s and 1940s. By the end of World War II, coal was supplying only half of the nation's energy. In 1952, its share was just one-third. By the end of the 1970s, coal was meeting less than a fifth of U.S. demand for energy. Oil imports were supplying another fifth.

'Saudi Arabia of Coal'

For the United States, coal is by far the top energy resource, representing 81 percent of fossil fuel reserves. That gives the nation 31 percent of the world's economically recoverable coal reserves.

With that base, said a key author of a May 1980 coal study, the United States could in the future become the "Saudi Arabia of coal." Carroll L. Wilson of the Massachusetts Institute of Technology and his colleagues on the World Coal Study urged a tripling of world coal consumption by the year 2000. The study was sponsored by 16 countries.

Another coal study, by the president's commission on coal, concluded that increased coal use was crucial to the nation's future. "There is an increasing awareness that the 1980s will be a decade of dangerous energy vulnerability," the commission said in its March 1980 report. "A proven energy production strategy for these years is essential. Stepped-up coal use is the practical solution."

Record Production of Coal

Coal production in 1980 was up to an all-time high of about 840 million tons, an 8 percent increase over the 1979 level of 776 million tons. Excess capacity was about 100 million tons, which means the industry could have produced that much more had there been demand. Continually rising oil prices, rules against utility and industrial use of natural gas and oil, and dwindling interest in nuclear power among utilities all benefit coal in the long run.

U.S. Coal Reserves: Leading States

	Million Tons		
	Underground	Surface	Total
Montana	70,958.9	49,610.1	120,568.9
Illinois	53,128.1	14,841.2	67,969.3
Wyoming	31,647.2	23,724.7	55,371.9
West Virginia	33,457.4	5,149.1	38,606.5
Pennsylvania	29,302.7	1,534.4	30,837.1
Kentucky	17,582.9	8,418.0	26,000.9
Ohio	13,090.5	6,139.8	19,230.2
Colorado	12,465.4	3,791.0	16,256.4
Total, U.S.	296,976.3	141,361.0	438,337.3

Source: Dept. of Interior, Bureau of Mines

Coal industry officials are hopeful about the future of their product, but argue that government policies have been hampering, not promoting, coal use. "All of the warm rhetoric we've been basking in since 1973, all of the energy policies, all of the 'coal is the cornerstone' and all that jazz, hasn't amounted to diddly squat," said Carl Bagge, president of the National Coal Association, in 1980.

Bagge contends that government policies — such as controls on oil and gas prices, anti-pollution laws, regulation of transportation and management of federal lands — restrict coal use.

"We see the projections" of increased coal use, Bagge said. "We're the eternal optimists. It's got to happen sometime. We've been saying that since 1947. We've been saying something's going to happen."

Environmental Controversies

Coal officials are particularly upset over what they consider unduly harsh federal clean air and other environmental regulations. Environmentalists say these are needed for the clean burning of coal.

The effects of coal burning on the environment and the impact of clean air rules on coal use were expected to be major issues in Congress in 1981, when the Clean Air Act of 1970 was scheduled for reauthorization.

When coal burns, the sulfur in it combines with air to form sulfur dioxide, a poisonous gas. A pollution control device called a scrubber can absorb much of the sulfur dioxide fumes. But scrubbers are expensive. Environmentalists worry that older plants, including those switched back to coal, are contributing enough sulfur dioxide to the atmosphere to increase the acidity of rainfall. Acid rain is considered a possible hazard to humans and to some crops. It can also make lakes too acidic to support life. *(Map, p. 110)*

Burning coal also leaves a residue of mineral particles, called ash. Some of those particulates escape into the air unless trapped by special equipment. This characteristic is the main reason coal is considered a dirty fuel.

Strip mining of coal can disturb the land, leaving gaping holes or squared-off mountaintops, with little vegetation. Underground mining can pollute ground water.

Another target of industry complaints has been the 1977 Surface Mining Control and Reclamation Act, which was passed after several years of controversy, including two vetoes. Designed to minimize the negative effects of surface mining, the law requires miners to restore land after mining by regrading it close to its original contours, replacing topsoil and revegetating the surface with native plants.

Industry officials have also focused on transportation, because that is a major factor in the cost and availability of coal. They have criticized the railroads for sharp rate increases and urged the government to promote coal slurry pipelines, which move a mixture of pulverized coal in water. Legislation under consideration would help pipeline builders gain rights-of-way across railroad properties.

One issue the coal industry has not had to deal with is government pricing and allocation rules. Unlike oil and gas, coal has not traditionally been subject to such government involvement in the marketplace.

The Future for Coal

Coal use has increased an average of 5 percent annually since 1977, up from the 3 percent annual growth rate of previous years. Consumption was expected also to increase by about 5 percent a year in the 1980s. Most projections of U.S. energy supplies suggest that close to 1 billion tons of coal will be produced annually by the United States by 1985, increasing to more than 1.2 billion tons by 1990.

The bulk of additional future production is expected to come from the West, primarily out of Montana and Wyoming, which developed a sizeable coal industry only in the 1970s. The coal there is low in sulfur and relatively inexpensive to mine because of the flat terrain and deposits near the surface. The Energy Department predicted in 1979 that western production would account for 47 percent of all U.S. coal production in 1995, compared to 25 percent in 1978. Coal reserves are concentrated there and in Illinois, with deposits in traditional producing states such as West Virginia, Pennsylvania and Kentucky showing the effects of years of production. (Chart of reserves by state, p. 68)

However, those states continued to lead coal production in 1978, with Wyoming fourth and Illinois fifth after Kentucky, West Virginia and Pennsylvania, in that order. (Chart of coal producing states, this page)

Utilities

The future of coal is closely tied to the utility industry.

Utilities are the major coal user, consuming 528 of the 776 million tons produced in the United States in 1979. If current plans are carried out, the relationship can only become closer.

In the next decade, utilities are scheduled to build 270 coal-fired plants, which will be consuming 400 million tons of coal annually by 1989. The conversion of existing plants from oil back to coal could increase coal consumption by about 30 million tons a year by 1985.

The only other major new contributor to electricity generation is expected to be nuclear reactors. But many utilities are reconsidering reactor plans because of doubts about nuclear safety. In 1979, the contribution of nuclear reactors to power generation dropped about 7 percent below the 1978 level, the first such decline ever. Extra generation from coal-fired plants made up the difference.

When utilities cancel orders for nuclear reactors, their chief alternative is additional coal-burning plants.

Many of the 270 new coal-fired plants planned by the utilities will replace existing facilities. However, some of the electricity they produce will be needed to meet expected growth in electricity demand. That means the utilities' plans could be affected, to the detriment of coal, if electricity use drops dramatically.

Electricity consumption, which increased an average of 7 percent a year until the early 1970s, grew by less than 3 percent in 1979. However, growth rates were much higher in the Southwest. The Edison Electric Institute projects that growth will average 4.3 percent in the next two decades.

One theory espoused by the National Coal Association is that consumers in some regions will find it more economical to use baseboard-type electric resistance heaters than their oil furnaces. This could increase electricity use.

Industry

About 21 percent of U.S. coal consumption in 1979 was by industry. The biggest potential for additional industrial coal use is boilers. The Fuel Use Act of 1978 prohibits the construction of large industrial boilers that use oil or gas.

U.S. Coal Production By States in 1978

| | Production (thousand short tons) | | |
	Under-ground	Surface	Total
Alabama	6,169	14,383	20,553
Alaska	—	731	731
Arizona	—	9,054	9,054
Arkansas	3	516	519
Colorado	4,511	9,303	13,814
Georgia	—	113	113
Illinois	24,841	23,760	48,600
Indiana	552	23,630	24,182
Iowa	108	342	450
Kansas	—	1,226	1,226
Kentucky			
Eastern	41,624	54,608	96,233
Western	17,860	21,596	39,456
Total	59,484	76,204	135,689
Maryland	382	2,616	2,998
Missouri	—	5,665	5,665
Montana	—	26,600	26,600
New Mexico	576	12,056	12,632
North Dakota	—	14,028	14,028
Ohio	11,897	29,340	41,237
Oklahoma	2	6,068	6,070
Pennsylvania	32,925	48,551	81,477
Tennessee	4,150	5,882	10,032
Texas		20,020	20,020
Utah	9,141	—	9,141
Virginia	21,511	10,435	31,946
Washington	—	4,708	4,708
West Virginia	65,216	20,099	85,314
Wyoming	708	57,620	58,328
Total	242,177	422,950	665,127

Figures may not add because of rounding.

Source: Department of Energy

Industrial purchase of boilers is expected to increase after the Environmental Protection Agency sets pollution control standards for coal-burning boilers. Those "new source performance standards" were expected to be issued in 1981.

Another industrial use of coal is to produce coke for steelmaking. Although production of coke accounted for close to 11 percent of 1979 coal consumption, the growth potential in the coke market is limited.

Coke is made by heating coal to about 2000° F in an airtight oven. The product, along with gases and wastes, is a hard, mostly carbon mass, which is then used in making iron and steel. The coke-making process requires coal with a high heat content, low ash and low sulfur content.

The steel industry has been reluctant to install pollution control equipment at its coke-making facilities. Instead, the industry is shutting down coke ovens and importing coke. About 4 million tons were imported in 1979, which is the equivalent of 6 million tons of bituminous coal.

The National Coal Association expects coal consumption by coke plants to stay at roughly the same level, 75 million tons, through 1990.

Synthetic Fuels

Perhaps the biggest limitation on the expansion of coal use is that it is a solid.

Coal can't be used in facilities designed for liquids or gases such as gasoline tanks. Boilers using coal are more expensive to build than gas or oil boilers. Coal also is more difficult and expensive to handle and transport, particularly compared to petroleum and gas that is sent through pipelines.

New technologies are being developed that either change coal to a liquid or gas, or improve coal in its solid form by removing pollutants and increasing the heat content by volume.

Coal is a hydrocarbon, like oil and gas, but has a much higher carbon content. The process used to create "synthetic fuels" from coal consists of two basic steps: the breaking, or cracking through heat and pressure, of heavy hydrocarbon molecules into lighter molecules, followed by the enrichment of those molecules with additional hydrogen.

No commercial synthetic fuels plants were operating in the United States, but Congress in 1980 voted to give $20 billion to a special government corporation set up solely to encourage commercialization of synthetic fuels. But even such a concerted effort probably would not result in operation of more than three to four plants by 1990.

The National Coal Association expects that coal demand from commercial synthetic fuels plants will range from 2 million to 30 million tons in 1990, with the most likely scenario projecting demand for 12 million tons.

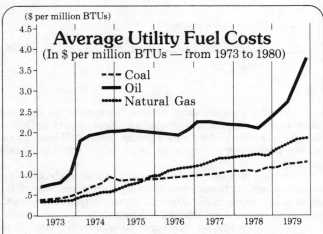

($ per million BTUs)

Average Utility Fuel Costs
(In $ per million BTUs — from 1973 to 1980)

- - - Coal
—— Oil
······ Natural Gas

The figures shown are nationwide averages for fuel delivered to utilities. Prices may be substantially higher or lower in particular areas and for fuels of particular kinds of qualities.

The figures shown *include* the costs of transportation (which have been going up rapidly for coal) but *do not include* the costs of storing or handling the fuel after delivery, or the capital and operating costs (including pollution control) for the power plants. Normally, these costs are higher for coal than oil or natural gas.

Source: *Federal Energy Regulatory Commission*

Exports

In the next decade, Japan and Western Europe could increase U.S. imports of coal for steam plants, such as utility generating stations. But coal exports will depend on transportation and production costs that could vary widely. About 9 percent of 1979 production was exported.

Although most current overseas exports are headed for coke plants, about 2 million tons in 1979 went to utilities and industry. The National Coal Association suggests that market could demand as much as 15 million tons by 1990.

SUBSIDIZING ALTERNATIVE FUELS

A feverish enthusiasm for synthetic fuels swept across Capitol Hill in the first half of 1979. Legislators prepared to hand over billions in federal aid to help commercialize technologies that turn coal into liquids, take oil from shale-like rock and squeeze energy from agricultural wastes. The enthusiasm had reached the White House by mid-July, when President Carter called for an $88 billion investment in synthetic fuels, "synfuels" as it was usually called. The new program was a great way for the president and Congress to let the public know they were doing something about energy, even though results would be a decade or more in coming — if then.

Advocates of energy from renewable sources, such as the sun, and of conservation scrambled to get on board what members of Congress were calling the "synfuels express." Senate Energy Committee Chairman Henry M. Jackson, D-Wash., attached to a synthetic fuels bill aid for conservation, solar energy, fuel from biomass (such as wood wastes) and a host of other energy programs. As an old hand at coalition building, Jackson knew "something-for-everybody" was a good way to get legislation through Congress.

The approach worked. By July 1980, Carter was signing a $20 billion, five-year authorization for energy subsidies, with most of the funds earmarked for synthetic fuels. Another $68 billion could be provided in 1984 if Congress approved. The victory capped a five-year push by many members of Congress for stepped-up aid to synfuels.

Beyond the Marketplace

In passing the bill, Congress endorsed the belief that the energy marketplace alone was not adequate to handle the nation's energy problems. It appeared that the risks of high-cost synfuels development were so great as to prevent private industry from getting involved in the next several years, or perhaps ever.

After deciding that synfuels were needed immediately as an alternative to imported oil, which might be cut off, Congress decided to offer billions of dollars in loans, loan guarantees and price guarantees to lure industry into the field in a big way, ahead of the market. The legislators said that if oil companies and other major firms still were not willing to undertake synthetic fuel production on their own, even with such guarantees, then the federal government would do it by contracting with private companies. That threat of federal competition, they agreed, might spur major oil companies, the most likely candidate for synfuels production, to get into the field.

The "carrots" dangled in front of the potential developers of synthetic fuels were the biggest yet offered by Congress for energy.

The 1980 legislation dwarfed other federal programs that directly subsidized energy development. (The price tag on decades-old indirect subsidies, such as the oil and gas percentage depletion allowance, foreign oil tax credits and the limit on oil imports from 1959-1973, probably totaled billions of dollars, but has been impossible to measure exactly.) In addition to aiding synthetic fuels, the synfuels bill provided low-cost loans for solar equipment by setting up a Solar Bank, loans and grants for alcohol fuels from biomass, and loan guarantees for geothermal energy. Additional subsidies in 1980 to fuels other than oil and gas included continuing support for existing research, development and demonstration; special programs such as the Solar Energy Research Institute; an exemption for gasohol from the federal excise tax on gasoline; and tax credits for production and use of energy from the sun, wind and heat trapped in the earth.

Nuclear power received a range of federal subsidies, including investment in research on breeder reactors, surveys of possible disposal sites for radioactive waste and safety investigations of reactor operations.

No Real Overview of Spending

Aid to energy development was scattered throughout the federal budget as of 1980, although most programs were concentrated in the Energy Department. The Synthetic Fuels Corporation also had a major share of funding.

Congress has seldom looked at overall energy spending to determine exactly what amount and share was going to each energy source. The programs have been authorized over the years in a string of bills, with the major blockbusters a 1975 authorization for the new Energy Research and Development Administration and the 1980 synfuels bill. General authority has also been provided by the Atomic Energy Act of 1954, the Federal Nonnuclear Energy Research and Development Act of 1974, and the Department of Energy Organization Act in 1977.

Basic Bills Never Passed

Congress would have a better overview of U.S. energy spending if the legislators had been able to pass the annual authorization for the Department of Energy prescribed in its 1977 charter. But by the end of 1980, Congress had been unable to pass a single authorization for the agency.

Although burdened by controversies over oil pricing and nuclear breeder reactors, these bills tended also to be enormously complex, with the allocation of funds set out in great detail. A further complication was that three House committees — Commerce, Interior and Science — shared responsibility for the legislation.

By 1980, the Senate Energy Committee had decided the line-by-line look at agency spending was more than it could handle each year, and instead drafted a broad authorization that set out general directions for the agency. Shifts in those general guidelines would be handled in future authorization bills, the committee decided. However, the House Commerce Committee's initial reaction to this approach was negative, as leaders such as Rep. John D. Dingell, D-Mich., preferred to keep a close eye

on agency affairs. Top Senate Energy Committee aides argued that detailed reviews and updates were of little value if they were never enacted into law, but to no avail.

Appropriations Panels Fill Void

The result of the continued impasse over the authorization was to give a major policy-making role to the Appropriations Committees in annual funding legislation. But Congress still had no real overview even of one fiscal year's energy programs because the Energy Department budget was split between two different appropriations bills: energy and water resources development (once known as public works) and interior, energy and related agencies (once known as interior). For example, nuclear programs were included in the energy and water bill, while those related to fossil fuels were part of the energy and interior bill.

Moreover, the full Appropriations Committees traditionally left most decisions on funding, for all government programs, to their subcommittees. Rarely did the full committees modify a bill drafted by a subcommittee. In this case, the energy programs were handled by the House and Senate Subcommittees on Energy and Water Development and the Subcommittees on Interior. As a result, the full Appropriations Committees did not give an overall look to energy spending. The Budget committees did, but they followed the recommendations of the standing committees, such as Senate Energy and House Commerce, and did not really set policy.

Solar Energy

Today's solar energy weather report: partly cloudy on Capitol Hill with little chance of sunny and pleasant conditions for the foreseeable future.

While Congress bestowed billions of dollars in federal largesse on synthetic fuels in 1980, solar energy and other renewable sources were left waiting in the wings. Programs did exist for renewables, so called because using the source does not deplete overall supplies, as does using oil and gas. Aid for renewables was in fact expanded by the same bill that set up the Synthetic Fuels Corporation. However, the programs hardly compared with the massive subsidies authorized for synthetic fuels.

It's not that energy from the sun, wind and agricultural wastes isn't popular in Congress. Alcohol fuels from biomass would probably give synthetic fuels a close race in the "most popular fuel" contest, and solar would get "most congenial." But Congress had not as of 1980 decided on a crash program for renewables, as it had for synthetic fuels.

Subsidies Seen as Crucial

Advocates of renewable fuels believe large subsidies are crucial, in part because of federal funding of other sources, such as nuclear and synthetic fuels. But there are other roadblocks for renewables, most notably the initial large capital investment required. For example, even though the lifetime operating costs of a solar heated home would be less than for a conventionally heated one, the need to shell out several thousand dollars at once often discourages installation of solar equipment.

Solar supporters think the government should help out because solar energy could reduce the nation's need for oil imports. They argue that the investment required is small compared with the multi-billion dollar backing necessary for synfuels plants. In addition, they argue that solar is a relatively benign fuel, while serious environmental questions remain about increased use of coal and production of synfuels, and doubts about safety plague expansion of nuclear power.

Doubt About Impact

As the various energy sources belly up to the federal bar, hoping for a hand-out, solar is hurt by three factors: skepticism that solar can make a major contribution to energy supplies; the nature of the energy source; and the newness of the industry.

Even many who favor aid to renewables argue that the contribution to total energy supply will be small in this century. Although the Carter administration called for a 20 percent contribution from solar by the year 2000, many officials admitted that was a lofty goal. The Electric Power Research Institute, which is funded by the utilities, predicted in 1980 that the share of energy from solar will be less than 5 percent by that date.

The basic character of solar energy also works against national action to promote it. Unlike other energy technologies, which run more or less the same wherever they are located, solar systems are heavily dependent on regional conditions. A solar system that works in Arizona may be completely inappropriate in Maine. This fact creates additional problems for any federal agency charged with devising a nationwide solar technology. Moreover, some very important factors in solar development, such as local building codes, are outside the scope of likely federal action.

Financial Problems

Although there is plenty of money to be made in solar energy, it hasn't been made yet. The whole industry was on the verge of financial collapse in 1978 when lengthy delays in enactment of solar tax credits caused consumers to postpone purchases of solar equipment. Other renewable sources, such as wind energy and ocean thermal systems, require major capital investment that users of small amounts of energy can't afford. In the late 1970s and 1980, though, utilities were getting more involved in using wind and biomass to generate electricity.

The economic weakness of renewables translates into a lack of lobbying strength. While some environmental groups also push for solar energy, only one group, the Solar Lobby, concentrates on congressional support for it. The Solar Lobby's small group of lobbyists is vastly outnumbered by the well-financed oil, coal and nuclear lobbyists.

"The solar groups, in terms of clout and financing, are pretty modest compared with their competitors," observed Denis A. Hayes, the former chairman of the Solar Lobby who in mid-1979 was appointed director of the Energy Department's Solar Energy Research Institute. The institute was called for in 1974, when Congress passed the Solar Energy Research, Development and Demonstration Act, the first major solar bill.

Little Mass Support

Despite overall popular support for solar energy as a concept, the public has not been exerting that much mass pressure on Congress for more solar energy, according to congressional staffers. An aide to one member noted

that mail into the office in support of solar energy was much more likely to come from individual amateur science enthusiasts than from any great number of people demanding immediate action.

Solar energy does have one advantage in Congress: virtually nobody is against it. Given the appeal of the sun's clean and unending energy, it is now hard to find anyone who says solar energy is a bad idea. Most solar advocates think they are hurt more by lack of interest than active opposition.

However, Gary DeLoss of the Environmental Policy Center argued in 1979 that the last three presidents, and congressional energy leaders, had in fact engaged in a "covert policy" of opposition to solar and conservation attempts because of the potential effects on demand for nuclear power.

"A really aggressive conservation plan would kill nuclear power. Carter and leading decision makers in power are reluctant to hurt the nuclear industry," he said.

However, Herb Epstein of the Solar Lobby had another view. "The issues of solar *vs.* nuclear haven't surfaced yet. Until you get to the point of spending more money on solar, or doing other types of things like mandatory solar standards, you won't really be able to draw the kind of political demarcation between the two," Epstein said.

Other Programs

In addition to ongoing research and demonstration programs, renewable sources benefit specifically from:

● Residential tax credits for solar, wind and geothermal equipment, equal to 40 percent of the first $10,000 in expenditures, with a maximum credit of $4,000. A 1980 liberalization of the credit replaced the original ceiling of $2,200 approved in 1978.

- Industrial tax credits for solar, wind or geothermal equipment of 15 percent, available through 1985. Like the residential credits above, this provision was included in the 1980 windfall profits tax act.
- Low-cost loans subsidized by a solar energy bank. All income levels were eligible for the $525 million authorized in fiscal years 1981 through 1983, although a larger subsidy was provided for lower income households. The bank was established by the 1980 Energy Security Act.

For residences with one to four units, the maximum subsidy would be 60 percent of cost for owners with income less than 80 percent of their area's median income; 50 percent for those with an income between 80 and 160 percent of the median and 40 percent of the cost for owners whose income exceeded 160 percent of the median. For a single-family dwelling, the maximum subsidy would be $5,000; for two-unit buildings, $7,500; for three- to four-unit buildings, $10,000; and for buildings with more than four units, $2,500 per unit or 40 percent of costs.

Commercial buildings, including some agricultural buildings, could receive subsidies of up to 40 percent of costs or $100,000. Builders could receive subsidies of up to 40 percent at the limits specified for owners.

- Authorization of $1.2 billion for loans, loan guarantees, price guarantees and purchase agreements designed to encourage production of alcohol and other fuels from biomass, which includes crops and crop residues, timber and timber waste, and animal waste. The goal of the program was production by the end of 1982 of at least 60,000 barrels a day of alcohol, or 920 million gallons a year. The goal for 1990 was that alcohol fuel production equal at least 10 percent of gasoline consumption, which could mean the use of gasohol in all cars. Gasohol is 10 percent alcohol and 90 percent gasoline. Administration of the program was split between the Agriculture and Energy Departments.
- Business tax credits equal to 11 percent of the cost of equipment producing electricity from small dams. The goal was to revive use of existing small hydropower projects that had fallen into disuse, and to tap existing dams to produce electricity.
- Business tax credits of 10 percent for property that used or produced energy from biomass, which is organic material such as sewage or crop residues.
- Exemption from the 4-cent-a-gallon federal excise tax on gasoline for fuels that were at least 10 percent alcohol. This provision in the 1980 windfall profits tax act extended an exemption granted in 1978 that would otherwise have expired in 1984. In addition, users of alcohol fuels who didn't buy at public pumps were given a tax credit of 30 to 40 cents a gallon of alcohol. The treasury secretary also was directed to waive or reduce exisiting regulatory requirements for distilleries if they were to produce alcohol that would be used as a fuel.

Renewables with Potential

Following are some of the most important non-nuclear, renewable energy sources with potential for development in the not-too-distant future.

Solar

There are four main types of systems that collect energy directly from the sun. They are:

Passive Systems. Passive systems, the simplest and oldest type of solar technology, use the design of a building itself to make most effective use of available energy from the sun. For example, houses with large windows or greenhouses facing south can obtain significant amounts of heat during the winter; houses with thick walls retain heat better, while at the same time keeping the interior cooler during the summer.

Active Systems. Active systems, such as one installed on the roof of the White House, use more sophisticated technologies to collect heat from the sun. The most common design involves heating a fluid by circulating it through collectors exposed to the sun. The heated fluid can then be used for space heating or, more easily, hot water production.

Photovoltaic. Photovoltaic systems convert solar rays directly into electrical energy. Long in use by the space program, the photovoltaic cells, usually made of silicon, are now still extremely expensive, although supporters hope government-encouraged mass production will bring down their unit cost.

Thermal. Thermal systems collect and focus the sun's rays in order to produce concentrated high temperatures. This heat can then be used to produce electrical energy, through steam-powered generation, or utilized directly in industrial processes.

Biomass

Biomass systems rely on plants to convert solar energy into usable form.

Wood, the oldest fuel, still supplies significant amounts of energy for home and industry. Although its high commercial price makes it more of a luxury for urban dwellers, wood is practical for home heating in heavily forested areas such as New England and the Pacific Northwest. Lumber and paper producers burn waste wood in their industrial processes.

Alcohol fuels, distilled from grain and other agricultural products, have been growing rapidly as an energy source in recent years. Gasohol was rarely available in 1977, but federal tax breaks and subsidies, as well as rising gasoline prices, encouraged production and sales in 1978-1980. More than 9,000 outlets sold gasohol in 1980.

Another form of biomass energy comes from waste products of cities and agriculture, which could be burned to run electric generators.

Hydroelectric

Hydroelectric power is the other form of indirect solar energy currently providing substantial amounts of energy.

Large hydroelectric facilities, such as Hoover Dam, supply 3 to 4 percent of energy consumption. However, the potential for creation of more such large projects is not great.

But thousands of small dams have energy potential not being fully realized. In the past, many of the small dam sites were used to supply local energy needs. They fell into disuse as regional electric generating systems were built. The Energy Department was trying in 1980 to get them back into operation. Each such facility might provide enough electricial power for up to 3,000 families.

Wind

Wind is another form of solar-created energy with a long history that fell into disuse during the era of cheap fossil fuels. Like falling water, wind is used to turn turbines which generate electric power. It can also be used directly to grind grain or pump water.

In addition to encouraging new small wind generators for farms and isolated areas, the Energy Department was looking into larger designs that could tie into utility systems. The largest unit, in Boone, North Carolina, has a rotor 200 feet long, with the potential for producing two megawatts of power.

Ocean

There are a number of different ideas floating around for harnessing the restless energy of the ocean to generate usable power. However, proposals to leash wave, tidal and ocean current energy will require much more research before they can be put into operation.

The concept nearest to practical application, according to the Energy Department, is called ocean thermal energy conversion (OTEC). This type of system, which is already in operation in waters near Hawaii, relies on the sharp temperature difference, as much as 40 degrees, between the warm surface waters and the cold waters near the ocean floor. A fluid with a low boiling point, such as ammonia, is vaporized by the warmth of the water, turning an electrical turbine. The gas is then cooled back into a liquid by the cold waters from below, and continually recycled.

Geothermal

A different type of renewable energy, not derived from solar rays, comes from the enormous amount of heat in the core of the earth. When this heat rises to near the earth's surface, it can be used to run steam-driven electrical turbines, or to supply heat directly to nearby buildings and industries.

In an area of California known as The Geysers, steam escaping from the earth has been used to run a power plant for two decades. However, such easily usable sources are not common, forcing scientists to look to hot brines in geopressurized reservoirs deep in the earth, and underground masses of hot, dry rock.

Gasohol: Energy from the Farm

Congress went on an alcohol fuel binge in the late 1970s and 1980. Tax breaks, loans and loan and price guarantees were among the ways the legislators chose to help spur production of alcohol fuels.

Their efforts seemed to be paying off. Gasohol, a mixture of 10 percent alcohol and 90 percent gasoline, was hardly available in 1977 and sold at only a few hundred outlets as of early 1979. By the end of 1980, more than 9,000 service stations sold the fuel, and total consumption for the year was expected to exceed 100 million gallons of alcohol, or 1 billion gallons of gasohol. A leading seller was Texaco.

The exemption for gasohol from the 4-cent-a-gallon excise tax on gasoline was a key boost to the industry because it helped make alcohol more cost competitive with gasoline. Alcohol was selling for about $1.75 a gallon, which was 30 to 50 cents more than gasoline. States also gave tax advantages to alcohol users and producers. By mid-1980, 25 states had exempted gasohol from all or part

of state excise taxes on gasoline. A year earlier, only eight states were providing such benefits. Ten states added to this break,* or substituted for it, an exemption for gasohol from all or part of state sales taxes. Several states also gave alcohol producers exemptions or reductions in property and income taxes.

In late 1980, the Energy and Agriculture Departments agreed to aid more than 30 producers who were expected to increase alcohol production by 500 to 700 million gallons in the early 1980s.

Used in Earlier Years

The use of alcohol as a fuel has a long history. Henry Ford designed the Model T to run on either gasoline, alcohol or a blend of the two. In the 1930s, service stations in a few Midwestern states sold an alcohol-gasoline blend

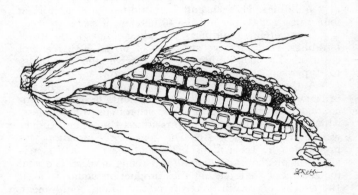

called Agrol. In World War II the government used ethanol made from grain, molasses and fruit to produce synthetic rubber and other war material.

The early interest didn't last, though, because of a hard economic reality: gasoline was much cheaper.

Rising gasoline prices in the 1970s sparked renewed interest in alcohol, and gasohol became the popular name for alcohol and gasoline mixtures. Gasohol can be substituted for gasoline without making adjustments in a car's engine. Consumers have been pleased with the fuel, with many contending that it makes their cars run better, probably because alcohol has a higher octane level than most gasoline.

Backed by Farmers

The most enthusiastic supporters have been individual farmers interested in lowering their own fuel bills and achieving a measure of energy independence. They could produce ethanol, a form of alcohol, from farm commodities and agricultural wastes.

"I look upon alcohol fuels as an opportunity for agriculture to become somewhat energy-independent," said Rep. Thomas A. Daschle, D-S.D., in 1979, a leading supporter of alcohol subsidies.

This grass-roots interest made the issue especially appealing to farm-state members of Congress. Experts agree that alcohol has the most potential in areas where large amounts of agricultural wastes are available. For example,

Louisiana could turn to bagasse, a leftover when sugar beets are processed. Iowa could depend on corn stalks. California might turn to orange peels or other wastes from food processing plants.

Politically Attractive

Subsidies for gasohol are politically attractive because they offer help for the nation's energy problems "without making anybody uncomfortable," said Sen. Patrick J. Leahy, D-Vt., in 1979. "Everybody wants to go home and say they solved the energy problem," said Leahy, a gasohol supporter, but "nobody really wants to come out in favor of mandating strict conservation measures, like requiring lower speed limits or lower home thermostat settings."

A critic of gasohol subsidies, Rep. Richard Kelly, R-Fla., also attributed the programs to vote-getting efforts. "It's especially attractive if you can go back home and say you can produce your own fuels in your own back yard and the government's going to loan you money to do it," said Kelly in 1979. "It sounds great, but I'm not sure that's the best way to invest capital."

Evidence of the broad congressional support for alcohol fuels was the Senate's willingness to endorse a $5 billion subsidy for alcohol fuels from biomass, with little debate and no record vote. The amendment by Agriculture Chairman Herman Talmadge, D-Ga., to the synthetic fuels bill was later watered down in conference.

The major controversies related to alcohol fuels have been worries that increased production would cut into food supplies and doubts about the wisdom of government subsidies. Federal government officials have emphasized production of alcohol fuels from wastes, which they say would not be a threat to food supplies. Critics of the subsidies have complained that the exemption for gasohol from the federal excise tax on gasoline will probably be valid long after the costs of producing alcohol fuel have become competitive with regular gasoline.

Major Producers

The biggest U.S. producer of alcohol fuel in 1980 was the Archer-Daniels-Midland Corp. of Decatur, Ill. A producer of large amounts of corn, ADM uses the starch from the corn to create alcohol. Other parts of the kernel are processed into corn oil and other products. The firm produces 50 million gallons of alcohol a year.

Two other producers are Georgia Pacific in Bellingham, Wash., which produces 4 million gallons a year, and Milbrew Inc., in Juneau, Wash., which produces 2 million gallons a year. The Milbrew plant uses cheese whey, a byproduct of cheesemaking that was once an undesirable waste product because it is a pollutant.

Several other companies either had or were considering adding alcohol production facilities in 1980. Publicker Industries had sold alcohol fuels produced in its Philadelphia plant and was expected to produce 20 to 24 million gallons in 1980. Joseph Minio, a company spokesman, said the plant could produce 60 million gallons of alcohol a year.

Researchers said in 1980 they were only two to three years away from developing commercially viable methods for converting cellulosic materials, like stalks, cobs and paper, into fermentable sugars that can be turned into alcohol. Such a conversion process would make it increasingly economical to turn municipal waste, for example, into alcohol.

Synthetic Fuels

The United States has enough coal to last 300 years. But chunks of coal cannot run automobiles.

That is one reason, among many, why the United States has found it difficult to use its coal resources to reduce oil imports. Half of U.S. oil consumption is used for transportation.

Coal can be converted into a liquid fuel, like gasoline. But the process has been prohibitively expensive. Even with the Organization of Petroleum Exporting Countries pushing world oil prices to close to $40 a barrel, synthetic fuel still is expected to cost more.

But President Carter and many in Congress decided cost should no longer be a barrier. They agreed to spend billions for a domestic industry that produces coal liquids and other substitutes for imported oil. Along with gases and liquids from coal, the term "synthetic fuels" usually refers to oil from shale-like rock, known as oil shale, and alcohol from biomass, such as agricultural wastes.

Although financing may be less of a problem for synfuels in the 1980s, major environmental questions remained unanswered at the end of 1980. The problems are discussed in the chapter on energy and environment.

Liquids from Coal

Coal can be converted to liquids by two principal methods:

Indirect. Heating the coal with steam and oxygen, which creates a gas, and then chemically changing the gas into a liquid. This is the method used in South Africa for the last 25 years.

Direct. Pulverizing coal with heat and pressure and then adding a solvent or catalyst to promote chemical reactions that lead to liquid byproducts. This method is more efficient and preferred over indirect liquefaction.

For years, the government and private industry have been working to improve the methods for converting coal to liquids. But high costs have prevented commercial marketing.

Despite these economic constraints, the Energy Department philosophy has been to support commercial development of coal liquefaction as an insurance policy against future oil embargoes.

In partnership with private industry, the agency has supported construction of pilot and demonstration plants in Tacoma, Wash., with a Gulf Oil Co. subsidiary; Baytown, Texas, with Exxon Corp., Carter Oil Co. and others; Wilsonville, Ala., with a Southern Co. subsidiary; and Catlettsburg, Ky., with Ashland Oil Co., and others. These plants are designed to produce less than 1,000 barrels of synfuels a day.

Larger plants, to produce the equivalent of 20,000 or more barrels a day, are planned for Morgantown, W.Va., and Owensboro, Ky., near coal fields. The Owensboro plant would produce a clean-burning solid instead of a liquid substitute. Each of these plants is expected to cost $700 million to build. A commercial plant producing 50,000 to 100,000 barrels a day is expected to cost $2 billion to $3 billion, although experts say accurate estimates are difficult. Reaching the daily production goal of 2.5 million barrels is expected to require 10 to 15 plants.

Coal liquefaction produces about 2.5 to 3 barrels of liquid or its equivalent from each ton of coal. That means production of 1.5 million barrels a day, or 547.5 million barrels a year, of coal liquids by 1990 would require additional coal production of up to 218 million tons a year.

Gases from Coal

In the early 1900s, before major oil discoveries and before pipelines brought natural gas to cities, gasified coal was used to fire ovens and street lamps. But the dirty, low-grade gas in use then is not what supporters of coal gasification are aiming for. Their product is comparable in quality to natural gas.

One coalition of pipeline companies and a gas company, Great Plains Gasification Associates, wants to market coal gas from a proposed $1.5 billion project in Mercer, N.D. The coalition was spearheaded by American Natural Resources Co. The Federal Energy Regulatory Commission (FERC) gave a go-ahead to the project in November 1979, overruling a decision made a few months earlier by a FERC administrative law judge.

The FERC judge had rejected the coalition's plan to require pipeline customers to pay rates that would cover costs of the Great Plains facility before it began operating and later even if they did not get gas directly from the project. FERC usually objects to having customers pay for a project before they start benefiting from it. The gas from the gasification plant was also expected to be more expensive, at least initially, than conventional gas.

The commissioners had been lobbied by the Carter administration for a ruling favorable to the project, which would be the first commercial-size synthetic fuel facility in the country.

Although the technology is well developed for making gas from western coal, eastern coal tends to cake and clog the gasifier equipment. To boost gasification processes for eastern coal, the Energy Department plans to help finance a demonstration plant.

Gasification of a ton of coal usually yields the equivalent of 2 to 2.5 barrels of oil, or roughly 12,000 to 15,000 cubic feet of gas.

Oil Shale

In a 16,500 square mile area straddling Colorado, Utah and Wyoming are deposits of oil shale that the administration estimates contain more recoverable oil than Saudi Arabia: between 400 billion and 700 billion barrels.

The hardened clay, which splits easily into layers, is permeated with oil. To extract the oil, the shale must be heated to extremely high temperatures — over 900 degrees. Then a ton of good quality shale yields about two-thirds of a barrel of oil.

If the production takes place above ground, it requires large amounts of water and yields massive amounts of leftover rock that must be disposed of. Once crushed, the rock expands in volume by about 20 percent, so it cannot be simply returned to where it came from.

To avoid this disposal problem, an "in-situ" method, an underground process for converting shale to oil, has been developed. An explosive is detonated within the shale deposit, triggering a slow-burning fire that releases the oil. The liquid then drips into a cavity below the heated deposit and is pumped out.

Four shale projects had been proposed as of 1980 by private concerns. Each would cost more than $1 billion. The White House in 1979 estimated the cost of shale oil at $25 to $35 a barrel, noting it probably would be "the first synthetic fuel to compete economically with imported

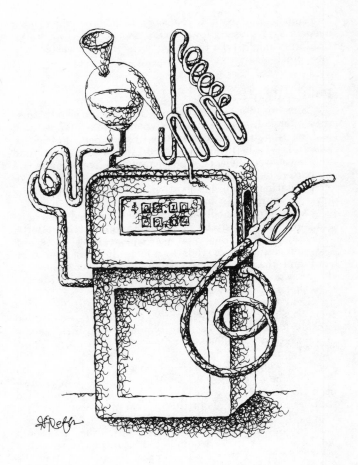

oil." Extensive oil-shale properties are held by Occidental Petroleum Corp.

Biomass

About 600 million tons a year of biomass are available annually for conversion to alcohol and fuel oil. Biomass includes farm and forest products or residues and municipal solid waste.

The best known product of biomass is gasohol, a mixture of gasoline and alcohol that can be used in automobiles. Most gasohol blends are 10-20 percent alcohol. Brazil has an ambitious program to promote gasohol.

Although some biomass plants simply burn wastes to create steam, a more sophisticated method of recovering energy is pyrolysis: heating the material in an oxygen-free chamber until it breaks down into gases, liquids and solids. Another method is fermentation of corn and wheat residues to produce ethanol. A ton of biomass yields .5 to 1.25 barrels of liquid fuel or its equivalent.

Background

Congress was first attracted to synthetic fuels in 1944, when experts were saying domestic oil reserves would last only another dozen years. The Synthetic Liquids Fuel Act was passed, providing $30 million over the next five years for research and demonstration plants that converted coal, oil shale, trees and vegetative matter into liquid fuels. A three-year, $30 million extension was approved in 1948, with another $27.6 million voted in 1950, when the authorization was extended through 1955.

In the years following expiration of the act, the Bureau of Mines, under its basic research authorization, continued its experiments with oil shale and liquefaction and gasification of coal. A special coal research bill was approved in 1960, setting up a new office of Coal Research in the Interior Department.

The oil embargo and price increases in 1973-74 renewed interest in synthetic fuels, which had still not been developed commercially in the United States. Extracting minerals from the ground and sending them through an expensive chemical process was certain to turn out a fuel much more expensive than even OPEC-priced oil, the researchers realized.

President Ford in his 1975 State of the Union message called on Congress to provide new incentives to spur production by 1985 of the equivalent of 1 million barrels a day of synthetic fuels. Although the market was not ready for synfuels, Ford thought the government should help along a new industry that might be crucial during future embargoes.

Loan Guarantees Used

The major method the Senate chose for encouraging synfuels production was loan guarantees, with up to $6 billion authorized. In addition, the government was directed by the Senate to undertake a joint project with industry to demonstrate "in situ" production of oil shale, a method that kept the processing underground.

However, the House was more skeptical of Ford's plans. When conferees retained the Senate provisions in an energy research and development bill, the House Rules Committee decided to allow separate votes on the questions of loan guarantees and oil shale demonstration. Both were opposed by an unusual coalition of liberals worried about federal benefits to industry and conservatives concerned about government interference in the marketplace. The House votes in December 1975, were 263-140 to strike the loan guarantees provisions and 288-117 against oil shale demonstration.

The House moves to kill the program came just a few months after Ford in September announced his proposal for an Energy Independence Authority.

The concept of the special corporation was developed by Vice President Nelson A. Rockefeller and his staff and endorsed by Ford despite reservations expressed by Treasury Secretary William E. Simon and Alan Greenspan, chairman of the Council of Economic Advisers. Ford wanted the corporation to have $25 billion in equity, with another $75 billion in government-backed borrowing authority. The five-member board of directors would report to Congress but have the power to make independent decisions about which projects to support. In addition to aiding synthetic fuels, the corporation could boost development of solar and geothermal energy, as well as conventional operations, such as electric utilities and oil pipelines.

Ford's proposal was later picked up and revised by President Carter, who in 1979 called for a quasi-governmental energy corporation to develop synthetic fuels.

Congress did not like Ford's proposal, but many legislators continued to push for special aid to synthetic fuels. A key supporter was Science and Technology Committee Chairman Olin E. Teague, D-Texas, also known as "Tiger." By threatening to tie up the House with parliamentary delays, Teague forced the House Rules Committee to grant a rule that allowed a floor vote on his controversial plan

for $3.5 billion in loan guarantees and $500 million in price supports for synthetic fuels. However, the House in September 1976 refused by a one-vote margin to allow a vote on the proposal. The vote was 192-193. The measure had support from the AFL-CIO, the U.S. Chamber of Commerce, the National Association of Manufacturers and the oil shale industry. Allied against it were the United Auto Workers, the Environmental Policy Center, the Sierra Club and Congress Watch, among others.

Hill Support for Projects

President Carter's 1977 energy plan had only a small place set aside for synfuels research and demonstration — not commercialization as Ford had wanted. Officials at the Office of Management and Budget even tried to cut back on the number of synfuels demonstration projects funded by the government, arguing they were redundant. But that type of synthetic fuels aid was supported by Congress, particularly by members from areas where the projects were located. For example, a Gulf Oil Co. demonstration plan in West Virginia, funded largely by the Energy Department, drew sharp criticism from some liberal Democrats and most Republicans on the House Commerce Committee. But their 1978 efforts to delete the funding for the project failed. Asked later about the location of the proposed Gulf plant, one opponent, Richard L. Ottinger, D-N.Y., responded that "of course" it was located in the district of Commerce Committee Chairman Harley O. Staggers, D-W.Va. "That's why [the committee] couldn't stop it," said Ottinger. Another opponent, Dave Stockman, R-Mich., called it "a deal in which the taxpayers get all the risk and Gulf gets any benefits." As for the chance of the project proceeding without federal aid, Dan Denning, a Washington representative of Gulf, said it wasn't possible because the fuel would be too expensive to market. "Our stockholders would go bananas and with good reason" if Gulf acted alone, Denning said. The project was funded.

1979-80 Legislative Action

Increasing support for synthetic fuels in the Department of Energy influenced Carter in April 1979, when he called for establishment of an Energy Security Fund, to be financed by revenues from the proposed oil windfall profits tax. Although the fund was to support mass transportation and help low-income families with energy costs, the bulk of the funds, $76 of every $100, were to spur development of new energy technologies and supplies, including synthetic fuels.

Congress did not like Carter's plans for a trust fund because it meant the members lost flexibility in — and even control over — decisions on how to spend federal revenues. However, synthetic fuels aid had come of age. In the spring of 1979, waiting lines at gasoline stations spurred Congress into a near frenzy over synfuels. It was their best chance for giving constituents what they apparently wanted: Action.

House, Senate Support Synfuels

A panel usually not involved in energy bills, the House Banking Committee, wrote the first synfuels bill, attaching it to an extension of the 1950 Defense Production Act. Majority Leader Jim Wright, D-Texas, steered it onto the floor. In late June, just before the legislators returned to their districts for the July 4 recess, the bill passed the

New Corporation Set Up to Spur
Commercial Development of Synfuels

The new United States Synthetic Fuels Corporation was designed to nudge private industry into the synthetic fuels business.

That nudge could cost U.S. taxpayers as much as $88 billion in the decade following approval of the authorizing legislation. But supporters of the corporation said it was unlikely the tab would be that high. Some contended that the synfuels industry would be so successful that it could cost the government very little.

The 1980 legislation setting up the corporation (PL 96-294) directed its seven-member board to provide loans, loan guarantees, purchase agreements or price guarantees to companies producing synfuels.

If a type of synthetic fuel ended up selling for less than the prevailing price of oil, then demand would soar and government expense would be minimal. But if cost overruns, higher coal prices or other factors made liquids from coal or other synfuels too high priced to compete on the open market, then the government could be forced to buy the costly fuel.

If necessary to the development of a synthetic fuels industry, the government could, as a last resort, contract with industry to build and operate a government-owned commercial facility. That would be the most expensive route because a full-scale plant could cost from $2 billion to $5 billion.

Interest in synfuels projects among private companies was high. The Energy Department in June 1980 received 951 applications for just $200 million in grants that companies could use to study the feasibility of commercial synfuels facilities or to push planned projects into final stages. If the projects were successful, the agency would have to be repaid for the grants, but the energy secretary could waive the repayment.

The grant money was provided in the fiscal 1980 interior appropriations bill, which made available to the Energy Department $2.2 billion of a special $19 billion reserve for synthetic and alcohol fuels. The reserve was set up in the same legislation.

A federal loan guarantee protects a private lender in case a company defaults on a loan. Federal price guarantees or purchase commitments require the government to buy a product or subsidize its selling price if the producer is unable to get an adequate return for the product on the open market.

The Energy Department continued to handle synfuels only until the new corporation was in operation.

The corporation was expected to operate as if it were a private enterprise, even though federally owned. Congress has asked for a comprehensive plan within four years to spell out how the corporation would achieve the synfuels production goals.

At that point, under the new synfuels legislation, Congress, using expedited procedures, could authorize $68 billion in addition to the $20 billion already provided. However, the legislators would still have to appropriate the funds annually.

The legislation directed the corporation, which had a life of 12 years, to work toward production by 1987 of the equivalent of at least 500,000 barrels a day of crude oil, increasing to 2 million barrels a day by 1992.

To give the corporation's board of directors freedom from political pressures in Congress, each member's term was for seven years. However, the appointments did have to be confirmed by the Senate. Unlike many presidential appointees, the board members could not be fired by the president. He could remove them only for neglect of duty or malfeasance in office.

House by a margin of almost 15-to-1. The public wants "bold action; they do not want timid action," said Wright. Authorized were $3 billion in price supports, as well as loans and loan guarantees limited in size only by a requirement for congressional review. Although critics had narrowly prevailed as recently as 1976, they were rolled over in 1979. Michigan's Rep. Dingell, key author of most major energy legislation, twice had tightening amendments rejected by lopsided majorities. He and others complained that Congress would have little control over the expensive programs. Ottinger joined in, "We are in effect telling the taxpayer we are going to 'roll out the barrel and damn the cost.'"

In the Senate, aid to synfuels was included in a package with solar energy, conservation and other energy sub-
sidy programs. As explained by Sen. J. Bennett Johnston, D-La., a senior Energy Committee member, "Many of our members were just not that interested" in synfuels.

Carter Gets on Bandwagon

Carter got on the bandwagon in mid-July. After rising oil prices boosted anticipated revenues from his windfall profits tax, Carter decided synfuels should benefit from a major share of the new income. The Energy Security Fund got its 10-year budget beefed up to $142 billion, with $88 billion going to a new Energy Security Corporation that would hand out the money for synthetic fuels development. Carter wanted production of 2.5 million barrels a day by 1990, a goal expected to require that 30 to 40 plants be in operation by then.

This time, the Senate, as opposed to the House in 1975 and 1976, was the skeptical body. Armed with expert testimony, the Banking and Budget Committees led the questioning of Carter's production goal as too ambitious, and the Senate Energy Committee also went along. The Energy panel, lead committee on the bill, decided to provide $20 billion initially for six to 12 pioneer plants, with a review of progress scheduled in five years, when further authorization of $68 billion was possible. They and the Finance Committee rejected Carter's plan linking the windfall tax revenues with synfuels development. No trust fund was set up, and the corporation was renamed the Synthetic Fuels Corporation.

The Senate Banking Committee, involved primarily because House Banking had drafted the original synfuels bill, took the opportunity to offer a scaled-down alternative to the Energy panel's bill. The measure that Banking completed in September provided only $3 billion for synthetic fuels, no special corporation and no authorization for federal ownership of synfuels plants. Their goal was to keep federal involvement in synfuels to a minimum.

On the floor in November, the Banking substitute was defeated, 37-57, despite support from an unusual coalition of business interests, oil companies and environmentalists. The Senate later insisted, 47-44, that the government have authority to own synfuels plants. The senators also tacked on enough other energy programs to turn the $20 billion legislation into a $34 billion package. Among the chief beneficiaries were gasohol, energy conservation and solar energy.

Conference action was slowed because the House wanted a chance to pass companion legislation to some of the titles in the Senate bill, such as the conservation and solar bank provisions. At first, the House had wanted to split up the massive bill, but the senators had refused, afraid support for the measure would fall apart if the package were broken apart. As it turned out, House conferees did a lot of original work in conference because the solar bank bill and others never reached the House floor. They had to work with a House synfuels bill that was very limited compared to the sweeping Senate proposal.

The Cookie Jar Bill

Conferees finished work in June 1980. Sen. Johnston was asked if the bill were not like a cookie jar, with something for everyone, and he agreed, but added, "All of the cookies are good for the country."

Carter signed the bill in a colorful ceremony on the White House lawn. The goal of the Energy Security Act of 1980 was for production of the equivalent of at least 500,000 barrels a day of crude oil by 1987, increasing to 2 million barrels a day by 1992. The new corporation could allocate funds through fiscal 1992. Its initial $20 billion authorization could be increased by Congress later by $68 billion, to a total of $88 billion.

The first chairman of the seven-member board of directors was John Sawhill, who had been deputy energy secretary in 1979-80, and earlier was a top energy official under Nixon and Ford until fired by Ford in October 1974 for support of higher gasoline taxes and other stiff conservation measures. *(Synthetic Fuels Corporation, box, p. 78)*

Soon after the 1980 bill was enacted, a new association opened its doors in Washington. The National Council on Synthetic Fuels Production represented the various companies involved in synthetic fuels that were anxious to get a share of the new federal subsidies. Chairman of the board of the organization was Walter Flowers, who as a representative from Alabama had served on the House Science Committee and helped draft legislation subsidizing research and development of synthetic fuels.

NUCLEAR POWER: MAJOR QUESTIONS REMAIN

When Congress was considering in 1954 whether to allow private industry to develop electricity from the still government-controlled nuclear fission, advocates of public power made a pitch for a federal nuclear electricity program. With a massive government investment, they said, the cheap power could be made available even more quickly across the nation — and at lower cost than if done by private industry. Their chief argument was that the government, at great expense, had developed the nuclear power program and thus the public should benefit. By letting private industry take over, they contended, the companies would get the major benefit of billions of dollars in public funds spent for present and future research and development.

The public power supporters lost the 1954 fight. Private industry was given responsibility for marketing nuclear power, and, in fact, the Atomic Energy Commission (later the Nuclear Regulatory Commission) was even prohibited from operating commercial nuclear power plants. But the AEC's development and promotion of nuclear power continued, along with regulation. As the commission cajoled the infant industry along, it was more as a booster than a watchdog.

By the mid-1970s, though, things were changing. The government continued to spend money on nuclear research and regulation, as predicted in the 1954 debate, but the earlier blind promotion of nuclear energy was tempered by concern about safety of reactors and disposal of nuclear wastes. Congress in 1974 abolished the Atomic Energy Commission, giving its regulatory functions to a new Nuclear Regulatory Commission, and its research and development to the Energy Research and Development Administration, which was later incorporated into the Energy Department.

Perhaps more significant for the new nuclear industry, though was the slump in electricity demand after the Arab oil embargo which, combined with rising fuel costs, put many utilities in a financial bind. Their solution was to cancel orders for nuclear reactors and put on hold any planning for new ones. Another blow to the industry was the Carter administration's opposition to completion of a breeder reactor demonstration project in Tennessee and to reprocessing. The breeder technology, which generates its own fuel, had been considered by the industry as the key to its future, with the demonstration project seen as crucial and timely.

Government was still favorably disposed to nuclear power, though, as a necessary energy source. The Carter administration decided to help by speeding the federal reactor licensing process, which industry had blamed for part of the 12-year lag between planning and operation of a reactor. In early 1979, the industry, which was by then living on back orders, was hoping for a boost from the licensing reform legislation. But in March 1979, came the accident at the Three Mile Island plant in Pennsylvania, the worst mishap in the history of commercial nuclear power.

To the existing financial difficulties then were added new public worries about safety and the prospect of expensive retrofitting of existing plants with new safety features. Though a group of senators interested in giving the industry a boost won Senate passage of a nuclear waste disposal bill in July 1980, the conference on the legislation was never completed. The outlook for the nuclear industry was bleaker than ever.

Though Congress indicated its continuing support for nuclear power after the Three Mile Island accident, many questions — both practical and philosophical — still faced the legislators in the 1980s. Congress had not given clear directions to the executive branch in years about issues such as disposal of radioactive wastes, the extent to which costly safety features should be required, changes in licensing procedures, standards for radiation exposure and allocation of the costs of accidents and of decommissioning plants. In addition, proponents of nuclear power still sought a hearty endorsement from Congress, while opponents looked for a vote halting expansion until controversies such as waste disposal had been resolved.

However, the majority of Congress apparently fell in neither camp as 1981 began. These moderates didn't want to abandon nuclear power, but they wanted operation of reactors and disposal of waste to be as safe as possible. Exactly what that meant, they weren't sure.

Background

That nuclear fission could be controlled was first demonstrated in 1942 by Enrico Fermi, who was conducting experiments at the University of Chicago. But it was 1951 before electricity was generated from nuclear power even on an experimental basis. The research was funded by the Atomic Energy Commission.

When Fermi was doing his research, responsibility for atom splitting still rested with the Army Corps of Engineers' Manhattan Project, which secretly developed the atomic bomb. Congress in 1946 shifted that responsibility to a new five-member civilian commission, the Atomic Energy Commission, which was directed to encourage development of atomic energy. To help oversee the new agency, Congress took the unprecedented step of providing in the law for a special joint legislative committee. The Joint Committee on Atomic Energy became one of the most powerful congressional panels ever to exist.

The same year the AEC lab first generated nuclear electricity, the commission set up an industrial participation program under which private companies could help develop electricity from atomic power, with the idea of eventually marketing it commercially. In 1953, Congress provided funding for a demonstration power plant, and the contract was awarded to Westinghouse, for the reactor, and to the Duquesne Light Company, for operation and construction of the plant. The facility was located near Shippingport, Pa., and went into operation in 1957.

The AEC could contract with utilities and power companies for development of nuclear power plants, but the 1946 act had made nuclear materials a government monopoly. Legally, only the government could own and operate the plants. As commercial production and sale of nuclear electricity more and more appeared feasible, the Eisenhower administration and Republicans in Congress sought to revise the 1946 law. Eisenhower had just made his "Atoms for Peace" speech to the United Nations in December 1953. But the bid for private industry development ran into opposition from Democrats who thought the government should retain some responsibility for commercial power development. The same groups that had fought for years over public versus private power renewed their debate, as the Democrats urged government-backed plants that would, they said, perform the same function as the Tennessee Valley Authority had in providing a basis on which to judge the performance of the private industry. Most notable was the chance to compare the rate charged. But the Republicans won, and the Atomic Energy Act of 1954 launched a new industry.

Under the act, the AEC would give a utility a permit to construct and then a license to operate a nuclear power plant. The AEC was to retain control of the nuclear fuel by leasing it to utilities and then taking it back. In 1964, however, Congress changed this procedure, authorizing sale to private industry of uranium enriched at government

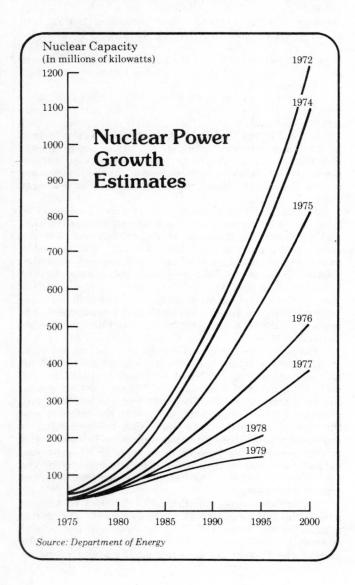

Nuclear Capacity
(In millions of kilowatts)

Nuclear Power Growth Estimates

Source: Department of Energy

Low-Level Wastes Piling Up

Congress in 1980 made it national policy for each state to be responsible for disposal of the low-level waste generated within its borders.

The National Governors Association was expected to work with states to develop regional storage sites. However, any interstate compacts or agreements would, under the Constitution, have to be ratified by Congress. The legislation passed in December 1980 said the regional groups after 1985 could exclude wastes from states that did not join a compact.

The provisions on low-level waste had been part of comprehensive nuclear waste disposal legislation, but several controversies kept that legislation from emerging from conference.

The much less controversial provisions on low-level waste were salvaged and cleared in a separate bill.

States Cutting Back Existing Sites

In the three states with existing disposal sites for commercial low-level waste in 1980, there had been efforts to close the nuclear waste dumps or cut back substantially on the amount of waste accepted.

Voters in Washington had in November approved an initiative to close the Hanford site to all out-of-state wastes, except for medical wastes, after July 1981. Nevada's Republican Gov. Robert F. List had vowed to close the site at Beatty, Nev. "There have been radioactive leaks all over our highways," said an aide to List, "and our federal transportation and packing regulations aren't being enforced."

South Carolina officials had announced they would in 1981 reduce the amount of waste from other states they would accept at Barnwell in their state. Barnwell was the only major storage site for nuclear waste in the East.

Barnwell cannot accept liquid wastes, so trucks must transport those to Hanford, Wash., from as far away as New England.

'Low-Level' Wastes

Low-level wastes are generated in every state. Basically, all wastes that are not produced in nuclear reactors or in the reprocessing of nuclear fuel are considered low-level wastes. Technically, these wastes are defined by what they are not — they are not high-level wastes or wastes contaminated by transuranics.

Some experts say the designation "low-level" leads to an erroneous impression that these wastes are not dangerous. In reality, some can be very radioactive and dangerous. Several organizations have recommended that these wastes be classified by the hazard they pose and not by where they come from. The Nuclear Regulatory Commission was considering such a change.

Commercial low-level wastes include contaminated paper, plastics, construction materials, tools, protective clothing, industrial wastes and contaminated trash produced by nuclear medicine.

Of the 100,000 cubic meters of low-level wastes buried each year in the three commercial dumps in the United States, about 43 percent comes from nuclear power plants, 25 percent from hospitals, 24 percent from industry and 8 percent from the federal government.

The Energy Department also buries about 50,000 cubic meters of low-level waste each year in its own dumps. According to James E. Dieckhoner, a low-level waste expert at the department, the federal government would not be inclined to accept commercial wastes if the three existing sites were closed. The three federal sites that could accept the material are adjacent to the existing commercial dumps, he said.

Three other low-level commercial dumps for spent nuclear fuel had already been closed. One, at Sheffield, Ill., was closed after it was filled in 1978. Two others, at West Valley, N.Y., and Morehead, Ky., were closed in 1975 and 1977 because of water contamination problems.

Ocean Dumping

For 25 years, until 1970, a great deal of low-level waste was put in metal barrels and dumped at 50 sites in the oceans.

Officials of the Environmental Protection Agency testified in 1980 that one-fourth of these barrels were leaking.

Experts disagree on the environmental effect of these leaks, but the publicity aroused the public in several states.

In California, Gov. Edmund G. Brown Jr. ordered state officials to monitor leaks by testing fish caught off the San Francisco coast near the Farallon Islands, where about 45,000 drums of radioactive wastes were dumped.

Dumping Stopped

At the three commercial dumps — Barnwell, S.C., Hanford, Wash., and Beatty, Nev. — low-level wastes are buried in trenches 40 feet wide, 20 feet deep and 600 feet long. Waste containers are dumped in and covered with dirt.

Nevada and Washington — claiming that federal regulations on the packaging and transportation of low-level wastes were being ignored — in 1979 ordered their dumping grounds closed for several weeks. This awakened other states to the impending crisis.

plants. The government still had responsibility for disposing of the wastes left after the fuel had been used. In addition, after no one assumed responsibility, Congress in 1978 provided federal funds for clean up of radioactive uranium "mill tailings" at abandoned mills and dumps.

Another obstacle to private development of nuclear electricity was removed in 1957, when Congress adopted an amendment to the 1954 law limiting industry liability to $560 million in case of a nuclear accident. The risk of a catastrophic accident had scared away private insurers. A 1957 report for the AEC by Brookhaven National Laboratory had said the cost of a "worst case" accident would be $7 billion. Under the 1957 law — the Price-Anderson Act — if what private insurance was available could not cover utilities for the $560 million, the government would make up the difference. The Act's sponsors were Rep. Melvin Price, D-Ill., and Sen. Clinton P. Anderson, D-N.M. Congress renewed the law in 1965 for 10 years, and again in 1975, extending the liability limit to reactors for which licenses had been granted as of Aug. 1, 1987.

While the AEC continued to prod along the infant nuclear industry, the commissioners did show some concern for public safety. In 1961, the AEC issued guidelines that required siting of reactors away from densely populated areas. However, within six years the siting rules had been relaxed, as the AEC had decided that safety features built into the reactor design were adequate protection.

The first nuclear reactor that produced electricity actually marketed by a utility was the Shippingport plant. But the first utility-owned reactor was the Dresden plant in Morris, Ill., owned by Commonwealth Edison Co. It began commercial operation in 1960. Two other plants of that era were the Yankee Nuclear Power Station in Massachusetts and Consolidated Edison's Indian Point.

As a whole, though, utilities were still dubious of the economic benefits of nuclear power. A turning point was a study done in 1964 for the Jersey Central Power and Light Co. Their proposed 620 megawatt plant at Oyster Creek would be cheaper to operate, the company said, than a similar sized plant fired with fossil fuels. As a result, they had selected the nuclear plant and would construct it without any federal assistance.

Also in the late 1960s, the reactor manufacturers began to offer special contracts to utilities that required the reactor builders to absorb any cost overruns or cost increases resulting from inflation. They wanted business, and they got it. The four reactor vendors were Westinghouse Electric Corporation, General Electric Company, Babcock & Wilcox Company and Combustion Engineering Inc.

State public utility commissions had responsibility for deciding whether a power plant, including a nuclear one, was necessary. If such a finding of need was made, then the commission issued a certificate of public convenience and necessity, which guaranteed the utility that it could charge ratepayers for construction and operating costs once the plant had gone into service. The AEC got involved usually only after this step.

The environmental movement prompted a major change in this procedure. A lawsuit was filed by opponents of the Calvert Cliffs plant, which the Baltimore Gas and Electric Company wanted to build on the Chesapeake Bay. Based on the National Environmental Policy Act (NEPA), the local environmentalists charged that the AEC, in issuing the plant permit and license, had not adequately considered the environmental impacts. In 1971, the federal circuit court in the District of Columbia ruled that the AEC had failed to comply with NEPA in this and other decisions. In the future, the court said, the AEC would have to ask four key questions: was there a need for power from the plant; was the site suitable; was nuclear energy satisfactory as a source for the plant; and were any additional safety precautions needed.

Nuclear Safety

Environmentalists and consumer advocates, such as Ralph Nader, kept raising questions about nuclear safety. At the same time, government officials continued to issue scenarios for the future that called for increasing reliance on nuclear power. Most were more realistic than a 1962 AEC report that said nuclear reactors would provide half of all electricity in the year 2000, but the role for nuclear power was expected to be significant by 1985. This optimism about nuclear growth was clouded, though, by increasing concern about nuclear safety.

In 1973 and 1974, when the Joint Atomic Energy Committee held hearings on nuclear safety, AEC officials contended that reactors were safe and that a special study they had commissioned would prove their point. The study, being directed by Norman C. Rasmussen of the Massachusetts Institute of Technology, peaked the interest of Congress. Those concerned about safety managed to add a special provision to a five-year extension of the Price-Anderson Act that they approved in 1974. If warranted by the Rasmussen report, the provision said, Congress could repeal the extension of the liability limit. However, President Ford did not like that restriction and vetoed the bill.

In late 1975, the Rasmussen report was completed. Called the "Reactor Safety Study (WASH-1400)," the report said an accident causing loss of reactor coolant, melting of the core and breach of the containment was likely to occur only once in 10 million years of reactor operation or, as the report declared, was as probable as a single meteorite striking an individual on earth.

Armed with that assessment, nuclear advocates easily won the 10-year extension of Price-Anderson, without a caveat related to nuclear safety.

In the meantime, however, Congress had moved to split the regulatory functions of the AEC away from its research and development functions designed to promote nuclear power. The legislators had finally recognized the difficulties of promoting industry growth and insuring safety at the same time. The Energy Reorganization Act of 1974 created the Nuclear Regulatory Commission and shifted the research to the new Energy Research and Development Administration (ERDA). Later, in 1977, ERDA's responsibilities were assumed by the new Department of Energy. Also in 1977, Congress reordered its own nuclear house, abolishing the Joint Atomic Energy Committee and spreading jurisdiction over nuclear power among eight House and Senate committees.

Troubled Nuclear Industry

In the wake of the Arab oil embargo, there was a quickening in the hopes of nuclear supporters. At first it seemed the new awareness of oil scarcity might be a boon to the still new nuclear industry. In 1975, there were 56 reactors in operation and more than 150 were in various

Most States Unprepared
For Nuclear Accidents

Most state and local authorities in areas around nuclear power plants are unprepared to protect residents against accidents involving the release of harmful radiation. At the same time there is no federal policy on providing the public with evacuation and other information about responding to a nuclear accident.

Those were some of the conclusions of a year-long study by the General Accounting Office, the investigative arm of Congress, released March 30, 1979.

The GAO report concluded that "people living near fixed nuclear facilities are not well informed about potential hazards nor about the actions that may be necessary to avoid or minimize radiation exposure."

NRC Criticized

The report criticized the Nuclear Regulatory Commission for failing to make emergency evacuation plans part of the process for licensing reactors.

The GAO also recommended that emergency planning zones around nuclear reactors be increased to 10 from five miles. The report said the NRC's criteria for emergency-planning areas "do not consider the more serious types of accidents that could occur and do not consider the public exposure levels that may require some protective action."

The agency said no single federal agency was prepared to direct an emergency evacuation in the event of a major disaster.

The report concluded that only 10 of the 43 states with commercial or military reactors met all of the NRC's emergency planning and preparedness standards.

It found that while 41 states have "some type of peacetime nuclear emergency plan," only nine had tested their plans in full scale drills and 16 had never tested their plans at all.

Annual Drills Recommended

The GAO recommended "annual emergency drills" involving state and local agencies and a coordinated federal, state and local effort to disseminate information to the public on the hazards of reactor accidents and protective actions that can be taken.

The investigative agency also found that utility operators have "discouraged efforts to inform the public" about the dangers posed by their reactors. "Facility operators did not appear concerned about the lack of information made available to the public. This reflects the attitude of most operators, namely, that there is little danger to the public from their facilities." The report said operators were "reluctant" to provide public information "for fear of creating public alarm that could result in new or prolonged . . . protest activities."

A similar attitude was found at the Department of Energy and at Defense Department facilities where the GAO said emergency preparedness is "almost nonexistent."

---

stages of development. But the surge of orders placed in the late 1960s and early 1970s had already started to dwindle. The embargo and resulting recession ended up curbing demand for electricity, the only outlet for nuclear energy. At the same time, higher bills for fuel forced utilities to scramble to stay out of the red financially. The result was a hold on plans for new power plants, including new nuclear reactors, which had turned out to be far more costly to build than the initial rosy predictions by reactor makers interested in drumming up business.

By early 1978, utilities had cancelled more than 30 earlier decisions to build reactors and deferred construction of dozens more. The slowdown gradually began to show up in government estimates of future nuclear generation. In 1972, the forecasts were for 1,200 gigawatts (GWe) of electricity in the year 2000 from nuclear power. (A gigawatt equals a million kilowatts.) In 1975, the projection had been cut by a third, to 800 GWe. In 1977, the Carter administration, perhaps more realistic than others, said nuclear capacity in the year 2000 would be only 380 GWe, less than half the 1975 projection. In 1978 and 1979, the forecasters did not try to see as far into the future. The

1979 prediction anticipated only that plants then operating or on order would be generating electricity by 1995. No new orders were expected, and even some cancellations of plants with construction permits were predicted. The anticipated capacity in 1995 was 148 GWe. (Chart of Nuclear Power Growth Estimates, p. 00)

By 1977, even the industry's leaders were conceding the future was cloudy. Craig Hosmer, president of the American Nuclear Energy Council, wrote in an October 1977 letter to a senior White House aide that unless new reactor orders came soon, "the U.S. nuclear industry will move quietly to extinction." Hosmer, a member of the House from 1953 to 1975, had once been ranking Republican on the Joint Committee on Atomic Energy.

Nuclear opponents shared that view in comments made in 1978. "The nuclear industry is dead in the water because they can't finance it — and we don't need it," said Mark Reis, Washington representative for Friends of the Earth, an environmental organization.

"It's like an endangered species," suggested Anthony Z. Roisman, an attorney with the Natural Resources Defense Council in Washington. "When it gets below a certain level, it cannot reproduce." Roisman cautioned that his group was not flatly against nuclear power. "Our position on nuclear power is that it is a last resort technology — which will not be needed," he said.

The already troubled nuclear industry was particularly frustrated by the Carter administration. The 1977 decision to cancel the plutonium-powered breeder reactor project at Clinch River, Tenn., and the ban on reprocessing of spent fuel to create plutonium had been blows to the industry, even though Congress kept pushing the breeder project. *(Box, p 86)*

But Energy Secretary James Schlesinger successfully urged the administration to suggest to Congress the reform of nuclear licensing, which was designed to satisfy industry complaints that government regulation was a major factor in the 12-year lag between a decision to build a reactor and its operation. "There are two White Houses instead of one," lamented Hosmer, the nuclear council president, in a 1977 speech. "There is the White House symbolized by Schlesinger and Co., where a courageous effort goes on.... And then there is that other White House, populated by no growth, counter-culture activists...."

The licensing bill, which had been the subject of intense, lengthy debate within the administration, provide a rallying point for the industry. It called for coordination between federal and state regulators on sites and on standardized reactor designs. More controversial were limits on public participation in licensing proceedings and a shift to the states of more regulatory burdens. The finding of need for power, for example, would have been left solely to the states, as would most environmental issues.

The licensing bill did not emerge from either a House or a Senate committee in 1978, but the industry planned to renew its efforts in the 96th Congress. Westinghouse and General Electric were preparing an intense lobbying campaign for 1979. The trade and research association for investor-owned utilities, the Edison Electric Institute, had planned to commit $5 million to a newspaper and magazine advertising campaign designed to win public support for nuclear reactors. The group spent $3.5 million in 1978.

However, 1979 turned out to be a very bad year for nuclear power.

In January, the NRC repudiated sections of the 1975 Rasmussen report. The commission had asked for a new safety study by a panel of scientists, known as the Risk Assessment Review Group, or the Lewis Panel, after its head, Harold Lewis, a physicist at the University of California. The Lewis report said the methodology used by Rasmussen was legitimate, but that the 1975 report was "inscrutable" to peer review.

Later that month, the Union of Concerned Scientists, the most respected of the groups critical of nuclear regulation, called on the government to shut down 16 U.S. reactors because of safety problems.

On March 13, the Nuclear Regulatory Commission ordered the temporary shutdown of five nuclear plants after it determined that a computer model used to determine their ability to resist earthquakes had been faulty. The same day a special 14-agency governmental review unit raised questions about the scientific and technical feasibility of safely disposing of radioactive wastes created by commercial reactors. The report called into question a matter the industry had long argued it would have no problem resolving.

Then came Three Mile Island.

Three Mile Island Accident

The problems at the reactor near Harrisburg, Pa., began at 4 a.m. on March 28, with a breakdown of water pumps that were part of the cooling system that kept water flowing over the fuel rods. Cooling is necessary because if the rods holding the uranium fuel pellets get too hot, the outside metal covering can melt, releasing radioactive fuel and other elements. In the worst case, the heat can crack the thick concrete walls of the reactor containment and release radioactivity outside the nuclear plant.

Several different mechanical problems contributed to the failure of the TMI cooling system, including poor overall plant design, but key factors were: the shutdown of two auxiliary cooling pumps for maintenance two weeks before the accident; the failure of relief valves to close properly, which allowed too much water to drain from the cooling system; and a struck pressure indicator, which gave operators in the control room erroneous information.

Of equal importance, later investigators said, were the actions of reactor operators, who turned off the emergency and primary cooling systems, thus unintentionally thwarting the built-in "defense-in-depth" against a failure of the cooling system. Their training had not prepared them for the series of events that took place at TMI. In addition, the utility, General Public Utilities Corporation; its subsidiary that operated TMI, Metropolitan Edison; and the reactor manufacturer, Babcock & Wilcox, were faulted for safety procedures and equipment. The Nuclear Regulatory Commission was criticized for its overall regulation of nuclear safety.

These findings were made in an October 1979 report by a presidential commission on the accident, headed by John G. Kemeny, president of Dartmouth College. In ad-

Status of Nuclear Power Plants

	1977	1978	1979	1980
Licensed to operate	65	70	70	68[2]
Licensed for testing[1]	—	—	—	1
Construction permits issued	78	88	91	85
Construction permits requested	59	37	25	11
Total	202	195	186	165

Figures are as of Sept. 30 of each year.

[1] After the March 1979 accident at Three Mile Island in Pennsylvania, licensing procedures were revised, adding another stage of review by the Nuclear Regulatory Commission after the testing period and prior to granting a commercial operating license.

[2] Does not include three plants shut down indefinitely: Three Mile Island in Pennsylvania; Humboldt Bay in California; and Dresden 1, in Illinois.

Source: Nuclear Regulatory Commission

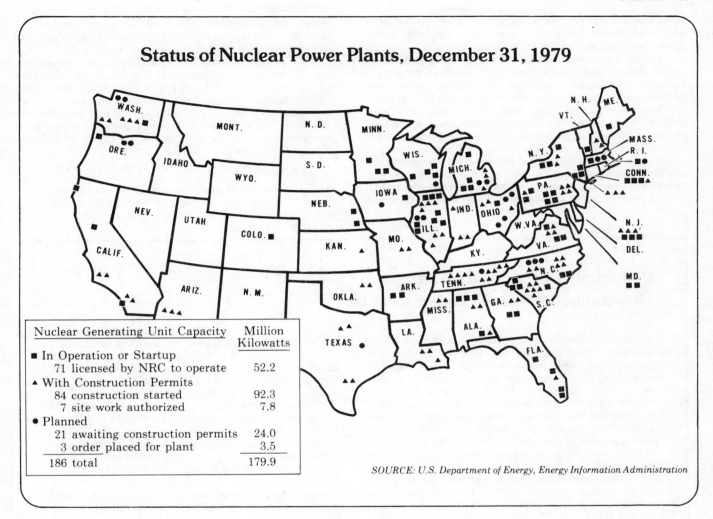

Status of Nuclear Power Plants, December 31, 1979

Nuclear Generating Unit Capacity	Million Kilowatts
■ In Operation or Startup	
71 licensed by NRC to operate	52.2
▲ With Construction Permits	
84 construction started	92.3
7 site work authorized	7.8
● Planned	
21 awaiting construction permits	24.0
3 order placed for plant	3.5
186 total	179.9

SOURCE: U.S. Department of Energy, Energy Information Administration

dition, most were supported by a study done for the NRC by Washington lawyer Mitchell Rogovin, as well as by a special Senate investigation by the Environment Subcommittee on Nuclear Regulation. (Details of Kemeny report, box, p. 89)

It was several weeks before the reactor had been cooled to the desired level. Cleanup of the contaminated reactor containment had still not been completed at the end of 1980. Also still unresolved was who would pay for the $900 million-plus cleanup operation, which an NRC report in late 1980 said could bankrupt Metropolitan Edison.

At the height of the crisis, officials had considered evacuating thousands of residents from the area because of the chance that the plant's nuclear fuel could overheat and "melt down," releasing dangerous radiation.

Pennsylvania Gov. Richard L. Thornburgh, R, March 30 did ask young children and pregnant women living within five miles of the plant to leave because of leaking radiation. They were joined by hundreds, possibly thousands, of others. Thousands more stayed home from work April 2, and most area schools closed.

Conflicting information about the accident and potential hazards from state, federal and utility company officials caused additional confusion, particularly in the

first two days after the incident. Eventually NRC official Harold Denton took charge.

Plans to handle such an emergency were being written on the spot, since apparently no evacuation plans had been ready prior to the accident.

The week's events left the public with a series of graphic images: top level government officials debating evacuation of a half million people; the voluntary evacuation of children and pregnant women; the federal government's deep involvement in the operation of the local utility; Pennsylvania's capital at Harrisburg temporarily reduced to a veritable ghost town as residents stayed inside; the Pentagon flying in tons of lead bricks to assist a team of government officials in bringing the overheated reactor under control, and the federal government flying in hundreds of thousands of bottles of potassium iodide to counteract absorption of radioactive iodine 131 in the event of a catastrophe. It was almost a week of news reports of industry spokesmen minimizing the safety risks of the accident, of contradictions by government officials taking a more cautious approach and of sharp challenges to both by nuclear experts and antinuclear groups.

Cautiously assessing the accident during its early stages, President Carter said the events "will make all of us reassess our present safety regulations ... and probably lead inexorably toward even more stringent safety design mechanisms and standards."

Pennsylvania Sen. Richard Schweiker, R, said the accident showed that "we have seriously underestimated both the safety problems associated with nuclear power generation and our ability to cope with a nuclear emergency."

A grimmer view came from Rep. Morris K. Udall, D-Ariz., who chaired the House Interior panel which handled most nuclear regulatory legislation. He declared, "The aura of confidence in nuclear energy has been shattered."

Industry officials reacted defensively, repeatedly referring to statements by Energy Secretary Schlesinger that "we will have to have nuclear power" to meet energy needs.

Charles F. Luce, chairman of Consolidated Edison of New York, predicted: "When the need is looked at with the alternatives, nuclear will remain an important part of our future."

"You can look at the situation in two ways," said an official with Westinghouse Electric Corp. who asked not to be identified. "From a technical viewpoint Three Mile Island is no problem. It sounds bad but there was no major accident.... From the political point of view it's next to a disaster. And public perception determines the political view.... It looks like this incident will have a profound effect" on the industry.

TMI Aftermath

In the months after the March accident, industry officials did not even mention licensing reform. The public

President Carter and Congress Deadlocked Over Breeder Reactor

Jimmy Carter first signaled his concern about proliferation of nuclear weapons during the 1976 presidential campaign. In April 1977, he banned reprocessing of nuclear spent fuel and called for a halt to construction of the breeder reactor project at Clinch River, Tenn. Both moves were designed to reduce the supply of plutonium available for bomb-making and to set an example for the rest of the world in non-proliferation. The breeder represented a move toward nuclear power based on plutonium, rather than uranium.

Four years later, Carter was still fighting with Congress over termination of the breeder project. The example he had hoped to set for the world had not been followed, as France, West Germany, Britain, Japan and also the Soviet Union moved forward with development of breeders. The president had also begun to emphasize another part of his argument against Clinch River: its high cost and outdated technology. Besides, he said, the slowed growth in electricity demand meant there would be no need for the breeder until 2020. There was time to develop a new, better design for a demonstration project, ideally using a fuel other than the plutonium that both fueled and was created by the liquid metal fast breeder reactor.

The congressional love affair with the Clinch River project was rooted in old predictions by the former Atomic Energy Commission and Joint Committee on Atomic Energy that the breeder was the wave of the future. Put in fuel and the breeder puts out more fuel, along with energy to produce electricity, they had been told.

The nuclear industry did not want to lose the actual, concrete demonstration of this long dream just because of Jimmy Carter's dreams about nuclear non-proliferation. The industry's years-old friendship with Congress paid off as the legislators again and again — four times in all — funded Clinch River anyway. They had similarly rejected amendments in 1975 and 1976 that cut funding for the projects. The action was also a reflection of doubt about the effectiveness of Carter's nuclear foreign policy.

What Congress never managed to do after 1976, though, was pass an authorization bill for the Clinch River project, which was usually part of the Department of Energy's annual authorization. Carter vetoed one bill, in 1977; he wanted the authorization for the project revoked, not continued and increased. Carter did not have to veto any other bills because Congress never got around to clearing other Energy authorizations during Carter's term. The authorizations usually got bogged down in fights related to oil pricing.

Carter tried to compromise with Congress, and made some headway in the Senate, but his pledge of new spending for breeder research, with a new demonstration project to be proposed in 1981, did not satisfy breeder proponents in Congress.

By the end of 1980, though, there was no concrete at the Tennessee site. The tug-of-war between Carter and Congress had kept the project on hold at an early stage. Components of the reactor were built and then stored at various places around the country. The failure by Congress to repeal the authorization, combined with continued appropriations for the project, forced Carter to spend about $15 million a month building and mothballing the components, but that was all he would do. The project, which had been initially authorized in 1971 and expected to cost $700 million when contracts were signed in 1973, was getting more and more expensive. Completing it was expected to cost more than $2.6 billion. The initial share to be paid by the consortium of utilities co-sponsoring the plant was $258 million; it had not changed.

mood was for more, not less, regulation of nuclear power.

Utilities stepped up their advertising campaign in support of nuclear power. "The safety system worked," was a headline in a full-page ad in *The New York Times*, bought by a group called America's Electric Energy Companies.

"One thing is certain," the advertisement continued. "What happened at Three Mile Island does *not* justify a halt to nuclear power development...."

The importance of public opinion to the future of nuclear power had led to a warning from the Kemeny Commission. "We are convinced that, unless portions of the industry and its regulatory agency undergo fundamental changes, they will over time totally destroy public confidence and, hence, they will be responsible for the elimination of nuclear power as a viable source of energy," the panel said.

The utilities that used nuclear power, along with other nuclear-related companies, took several steps they hoped would improve nuclear safety and public opinion.

They set up an Institute of Nuclear Power Operations in Atlanta to serve as an in-house regulator of safety. The institute was to certify utility training programs for plant operators, use auditors to monitor reactor operations and distribute information about potential problems. Its initial annual budget was to be between $11 million and $12 million.

"Altogether it will be a kind of watchdog," said Carl Goldstein of the Atomic Industrial Forum, an international association of companies involved with nuclear power. The institute would "prod a utility into action" if a deficiency were found, he said.

The utilities also set up a mutual insurance program to help cover the costs of buying more expensive substitute electricity in the event of an accident or shutdown.

One sanction the institute would have against plants that did not meet safety requirements would be to keep them out of the insurance program, Goldstein said.

Still another industry program developed in response to the Three Mile Island accident was the Nuclear Safety Analysis Center, which was to be part of the Edison Electric Institute. The center was to concentrate on technical analysis and long-term research on reactor safety and operations.

Congressional Reaction

In Congress, the initial reaction to the Three Mile Island accident was a spate of hearings and investigations, led primarily by the House Interior and Senate Environment and Public Works committees, which had jurisdiction over the NRC and nuclear regulation. Rep. Udall chaired Interior, as well as its energy subcommittee. Sen. Gary Hart, D-Colo., chaired the Nuclear Regulation Subcommittee. Both men had not hesitated in the past to criticize the nuclear industry or the NRC, and were expected to push for additional federal controls. They were countered by nuclear advocates, who still sought to boost the industry's fortunes and thus downplayed the accident. For example, Rep. Mike McCormack, D-Wash., said the Three Mile Island incident was not unexpected by nuclear experts. He then cited the lack of injury as a demonstration of the safety of nuclear energy. "Nuclear power is still hundreds of times safer than coal," said McCormack, referring to the deaths of coal miners and other problems.

When faced with such divergent views and such complicated and controversial questions, Congress usually

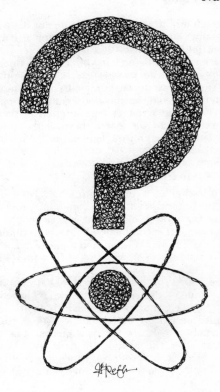

takes several years to pass major legislation. The impasse is prolonged further when the signals from the American public are mixed, as they have been on nuclear power. As Udall put it, "People tell you they are willing to have nuclear power, and then they say, 'But don't put it in my neighborhood.'"

The middle ground usually necessary to pass legislation was not obvious in the months after the TMI accident. Improved emergency preparedness and stiffer fines for violators of NRC rules were the most Congress could agree on. A bold Senate plan to shut down reactors in states without approved evacuation plans was watered down in conference in 1980, so that in an uncooperative state, a utility could submit a plan of its own to the NRC, thus reducing the chance of reactor shutdowns.

During 1979 action on the same bill, a move by nuclear critics to pass a six-month moratorium on NRC issuance of new construction permits failed badly. The Senate vote, in July, was 35-57; the House vote, in November, was 135-254. Supporters had argued that safety problems should be resolved first, before further industry expansion. But opponents said a moratorium by Congress would be the death knell for the nuclear industry.

Carter Response

In his first response to the Kemeny Commission, in December 1979, which was also his first detailed statement on nuclear power since the accident, President Carter urged a resumption of plant licensing by the NRC as soon as possible, but no later than six months. Safety was important, "my top priority," Carter said, but he continued, "We cannot shut the door on nuclear power for the United States."

Nuclear power was "critical if we are to free our country from its overdependence on unstable sources of high-priced foreign oil," Carter said. "We do not have the luxury of abandoning nuclear power or imposing a lengthy moratorium on its further use.

"As I have said before, in this country nuclear power is an energy source of last resort," Carter said. "By this I meant that as we reach our goals on conservation, on the direct use of coal, on development of solar power and synthetic fuels and enhanced production of American oil and natural gas, as we reach those goals, then we can minimize our reliance on nuclear power."

Safety Debate Continues

The question of a moratorium had been ducked by the Kemeny Commission. The 12 members failed to agree on whether the growth of nuclear power should be halted until the changes it recommended have been made. Though eight commission members wanted a pause in construction, they could not agree on what events would lift a moratorium.

In the midst of congressional debate on the issue, the NRC made a decision on its own. The commission Nov. 5 announced that it would continue to hold off for an indefinite period on the issuance of operating licenses and construction permits for new plants. The NRC had decided just after the March accident to delay licensing for a few months in order to concentrate on the TMI accident. The NRC action continued what was essentially a *de facto* moratorium.

"Our first and most important responsibility is to apply those remedies and lessons [from Three Mile Island and the Kemeny report] to the operating plants," said NRC Chairman Joseph Hendrie at a Nov. 5 congressional hearing. "We have a pause in licensing. I've been trying to stay away from the word 'moratorium.'"

The delay in licensing immediately affected four newly constructed plants that were ready or almost ready to start up. The plants were Salem 2 in New Jersey, North Anna 2 in Virginia, Diablo Canyon in California and Sequoyah 1 in Tennessee.

The "pause" in licensing ended in August 1980, when the first post-TMI license was issued to the North Anna 2 unit, a Virginia Electric and Power Co. plant. The NRC moratorium was months longer than that sought by congressional proponents of the unsuccessful moratorium amendments.

As the NRC and other federal officials have tried to deal with nuclear power, they have been hampered because major policy — and philosophical — questions about nuclear power have not been addressed by Congress in years. Without some signal from the legislators, the nuclear regulators will go only so far in forcing expensive safety improvements.

For example, NRC officials have received little guidance on how to balance possible risks to the public against the costs to utilities of making safety improvements. Congress had never expanded on the few words in the 1954 Atomic Energy Act that said there should be "adequate assurance of no undue risk" from nuclear power.

"Congress needs to say either we want it [nuclear power] under the following conditions or we don't want it," said one NRC official. "Lacking those kinds of decisions, we're all in a quandary — and nuclear power is slowly going down the tubes."

Though most legislators generally agree that safety must be improved, they are less united on just how to accomplish that. And safety questions tend to breed other, politically loaded questions.

For example, if evacuation plans are required but are not feasible for a reactor near a major city, does that mean the plant should be shut down?

If better designed control rooms could prevent accidents, does that mean existing plants should be retrofitted, at great expense?

If agreement is reached that safety must be improved, does that mean no additional reactors should be built until the new safety rules are in place?

The Kemeny report made it clear that the future of nuclear power is a political question.

"The ultimate resolution of the question involves the kind of economic, environmental and foreign policy considerations that can only be evaluated through the political process," the commission said.

Nuclear Waste

One of the most difficult political questions facing Congress has been disposal of radioactive nuclear wastes.

The government has always had responsibility for handling military wastes from nuclear weapons programs and since 1954 has been responsible for wastes generated by commercial nuclear power. But after four decades of waste generation, no permanent disposal had been provided for the materials, some of which remain radioactive for more than a thousand years. Instead, by the late 1970s the federal government had built a poor record of waste management. Leaks had developed in 1973 from tanks of high-level military waste stored at Hanford, Wash. Plans to store waste at a Lyons, Kan., salt deposit had to be abandoned when investigators discovered penetration of the site by wells drilled during oil and gas exploration. In the meantime, the government's inept dealing with local and state officials had sparked heated local opposition to the plans. Another stab at salt deposits was made in northern Michigan. Again, political opposition developed, leading the government to give up the sites. The agency had neglected to inform the state government that its surveys were only preliminary. When state officials found safety criteria inadequate, the governor asked federal officials to leave.

Gus Speth, a member of the White House Council on Environmental Quality, summed up concerns about the government's track record in a well-publicized September 1977 speech: "Perhaps the waste problem is manageable in theory; perhaps not. I hope it is. But many things that are theoretically doable never get done. Certainly the sorry history of radioactive waste management in this country to date provides no basis for confidence that things will work out." Speth went on to suggest setting a near-term deadline for resolving the waste question; if the deadline were not met, no new licenses would be issued.

Congress has not gone that far in linking waste disposal with continued nuclear development, as critics demanding it have been clearly in the minority in Congress. But nuclear advocates had begun to realize by the late 1970s that inaction on nuclear waste was becoming a serious liability to the nuclear industry. The Carter administration held the same view, and its officials concluded that public opposition was a bigger problem than the remaining technical questions about isolating materials from air, water

Three Mile Island Commission Critical of Nuclear Regulation

The presidential commission that studied the Three Mile Island accident issued on Oct. 30, 1979, the most critical government assessment to date of nuclear power.

"If the country wishes, for larger reasons, to confront the risks that are inherently associated with nuclear power, fundamental changes are necessary if those risks are to be kept within tolerable limits," said the 12-member commission.

The panel, called the Kemeny Commission after its chairman John Kemeny, president of Dartmouth College, spent six months on its study, which cost $3 million.

Carter established the commission.

Because of shortcomings it found in utility operation and government regulation of nuclear power, the commission said an accident such as the one at Three Mile Island was "eventually inevitable." And even if changes were made, the panel said, a similar accident could occur.

"Our findings do not, standing alone, require the conclusion that nuclear power is inherently too dangerous to permit it to continue and expand as a form of power generation," the report said. "Neither do they suggest that the nation should move forward aggressively to develop additional commercial power."

Major Recommendations

The commission's major recommendations were that:

● Requests for operating licenses and construction permits be reviewed by the Nuclear Regulatory Commission (NRC) on a case-by-case basis to make sure that 1) new safety standards recommended by the commission had been incorporated in the plant; 2) the plant operator could meet more stringent qualifications for reactor management and operation, and 3) state and local emergency response plans for handling accidents had been approved.

● The five-member, independent NRC be abolished and replaced with an executive branch agency headed by a single administrator appointed by the president. A 15-member oversight committee on reactor safety would review the agency's performance and consider the overall risks of nuclear power.

● Government regulation of nuclear power concentrate on safety, instead of on licensing. "Where additional safety improvements are not clearly outweighed by cost considerations, there should be a presumption in favor of the safety change," the report said.

● Oversight of plant operation be upgraded, including establishment of government-accredited schools for training reactor operators and periodic review of licensees to be sure they are complying with government standards.

● New plants be located in areas remote from population centers "to the maximum extent feasible."

● The government expand its research on the effects of radiation. This recommendation came despite the commission's finding that most radiation resulting from the accident was contained within the reactor. The report noted that the major health effect was mental stress, which was found to be "quite severe" among those living within the vicinity of Three Mile Island.

Carter Response

In responding to the recommendations Dec. 7, President Carter:

● Proposed reorganization of the Nuclear Regulatory Commission, with more authority given to the chairman. Congress in 1980 approved the reorganization plan.

● Announced the removal as chairman of Joseph Hendrie, with Commissioner John Ahearne to serve as acting chairman until a new chairman could be appointed when a vacant seat opened up in June 1980. Carter later indicated he would appoint as chairman Albert Carnesale, a Harvard public policy professor trained as a nuclear engineer. But political considerations in an election year worked against Carnesale's confirmation, and the seat remained vacant for most of 1980. Ahearne continued to act as chairman through the last months of the Carter administration.

● Proposed establishment of a five-member expert advisory committee to monitor how the NRC, other federal agencies, the states and utilities carried out the recommendations of the commission relating to safety.

● Asked the NRC and other agencies to accelerate a program to place a resident federal inspector at every reactor site. He also asked the NRC to study the need for a federal presence, of either people or instruments, in the control room of operating reactors.

● Directed the Federal Emergency Management Agency to assume responsibility for evaluating and monitoring the plans of state and local governments and other organizations for responding to nuclear emergencies.

and human contact for several centuries. The solution they proposed was a methodical exploration of possible waste sites, with federal officials cooperating fully with the state and local governments.

In Congress, though, the sentiment has been for a better defined state role. The majority apparently feel that a state should be able to veto waste disposal if Congress went along with its action. Then, the problem of having all of the states refuse would be avoided and a federal role would be retained, they reasoned. But if a state truly did not want the radioactive waste, it is not likely a vote by Congress could force the citizens to accept it.

Both the House and Senate in 1980 passed comprehensive nuclear waste legislation for the first time. However, the bills died in conference. Further action was expected in the 97th Congress.

Types of Waste

Nuclear waste comes in a variety of forms that present varying degrees of danger.

High-level Wastes. High-level wastes are highly radioactive liquids generated when used nuclear reactor fuel is reprocessed. No commercial reprocessing was underway in 1980, but the government continued to reprocess fuel for military uses. More than 80 million gallons of these high-level wastes had been generated through 1980. They are stored at sites in Washington state, Idaho, South Carolina and New York.

Transuranic Wastes. These are produced in the reprocessing of nuclear fuel and the production of nuclear bombs. While not as intensely radioactive as high-level wastes, transuranic wastes take far longer — many thousands of years — to decay to a safe form.

Low-level Wastes. Low-level wastes are generated from all activities using radioactive materials. They include protective clothing, hand tools, rags, vials and a variety of solutions, many from medical uses. Only three states had disposal facilities for commercial low-level wastes in 1980, and officials were threatening to close them down or at least limit acceptance of waste from out-of-state.

Uranium Tailings. This waste from mills and mines contains naturally occurring radioactive materials. Hugh piles of these tailings, in the form of fine sand, have been dumped at abandoned mills and mines in 11 states.

Spent Nuclear Fuel. Spent nuclear fuel is not classified as waste because it still contains minerals that could be reused, but if it were classified, it would be a high-level waste. Because of the ban on reprocessing by President Carter, and earlier failures of commercial reprocessing, utilities must keep racks of spent fuel assemblies in pools of water near their reactors, and some of those pools are filling up.

Carter Proposal

In 1978, President Carter established an Interagency Review Group to examine the nuclear waste problem. Based on its March 1979 recommendations, he issued what the White House called a comprehensive national policy on nuclear waste management in February 1980.

It took nearly a year to issue the policy because of intense fighting within the administration between environmentalists in the Council for Environmental Quality and nuclear power advocates in the Energy Department.

Carter established a State Planning Council of state, local and federal officials to deal with the nuclear waste issue, with Gov. Richard W. Riley, D-S.C., as chairman. Carter said the siting, design and construction of nuclear dumps would be based on the principle of "consultation and concurrence" with the states, although what this means has never been precisely defined.

Carter's plan called for permanent geologic disposal of nuclear wastes. Following the requirements of the National Environmental Policy Act (NEPA), the federal government would evaluate four or five potential sites in a variety of different types of rock formation, selecting one site for development by 1985, with a goal of having it operational by the mid-1990s. Carter insisted nuclear garbage dumps would be licensed by the Nuclear Regulatory Commission (NRC).

To the delight of environmentalists, Carter said spent nuclear fuel would continue to be the responsibility of the utilities until a permanent federal geologic repository was built. To their dismay, however, he said the administration would press for passage of its legislation to build away-from-reactor (AFR) facilities to store the spent fuel that utilities do not have room for.

Carter also said the administration would work with the states through the planning council to establish a regional network of low-level waste disposal sites. He asked Congress to permanently authorize the council.

Senate Bill

Carter's formal proposal came more than a month after the Senate Energy Committee had reported a substantially different nuclear waste bill. Instead of emphasizing permanent geologic storage of radioactive wastes, the committee bill called for putting high-level wastes in above-ground vaults for as long as 100 years or more. The wastes could be monitored and even retrieved, if necessary or profitable. Geological investigations were to continue.

Sen. J. Bennett Johnston, D-La., prime sponsor of the bill, said encasing the wastes in steel casks and monitoring the facility would be safer than permanent, underground storage. Above-ground facilities could be built anywhere, Johnston noted, since no special geology is required; he suggested using tunnels at the federal atomic test sites in Nevada.

He later called it "not just safe disposal, but disposal that is so safe that even the most skeptical anti-nuclear person will be convinced that these wastes will not contaminate the water supply or shoot him with a death ray while he lies asleep at night."

As soon as the committee approved the bill, Johnston issued a press release in Louisiana saying his proposal had ensured that nuclear wastes would not go to Louisiana salt domes, which had been a prime candidate for such repositories. "The bill would help to assure that Louisiana does not become a dumping ground for the nation's nuclear waste," the release said.

The bill provided for AFR storage of spent fuel for utilities, as proposed by the administration in 1979. The government would take over the responsibility for storing spent fuel until a permanent geologic site was available. The utilities would pay a one-time fee, but would retain rights to the spent fuel if reprocessing were later allowed.

The storage vaults for high-level waste were exempted from NEPA provisions that require an environmental impact statement before a site is decided upon. The impact statement eventually written would not have to consider alternative facilities, and the NRC in its licensing process also could not review alternatives, as it normally does.

Nuclear Waste Storage Sites

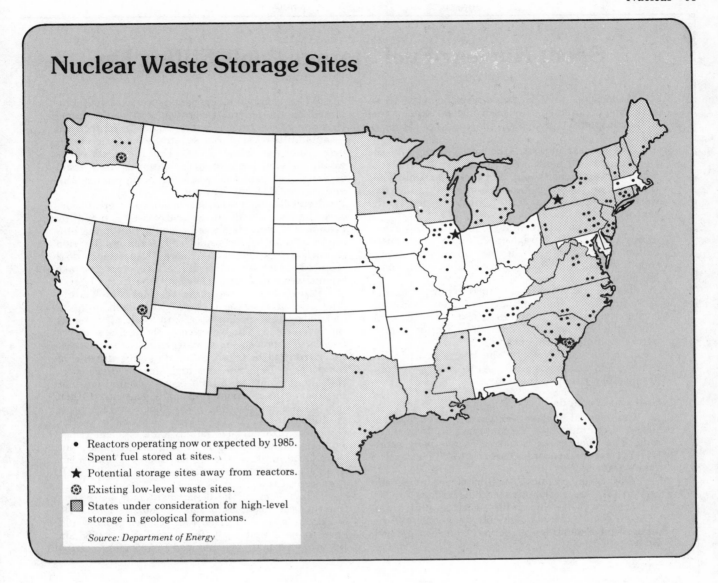

- • Reactors operating now or expected by 1985. Spent fuel stored at sites.
- ★ Potential storage sites away from reactors.
- ⊛ Existing low-level waste sites.
- ▦ States under consideration for high-level storage in geological formations.

Source: Department of Energy

The measure also authorized the State Planning Council. It said the states would participate in decisions on where to store wastes, but left details to be handled by floor amendment.

The Senate passed the bill July 30 by a vote of 88-7, five days after the Senate Environment Committee reported a bill emphasizing permanent disposal. The Environment proposal would have set a specific timetable for the government to follow to have a permanent geologic disposal site in operation by the year 2000. If the site were not established by then, the NRC could not issue construction permits or operating licenses for new nuclear power plants.

The Environment bill, sponsored by Sen. Gary Hart, D-Colo., was not considered by the Senate. Hart criticized the Energy Committee's approach as neglecting the ultimate disposal of the waste, saying it left the problem to future generations. However, the surface storage in the Energy bill was not challenged on the Senate floor.

Hart and Sen. Alan K. Simpson, R-Wyo, attempted unsuccessfully to amend the Energy bill to insist that util-

ities, not the federal government, have the primary responsibility for storing spent fuel. The amendment would have required utilities to expand their existing storage at reactor sites before they could be eligible for federal AFR storage. But Johnston said the amendment would kill the bill, and the Senate tabled it by a 51-44 vote.

The Senate added a provision giving states authority to veto storage of nuclear wastes within their borders if their objection were upheld by either the House or Senate. However, this section would not apply to AFR spent fuel facilities.

House Bills

In the House, leaders of two of the three committees involved in the legislation reached a last-minute compromise in mid-November. Though they managed to get their comprehensive waste bill through the House, the legislation died in conference. Congress did pass a separate bill enacting the relatively non-controversial title dealing with low-level wastes. *(Low-level wastes, box, p. 81)*

Spent Nuclear Fuel Storage Pools Filling Up . . .

A decision must be made soon on what to do with growing quantities of used nuclear reactor fuel at power plants throughout the country. *(Map, p. 91)*

The nuclear industry, the utility lobby and the Department of Energy were saying in 1980 that the federal government should take the responsibility for this fuel and store it until permanent radioactive waste repositories are built toward the end of the century.

However, environmental groups called this away-from-reactor (AFR) storage approach an unwarranted bailout of the utilities; they say spent fuel storage should remain the responsibility of the nuclear power industry.

The Senate voted in July 1980 to put the burden of storing spent fuel on the government, while allowing the utilities to retain title to it in case reprocessing were allowed later. The Carter administration supported this position.

The bill considered by the House in early December had no provision for AFR storage. A compromise had dropped the issue.

Storage Methods

Commercial nuclear reactors are fueled with enriched uranium which is contained in long metal rods. The nuclear reaction creates relatively short-lived fission products and what are called "transurancis."

The fission products, such as strontium-90 and cesium-137, are radioactive and hazardous for 300 to 600 years. The transuranics, such as plutonium-239, are even more radioactively dangerous and remain so for a much longer period — at least 245,000 years.

When commercial nuclear power was first promoted by the federal government, it was assumed that spent fuel from reactors would be reprocessed — an additional step that separates the fission products from the transuranics. The fission products would be stored and the transuranics used again as fuel. The spent fuel would again be reprocessed, and the cycle would continue.

Reprocessing never became a commercial success, however, and subsequently was banned by President Carter. He argued that the plutonium produced in reprocessing could lead to the proliferation of nuclear weapons. (The Energy Department does reprocess spent fuel from military reactors to make atomic weapons for the Defense Department.)

Periodically, a portion of the fuel core of a nuclear reactor must be replaced with fresh uranium fuel. The spent fuel is stored in pools of water at the reactor site. The water cools the fuel and serves as a barrier preventing the escape of radioactivity.

According to Owen Gormley, acting director of the Energy Department's fuel storage division in 1980, most plants were built on the assumption that they would store spent fuel for a year or so, then ship it to a reprocessing plant. Their storage pools are filling up.

Some utilities have put in more efficient racks, enabling them to store more fuel in the pools, but there is a limit to that. The Energy Department in 1980 said 27 nuclear plants would require AFR storage by 1985.

Critics suggest the department may be overestimating the need, as it has in the past. In 1979, for example, it said 1,180 tons of spent fuel would have to be stored away from reactors by 1985; in 1980 that estimate was reduced to 755 tons.

The compromise agreement between Interior Chairman Morris K. Udall, D-Ariz., and John D. Dingell, D-Mich., chairman of the Commerce Subcommittee on Energy and Power, had by-passed the Science Committee, which had drafted its own, much different waste bill. Key sponsor of the Science bill had been Mike McCormack, D-Wash., who had just lost his re-election bid Nov. 4.

The Science bill had been reported first, in July, and called for demonstration of underground waste disposal at four sites by 1990. Under the bill, the projects were exempted from requirements of the National Environmental Policy Act and from NRC licensing. No public hearings were required on site selection. Environmental groups warned that the demonstration projects could be converted later to full-scale repositories, without having undergone full environmental and safety reviews.

Commerce and Interior reported their versions of the waste bill in August and early September. Commerce provided for the four demonstration sites, but required they be closed in the year 2000.

Interior rejected the idea of unlicensed test sites and set out a detailed schedule for the Energy Department to follow in developing a licensed, full-scale, geologic waste repository, to be operational by about 1996. The committee argued that test sites could not demonstrate the ability to safely isolate wastes for more than a few years, a very short time considering the long period that nuclear wastes remain dangerous. Meanwhile, the emphasis on these demonstration sites would delay work on permanent repositories. That work, primarily the testing of different geologic formations to isolate the waste from man and the environment, should proceed, the panel said.

This approach, based on the recommendations of the president's Interagency Review Group, would require the government to select four candidate sites for repositories by 1985, submit plans for them to the NRC, have the

. . . As Debate Grows Over Permanent Waste Sites

Utility engineers have come up with several different methods for increasing the capacity of storage pools. They can stack the rods differently, for example, or add other materials that prevent interaction among the radioactive matter in the rods.

"Any totals are always going to be funny numbers," Harold Denton, director of nuclear regulation for the Nuclear Regulatory Commission, said in April 1980. Asked if the utilities were about to run out of storage, Denton said, "I'm not going to cry 'wolf.' "

Carter Position

However, the Carter administration took the position that no commercial reactor should be required to shut down because of lack of space to store spent fuel. The options are for utilities to build their own additional storage facilities, or for the government to provide centralized storage. The first option would require a large economic commitment by utilities in uncertain times, Gormley said — the future of nuclear power is not clear, and commercial reprocessing again could be initiated. The Carter administration chose the second option.

The Energy Department was exploring three sites where federal AFRs could quickly be established:

- The Barnwell Nuclear Fuel Plant, Barnwell, S.C. This plant, owned by Allied General Nuclear Service, was intended as a reprocessing facility but was caught in the reprocessing ban and has never been used. The storage pool there could store 1,750 metric tons of fuel.
- The Morris Operation, Morris, Ill. This plant, owned and operated by General Electric, also was designed to be a reprocessing plant, but never reprocessed any fuel because of design problems. It has been used for several years as a commercial AFR to store fuel from GE reactors. It already holds about 350 tons of spent fuel and could store about 1,100 tons altogether.
- The Western New York Nuclear Service Center, West Valley, N.Y. This plant, owned by a subsidiary of Getty Oil, was the only commercial reprocessing facility that ever operated in the United States. It could store 1,500 tons of fuel; it already holds 165 tons. Congress in 1980 passed legislation providing federal aid to help clean up the high level wastes at West Valley.

While environmental lobbyists generally agree with Carter's overall nuclear waste policy of building safe, permanent, geologic repositories, they vigorously disagree with the need for AFRs.

Federal AFRs would be a "taxpayer bailout" of the nuclear industry, according to a September 1980 memo to House members from environmental lobbyists. The utilities would shoulder none of the responsibilities for the wastes while retaining the potential benefits remaining in the spent fuel, the memo said. In addition, it said, AFRs would cause a large increase in the amount of nuclear waste that must be transported over public roads, some through heavily populated areas.

A senior official with the Carter administration's Council for Environmental Quality said there had been an effort within the administration to clarify the president's policy on AFR storage, making clear that the utilities must do as much as they could to store the fuel before the government would take it. That effort was sidetracked by the election, he said.

president nominate one site for a permanent repository in 1988, along with a final environmental impact statement, have the NRC make a final decision on a construction permit in 1992 and begin operating the repository in 1996.

A state could veto the site selection of the repository if either house of Congress passed a resolution agreeing with the state, under the Interior bill.

In addition to reporting a companion to the Science bill, Commerce also reported legislation emphasizing permanent disposal, as a companion to the Interior approach. Interior had put its provisions in two different bills: one to accompany the Science bill, which had been referred to Interior and Commerce, and one of its own that was referred only to Commerce.

The November compromise worked from these Commerce and Interior versions, dropping the idea of underground demonstration projects and abandoning any provision for surface, vault-type storage. A sticking point was the question of state veto rights over waste sites. Commerce required both houses to agree with a state on blocking a waste dump within its borders. Interior said if either house went along, the state veto would be upheld. The November compromise adopted the Interior position, giving states more authority.

On the House floor in early December, the question of state rights was the most controversial. An amendment was offered by Peter H. Kostmayer, D-Pa., to let a state's veto of a disposal site stand unless both houses of Congress voted to override it. But the amendment failed, 161-218, leaving intact the compromise in favor of one-house approval of a state veto.

The approach by the House bill was much closer to the Senate Environmental proposal than the Energy panel bill that had been approved by the Senate. The House Interior and Commerce compromise had left out any provision for away-from-reactor storage, which was included in the Senate bill and sought by the nuclear industry and the Carter administration. However, the issue that proved most intractable to the conferees was the question of state authority over disposal of nuclear wastes from military activities. Though the Senate had voted to give states limited authority over military waste disposal, Energy Chairman Henry M. Jackson, D-Wash., refused to allow any state say over military wastes. Jackson, a senior member of the Armed Services Committee, feared a precedent would be set for a state role in other military decisions. His unyielding position doomed the conference.

Over the last several months of the session, what progress was made on nuclear waste legislation was achieved almost totally behind closed doors. The House bill was a compromise produced privately by Udall and Dingell. The negotiations between them and key senators were conducted in the privacy of Jackson's Capitol suite, not in an open conference committee. And additional proposals offered by senators and their staffs were handled privately.

Administration Faulted

The Carter administration was widely criticized for its lobbying role.

"They did an abysmal job," said David Berrick, a lobbyist for the Environmental Policy Center. Carter's policy is "a good blueprint," he said, but the administration had not worked to sell it on Capitol Hill and Congress had marched in the opposite direction.

"The administration was all over the place," added a House Commerce Committee staffer. In the Senate, it accepted things it previously opposed, such as non-geologic disposal of high-level wastes, to get away-from-reactor (AFR) storage and the State Planning Council, the aide said. "Then they came over [to the House] and were different. No one in the House is enthusiastic about AFRs or the state council. We were offering nothing they wanted, so they said just pass a bill and get to conference."

In early September, presidential adviser Stuart E. Eizenstat sent Udall a letter calling for a bill with four main features: licensed geologic disposal; active, but unspecified, participation by the states; AFR storage until permanent disposal is available, and full NEPA environmental reviews.

The White House opposed McCormack's unlicensed demonstration bill and would fight any compromises on NEPA, Eizenstat said.

But, according to staff members and published reports, later in September, when the committees were having trouble reaching a consensus, Acting Energy Under Secretary C. Worthington Bateman was lobbying for the House to pass any bill so the legislation could move to conference. This led environmental groups to pressure the White House into pulling Bateman back and assuring Congress it would not accept bad legislation.

Energy Department lobbyists admit they did not push the waste legislation very hard. "It was not established as a very high priority here," one said. "There was not a solid administration position on several waste issues, plus we were afraid to pressure the committee chairmen, who also handle our annual authorization bill."

According to Sen. Johnston, the administration "was a non-player" on the waste bills.

5

Emergency Preparedness

Three important steps taken as the "Energy Crisis" decade of the 1970s came to an end made the United States better prepared for serious oil shortages in the 1980s than it had been in 1973, when Arab members of the Organization of Petroleum Exporting Countries (OPEC) cut off supplies to the West.

First, a contingency plan for gasoline rationing dated July 30, 1980, became a part of the president's emergency powers to deal with a future national fuel shortage. Second, the states in 1979 were given the authority to draft their own standby energy conservation plans. Third, Congress issued a directive to the federal government in 1980 to accelerate the storage of oil in a strategic petroleum reserve that would be available during fuel emergencies.

Nevertheless, major problems remained.

● Officials at the Economic Regulatory Administration, a branch of the Energy Department, were still working out the details of the gas rationing scheme. It was expected to be ready by September 1981. Even so, the logistical nightmare of rationing, better understood in 1980 than earlier, had cooled enthusiasm among many rationing proponents in Congress for this scheme as a workable tool during emergencies.

● As for state conservation plans, only two formal proposals by states had been submitted to the Energy Department by the end of 1980. The federal plan, which could be imposed on a state in an emergency if the state's conservation efforts failed, was still not in final form.

● The Strategic Petroleum Reserve held 108 million barrels of oil at the end of 1980. The price tag on putting into storage the entire 1 billion barrels mandated by a 1975 law was from $5 billion to $11 billion for the extra storage capacity and $50 billion for the oil, although the oil costs presumably could be recovered if and when the reserve was tapped. The size of the initial outlay raised serious questions about whether the United States could afford to meet the 1975 law's goal. However, the Congressional Budget Office, which provided the cost estimates in a June 1980 report to Congress, said a reserve of 1 billion barrels could avert a loss of $205 billion in gross national product (GNP). This was the estimated loss that could be expected from a year-long foreign supply interruption of 3 million barrels a day.

It appeared that only another crisis, or the immediate threat of a crisis, would prompt a new look at emergency preparedness and another round of efforts to make improvements. Even then, it was questionable whether Congress would be willing to legislate more conservation programs. A hint of its disinclination toward strong action was provided by a 1979 law, the Emergency Energy Conservation Act, which gave the president more responsibility for drafting a standby rationing plan and the states more responsibility for handling emergency conservation efforts. Congress simply did not want to give even the appearance of telling Americans to use less energy.

Conservation, Rationing

The energy crisis precipitated by the Arab oil embargo in October 1973 prompted the president and Congress to focus immediately on the need for emergency measures and new executive powers.

President Nixon asked in November 1973 for a range of emergency powers, including authority to reduce speed limits, require lower temperatures in buildings, limit energy consumption by public and commercial establishments and restrict non-essential outdoor use of fuel, such as neon lights on advertisements.

The first effort to enact these authorities in an energy emergency act became bogged down in disputes over limits on oil company profits and then in an oil price control fight that led to a Nixon veto of the bill in 1974.

When the lack of abundant, cheap energy turned out to be not a short-term crisis but a long-term problem, Congress shifted its attention from crash efforts to issues such as oil and gas pricing, conservation and development of alternative fuels.

However, as part of its major 1975 energy bill, the Energy Conservation and Policy Act (EPCA), Congress did include two provisions relating to emergency preparedness. The two directives to the executive branch required establishment by 1982 of a strategic petroleum reserve of 1 billion barrels of oil that could be drawn on in an emergency, and the preparation by June 1976 of contingency plans for conservation and gasoline rationing; the standby plans had to go to Congress for approval.

President Ford submitted standby plans in early 1977, just before leaving office, but the Carter administration withdrew the proposals, preferring to write its own.

Energy policy was one of Carter's earliest priorities. It was launched in April 1977 with announcement of a national energy plan, but it required a renewed sense of crisis, the Iranian revolution in early 1979, to shift attention back to emergency preparedness. At the time, the Strategic Petroleum Reserve held only 70 million barrels of oil, and even that could not be used because no pumps were in place to lift it out of the Louisiana salt domes where it was stored. In addition, the contingency plans Congress had asked for in 1975 still hadn't been formally submitted.

The new concern about emergency preparedness was heightened in February 1979 when Energy Secretary James R. Schlesinger warned that loss of Iranian oil from the world market was "prospectively more serious" than the Arab oil embargo. He called for preparation of contingency plans. However, other Carter administration officials cautioned against moving too quickly with mandatory steps to cut oil demand. With rationing, for example, which the administration considered a last resort, "the government would be trying to tell millions of people how to manage their lives. I don't think we'd be very good at that," David J. Bardin, administrator of the Economic Regulatory Administration, said in February 1979.

Carter's Proposals

The Carter administration Feb. 27 sent Congress three standby plans for conservation and a contingency proposal for rationing gasoline. The rationing plan was similar to one proposed in June 1978 and discussed subsequently at public hearings.

Under EPCA, the 1975 law, both houses would have to approve each of the plans within 60 days; otherwise a plan was considered rejected. Congress could not amend a plan, although the administration could offer amendments. Once the plans had been approved, Congress would still get another look at rationing. The 1975 law gave either house 15 days to veto any move to put a rationing plan into effect. However, the president could carry out any of the standby conservation plans without congressional consent. The plans proposed by Carter called for:

● Restrictions on weekend sales of gasoline.
● Controls on thermostats in non-residential buildings, with 80 degrees the lower limit for cooling and 65 degrees the upper limit for heating.
● Limits on some lighted advertising.
● Rationing of gasoline, as a last resort. Coupons would be distributed to vehicle owners. They could be sold legally on an unregulated "white market."

Carter did not ask for power to restrict commuter parking as energy officials had suggested. Their proposal had been to close a certain percentage of garage and lot spaces during early morning hours, presumably forcing commuters to carpool or use public transportation. Parking lot and garage owners complained loudly about the plan, which a spokeswoman for the National Parking Association had said would "single us out and put us out of business."

Everybody Objects

The conservation and rationing plans submitted to Congress also ran into opposition. The tourism industry strongly opposed the proposal to restrict weekend gasoline sales. Such closings would "single us out unfairly," said Albert L. McDermott, Washington representative for the American Hotel and Motel Association. During the 1973-74 Arab oil embargo, when many stations were closed on Sunday, the tourism industry lost $717 million in revenues, McDermott said. His organization sent a telegram to President Carter noting that hotels and motels were happy to do their fair share, but "if we are, for all intents and purposes, to go without business for one or two days of the week, then a similar sacrifice should be borne by others."

Gardner McBride, executive vice president of the Building Owners and Managers Association, objected to the thermostat controls. Because of the way heating and cooling systems were designed in large buildings, lower winter settings would in many cases mean running air conditioning, he said. "What we need are directives to curb energy uses, but we don't need arbitrary numbers to work against," McBride said.

The limit on non-essential outdoor advertising was ridiculed by businesses and many members of Congress because of the small reduction in oil use expected: an estimated 4,000 barrels a day. The administration had called it "an especially conspicuous and visible form of energy consumption during an emergency."

Worries about the possibility of gasoline rationing and other restrictions on driving prompted the National Automobile Dealers Association in late 1978 to start an extensive national advertising campaign with the theme, "Help us protect your freedom to drive." The campaign was financed by the association, Chrysler, Ford, General Motors and others, who contributed to a new corporation called The Automobility Fund. "Don't take your wheels for granted," stated one advertisement that appeared in February issues of national magazines. "There are people in government, and others, whose only answer to our environmental and energy problems is to restrict use of the automobile.... Join with us.... Because if you don't speak up today, your freedom to drive may be restricted tomorrow."

During their deliberation on the conservation proposals in April 1979, both the House Commerce and Senate Energy committees rejected the plans to restrict weekend sales of gasoline and limit outdoor lighted advertising. Only the plan to restrict heating and cooling in non-residential buildings was approved by the panels and later by Congress. Carter imposed thermostat restrictions July 16, 1979, although he changed the 80 degree air conditioning limit to 78 degrees.

The Rationing Controversy

Rationing was another contentious matter. A last-minute pledge by the Carter administration to keep rural states from being shortchanged succeeded in getting the rationing plan approved that same April by the Senate Energy Committee by a one-vote margin. However, when the pledge was put into writing May 7, as a formal amendment to the plan, the Energy Committee was displeased and reversed itself, voting against the plan on May 8.

Later the same day, the administration came up with yet another amendment. The third plan allocated gasoline almost solely on the basis of historical consumption patterns, whereas the original rationing plan had used those criteria for half the allocation and had divided the rest of available supply equally among vehicles regardless of where they were registered. The intent was to give a fair share to those most dependent on cars for transportation.

After the second revision, the plan squeaked by the Energy Committee by one vote.

"We've been operating by trial and error — mostly

error," committee Chairman Henry M. Jackson, D-Wash., said later, describing the hurried changes. "It's an open secret we've been in a hell of a mess." Why did the administration present still another plan? "I advised them they were dead in the water by a vote of two to one," Jackson explained.

There was little time left before the May 11 deadline for congressional action. In the Senate May 10, Jackson argued that the alternative to rationing in an emergency was "anarchy at the gasoline pump." The plan was approved, 58-39.

In the House, the Commerce Committee twice narrowly rejected the plan, but on May 1 agreed to send it to the floor without recommendation. Even supporters agreed the plan was flawed. "But I believe the national interest requires [it] be set in place," said Rep. John D. Dingell, D-Mich. Opponents were harsh. Rationing, argued Rep. Dave Stockman, R-Mich., would be "just like Monopoly — everybody gets funny money." Rep. Clarence J. Brown, R-Ohio, said, "It will bring controls into our lives as never before."

On the floor, critics continued their attacks. Even those not usually opposed to standby rationing plans argued against the final Carter proposal. The two revisions made it difficult for members to obtain accurate information about how the plan would affect their districts. "They told us this is the only plan; obviously there were two others after they told that to the Senate," said Rep. George Miller, D-Calif.

Parochial concerns dominated debate, with members questioning whether the plan would shortchange rural residents, or farmers, or suburbanites, or oil drillers — in short, whoever each member considered important. In a plea for a favorable vote, House Speaker Thomas P. O'Neill Jr., D-Mass., likened the decision to the military draft vote prior to World War II, when "weakling after weakling" stood up to oppose the draft because it wasn't popular

at home. After Pearl Harbor, O'Neill said, "they walked the streets with their heads down." He urged the House to "act in the national interest" and reminded them that "this is the only plan you have."

The Democratic leadership, however, was not able to turn out the vote on the volatile question. The House voted 158-246 against the plan, with 106 Democrats voting against Carter's proposal. Only seven Republicans voted for it.

After rejecting two of the three conservation plans, the Senate Energy Committee decided in May that a new procedure was needed for emergency preparations. The bill they drafted didn't deal with rationing, but the House later added rationing provisions. The Senate bill, easily approved June 5, gave the president broad authority to take steps to curb energy use during emergencies, but allowed states to avoid the federal sanctions by coming up with effective plans of their own. Conservation targets for the nation and each state could be set by the president.

The House Commerce Committee added rationing authority to the bill, giving the president sole responsibility for drafting a standby rationing plan. Implementation of a plan still could be vetoed by either house. In addition, the committee said the president could not impose rationing unless there were a 20 percent shortage of gasoline, and it specified that federal conservation plans could not be imposed on uncooperative states unless a state experienced a 10 percent or greater shortfall of petroleum.

Although a major committee rationale for the bill had been the desire to shift to the president more responsibility for drafting a standby plan, the House had other ideas. It adopted an amendment by Rep. Benjamin A. Gilman, R-N.Y., to give either house a veto over the standby plan. The July 25 vote was 232-187, with 80 Democrats voting with Gilman. Carter later said the action "illustrated once again the timidity of Congress in dealing with a sensitive political issue."

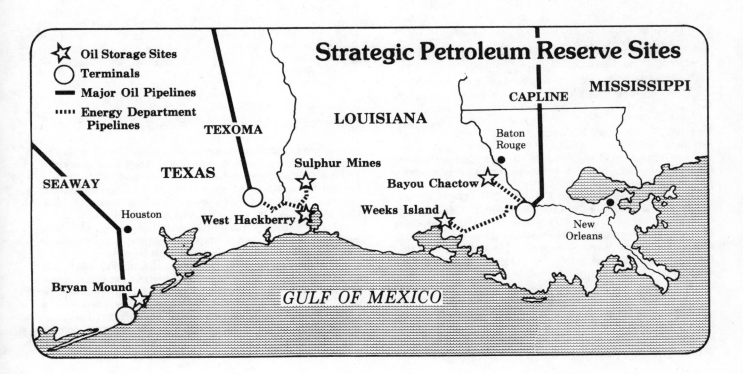

Strategic Petroleum Reserve Sites

☆ Oil Storage Sites
○ Terminals
▬ Major Oil Pipelines
····· Energy Department Pipelines

The Democratic leadership scrambled to line up votes for the Commerce approach. When the bill was considered again July 31, the House reversed itself, voting 234-189 for an amendment by Majority Leader Jim Wright, D-Texas, that restored the language giving most responsibility for a rationing plan to the president and deleting the veto provision. The House also gave either house a chance to veto federal imposition of conservation plans on a state that failed to achieve its conservation goals.

After losing the second rationing vote, Republicans offered and won approval of a string of amendments giving special treatment to certain industries. For example, the food and fiber industry was given an exemption from conservation rules, and a special set-aside of fuel was established for farmers and commercial fishermen. An example of the members' skittishness about being on record in favor of restrictions on energy use, especially when related to driving, was a vote on a provision simply suggesting to the president that he consider restricting automobile use to six days a week during shortages. The "sticker" plan, which let the driver choose and display his non-driving day on a window sticker, was overwhelmingly defeated, 3-413.

The bill was finally passed Aug. 1 by a 263-159 vote.

In conference, the Senate conferees proved reluctant to give up their chance to review a standby rationing plan. After all, they had forced two revisions by the administration. By mid-September 1979, the conferees had worked out a compromise: A standby plan would be considered approved 30 days after submission to Congress unless both houses voted against it. Although their joint resolution could be vetoed by the president, Congress could override the veto.

The conferees retained the House prohibition on rationing unless there were a 20 percent shortage, but they allowed Congress to waive that restriction. In the conservation section, the House provision for a one-house veto was dropped. In states with approved conservation plans, a state would have 90 days to meet its conservation goal before the effort was considered a failure and the federal plan could be imposed. For states without approved plans, no such restriction applied.

The Senate adopted the conference report Oct. 17. In the House Oct. 23, a new mood of conciliation prevailed, in sharp contrast to past partisan wrangling on the subject.

"I think the spirit of cooperation springs from the fact that we do have a continuing energy shortage and probably will have for many years to come," said Rep. Clarence Brown, a key Republican conferee who had fought rationing legislation in the past. "We have come to a general agreement that we must have both production and conservation because of the finite nature of our energy resources."

Another conferee, Rep. Toby Moffett, D-Conn., also noted a new common ground on energy. "Many of us who at one time talked rather casually about imposing rationing have come to the conclusion that indeed rationing should be a last resort," he said. He pointed out that the new bill provided a role for Congress, but "does not put Congress in the position of being an obstructionist force."

The vote on the conference compromise was 301-112.

The surprisingly wide margin did not mean the rationing battle was over, however. The Energy Department in December 1979 proposed a new rationing plan and held public hearings. Carter formally submitted the plan to Congress June 13, 1980. *(Box, p.100)*

On July 30, the last day for congressional action, Brown led the House fight against it. However, his motion to force a vote on the new plan was defeated, 205-209. The House was clearly still uncomfortable about showing up on the "yes" side of a gasoline rationing vote of any sort.

In the Senate there was less opposition, as senators voted 31-60 against a motion to allow a vote on rejecting the plan. A rationing plan was legally in place.

Implementation of Conservation Plans

Getting the details of the rationing system worked out was expected to take much longer, though, with completion not expected before September 1981. The Energy Department had wanted $103 million to prepare the system, but Congress provided only $51 million. That meant no new coupons were printed; instead, the agency planned to use coupons left over from the mid-1970s and stored in Pueblo, Colo. Once rationing began, additional coupons could be printed. Lack of funds also forced the department to abandon its plan to issue rationing "checks" to vehicle owners that would be cashed in for actual coupons at banks or other outlets. The scheme called for vehicle owners to take their registration slips to the post office or some other outlet, where a basic coupon allotment would be provided.

The conservation plans also were incomplete at the end of 1980. The 1979 law didn't require states to submit their plans until an emergency had been declared, but it encouraged them to draft plans in advance. Only two states, Nebraska and Missouri, had submitted their plans by the end of 1980, although more than 25 others had contacted the Energy Department about their planning. To encourage states to act before an emergency existed, the department in December 1980 offered each state $29,000 to aid in planning.

The states also were offered funding for development of rationing plans related to distribution of a special state allocation of gasoline provided for in the federal rationing plan. The $8 million was made available to help states figure out how they would distribute the extra gasoline set-aside for priority needs and for those with special requirements for gasoline.

Strategic Petroleum Reserve

When Congress decided in 1975 to put 1 billion barrels of oil into storage as a reserve for emergencies, it seemed to be a straightforward idea. The chairman of the Senate Budget Committee did warn that the Strategic Petroleum Reserve might cost "well over $6 billion over its life." Generally, though, the idea was well received, and the program seemed to be moving forward smoothly, with Louisiana and Texas salt domes, conveniently located near pipelines and oilfields, chosen as storage sites.

By the end of 1980, however, the reserve held only a couple of weeks replacement if imports were interrupted, and the cost was expected to exceed $60 billion. At the existing rate of storage, 100,000 barrels a day, the 1 billion barrels would not be in place until about 1998. The price tag was beginning to raise doubts about whether the reserve was worth it. Questions also persisted about the international reaction, as Saudi Arabia had previously hinted

To preserve its oil lifeline, emergency preparedness steps were taken by the United States: a standby gasoline rationing plan was adopted; states were given authority to draft their own standby energy conservation plans; and a petroleum reserve was created to store oil for future needs.

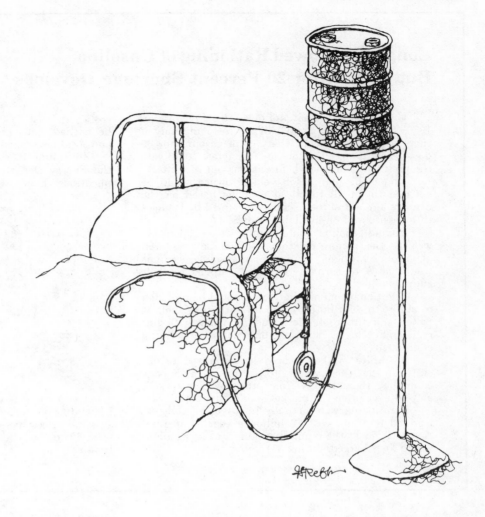

that U.S. purchases of imported oil for the reserve would prompt a cutback in the Saudi production level, which was more than 10 million barrels a day at the end of 1980. In addition, U.S. allies had been worried that the greater demand would force them to pay more for oil. Because supplies were not tight at the end of 1980, it was unclear whether diverting 100,000 barrels a day to the petroleum reserve would prompt Europeans and others to object.

Complications at the Start

The concept of storing oil in the ground seemed fairly simple and, in fact, had been done before. West Germany, for example, has a petroleum reserve. But a system of buying, storing and distributing the oil is complicated, as Energy Department officials found out. And no one had tried it before on such a large scale or with such an ambitious timetable.

The Energy Department wanted to store the oil underground near existing oil distribution systems so it could be used in an emergency. The Gulf Coast was a major distribution center, which also had large salt domes that could serve as storage sites. The agency identified five such sites in Louisiana and Texas that the Energy Department could connect to existing major pipelines by building smaller connector lines. Additional sites, needed

to complete the program, could be located in other parts of the country. *(Map of sites, p. 97)*

At the outset, the department had to build a 67-mile, $78 million pipeline in Louisiana between a storage site at Weeks Island and the St. James tanker terminal. The terminal feeds into the Capline pipeline, a major commercial artery that goes to Illinois. The department's pipeline is used to bring oil to the storage site and to take it out in an emergency.

The Weeks Island storage was in caverns that were created by the Morton Salt Co. when it mined rock salt.

Although the Weeks Island site was ready to accept the oil, other salt caverns were not because they had been used by chemical companies. Unlike Morton, the other companies were not interested in dry salt, but wanted salty water — brine — that they used in chemical processes. These firms, such as Dow Chemical Co., which owned Bryan Mound in Texas, pumped water into the dome, where it mixed with the salt to become brine. The brine was then pumped out and transferred to chemical plants. But not all the brine was removed from the caverns and, as oil was pumped in, the brine was displaced. As the salty sludge was pushed out of the caverns, the Energy Department had to find ways to dispose of it.

"Five months ago I did not know what the hell brine

Congress Allowed Rationing of Gasoline
But Only After 20 Percent Shortage Develops

Under the proposal approved by Congress in 1980, the president could call for rationing only if there were a 20 percent shortage of gasoline for 30 days. Even then, either house of Congress could veto the president's decision before it was put into effect.

Under the plan, each vehicle owner would be entitled to an allotment of coupons based on the average amount of fuel usually consumed by vehicles in his state and on available supplies.

Buying gasoline would require that coupons, as well as the money for the gasoline, be presented at gasoline stations. To get more gasoline, stations would have to turn in the used coupons to their suppliers.

Additional coupon allotments would be provided to states to distribute to priority activities, such as police and fire protection, and for firms with unregistered vehicles, such as construction or farming equipment.

A "white market" would be permitted to operate, so that those willing to pay for extra coupons could buy them legally from others willing to sell, at whatever price the market would support.

If rationing were actually imposed, officials estimated it would cost $2 billion a year to operate. A special fee at the pump, probably 2 cents a gallon, would be charged during rationing to cover those costs. At least 5,000 new federal employees would be needed, plus another 5,000 or more new state and local government workers.

In a June 1980 report to Congress on the plan, the Energy Department outlined some of the complications. Every three months, 153 million ration  checks would be mailed: one for each registered vehicle. Motorcycles would get one-quarter of a car's coupon allotment and mopeds would get one-tenth. "It would involve, in effect, creating an entirely new currency, complete with "checking accounts," the report said.

Extra coupons could be bought and sold freely. Depending on the demand for gasoline and how much gasoline prices increased, a coupon would be worth from $2 to $5, according to Energy Department estimates.

---

was," Joseph Deluca, a deputy assistant secretary in charge of the program, told Congress in December 1978. "Now I live with it."

Deluca, a retired Air Force general, had become the program's third manager in July 1978. He resigned at the end of February 1979, for personal reasons, and the fourth manager, J. R. Brill, took over in March. However, he retired in September because of health. Harry A. Jones became the program's fifth director in October 1979.

The changing cast of characters didn't help the struggling program. The most embarrassing failure was not that only 70 million barrels were in storage by early 1979, but that the oil could not be extracted because no pumps were in place. Deluca said in his 1978 testimony that pumps had been a low priority earlier in the program because of the idea that "the earlier the oil is acquired and stored, the lower the real cost to the United States." The pumps were working by the summer of 1979.

Storage Problems

Other problems plagued the department in its early efforts to store oil and construct a system to extract and transport it in an emergency. The mishaps included:

● A fire at one of the storage sites. While a contractor was repairing equipment at West Hackberry, La., too much pressure built up and there was an explosion. The oil spewing from the storage site caught fire.

● Several storage caverns that turned out to be smaller than expected. As a result, the government paid an extra $8 million to the owners of oil tankers that had to wait in the Gulf of Mexico because not enough storage space was available to hold the oil.

● Underground wells that could not "swallow" salty water displaced from the caverns as fast as planners had predicted, which caused delays in the program. The Energy Department later acquired a permit to dispose of some brine in the Gulf of Mexico.

In addition, storage costs, originally estimated at less than $1 a barrel, had risen to $3.50 a barrel in early 1979. The average had dropped to $3 a barrel by the end of 1980.

● The price of oil escalated even more sharply, more than doubling from $13 to $30 or more a barrel, between late 1978 and early 1980. By the end of 1980 the price was $35 a barrel.

The problems with the reserve prompted Energy Secretary Schlesinger to admit in early 1979 that the program had once suffered from "bad management," but he cited improvements under Deluca. Rep. Dingell, who chaired hearings on the program, was more blunt in late 1978.

"Clearly the failures in the program are management failures," he said.

World Oil Disruptions

Management, however, wasn't the only problem. In early 1979, just as it appeared the management snags had been worked out, the world oil market was severely disrupted by cutbacks in Iranian oil production that followed Iran's revolution. In the ensuing months, Saudi Arabia attempted to act as a stabilizing force in the world market by increasing production and arguing at OPEC meetings against sharp price hikes. Then, and even after the market stabilized, Saudi officials worried that additional U.S. purchases for the reserve would further tighten oil supplies, making it more difficult for Saudi Arabia to resist price hikes sought by other OPEC members. In addition, some political groups in Saudi Arabia wanted production cut back. A U.S. move to fill the reserve would make it politically difficult for Saudi officials to justify continuation of the higher production level. Saudi officials also were concerned that U.S. conservation efforts might lag if the reserve were available to ease the fear of shortages.

In March 1980 Energy Secretary Charles W. Duncan Jr. went to Saudi Arabia to discuss the reserve and other issues with Sheik Ahmed Zaki al-Yamani, the Saudi oil minister. Yamani reiterated his country's intention to cut production if further oil supplies were diverted to the reserve. At the time, it had been a year since any oil was purchased for the storage program.

Another U.S. official visited Saudi Arabia that spring. A freshman senator, Bill Bradley, D-N.J., had wanted to hear the Saudi viewpoint in person, so he traveled to the Middle East in April. Bradley returned convinced that the advantages of the reserve far outweighed any disadvantages. The probability of an interruption in oil supplies in the next few years, Bradley said, made the reserve essential to the nation's energy security.

As for the threat of a production cutback by the Saudis, Bradley said, "I'm not so sure that there won't be that reduction anyway."

Even if the Saudis did cut back, Bradley said, filling the reserve would help the Saudis understand that we know what our national security interest is, articulate it and accept the consequences. And in future dealings, I think it might strengthen the relationship."

Order To Fill the Reserve

Bradley and Sen. Robert Dole, R-Kan., teamed up in 1979 to sponsor an amendment to the synthetic fuels bill, later enacted as the Energy Security Act of 1980. Their amendment directed the president to put at least 100,000 barrels of oil a day into storage. As a conferee on the legislation, Bradley continued to lobby for the provision. Even though the administration opposed it, Bradley found his colleagues sympathetic. All agreed the reserve was vital to emergency preparedness.

However, Dingell, one of the House conferees on the bill, warned that the administration might ignore the directive. His solution was to link the reserve to production from U.S.-owned oil fields, chiefly those at Elk Hills, Calif., where output averaged about 160,000 barrels a day. If the government within six months had not started putting at least 100,000 barrels a day into the reserve, then the Elk Hills oil would have to be used to fill the reserve or it would have to be swapped for other oil destined for the reserve, according to the final version of the bill. If the directive were not carried out, Elk Hills production would be halted.

The requirement got results. Unwilling to lose the revenues from Elk Hills, the government again started filling the reserve on Sept. 23, 1980, at the rate of 100,000 barrels a day.

The Environment Conflict

6

Environmentalists considered themselves fortunate that their movement was well-established on Capitol Hill long before the 1973-74 Arab oil embargo made energy a top national concern. The momentum they had developed with passage of major laws such as the National Environmental Policy Act in 1969, clean air in 1970 and clean water in 1970 and 1972, helped push through other major legislation after the embargo. In 1974, Congress set national standards for safe drinking water. In 1976, the legislators passed new rules for management of federal lands, including the designation of wilderness areas, controls on toxic substances and restrictions on hazardous waste disposal.

In 1977, the Carter administration, which was sympathetic to environmental protection, helped win enactment of legislation that had been under consideration for several years, including controls on strip mining of coal and a strengthening of the clean air and water laws. In 1978, Congress approved new environmental controls and leasing procedures for development of energy offshore on the outer continental shelf.

The tide began to turn in 1979. Complaints from energy developers about red tape and unrealistic pollution control standards received more attention as oil prices skyrocketed and lines developed at gasoline pumps in the spring of 1979. These developments, caused in part by the Iranian revolution that overthrew the pro-Western government of Shah Mohammed Reza Pahlavi, reminded Congress that the United States still was quite dependent on insecure foreign supplies.

When Jimmy Carter, a president with high marks from environmentalists, proposed in July 1979 that a special board be set up to resolve conflicts between energy and environment demands, the evidence was unmistakable: The environmental decade was over. The only aberration in this trend was the enactment in December 1980 of the Alaska Lands Act and "superfund" legislation which set up a $1.6 billion fund to pay for cleanup of toxic dumps and chemical or oil spills until liability could be assessed. A factor in passage was the view of environmentalists that they were unlikely to do better in the future and might do worse as energy concerns increased.

Environmentalists expected the attack on the laws they had supported to intensify in the 1980s, especially with the election to the presidency of Ronald Reagan who had frequently blamed environmental controls for much of the nation's energy problem. A special target during his election campaign was the Clean Air Act, scheduled for renewal in 1981. Reagan's support for nuclear power also was expected to affect planning for disposal of radioactive wastes from nuclear power, another energy and environment conflict discussed in an earlier chapter.

The tension between energy and environment falls into five major subject areas:

● Restrictions on oil and gas drilling, on coal mining and on other energy development on federally owned lands, primarily in the West and Alaska.

● Limits on air pollution, including tight rules that prevent "significant deterioration" of areas with clean air.

● The need for a special federal board to reduce red tape and to resolve conflicts between environmental laws and priority energy projects. The House in 1980 killed legislation setting up an Energy Mobilization Board to expedite such projects.

● The effect of environmental controls on the increased use and production of coal, a step considered crucial to reducing oil imports.

● Potential conflicts between protection of the environment and development of synthetic fuels.

Energy from Federal Lands

One target of the lobbying by major energy industry associations such as the American Petroleum Institute and the National Coal Association was the restrictions on energy development on federal lands. The energy industry was particularly frustrated by the administration of public lands under President Carter's interior secretary, Cecil D. Andrus, who in 1977-80 brought the viewpoint of an environmentalist to an agency long dominated by the developers' philosophy. He favored strip mining controls, fought to protect Alaska's wilderness and sought federal controls on how lessees searched for and produced energy on public lands.

Because the interior secretary has such great latitude over the resolution of so many land management issues, the energy industry was extremely pleased with Reagan's choice for the job, James Watt. As a lawyer for a Western energy association, Watt had challenged in court many government decisions that went against the association's business orientation.

Vast Energy Potential

Moreover, efforts begun in the late 1970s to revise land management laws were expected to reach fruition with the backing of the Reagan administration. The reason for the continued attention to legislation was the vast potential energy supplies located on federal property. Federal lands, including the outer continental shelf, held an estimated 37 percent of all undiscovered oil and 43 percent of undiscovered natural gas. About 40 percent of coal reserves and 80 percent of recoverable Western oil shale were located on federal lands.

Of total land in the 50 states, the federal government owned about 775 million acres, or one-third, with most of the government property located in the West and Alaska. On the outer continental shelf, the federal government controlled 528 million acres of submerged lands. Two-thirds of this land was off the coast of Alaska.

Principal land management legislation of the 1970s included the:

● Federal Land Policy and Management Act of 1976, which included a directive to the interior secretary to recommend designation of wilderness areas on public lands. While the studies were underway, 174 million acres of wilderness areas were withdrawn from energy and other development.

In November 1980, all but 24 million acres were released from any special restrictions on their use.

● Outer Continental Shelf Lands Act Amendments of 1978, which tightened environmental controls on offshore drilling and production, attempted to open offshore areas to companies other than the major oil companies and increased state participation in federal leasing decisions.

● Alaska Lands Act of 1980, which set aside about 104.3 million acres of federal land in Alaska as parks, refuges and other types of conservation areas, with energy development restricted in most instances. The law more than doubled the size of the country's national park and wildlife refuge system, and nearly tripled the amount of land designated as wilderness.

Mixed Record by Industry

On federal land that is open to energy exploration, industry has a mixed record, particularly in coal production. New coal leasing was halted in 1971, but was expected to resume in 1981 under a plan developed by Secretary Andrus. The leasing moratorium was prompted by a 1970 Interior Department study showing that coal production by federal lessees had drastically decreased in recent years. The acreage of public lands under lease for coal development had increased almost tenfold from 1945 to 1970, the report said, but production of coal from leases had declined from 10 million tons in 1945 to 7.2 million tons in 1970. As of 1974, only 59 of the 533 active federal coal mining leases were producing coal. A new coal leasing law enacted in 1976 over President Ford's veto required better production performance by coal lessees and also set out procedures designed to improve competition for leases.

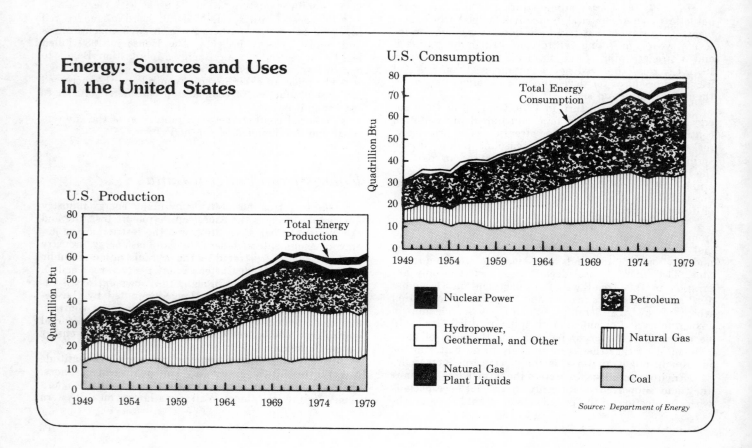

Energy: Sources and Uses In the United States

U.S. Production

U.S. Consumption

Nuclear Power   Petroleum

Hydropower, Geothermal, and Other   Natural Gas

Natural Gas Plant Liquids   Coal

Source: Department of Energy

Clean Air Standards

Although the energy industry had complaints about many aspects of the Clean Air Act, a special target was the provision added in 1977 to prevent the pollution of areas with air cleaner than the national standard. Industry officials said this clause was a particular hindrance to energy development in the West. They expected support from the Reagan administration to change the law.

The PSD Rule and Its Impact

The "prevention of significant deterioration" clause, or "PSD," in the 1977 provision meant that in certain areas limits on air pollution were much stricter than the national standard, which was considered the minimum cleanup level. National parks, wilderness and other "pristine" areas were immediately put into this special category, which was later expanded to include rural counties and other areas with limited industrial development. Visibility could even be a reason for restricting emissions near scenic areas, with states authorized to set stricter standards in such cases. Under the act, states were responsible for carrying out the law through federally approved state implementation plans.

Some additional discharges were allowed in such areas to accommodate growth, but pollution was not permitted to reach the national standard for clean air. Supporters of the provision had argued in 1977 that they wanted "clean growth." Opponents called the approach "no growth."

The effect of the requirement was to force industries seeking to locate in such "PSD" areas, called Class I and Class II, to use the best pollution control technology possible. Once the limit on the additional allowable pollution had been reached, no more pollution would be permitted. A new industry would have to improve the cleanup at an existing source of pollution — such as a factory — regardless of whether it owned it or not, in order to get a permit to emit pollutants at any level. The same procedure was used in areas that did not meet the minimum national standard, such as the Los Angeles Basin.

The 1977 amendments to the Clean Air Act, which had been debated by Congress in earlier years, were prompted by a 1972 Supreme Court decision that ruled that the original 1970 law required protection of air quality in areas where air was cleaner than the national standards. Regulations issued by the Environmental Protection Agency to carry out this directive were extremely controversial, and Congress tried to clarify the policy and simplify the rules through the 1977 amendments. Many of the regulations to carry out the "PSD" provisions still were being written at the end of 1980, as standards for only two pollutants were in place.

Energy industry officials pointed repeatedly to the "PSD" rules as a major roadblock to energy development. They contended that the provision would hamper construction of additional coal-burning power plants in the West and development of synthetic fuels.

Limits on Synfuels Development

Specific regions where development of synthetic fuels was thought to be jeopardized by the clean air standards were:

- Oil shale development in Colorado and Utah.
- Coal liquefaction in Montana and Wyoming.
- Extraction of heavy oil in Kern County, Calif.

An Energy Department review of siting limitations for future coal liquefaction plants found only 13 percent of counties in coal-producing states to have adequate coal to support a 100,000 barrel-per-day facility for 25 years. And the number of eligible counties declined by 75 percent, to 41 counties, when air quality limitations were considered. The areas eliminated either had been designated as having especially clean air and were covered by "PSD" rules or were those not in compliance with national standards. In either case, additional pollution was tightly restricted. In addition, some counties, primarily in the East, were made ineligible by rough terrain that would trap pockets of very polluted air in violation of minimum national air quality standards.

Despite these restrictions, the study concluded that the remaining sites could support an industry producing 1.5 million barrels a day of liquids from coal.

Reagan Position

As a candidate, Reagan had planned to outline his proposed changes to the Clean Air Act in an October 1980 speech to out-of-work steelworkers and coal miners in Steubenville and Youngstown, Ohio. However, Reagan did not stick to his written text.

Instead he made off-the-cuff remarks about air pollution that later touched off a flurry of angry newspaper editorials and denunciations from environmentalists who charged that Reagan was "out of touch with reality."

The written speech, which wasn't delivered, said that air pollution had been "substantially controlled." Although air pollution had been decreasing overall, some cities still were suffering. While Reagan was making his remarks, Los Angeles was experiencing one of its worst smog alerts ever.

Reagan vs. the Environmentalists

But Reagan's ad-lib comments caused the biggest ruckus. He quipped that the Mount St. Helens volcano had probably dumped more sulfur dioxide into the air than was released in 10 years of "automobile driving or things of that kind."

Reagan had confused his chemistry. Cars weren't regulated for sulfur emissions. They were regulated for carbon monoxide, hydrocarbons and oxides of nitrogen. Power plants emitted sulfur dioxide, but about 40 times as much as the volcano, said the Environmental Protection Agency (EPA).

Then Reagan repeated one of his favorite themes — that money was being wasted on automobile pollution control devices because nearly all air pollutants came from trees and decaying plants. "Growing and decaying vegetation in this land are responsible for 93 percent of the oxides of nitrogen," said Reagan.

Actually, plants and trees emit *nitrous* oxide, a harmless gas. Oxides of nitrogen come from man-made sources such as power plants and automobiles.

Angry environmentalists called a hasty press conference in Washington to charge that Reagan's comments showed he was uninformed on environmental issues.

Joe Fontaine, president of the Sierra Club, rebutted Reagan's claims that environmental regulations had caused most of the plant closings in the steel industry. Plant obsolescence and the dumping of foreign steel, not environmental laws, had caused the industry's ills, Fontaine said.

Reagan's Undelivered Proposals

Reagan's undelivered speech had outlined a six-point program for streamlining federal regulations and the Clean Air Act. He called for replacing rules specifying certain procedures with performance standards, which were more flexible. Besides requiring cost-benefit tests for new regulations, he called for adding automatic expiration dates, giving Congress veto power over them and updating existing rules to reflect new scientific knowledge.

A spokesman for the regulatory reform office at EPA said later that new environmental regulations were already being reviewed on a regular basis for their impact on the economy. However, he said that applying a cost-benefit test to health-based standards would be difficult because there was no way to quantify benefits.

"How do you put a price on better visibility and less coughing; how do you put a price on a life?" asked Michael Levin, chief of EPA's regulatory reform staff.

Reagan in California

As governor of California, Reagan signed one of the toughest air pollution control laws in the country. But before he signed it he insisted that it call for local, rather than state, control over stationary sources of pollution. As a result, the law was poorly enforced, according to later investigations by Democratic Gov. Edmund G. Brown Jr.'s administration.

He also fought the development of mass transit, despite the heavy auto pollution in California. This situation led later to rejection of California's air pollution control plan by the EPA during the Nixon administration.

Reagan also fought the state Legislature's attempt to require pollution devices on used cars. When the state Air Resources Board tried to implement the law, Reagan fired two of its members and replaced them with people who agreed with him.

Energy Mobilization Board

From the start, environmentalists were wary of the proposed Energy Mobilization Board, a federal entity expected to put key energy projects on a "fast track" through the bureaucracy. Their fear was that the board would chose energy development over environmental protection. Also concerned about the board were state and local governments, who saw the new federal power as a threat to their rights.

After a year of congressional consideration, and bitter fights in the House and Senate, the environmentalists and states' rights advocates in mid-1980 were still trying to weaken the board's powers, but it was an uphill battle. The EMB, as the board was called, apparently was heading for victory. The mood in Congress had clearly swung toward energy and away from the environment.

The Surprising House Vote

Then the House, to the astonishment of many observers, voted June 27 by a margin of almost 2-1 to kill the legislation. The same concerns raised earlier had prompted many Democrats — 107, to be exact — to go against Carter and vote to defeat the board. The key to the board's defeat, though, was the GOP. Only nine of 134 Republicans voting on the question supported the board. A major factor in the Republican opposition was a flurry of lobbying just two to three days before the vote by Reps. Thomas B. Evans Jr., R-Del., John H. Rousselot, R-Calif., and other leading Reagan supporters. They had urged their colleagues to vote against the board, which Reagan had opposed during the campaign. Many already had doubts about the wisdom of expanding the federal bureaucracy. A side benefit for them was that defeat of the board would embarrass Carter, who had ranked the board with synthetic fuels and the oil excess profits tax as his top energy priorities.

That Reagan had helped defeat the board was little consolation for the Democratic opponents worried about environmental protection. Reagan's views were along the lines of those held by Rep. Phil Gramm, D-Texas, who favored a powerful board. "We should not fool ourselves into thinking we can expedite these projects just by cutting red tape," said Gramm during Commerce Committee action on the bill. "We need circumvention of substantive language — the problem is with the laws."

The environmental laws were seen by most Republicans as a principal obstacle to energy development, and they expected to have ample opportunity to change them in the 97th Congress. However, that was likely to be a time-consuming process, so the board idea could be revived. The board itself generally enjoyed support in Congress, although some members were concerned that it would add another layer of bureaucracy. A question they wrestled with for months was how much power the board should have to reconcile conflicts between energy and environment. Specifically they asked whether the board should be able to modify substantive laws, such as clean air standards, or only procedural rules, such as the time period set aside for public hearings, in order to expedite energy projects.

Rationale for a Board

Even before President Carter in mid-July 1979 asked that the board be established, Congress was considering ways to cut red tape for energy projects. Legislators generally agreed that bureaucratic delays were hindering construction of major refineries, power plants and other facilities needed to provide energy for the nation.

The siting of a coal-burning power plant, for example, usually took several years. A refinery proposed for Virginia in 1969 was held up first by delays in obtaining state and local permits and later by disagreements among federal agencies. Companies seeking to build major pipelines had insisted on special legislation, such as the Trans-Alaskan Pipeline Authorization Act of 1973, for oil, and the Alaska Natural Gas Transportation Act in 1977.

Although duplicative reviews and paperwork snarls were a factor, decisions about major energy facilities took longer also because they were more difficult. In addition, local communities had become more aware of the disadvantages of projects they once welcomed without question.

"There was a period when energy facilities were viewed as providing unblemished benefits for local and state economies," said a mid-1979 study by the National Governors' Association. "Those days have passed."

Power plants and pipelines may mean jobs for area residents, but they also may burden the community by increasing the cost of education and other services. And pollution could threaten a local industry, such as fishing. Besides, the benefits from the project might end up going to a city hundreds of miles away that shared none of the disadvantages.

Local residents, increasingly aware of these costs, learned to speak up.

Anyone Can Say No

However, national energy policymakers argued that someone must accept a refinery, someone must give a pipeline a right-of-way, someone must make room for a synthetic fuels plant.

"We have reached the stage of participatory democracy where almost everyone in the society can say 'no,' but no one can say 'yes,'" former Energy Secretary James R. Schlesinger once lamented.

Senate Energy Committee Chairman Henry M. Jackson, D-Wash., later expressed a similar idea. "In fighting the threat of oil dependence, the greatest obstacle to success is ourselves," he said on the Senate floor. "We have created an institutional crisis in this country. We no longer can get anything done. Everyone has the power to delay decisions on energy projects, and too many decision-makers are unwilling to decide."

Yet, the decisions usually are very difficult. "And if something is difficult or controversial, we tend to postpone it," said Bert Carp, deputy assistant to the president for domestic policy. The role of the Energy Mobilization Board, Carp said in September 1979, will be "to say 'Let's make a decision, and let's mean it.'"

"If we don't have a board, where will the major energy facilities we need be built?" asked Carp. "They won't. And it's not because people say 'no,' but because they don't want to make a decision."

Powers of the Board

Legislation setting up a board was considered by various committees of the House and Senate during the 96th Congress, but the House Commerce and Senate Energy panels dominated the debate. Their proposals prevailed over efforts in both houses to weaken the powers of the board. Environmentalists and states' rights advocates failed again.

The final House-Senate conference agreement on the legislation, reached in June, ended up calling for a three-member Energy Mobilization Board. Firms building pipelines, synthetic fuels plants or other energy projects could apply to the board for priority status. Once a project had been granted special status, the board could order federal, state and local agencies to set deadlines for their decisions on permits for the project. If an agency missed a deadline the board could act in place of the agency. The project could also be exempted by the board from laws or regulations written after priority status had been requested or after construction had begun. If the board wanted to exempt a project from federal laws already on the books, the board would have to get permission from Congress and the president. Judicial review of board decisions was limited.

The conference agreement was similar to Carter's original proposal, although he had not sought authority for the board to tamper with existing substantive laws.

In the Senate the opposition to the bill had centered on two aspects of the board's power:

● The so-called "grandfather" clause, which gave the board authority to waive any laws or regulations enacted after construction began on a priority project.

● The board's authority to step in and make decisions for federal, state and local agencies that missed deadlines for actions related to a priority project.

Two veteran senators, Edmund S. Muskie, D-Maine, and Abraham Ribicoff, D-Conn., offered a substitute in which the board could not have waived any laws; instead, it would have had to take a tardy agency to court in order to force a decision; it would not have been able to step in and act for the agency. Under the substitute, only eight projects a year would have been allowed priority status instead of an unlimited number.

Favoring the substitute were several Senate Republicans, who were worried about states' rights. They were joined by many liberal Democrats. The major state and local government associations and environmental groups were on their side.

"If members of the Senate believe that a project can be forcibly rammed down the throats of an objecting public, they are deceiving themselves," said Sen. Robert T. Stafford, R-Vt. "Federal force will not expedite projects; it will delay them."

Muskie was particularly upset at the grandfather clause. "Once you turn the first shovelful of earth on a project, anything you learn about its environmental effects, however toxic, dangerous or damaging to the health, goes by the board," Muskie said. "You cannot do anything about it. This is the grandfather clause."

Those opposed to the substitute were disdainful of the weaker board. "No Energy Mobilization Board is better than the impotent board created by the substitute bill," said Energy Chairman Jackson.

The substitute was defeated on a 58-39 procedural vote.

In the House, the chief sponsor of the alternative proposal was Interior Committee Chairman Morris K. Udall, D-Ariz. His panel initially had drafted a bill that required congressional approval even for a waiver of procedural requirements and allowed the federal government to act in place of federal agencies only, not state and local authorities. But Udall and his allies realized a somewhat stronger board might win enough votes on the floor to defeat the Commerce Committee's bill, which allowed the board, with consent from the president and Congress, to waive any law or rule standing in the way of a priority project.

Therefore, Udall revised his bill. The board was given a chance to take a federal agency to court to get a decision, but also was authorized to ask the president to decide in place of a state or local agency still unwilling to act. Procedural requirements, such as shortening a timetable for hearings, could be changed without going to Congress. A law passed after a project was under construction could be suspended.

The vote rejecting the substitute was close, 192-215, especially considering that Udall was fighting his own Democratic leadership. But the rhetoric of the bill's author, John D. Dingell, D-Mich., Majority Leader Jim Wright, D-Texas, and others apparently had some effect. Wright promised that the board could get rid of unnecessary regulations written by bureaucrats with "a thirst to write laws without the inconvenience of running for Congress." The substitute, Dingell said, should be known as the "slowtrack, side track, massive litigation and lawyers full employment act of 1979."

But Udall said of the Commerce Committee bill that eventually was passed by the House: "This bill is a formula for dismantling the environmental, health and safety laws put together in the appropriate committees in this Congress in the past 20 years."

Udall's ranks of supporters had been depleted when key sponsors of the Commerce bill, and then the House, accepted an amendment prohibiting the board from waiving state or local laws. The vote was 415-1.

The Carter administration was severely criticized for its lobbying on the bill and for its inconsistent position on the question of whether the board should be empowered to suggest waivers of substantive laws — such as clean air standards — as provided in the Commerce Committee's version. Even top environmental officials within the administration complained about the Energy Department's support of the Commerce bill instead of the Udall substitute. The department's theory was that administration officials could work to remove the offensive aspect of the Commerce bill — the waiver of substantive law — in a House-Senate conference. And the department considered the board established by the Udall substitute to be too weak.

Increased Coal Use

Although the United States has abundant supplies of coal, producing and using that coal could increasingly conflict with protection of the environment.

When Congress agreed in 1977 to put federal controls on the strip mining of coal, the landmark law ended several years of debate, or so it seemed. In only two years, however, opponents had won Senate approval of an amendment that supporters of the 1977 law argued would gut the act. The House never considered the amendment, but further fights were expected in the future as coal producers sought revisions in — or repeal of — the act.

In another area, air pollution controls, utilities complained about rules issued in May 1979 under the 1977 clean air amendments that limited emissions from power plants built after 1978. The utilities and the coal industry planned to work in the 97th Congress for revisions in the clean air law in order to ease these "new source performance standards" and other emission controls that, they said, hindered increased coal use. In addition, they were gearing up to fight moves to tighten controls on pollution from existing plants and to reduce acid rainfall, which critics charged was caused principally by coal emissions.

Still a third arena of conflict between environmentalists and proponents of increased coal use was the leasing procedures for coal development on federal lands, as discussed above on p. 103.

Strip Mining Controls

In the East, much of the damage to the coal fields already had been done. Only half of the strip-mined land there had been reclaimed as of 1977. In the West, strip mining was expected to be the chief means of extracting the vast deposits of coal. And extraction by that method throughout the United States was expected to increase dramatically: in 1970, about 44 percent of U.S. coal production came from surface mines; by 1976, the share was 56 percent; by 1978, 64 percent.

Enactment of the Surface Mining Control and Reclamation Act in August 1977 ended several years of congressional consideration. It had been a goal of environ-

mentalists for more than a decade. The House approved a bill in 1972, but the Senate did not act. President Ford pocket-vetoed a bill in 1974 after the 93rd Congress had adjourned. In May 1975 Ford vetoed another bill, and the House failed to override the veto by just three votes. Twice in 1976, with the chance of a veto uncertain, the House Rules Committee prevented strip mining bills from reaching the floor.

Although it was clear from the beginning that Carter favored strip mining control legislation, the bill he signed was slightly weaker than some of the earlier versions. Coal companies, facing the inevitability of strip mining rules, lobbied for certain exemptions and simplified procedures and, in some cases, they won. They were particularly successful in the Senate, where leadership for a strong bill had been weaker than in the House, where Udall made passage a top priority. In addition, the coal industry had powerful friends in the Senate, such as Majority Leader Robert   Byrd Jr., D-W.Va.

Environmentalists Pleased

As finally enacted, however, the bill pleased environmentalists for the most part. Coal mining lobbyists were unhappy, but relieved that certain exemptions and variances had been allowed. Senate and House conferees generally felt they had reached a good compromise. The 1977 law:

● Set standards for environmental protection at major coal surface mining sites, including requirements for restoration of topsoil, revegetation with native plants, regrading to original contours and protection of water supplies.

● Provided for joint responsibility and enforcement by the states and the federal government.

● Established a self-supporting Abandoned Mine Reclamation Fund to restore lands ravaged in the past by uncontrolled mining operations.

● Protected certain lands regarded as unsuitable for surface mining, such as fertile Western farmland in alluvial valley floors.

Implementation of the law moved slowly, as federal standards had to be written and then state plans submitted and approved by the Interior Department. When Congress began considering whether to extend the deadline for submission of state plans, opponents of the law seized the opportunity to suggest major amendments.

The thrust of the legislation passed by the Senate in September 1979 was to allow states to design their strip mining regulations without following the 151 pages of tough federal regulations written by Interior's Office of Surface Mining. Instead, the states would only have to make their strip mining plans conform to the act itself.

Opponents of amending the act said it would mean several years of court challenges because the federal government, without a set of regulations, would have little legal basis for approving or rejecting a state plan. That, they charged, would delay additional coal production. Also, without minimum federal standards, mining companies would shop around for a state with weak controls, a situation the original act was specifically designed to discourage, said Senate Energy Chairman Jackson. Another opponent of amending the act, Sen. John Melcher, D-Mont., said exempting states from a set of regulations was "reckless" and "unprecedented."

But supporters of the amendments said the federal rules were so overly specific that they had "usurped" state authority and required "state-level clones" of the federal plan in order for states to win approval from the Interior Department. This, they said, was not the intent of the 1977 law. Those were the phrases used by Sen. Mark O. Hatfield, R-Ore., who joined others in successfully urging passage of the 1979 amendments. Two senators who helped win votes for the changes were the two Democratic senators from West Virginia, Byrd and Environment and Public Works Committee Chairman Jennings Randolph. Another aggressive lobbyist was West Virginia Gov. John D. (Jay) Rockefeller, also a Democrat.

However, the overwhelming 68-26 Senate vote Sept. 11, 1979, turned out to be futile because Udall refused to consider the legislation in his House Interior Committee.

In the 97th Congress, though, Udall was expected to have less control over a more conservative Interior panel. Although Interior Secretary Andrus had been a strong supporter of the strip mining law and had hinted that the Carter administration would have vetoed the Senate bill, Reagan's appointee for Interior, James Watt, had no similar commitment to the 1977 law. In fact, Reagan's transition team received in December 1980 a proposal from the leading coal industry associations for a new set of amendments to the strip mining law. Although passage of this "substitute" could prove difficult, amendments to the 1977 act seemed increasingly likely to win congressional approval.

Air Pollution from Coal Burning

The Clean Air Act controlled three emissions from coal-burning plants — sulfur dioxide, nitrogen oxides and particulates (or soot). Another emission, carbon dioxide, was not controlled, but was considered to have a detrimental effect on the environment.

The pollution standard that evoked the greatest controversy was that regulating sulfur dioxide.

Sulfur Dioxide

Sulfur dioxide is a gas that causes respiratory difficulties and can mix with other air pollutants to cause coughs, colds, bronchitis, asthma and emphysema.

Sulfur dioxide can be controlled by washing the coal before burning it or by using smokestack "scrubbers," devices that remove the sulfur from the gases before they are emitted from the stack.

The Environmental Protection Agency in June 1979 issued rules governing sulfur emissions from power plants that require the use of scrubbers on the smokestacks of all new power plants built after 1978. The standard required utilities to remove up to 90 percent of the sulfur dioxide from their emissions before they were spewed into the air.

The requirement had been controversial because industry claimed it could not achieve 90 percent removal on a continuing basis. Utilities wanted to see the standard lowered to about 85 percent removal.

Another reason the sulfur standard was controversial was because scrubbers cost a lot. A scrubber for a 500 megawatt power plant could cost $50 million, according to the Edison Electric Institute, an industry research organization.

Despite the high cost of scrubbers, environmentalists argued that the price to society of uncontrolled sulfur emissions also was high. One cost analysis done by a University of Washington environmental economist found that an un-

controlled 500 megawatt coal-fired plant can cause environmental damage of from $7 million to $50 million a year.

The figure included damage to lakes, buildings and vegetation, decreased visibility caused by acid rain and increased mortality allegedly caused by acid sulfates.

Closely related to the issue of putting scrubbers on new coal-burning power plants was the problem of the millions of tons of pollutants being spewed into the air from existing power plants.

The new scrubber standards applied only to future power plants. Older plants still were controlled by individual state air pollution control plans, developed to enforce the Clean Air Act.

Many of those state plans — particularly in the Midwest — allowed utilities to build tall smokestacks in order to get around the local pollution limits. By spewing their pollutants high into the air via tall stacks, the companies could burn dirtier coal — without having to install pollution control devices — and still meet local health standards.

For example, sources in Ohio alone emitted almost 9,000 tons of sulfur dioxide each day, almost twice as much as was emitted by sources in all the New England states, New York and New Jersey.

Existing plants spewed an average of up to 6.5 times as much pollution into the air as that allowed new plants under the clean air standards. The EPA estimated that, by the year 2000, as much as 70 percent of the sulfur dioxide emitted will be coming from power plants built before 1970.

Another potential problem with older plants is that many utilities may delay retiring their older plants because of the high cost of new scrubber-equipped plants.

"A number of utilities may now be planning to artifically extend the life of their existing generating plants from a normal expected life of approximately 35 years to perhaps 50 or even 60 years," Robert Rauch, staff attorney for the Environmental Defense Fund, told the House Commerce Committee's Oversight Subcommittee in February 1980.

"If this occurs on a widespread scale, it will eliminate any chance of reducing present sulfur dioxide levels in the rest of this century," Rauch warned. "In short, controls on new power plants simply are not enough. The key is emissions from existing facilities."

To control those older plant emissions, EPA was urged to: establish a sulfate standard, require early retirement of older plants or use several other tools available under the Clean Air Act.

Nitrogen Oxides

Direct exposure to nitrogen oxides is believed to increase the risks of acute respiratory disease and susceptibility to chronic respiratory infection.

Nitrogen oxides can mix with other pollutants to form urban smog, which reduces visibility and can aggravate respiratory diseases such as bronchitis and pneumonia. Coughing, eye irritation, headaches and sore throats are common complaints during smog episodes.

EPA research indicated that nitrogen oxides could become one of the most troublesome air pollutants of the 1980s. In 1980, more than 20 million metric tons of nitrogen oxides were polluting the air annually. Half of it came from cars and trucks and half from coal- and oil-burning plants, EPA said.

But by 1985, vehicles are expected to contribute only 30 percent of the total, with industry and utilities contributing 70 percent.

If present trends continued, nitrogen oxide emissions could increase by 50 percent over the next 20 years, while sulfur dioxide emissions are expected to stabilize. That's because emission control technologies developed so far have provided only a 50 percent reduction in nitrogen oxide emissions, while sulfur dioxide controls can achieve 90 percent reductions.

One way of controlling nitrogen oxides is by fine-tuning the combustion process, much like tuning a car. EPA and the coal industry are researching new methods of controlling nitrogen oxides.

Particulates

Particulates are solid particles such as dust, soot or smoke, which irritate the lungs.

The smaller the particle, the more likely it is to lodge in the inner-most parts of the lung. Scientists are concerned that the smaller particles can carry traces of toxic metals released when coal is burned. Particulates can contain traces of up to 27 toxic metals — such as arsenic, cadmium, mercury, and uranium. But it is not known whether these are emitted in large enough quantities to harm the lungs or the environment. They also contain small amounts of radioactivity.

Because of their light-scattering properties, these smaller particles also contribute to reduced visibility.

About 99.5 percent of the larger particulates can be controlled, but only about 80 percent of the smaller particles are controllable.

Environmentalists in May 1980 petitioned EPA to develop a national health standard for fine particulates. In the meantime, new technologies are being tested for controlling the finer particulates.

Acid Rain

Although sulfur dioxides and nitrogen oxides can cause health and environmental damage in the area surrounding a polluting power plant, many utilities installed tall stacks that throw the pollutants high into the air, thus protecting local residents.

Some scientists are concerned that when these pollutants are transported long distances in the upper atmosphere, they are transformed into sulfates and nitrates, which can be even more dangerous than are the original emissions.

Sulfates and nitrates may cause two serious — and costly — environmental problems: respiratory illness (including, possibly, lung cancer) and acid rain.

Although there are a number of unanswered questions about all the factors that cause acid rain, there is little argument that the major contributors are sulfates and nitrates.

Scientists have found that when sulfates and nitrates combine with moisture in the atmosphere they form acidic droplets. The droplets eventually form rain, snow or sleet high in acidity, sometimes as acidic as lemon juice or vinegar.

When the acid enters lakes, either in rainfall or as runoff through lakeside soils, entire ecosystems can be affected. The acid can cause fish egg cases to dissolve and can destroy lake food chains. Aquatic plant life slowly comes to a halt.

Toxic metals, such as mercury, extracted from the lakeside soil by the acid runoff can contaminate fish. Aluminium, which is broken down in the soil by the acid runoff, can destroy the gills of fish.

Eventually, the lakes become deceptively crystal clear — totally devoid of life except for algae.

First discovered in Scandinavia in the 1950s, acid rain was blamed for fish kills in New York's Adirondack Mountains, where 90 percent of the lakes contained no fish in 1980.

Scientists believe that acid rain first appeared in Scandinavia and the Adirondacks because those areas were once covered by glaciers and thus have thin soil covers. The shallow soils cannot buffer the effects of the acid. The phenomenon appears to be spreading. Lakes in the Blue Ridge and Colorado mountains have also begun to show signs of increased acidity.

Scientists believe the phenomenon has just begun showing up because it results from the cumulative effect of sulfur buildup over many decades of coal and oil burning.

"The natural buffering capacity of the rocks, soils and lakes has been used up," explained Dr. Ian Marceau, staff director of the House Science and Technology Subcommittee on Natural Resources and the Environment. He said that more research is needed on the effects of acid rain on agriculture and forests.

"The signs indicate we could be facing potentially alarming economic problems caused by a reduction in crop yields and interruption of the food chain," he warned. "But, so far, totally inadequate work has been done on these effects."

In 1980, EPA began studying the long-term effects of acid rain on crop yields. Early results showed that half the crops tested thrived in the more acidic environment, while the rest showed signs of leaf and root damage and stunted growth.

But Dr. Marceau warned that although some plants may thrive in the acidic environment, it could mean that the acid was robbing the soil of its natural nutrients and feeding them to the plants faster than normal. That could speed up plant development in the short run, but completely wear out the soil over a long period of time, he said.

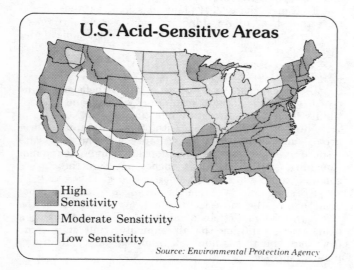

U.S. Acid-Sensitive Areas

High Sensitivity
Moderate Sensitivity
Low Sensitivity

Source: Environmental Protection Agency

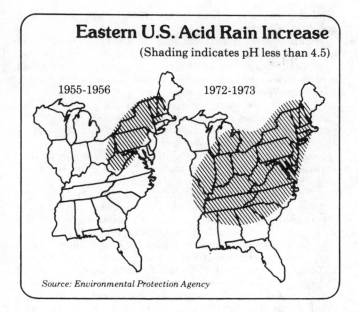

Eastern U.S. Acid Rain Increase

(Shading indicates pH less than 4.5)

1955-1956   1972-1973

Source: Environmental Protection Agency

of the University of Washington and Dr. Guy Orcutt of Yale University presented other evidence that sulfates are deleterious to human health.

After analyzing more than two million death certificates, they found that sulfates may account for up to 187,686 deaths a year in the United States. Even by conservative estimates, the authors said, sulfates account for more than 150,000 deaths annually.

The statistical evidence that links sulfates with mortality is extremely controversial. The Office of Technology Assessment (OTA) reviewed some of the criticisms of the evidence. OTA researchers concluded that critics' arguments were insufficient to reject claims that significant health damage is caused by existing levels of the pollutants.

"It is not entirely clear, however, that sulfates are the culprit, or the only culprit," said OTA's Alan Crane. He said that the tiny particulates also emitted from coal-burning plants, which are suspected of carrying the largest amount of toxic metal residues, may be the biggest contributor to respiratory diseases.

Carbon Dioxide

Carbon dioxide buildup in the atmosphere is blamed on deforestation and the burning of fossil fuels, primarily coal, oil and natural gas.

A Department of Energy study warned that man's burning of fossil fuels could double the amount of carbon dioxide in the air over the next 50 to 75 years.

That could trap more of the sun's rays and create a "greenhouse effect," increasing world temperatures and altering the Earth's climate, the study said in 1979.

The threat is increased if there is a shift to more coal use. Coal combustion yields 25 percent more carbon dioxide than oil and 67 percent more than natural gas, due to the greater amount of fixed carbon in coal.

Some scientists have warned that significant increases in coal use possibly could result in melting of the polar icecaps, flooding of coastal cities and alteration of rainfall patterns that would drastically affect agriculture.

Other scientists, however, claimed that if the carbon dioxide buildup did increase the Earth's temperature, it simply would create more clouds that would cool off the Earth, canceling the effects of the carbon dioxide.

Although scientists disagree on what the effects of increased carbon dioxide buildup will be, they do agree that it is something that should be studied.

"Although it does appear that some time remains before the hard decisions have to be made, carbon dioxide could conceivably represent an ultimate and, possibly, uncontrollable constraint on coal development," said the OTA's Crane.

A study prepared for the Council on Environmental Quality concluded that sound conservation practices are the first step toward controlling carbon dioxide buildup.

Another CEQ study, issued in January 1981, pointed out that many scientists have concluded that, if the burning of fossil fuel increases at a rapid rate in the decades ahead, the accompanying increases in carbon dioxide "will lead to profound and long-term alteration of the earth's climate . . . with far-reaching adverse consequences, affecting our ability to feed a hungry and increasingly crowded world. . . ."

Synthetic Fuels

Development of synthetic fuels is expected to cause a host of environmental problems that will require ex-

The coal industry argued that more study is needed before Congress acts to control acid rain.

The Electric Power Research Institute (EPRI), which had spent $5 million on acid rain research as of 1980, said it had found no simple relationship between acid precipitation levels and ecological damage.

"A simple cause and effect cannot be quantified," said Dr. Ralph M. Perhac, acting director of EPRI's environmental assessment department. "If we don't know what or how much damage is due to acid rain, we don't know what sort of control would minimize the damage."

Acid Dust

Although most media attention has concentrated on damages to fish and vegetation caused by acid rain, scientists are becoming increasingly concerned about the direct health effects on humans of dry acid fallout in the form of sulfates and nitrates.

Not all sulfates and nitrates mix with rain, sleet or snow to form acid rain. Some, after traveling long distances, float back down to earth as "acid dust," which is then inhaled by people.

Acid sulfate particles can lodge in the lungs and contribute to chronic bronchitis, emphysema and asthma. Also, some scientists fear the particles mix with other pollutants in the air to cause lung cancer.

Dr. Leonard Hamilton, director of biomedical and environmental research at Brookhaven National Laboratory, said sulfates have a "corrosive" effect on the lungs over a long period of time, bringing on or exacerbating respiratory illnesses.

"We have found that in 1975 there were 7,500 to 120,000 deaths caused by coal-fired power plants. If we don't put controls on those plants, or replace them with new plants, that rate will probably continue," he said.

He predicted that if only 40 power plants were converted to coal use under a proposed coal conversion bill, the resulting acid sulfate fallout would cause at least 1,000 premature deaths a year.

Another study, conducted by Dr. Robert Mendelsohn

tensive and probably expensive mitigation efforts. In most cases, the specific environmental effects have proven difficult to pinpoint because the technology is still being developed.

The environmental impacts of synthetic fuels development that have already been identified include:

• Air pollution, including emissions of sulfur dioxide, nitrogen oxide, particulates and carbon dioxide. Carbon dioxide emissions could be multiplied because some processes, such as coal liquefaction, require the fuel to be burned twice.

• Heavy demand for water, which could cause problems in the arid West where most development of synthetic fuel is expected to occur. Although most development plans call for zero discharge of pollutants, toxic substances could prove difficult to extract fully, and underground conversion of oil shale, called in situ processing, could affect ground water supplies.

• Disposal of tons and tons of solid waste that could include toxic materials. The volume of waste from shale, for example, is expected to exceed 150,000 tons a day from a plant producing 100,000 barrels of liquid fuel a day. Underground injection of wastes was restricted by the 1974 Safe Drinking Water Act, and disposal of hazardous wastes was controlled by the Resource Conservation and Recovery Act.

• Land alteration from strip mining of coal and mining of shale that could lead to water pollution, soil erosion and loss of farm land.

• Carcinogens from coal liquefaction that could affect workers and those using or transporting the fuel.

Some states have environmental laws that could affect synfuels development. For example, Colorado has standards for "prevention of significant deterioration" in air quality that are more stringent than the national rules. Colorado also has tough reclamation and solid waste disposal laws. Wyoming has tightly controlled industrial siting and protected groundwater with detailed regulations. Nebraska residents once objected in court to an energy facility because it required water to be withdrawn in Wyoming that they said would adversely affect Nebraska.

Another environmental consequence of synthetic fuels development is the expected rapid growth of the small towns that characterize the counties suitable for coal liquefaction, oil shale and other synfuels production.

An Energy Department report in July 1979 estimated that each 100,000 barrel-per-day facility would require 10,000 to 20,000 people, either directly as employees or indirectly. This type of increase in many rural counties would double the population in a few years, requiring a quick expansion of schools, sewage treatment plants, housing and roads. Possible environmental consequences of rapid, uncontrolled development are difficult to quantify, but they include air and water pollution, loss of natural vegetation and improper disposal of solid wastes.

7

Energy Policymakers

A traditional way to give the appearance of doing something is to reorganize.

The federal government succumbed to that temptation in the 1970s, as the pressure mounted for officials to do something about the nation's energy problems. The federal energy bureaucracy was the target of most efforts, although Congress itself was not immune to the efforts of the re-organizers.

The fruits of the efforts were a Cabinet-level energy agency, the Department of Energy; an independent regulatory body within that department, the Federal Energy Regulatory Administration; and a nuclear agency concentrating on regulating, not promoting, nuclear power, the Nuclear Regulatory Commission. The Energy Department has been much-maligned, and the criticism prompted a threat from Ronald Reagan during his presidential campaign that he would dismantle the agency if elected. However, as Reagan prepared to take power in Washington, his energy advisers appeared to be backing away from that promise.

The most dramatic change in congressional energy decision-making was abolition of Congress' Joint Committee on Atomic Energy in 1977, with jurisdiction over nuclear matters divided among three Senate and five House committees. As part of an overall Senate reorganization not prompted solely by energy-related concerns, the Senate Interior Committee was revamped and its jurisdiction expanded so that most energy matters came before it as a renamed Senate Energy Committee. However, the Senate Environment and Public Works Committee handled nuclear regulation and safety, and several panels shared responsibility for other issues.

In the House, a special energy committee was considered in 1977 and then recommended in 1980 by a House Select Committee on Committees. But the House rejected the idea, preferring instead to give the Commerce Committee principal responsibility for energy. Other key House energy panels were the Interior and Science and Technology committees.

In the executive branch and in Congress, decisions about reorganization have usually kep some energy-related matters outside the jurisdiction of any new, consolidated energy organization. The rationale has been that conflicts between matters such as protection of federal lands and energy development on those lands, use of nuclear energy and safe operation of nuclear reactors and increased coal mining and regulation of strip mining, would be better handled by putting responsibilities in different agencies. Even though it might be less efficient, the disputes would be brought out into the open and resolved in public, rather than within the confines of a bureaucracy where the more powerful private interests might prevail over the consensus of the public good. That is why Interior still leased federal lands, although Energy had some responsibilities, and why the Atomic Energy Commission was disbanded, because it had handled both promotion and regulation of nuclear power. The Senate Environment Committee regulated nuclear safety, while Senate Energy could recommend legislation encouraging expansion of nuclear use. House Interior and Commerce played similar roles.

Many of the conflicts have been between energy and environmental concerns. The trend has been to keep separate the agencies designed to achieve the goals of enhancing energy conservation and production, and protecting the environment. The Carter administration's proposed Energy Mobilization Board was designed to end the often time-consuming, interagency disputes and give a special board responsibility for arbitrating conflicts. The failure of Congress to approve the board was in part a rejection of this attempt to change the past practice of encouraging tension among the different agencies. The refusal by the House to create an Energy Committee reflected the same concerns, although there were other factors, too.

The leaders of agencies and committees usually influence decisionmaking. The first three energy secretaries brought different personalities, means of operating and ideas to the job, and thus affected the role assumed by the department and the policies it made. In the House and Senate, two energy leaders in the late 1970s and 1980 — Rep. John D. Dingell of Michigan and Sen. J. Bennett Johnston of Louisiana — emerged from the principal energy committees, House Commerce and Senate Energy. Although not committee chairmen at the time, their positions as subcommittee chairmen gave them ample opportunity to have a major role in energy policymaking. A look at their convictions and style provides important clues to congressional attitudes toward energy.

However, every member of Congress is an energy policymaker because of votes cast on the House and Senate floors. Influenced in part by party philosophy and by the interests of their state or district, the legislators make several major policy decisions each session. Attempting to sway their votes is a sophisticated, well-financed lobby of energy interests. For oil and gas interests, more than 130 different political action committees were making campaign contributions as of late 1979. A review of those groups and their major contributions provides some insight into their efforts to influence energy-policymaking.

Energy Bureaucracy

The energy bureaucracy was born in the late 19th century, when the Bureau of Mines was established. Although at first oriented towards research and development of minerals and coal, the agency added an oil division in 1915. During World War I, a U.S. Fuel Administration was set up to regulate the petroleum industry, with supplies reserved for top priority uses. Leader of that effort was Mark Requa. A similar responsibility was given during World War II to Harold Ickes, who as interior secretary and in other posts had been a key figure in oil policymaking during the New Deal. After the war, an oil and gas division was set up within the Interior Department.

Another branch of the federal energy bureaucracy was established in 1920, when the Federal Power Act set up a commission to oversee development of hydropower projects. The federal role was based on longtime federal authority over the nation's navigable rivers and streams. The Federal Power Commission was given additional responsibility in 1935 to regulate interstate sale of electricity at the wholesale level, and in 1938 to perform a similar function for natural gas. The authority over natural gas was further expanded by a 1954 Supreme Court ruling that directed the FPC to regulate price setting at natural gas wellheads.

Even before the FPC was set up, the interior secretary had been given authority to sell electricity not needed to pump irrigation water at Bureau of Reclamation water projects. The bureau had been established in 1902 to make profitable agriculture possible in the arid West. The authority to sell electricity was provided in 1906.

In 1909, another dam-building agency, the Army Corps of Engineers, was directed to consider electricity production as a benefit when considering navigation projects. By 1924, hydropower had become a rationale in itself for Corps of Engineers projects.

The next wave of bureaucracy building came as part of the New Deal. Hoping to provide electrical power to rural Appalachia and at the same time a yardstick by which to measure the performance of privately owned utilities, Congress in 1933 set up the Tennessee Valley Authority. Soon after, the Bonneville Power Administration was established in the Pacific Northwest to market power from a Corps of Engineers project on the Columbia River at Bonneville. Later, other regional power marketing administrations were set up. In 1935, the Rural Electrification Administration was created to promote the marketing of electricity in rural areas.

The creation of the Atomic Energy Commission in 1946 added still another arm to the federal energy bureaucracy, although it was several years before electricity was produced by nuclear power.

A growth in environmental awareness as much as attention to energy prompted Richard Nixon in 1971 to ask Congress for a new Cabinet agency for environment and energy: the Department of Natural Resources. But the plan received less than a lukewarm reception on Capitol Hill.

In his 1973 response to the Arab oil embargo, Nixon again asked for a new Cabinet agency, this time to be called the Department of Energy and Natural Resources, which Nixon wanted as a replacement for the Interior Department.

Perhaps because he knew a separate Cabinet-level agency would be difficult to achieve, Nixon also asked for two other new agencies: a temporary Federal Energy Administration to be responsible for management of short-term energy problems and an Energy Research and Development Administration to handle energy research and development.

Congress agreed in mid-1974 to set up the FEA, passing the Federal Energy Administration Act of 1974. Later, additional powers for the agency were provided in the Energy Supply and Environmental Coordination Act of 1974. The new agency, originally expected to have a life of two years, was directed to handle oil price regulation and allocation, develop and impose mandatory energy conservation measures in emergencies, gather information on energy and project future use patterns, study the potential of conservation, order utilities capable of using coal to make the switch and recommend improvements in public transportation.

ERDA was established later in 1974, after Gerald R. Ford became president. The Energy Reorganization Act of 1974 took nuclear research and development functions from the Atomic Energy Commission, fossil research from Interior and solar and geothermal development from the National Science Foundation. Most of the staff and budget came from the AEC. The remaining regulatory functions of the AEC were given to a new agency, the Nuclear Regulatory Commission. The argument was that nuclear promotion and regulation should be handled separately. In addition, a new agency seemed appropriate to consolidate the government's overall energy research efforts, which were expanded in reaction to the quadrupling of oil prices and worries about shortages.

As one of his last acts, Ford in early 1977 sent Congress a proposal for a new Energy Department. In March President Jimmy Carter also asked for a Cabinet agency for energy, and his plan took precedence. The Energy Department was to take on overall energy research, development, commercialization and regulatory functions except regulation of nuclear power.

Congress was receptive to Carter's plan, which was considered by the Senate Governmental Affairs and House Government Operations committees. The major controversy was over Carter's proposal to give the energy secretary responsibility for pricing of oil and natural gas and for leasing of federal lands for energy development.

The Senate put the price-setting responsibility for gas under an independent regulatory agency within the Energy Department, which was to be called the Federal Energy Regulatory Commission. Essentially, the FPC would be placed within the organization chart of the Energy Department, but remain independent. The senators also kept most authority over leasing in the Interior Department, giving the Energy Department directives to foster competition for leases and set production rates.

Although these changes had been recommended by the Senate committee, in the House the controversies spilled onto the floor in June. Attention was focused on the proposal to give the energy secretary authority for oil and gas pricing. The bill would "vest far too much power in a single individual," said Rep. John D. Moss, D-Calif. Another plea for revision was made by Rep. John D. Dingell, D-Mich. "The age of kings, my colleagues, expired with the French Revolution," he said. "And I beg you not to set up a new king here in Washington." An amendment establishing an independent regulatory agency within the department was adopted, 2-to-1. The House also split leasing between Interior and Energy, as did the final bill. Action was completed in early August.

James R. Schlesinger

The first secretary of energy was James R. Schlesinger, who had been serving as Carter's energy "czar" in the White House. He and his staff had drafted the 1977 national energy plan unveiled that April. Carter signed the energy agency bill Aug. 4, and the Schlesinger appointment was confirmed that same day.

Schlesinger was a controversial, very visible energy secretary. A familiar sight on Capitol Hill in 1977 and 1978 was Schlesinger, his pipe smoking and his square chin jutting out as he tried to tug Carter's energy plan through a recalcitrant Congress. Schlesinger made news again in early 1979 when he warned of severe oil shortages because of cutbacks in Iranian production and urged new attention to emergency rationing and conservation plans.

James Rodney Schlesinger was born in New York City Feb. 15, 1929. He was a summa cum laude, Phi Beta Kappa graduate of Harvard University (1950), where he also earned his masters (1952) and doctorate (1956) degreees, all in economics. Fron 1953 through 1963, he taught at the University of Virginia and during those years also served terms as a consultant to the Naval War College and the Federal Reserve System's Board of Governors. Officers of the Rand Corporation, a national security think tank in Santa Monica, Calif., invited Schlesinger in 1963 to become a senior member, and by 1967 he was Rand's director of strategic studies. From 1965 to 1969 he doubled as a consultant to the federal Bureau of the Budget. He entered that agency as assistant director in 1969 and continued to be responsible for national security and energy when it became the Office of Management and Budget.

Schlesinger held top federal jobs for the next several years. He was chairman of the Atomic Energy Commission from August 1971 through February 1973, and director of the Central Intelligence Agency from then until July, when he became secretary of defense, a post from which Ford fired him in November 1975. Schlesinger had complained about Ford's detente efforts and urged increased spending for arms to counter the Soviet Union.

Schlesinger's unqualified support of nuclear power as AEC chairman made him immediately suspect as energy secretary in the eyes of nuclear critics, but his policy decisions relating to that fuel were somewhat balanced by cautious officials elsewhere in the Carter administration. His attention to the 1977-78 energy legislation, which did not deal with nuclear, also left him little time to focus on that energy source.

Schlesinger was popular on Capitol Hill, with even critics finding his outspokenness a refreshing change.

Schlesinger resigned as energy secretary July 20, 1979, just days after Carter's return from a soul-searching retreat at Camp David, Md. Although Schlesinger apparently was not fired, the Energy Department during his tenure had been criticized as poorly managed, and Carter aides had also grumbled about his performance as secretary.

Charles W. Duncan

Carter's replacement for Schlesinger was a deputy defense secretary who seemed a mild-mannered organization man next to his flamboyant predecessor. That was the image Carter sought, along with management expertise, when he chose Charles W. Duncan as the second energy secretary.

Duncan's principal responsibility had been financial management of the Pentagon. He brought to that job a record as a successful businessman with neithr political experience nor any special expertise in military matters.

Duncan was born in Houston on Sept. 9, 1926, and graduated from Rice University in 1947 with a B.S. in chemical engineering. He later did graduate work in management techniques at the University of Texas. His first job was with the Humble Oil and Refining Co. In 1948, he joined the family firm, Duncan Foods Co., producers of Maryland Club Coffee. In 10 years, he had become company president. In 1964, Coca-Cola Co. bought Duncan Foods, and Duncan became an executive and director of the parent firm. As part of the acquisition agreement, he received one of the largest individual blocks of Coca-Cola stock, 170,000 shares. Duncan was president of the Atlanta-based company from 1971 to 1974, a period coinciding with Carter's tenure as governor of Georgia. However, Duncan was not known as a close adviser or political supporter of the president. At the time he was chosen for the defense post, Duncan was serving as a director of Coca-Cola and held other business posts.

Duncan's one-and-a-half years as energy secretary were marked by a lowered profile for the agency, with major policy decisions concentrated at the White House and the Office of Management and Budget, as they had been before the Department of Energy was established. Two key aides there were Elliot Cutler and Katherine Schirmer.

James B. Edwards

In choosing former South Carolina Gov. James B. Edwards to be his energy secretary, President-elect Reagan found someone who shared his basic philosophy: get government out of the way so private industry can produce more energy.

But other than being a fervent supporter of nuclear power, Edwards has not been involved in or taken public positions on most major energy issues.

Edwards was to head a three-year-old, $10 billion-a-year agency often criticized by Republicans and Democrats alike for bureaucratic ineptness. Edwards said he was not an energy expert but a "problem solver."

Edwards, an oral surgeon who also was considered to head the Department of Health and Human Services, said that as governor, he was heavily involved in energy. He chaired an energy subcommittee of the National Governors' Association in 1978.

Environmental groups were unhappy with his nomination because of his strident pro-nuclear position.

Edwards was selected after Southern senators, led by Strom Thurmond, R-S.C., complained that the South had been ignored in Reagan's initial Cabinet selections.

Shortly before he was named, Edwards said, "I'd like to go to Washington and close the Energy Department down and work myself out of a job." Abolishing the department was an early Reagan campaign pledge, but at a press conference Dec. 22, 1980, Edwards ducked the question, saying he needed direction from Reagan before making any decision on dismantling the department.

Edwards has said, "The less the federal government has to do with problems, the better I like it."

However, at his Senate confirmation hearings in January 1981, Edwards said his interest in abolishing the department had diminished. He told members of the Senate Energy Committee: "There has to be some sort of focus for energy policy. We'll have a Department of Energy until you gentlemen [in Congress] decide otherwise."

Edwards' 1974 election as South Carolina's first Republican governor since Reconstruction was regarded as something of a fluke. He defeated retired Army Gen. William C. Westmoreland in the primary, but was expected to lose the general election to Democrat Charles (Pug) Ravenel. However, state courts ruled Ravenel off the ballot because he did not meet residency requirements, and Edwards faced a weaker opponent, former Rep. William Jennings Bryan Dorn. Dorn failed to unite his party, and Edwards won with 50.9 percent of the vote.

As governor, Edwards strongly supported Reagan's 1976 bid for the Republican presidential nomination against President Ford. But in 1980, he, like Thurmond, backed John B. Connally. When Connally quit the race after losing the South Carolina primary, Edwards helped Reagan carry the state in November.

William Brantley Harvey Jr., lieutenant governor under Edwards and a Democrat, described him as a "committed conservative" and "completely honest and fair." State GOP Chairman George Graham called him "a great one-on-one politician," good at "disarming his enemies."

Lamar Priester, state energy director under Edwards, said Edwards was often frustrated by the long time it took the Energy Department to get things done. He said Edwards considers energy the "basic thread of this country's economic base" and believes improved energy production is necessary to provide jobs for young Americans.

Edwards has been an unabashed supporter of nuclear energy. As governor, he created a state Energy Research Institute which studied ways to expand nuclear power. It recommended building a 12-reactor nuclear power park in the state to supply electricity for the region, but the controversial project was not built.

Edwards' strong backing for renewed commercial reprocessing of nuclear fuel was the position that most dismayed environmental groups. Presidents Ford and Carter banned reprocessing, which involves turning burned nuclear reactor fuel into fresh fuel, plutonium and highly radioactive liquid waste. The ban was based on the fear that the plutonium could be used to produce nuclear weapons.

Edwards said in 1977 that "this idea that a high school kid can go into the kitchen and manufacture a plutonium bomb is hogwash." He promoted a reprocessing facility that was built in South Carolina but never operated because of the ban. Testifying before a Senate subcommittee in 1978, he said reprocessing would reduce U.S. dependence on foreign oil.

At a hearing in 1978, he said "the only answer we have [to the U.S. energy shortage] is nuclear energy," which he described as safer than oil, coal or natural gas.

He also urged that something be done about radioactive waste. "Everyone has wanted to put it off, and we are getting constipated with nuclear waste and have no real way to dispose of it so we can move ahead [with nuclear power]. Let us do something, even if it isn't the ideal situation in years to come. We can move back and correct it as technological advances are made," he said.

Edwards said he was happy to have the millions of gallons of highly radioactive waste from making nuclear weapons because without it "we would probably all be slaves working in the Siberian salt mines today."

Edwards was born June 24, 1927, in Hawthorne, Fla. He received a B.S. degree from the College of Charleston in 1950 and a D.M.D. from the University of Louisville School of Dentistry in 1955. He went to sea with the U.S. Maritime Service during World War II and served as a Navy dentist from 1955-57, remaining in the Naval Reserve until 1967.

Associates credited Edwards with building his local Republican organization almost from the ground up. He chaired the Charleston County Republican Party from 1964-69. In 1971, Edwards ran for Congress and lost. In 1972 he was elected to the state Senate, and in 1974 he won the governorship. In 1978, prohibited by law from seeking a second term, he returned to his dental practice in Charleston. The day after being named to Reagan's Cabinet, he performed a full day of surgery.

KEY HILL FIGURES: DINGELL, JOHNSTON

The leaders of executive branch agencies and congressional committees usually are the most important individuals in forming energy policy. But occasionally others play equally significant roles. In the House and Senate during the 1970s, two leaders on energy issues emerged from the principal energy committees, Senate Energy and House Commerce. Although not committee chairmen at the time, their positions as subcommittee chairmen gave them ample opportunity to have a major role in energy policymaking. Following are profiles of these two individuals: Rep. John D. Dingell, D-Mich., and Sen. J. Bennett Johnston, D-La.

Dingell: Stubborn, Abrasive, And at Center of Energy Issue

"John Dingell in a legislative fight is the best friend you can have if he's on your side, and the worst enemy you can have if he's on the other side," said James Free, a White House lobbyist for President Carter, in 1979. "He takes it all very hard."

"Whatever side he ends up on, he just goes all out. He doesn't like to give ground," comments Howard Paster, a lobbyist for the United Auto Workers Union.

In the House, where members usually treat colleagues with deference and yield gracefully when out-gunned, John D. Dingell, D-Mich., turned an abrasive manner and a stubborn refusal to quit fighting into assets that produce power and victories.

To keep a conference committee in session for weeks without compromising, to dress down a colleague on the House floor or to badger a witness at a hearing is all in a day's work for Dingell if a point can be proved or a victory scored.

"I've been sent here to serve my constituents well," Dingell told a reporter in 1979. "Occasionally I'm going to have to do ugly things that hurt me politically because they're right. But I was sent here to win."

Although it is rare for even a full committee chairman in the House to become well known, Dingell attracted significant national recognition from his platform as chairman of a single subcommittee — the House Commerce Subcommittee on Energy and Power.

His strong views, forceful personality and unwillingness to bend in a fight earned the Michigan Democrat an important role in the national energy debate and a reputation as a formidable legislative artisan.

But they also earned him a reputation as one of the meanest men to tangle with in the House.

Keys to Effectiveness

To friend and foe alike, John Dingell is seen as tenacious in his beliefs, thorough and tireless in his work and intensely loyal to his friends. The combination made him an extremely effective legislator, many colleagues say.

"You've got to give him credit for his diligence, his hard work and his tirelessness," commented Interior Committee Chairman Morris K. Udall, D-Ariz., who frequently was on the opposite side of key energy controversies from Dingell.

"He's one of the most effective members of the House. There aren't many subcommittee chairmen who have as much influence as the committee chairmen, but he's one of them," Udall said.

Dingell's ability to move legislation through his committee to the floor was universally acknowledged. By all accounts, he did so not only by combativeness but also by thorough knowledge of the subject and a remarkable ability to mold coalitions.

Dingell begins work on an issue by immersing himself in it. He thoroughly studies the controversies by reading and by briefings from his staff — a diverse and seasoned group that many people on Capitol Hill consider one of the most effective staffs in the House.

"When he sinks his teeth into a subject, you know he'll learn all the ramifications of that subject before beginning to work on it," said Wayne Smithey, Washington vice president of the Ford Motor Co. and a long-time acquaintance.

Even before markup begins, Dingell tries to lay a solid foundation by getting a variety of individuals and groups behind a proposal. "I think the whole key to his leadership is in building coalitions," said Phil Gramm, D-Texas, a member of Dingell's subcommittee first elected to the House in 1978. "He makes everybody think they're a part of things."

To assemble a coalition, Dingell begins a process of behind-the-scenes horse-trading, working across both ideological and party lines — both inside and outside of Congress — to garner support for his views. "He works incredibly well with the other side of the aisle," commented White House lobbyist Free.

Never Waivers

During the early stages, Dingell is willing to listen to all points of view, colleagues say. To fashion a successful coalition, he'll even accept views he doesn't necessarily agree with. But once he's closed the deal and made up his mind to support it, the situation changes.

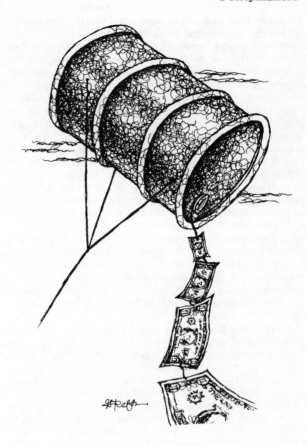

"Once the bargain is struck, you know he's going to stick to it," said the UAW's Paster. "John will never waiver from his convictions on an issue. He never tap-dances on both sides."

Fellow Commerce Committee member Lionel Van Deerlin, D-Calif., commented in 1979: "You're never in any doubt about whether he's going to be for you or against you."

Tired of Being Bullied?

Dingell's unwillingness to bend has earned him some important legislative victories. Refusing to cut a deal too soon often has served him well in wearing down the other side in order to win important concessions.

But this stubborn streak also has created problems for Dingell. Some of his colleagues, tired of being bullied and tired of his tenacity, now try to work around Dingell on important energy matters, and a few are mulling ways to clip his jurisdiction.

Synthetic fuels legislation is a case in point. Leaders of the House Banking Committee drafted a very narrow version of the synfuels bill in 1979. Reportedly one of their goals was to keep it out of Dingell's Energy and Power Subcommittee. The bill was written to go from the Banking Committee directly to the House floor because Dingell had helped defeat similar bills in 1975 and 1976.

A series of Dingell floor amendments to the synthetic fuels bill were strongly opposed by Banking Committee leaders, essentially to keep Dingell out of the conference committee negotiations, according to committee aides.

When Dingell and fellow Merchant Marine Committee member John B. Breaux, D-La., plunged into the debate in the 96th Congress over Alaska lands legislation by offering an alternative to the bill approved by the Interior Committee, Dingell's belligerent manner of debating cost him votes, in the opinion of some of his colleagues.

An attempt to characterize the Interior bill as anti-gun and anti-hunter in order to bring the forces of the National Rifle Association into the fray also contributed to Dingell's loss, some members suggested. Despite Dingell's tenaciousness and blistering attacks on his foes, the Interior Committee bill won by a hefty margin.

"A number of his colleagues feel he overdid it a little bit on the Alaska lands debate," a fellow Democrat commented. "If he had left more of the debating to John Breaux, I think his side might have picked up some more votes."

The ultimate counterattack by members angered over Dingell's tactics would be a revamping of committee jurisdictions to take away some of his power. But a recommendation to do that was rejected in 1980.

Dingell also was well known for a tendency to berate and intimidate witnesses holding views with which he disagreed.

"He can be a dreadfully bullying interrogator at public hearings," commented a fellow Democrat who knows him well. Some administration officials who have been stung by a Dingell dressing-down on the witness stand say his attitude harms the public interest by robbing the hearing record of a wide spectrum of views on an issue.

Dingell admits he can be belligerent at hearings, but says he only raises his voice if a witness is "dissembling." He said "no one who has ever appeared before the committee has been castigated for telling the truth. I can recall many who have been castigated for not telling the truth."

A Child of the House

John Dingell's first introduction to the House was as a child of five, led by his father, Rep. John D. Dingell Sr., D-Mich. (1933-55). His memory of his father has continued to be major influence on him, Dingell said. His father's picture, he noted, stands on a cabinet directly behind his desk "so he can keep an eye on me."

Dingell became a page in the House at age 12, and practiced law until his father's death in 1955. He successfully ran for his seat in a December 1955 special election, and became the youngest House member of the 84th Congress. Since that time, his seat has never been in serious jeopardy.

Dingell characterizes his politics as "middle-of-the-road," but his colleagues say he is hiding a true liberal bent on most issues. Congressional Quarterly presidential support and party support studies consistently show him to be at least as loyal to his party and to Democratic presidents as the majority of his fellow Democrats.

During his congressional career, he traditionally has been a strong environmental and consumer advocate. As chairman of the Merchant Marine Fisheries and Wildlife Conservation Subcommittee in the 1960s, he played an important role in the drafting of landmark legislation on protection of endangered species and environmental policy.

He has been a vigorous supporter of civil rights and health bills. And he has introduced national health insurance legislation in every Congress.

Energy Role

In the energy area, Dingell has played a key role since he assumed the chairmanship of the Energy and Power Subcommittee in 1975, the year the panel was set up. "He's probably got a better understanding of the energy problem here and abroad than any other member of Congress," commented Wayne Harmon, congressional relations director for Gulf Oil Co.

He became chairman after he and other top Commerce Committee Democrats engineered a coup early in the 94th Congress that robbed Chairman Harley O. Staggers, D-W.Va., of many of his powers and redistributed them to the subcommittee chairmen.

In the coup, the jurisdiction of the Communications and Power Subcommittee, chaired at that time by Rep. Torbert H. MacDonald, D-Mass. (1955-76), was split in two and Dingell was given the new energy panel.

In his years as chairman, Dingell has found himself at the center of the fight over energy pricing.

In 1975, he was a leading opponent of the Ford administration's plan to decontrol oil prices. Dingell, along with many other Democrats, preferred instead to use tax penalties and credits to discourage oil consumption. But that approach failed, and the Michigan legislator became one of the principal authors of a complicated compromise that allowed oil prices to rise gradually.

That much-maligned law, the Energy Policy and Conservation Act, governed oil pricing and allocation through Sept. 1, 1981. Even the Energy Department has admitted that the law and regulations implementing it contributed to gasoline lines this past summer. The myriad definitions for different types of oil gives the oil industry nightmares.

But the compromise, despite its flaws, was apparently the only way that Dingell and others could prevent immediate decontrol of oil prices.

Natural Gas Pricing Debate

Another major battle over energy pricing occurred in 1977 and 1978. The subject was another longstanding energy controversy: controlling the price of natural gas.

Dingell opposed an end to existing gas price controls. When a House and Senate conference deadlocked for months on the issue, Dingell played a key role in drafting a compromise that allowed price controls to be lifted gradually. Like the oil pricing rules, the scheme for natural gas pricing was incredibly complicated. Even Dingell and other supporters admitted the bill had problems. As Commerce Chairman Staggers put it, "This is the best thing we could come up with."

In 1979, Dingell's subcommittee again became the arena for skirmishes over pricing. But he managed to fight back moves both to decontrol oil prices immediately and to restore the oil price controls the Carter administration began gradually lifting in June of that year.

Opponents of oil decontrol admitted in 1979 they cannot win in the House or Senate. Years of congressional fighting over energy pricing appear to be almost over. John Dingell's major focus of teh past few years has become history.

Change in Energy Stance?

Dingell's ultimate acceptance of decontrol — and a growing emphasis on encouraging energy supply — have prompted some observers to suggest that Dingell has become more pro-oil-industry in recent years.

Energy Policymaking in Congress: A Competition Among Committees

Several committees in the House and Senate have a say in energy-related decisions and policymaking.

Although there are primary committees in each house that are the most involved with energy matters, others can claim jurisdiction over certain issues, and usually attempt to do so because of the intense interest in energy legislation.

Decisions about which committees a bill is referred to are made by the House parliamentarian on the Speaker's order, and by the Senate president. Because the lines dividing the jurisdictions are often blurred or overlap, the referral is usually a question of judgment, with a heavy dose of politics.

A Variety of Reasons

The rationale for involvement in energy varied widely. For example, the Agriculture panels drafted bills and floor amendments to promote production of alcohol fuels from forest and farm products and wastes. Committees responsible for small business investigated complaints by owners of independent service stations that the major oil companies were withholding their supplies. The banking committees shared responsibility for the 1980 Energy Security Act because the House Banking Committee originally attached its bill to a 1950 law, the Defense Production Act, within their jurisdiction. The solar and conservation banks in the synthetic fuels bill would have been in their territory anyway if handled separately.

Responsibility for coastal zone management and the oceans often involved the Senate Commerce and the House Merchant Marine and Fisheries committees in decisions about offshore energy development. The Senate Governmental Affairs and House Government Operations committees wrote the Energy Department legislation and usually played a role in matters affecting the relationship between the federal government and the states, such as the question of whether a state can veto federal plans to store nuclear waste within its border.

Wide Energy Jurisdiction

The Senate Energy Committee handled overall energy policy, such as matters affecting production and consumption. Specifically, the panel was responsible for oil and gas regulation, energy research and development including commercialization of nuclear power, hydropower and preparedness for energy shortages. The committee also was responsible for natural resources and public lands, which meant it handled decisions related to oil and gas leasing on federal lands, strip mining controls and energy development in parks and other protected areas.

Because there were so many conflicts between energy and the environment, the panel responsible for overall environment policy often influenced energy policy. The Environment and Public Works Committee considered energy as part of decisions on water and air pollution, controls on toxic substances and disposal of solid wastes, to name a few issues. The committee was directly involved in regulation of nuclear power, for which it was primarily responsible.

In the House, the major lines of responsibility were tangled among three committees: Interstate and Foreign Commerce, Interior and Science and Technology. Both Commerce and Interior had dual responsibility over some energy and environmental issues, with no "purely" environmental panel, as in the Senate. However, Interior usually played that role because of its overall jurisdiction over natural resources, including public lands.

Regulation of air pollution and toxic substances was handled by the Commerce Committee, water pollution by the Public Works Committee and fish and wildlife by the Merchant Marine Committee.

Interior's energy functions included responsibility for energy development on public lands, coal mining and general regulation of the nuclear industry. Many of these issues required consideration of conflicts between energy and environment. The Energy Mobilization Board legislation, that the 96th Congress failed to pass, which would have put priority  energy projects on a "fast track" through the bureaucracy, was an Interior responsibility, although it was also referred to Commerce. Interior's Energy and Environment Subcommittee was the principal panel for most energy legislation.

Commerce handled laws dealing with energy regulation in general including supply and conservation, interstate transmission of electric power, emergency preparedness and regulation of nuclear facilities. Its Energy and Power Subcommittee, established in 1975, usually drafted energy bills.

Science and Technology was responsible for overall energy research and development and had two principal energy subcommittees: Energy Development and Applications, and Energy Research and Production.

"I don't find that controls are protecting people any more," Dingell told the Associated Press in June 1979. "They are causing great distortions in supply. They've had a very adverse effect on construction of new refineries. They're driving a lot of people in business up a wall."

"He's still a good environmentalist," Rep. Udall remarked, "but I think he now views the country as having overdone it a little on the environmental side and now having to do more to increase energy production. On a couple of things, he's changed in emphasis."

Dingell denies this. In a 1979 interview, he said he remained an environmentalist and still would prefer extensive government control over energy pricing if he could have his way.

But he acknowledged that the time for a pervasive government presence in the energy industry has passed. "I see no good sense in fighting a war that is lost," he said. "So I choose to go and do the things I still can do to achieve energy independence and help consumers."

'New Ways Perplex Me'

Despite the tough talk, Dingell said he's not unconcerned about his tough-guy image. But he believes his behavior is necessary to accomplish what he thinks is right.

"I won't tell you that I don't worry about the subject of my tenacity," he said. "But you must try to seek a balance between what you believe and what you can get accomplished. Then, there is also a third duty — to move legislation and see that the national problems are cured."

"The House has changed," Dingell added. "I've watched the responsibilities grow. I've watched the workload and the budget grow. I still think I'm a child of the House, but the new ways of this place and some of the attitudes of my colleagues perplex me.

"In my father's time, the most important measure of a man's worth was his sincerity. Now it's not so rigorously applied. People fashion their views on how they will play back home. I hear very little of the term 'sincerity' today."

J. Bennett Johnston:
Streak of Riverboat Gambler

J. Bennett Johnston was pressing his fellow Senate conferees to accept his compromise on a major energy bill.

But they balked. "We need more time to study this," said one, adding that he held enough proxies — votes from absent senators — to defeat Johnston's proposal.

Johnston, his move at an informal consensus thwarted, lost his temper.

"Proxies?" asked the Louisiana Democrat. "I'll go out and get some proxies. And I'll break arms if I have to."

By the next day, tempers had cooled, and the Senate conferees met to talk strategy. Johnston, according to those present, managed to soothe conferees who had been upset. A consensus was restored. But the sour note lingered. "He slipped," said an aide. "He should be more careful."

Most of the time Johnston is more careful — artful, in fact, in the gentlemanly ways of the Senate. But there's a streak of the riverboat gambler who'll bluff and bully when dealt a bad hand.

The junior senator from Louisiana emerged as a key power broker on energy matters in the late 1970s and 1980. A ranking member of the Senate Energy Committee, he chaired many committee sessions, managed bills on the floor and moderated conference sessions on major energy legislation. Although Sen. Henry M. Jackson, D-Wash., was chairman of the Energy Committee, he was focusing his activities on the Armed Services Committee, especially in 1979 and 1980, and so turned to Johnston to take over some of his responsibilities on the Energy Committee.

As the 96th Congress drew to a close, it appeared Johnston would have a chance to get the title of energy chairman. But the November 1980 election gave Republicans the majority in the Senate, and James A. McClure, R-Idaho, became chairman of the Energy Committee. However, Johnston was certain to remain a leading participant in energy policy decisions and negotiations.

* * * * *

"Oil-state senator." That's the shorthand way Bennett Johnston is described in many national new stories. But he'd rather not be thought of like that.

"I think that's inaccurate," Johnston told a reporter in a 1980 interview. "It's simply not true. I have voted many times against the position of big oil."

He cites as an example his support for government ownership of synthetic fuels plants, which could turn coal into a liquid or gaseous fuel. The oil companies fought giving the government that authority.

Another example Johnston uses is his vote for final passage of the oil windfall profits tax. That vote cost Johnston a perfect voting record on the list of issues supported by the major association of independent producers, the Independent Petroleum Association of America. He scored 88 percent. The voting study is the only one by a major oil and gas association. But key votes on energy issues show Johnston consistently voting the industry position.

Johnston admits he favors policies that encourage more oil and gas production. "I believe that not just because I'm from Louisiana, but because I think it's right," he said. "Please understand, I'm not trying to represent that I'm non-political. There's not a person up here who's non-political. And we get elected just like everybody else."

The implication was that no Louisiana senator could ignore the oil and gas interests. But there's another angle noted by a Carter administration lobbyist: "Unlike some of his colleagues from energy producing states, he recognizes there are a hell of a lot of energy consumers in his state — far more consumers than producers."

* * * * *

Chairing a meeting requires a different approach from just being a participant. "That doesn't mean you can't have your own agenda, but you must faithfully represent your Senate conferees and the compromises that have been made," Johnston said.

"If people recognize you're going to deal with them fairly, that if you have a difference you'll not cut them off at the pass in a sneaky way, then they'll have more confidence in dealing with you and letting you represent the Senate's views."

This effort to be fair did not go unnoticed. "People have been surprised at his evenhandedness," said a Senate colleague of how Johnston operated as chairman.

Nuclear Regulatory Commission: 'Nobody Is Running the Show'

Even after it lost its dual responsibility for promoting and regulating nuclear power in 1974, the Nuclear Regulatory Commission continued to have problems. The presidential commission that studied the 1979 accident at Three Mile Island nuclear power plant in Pennsylvania was sharply critical of the NRC.

"The totality of our findings is that no one is running" the NRC, said Chairman John Kemeny.

"We find the NRC is not necessarily a mismanaged agency — it is an unmanaged agency," said Harry McPherson, a member of the Kemeny Commission and a Washington lawyer who worked in the Johnston administration. "Nobody is running the show down there."

Patrick E. Haggerty, another Kemeny member and general director of Texas Instruments Inc., was also critical. "You not only have five people on top; you have departments underneath that are not coordinated. The thing is legislated for confusion."

In addition to having a complex, unwieldy organizational staff structure, the NRC also was hampered by the fact that its five members split on issue after issue. Two commissioners — Chairman Joseph Hendrie and Richard T. Kennedy — usually leaned toward the industry; two others — Peter Bradford and Victor Gilinsky — usually opposed the industry, and the fifth and newest member — John Ahearne — usually cast the "swing" vote.

An example of dissension within the commission came up at a House Commerce hearing in November 1979 where four NRC commissioners testified. When asked about the role of the executive director in managing the NRC, Gilinsky said, "This executive director does not have the backing of the majority of this commission." Hendrie, quickly interrupting, disagreed. "I have great confidence in the executive director," he said.

Later that day, the executive director, Lee V. Gossick, a retired Air Force general, resigned.

At the same hearings, Hendrie responded to several questions by saying he would have to let each commissioner speak for himself. "I would be surprised if that were not the case," replied an exasperated Albert Gore Jr., D-Tenn., who was chairing the session.

Most NRC commissioners didn't want to abolish the agency, as suggested by the Kemeny panel, but they agreed that improvements were needed. In 1980, the NRC was reorganized and received a new chairman, who was given more management authority than the other four commissioners.

"The current situation at the NRC is analogous to the results that one would expect from hitching five horses to different points around a sled," Bradford wrote in a November 1979 letter to the White House.

"The fact that the sled does not move steadily forward does not tell you very much about the relative strength of the horses. It does raise questions about the intentions of the teamster."

Gilinsky warned that an "agency in the executive branch would be under much more pressure to fall in line with the administration." A body such as the commission can more accurately reflect a public that is "strongly divided on these questions," he said.

Ahearne endorsed having a single administrator. Although some observers compared the Kemeny proposal for a single administrator with the Environmental Protection Agency, Sen. Gary Hart, D-Colo., said the comparison wasn't valid. "Congress has established the nation's environmental policy in great detail," Hart said. "The same is not true for nuclear power."

All agreed that putting the NRC in one building would improve its operation. The commissioners were located in a downtown Washington office while most of the staff was a dozen miles away in Bethesda, Md. In all, the agency was spread among eight buildings.

Another senator explains that Johnston is "not a purist — he likes to get things done." That means, the senator said, that Johnston is "ready to compromise, rather than getting his own way every time."

But Johnston does like to be on the winning side. He appreciated the power of the chair. "You'll know that he's chairman," said an environmentalist. "But his will be an iron fist covered with a glove."

Johnston has strong views and argues forcefully for them. But he was keenly aware that as chairman he had to work with both critics and supporters of his views.

He operates with confidence, sometimes with flamboyance. He has a bright red velvet sport coat that he wears to work in the December holiday season. Often a long cigar juts from the side of his mouth.

A former House aide is appreciative of his personal skills. "He's given to folklore and witticisms — just the right touch in a meeting where everybody is trying to be serious," he said.

In tense negotiating sessions, said another congressional staffer, "Bennett can come up with some story to break the tension."

"Really, I enjoy the job," Johnston said, asked about the time he spent in meetings and reading documents. "It does not seem like hard work to me because I thoroughly enjoy legislation."

Even the hours and hours of committee and conference sessions?

"That's high drama to me," Johnston replied, smiling broadly.

"I don't mean that every single conference is. But ours on energy, they move, decisions are made, and that's the way I like to conduct a conference — to keep it moving, not let it bog down. Part of the challenge is to keep the process moving."

Johnston is patient. An environmental lobbyist who has worked closely with him put it this way: "Some people try to get what they want by screaming. Johnston will just sit down in one of those chairs and endure just hours of interminable, brutal boredom."

The lobbyist said Johnston was one of the most skillful negotiators in the Senate. "Bennett has a fairly good grasp of what's important and what's not important. He knows the process. He knows how to graciously give up on a headline item and then win it all back in the fine print."

A legislative aide less enamoured of Johnston had another description of his negotiating technique: "He throws people a few bones and then they let him carry the ball the rest of the way."

"It's all gentlemanly stuff," said a House staff member. "He pushes. Other people allow themselves to be used. He fills the vacuum. He comes into the room and va va va voom." Things just start to happen, she said.

Johnston isn't embarrassed or uncomfortable while talking to a reporter about his statement that he would "break arms" to get his way.

His theory is that Senate conferees have to work together for the Senate position to prevail. "Everybody has to hang together on what the game plan or position is," he explained. "I was exasperated at that particular time because I thought [the senator's objection in the energy mobilization board conference] was a departure from our game plan.

"Sometimes," he added, "you have to be a little more blunt than others."

Asked if he regretted the statements he made, Johnston said he didn't. "No, because I thought that was the proper thing at the proper time," he said, noting that the exchange hadn't been personal. "I try to run the conference with a sort of unanimous consent," Johnston added, explaining why he does not like voting formally, with roll-call and proxy votes. "We work our game plan, but that changes and modifies as we go along."

* * * * *

"Would you like some of the grape?" Johnston asked, extending a glass of white wine to a reporter. Etched on the glass was the Senate seal and below that Johnston's signature.

The office, off of a little-used corridor of the Capitol, was Johnston's "hideaway," a perquisite reserved for the Senate's most senior members.

A huge crystal chandelier sparkled over the luncheon table, set up for Johnston, two top aides and a few energy reporters. A refrigerator and bar were tucked neatly into a corner.

"You should have seen this place," said Johnston, pressed about his elegant surroundings. The previous tenant had let his staff use the office, and Johnston inherited shabby desks and dingy walls. He was obviously pleased at the new decorations — and at joining the club of those senior enough to enjoy such a privilege.

Over lunch, for more than an hour, Johnston smoothly answered questions about pending energy bills and ideas for the future. Comfortable, making light jokes, Johnston appeared completely at ease and confident.

The impression was of a man in control.

* * * * *

When Bennett Johnston came to Congress in 1972, he was assigned to the Interior Committee, which later became the Energy Committee. At that time, its activities were oriented toward federal lands in the West, but it did have jurisdiction over offshore areas. That was important to Louisiana, which thought the federal government was claiming more than its share of the underwater oil fields in the Gulf of Mexico.

"I tried to discourage him from joining that committee," admits Charles McBride, his top aide at the time and now a Washington political consultant. It was not a great assignment.

But just a year later the energy crisis began when the Arab oil-producing countries refused to ship oil to the United States.

And the Senate, in its 1977 reorganization, built on the Interior Committee's involvement in energy-related areas and revamped it as the Energy Committee.

Its first major task was handling President Carter's energy program. Most of his proposals were within the jurisdiction of the Energy Subcommittee on Regulation. The chairman: Bennett Johnston. It was a marvelous opportunity for a freshman senator.

Johnston's other committee was Banking. But he lobbied for a seat opening up on the Appropriations Committee in 1975. He got it. By 1978, he was chairman of the Public Works Subcommittee. In 1979, the name of that panel had been changed to the Energy and Water Development Subcommittee. Although the water projects they control get the most attention, the subcommittee also oversees more than half of the Energy Department budget and the Nuclear Regulatory Commission.

In addition to that impressive list of committee jobs, Johnston is a member of the Senate Budget Committee.

But the Energy Committee seat is clearly Johnston's most important assignment. He admits he has been "very lucky."

"But, of course, you've got to understand luck and timing are the essence of politics," he said.

Asked if there's any way to help luck along, Johnston replied, "You work like hell and make your best judgment and hope it all works out. If you're lucky, it does. Luck itself is not going to put you in the right position. But if you do the rest of it, then. . . ."

* * * * *

It was about midnight, April 21, 1978. Key members of the natural gas conference were putting the final touches on an agreement they had been negotiating for months. With Energy Secretary Schlesinger, they were gathered in the office of Energy Chairman Jackson. The points of dispute were being resolved and ticked off, one after another.

But Bennett Johnston was unsure about the effect of a certain detailed provision. He needed advice. Johnston telephoned Harry Barsh, who was the Washington representative for the state of Louisiana and a man intimately familiar with the natural gas industry.

Those present described Jackson as livid. "Do you know who he's calling?" he asked.

Eventually, Schlesinger got on the phone with Barsh, discussing the details of the agreement and working it out.

Johnston had surprised those present by admitting so blatantly his dependence on an outsider, particularly a man linked to the gas industry. Of course, everyone else also had advisers. But they didn't put them on the telephone with the energy secretary in the wee hours of the morning.

Those familiar with the incident, and with Johnston's work since, say it was an important learning experience for the freshman senator. Johnston, said one adviser, would never again put himself in such an embarrassing position in front of his peers.

* * * * *

The same, drawn-out negotiations over natural gas later provided another glimpse at Johnston's way of doing business. Although he supported the compromise and was a key participant in developing it, Johnston refused to vote for or sign the conference report. His reason was simple: home-state politics.

"My vote was not necessary to pass it," Johnston said, painting a background for his decision. "I voted against it partly because of a couple of provisions, small ones I didn't think were right. But more importantly, I voted against it because the people in my state opposed it."

When signatures for the conference report were being collected in August, Johnston was in the midst of his re-election campaign. A relatively unknown challenger, Democratic state Rep. Louis (Woody) Jenkins, was making a stronger than expected bid for Johnston's seat.

The very conservative Jenkins was criticizing Johnston for going along with high taxes and big spending — and for even considering a natural gas compromise that didn't immediately end price controls.

Johnston won the primary with 59 percent of the vote, a much smaller margin than had been originally predicted. Under Louisiana's system, with a non-partisan primary, that meant he was unopposed in the November general election.

* * * * *

The Duke University sophomore is quite skeptical of nuclear power. But he keeps getting material in the mail — background papers and so forth — from Washington.

They're from his father, Bennett Johnston, who says he just wants to be sure his son, Bennett Jr., has enough information.

The two Johnstons disagree about nuclear energy and have had lively discussions. But the pro-nuclear senator isn't interested in squashing his son's ideas. "It doesn't bother me that he doesn't share my views," Johnston said, adding, "He'll come around to the right view, hopefully the right view. But I want him to be intellectually curious."

* * * * *

Johnston has four children: two sons and two daughters. Friends say he regularly takes the family away, usually to the beach for a week or so, in order to keep in touch.

Aides and others who know Johnston's wife, Mary, praise her warmly for her charm and strong character. "She's one of those steel magnolias," said a family friend.

Johnston's father was an important influence. A lawyer, he had four daughters. Then Bennett was born. The family was supportive, encouraging its youngest member to be an achiever, to do better than just average.

The lesson stuck. Not a brilliant student, Johnston was quick. He went to law school at Louisiana State University, and then practiced with his father. In only a few years, he was involved in politics, winning a seat in the state House at the age of 32 and moving to the state Senate at the age of 36.

After eight years in state politics, Johnston went for the big prize in Louisiana: the governorship. His 1971 campaign against fellow Democrat Edwin W. Edwards was one of the most colorful, bitterly fought battles in the state's history. Edwards won the primary runoff by a margin of less than 5,000 votes out of more than 1 million cast.

Johnston's campaign hardly missed a beat. In 1972, he filed a challenge to the U.S. Senate seat held by 81-year-old Democrat Allen J. Ellender.

It was another tough race for Johnston. The vote was expected to be close. But, just a month before the primary, Ellender died. Although many urged that filing be reopened so others would have a chance to enter, the state election panel refused. That gave Johnston a clear shot at the nomination.

Edwards had played a role in keeping others out of the primary race. He did another favor for Johnston after the November election. Edwards had appointed his wife to Ellender's Senate seat. She stepped down, so that Johnston could be sworn in Nov. 14, weeks before most other freshman senators would take office. Bennett Johnston automatically had seniority, a crucial ingredient for Senate success.

* * * * *

Despite Edwards' largesse to Johnston, the flamboyant governor gave the senator little peace in his first term. He left open the possibility that he would challenge Johnston for the Senate seat in 1978.

"He needled Bennett every chance he got," said one Louisianan.

The two men had sharply different personalities. Edwards, who liked to wear double-knit leisure suits, was an old-style backslapping politician. Johnston, who favored conservatively tailored clothes, was somewhat aloof.

Most of the time, Edwards kept his hand in Johnston's affairs from a distance. Once, though, on a visit to Washington, he breezed into Johnston's Senate office followed by an entourage of reporters and aides. "I'll keep this person," he said, "and this one." All through the maze of offices he walked, pointing out which employes would stay if Edwards took over the Senate seat.

That sort of shenanigan is part of the past. Johnston won a second term, easing any sense of obligation he might have felt toward Edwards for that first Senate term and the early appointment. Johnston also feels more secure about his standing with the voters.

And Edwards, currently out of office because Louisiana doesn't allow a third consecutive term as governor, has another target for his formidable attentions. Republican Gov. David Treen, elected in 1979, runs into Edwards everywhere. The former governor is organizing legislators and plotting his 1983 campaign, when he'll be eligible to run again.

* * * * *

More at ease in terms of Louisiana politics, Johnston is also more at ease within the Senate.

He was essentially the Energy chairman in 1979 and 1980. His standing among his colleagues went up considerably as committee bills were passed, relatively unscathed, by the full Senate. As a key conferee, he had more influence than any other senator on the final version of important energy legislation. And he is no longer obscured by the shadow of Louisiana's senior senator, Russel B. Long.

Johnston watchers say 1979 was the year Johnston emerged as a mature senator. "He quit doing dumb things," said one lobbyist.

A friend agreed, but admitted there was one exception. Johnston called for a 50-cent-a-gallon gasoline tax in the fall. "He caught holy hell in his state," he said.

Johnston said that was when his press secretary earned his salary. The calls and letters were not favorable.

But the gasoline tax idea is an indication that Johnston is thinking, trying to come up with new energy policies and ideas.

When he comes up with a new concept, he isn't hesitant about pushing ahead with it. In the spring of 1979, Congress rejected President Carter's proposed standby gasoline rationing plan, largely for parochial reasons. Everyone wanted to be sure his state or district got a fair deal. That reaction made Johnston believe more strongly that states should be given a larger role in the national energy conservation effort. He drafted a bill doing just that. Several months later, it was signed into law.

Another example of original thinking is his attempt to get the government to set goals for energy consumption, with a certain amount expected to come from coal, from oil and from other energy sources.

"I really believe this country will never have an energy policy until it at least gets an idea of where it's going," he said. "What my targets and goals do is require the government and Congress to sit down in a disciplined way

and try to assess costs, environmental problems, strategic problems, both defense-wise and from the standpoint of the economy, availability problems, lifestyle, all those things."

The goals might not be met, and they could be revised and updated annually. But at least it would be a start, Johnston said. "As it is now, we make statements which amount to sort of goals or wishes and then those are not fulfilled — but you don't even know when they're not fulfilled."

Johnston thinks it's important to figure out how much energy is needed and how to provide it. He realizes it's not a perfect process. "I just want everybody to focus in. If we put the wrong numbers in those projects, it's not going to distress me and make me feel like the bill is a mistake.

"Each person that participates in that has learned something."

ENERGY PACS: POWER IN ELECTIONS

More than 130 political action committees (PACs) affiliated with oil and gas interests wre registered with the Federal Election Commission as of November 1979 — nearly seven times as were registered at the beginning of 1976.

The 133 PACs listed as "active" in FEC records had contributed more than $2.6 million to House and Senate candidates since 1977, according to a November 1979 study by Congressional Quarterly.

Despite the rapid increase in the number of PACs affiliated with oil and gas interests, contributions by these campaign financing committees accounted for only a small portion of PAC spending generally and made up only a fraction of the total contributions received by individual political candidates.

Probably more important than the actual amounts that oil and gas PACs had contributed by the end of 1979 was the sizable growth in the number of these political committees and the formidable role they could play in future campaign financing.

PACs are the political arms of corporations, labor unions and other groups that collect donations and contribute the proceeds to political campaigns. While an individual can give only $1,000 to a single candidate in any primary, runoff or general election, PACs may contribute up to $5,000.

PAC Diversity

CQ's survey of energy-related PACs identified 138 committees that were affiliated at some time after 1975 with corporations, trade associations or private investors having substantial oil and gas interests. Five of the PACs subsequently terminated their activities.

Of the 133 remaining PACs, the vast majority, 119, were established after the FEC issued a ruling in 1975 making clear that corporations could establish and administer political action committees.

PAC Growth, 1974-78

Figures indicate the number of political action committees (PACs) registered with the Federal Election Commission at the end of each calendar year.

	1974	1975	1976	1977	1978
Corporate	89	139	433	570	808
Labor	201	226	224	234	217
Trade, membership, health	318	357	489	438	451
Non-affiliated	—	—	—	110	165
Cooperative	—	—	—	8	12
Total PACs	608	722	1,146	1,360	1,653
Oil and Gas*	12	19	70	93	128

* Oil and gas PAC figures are based on CQ's identification of PACs with energy interests and are included in the overall totals.

Source: Non-energy PAC figures, Federal Election Commission.

Although only one major oil corporation had a PAC prior to 1975, and only 18 other oil and gas PACs were in operation by the end of 1975, there were 70 operating at the end of 1976, 93 by the end of 1977 and 128 by the end of 1978. *(Box, facing page)* ·

The 133 active oil and gas PACs identified by CQ were affiliated with corporations and associations in virtually every segment of the oil and gas industry, including exploration, drilling, refining, transmission, manufacturing of oil field equipment and providing oil field services.

The survey identified 59 oil and gas PACs affiliated with companies having substantial interests in crude petroleum and natural gas production.

The oil and gas interests of these and most of the other PACs in the survey were drawn from "standard industrial classification" data listed by Standard & Poor's Register of Corporations.

Most Majors Represented

Eight of the top 10 oil companies had PACs as of late 1979 and had given more than $474,000 to Senate and House candidates since 1977.

Contributions since 1977 made by these "majors" — defined as such in terms of their annual sales by *Fortune* magazine — broke down as follows:

- Standard Oil of Indiana (Amoco) $171,850
- Atlantic Richfield, $70,278
- Texaco, $57,700
- Shell Oil Co., $51,170
- Tenneco Inc., $50,971
- Standard Oil of California (Chevron), $45,560
- Continental Oil Co., $24,850
- Mobil, $1,900.

Exxon, the nation's largest oil company, and Gulf Oil had not established PACs. Gulf was not, however, inactive in the campaign financing arena. In 1978 a Gulf official admitted that the corporation made nearly $4 million in illegal contributions to political candidates between 1962 and 1973.

In terms of their aggregate spending since 1977, oil and gas PACs provided only a small percentage of the overall receipts in the campaigns in which they participated.

Only 17 of the PACs identified by CQ contributed more than $50,000 to congressional and senatorial candidates, and only three committees contributed more than $100,000. The oil and gas PAC contributions represent only a portion of the total oil and gas money flowing into congressional campaign coffers. Large numbers of executives of oil and gas companies who finance the 133 oil and gas PACs also made individual contributions to candidates sympathetic to industry energy objectives.

An investigation by the *Tulsa Tribune* revealed that one oil-state Senate candidate who made a policy of refusing PAC contributions, David L. Boren, D-Okla., was elected in 1978 with about 37 percent of his primary and general election contributions coming from individuals with oil connections. Of Boren's total $872,107 in receipts, fully $320,000 came from oil interests, the newspaper said.

A 1979 *Washington Post* survey of campaign contributions to members of the Senate Finance Committee found that 12 of the 20 committee members had received at least $370,200 from "clearly identifiable" oil industry contributions since 1977.

The CQ survey identified an additional $62,600 in oil and gas PAC contributions to Finance Committee members from the 133 identified oil and gas PACs since 1977. The Finance Committee handled the oil windfall profits tax that was passed in 1980.

More than $65,000 in contributions from oil and gas PACs have gone to members of the Senate Energy Committee since 1977, the CQ survey found.

In the House, members of the Ways and Means Committee and the Commerce Subcommittee on Energy and Power, the two key panels writing energy legislation, received $94,700 and $138,000, respectively, from the PACs.

More PACs, More Spending

A study done by Common Cause, the self-styled citizens' lobby, concluded that the growth in the number of PACs has been accompanied by substantial increases in PAC spending.

The Common Cause study found that campaign spending by energy PACs (oil, gas and coal) totaled only $183,000 in 1974 (when the group identified 12 energy PACs), but grew to $783,606 in 1976 (when it counted 67 PACs) and $1.9 million in 1978 (when it identified 110).

The study released in October 1979 identified 110 PACs affiliated with companies Common Cause said had substantial energy interests.

Figures in the Common Cause study differed from CQ's survey, which used a different methodology in identifying oil and gas PACs and did not include PACs affiliated with coal interests.

The growth in energy PACs parallels closely the general growth in non-candidate political committees.

Corporation, labor union and trade association PACs grew from 722 in 1975 to 1,146 at the end of 1976, to 1,360 at the end of 1977 and 1,653 at the end of 1978. At the time of CQ's 1979 study, there were more than 1,840 PACs registered with the FEC.

In terms of spending, FEC records show that PACs contributed $12.5 million to candidates in federal elections in 1974, $22.6 million in 1976 and $35.1 million in 1978. As a percent of total contributions received by House candidates in those races, PAC money accounted for 18 percent in 1974, 22 percent in 1976 and 25 percent in 1978.

Senate Study

In an effort to identify where oil and gas PACs targeted their money, CQ examined PAC contributions in all 35 1978 Senate races. *(Senate chart, p. 127)*

The aggregate oil and gas contribution totals per candidate were arrived at using a computer to separate by senatorial candidate Federal Election Commission spending reports on 133 oil and gas PACs. The raw FEC data is compiled from reports required by law to be filed by candidates' committees.

Not surprisingly, a large percentage of oil and gas PAC funds in those Senate races went to Republicans and Southern Democrats with strong pro-industry voting records. Of the top 20 recipients of oil and gas PAC money identified in the CQ survey, 18 were Republicans and two were Southern Democrats. Taking all 35 races together, Republicans received $659,640 and Democrats $169,905. Incumbents were also favored, receiving a total of $363,624 while challengers received $178,433.

Contributions by specific PACs to individual candidates generally were less than $1,000 — a figure that was also true for oil and gas PAC contributions to candidates for the House.

The top 10 oil and gas PAC recipients were: 1) William L. Armstrong, R-Colo., $66,933; 2) John Tower, R-Texas, $53,499; 3) J. Bennett Johnston, D-La., $49,015; 4) Robert P. Griffin, R-Mich., $36,725; 5) Howard H. Baker Jr., R-Tenn., $34,455; 6) David Durenberger, R-Minn., $33,550; 7) Nancy Landon Kassebaum, R-Kan., $33,025; 8) James D. Martin, R-Ala., $30,050; 9) Alan K. Simpson, R-Wyo., $29,200, and 10) Jeffrey Bell, R-N.J., $28,905. Only Griffin, Martin and Bell lost. Griffin was an incumbent senator; the other two were not.

Six of the top energy PAC recipients reported more than $1 million in overall receipts in their 1978 campaigns. There were 21 million-dollar campaigns in 1978.

Armstrong, the top recipient of oil and gas PAC dollars in a Senate race, unseated Floyd Haskell, D-Colo., who received only $2,200 from energy PACs. Haskell, a liberal who was frequently at odds with the oil industry, was a member of the key Senate committees with jurisdiction over energy legislation, Finance and Energy.

In voting studies on key energy votes during the 95th Congress, the Atlantic Richfield Company determined that Haskell voted with the industry only 20 percent of the time. The Independent Petroleum Association of America gave Haskell a pro-industry rating of 35 on a 100-point scale.

In the 1978 Senate elections, oil and gas PACs financed winners in 24 of 34 contests. In the 21 races involving incumbents, energy PACs favored officeholders 13 times. Eleven of those incumbents won their bids for re-election. Energy-related PACs were even more successful in choosing winners in races involving open seats. In the 13 contests for open seats, they picked winners in eight.

More in the Future

There was every reason to believe that energy PACs would play an increasing role in future elections. However, Bill Wiley, vice chairman for Amoco PAC, and other oil and gas officials downplayed the importance of oil and gas PAC spending.

Wiley cited Sen. Tower's $4.2 million 1978 re-election race, in which the Texas Republican received $53,499 in energy PAC funding, as an example of the minimal role oil and gas PACs were playing in federal elections.

According to Wiley, oil and gas PACs haven't made their mark. He said, "1978 was the first election where [energy PACs] were really involved," and many PACs didn't get started until the 1975 FEC ruling made it clear that they could.

Amoco PAC, the leading contributor among oil and gas PACs surveyed by CQ, "started earlier and worked harder at soliciting" than other energy PACs, Wiley said, explaining the group's $171,000 in contributions since 1977.

Edwin McGhee, secretary of the Drilling Contractors PAC, also minimized the role of oil and gas PACs in federal elections.

"We harbor no illusions that the contributions we're making are going to win us any votes. . . . The only thing they've gotten us are a lot of invitations to fund-raisers."

McGhee said his PAC was established as a reaction to "the very adverse climate in Washington towards the petroleum industry."

Not everyone, however, is as sanguine about the growth of energy PACs as some of the industry's spokesmen.

Common Cause Vice President Fred Wertheimer agrees that oil and gas PACs have not yet accounted for a significant amount of campaign spending. But Wertheimer insisted their number is more significant than the amount of dollars they've contributed.

Wertheimer said that because many of the oil and gas PACs are still in the "incubation stage," PAC contributions would increase. "It's a building-block situation. Like the United Way, you have to get people used to giving."

Common Cause had been lobbying Congress for several years for financing of elections from federal tax funds to eliminate the existing system of private funding.

Although the increase in the number of oil and gas PACs slowed, new ones continued to be organized in 1980.

A spokesman for one of the two major oil companies that had not yet established a PAC, said in 1979 the company was considering creating one. He said his firm was aware that critics of the industry would attack the creation of new PACs, charging it was further evidence that big oil was "wielding too much influence." On the other hand, he said, supporters of creating a PAC believe the company should "help those who are pro-business" because big oil "can't make any more enemies than it already has."

Fears of adverse public reaction led Gulf Oil, which has suffered from negative publicity about its illegal campaign contributions, to decide against forming a PAC. Gerald Thurmond, Washington council for Gulf, said that while corporate contributions are now legal, "the public doesn't perceive the legality of them."

PAC Money in 1977-78 Senate Races

	PAC Contributions			
	Energy PAC	Corporate PAC	Total PAC	Total Receipts
ALABAMA				
(Six-year term)				
Howell Heflin (D)†	7,300	30,250	124,400	1,107,015
Jerome B. Couch (P)	0	NA	NA	NA
(Two-year term)				
Donald Stewart (D)†	3,750	15,069	184,685	823,619
James D. Martin (R)	30,050	65,890	97,132	539,267
ALASKA				
Donald W. Hobbs (D)	0	0	100	15527
Ted Stevens (R)†*	15,900	65,224	170,724	366,895
ARKANSAS				
David Pryor (D)†	7,780	40,430	97,280	802,861
Thomas Kelly Jr. (R)	100	100	300	16,210
John G. Black (I)	0	0	0	32,863
COLORADO				
Floyd K. Haskell (D)*	2,200	20,155	213,435	658,657
William L. Armstrong (R)†	66,933	175,021	310,930	1,163,790
DELAWARE				
Joseph R. Biden Jr. (D)†*	500	13,350	126,100	487,637
James H. Baxter (R)	750	2,350	9,923	207,637
GEORGIA				
Sam Nunn (D)†*	10,800	73,615	135,145	708,417
John W. Stokes (R)	0	1,000	1,000	7,291
IDAHO				
Dwight Jensen (D)	0	0	17,500	55,163
James A. McClure (R)†*	27,125	76,475	161,873	378,084
ILLINOIS				
Alex R. Seith (D)	1,700	6,964	27,214	1,370,457
Charles H. Percy (R)†*	19,445	112,504	217,710	2,185,153
IOWA				
Dick Clark (D)*	200	10,550	214,777	862,635
Roger Jepsen (R)†	16,450	64,515	156,072	738,581
KANSAS				
Bill Roy (D)	1,550	16,050	194,643	824,537
Nancy Kassebaum (R)†	33,025	69,245	121,721	864,288
KENTUCKY				
Walter Huddleston (D)†*	9,615	41,569	152,664	395,557
Louie R. Guenthner (R)	0	2,150	2,750	77,012
LOUISIANA				
J.Bennett Johnston(D)†*	48,515	118,205	206,705	983,343
MAINE				
William D. Hathaway (D)*	0	18,400	166,594	423,499
William S. Cohen (R)†	16,900	82,815	157,551	658,254
Hayes E. Gahagan (I)	0	500	2,927	115,903
MASSACHUSETTS				
Paul E. Tsongas (D)†	800	10,200	45,350	772,513
Edward W. Brooke (R)*	5,425	41,875	203,767	957,252
MICHIGAN				
Carl Levin (D)†	100	11,744	206,291	994,439
Robert P. Griffin (R)*	36,725	211,312	307,944	1,691,534
MINNESOTA				
(Six-year term)				
Wendell R. Anderson (D)*	100	17,664	198,847	1,155,562
Rudy Boschwitz (R)†	25,550	152,292	261,257	1,902,861
(Four-year term)				
Robert E. Short (D)	1,000	8,745	40,295	1,982,442
David Durenberger (R)†	33,550	161,140	250,448	1,073,135

	PAC Contributions			
	Energy PAC	Corporate PAC	Total PAC	Total Receipts
MISSISSIPPI				
Maurice Dantin (D)	7,200	29,955	64,705	874,590
Thad Cochran (R)†	23,380	90,485	185,230	1,201,259
Charles Evers (I)	0	0	0	142,684
MONTANA				
Max Baucus (D)†	1,445	24,922	168,220	668,189
Larry Williams (R)	24,453	33,078	84,216	352,848
NEBRASKA				
J. James Exon (D)†	2,750	16,900	63,250	262,404
Donald E. Shasteen (R)	800	8,950	16,349	222,190
NEW HAMPSHIRE				
Thomas J. McIntyre (D)*	350	20,150	102,450	298,608
Gordon Humphrey (R)†	7,650	18,900	89,126	366,632
NEW JERSEY				
Bill Bradley (D)†	5,900	25,700	192,896	1,689,975
Jeffrey Bell (R)	28,905	64,100	166,263	1,432,924
NEW MEXICO				
Toney Anaya (D)	0	1,000	48,505	175,659
Pete V. Domenici (R)†*	24,450	81,201	150,401	925,622
NORTH CAROLINA				
John R. Ingram (D)	0	0	10,042	261,982
Jesse Helms (R)†*	24,110	129,949	271,290	7,463,282
OKLAHOMA				
David L. Boren (D)†	800	300	800	779,544
Robert Kamm (R)	1,700	5,150	31,664	444,734
OREGON				
Vern Cook (D)	0	0	6,050	38,977
Mark O. Hatfield (R)†*	8,060	29,783	90,633	277,059
RHODE ISLAND				
Claiborne Pell (D)†*	500	9,350	75,945	398,898
James G. Reynolds (R)	500	2,650	5,650	85,615
SOUTH CAROLINA				
Charles D. Ravenel (D)	1,100	9,150	144,644	1,145,542
Strom Thurmond (R)†*	24,100	113,578	216,890	1,753,628
SOUTH DAKOTA				
Don Barnett (D)	0	0	67,404	152,665
Larry Pressler (R)†	21,750	74,724	177,345	489,983
TENNESSEE				
Jane Eskind (D)	0	1,500	26,930	1,906,603
Howard H. Baker Jr. (R)†*	34,455	189,283	344,683	1,946,071
TEXAS				
Robert (Bob) Krueger (D)	25,650	76,687	157,112	2,431,204
John G. Tower (R)†*	53,499	251,519	392,722	4,264,015
VIRGINIA				
Andrew P. Miller (D)	10,750	38,830	157,404	850,313
John W. Warner (R)†	10,350	56,325	108,144	2,907,073
WEST VIRGINIA				
Jennings Randolph (D)†*	12,050	71,100	240,250	732,484
Arch A. Moore Jr. (R)	14,350	61,825	111,975	474,218
WYOMING				
Raymond B. Whitaker (D)	0	0	0	143,051
Alan K. Simpson (R)†	29,200	62,730	124,385	442,484

*designates incumbent.
†designates winner.
P designates Prohibition candidate.
I designates Independent candidate.
NA indicates figures not available.

Source: Energy Pace figures compiled from Federal Election Commission computer data. Other figures from FEC contribution studies.

Oil and Gas PAC Contributions

PAC Name	Affiliation	Date Organized	Energy Interest‡	Contributions, 1/1/77-10/1/79		
				Senate	House	Total
ACBL-Jeffboat PAC	Texas Gas Transmission Corp.	15June77	k	$ 2,900	$ 5,205	$ 8,105
ANR PAC	American Natural Resources Co.	2July76	a,i,k	6,550	25,780	32,330
Allied Chemical PAC	Allied Chemical Corp.	25May78	a,b,f,k	8,200	6,400	14,600
Amarex Employes PAC*	Amarex Inc.	18Oct76	a	0	0	0
Amax Concerned Citizens Fund	Amax Inc.	6Feb76	a	19,850	23,600	43,450
American Petrofina PAC	American Petrofina Inc.	15May79	a,f,n	0	0	0
American Petroleum Refiners Association PAC	American Petroleum Refiners Association	10Oct77	q	23,700	11,750	35,450
Amoco PAC	Standard Oil Co. of Indiana	17Aug76	a,f	77,200	94,650	171,850
Ashland Oil PAC for Employees	Ashland Oil, Inc.	23Feb77	a,f	21,350	29,800	51,150
Associated Citizens PAC	Pennzoil Co.	17Aug76	a,f	12,681	10,315	22,996
Babcock & Wilcox Good Government Fund	Babcock & Wilcox Co. (subsidiary J. Ray McDermott & Co.)	7Sept76	g	8,600	12,550	21,150
Bechtel PAC	Bechtel Corp.	25Sept78	d	6,000	1,600	7,600
Better Government Committee	Mountain Fuel Supply	19June78	a	1,000	2,250	3,250
Brown Builders PAC	Brown and Root Inc. (subsidiary of Halliburton Co.)	25Sept75	d,g	32,545	58,680	91,225
Businessmen for Good Government	South Carolina Oil Jobbers Association	31Mar76	q	1,075	2,150	3,225
CONPAC	Consolidated Natural Gas Service Co. Inc.	19Oct76	k	2,900	7,975	10,875
Cabot PAC	Cabot Corp.	26Feb76	a,g,k	7,325	4,950	12,275
Celanese PAC	Celanese Corp.	13Jan78	f	6,750	11,900	18,650
Chem-Fed	Chemtech Industries	7Sept78	m	0	950	950
Chevron Committee for Political Participation	Standard Oil Co. of California	15Oct75	f,m,o	13,360	32,200	45,560
Cities Service PAC	Cities Service Co.	23Jan76	a,b,f	13,150	22,100	35,250
Coastal States Employee Action Fund	Coastal States Gas Corp.	7Apr78	a,b,f,k	5,650	17,100	22,750
Columbia Employees Political Action Fund	Columbia Gas Transmission Corp.	2Aug76	k	10,200	22,885	33,085
Columbia Gas Distribution Employees Political Action Fund	Columbia Gas Co.	28July76	k	800	1,239	2,039
Columbia Gas Employees Political Action Fund	Columbia Gas Co.	27July76	k	9,915	21,000	30,915
Combustion Engineering PAC	Combustion Engineering Inc.	25June76	g	6,350	7,500	13,850
Committee for Free Enterprise & Responsible Government	Koch Industries, Inc.	28Sept78	h,i,m	3,000	500	3,500
Committee of Concerned Citizens	Southern Union Co.	5July77	a,f,k	2,450	3,075	5,525
Concerned Citizens Fund	Atlantic Richfield Co.	23Oct75	a,f,m,o	30,632	39,646	70,278
Connecticut Natural Gas PAC	Connecticut Natural Gas Corp.	10July78	k	0	114	114
Conoco Employees Good Government Fund	Continental Oil Co.	26Feb76	a,f	8,800	16,050	24,850
Consolidated Executives Voluntary Non-Partisan Political Fund	Consolidated Gas Supply Corp.	23Oct72	k	900	1,750	2,650
Cooper Industries PAC	Cooper Industries, Inc.	14July78	g	12,250	14,800	27,050
Dallas Energy PAC	+	7Nov77	e	20,500	44,500	65,000
Datotek Better Government Committee	Entex, Inc.	22Sept78	k	1,000	0	1,000
Diamond Shamrock Corp. Voluntary Political Contribution Plan	Diamond Shamrock Corp.	3May78	a,f	5,450	4,700	10,150

‡ The energy interests indicated in this column are drawn largely from standard industrial classifications listed by Standard & Poor's Register of Corporations, 1979, and the Dun and Bradstreet Million Dollar Directory, 1979.

In a limited number of cases information on companies was obtained through interviews with company or association officials or other sources knowledgeable about energy related political action committees.

Some of the companies listed may have interests in addition to the energy interests noted.

Where subsidiary companies are listed, energy interests are those of the parent company.

* indicates committee no longer operating.

+ indicates an independent PAC that is not affiliated with a particular company or trade association.

KEY:
a crude petroleum and natural gas.
b natural gas liquids.
c drilling oil and gas wells.
d oil and gas field exploration services.
e miscellaneous independent oil and/or gas interests.
f petroleum refining.
g oil field machinery and equipment.
h crude petroleum pipe lines.
i refined petroleum pipe lines.
j pipe lines.
k natural gas transmission and/or distribution.
l mixed, manufactured or liquified gas production and/or distribution.
m petroleum bulk stations and terminals.
n petroleum and petroleum products wholesalers.
o gasoline service stations.
p oil royalty companies.
q trade association.

PAC Name	Affiliation	Date Organized	Energy Interest‡	Contributions, 1/1/77-10/1/79		
				Senate	House	Total
Domestic Petroleum Council PAC	Domestic Petroleum Council	14Mar77	q	$ 8,550	$ 8,825	$ 17,375
Dow Eastern Employees PAC	Dow Chemical U.S.A.	21Oct75	d	2,300	8,000	10,300
Dresser Industries PAC	Dresser Industries Inc.	27Sept76	g	21,548	39,449	60,997
Drilling Contractors PAC	International Association of Drilling Contractors	12Aug76	q	12,300	104,800	117,100
EN PAC	Kansas-Nebraska Natural Gas Co., Inc.	12Sept78	a,k	950	1,700	2,650
East Ohio Gas Employees Voluntary Good Government Association	East Ohio Gas Co.	22Feb74	k	300	1,200	1,500
Effective PAC	Pogo Producing Co.	14July78	a	3,700	600	4,300
Employees of Mustang PAC	Mustang Fuel Corp.	25Aug78	a,c,d,j,k	0	0	0
Enserch Employees' Political Support Association	Enserch Corp.	6Feb76	a,d,k	5,500	19,700	25,200
Entex Better Government Committee	Entex, Inc.	25Nov77	a,k	4,550	11,400	15,950
Ethyl Corp. PAC (ECPAC)	Ethyl Corp.	9Feb78	a,d	8,250	5,050	13,300
Florida Gas Federal PAC	Florida Gas Co.	14Oct76	a,d,f,k	550	6,000	6,550
Fluor Public Affairs Committee	Fluor Corp.	19Apr72	c	27,125	30,775	57,900
Forest PAC	Forest Oil Corp.	31Mar78	a	1,700	1,100	2,800
Free Enterprise PAC	National Association for Free Enterprise	7Sept76	e	0	0	0
Freeport Citizenship Committee	Freeport Minerals Co.	6Aug76	a	16,450	19,900	36,350
GLOMARPAC	Global Marine Inc.	17Oct78	a,c,d	0	0	0
Gas Employees PAC	American Gas Association	15May72	q	5,025	8,450	13,475
Getty Oil Co. PAC	Getty Oil Co.	15Mar76	a,f,n,o	19,950	40,150	60,100
GoldPAC	Goldrus Drilling Co.	12Apr76	c	16,000	23,000	39,000
Good Government Fund	Pacific Gas & Electric Co.	16May75	k	2,150	11,530	13,680
Gulf Resources & Chemical Corp. PAC	Gulf Resources & Chemical Corp.	9Mar76	a	7,650	7,225	14,875
Hawaii Automotive & Retail Gas Dealers Association PAC*	Hawaii Automotive & Retail Gas Dealers Association	14Feb77	q	0	100	100
Halliburton PAC	Halliburton Co.	6Feb76	d,g	8,750	11,450	20,200
Houston Oil & Minerals Good Government Fund	Houston Oil & Minerals Corp.	23Feb76	a,b	8,700	8,500	17,200
Howell Corp. Political Awareness Committee	Howell Corp.	30Mar76	a,d,p	0	0	0
Hughes Tool Co. PAC	Hughes Tool Co.	17Apr72	g,d	1,200	1,225	2,425
Hunt Energy Corp. PAC	Hunt Energy Corp.	29Sept78	d	0	0	0
IMPAC	+	1Sept76	e	21,500	22,430	43,930
Illinois Marketers PAC	Illinois Petroleum Marketers Association	3June78	q	700	2,600	3,300
Independent Gasoline Marketers Council PAC	Independent Gasoline Marketers Council	6Oct76	q	400	1,900	2,300
Independent Energy Fund	National Council Associates	22June76	q	1,300	3,600	4,900
Indiana Service Station Dealers PAC	Indiana Service Station Dealers Association	30Sept76	q	0	1,500	1,500
Kerr-McGee Corp. PAC	Kerr-McGee Corp.	27Sept72	a,c,f,m	1,700	2,900	4,600
Lehigh Oil PAC	Lehigh Oil, Inc.	6Apr78	o,m,n	0	670	670
Lovaca Gathering Co. PAC	Coastal States Gas Corp.	4May79	a,b,f,k	0	0	0
Mapco Inc. PAC	Mapco Inc.	30Jan76	a,b,i,n	19,150	34,250	53,400
Marathon Employees PAC	Marathon Oil Co.	25Feb76	a,f,h	9,750	13,250	23,000
Meridian Public Affairs Committee	+	27Mar74	k	100	4,775	4,875
Michigan Petroleum PAC	+	27Dec77	e	2,750	12,850	15,600
Midland Committee	Dow Chemical U.S.A.	24June77	d	12,050	18,850	30,900
Mitchell Energy & Development PAC	Mitchell Energy & Development Corp.	24Feb78	a,b,c,k,p	1,800	7,350	9,150
Mobil Oil Corp. PAC (Mobil PAC)	Mobil Corp.	17May78	a,f	1,050	850	1,900
NCPR-PAC	National Congress of Petroleum Retailers	1Sept76	q	0	800	800
NFG FedPAC (National Fuel Gas PAC)	National Fuel Gas Corp.	19Dec77	a,b,k	400	2,450	2,850
NL Executives Non-Partisan Fund	NL Industries, Inc.	1974	g	6,300	10,400	16,700
National Oil Jobbers Council Small Businessmen's Committee	South Carolina Oil Jobbers Association	12Mar76	q	9,150	10,575	19,725
North Texas PAC	+	3Nov77	e	9,000	29,000	38,000
Northeast Utilities PAC	Northeast Utilities Service Co.	25Aug78	k	200	1,850	2,050
Northern Political Action	Northern Natural Gas Co.	20Oct78	k,n	2,300	800	3,100
Northwest Energy PAC	Northwest Energy Co.	2Apr79	k	0	0	0

PAC Name	Affiliation	Date Organized	Energy Interest‡	Contributions, 1/1/77-10/1/79		
				Senate	House	Total
OXYPAC	Occidental Petroleum Corp.	22Dec77	a,f	$ 19,500	$ 50,000	$ 69,500
Offshore Co. PAC	Offshore Co.	27Oct76	c,g	0	0	0
PARPAC	Parker Drilling Co.	11May79	c	0	0	0
PEPIC	Peoples Natural Gas Co.	17Feb76	c	0	1,250	1,250
PG-PAC	Peoples Gas Co.	14Aug78	l	0	3,100	3,100
Pacific Lighting Political Assistance Committee	Pacific Lighting Corp.	17Sept73	k	9,200	26,640	35,840
Pacific Resources PAC	Pacific Resources Inc.	17May77	l	300	2,850	3,150
Panhandle Eastern System PAC	Panhandle Eastern Pipe Line Co.	8June76	k,l	11,000	18,100	29,100
Panhandle Energy PAC	+	12Aug76	e	2,500	8,500	11,000
PasPAC	El Paso Co.	27Apr78	a,k	7,500	5,700	13,200
Permian Basin PAC	Permian Basin Petroleum Association	7Feb78	q	500	9,000	9,500
Petroleum Exploration Production Political Committee of California South	+	28Aug78	e	0	0	0
Petrolane PAC	Petrolane, Inc.	30Apr76	d,n	5,200	9,500	14,700
Petroleum Producers of East Texas PAC	+	30Sept77	e	2,000	10,000	12,000
Phillips Petroleum Co. PAC	Phillips Petroleum Co.	22Aug79	a,d	0	0	0
Pine Tree Political Committee	Santa Fe Industries, Inc.	15Oct74	a,h	400	6,650	7,050
Pipeliners Voluntary Fund*	+	15Mar77	q	0	0	0
Political Awareness Fund	Union Oil Co. of California	14Apr72	a,f,m,o	38,300	66,180	104,480
Political Support Association	Houston Natural Gas Corp.	29Oct73	a,k,l	4,750	12,500	17,250
Propane Industry PAC	National LP-Gas Association	19Aug77	q	3,900	5,700	9,600
Quaker State Political Participation Fund	Quaker State Oil Refining Corp.	12May78	a,f	500	3,900	4,400
Raytheon PAC	Raytheon Co.	13June78	d	13,975	4,150	18,125
Reading & Bates PAC	Reading & Bates Offshore Drilling Co.	11Apr77	a,c	600	1,500	2,100
SEDCO PAC	SEDCO, Inc.	8Dec76	c,g	5,950	14,050	20,000
SFI PAC	Santa Fe International	17Apr78	a,c,d	0	1,300	1,300
Service Station Dealers Association PAC	Service Station Dealers Association Michigan, Inc.	17Mar78	q	100	650	750
Service Station Dealers for a Responsive Government	Gasoline Retail Dealers Association-N.H. & Vt.	31July79	q	0	0	0
Shell Employes Political Awareness Commitee	Shell Oil Co.	8Apr76	a,f,h	16,975	34,295	51,270
Skelly Oil Co. PAC*	Skelly Oil Co.	5Sept77	a,f,n,o	0	0	0
Small Producers for Energy Independence PAC	Council of Active Independent Oil and Gas Producers	7Jan76	q	14,000	48,700	62,700
Sohioans Civic Contribution Fund SUPAC	Standard Oil Co. of Ohio	6Jan76	a,f	6,150	12,910	19,060
Southern Natural Resources, Inc. PAC	Southern Natural Resources, Inc.	23July76	a,c,k	11,000	8,100	19,100
Southland Royalty Co. PAC	Southland Royalty Co.	6Dec78	p	0	0	0
Southwest Gas PAC	Southwest Gas Corp.	4Apr77	k	250	1,500	1,750
St. Joe Minerals Political Assistance Committee	St. Joe Minerals Corp.	12Mar76	a	13,900	21,150	35,050
Sun Co. Inc. PAC	Sun Co. Inc.	31Jan77	a,f,m	24,350	50,000	74,350
Ten-PAC PAC	Earth Resources Co.	19Dec78	f,o	0	0	0
Tenneco Good Government Fund-Federal	Tenneco Inc.	17Mar78	a,f,k	18,000	32,971	50,971
Texaco Employees Political Involvement Committee	Texaco Inc.	16Dec75	a,f	24,775	32,925	57,700
Texas Eastern PAC	Texas Eastern Gas Transmission Co.	5Jan76	k	9,300	9,150	18,450
Texas Gas Transmission PAC	Texas Gas Transmission Corp.	17Oct75	a,c,k	3,600	8,350	11,950
Texas Oil for Texans*	+	27Apr76	q	0	0	0
TexasGulf PAC	TexasGulf Inc.	30Apr76	a	2,000	7,050	9,050
Transpac	Transco Companies, Inc.	13Apr78	a,k	2,800	8,000	10,800
True Responsible Government Committee	True Oil Purchasing Co.	25Feb76	a,c	2,225	5,675	7,900
United Energy Resources PAC	United Energy Resources, Inc.	8July77	a,k	12,850	5,175	18,025
WNGPAC Federal	Washington Natural Gas Co.	17Oct77	i,k	450	2,390	2,840
Western Co. of North America SAFEPAC	Western Co. of North America	29Apr77	c,d	6,000	10,350	16,350
Williams Companies PAC	Williams Companies	13Apr76	i,k	5,429	11,800	17,229
Workover & Well Servicing Action Commitee	Association of Oilwell Servicing Contractors	21June76	q	4,000	17,800	21,800
Zapata PAC	Zapata Corp.	24Jan78	c	1,500	2,900	4,400
TOTALS				$971,560	$1,705,854	$2,677,414

Energy Legislation
Chronology of Events, 1973-1980

1973

Highlights

Alaska Oil Pipeline

The Trans-Alaska Pipeline Authorization Act (PL 93-153) overrode environmental challenges to the pipeline, which was expected to carry 2 million barrels of crude oil a day from Alaska's frozen north to its ice-free southern port of Valdez. From there, tankers would deliver the oil to the West Coast.

Mandatory Oil Allocation and Pricing

The Emergency Petroleum Allocation Act (PL 93-159) required the president to set up systems for allocating and pricing oil and oil products in the hope of distributing available fuel equitably. This bill was Congress' initial thrust into federal regulation of the complex petroleum market.

Daylight Saving Time

In a move to save energy, Congress instituted year-round daylight saving time (PL 93-182).

Energy Conservation

Determined to force Americans to use less energy, the Senate approved a national energy conservation program requiring improvements in automobile fuel efficiency and mandating labels on major household appliances that described expected operating costs. The House did not act on the bill in 1973, but many of the concepts were later included in the major energy policy act (PL 94-163) enacted in 1975.

Natural Gas Deregulation

One of Congress' longest running debates was reopened in 1973 when the Nixon administration proposed an end to price controls on new discoveries of natural gas. But, despite industry arguments that decontrol would lead to increased production, consumer advocates managed to prevent action in either house. After bitter wrangling, a compromise was finally enacted in 1978 (PL 95-621).

Emergency Energy Powers

Frustrated with the chaos in the petroleum market and partly in response to proposals from the Nixon administration, Congress sought to broaden the federal government's energy powers. But the legislators retained for themselves authority to block the president each time he proposed using his new authority. The bill hit a snag when the House insisted on language suggesting regulation of excess profits in the oil industry. The Senate, at the urging of oil-state senators, opposed that provision.

Highway Speed Limit

An an energy conservation measure, Congress set a nationwide speed limit of 55 miles per hour (PL 93-239).

Energy Reorganization

President Nixon made the first of many presidential attempts to solve the energy problem by reorganizing the federal energy bureaucracy. Congress began to work on his scheme, but the legislators had their own ideas.

The Year in Review

At first glance, the congressional response to the energy crisis appeared impressive. Three weeks after the Arab oil producers imposed their embargo Oct. 18, 1973, two major energy measures arrived at the White House for the president's signature.

President Nixon signed both. One — clearing the way for construction of the Alaska oil pipeline — he had sought. The other — directing him to impose a mandatory fuel allocation system on the nation — he had opposed and signed reluctantly.

This running start for Congress was deceptive. Both measures were already in the final stages of the legislative process when the embargo was imposed. The only other energy bills cleared by Congress in 1973 were two conservation measures requested by Nixon in his Nov. 7 address announcing Project Independence. One of these lowered the speed limit nationwide to 55 miles per hour; the other instituted daylight saving time year-round.

The House and Senate each passed a number of other energy measures in December, but none was enacted. They wanted to reorganize the federal energy structure, provide the president with special emergency powers over energy production and use, encourage conservation and accelerate energy research. The lack of coordination between the two chambers produced a confusing crisscross of similar provisions in differing bills, and Congress adjourned without completing action.

During the year, Congress had worked on several major energy issues that either had been debated in the past or promised to come up again and again in the future. Topics included natural gas deregulation, conservation policy and reorganization of the federal energy bureaucracy.

The scramble at the end of 1973 to give the president emergency powers was an early indication of the problems that would continue to impede the congressional effort to formulate an energy policy. Both chambers approved versions of emergency legislation in December, with the House including a windfall profits restriction that was not part of the Senate bill.

Conferees worked feverishly to compromise the differences; congressional leaders prolonged the session, hoping to complete work on the bill. On Dec. 21, the Senate moved to consider the conference report, only to have it blocked by senators from oil-producing states who filibustered against the windfall profits provision. Finally, Senate leaders dropped the provision and won approval of a compromise.

Late in the evening the House received the revised version of the conference bill. Outraged by what they considered a high-handed Senate move, the House voted resoundingly three times to insist on the windfall profits provision and to reject any compromise. Tired and angry, members of Congress gave up their effort for this session and adjourned Dec. 22.

Alaska Oil Pipeline

In the first major legislation enacted after the imposition of the Arab oil embargo, Congress overrode environmental challenges blocking construction of a huge oil pipeline to carry 2 million barrels of crude oil a day from Alaska's frozen north to the rest of the United States.

As signed by President Nixon Nov. 16, 1973, the Trans-Alaska Pipeline Authorization Act (S 1081 — PL 93-153) directed the interior secretary to move immediately to authorize construction of the 789-mile pipeline connecting the oil-rich North Slope with the ice-free port of Valdez. Tankers were to carry the oil from Valdez to the West Coast.

PL 93-153 disarmed pipeline opponents of their most effective weapons — the National Environmental Policy Act of 1969 and the Mineral Leasing Act of 1920.

Alarmed by the potential danger the pipeline posed to the Alaskan tundra and wildlife, and by the increased possibility of oil spills from the tankers it fueled, environmental groups sought to block federal approval of its construction.

Their initial challenges were based on the 1969 law, which required thorough examination of the environmental impact of all major federal actions. But the court ruling that had stymied construction was based on the older mineral leasing law, which limited to 50 feet in width the rights-of-way that could be issued across federal lands. The oil companies planning to build the pipeline had requested widths up to three times that size.

Congress moved actively into the pipeline dispute early in 1973, after the Nixon administration asked for legislation waiving the 50-foot limit. The pace of congressional activity quickened in April after the Supreme Court turned down the government's request that it overrule the lower court.

PL 93-153 removed the 50-foot limit and barred any future challenges to the pipeline based on the 1969 law. It provided expedited procedures for consideration of any other court challenges to construction of the pipeline.

The Senate approved its version of the bill in July; the House, in August. Conferees finished work in mid-October, just as the Arab members of the Organization of Petroleum Exporting Countries (OPEC) moved to impose the embargo.

Nixon prodded Congress to complete action on the bill when he addressed the nation Nov. 7 to announce Project Independence. Alaskan oil was a major component of the nation's effort to attain energy independence. Within a week of Nixon's speech, the pipeline bill was on his desk for his signature.

Senate Action

The Senate Interior Committee reported the bill (S 1081 — S Rept 93-207) June 12. The measure authorized the interior secretary to grant rights-of-way across public lands without restriction as to width and requested the president to begin negotiations with Canada to determine the feasibility of a trans-Canada pipeline.

Floor Action. The Senate approved the bill July 17 by a vote of 77-20. But first the senators added controversial language immunizing all future federal actions regarding construction of the pipeline from further court challenge under the National Environmental Policy Act of 1969 (NEPA).

The NEPA amendment, proposed by the two senators from Alaska, Democrat Mike Gravel and Republican Ted Stevens, was adopted by a 49-48 vote. It was a victory for the oil companies and the Nixon administration, ensuring that the pipeline would be delayed no longer by litigation or court orders resulting from such challenges.

By approving this amendment, the Senate declared all actions taken by the interior secretary and other federal agencies regarding the pipeline, related highways and airports to be in compliance with the 1969 act. Gravel said that Congress, in approving this language, was simply stating that the environmental impact statement filed on the pipeline was sufficient to fulfill the requirements of the law. Interior Committee Chairman Henry M. Jackson, D-Wash., disagreed and argued against the amendment, saying that it was beyond the power of Congress to foreclose further judicial review of such matters.

After the Senate voted to adopt the amendment, Gravel routinely moved for reconsideration of the vote and, as was customary, a move was made to table that motion and thus close the matter. The vote to table was a tie, 49-49. In the case of a tie, a motion fails. But Vice President Spiro T. Agnew, who was presiding over the Senate, broke the tie, voting for the motion and thus confirming Senate

Courts Blocked
Alaska Oil Pipeline

Atlantic Richfield Company struck oil on the North Slope of Alaska in the summer of 1968. Subsequent exploration located billions of barrels of proved reserves of oil, and estimates of the potential there ran higher than 100 billion barrels, more than all other known U.S. oil reserves combined.

The major obstacle to development of this oil was its location: how could it be transported to its markets, all far to the south?

A consortium of oil companies was formed, first known as the Trans-Alaska Pipeline System and later as Alyeska Pipeline Service Company. The companies, involved directly or through subsidiaries, were Atlantic Richfield, Amerada Hess Corporation, Standard Oil Company (New Jersey), British Petroleum, Mobil Oil Company, Phillips Petroleum Company, Union Oil Company of California and Home Oil Company of Canada, which later withdrew from the group.

The consortium applied for permits from the Interior Department to build an access road and the pipeline to Valdez, much of which would run across federal lands.

Environmental groups wasted little time. In April 1970, three of them — the Wilderness Society, Friends of the Earth and the Environmental Defense Fund — won a federal district court order forbidding the interior secretary to issue the permits until a full environmental impact statement had been prepared on the pipeline and alternative methods of transporting the oil.

It was two years before such a statement was completed and released. When made public in March 1972, it filled nine volumes. In May of that year Interior Secretary Rogers C. B. Morton said he intended to issue the permits. In August, the federal

court lifted its order forbidding him to issue the permits. The environmentalists appealed.

The result of their appeal was a February 1973 decision by the court of appeals, District of Columbia circuit, forbidding Morton to issue the permit. The basis for the prohibition was the 1920 Mineral Leasing Act, which limited rights-of-way across public lands to 50 feet in width.

The Nixon administration appealed to the Supreme Court to overturn the court of appeals. On April 2, the Supreme Court upheld the court of appeals' order. The only remaining avenue of relief was Congress, which could change the 1920 law on which the court decisions were based.

adoption of the amendment.

The other major point of controversy concerned an alternate route across Canada.

Sens. Walter F. Mondale, D-Minn., and Birch Bayh, D-Ind., offered an amendment to delay construction of any Alaska pipeline for at least a year while the Canadian route was studied. They argued that the proposed Alaska pipeline would take oil only to the West Coast — and from there possibly to Japan. By using the Canadian route instead, the Alaskan oil would be linked with two U.S. pipelines, one to the West Coast and one to New York, thus delivering Alaskan oil nationwide, they said.

However, opponents argued that consideration of a trans-Canada pipeline would only delay the shipment of North Slope oil and that such a pipeline was risky because it would not be under sole U.S. control. The Senate rejected the amendment, 29-61.

House Action

The House Interior Committee July 28 reported its Alaska pipeline bill (HR 9130 — H Rept 93-414), less than two weeks after Senate passage of S 1081. As reported, HR 9130 amended the 1920 Mineral Leasing Act to allow grants of rights-of-way wider than 50 feet, directed the interior secretary to grant the rights-of-way for the Alaska pipeline and declared the pipeline to be in compliance with NEPA.

Floor Action. The House Aug. 2 approved HR 9130 by a vote of 356-60, after rejecting an effort to remove the provision prohibiting further NEPA challenges. The amendment deleting that section, proposed by John Dellenback, R-Ore., and Wayne Owens, D-Utah, was rejected on a close roll call vote of 198-221 (R 65-120, D 133-101).

Final Action

The conference report (H Rept 93-624) declared that Congress had determined that the trans-Alaska pipeline should be built without further delay and that federal officials should have no discretion to postpone it.

The conferees retained several Senate amendments to S 1081 that were strongly opposed by the business community and the administration, even producing veto threats late in October. The problem provisions gave the Federal Trade Commission more authority to take its antitrust efforts to court, required confirmation of persons named to certain energy-related posts and transferred to the General Accounting Office from the Office of Management and Budget the authority to screen requests from federal agencies for information from the business community.

After refusing, 162-213, to strike out these provisions, the House Nov. 12 adopted the conference report by a 361-14 vote.

The Senate adopted the conference report, 80-5, on Nov. 13, clearing the bill for the White House.

Nixon signed the measure Nov. 16.

Provisions

As signed into law, PL 93-153 contained major provisions that:

Trans-Alaskan Pipeline

● Required the interior secretary to authorize construction of the trans-Alaskan pipeline.

● Provided that all actions necessary for completion of the pipeline be taken without further delay under the National Environmental Policy Act of 1969.

● Restricted judicial review 1) to the constitutionality of the act, 2) to actions taken under the act that violated constitutional rights and 3) to actions that went beyond the authority granted by the act.

● Provided expedited procedures for consideration of such challenges to the pipelines and the law.

● Provided liability of up to $50 million for each incident for damages resulting from pipeline construction or operations that affected the subsistence or income of Alaskan natives.

● Held the pipeline owners liable for the full costs of controlling and removing any pollution caused by the pipeline.

● Established liability without regard to fault of up to $100 million for each incident of oil spills from vessels carrying oil from the pipeline unless the oil spills were caused by acts of war or actions of the United States.

● Limited liability for oil spills to $14 million for owners of vessels transporting crude oil.

● Established a Trans-Alaskan Pipeline Liability Fund to meet claims of more than $14 million.

● Provided that oil companies using the pipeline pay into the fund five cents for each barrel loaded on vessels until the fund reached $100 million.

● Directed the president to ensure the equitable allocation of Alaskan North Slope crude oil among all regions of the United States.

● Authorized semiannual advance payments of $5 million starting in fiscal 1976 for the Alaska Native Fund, pending delivery of North Slope oil to the pipeline, and limited total payments to $500 million.

● Authorized the president to negotiate with Canada concerning an alternative pipeline to carry North Slope oil across Canada to the midwestern United States.

Rights-of-Way

● Permitted the interior secretary to authorize rights-of-way wider than 50 feet, in addition to the ground occupied by pipelines and related facilities, if necessary.

● Provided that no domestically produced crude oil transported through any pipeline crossing federal land could be exported unless the president found and reported to Congress that such exports 1) would not diminish oil supplies in the United States and 2) would be in the national interest.

● Provided that such exports would be prohibited if Congress disapproved the president's findings by concurrent resolution within 60 days after receiving the report.

Miscellaneous Provisions

● Required Senate confirmation of the director of the White House Energy Policy Office and the head of the Interior Department's Mining Enforcement and Safety Administration, including the incumbents.

● Permitted the Federal Trade Commission (FTC) to go to court to enforce its own subpoenas and to seek temporary injunctions to avoid unfair competitive practices.

● Permitted the FTC to prosecute cases under its jurisdiction after consulting with the U.S. attorney general and giving him 10 days in which to take the action proposed by the FTC.

● Transferred from the Office of Management and Budget to the General Accounting Office the authority to review regulatory agency requests for information from businesses and corporations.

● Exempted from price controls under the Economic Stabilization Act of 1970 and from subsequent fuel allocation programs the sale of oil and natural gas liquids from wells producing no more than 10 barrels daily.

● Advanced the effective date of the Ports and Waterways Safety Act of 1972 (PL 92-340) with respect to U.S. vessels engaged in coastal trade to June 30, 1974, from Jan. 1, 1976. (The 1972 act established construction standards for tankers to prevent pollution.)

● Specified that the rest of the act would not be affected if any provision were held invalid.

Oil Allocation, Pricing

To spread scarce fuel supplies evenly, Congress in 1973 insisted that the president impose mandatory controls allocating oil and oil products among different regions of the nation and sectors of the petroleum industry.

The Nixon administration first opposed this legislation, but its objections weakened as the failure of voluntary allocation efforts became obvious. By the time Congress cleared the Emergency Petroleum Allocation Act (S 1570 — PL 93-159) for the White House in mid-November, President Nixon had already announced mandatory allocation systems for propane, heating oil, jet fuel and diesel fuel. Earlier in 1973, Congress had given the president discretionary power to set up such systems (S 398 — PL 93-28).

PL 93-159 required the president to set up within 30 days a comprehensive allocation program for oil and oil products.

In provisions that would become increasingly controversial as the price of foreign oil rose precipitously over the following months, PL 93-159 also directed the president to set prices — or to set out a formula by which they should be determined — for crude oil and refined petroleum products. Retailers could pass on to consumers increases in wholesale prices. Most oil exports were banned.

PL 93-159 also offered protection for independent retailers and refiners by requiring that they receive as much oil or oil products as they had in 1972 — or a proportional amount, if supplies were lower than in 1972. Independent marketers supported a mandatory allocation system, saying that many of them were forced out of business when suppliers cut off oil deliveries altogether. The major oil companies opposed any mandatory allocation system.

The Senate approved S 1570 in June. The House passed its version of the bill Oct. 17 — the day that Arab nations announced their plans to curtail oil production and exports to the United States.

Conferees Nov. 10 filed their report on the bill. The final version of S 1570 stated that shortages of oil, caused by inadequate domestic production, environmental constraints and insufficient imports, were imminent and would create severe economic hardships constituting a national energy crisis. The purpose of the mandatory allocation system, S 1570 stated, was to minimize the adverse impact of these shortages on the American people and their economy. The House Nov. 13 adopted the conference report; the Senate Nov. 14. Nixon signed the bill Nov. 27.

Background

Demands for a mandatory allocation program for oil and oil products escalated in 1973 as mid-winter fuel shortages were succeeded by summer gasoline shortages and finally by the Arab embargo on oil shipments to the United States following the Middle East war in October.

In April, Congress included in the Economic Stabilization Act Amendments of 1973 (S 398 — PL 93-28) a Senate amendment giving the president discretionary authority to allocate petroleum products. The act also empowered the president to control prices — including oil prices — until April 30, 1974.

The administration May 10 announced "voluntary" guidelines to assure that independent gasoline stations and other oil product purchasers would not suffer a cutoff in their supplies. Under the plan, suppliers were urged to sell to their customers the same percentage of refinery output and crude oil supplies that they sold in 1972. An administration spokesman said that if the voluntary guidelines were not effective, "more stringent measures" would be applied.

The administration resisted imposition of a mandatory allocation program, but by autumn it was clear that the voluntary program had failed.

On Oct. 2, the administration announced a mandatory allocation program for propane gas, followed Oct. 2 by a similar program — effective Nov. 1 — for heating oil, kerosene and jet and diesel fuels.

Senate Action

The Senate Interior Committee May 17 reported S 1570 (S Rept 93-159), stating that something more than the discretionary authority provided by PL 93-28 was necessary. The fuel shortage, the committee report said, was "so imminent that executive discretion as to whether or not to implement mandatory allocation measures is no longer warranted." The bill directed the president to draw

White House Energy Advisers

The White House post of chief energy adviser had three different occupants and almost as many different names in 1973. The confusion was only the beginning of a long struggle to find the best way for the bureaucracy to deal with the nation's growing energy problem.

In February, President Nixon named Charles J. DiBona as his special consultant on energy. In June, DiBona became deputy director of a new Energy Policy Office set up in the White House. The director of the new office was John A. Love, a Republican who resigned as governor of Colorado to take the post.

But Love found himself ignored by the president and at odds with the Treasury Department, which also had definite ideas about how to deal with the energy problems. As a result, in December, Love and DiBona resigned.

The following day — December 4 — Nixon asked Congress to create a separate energy agency, to be called the Federal Energy Administration. In the interim, Nixon reorganized the White House Energy Policy Office as the Federal Energy Office and named as its chief William E. Simon, deputy secretary of the Treasury. John C. Sawhill, an associate director of the Office of Management and Budget, was appointed Simon's deputy.

up a plan for a mandatory fuel allocation system within 60 days of its enactment. The authority granted by S 1570 would expire Sept. 1, 1974.

Floor Action. The Senate June 5 passed S 1570, 85-10. The bill required the president to submit to Congress within 30 days a plan for a mandatory fuels allocation system, giving priority to supplying public health facilities, public utilities and agricultural production and distribution systems.

During debate on S 1570, the Senate adopted amendments guaranteeing small independent oil companies continuing supplies of fuel, reducing to 30 days the time for preparation of the president's plan and changing the act's expiration date to March 1, 1975. The Senate rejected amendments that would have excluded independent oil producers from the allocation formulas and that would have allowed oil companies to sell fuel at free market prices, free of price controls. Both amendments were proposed by Dewey F. Bartlett, R-Okla. The first was rejected 42-51, after Senate Interior Committee Chairman Henry M. Jackson, D-Wash., warned that one-third of all petroleum producers could slip through the loophole it created. The second was rejected 21-71.

House Action

The House Interstate and Foreign Commerce Committee Sept. 29 reported its allocation bill (HR 9681 —

H Rept 93-531). The bill required the president to submit plans for an allocation system within 10 days of enactment and implement them 15 days later. The system set up under the legislation was to be effective through Feb. 28. 1975.

Floor Action. The House Oct. 17, by a 337-72 vote, passed HR 9681, over objections from the Nixon administration that it did not give the president sufficient flexibility to administer an effective allocation program.

During consideration of the bill, the House rejected several amendments backed by the oil industry, which generally opposed a mandatory allocation system. J. J. Pickle, D-Texas, wanted to prohibit the allocation of crude oil at the producer level unless it was necessary to assure the maintenance of public services, agricultural operations and competition in the oil industry. The Pickle amendment was rejected, 136-245.

The House subsequently rejected, 152-256, an amendment proposed by John M. Ashbrook, R-Ohio, that would have made the General Accounting Office, rather than the Federal Trade Commission, the monitor of the allocation program. It also rejected, by voice vote, an amendment moving the program's expiration date up to April 30, 1974.

Final Action

Conferees Nov. 10 filed their report on S 1570 (H Rept 93-628), agreeing that it was imperative for the federal government to intervene in the marketplace to preserve competition and to ensure an equitable distribution of scarce supplies of oil and oil products.

The House Nov. 13 adopted the conference report, 348-46. The Senate Nov. 14 cleared the measure for the White House by adopting the report, 80-3.

Provisions

As signed into law, PL 93-159, the Emergency Petroleum Allocation Act of 1973:

● Directed the president to issue regulations for the allocation and pricing of crude oil and oil products within 15 days of enactment and to put the regulations into effect 15 days after they were issued.

● Gave the president an additional 15 days to put into effect allocation regulations covering gasoline and products covered by the allocation program established by the president under the Economic Stabilization Act of 1970 (PL 91-379). The president's allocation program covered propane, home heating oil and jet and diesel fuels only.

● Established as objectives that were to be considered in issuing the regulations the following: maintenance of all public services, agricultural operations and public health, safety and welfare; preservation of competition in the oil industry; equitable allocation and pricing of oil and oil products; and allocation of enough oil to ensure the exploration, production and transportation of new fuel supplies.

● Permitted retailers to pass on to their customers increases in the wholesale price of oil and oil products.

● Required the same base period to be used to compute all price markups.

● Required that oil and oil products be allocated to each user in an amount not less than that supplied to them during the corresponding period of 1972.

● Provided for proportional reductions of supplies to each user if the total supply of oil was less than that for a corresponding period of 1972.

● Required the president to give special consideration in allocating oil and oil products to anyone whose use of other fuels had been curtailed or terminated in compliance with an order of a federal or state agency.

● Directed the president to make equitable adjustments in the program to account for any increases in total supply for the entry into the market of new users.

● Directed the president to the extent practicable and necessary to allocate propane in a way that did not deny supplies to industrial users with no alternative supply of fuel.

● Required that all oil and oil products produced or refined within the United States be totally allocated within the United States to the extent practicable and necessary to carry out the act.

● Exempted from price and allocation regulations oil from wells that produced 10 barrels or less of oil daily.

● Permitted the president to exclude from the allocation program crude oil at the producer level if he found such allocation was unnecessary to meet the objectives of the act.

● Permitted the president to exempt from the allocation program for a period of 90 days oil and oil products for which he found no shortages and where such an exemption would not reduce the supply of other oil products.

● Provided that either the House or the Senate could disapprove such an exemption from the allocation program by a simple resolution of disapproval passed within five days of receiving notice from the president of the proposed exemption.

● Provided for the same fines and injunctive relief as were authorized under the Economic Stabilization Act of 1970: a fine of up to $5,000 for each willful violation, and a fine up to $2,500 for civil penalties, for each violation; the attorney general could seek injunctions to prevent violations of the act.

● Made compliance with regulations issued under the act a defense in breach of contract and federal antitrust cases.

● Directed the Federal Trade Commission to monitor the allocation program during the first 45 days that it was in effect, and to report to Congress and the president within 60 days on the effectiveness of the act and the actions taken under it.

● Terminated the act at midnight, Feb. 28, 1975.

Emergency Energy Powers

Despite strenuous efforts, Congress in 1973 failed to pass a bill (S 2589) giving the president broad emergency powers to control the production and consumption of energy. The key dispute was over a restriction on oil industry profits, which the House insisted on, and the Senate refused to accept.

The Energy Emergency Act was introduced Oct. 18, the day after Arab leaders indicated their intention to cut off exports of oil to the United States. Eventually incorporated into the bill were a number of the special powers that President Nixon requested in his Nov. 7 Project Independence address. Among them were the power to reduce speed limits, restrict the non-essential outdoor use of fuel, restrict energy-use advertising, require lower indoor temperatures, limit fuel consumption by public and commercial establishments, order industries and utilities to change types of fuel and require refineries to adjust the

Nixon Outlines 'Project Independence'

"We must . . . face up to a very stark fact: We are heading toward the most acute shortages of energy since World War II," President Nixon warned the nation in a televised address on Nov. 7, 1973, two weeks after the imposition of the Arab oil embargo.

"In the short run, this course means that we must use less energy. . . . In the long run, it means that we must develop new sources of energy which will give us the capacity to meet our needs without relying on any foreign nation," Nixon continued.

"Let us unite in committing the resources of this nation to a major new endeavor, an endeavor that in this bicentennial era we can appropriately call 'Project Independence,' " the president said. "Let us set as our national goal, in the spirit of Apollo, with the determination of the Manhattan Project, that by the end of this decade we will have developed the potential to meet our own energy needs without depending on any foreign energy sources. . . . We have an energy crisis, but there is no crisis of the American spirit."

The following day, Nixon sent a message to Congress announcing the administrative actions he had taken to deal with the crisis and asking Congress to:

● Authorize restrictions on public and private consumption of energy.

● Authorize a national 50-mile-per-hour speed limit.

● Provide that steps taken under energy emergency authorities be exempted from the requirements of the National Environmental Policy Act.

● Give federal regulatory agencies emergency powers to adjust the operations of transport carriers to conserve fuel.

● Empower the Atomic Energy Commission to grant nuclear power plants temporary operating licenses for up to 18 months.

● Authorize full production from the Elk Hills Naval Petroleum Reserve and exploration and development of the other reserves, including the Alaskan reserve.

● Permit year-round establishment of daylight saving time.

● Authorize the president to order power plants and other installations to switch from using oil to using coal.

● Authorize the president to allocate and ration energy supplies.

● Provide additional authority for using funds from the federal highway program for mass transit capital improvements.

● Authorize the Federal Power Commission to suspend the wellhead price regulation of new natural gas during the energy emergency.

● Empower the president to exercise any authority contained in the Defense Production Act, the Economic Stabilization Act and the Export Administration Act, even though those acts may have otherwise expired.

To move toward the long-term goal of energy independence, Nixon requested congressional action to:

● Authorize construction of the Alaskan oil pipeline.

● Permit the competitive pricing of new natural gas.

● Set up a Department of Energy and Natural Resources.

● Simplify procedures for siting and approving electric energy facilities.

● Set up procedures for approving construction and operation of deepwater ports.

● Create an Energy Research and Development Administration to direct a $10 billion program designed to achieve energy self-sufficiency by 1980.

---

mix of products they manufactured. But — in a provision opposed by the administration — Congress retained for itself the power to block the implementation of such measures.

Senate Action

Senate Interior Committee Chairman Henry M. Jackson, D-Wash., introduced S 2589 Oct. 18. After two closed-door sessions with White House Energy Policy Office Director John A. Love, an 11-hour hearing the day after Nixon's address and two mark-up sessions, the bill was amended and reported Nov. 13 by the Interior Committee (S Rept 93-489).

S 2589 required the president to issue within 15 days regulations for rationing and conserving fuel supplies. Within 10 days after being implemented, the regulations would have to result in a 10 percent reduction in con-

sumption; within four weeks, consumption would have to be cut by 25 percent. The bill granted the president much of the emergency authority he requested in his speech, but gave Congress 15 days to disapprove the exercise of these powers.

The Senate Nov. 19 passed S 2589 by a 78-6 vote. The most controversial amendment dealt with imposition of gasoline rationing. Sen. Floyd K. Haskell, D-Colo., proposed that rationing be put into effect by Jan. 15, 1974. His amendment was rejected, 40-48. Opponents, including the Nixon administration, had argued that rationing should be used only as a last resort.

Before passing the bill, the Senate did make several major changes. Among them were amendments allowing the relaxation of clean air standards during the energy emergency, deleting the authorization for producing oil from the naval reserves, providing unemployment benefits for persons laid off because of fuel shortages and providing some defense against charges of antitrust violations by persons or companies working together to comply with the emergency energy program.

House Action

The House Commerce Committee Dec. 7 reported its version of the energy emergency measure (HR 11450 — H Rept 93-710), making clear its intent to preserve a strong congressional role in the exercise of these emergency powers.

The committee's bill set up a Federal Energy Administration to administer the fuel allocation program and other federal energy programs. The agency was directed to submit within 30 days energy conservation plans to Congress for its approval. The bill also allowed some easing of clean air standards during the emergency, prohibited any major fuel-burning installation from using oil or natural gas if it could use coal and restricted windfall profits by fuel sellers by providing for hearings by the Renegotiation Board on suspected excess profits.

After three days of debate, the House Dec. 15 passed the Energy Emergency Act, 265-112. Sixty-four amendments were considered during debate on the measure; 37 were adopted. Some members criticized the bill for giving the president too much power; others for giving him too little. Since there was no national energy policy, said Richard T. Hanna, D-Calif., House members working on this bill were "like a bunch of blind men trying to put together a jigsaw puzzle in the bottom of a sack in the middle of the night."

The House rejected an amendment that would have replaced the requirement for congressional approval of energy plans with a weaker provision giving Congress 15 days to veto a presidential proposal. It also adopted an amendment requiring the president to submit any rationing proposals to Congress for final approval.

The excess profits provision was the target of a number of amendment efforts. In the major vote on this issue, the House rejected, 188-213, an amendment that would have permitted the president to define reasonable profits, to propose regulation of excess profits and to give industry incentives to reinvest profits in research and exploration. The amendment would have eliminated the role of the Renegotiation Board.

Proposals to suspend environmental protection standards during the energy crisis — in particular those controlling auto emissions — provoked some of the hottest debate on the bill. The House refused to suspend clean air requirements altogether during the emergency, but did agree to postpone the effective date for some of them. On a vote of 180-210 (D 78-137; R 102-73) the House Dec. 14 rejected an amendment proposed by Louis C. Wyman, R-N.H., to suspend auto emission controls until Jan. 1, 1977, or whenever the president said the fuel shortages were over. This was the most far-reaching of proposals to relax these standards.

Conference Action

Conferees reached agreement Dec. 20 after a week of intense negotiations; the conference report (S Rept 93-663) was not available as the House and Senate attempted to complete action on the bill before adjournment. On the major point of controversy, conferees retained the House windfall profits provisions and added language directing the president to set prices for crude oil and oil products which would avoid windfall profits. The conference version of the bill gave Congress a veto over energy conservation plans proposed before July 1, 1974, and required its affirmative approval of plans proposed after that date.

Senate Debate. Oil state senators, led by Russell B. Long, D-La., and Paul J. Fannin, R-Ariz., expressed their opposition to the windfall profits language by a filibuster against the conference version of S 2589. When Senate leaders attempted to bring it up for consideration Dec. 21, Long argued that the Finance Committee, of which he was chairman, should have held hearings on the provision. Fannin argued that the language would inhibit the industry's search for new sources of oil.

While the Senate voted three times to reject a motion to recommit the bill with instructions to add language barring shipments of oil for military operations in Southeast Asia, Senate leaders met in the cloakroom and drafted a compromise version of S 2589, omitting the windfall profits section. The Senate then agreed to tack this compromise on to S 921, a non-controversial wild and scenic rivers bill already approved by the House. The compromise was approved Dec. 21, 52-8.

House Debate. A confused and angry House took up the compromise measure late on Dec. 21. Commerce Committee Chairman Harley O. Staggers, D-W.Va., expressed outrage at the Senate action on windfall profits: "The Senate considers the House . . . its doormat." Instead of considering the compromise attached to S 921, Staggers first offered a substitute bill which consisted of the conference version of S 2589 with a modified windfall profits provision. He moved that the House suspend the rules and approved the substitute bill. The motion failed by seven votes to obtain the two-thirds majority needed for approval. The vote was 169-95; 176 votes were needed. The House then defeated 22-240, a Staggers motion that it approve the conference version without a windfall profits section.

The final vote came early on Saturday morning, Dec. 22, the last day of the 1973 session. Staggers moved that the House suspend its rules and accept the Senate compromise, an action which would have sent S 921 to the White House. The motion failed utterly on a vote of 36-228 (R 28-79; D 8-149). Congress then adjourned without further efforts to pass the energy emergency bill. The bill was eventually cleared in 1974 and then vetoed by Nixon.

Highway Speed Limit

Congress late in December gave final approval to a measure (HR 11372 — PL 93-239) lowering the maximum speed limit on the nation's highways to 55 miles per hour until June 30, 1975.

President Nixon Nov. 7 had asked Congress to empower him to set a nationwide speed limit of 50 miles per hour. After protests by truckers that their vehicles would operate less efficiently at the lower speed, Nixon amended his request to allow truckers to operate at 55 miles per hour.

As approved by Congress, PL 93-239 used the leverage of federal highway funds to persuade states to lower their speed limits to 55 miles per hour for all vehicles. Advocates of the measure said it would save 130,000 to 165,000 barrels of gasoline each day.

Nixon Pushed to End Controls on Gas Prices

Despite the boost of administration support, the oil and gas industry push for an end to federal regulation of natural gas prices did not move past the hearing stage in Congress in 1973.

The Senate Commerce Committee held hearings in October and November on a Nixon administration proposal (S 2408, HR 7507) to end price regulation for all newly discovered gas.

Administration and industry officials argued that deregulation would give the industry new incentive to explore and develop new sources of natural gas. They warned that the nation's reserves of this fuel were shrinking and that a shortage was likely.

Consumer-oriented witnesses expressed skepticism about the validity of any shortage, questioning the industry-supplied estimates of natural gas reserves and the effectiveness of price increases as a spur to exploration.

Senators did get a chance to vote on gas deregulation during floor action on another energy bill. They rejected deregulation by a margin of two votes.

Background

Since 1954, the Federal Power Commission (FPC) had regulated the wellhead price of natural gas sold outside the state in which it is produced. In that year the Supreme Court ruled, to the dismay of gas producers, that Congress had granted the FPC this price control authority as part of the Natural Gas Act of 1938 *(Phillips Petroleum Co. v. Wisconsin)*.

Gas sold within the state of its production was not subject to federal regulation and could be sold at whatever price the market would bear.

Just two years after the Supreme Court decision, oil and gas producers won passage of a bill ending this regulation.

But after Sen. Francis R. Case, R-S.D. (1951-62), disclosed that he had been offered campaign funds — an offer he regarded as a bribe in return for a vote for deregulation — by an oil company attorney, President Eisenhower vetoed the bill, which he otherwise approved.

This scandal caused Congress to shy away from deregulation measures in later years.

Natural gas is the cleanest of the nation's fossil fuels and, due to federal regulation, it was the cheapest as well through the 1960s and 1970s.

Not surprisingly, consumption of natural gas increased steadily, particularly in the industrial sector, as environmental awareness enhanced the attractiveness of this cheap, pollution-free fuel.

By 1973, natural gas accounted for 32 percent of the energy consumed in the United States. But five years earlier, in 1968, the rate at which new reserves of natural gas were discovered had begun to fall behind the rate of their consumption. From 1966 to 1973, the nation's reserves of natural gas decreased by 20 percent.

In 1972, the FPC moved to encourage exploration, adopting an optional pricing procedure that allowed certain gas to be sold at more than the regulated price. Gas drilling began to increase.

In April 1973, President Nixon asked Congress to end FPC control over the price of natural gas from new wells, gas newly dedicated to interstate sales and gas from old wells, once the existing contract for its sale expired. Nixon re-emphasized this request in his Project Independence message to Congress later in the year.

Hearings

Interior Secretary Rogers C. B. Morton, White House Energy Office chief John A. Love, and FPC Chairman John N. Nassikas testified in favor of the administration proposal at the Commerce Committee hearings. Love pointed out that the low price for natural gas — 22 cents as compared to 72 cents for an equivalent amount of domestic oil — was contributing to its increasingly inefficient use by industry. Morton noted that the administration bill would retain for the Interior Department the power to set price ceilings to keep the natural gas prices from rising too sharply.

Testifying in favor of immediate deregulation, rather than the gradual process envisioned by the administration, were five Republican senators from producing states: John G. Tower of Texas, Paul J. Fannin of Arizona, Clifford P. Hansen of Wyoming, and Dewey F. Bartlett and Henry Bellmon, both from Oklahoma.

David S. Schwartz, assistant chief of the FPC office of economics, and James T. Halverson, director of the Federal Trade Commission's (FTC) bureau of competition, cast doubt on the assumptions underlying the deregulation proposals. Schwartz said that the oil and gas industry was insufficiently competitive to keep prices down to a reasonable level, without continued regulation. He warned that deregulation in a time of shortages would result in skyrocketing prices for gas and other fuels.

Floor Vote

Though the committees with jurisdiction over natural gas pricing did not send legislation to the floor, the question came up in the Senate during action on the proposal (S 2776) for a Federal Energy Administration. Sen. James L. Buckley, Cons. R-N.Y., offered as an amendment the Nixon administration's gas deregulation plan. The Senate narrowly rejected the amendment, voting 45-43 to table it.

Daylight Saving Time

Congress in December approved an administration request to institute year-round daylight saving time (HR 11324 — PL 93-182). President Nixon included this proposal in his Nov. 7 energy message. Officials estimated that the time change could save 2 to 3 percent in fuel consumption a year. PL 93-182 provided for year-round daylight saving time through the winters of 1973-74 and 1974-75.

1974

Highlights

Energy Reorganization

Two new energy agencies were created. The Federal Energy Administration (FEA) was set up to manage federal efforts to deal with energy shortages (PL 93-275). Responsibilities included allocation of oil, gathering of energy data, conservation programs and, from a separate law (PL 93-319), programs to require utilities to burn coal.

Another bill, the Energy Reorganization Act (PL 93-438), established the Energy Research and Development Administration (ERDA), which consolidated all federal energy research in one agency. The Atomic Energy Commission (AEC), which had handled nuclear power development, was abolished and its regulatory functions assumed by a new Nuclear Regulatory Commission (NRC).

Energy Research

To emphasize its support of all energy sources, not just nuclear power, Congress passed the Federal Non-Nuclear Energy Research and Development Act (PL 93-577). The law called for a decade-long, $20 billion investment in conservation, solar energy, geothermal, liquids from coal and a variety of other energy sources.

Highway Speed Limit

Congress made permanent the national highway speed limit of 55 miles per hour, a rate first set in 1973. The provision was included in a law (PL 93-643) continuing federal aid to highways.

Daylight Saving Time

In response to public complaints about year-round daylight saving time, Congress approved legislation (PL 93-434) restoring standard time for the months of November, December, January and February.

Oil Allocation and Pricing

Congress extended for six months the Emergency Petroleum Allocation Act of 1973 (PL 93-159), which authorized the president to control the allocation and pricing of oil and oil products. The expiration date was extended from Feb. 28 to Aug. 31, 1975.

Geothermal Energy

Confident that the heat trapped beneath the earth's surface could be tapped commercially, Congress authorized federal loan guarantees of up to $50 million to utilities and private industry for development of electricity from geothermal energy (PL 93-410).

Solar Research and Demonstration

The Solar Energy Research, Development and Demonstration Act (PL 93-473) called for a broad federal program of research into and commercialization of solar energy, with $75 million authorized for fiscal 1976 to plan and begin the program. Demonstration projects costing up to $20 million were authorized. Also established was a Solar Energy Research Institute (SERI). Another solar law (PL 93-409) authorized a five-year, $60 million program to demonstrate the feasibility of heating and cooling buildings with solar energy.

Deepwater Ports

By approving a licensing procedure, Congress cleared the way for construction and operation of deepwater ports in international waters off U.S. coasts. The ports were to receive huge oil tankers too large for all but two existing U.S. ports. The Deepwater Port Act (PL 93-627) authorized the transportation secretary to issue licenses if environmental specifications were met and if adjacent coastal states did not object.

Energy Emergency Act

Unhappy with its low ceilings on oil prices, President Nixon in March vetoed the Energy Emergency Act (S 2589), which contained many presidential powers he had earlier requested. He also labeled unworkable its provisions giving unemployment benefits to workers who lost their jobs because of energy shortages.

Strip Mining

Conflicts between energy and environmental concerns were to confront Congress again and again. In 1974, President Ford pocket-vetoed legislation (S 425) setting minimum environmental standards to be followed in the strip mining of coal. The coal industry had opposed the bill.

The Year in Review

Reorganization of the federal energy bureaucracy was the major energy-related accomplishment of the second session of the 93rd Congress.

By mid-1974, Congress had agreed to set up a new Federal Energy Administration (FEA) to manage federal efforts to cope with fuel shortages. It was expected to be a temporary agency.

Later in the year, the legislators unified many federal energy research programs in a new Energy Research and Development Administration (ERDA). Nuclear research, formerly handled by the Atomic Energy Commission, was combined with research on other sources, such as coal and solar, which previously had been scattered among various agencies.

The Atomic Energy Commission (AEC) was abolished, and its responsibility for regulating the nuclear power industry was given to a new body, the Nuclear Regulatory

Commission (NRC). All three agencies — FEA, ERDA and NRC — officially opened their doors in January 1975.

Though the bulk of ERDA's funds and personnel were to come from AEC, Congress wanted to emphasize that work on other sources of energy was equally important. In a sweeping policy statement, Congress declared a commitment to a decade-long, $20 billion effort to develop non-nuclear energy, such as that from heat trapped underground, the sun, shale, coal and even garbage.

The Arab oil embargo was lifted in March 1974 and, with its end, the sense of crisis vanished. The Energy Emergency Act, left dangling at the end of the 1973 session, was finally cleared in February, only to die of a veto in March. Efforts to revive it failed.

Congress did extend several other measures initially adopted during the embargo — among them the 55-mile-per-hour speed limit and the emergency fuel allocation system. It also cleared a measure authorizing the construction of deepwater ports to receive the supertankers loaded with imported oil for the United States.

New Energy Agencies

Congress in 1974 set up two new agencies as it reorganized the federal energy structure.

In May President Nixon signed a measure (HR 11973 — PL 93-275) creating a temporary Federal Energy Administration (FEA) to manage federal efforts to deal with fuel shortages. The FEA replaced the Federal Energy Office, which Nixon had created late in 1973.

In October, President Ford signed a second reorganization measure (HR 11510 — PL 93-438). The Energy Reorganization Act of 1974 created a new Energy Research and Development Administration (ERDA) to direct federal research into the better use of existing fuels and the development of new sources of energy. ERDA took over most of the functions of the old Atomic Energy Commission, which was abolished by PL 93-438, plus programs from the Interior Department, the National Science Foundation and the Environmental Protection Agency.

Federal Energy Administration

The agency created by the Federal Energy Administration Act was less powerful than Nixon had proposed. Rather than giving it broad authority to deal with the problems of energy shortages, Congress limited FEA powers to those specifically granted by law.

The Senate had approved its FEA bill (S 2776 — S Rept 93-634) on Dec. 19, 1973, by an 86-2 vote. To provide a data base for energy policy decisions, S 2776 directed the FEA to undertake a massive energy information-gathering effort. The bill provided for public disclosure of much of this information and directed the General Accounting Office to monitor the new agency's operations.

Also in 1973, the House had approved provisions setting up a federal energy agency, but they were attached to the emergency energy bill, which was bogged down in controversy. As a result, another bill, drafted by the Government Operations Committee, emerged as the primary House reorganization measure. The bill (HR 11793 — H Rept 93-748) was reported Dec. 28, and gave the proposed FEA a wide range of enumerated powers — to stimulate energy development, to control excess profits and to impose energy conservation programs.

Nixon Reorganization Plan

President Nixon had in 1973 proposed a comprehensive reorganization of executive branch energy functions.

Nixon's proposal had three parts:

● To administer federal efforts to cope with energy shortages, he asked Congress to create a Federal Energy Administration empowered to take all actions its chief deemed necessary to meet the nation's energy requirements. Nixon signed the FEA bill in May 1974.

● To spearhead the federal energy research effort, Nixon asked Congress to unify the energy research and development units of the Atomic Energy Commission (AEC), the Interior Department, the Environmental Protection Agency (EPA) and the National Science Foundation (NSF) in an Energy Research and Development Administration (ERDA). President Ford signed the ERDA bill in October 1974.

● To unify the other federal energy and resource units scattered throughout the government, Nixon revived his proposed Department of Natural Resources — which had received scant attention when first proposed in 1971 — and asked Congress to create a Cabinet Department of Energy and Natural Resources, replacing the Interior Department. But this proposal never got to the floor of either chamber.

The House passed HR 11793 March 7, 353-29. The Senate approved the bill March 13 after amending it to substitute the text of S 2776.

Final Action

Conferees filed their report on HR 11793 (H Rept 93-999) April 23, emphasizing the short-term nature of the new agency and the circumscribed nature of its powers. The life of the agency was scheduled to end June 30, 1976.

The House adopted the report April 29, 356-9. The Senate adopted it by voice vote May 2, clearing the bill for President Nixon who signed it May 7.

Provisions

As signed into law, the major provisions of PL 93-275:

● Established a Federal Energy Administration (FEA) to manage short-term fuel shortages.

● Made the agency's administrator, two deputy administrators, six assistant administrators and general counsel subject to Senate confirmation.

● Granted the administrator authority to take actions delegated to him by Congress or the president under specific laws. PL 93-275 also granted specific powers, including authority to develop plans for dealing with energy short-

Two Narrow Defeats For Oil Price Controls

In both the House and Senate, energy reorganization legislation (HR 11793) attracted amendments from advocates of price controls on oil.

The Senate in December 1973 narrowly rejected an effort to place a ceiling both on the cost to consumers of oil and oil products and on the oil industry's profits during the energy emergency. Walter F. Mondale, D-Minn., proposed an amendment limiting the price of gasoline and other petroleum products to an amount equal to the actual increase in the cost of producing them. The amendment was tabled, and thus killed, on a 47-44 vote. Ten Republicans and 34 Democrats went along with Mondale.

Debate over oil price controls also dominated House consideration of the FEA legislation. John D. Dingell, D-Mich., led the fight to salvage the price control provisions of the Energy Emergency Act (S 2589).

That bill was vetoed by President Nixon March 6, 1974, and the Senate voted the same day to sustain the veto. But later on March 6, Dingell offered an amendment to the FEA bill that would have rolled back the price of most domestic oil to $5.25 a barrel.

Dingell was scathing in his criticism of the "scandalous level" to which oil prices had risen and the "grotesque and outrageous profits" thus generated for the oil industry. Opponents of the amendment said it would guarantee a presidential veto for HR 11793.

The Dingell amendment was modified by Bob Eckhardt, D-Texas, to exempt from price controls those producing up to 30,000 barrels per day of new oil. Eckhardt said this would encourage small independent oil producers to continue searching for and developing new sources.

The House approved the price control amendment March 6, 218-175 (R 61-115; D 157-60), but reversed itself the following day, rejecting the amendment, 163-216 (R 34-136; D 129-80). Fifty members evenly divided between the two parties switched from support to opposition, including a sizable number of freshmen and Southern Democrats.

ages, to prevent unreasonable profits in the energy industry and to impose mandatory energy savings measures.

● Transferred to the new agency from the Interior Department the offices of petroleum allocation, energy conservation, energy data and analysis, and oil and gas. The energy division of the Cost of Living Council also was transferred to the new agency.

● Gave the Cost of Living Council five days to approve or disapprove proposed actions dealing with energy prices.

● Gave the Environmental Protection Agency five days

to comment on, but not veto, energy policies which could affect environmental quality.

● Provided for judicial review of agency actions.

● Gave the agency's administrator and the General Accounting Office (GAO) authority to compel energy suppliers or major energy consumers to produce information.

● Directed the GAO to monitor and evaluate the agency's actions.

● Directed the administrator to provide access for the public to all information except that which could be excluded from public reports to the Securities and Exchange Commission.

● Directed the president to report to Congress six months before the act expired on 1) his recommendations for a permanent federal energy organization and 2) whether the FEA should be continued, terminated or reorganized.

● Directed the FEA administrator to report within one year of enactment on the nation's oil and gas reserves and annually on the FEA's activities and on estimates of the nation's future energy supplies.

● Directed the administrator to submit a comprehensive energy plan within six months of enactment.

● Required the administrator to conduct a comprehensive review of foreign ownership of domestic energy sources and supplies.

● Authorized appropriation of $75 million for fiscal 1974 and $200 million for each of fiscal 1975-76.

● Provided that the act would expire June 30, 1976.

Energy Research and Development

Congress in 1974 created a new billion-dollar agency to take the lead in research and development of new energy sources. President Ford Oct. 11 signed a measure (HR 11510 — PL 93-438) creating an Energy Research and Development Administration (ERDA) expected to have a budget of $2.6 billion in 1975 and a staff of more than 7,000 employees.

Ford had labeled the bill his top-priority energy measure; he signed it the day after Congress completed work on it.

ERDA took over the nuclear power development functions of the Atomic Energy Commission (AEC), which was abolished by PL 93-438. A new Nuclear Regulatory Commission was created by the bill to take over AEC's safety and regulatory responsibilities.

The bulk of ERDA's budget ($2.2 billion) and staff (6,000) was to come from the AEC. Yet, the new agency was oriented more toward energy conservation, environmental protection and nuclear safety than President Nixon had initially proposed. When the House considered the bill in December 1973, it rejected all but one of a series of amendments attempting to broaden the agency's focus beyond nuclear power. But the Senate and conferees included language designed to encourage a broad approach. In addition to the AEC programs, ERDA acquired fossil fuel energy research programs from the Interior Department and geothermal and solar energy development programs from the National Science Foundation.

Senate Action

The Senate passed its version of the ERDA bill (S 2774 — S Rept 93-980) by voice vote Aug. 15 after unanimously agreeing to incorporate in the bill the bulk of another bill (S 1283) calling for a 10-year, $20 billion nonnuclear energy research and development program. The Senate had passed S 1283 in December 1973.

A number of provisions designed to ensure fair representation of and funding for non-nuclear energy programs were inserted in the bill by the Senate Government Operations Committee, which reported it June 27. These included the requirements that the ERDA administrators be generalists, that separate energy conservation and safety programs be set up and that no energy program receive less than 7 percent of ERDA's annual funds.

In addition to the inclusion of language calling for the massive non-nuclear energy research program to balance the AEC's nuclear programs that ERDA would receive, the Senate bill differed from the House measure in abolishing the AEC, rather than simply renaming it, and in creating a new regulatory body called the Nuclear Safety and Licensing Commission. The Senate bill did not transfer to ERDA Environmental Protection Agency (EPA) programs to develop a low-pollution automobile engine and technology to control pollution from power and industrial plants. But it did create a Council on Energy Policy in the White House, an administration-opposed step that the Senate had approved three times in 1973.

The Senate also amended its ERDA bill to provide that the nation would return to standard time, from daylight saving time, for the period from late October 1974 through February 1975. Congress in 1973 had provided that the nation would be on daylight saving time year-round until April 1975. Only a small amount of energy had been saved by this move, said Robert Taft Jr., R-Ohio, the sponsor of the amendment, while the lives of small children were endangered as they walked to school in the dark.

Final Action

Conferees filed their report on the bill (H Rept 93-1445) Oct. 8.

They dropped from the final version the non-nuclear research programs added on the Senate floor, explaining that legislation containing such provisions (S 1283) was already in conference with a similar House bill (HR 13565).

Otherwise, the conference version of the bill resembled that approved by the Senate. Conferees compromised by agreeing to language abolishing the AEC and creating a new structure for a new Nuclear Regulatory Commission, and by transferring part of the EPA automobile engine research program to ERDA.

Conferees dropped the Senate provision for a White House Council on Energy Policy, the Senate language requiring a basic 7 percent share of ERDA funds for each energy program and the daylight saving time repeal. Congress Sept. 30 had cleared legislation (HR 16102 — PL 93-434) returning the nation to standard time for the four winter months.

The House adopted the conference report on HR 11510 Oct. 9 by a vote of 372-1. The Senate cleared the bill Oct. 10 by voice vote.

Provisions

As signed into law, the major provisions of PL 93-438:

ERDA Establishment

● Established an Energy Research and Development Administration (ERDA) within 120 days of enactment of PL 93-438.

● Provided that the ERDA administrator, deputy ad-

ministrator and six assistant administrators be appointed by the president and confirmed by the Senate.

● Established six program areas, one under each of the assistant administrators, for fossil energy, nuclear energy, environment and safety, energy conservation, solar, geothermal and advanced energy systems, and nuclear weapons programs.

● Required the administrator and his deputy to be specifically qualified to manage the full range of energy research and development programs; prohibited appointment of military officers to either position until two years after retirement.

Program Transfers

● Abolished the Atomic Energy Commission (AEC) and transferred all of its functions, except licensing, regulation and safety, to ERDA. Regulatory functions were transferred to the Nuclear Regulatory Commission.

● Transferred to ERDA from the Interior Department the programs of the Office of Coal Research, the fossil

---

Additional FEA Powers

The Federal Energy Administration (FEA) was granted additional powers and responsibilities later in 1974 when Congress passed the Energy Supply and Environmental Coordination Act (HR 14368 — PL 93-319). A major new goal for the agency was to encourage utilities to use coal.

Many of the act's provisions had been part of the ill-fated Energy Emergency Act. But when the issue of oil price controls appeared to doom that bill (S 2589), the section on FEA was split off into a separate measure (HR 14368).

Along with the FEA powers, the act also delayed certain clean air standards.

For FEA, the act provided authority to prohibit the burning of oil or natural gas by utility power plants capable of using coal. The agency was directed to allocate coal, if necessary, to those plants ordered to make the switch. Congress also directed FEA to require that new power plants be designed to burn coal.

The measure also:

● Directed FEA to report to Congress within six months on the potential for energy conservation.

● Directed the transportation secretary to recommend within 90 days a plan for saving energy by improving public transportation.

● Ordered the FEA administrator and the transportation secretary to report within 120 days on the feasibility of requiring a 20 percent improvement in new car mileage by 1980.

● Directed FEA to gather and make public any information considered necessary in order to make energy policy decisions and gave the agency subpoena power to obtain that information.

fuel research of the Bureau of Mines and underground electric transmission research.

● Transferred to ERDA from the National Science Foundation (NSF) the geothermal and solar heating and cooling development programs. NSF retained control of basic research on the conversion of solar energy for generating electricity from central power stations.

● Transferred to ERDA from the Environmental Protection Agency (EPA) authority for research and development of an alternative automobile power system. EPA would retain research authority related to monitoring and control of air pollution from automobiles.

Energy Policy Coordination

● Established in the White House a temporary Energy Resources Council to ensure coordination among federal energy agencies and to advise the president and Congress.

● Directed that the council be composed of the secretary of interior, the federal energy administrator, the ERDA administrator, the secretary of state, the director of the Office of Management and Budget and other federal officials.

● Provided that the council would terminate upon creation of a permanent department for energy or natural resources or within two years, whichever occurred sooner.

Nuclear Safety

● Established a five-member Nuclear Regulatory Commission, appointed by the president, to take over the AEC's safety, licensing and regulatory powers.

● Created an Office of Nuclear Reactor Regulation and an Office of Nuclear Regulatory Research.

● Upgraded the AEC's regulatory division into an Office of Nuclear Material Safety and Safeguards.

● Made the safety office responsible for protecting commercial facilities against threats, sabotage or theft of nuclear materials.

● Directed the office's director to make a study and report on whether the office should establish a security force to protect facilities and fuels.

● Required employees of firms regulated by the commission to report immediately to the commission any violation of the Atomic Energy Act or any cases of facilities having a safety defect that could create a substantial safety hazard.

● Directed the commission to report quarterly to Congress on any abnormal occurrences at licensed nuclear facilities; such incidents would have to be reported to the public within 15 days of an occurrence.

Future Energy Reorganization

● Directed the president to report to Congress by June 30, 1975, his recommendations for further reorganization of federal energy activities.

Non-Nuclear Energy Research

Nuclear energy had benefitted for years from federal dollars, but Congress was dissatisfied with the limited funding given to other energy sources. To bring a better balance to federal energy programs, Congress in 1974 approved legislation (S 1283 — PL 93-577) calling for a decade-long program of non-nuclear energy research and development.

The act established broad policy guidelines for research and development in non-nuclear energy to parallel the nuclear energy policy established by the Atomic Energy Act of 1954 (PL 83-703). The law declared that the nation's energy problems required federal investment of $20 billion over a 10-year period to develop non-nuclear energy. However, no specific plan for spending the money was provided.

Among the activities expected to receive the aid were efforts to develop energy from garbage, improve automobile efficiency, tap geothermal energy, make liquid fuels from coal and generate power from the sun.

The administrator of the new Energy Research and Development Administration (ERDA) was directed to send Congress by mid-1975 a comprehensive plan for meeting the nation's energy needs in the short-term (through the early 1980s), the mid-term (through the year 2000) and the long-term (beyond the year 2000). Annual updates were required.

The Nixon administration opposed the legislation as unnecessary, but the executive branch reversed its position under President Ford. The Senate approved the measure in December 1973, and the House passed its version in September 1974. After final action in December, Ford signed the Federal Non-Nuclear Energy Research and Development Act of 1974.

Senate Action

The Senate bill (S 1283 — S Rept 93-589), approved Dec. 7, 1973, by an 82-0 vote, focused immediate efforts on coal, the nation's most abundant fossil fuel. The legislation called for federal research on improving methods for mining coal and for turning coal into gas-like and oil-like "synthetic" fuels. Emphasis was placed on government-industry cooperation to demonstrate the commercial feasibility of new energy sources, such as underground heat (geothermal), oil shale (from rocks) and synthetic fuels.

House Action

The House Sept. 11 approved its version (HR 13565 — H Rept 93-1157) by a 327-7 vote. Though the Interior Committee had written specific authorizations into the bill, the full House replaced those with a statement of congressional finding that $20 billion should be invested in non-nuclear programs over the next decade. The change resolved a jurisdictional fight between the Interior panel and the Science Committee.

During floor action, Craig Hosmer, R-Calif., unsuccessfully offered more than a dozen amendments, most of them aimed at de-emphasizing the role to be played in the program by energy conservation and environmental considerations. Hosmer was the ranking Republican on the Interior Committee.

Conference Action

Conferees Dec. 11 filed their report (H Rept 93-1563). The most difficult issue facing them had been the patent policy to cover the technologies developed under S 1283. The administration objected to Senate language requiring the federal government to retain the rights to all the technologies and to license them on a non-exclusive basis. The House bill called for a study and report on the adequacy of existing patent law. Conferees modeled the final patent provisions on policy governing work done for the National Aeronautics and Space Administration, similar to the Senate language but less restrictive.

Early Message Outlined
Nixon's 1974 Energy Program

In an effort to spur Congress to deal with the energy crisis, President Nixon broke tradition to send his 1974 energy message to Congress Jan. 23, 1974, even before the State of the Union message. "No single legislative area is more critical or more challenging to us as a people," the president said.

Nixon set out a long list of measures he requested Congress to approve. Among them were:

● A special energy emergency act permitting restrictions on private and public consumption of energy and temporary relaxation of Clean Air Act requirements for power plants and automobile emissions.

● A windfall profits tax to prevent private profiteering from raising fuel prices.

● Unemployment insurance to help persons losing jobs because of the energy crisis.

● Establishment of a Federal Energy Administration.

● A requirement that major energy producers provide a full and constant account to the government of their inventories, production and reserves.

In addition to these short-term measures, Nixon asked Congress to approve:

● Deregulation of the price of new discoveries of natural gas.

● Temporary production of oil from the Elk Hills reserve.

● Legislation permitting coal surface mining in an environmentally safe manner.

● Legislation allowing construction and operation of deepwater ports.

● Expansion of the investment tax credit for all exploratory oil and gas drilling.

● Revision and consolidation of federal mineral leasing laws.

● Establishment of an Energy Research and Development Administration and a Department of Energy and Natural Resources.

● Elimination of the tax depletion allowance for foreign oil and gas resources developed by U.S. companies, but retention of the allowance for domestic oil and gas resources.

● Acceleration of the procedure for licensing and building nuclear power plants.

● A requirement for energy efficiency labeling of products.

● Streamlining of site selection procedures for energy facilities.

Nixon said he had ordered acceleration of federal leasing of outer continental shelf oil and gas resources, with plans to lease 10 million acres in 1975. He reported that the administration would act quickly on proposals to build the Alaska oil pipeline, study what incentives might be needed to encourage domestic production of synthetic fuels and propose increased federal aid for mass transit and energy research.

In his September 1974 message to Congress on legislative priorities, President Ford endorsed Nixon's proposals for creation of the Energy Research and Development Administration; deregulation of new natural gas; authorization of deepwater port construction; passage of energy tax changes relating to windfall profits, tax depletion and foreign tax credit provisions affecting oil companies, and approval of production of oil from Elk Hills.

Final Action

The House Dec. 16 adopted the conference report by a 378-5 vote. The Senate cleared the bill for the president Dec. 17, adopting the conference report by a vote of 91-1.

Provisions

As signed into law, the major provisions of PL 93-577:

● Declared that the nation's energy problems required a 10-year federal investment of $20 billion for non-nuclear energy research and development.

● Made it the policy of Congress to develop on an urgent basis the technological capability to support the broadest range of energy policy choices through conservation and the use of domestic energy resources in socially and environmentally acceptable ways.

● Emphasized that the research and development programs should give primary consideration to energy conservation, environmental protection, development of renewable resources and water requirements of new technologies.

● Directed that the program should 1) facilitate the commercial development of adequate energy supplies for all regions of the United States; 2) consider the urgency of the public need for the technologies supported; 3) ensure that the problems treated had national significance and 4) direct federal support to areas which might not attract private capital.

Planning and Programming

● Directed the ERDA administrator to send to Congress by June 30, 1975, a comprehensive plan and program designed to solve short-term energy problems through the early 1980s; middle-term problems through the year 2000; and long-range problems beyond the year 2000.

● Specified that non-nuclear aspects of the plan should focus on 1) agricultural and other wastes; 2) the reuse and recycling of materials; 3) improved efficiency of automobile engines and 4) improvement in the design of homes and buildings.

● Directed that the research program also stress the development of low-sulfur fuels; improved methods of producing and delivering electrical energy; the development of synthetic fuels from coal and oil shale; and improved methods for recovering petroleum.

Forms of Federal Assistance

● Authorized federal assistance in the form of joint federal-industry corporations; contracts; federal purchases or price guarantees of products from demonstration plants; loans to non-federal entities and incentives for inventors.

● Provided that joint government-industry corporations or price supports could not be implemented unless authorized by an act of Congress.

● Authorized the administrator to provide assistance for projects to demonstrate the commercial feasibility of new energy technologies.

● Limited to $50 million the amount of federal assistance that could be appropriated for any project without a specific authorization by Congress.

● Directed the administrator to report to Congress on any project for which the federal contribution exceeded $25 million.

Patent Policy

● Required that the federal government retain the rights to any technologies developed under the act and directed the government to grant licenses for use of technologies on a non-exclusive basis.

● Permitted a waiver of federal rights if such waiver would make the benefits of the technology quickly and widely available to the public; would promote the commercial use of the technology; would encourage participation of private persons in the energy research program; and would foster competition.

● Permitted the administrator to grant exclusive licenses for a technology if it promoted the interests of the general public; if the desired use of the technology had not occurred under a non-exclusive contract; or if an exclusive license was needed to encourage the investment of private risk capital in development of the technology.

● Prohibited the granting of an exclusive license if the grant tended to substantially lessen competition.

Environmental Evaluation

● Directed the Council on Environmental Quality to evaluate the application of non-nuclear energy technologies supported under the act for their adequacy of attention to energy conservation and environmental protection.

● Directed the Water Resources Council, at the request of the ERDA administrator, to assess the water resource requirements and the availability of water for energy technologies which were supported under the act.

Reports to Congress

● Directed the administrator to send to Congress each year at the time the president's budget was submitted a report on the activities supported during the previous fiscal year and a detailed description of the nuclear and non-nuclear energy plan then in effect.

Authorizations

● Authorized annual appropriations of $500,000 for the environmental evaluation and $1,000,000 for the water resource evaluation.

Energy Emergency Act

The ill-fated Energy Emergency Act (S 2589) died a slow death in the first months of the 1974 session. The immediate cause of death was a presidential veto, complicated by a fading sense of crisis after the end of the Arab oil embargo in March.

In 1973, the measure — which gave the president special powers he had requested to control the production and consumption of energy in an emergency — had been approved by both chambers and a conference committee. But final action on the bill was stalled on the next-to-the-last day of the session when oil state senators filibustered against language that would have limited the profits made by oil companies from the "windfall" of skyrocketing oil prices.

In addition to the energy emergency powers and the windfall profits provisions, S 2589 also permitted a temporary loosening of clean air standards. When Congress reconvened in 1974, an unusual coalition formed in the Senate — oil-state senators and conservation-minded senators — to send the measure back to conference.

In February the Senate approved the second conference version, which substituted a ceiling on oil prices for the windfall profits provision. Both the Nixon administration and the oil industry opposed the price ceiling provisions. The House then cleared this version for the White House after forestalling a move to send the bill back to conference for a third time.

President Nixon vetoed the bill March 6, citing as particularly objectionable the price ceiling provisions and those providing unemployment benefits for workers losing their jobs because of energy shortages. The Senate sustained the veto, 58-40, the same day.

Revised versions of the energy emergency bill (HR 13834, S 3267) reached the House and Senate floors in May. But after the House refused to pass the bill, the effort to revive the measure died. The clean air provisions and those granting new powers to the Federal Energy Administration were enacted as separate legislation (HR 14368 — PL 93-319).

Senate Recommittal

The Senate Jan. 29, by a 57-37 roll-call vote (R 32-7; D 25-30), recommittal S 2589 to conference.

Supporters of the bill said "an unholy alliance" of senators was responsible for recommitting S 2589. Offered by Gaylord Nelson, D-Wis., recommittal motion brought together three groups: some conservation-minded senators — mostly Northern Democrats — who wanted less stringent modifications in the 1970 Clean Air Act's standards, oil state senators who wanted the windfall profits limitations expunged and backers of Nixon, who wanted everything dropped from the bill except the basic authority to impose rationing and conservation programs and provisions easing the federal clean air regulations.

Henry M. Jackson, D-Wash., floor manager of the conference report, declared the 57-37 vote "a victory for the oil industry."

Nelson, a member of the Finance Committee, asserted that enactment of the windfall profits section would play "a gigantic con game on the American people."

Nelson argued that the provision, as written into S 2589, was not a tax but rather a method to limit prices and provide for consumer appeals through the Renegotiation Board, which was created during the Korean War to recapture excess profits from the defense industry. Consumers could petition the board for a roll-back of prices and rebates of excessive profits, Nelson said. He contended that any of the nation's 220,000 service station operators could be hauled before the board if a customer complained.

Jackson defended the windfall profits provision, saying that it would serve as "a burr under the saddle" to get Congress to pass legislation dealing more effectively with excess profits in the oil industry.

Nelson criticized S 2589 for allowing a five-year delay in meeting air pollution standards. But Edmund S. Muskie, D-Maine, chairman of the Senate Public Works Subcommittee on Air and Water Pollution, argued that the conference provisions modifying the Clean Air Act were superior to those originally approved by the Senate.

Second Conference Action

Forced to reconvene by the Senate action, conferees wrote a second report (S Rept 93-681), filing it Feb. 6. Junking the windfall profits restriction, they replaced it with language setting the price of all domestic crude oil at $5.25 per barrel. "Meteoric increases" in oil prices had become "one of the most serious . . . aspects of the energy emergency," conferees asserted, pointing to the 150 percent increase from October to December 1973 in the price of the fuel oil used by electric utilities.

Regulators Ease
Gas Price Controls

Again in 1974, administration urging failed to propel natural gas deregulation measures (S 2408, HR 7507) beyond the committee hearing stage. But reports of a worsening shortage of this fuel kept the matter alive. In addition, the Federal Power Commission (FPC) moved boldly to revise and increase the price ceilings that the administration and industry sought to scrap.

President Ford told Congress Oct. 8 that deregulation to increase domestic energy supplies was his No. 1 energy priority. The Senate Commerce Committee, which began hearings on the issue in 1973, continued them early in 1974. Hearings resumed again in December after their staff had drafted a new bill that directed the FPC to set a flat and final price between 40 and 60 cents per thousand cubic feet (mcf) for new natural gas.

Interior Secretary Rogers C. B. Morton opposed the new bill as inadequate, saying that it "tries to regulate our way out of something we've regulated our way into." FPC Chairman John N. Nassikas agreed with Morton that deregulation would provide the necessary incentive to spur increased production, but he urged that the FPC be given authority to reimpose price ceilings if new gas supplies did not result from higher prices.

FPC Actions

Under Nassikas, selected by President Nixon in 1969 to head the FPC, that agency had already allowed prices to rise in the various areas, granting exemptions from price ceilings for small producers, for emergency sales and for producers who chose to use certain optional pricing alternatives.

On June 21, 1974, the FPC took its boldest step, abolishing the area rates and replacing them with a single nationwide rate of 42 cents per mcf for new gas. This was nearly double the maximum price allowed before 1969. The new rate had a built-in escalator of 1 percent per year. It applied to all gas sold from wells going into production after Jan. 1, 1973, and all gas contracted for interstate sales after that date. The new rate applied to onshore and offshore gas, and to oil-well as well as gas-well gas.

Six months later, in December, the FPC again raised the rate — to 50 cents per mcf — squarely in the middle of the range which the Commerce Committee draft measure prescribed.

The Intrastate Problem

But even this new higher price, argued proponents of deregulation, was not enough. Interstate gas purchasers still could not effectively compete with those in the unregulated intrastate market. A Library of Congress report issued in November bore out this fact. The percentage of gas production sold interstate had slipped from 55 percent in 1972 to 53.5 percent in 1973. Intrastate prices ranged between $1.00 and $1.25 per mcf and even as high as $2.00 per mcf.

"The fact is," concluded the study, "that the interstate market is losing out to the unregulated intrastate market. Notwithstanding, gas production as a whole has virtually not grown at all since 1969."

But the study was skeptical about the argument that deregulation and resulting price increases would spur production: "Our recent experience with oil may serve as a guide here. The price of new oil, that is, the incentive price for generating new production, has increased three-fold in the past year. Nevertheless, production continues to decline. Indeed, it is 700,000 barrels per day lower than it was a year ago."

The price ceiling adopted by conferees was that already imposed on 71 percent of all domestic crude oil by the Cost of Living Council, acting under the authority of the Economic Stabilization Act. Crude oil exempt from this ceiling — oil from new wells and oil from low-producing wells — was selling for about $10.35 per barrel, conferees said. It was the price of this exempt oil that would have to be rolled back. Conferees also included language in the bill allowing the president to increase the price of oil that was costly to produce — up to about $7.09 per barrel.

Conferees expanded the unemployment benefits provision to cover all workers losing their jobs because of energy shortages, not only those losing their jobs because of actions taken under S 2589.

The Senate Feb. 19 approved the second conference report by a 67-32 vote — just one more than the two-thirds majority needed to override the veto that Nixon threatened. Before adopting the report, the Senate, by votes of 38-60, 37-62 and 37-62, rejected efforts to send the bill back to conference to remove the price ceiling requirements.

The House Feb. 27 adopted the conference report by a 258-151 vote — 15 short of a two-thirds majority. Earlier, the House had forestalled the possible death of the bill — or a third conference — by agreeing to let the House vote separately on three controversial provisions. Usually on a conference report just one vote — to accept it or reject it — is allowed.

In subsequent votes, the House refused, 173-238, to delete the oil price ceiling from the bill and refused, 66-343, to delete language allowing Congress to veto presidential plans to conserve energy. The legislators also rejected, 199-211, a move to strike out language authorizing the president to impose rationing. On this last vote, and on final passage, the margin of victory was provided by Republicans, preserving the conference language despite administration and oil industry opposition.

Provisions

As sent to the president, key provisions of the Energy Emergency Act:

• Authorized the president to draft a rationing plan for oil and oil products, but provided that rationing be used to limit energy demands only if all other means failed.

• Set up a Federal Energy Emergency Administration and authorized its chief to implement energy conservation plans, to require power plants to use coal rather than oil or natural gas, to propose a means of allocating energy-related materials and to require maximum production from public and private oil fields.

• Provided Congress with the power to veto energy conservation plans proposed before Sept. 1, 1974, and required that subsequent conservation plans be approved by Congress.

• Directed the president to reduce to $5.25 per barrel the price of domestic crude oil presently exempt from price controls, allowing increases to $7.09 per barrel for domestic crude oil that cost more to produce.

• Authorized $500 million for grants to states to pay unemployment benefits to people losing their jobs due to fuel shortages.

• Postponed until 1977 the scheduled 1976 limits on automobile emissions of hydrocarbons and carbon monoxide mandated by the Clean Air Act; permitted the Environmental Protection Agency (EPA) to grant another year's delay; delayed to 1978 the standard for nitrogen oxide; authorized EPA to suspend until Nov. 1, 1974, fuel and emission standards for industrial and electrical facilities and waived those standards through Jan. 1, 1979, for facilities ordered to convert to use of coal.

• Exempted for one year actions taken under the act from the environmental impact statement requirement of the National Environmental Policy Act.

● Provided for expiration of these authorities and for termination of the Federal Energy Emergency Administration on May 15, 1975.

Veto

President Nixon March 6 vetoed the bill, saying that "after all the hearings and speeches, all the investigations, accusations and recriminations, the Congress has succeeded only in producing legislation which solves none of the problems, threatens to undo the progress we have already made and creates a host of new problems." Nixon said the price ceiling was so low that the oil industry would be unable to sustain its present level of production. Furthermore, the unemployment provisions were unworkable and inequitable, Nixon said.

Senate Action. The Senate that day sustained the veto, 58-40. Voting in support of the president were six senators who two weeks earlier had voted to adopt the conference report. They were Democrats John Sparkman of Alabama, J. Bennett Johnston Jr. and Russell B. Long, both of Louisiana, and John L. McClellan of Arkansas, along with Republicans Hugh Scott of Pennsylvania and James B. Pearson of Kansas.

In the debate preceding the vote, Jackson challenged the assumption that price and production were linked so closely. "In February 1973," he said, "the domestic oil industry was producing 9.4 million barrels of crude oil per day at an average price of $3.40. In February 1974 it produced 9.2 million barrels a day at an average price of $6.95. . . . Crude oil prices have doubled and crude oil production has not increased one whit."

Defenders of the veto argued that the price rollback would increase U.S. reliance on oil imports. "Every barrel of domestic oil that the industry cannot afford to produce at $5.25 . . . a barrel will be imported," said Paul J. Fannin, R-Ariz. A vote to override the veto, said Dewey F. Bartlett, R-Okla, would be a vote "for continued long lines at the filling stations . . . for more unemployment . . . for less productivity."

Revival Efforts

A final effort to enact an energy emergency bill collapsed May 21, when the House by a vote of 191-207 (R 30-147; D 161-60) refused to approve a revised version (HR 13834).

William E. Simon, head of the Federal Energy Office, had told the House Interstate and Foreign Commerce Committee early in April that the nation no longer needed the measure because the Arab oil embargo was over.

But the Senate Interior Committee disagreed and April 19 reported out a revised bill (S 3267 — S Rept 93-785). Left out were the controversial oil price ceiling provisions. However, the House Commerce Committee, in its new version (HR 13834 — H Rept 93-1014), required a ceiling on the price of both domestic and imported oil.

The Commerce Committee split off from its controversial bill the provisions dealing with clean air, coal conversion and energy information. These were included in another bill (HR 14368) later enacted as the Energy Supply and Environmental Coordination Act of 1974 (PL 93-319).

The new Commerce bill was brought to the House floor May 21 under suspension of the rules. That meant that a two-thirds majority was needed to pass the bill; it did not obtain even a simple majority. The Senate,

which had begun debate on its version, suspended further action on the bills.

The lopsided defeat was a sharp contrast to the mood just a few months earlier, when members had feverishly fought for the right to slap federal price controls on the oil industry. Presidentially imposed controls had been viewed as inadequate.

One factor in the changed attitude was the preference of some members for new taxes on the oil industry as the better way to exert control. The Ways and Means Committee was working on legislation at the time, but no bill was to emerge from the panel in the 93rd Congress.

But also behind the defeat was a more important factor — a sense that the crisis was fading. Winter was over, and so was the embargo, which the Arabs had ended in March. James T. Broyhill, R-N.C., explained that the earlier price control provisions had been written "in a different year and a different time and under different circumstances than exist today." Like many of his colleagues, Broyhill switched his vote, lining up against oil price controls.

1975

Highlights

Energy Policy

Hoping to put in place the first overall national energy policy, Congress passed the Energy Policy and Conservation Act (PL 94-163). The most important element was the continuation of oil price controls, which Ford agreed to despite his earlier efforts to allow higher prices; however, the law also provided for the end of those controls by October 1981. The bill also gave the president standby powers to use during fuel shortages, mandated improved automobile fuel efficiency and set up a strategic petroleum reserve.

Energy Research

Congress approved legislation (PL 94-187) authorizing specific energy research programs for the new Energy Research and Development Administration. Opponents of the major nuclear demonstration project — the liquid metal fast breeder reactor at Clinch River, Tenn. — failed in their bid to slow work on the project. Also unsuccessful was an attempt to provide $6 billion in federal loan guarantees to private companies developing synthetic fuels, such as liquids from coal.

Nuclear Accident Insurance

In the face of increasing criticism of nuclear energy, Congress extended for 10 years the legal limit on the nuclear industry's liability for an accident. The continuation (PL 94-197) of the Price-Anderson Act required federal subsidies so that the combination of private and federal insurance would provide accident coverage of up to $560 million, which was the liability limit. The assumption was that a nuclear accident was extremely unlikely.

Import Fee

President Ford found himself opposed both by Congress and the courts when he tried to raise by $3 the fee on oil imports. Ford managed to impose a $2-per-barrel fee hike, but rescinded that in December when he and Congress agreed on the Energy Policy and Conservation Act.

Energy Taxes

The House Ways and Means Committee tried unsuccessfully to win passage of major legislation using the tax system to force changes in U.S. energy habits. The House passed the bill. But committee provisions such as a 23-cents-a-gallon gasoline tax, taxes on gas-guzzling cars and stiff oil import quotas proved too controversial and were easily defeated or watered down by the House. The Senate did not act.

Congress, in a tax cut bill (PL 94-12), did repeal the 22 percent depletion allowance for major oil companies, a change expected to cost industry $2 billion a year.

Energy Independence Authority

The Ford administration wanted Congress to set up a special corporation to hand out federal subsidies to private industry to encourage energy development. Both new and conventional energy sources could receive aid from the Energy Independence Authority, which was to have $25 billion in equity and $75 billion in government-backed borrowing authority. But liberals thought it was a handout to big business, and conservatives saw the plan as more bureaucratic interference in the marketplace. That combination doomed the proposal.

Natural Gas Deregulation

Senate passage of natural gas deregulation was the first major step toward decontrol in almost 20 years.

Strip Mining

For the second time, Ford vetoed strip mining legislation; the House sustained his action. Opponents argued the environmental protection bill would inhibit coal production, a needed energy source.

The Year in Review

Congress in 1975 came face-to-face with the full difficulty of writing a national energy policy. After a year of sustained effort, the 94th Congress passed a mammoth energy policy bill of uncertain effect. It also cleared the first authorization legislation for the new Energy Research and Development Administration (ERDA), and a bill extending the federal program of insurance for the nuclear power industry.

President Ford seized the initiative early in the year, sending a multi-part energy package to the new Congress in January. Ford's conservation strategy was based on still higher energy prices. He proposed to tack on an additional $3 in import fees to every barrel of imported oil and to lift federal controls holding down the price of domestic oil. If energy were more expensive, his reasoning ran, both production and conservation would be encouraged.

Caught off guard, Congress tried to buy time. It quickly moved to suspend the president's power to raise the oil import fee and urged Ford to delay his planned oil decontrol proposal. Democratic leaders huddled to formulate an alternative energy plan less damaging to the already weak economy and less painful for the already pressed consumer.

The heavily Democratic Congress seemed ready to move boldly. In March it sent the White House a tax bill that, among other provisions, repealed for major oil producers the long-cherished depletion allowance for oil and gas, thereby increasing the oil companies' federal taxes by an estimated $2 billion in 1975. When Ford compromised on further import fee increases and decontrol moves in March, agreeing to delay them, Sen. John O. Pastore, D-R.I., head of the Senate energy task force, spoke optimistically of congressional ability to come to grips with the energy problem: "If we can't resolve this in 30 days, we can't resolve it at all."

In June, however, the House dealt such enthusiasm a body blow, overwhelmingly rejecting any increase in gasoline taxes, the cornerstone of an energy tax bill that had been heralded as the basis for the Democratic energy policy. When finally passed by the House, the measure received little attention in the Senate.

The focus of congressional energy activity shifted to an energy policy measure, which moved to the House floor in July and immediately bogged down in a dispute over whether to extend, expand or end the existing system of federal controls on the price of domestic oil. The authority for these controls was to expire Aug. 31. Eventually cleared and reluctantly signed by Ford in December, the bill was an amalgam of energy measures; it extended oil price controls until Sept. 30, 1981.

Congress also approved the first authorization bill for ERDA after weathering storms over the wisdom of proceeding with the premier nuclear energy project — the Clinch River breeder reactor — and over giving government aid to industry to encourage development of synthetic fuels. In addition, despite the vigorous opposition of the critics of nuclear power, it granted a 10-year extension of the existing federal program of insuring industry against a nuclear accident.

Congress passed, Ford again vetoed, and the House sustained the veto of a bill to regulate strip mining. Congress also took the first full step in almost 20 years toward deregulation of natural gas with Senate passage of such a measure. Also in the legislative pipeline at the end of the 1975 session were bills to unlock the naval petroleum reserves for production, to set new standards for leasing federal resources offshore and in the West for development, and to modify clean air requirements.

Energy Policy

"This legislation puts into place the first elements of a comprehensive national energy policy," President Ford said Dec. 22, announcing his decision to sign S 622 (PL 94-163), the Energy Policy and Conservation Act.

"The time has come to end the long debate over national energy policy," Ford said, explaining why he opted for signing the bill in the face of intense opposition from conservative Republicans, oil-state representatives and the oil industry. The bill was "by no means perfect," Ford conceded, but it "provides a foundation upon which we can build a more comprehensive program."

Most controversial was the bill's requirement that Ford

Summary of Provisions
In Major 1975 Energy Act

The key elements of the energy program contained in PL 94-163 included:

● Expanded authority of the Federal Energy Administration (FEA) to order major power plants and fuel burning installations to switch to using coal in place of oil or natural gas, and a new program of loan guarantees to encourage development of new underground mines producing less-polluting forms of coal. (Title I)

● Increased presidential authority to control the flow of energy supplies and energy-related materials. This included the power to restrict exports of these items; to allocate scarce supplies; to require increased oil and gas production; to require refineries to adjust the relative proportions of fuel oil or refined products they produce; and to order companies engaged in the oil business to accumulate, maintain or distribute certain levels of oil and petroleum product inventories. (Title II, IV)

● A new measure of protection for the United States in the event of another oil embargo or unexpected interruption of foreign policy supplies, provided through creation of a national strategic petroleum reserve of 1 billion barrels of oil and petroleum products, sufficient to replace three months' oil imports. (Title II)

● An arsenal of standby powers for use by the president under congressional review in case of an energy emergency or if needed to fulfill U.S. obligations under the international energy agreement, including the power to order national energy conservation measures and gasoline rationing. (Title II)

● Mandatory federal fuel economy standards for new automobiles manufactured or imported in any model year after 1977, targeted to reach an average fleet-wide fuel economy level of at least 26 miles per gallon by 1985. (Title III)

● A federal energy testing and labeling program for major consumer products from refrigerators to television sets. (Title III)

● Continued federal price controls on domestic oil into 1979, eventual conversion of the price control authority into a standby power, and an immediate rollback of domestic oil prices to an average per-barrel price of no more than $7.66. (Title IV)

● Authorization for federal audits of all persons and companies required to submit energy information to the federal government (except the Internal Revenue Service) and of all vertically integrated oil companies, to verify the information they report. (Title V)

---

continue federal controls on the price of domestically produced oil. The legislation even required an extension of those controls to new oil discoveries, which had not previously been subjected to price limits. A ceiling of $7.66 was set on the average price per barrel. The president could increase this figure by up to 10 percent a year to reflect inflation or to encourage production.

However, the legislation did provide for the eventual end to oil price controls. Mandatory controls were continued until June 1, 1979. After that, the president could extend the controls on his own authority until Sept. 30, 1981. On that date, the controls would end automatically.

By signing the bill, Ford acknowledged defeat — at least for the short term — of his effort to cut consumption and increase production by allowing oil prices to rise. This "conservation-by-price" philosophy had marked the major difference between the positions taken by the administration and by congressional Democrats.

Pricing was just one element, albeit the most controversial, in the multi-part energy bill. The measure also provided to the president standby authorities that could be used in an emergency to control energy production and use; required automobile manufacturers to improve fuel efficiency; mandated the labeling of major appliances to show anticipated energy costs and directed the president to establish a strategic petroleum reserve — a stockpile of oil to be used in an emergency.

The Senate had approved these provisions in four separate pieces of legislation, while the House combined them in one omnibus energy policy bill. Conferees used the House approach.

Senate Action

Oil Price Controls

The Senate April 10 approved legislation extending price controls on domestically produced oil. The vote was 60-25.

The bill (S 622 — S Rept 94-26) also equipped the president with a variety of powers to use in an energy emergency, including the authority to ration gasoline, restrict fuel exports and otherwise control the nation's production and use of energy. Many of these powers had been requested by President Nixon and then, in early 1975, by President Ford. However, the legislation did retain for Congress the right to review the presidential plans and, in some cases, the decision to put them to use.

Conservation was also addressed in the legislation. The president and the Federal Energy Administration were directed to adopt programs designed to cut domestic energy consumption by at least 4 percent a year, an amount equal to about 800,000 barrels of oil a day. A White House-backed effort to strike this provision failed, 25-60.

The continuation of oil price controls was accomplished by extending and revising the law governing the existing controls.

The expiration date for the price control law — the Emergency Petroleum Allocation Act of 1973 (PL 93-159) — was extended from Aug. 31, 1975, to March 1, 1976. The revised system of controls required the president to impose a price ceiling on all domestic oil — even oil from new discoveries. "New" oil had not been covered previously and as a result was selling for more than twice the price of "controlled" oil. The allowable price under this new scheme was to vary depending on the type of oil and when it was discovered.

During debate on the measure, the Senate four times, by margins of almost 3-to-1, rejected efforts to decontrol oil prices. The only concession made to those arguing for higher prices was an agreement to raise the price ceiling for hard-to-get oil recovered by special, expensive techniques.

Fuel Efficiency

The Senate July 15, by a 63-21 vote, approved mandatory fuel efficiency standards for automobiles.

American automobile manufacturers were required to double the fuel efficiency of their average new car by 1985, to 28 miles per gallon from the 1974 average of 14 miles per gallon. The fuel efficiency measure (S 1883 — S Rept 94-179) had been reported June 5 by the Senate Commerce Committee.

By passing the bill, the Senate rejected the auto industry's approach: a promise to improve fuel efficiency voluntarily in exchange for a five-year delay in the final auto emission standards, then scheduled to take effect in 1978. President Ford asked Congress in January for this delay, saying he had accepted the commitment by General Motors, Ford and Chrysler to improve their average fuel efficiency to 80 percent by 1980 — to 18.7 miles per gallon. Under S 1883, the average fuel efficiency of all new cars had to be at least 21 miles per gallon by 1980.

The legislation also authorized a research and development program in the Department of Transportation to develop a prototype gasoline-powered car that was fuel-efficient, non-polluting, safe and feasible for mass production.

Energy Labeling

The Senate July 11 approved a measure (S 349 — S Rept 94-253) requiring manufacturers to label large household appliances and automobiles to indicate the cost of the energy needed to run them. The vote was 77-0.

President Ford had requested efficiency labeling requirements as part of his comprehensive energy plan. They were intended to give consumers the information needed to compare the energy cost of different products.

Strategic Oil Reserves

The Senate July 8 approved a measure (S 677 — S Rept 94-260) authorizing creation of a strategic reserve of oil to cushion the nation against the impact of future interruptions or reductions in oil imports. The vote was 91-0.

President Ford had proposed creation of such a reserve as part of his energy program.

As approved by the Senate, S 677 authorized the creation of a stockpile of crude oil sufficient to replace oil imports for a period of 90 days. This amount was to be accumulated by the Federal Energy Administration (FEA) over a period of seven years from oil wells on federal lands, from the naval petroleum reserves (if production there were authorized), as royalties from future production from federal lands, including the outer continental shelf, and from purchases or exchanges of oil. The bill also authorized creation of regional reserves of petroleum products.

House Action

When the House Sept. 23 approved its omnibus energy bill (HR 7014), the legislators were endorsing many of the concepts contained in the four separate Senate-passed measures.

The 255-148 vote to pass the legislation followed closer votes on unsuccessful amendments seeking to end oil price controls and to water down conservation goals in the bill.

To the frustration of many members, action on the bill was spread over a two-month period. Debate began July 17.

The multi-part bill had been drafted by the Commerce Subcommittee on Energy and Power, which had called for a gradual phasing out of oil price controls. But the full Commerce Committee — by a one-vote margin — had rejected decontrol and instead extended controls, including a rollback in the price of newly discovered oil to $7.50 a barrel. The panel July 9 reported the bill (H Rept 94-340).

During floor action, an attempt was made July 23 to restore the subcommittee decontrol language. It failed by 18 votes, 202-220. But later that afternoon, the House decided, on a vote of 215-199 (R 125-15; D 90-184), to take all the oil pricing provisions out of the bill.

However, in August, the House reversed itself again, voting 218-207 to set up a three-tiered oil price control system: $5.25 per barrel for old oil, $7.50 per barrel for new oil and up to $10.00 per barrel for hard-to-produce oil. A later amendment added still another tier, allowing some oil produced by independent companies to sell for up to $11.50 per barrel.

Republicans, who generally opposed controls, also fought against other sections of the bill. But the House refused to strike the provision requiring a 2 percent reduction in gasoline consumption over a three-year period. Critics called this the "long lines" provision, charging that it would cause a recurrence of the long lines at gasoline stations common during the Arab oil embargo. The vote was 150-239.

The House also refused, 146-254, to delete provisions authorizing the president in certain instances to act as the exclusive agent for the nation's purchases of foreign oil.

By a 117-284 vote, the legislators rejected a move to strike the 28-miles-per-gallon auto efficiency goal for 1985.

Adding still another controversy to the unwieldy bill, the House adopted an anti-busing amendment, phrased in terms of conserving fuel by prohibiting its use to transport children to pubic schools other than the closest appropriate school to their home. First adopted by voice vote, the House reaffirmed its addition to the bill by a three-vote margin, 204-201, Sept. 23.

House Provisions. As passed by the House, the bill contained provisions:

● Granting the president standby energy emergency powers to be exercised with congressional consent, including the power to impose gasoline rationing and to prescribe energy conservation plans.

● Authorizing creation of a national civilian strategic petroleum reserve of up to 1 billion barrels of oil and petroleum products.

● Extending oil price controls on domestic crude oil indefinitely, setting up a four-tier system of oil price ceilings. Ceilings would range from $5.25 per barrel for flowing oil to $11.50 per barrel for some of the new oil produced by independent producers.

● Establishing a mandatory gasoline allocation program requiring the president to hold down the domestic consumption over the next three years.

● Setting fuel economy standards for domestic passenger cars, ranging up to 28 miles per gallon by 1985, and establishing an energy labeling and energy standards programs for major household appliances.

● Extending the coal conversion authority of the Federal Energy Administration (FEA) until June 1977, and authorizing FEA to prohibit the use of natural gas as boiler fuel for generating power.

● Prohibiting the use of any gasoline or diesel-powered vehicle for busing school children to schools beyond their neighborhood school.

● Authorizing the General Accounting Office to verify through audits of the books of oil producers any reports those producers were required to submit to the government and directing the Securities and Exchange Commission to set out uniform accounting standards for oil and gas producers to use in reporting their energy data.

● Barring joint ventures by major oil companies to develop oil, gas, coal or oil shale resources on federal lands.

Conference Action

After various procedural maneuvers to link the four Senate bills with the House bill, the massive piece of legislation was sent to conference Oct. 1.

"We have a big problem on our hands," said Interior Committee Chairman Henry M. Jackson, D-Wash., admitting he had made the understatement of the day. "But we have brought together all of the problems, except a few remaining, into one forum."

On the chief controversy — oil pricing — conferees scrapped both the House and Senate provisions setting up tiers of prices, and substituted a system giving the president the flexibility to adjust prices for various categories of oil to optimize production, so long as the average per barrel price for domestic oil did not exceed $7.66. This average could be adjusted to reflect inflation and to encourage production from certain areas, but the combined increase in any one year could be no more than 10 percent. Conferees agreed to extend mandatory price controls for 39 months and to provide the president with standby authority to continue controls until Sept. 30, 1981.

Among other actions, conferees dropped from the bill the House-approved gasoline allocation program requiring a 2 percent reduction in consumption of gasoline from the volume used in 1973-74. They also discarded the House anti-busing provision and banned joint ventures by major oil companies on the outer continental shelf, instead of on all federal lands as the House had proposed.

Agreement was reached in mid-November, but the work of drafting the language of the final provisions and writing the conference report consumed almost a month. The conference report was filed Dec. 9 (H Rept 94-700, S Rept 94-516). None of the Republican conferees signed

it — nor did three of the Democratic senators: J. Bennett Johnston Jr., La., James Abourezk, S.D., and Ernest F. Hollings, S.C.

Final Action

The final House and Senate votes on S 622 were relatively close, reflecting the disagreements and divisions which continued to plague Congress as it attempted to deal with energy.

"This, perhaps, has been the most parochial issue that could ever hit the floor," said House Majority Leader Thomas P. O'Neill Jr., D-Mass., as his colleagues took up the conference report Dec. 15. "It is extremely difficult to write an energy bill. We in New England who depend upon so much Arab and Venezuelan oil, feel differently about the legislation from those members from Texas, or Oklahoma, or California, or Louisiana, or from the Tennessee Valley Authority section. We feel differently from those in the Northwest where there is an abundance of natural gas."

The House still wasn't satisfied with the conferees' agreement. By a 300-103 vote, the legislators struck provisions — originally part of the Senate fuel efficiency measure — providing loans and grants to encourage the development of advanced automotive technology. Rep. Olin E. Teague, D-Texas, chairman of the House Science and Technology Committee, had objected to their inclusion in the bill because they fell within his committee's jurisdiction and it had not considered them. By making this change in the bill, the House rejected the conference report.

The House then voted, 215-179, to block efforts to make further changes in the oil price provisions.

The final step was a motion, adopted 236-160, to approve and return to the Senate a clean bill (S 622) containing all the language approved by conferees except the automotive technology program and language expanding a loan guarantee program for coal mines.

The Senate cleared S 622 for the president Dec. 17 on a vote of 58-40 (R 8-30; D 50-10), concurring in the House changes in the conference bill.

In neither chamber did these final votes demonstrate sufficient strength to override a presidential veto, should one have been cast. Federal Energy Administrator Frank G. Zarb Dec. 18 said he still did not know if Ford would sign the bill.

Zarb had had a hand in developing the conference version and had urged the president to sign the bill. Ending weeks of suspense about his decision, Ford did so Dec. 22.

Provisions

PL 94-163, the Energy Policy and Conservation Act, established a national energy policy designed to 1) maximize domestic production of energy and provide for strategic storage reserves of oil and petroleum products; 2) minimize the impact of disruptions in energy supplies by providing for emergency standby measures; 3) provide for a level of domestic oil prices that would both encourage production and not impede economic recovery; and 4) reduce domestic energy consumption through voluntary and mandatory energy conservation programs.

The bill's short-term objectives were protective: to reduce the economic and social impact of higher foreign oil prices and any accompanying shortages. Its long-term

Extending Oil Price Controls: A Long Story

Enactment of the Energy Policy and Conservation Act (S 622 — PL 94-163) ended a year-long debate on the question of extending federal controls holding down the price of domestic oil.

As signed by President Ford, S 622 set $7.66 as the average maximum per-barrel price for domestic oil, more than a dollar below the current average per-barrel price of $8.75. The president could adjust prices for various categories of oil so long as the average price was not exceeded. S 622 continued mandatory federal oil price controls until June 1, 1979. After that date, the controls could be continued with presidential discretion until Sept. 30, 1981. On that date, the law provided for the end to the price controls.

President Nixon imposed price controls on domestic oil in 1971, under authority granted him by the Economic Stabilization Act. In 1973, Congress shifted authority for these controls from that act, which expired in 1974, to the Emergency Petroleum Allocation Act. Authority for the controls was extended in 1974 until Aug. 31, 1975.

Under the price control system, most domestic oil was classified as "old" (that produced from wells existing in 1973 at a rate equal to 1972 production) or "new" (that produced from newly drilled wells or from old wells in excess of the 1972 volume). Old oil was subject to a price ceiling of $5.25 per barrel in 1975; new oil was not subject to any price ceiling. Old oil accounted for about 60 percent of all domestic oil production in 1975.

Administration Proposals

President Ford in his 1975 State of the Union message said he would remove all controls on the price of domestic oil April 1. Under the 1973 law, either house of Congress could block this move by adopting a resolution of disapproval within five days of the president's formal proposal.

As negotiations began, Ford delayed and modified his decontrol plan. On April 30, he announced a 24-month phase-out of controls to begin in June. But a formal decontrol proposal was not sent to Capitol Hill until mid-July; it provided for a 30-month phase-out period and a price ceiling of $13.50 on all domestic oil.

Congressional Response

The tug-of-war on oil price controls then proceeded along these lines:

● Congress July 17 sent Ford a bill (HR 4035) which:

　　1) Extended oil price controls to Dec. 31, 1975.

　　2) Extended the congressional review period from five to 20 days.

　　3) Directed Ford to set a ceiling of no more than $11.28 per barrel for new oil.

The Senate May 1 had approved its version of the bill, 47-36 (S 621 — S Rept 94-32); the House June 5 approved HR 4035 (H Rept 94-65), 230-151. Conferees filed their report (H Rept 94-356) on the measure July 14 with no Republican signatures. The Senate adopted the conference report July 16, 57-40; the House July 17, 239-172.

● Ford vetoed HR 4035 July 21 as allowing "a drift into greater energy dependence." Hill leaders, lacking the votes to override, shelved the measure.

● Responding with a veto of its own, the House July 22 voted 262-167 to adopt a resolution (H Res 605) to block Ford's 30-month oil decontrol plan.

● Ford July 25 proposed still another decontrol plan that would phase out oil price controls over a 39-month period.

● The House July 30 vetoed this second plan, adopting a resolution of disapproval (H Res 641) by a vote of 228-189.

● Congress July 31 completed action on another price control extension measure (S 1849), simply extending until March 1, 1976, the price control authority under the Emergency Petroleum Allocation Act which would otherwise expire Aug. 31. The bill was not sent to the White House until Aug. 28, in order to prevent a pocket veto during the summer recess. The Senate had approved the bill (S Rept 94-220) July 15, 62-29; the House approved it, 303-117, July 31 without change.

● Ford vetoed S 1849 Sept. 9, but said that if his veto were sustained he would agree to a temporary 45-day extension of controls. The Senate Sept. 10 sustained the veto by six votes, 61-39.

● Congress Sept. 26 sent Ford a bill extending oil price control authority until Nov. 15 and providing that controls would be retroactively effective for the period since Aug. 31. Ford signed the bill (HR 9524 — PL 94-99) Sept. 29. The House had approved it by voice vote Sept. 11; the Senate approved it with amendments 72-5, Sept. 26; the House accepted the Senate changes the same day, 342-16.

● By this time, conferees on the policy bill (S 622) were at work. To give them more time to work out differences among themselves and with the administration, Congress and Ford agreed in November on one last temporary extension of oil price controls. Congress Nov. 14 sent Ford a bill (S 2667) extending those controls to Dec. 15; Ford signed the bill (PL 94-133). The next step was passage of S 622.

aims were more positive: to increase available domestic energy supplies and the efficiency with which they were used.

To achieve these goals, PL 94-163 contained the following major sections and provisions:

Title I — Domestic Energy Supplies

To encourage increased use of coal, Title I:

● Extended to June 30, 1977, from June 30, 1975, the authority of the Federal Energy Administration (FEA) to order power plants and other major fuel-burning plants to convert from use of oil or natural gas to use of coal.

● Authorized loan guarantees to small coal operators opening up new underground coal mines.

To ensure domestic energy supplies, Title I:

● Authorized the president to restrict exports of coal, crude oil, natural gas, residual fuel oil, any refined petroleum product, any petrochemical feed stock, equipment or material necessary for domestic energy production or domestic consumption.

● Required the president to bar the export of crude oil or natural gas produced in the United States but allowed him to permit exemptions in the national interest.

● Amended the Defense Production Act (PL 81-774) to authorize the president to allocate supplies of materials and equipment essential for domestic energy needs; this authority would expire Dec. 31, 1984.

● Required the interior secretary to ban joint bidding for rights to develop oil or natural gas on the outer continental shelf by any joint venture in which two or more major oil companies or their affiliates participate.

● Authorized the president to require production from domestic oil and gas fields at the maximum efficient rate or at a temporary emergency rate above that maximum during an energy supply emergency.

● Authorized creation of a strategic petroleum reserve of 1 billion barrels of oil and petroleum products within seven years of enactment of PL 94-163, including an early storage reserve of 150 million barrels accumulated within three years after enactment; directed FEA to submit to Congress, by Dec. 15, 1976, a plan for development of the strategic reserve, which could be vetoed by either chamber of Congress within 45 days.

● Granted the FEA administrator a wide range of powers including that of condemnation, to use in implementing the reserve plan; authorized use of supplies from the reserve in a severe energy supply interruption or when required by international obligations; authorized necessary appropriations for creation of the early storage reserve, and $1.1 billion for the strategic reserve.

Title II — Standby Authorities

Title II equipped the president with standby authority to deal with future energy supply emergencies through provisions which:

● Authorized the president to prescribe national energy conservation and gasoline rationing plans; required the president to submit to Congress contingency plans for exercising these powers within 180 days of enactment of S 622; provided that the plans had to be approved by both chambers within 60 days in order to become potentially effective.

● Allowed Congress to block implementation of a rationing plan if, when the president sent Congress a finding that it was necessary to put the plan to use, one chamber

disapproved that finding within 15 days; limited the effective period of a plan to nine months.

● Authorized the president to take or order such actions necessary to fulfill U.S. obligations in international oil allocation under the international energy programs.

Title III — Energy Efficiency

To improve the efficiency with which U.S. automobiles consume fuel, Title III amended the Motor Vehicle Information and Cost Savings Act to add provisions that:

● Required that the average fuel economy for passenger cars manufactured or imported by any one manufacturer in any model year after 1977 be no less than:

18 miles per gallon in 1978
19 miles per gallon in 1979
20 miles per gallon in 1980
27.5 miles per gallon in 1985 and succeeding years.

● Directed the transportation secretary to set standards for the interim, 1981-1984, at the maximum feasible average fuel economy level which would result in progress toward the 1985 standard, which the secretary could adjust downward to 26 miles per gallon if necessary.

● Authorized the secretary to adjust the average fuel economy downward as it applies to a certain manufacturer if he finds that other federal standards — such as clean air requirements — reduce the fuel economy of the cars produced by that manufacturer despite the application of a reasonably selected technology to prevent such a fuel economy reduction.

● Required labeling of cars manufactured or imported in any year after model year 1976 to indicate fuel economy performance.

● Set penalties at $5 per 0.1 miles per gallon for every 0.1 miles by which a manufacturer's average failed to meet the standard, multiplied by the number of cars produced by that company; gave a credit in the same amount to any manufacturer for any year in which his average fuel economy exceeded the standard.

Consumer Product Efficiency

Title III also:

● Authorized FEA to set up an energy testing, labeling and standards program for other major consumer products.

● Directed FEA to set energy efficiency targets for these products, designed to achieve an aggregate improvement of at least 20 percent in efficiency by 1980 over similar products manufactured in 1972; required FEA to set enforceable energy efficiency standards for products which failed to meet those targets.

Conservation Programs

To encourage conservation on other fronts, Title III:

● Authorized a three-year, $150 million program of federal grants to assist states in developing and carrying out energy conservation programs to reduce their consumption by 5 percent below the expected level for 1980; required certain elements in any state plan in order for the state to receive federal funds, which included establishing building efficiency standards and allowing right turns after a stop at a red light.

● Directed FEA to set voluntary energy efficiency improvement targets for the 10 most energy-consumptive industries in the country.

● Directed the president to develop and implement a 10-year conservation plan for the federal government.

Title IV — Oil Pricing

Title IV amended the Emergency Petroleum Allocation Act of 1974 (PL 93-159) with new provisions which:

● Required the president, within two months of enactment, to set a ceiling price for the first sale of domestic oil which would keep the average per-barrel price for all domestic oil at $7.66 or less for 39 months.

● Allowed the president, within that required average price, to allow the price of "old crude oil production" to increase if such would result in increased production or was needed because of declining production. ("Old oil" was defined as the amount of oil produced from a well or field equal to the volume produced from that source in 1972. "Old crude oil production" was defined by PL 94-163 as the volume of oil produced from a well or field in a month, equal to or less than the volume of "old oil" produced and sold from that source in September, October and November 1975, divided by three.)

● Granted the president authority to set particular ceiling prices for certain categories of domestic oil.

● Allowed the president to adjust the ceiling price for domestic oil to: 1) take inflation into account, and 2) to encourage production either from high-cost, high-risk properties, through the use of enhanced recovery techniques, or from marginal properties, including stripper wells, through sustaining production; limited any adjustment for encouraging production to that permitting an increase of no more than 3 percent per year in the average first-sale, per-barrel price of domestic oil; provided that the total increase in the average ceiling price in any one year resulting from the inflation adjustment and the production incentive adjustment could be no more than 10 percent; allowed the president to propose that the 3 percent and the 10 percent limit be raised, and provided that either house of Congress could disapprove such a proposal within 15 days.

● Required the president to report to Congress by Feb. 15, 1977, on the impact of these price ceilings and changes on the economy and the nation's fuel supply; specified that at that time the president could also propose to continue or modify the incentive adjustment factor or the limits placed on it, a proposal which could be vetoed by either chamber within 15 days; if such a proposal did not take effect then, the power to adjust the ceiling price to encourage production would expire.

● Required the president, by April 15, 1977, to report to Congress on the adequacy of the incentive provided under existing price ceilings for development of Alaskan oil; directed the president — if he found the ceilings inadequate — to propose exemption of up to 2 million barrels per day of Alaskan oil from those price ceilings and from the calculation of the average domestic oil price and to propose another ceiling price for this exempted oil no higher than the highest average price allowed for any other class of domestic oil; either chamber could veto such a proposal within 15 days.

● Repealed language requiring allocation of all domestic oil production for domestic use and exempting low-producing stripper wells from price controls.

● Required that all decreases in oil costs be passed through to the consumer at the retail level on a dollar-for-dollar basis; limited to 60 days the period during which oil producers could "bank" increased crude oil prices before passing them on to the consumer.

● Required an equitable distribution, across the range of oil products, of the costs of crude oil.

● Forbade the president from using any authority under the Emergency Petroleum Allocation Act or the Energy Policy and Conservation Act to set minimum prices for crude oil or petroleum products.

● Exempted from the entitlements program — for the first 50,000 barrels per day of their production — small refiners who on and after Jan. 1, 1975, had refining capacity of no more than 100,000 barrels per day.

● Set penalties for violations of the pricing sections of the Emergency Petroleum Allocation Act: for non-willful violations, civil fines up to $20,000 per day for producers and refiners, up to $10,000 per day for wholesale distributors, and up to $2,500 per day for retail distributors; for willful violations, up to one year in prison or fines of up to $40,000 per day, $20,000 per day and $10,000 per day respectively.

● Authorized the president to submit to Congress a plan granting the federal government the exclusive right to purchase foreign oil and petroleum products for import into the United States; the plan would take effect if not disapproved by either house within 15 days.

● Authorized the president to require adjustments in the operations of domestic refineries with respect to the relative proportions of residual fuel oil or other refined products produced, and to require adjustments in the amounts of oil or petroleum products held in inventory by any persons engaged in importing, producing, refining, marketing or distributing such products, including direction that inventories be distributed to certain persons at specified rates or that inventories be accumulated to certain levels and at certain rates.

● Prohibited the willful hoarding of petroleum products during a severe supply interruption by any person engaged in any aspect of petroleum production or distribution, except as required by the strategic petroleum reserve provisions of Title I.

● Provided for conversion of the mandatory pricing requirements of the Emergency Petroleum Allocation Act to discretionary authority 40 months after the new ceiling price provisions took effect; provided for expiration of these standby powers of the Allocation Act on Sept. 30, 1981.

Title V — General Provisions: Energy Data

To provide data upon which energy policy decisions could be made, Title V:

● Authorized the General Accounting Office, headed by the comptroller general, to conduct verification audits of the records of 1) any person required to submit energy information to the FEA, the Interior Department or the Federal Power Commission (FPC); 2) any person engaged in production or distribution of energy (except at the retail level) who has furnished energy information to a federal agency, with the exception of the Internal Revenue Service (IRS), which that agency is using; 3) any vertically integrated oil company.

● Authorized such audits if requested by any congressional committee with legislative or oversight responsibilities in the energy field or with regard to laws administered by the Interior Department, the FEA or FPC; the report on such an audit would be committee property.

● Granted the comptroller general the power of subpoena, access to energy information possessed by any federal agency except the IRS and other related powers for use in the audits; provided civil penalties of up to $10,000 per day for failure to provide information sought in such an audit.

●Stated that any information obtained through these audits and related to geological matters, disclosure of which would result in significant competitive disadvantage to the owner, could be given only to a congressional committee; unauthorized disclosure could be subject to the penalties specified for violations of the Emergency Petroleum Allocation Act.

●Directed the Securities and Exchange Commission (SEC) to prescribe rules to assure development and observance of uniform accounting practices for persons engaged in domestic oil or gas production.

●Extended to Dec. 31, 1979, from June 30, 1975, the provision of the 1974 Energy Supply and Environmental Coordination Act (PL 93-319) which required energy-producing companies to supply production and reserve data to FEA.

In other administrative provisions, Title V:

●Required all FEA or Interior Department employees to disclose, by Feb. 1, 1977, any financial interest in coal, natural gas or oil production or property.

●Set penalties for violations of Title I, Title II, the oil recycling provision of Title III, Title V and for failure to comply with an energy conservation plan at up to $5,000 for a non-willful violation; up to $10,000 for a willful violation; and up to $50,000 and/or six months in prison for a willful violation following a penalty for a non-willful violation.

●Provided that Titles I and II, with certain exceptions noted in individual provisions, would expire June 30, 1985.

Nuclear Accident Insurance

Congress in 1975 approved a 10-year extension (HR 8631 — PL 94-197) of the program of federal insurance against a nuclear power accident. PL 94-197 extended the program until Aug. 1, 1987, and provided for a phase-out of the government's role as insurer as the amount of available private insurance and the number of operative nuclear power plants increased.

The insurance program, created by the Price-Anderson Act, was set up in 1957 as an amendment to the Atomic Energy Act of 1954. It was designed to assure the public of compensation for any damages resulting from a nuclear power accident and to limit the liability of the industry for damages from a single accident. It required nuclear power plants to obtain the maximum private insurance coverage available. It limited the industry's liability to $560 million for a single accident; the government agreed to pay the difference in damages between the amount covered by private insurers and that limit.

During consideration of measures extending the insurance program in 1974 and 1975, the liability limit came under attack by critics who argued that it was unnecessary if nuclear power was as safe as the industry claimed, and that it prevented adequate recovery for damages if a severe nuclear accident did occur.

But both the House and the Senate in 1975 rejected efforts to eliminate or increase this liability limit. However, they did require that this ceiling rise gradually as the number of nuclear power plants increased.

Background

The liability limit had provided the reassurance to the public that had been needed in 1957 to encourage development of the infant nuclear power industry. The law (PL 85-256) was named for Rep. Melvin Price, D-Ill., and Sen. Clinton P. Anderson, D-N.M.

As the amount of insurance obtainable from private sources increased (from $60 million in 1957 to $110 million by 1974), the government's liability decreased, but the $560 million limit on the industry's liability remained in place. The federal government had never paid any claims under the act because there had been no accidents. Thus the system had actually produced revenue for the government because the power plants paid a fee for the government's backing. From 1957 to 1975, these fees totaled $5.6 million.

Spurred by the frequent pronouncement by government officials that nuclear power would be the prime energy source of the future, environmentalists and consumer spokesmen began in the early 1970s to question the safety of expanding nuclear power production. This concern was enhanced in 1973 by the leak of 115,000 gallons of liquid radioactive nuclear waste from an Atomic Energy Commission (AEC) facility at Hanford, Wash.

The Joint Atomic Energy Committee began hearings in 1973 on the safety issue. AEC officials testified that nuclear reactors were safer than other means of generating energy. They expressed confidence that this assessment would be supported by the results of a new study of reactor risks, directed by Norman C. Rasmussen of the Massachusetts Institute of Technology, due for completion in 1974.

When the Joint Committee resumed hearings early in 1974, critics of nuclear power testified, rebutting the AEC position. Consumer advocate Ralph Nader called nuclear power a form of "technological suicide." Henry W. Kendall, a nuclear physicist speaking for the Union of Concerned Scientists, cited the Hanford leak and other recent accidents as illustrative of the need to halt construction of new nuclear plants.

Joint Committee member Rep. Mike McCormack, D-Wash., a nuclear research chemist associated with the Hanford project for 20 years before his election to Congress in 1970, took issue with Kendall's statements as "reckless and irresponsible."

Anxious to hear from the Rasmussen report, Congress in 1974 had added a condition to its five-year extension of Price-Anderson (HR 15323). The legislation contained a provision giving Congress the right to repeal the extension — even after the president had signed it — if such action were warranted by results of the Rasmussen study.

That provision prompted a veto from Ford on Oct. 12, 1974. Although he supported extension of Price-Anderson, Ford argued that the bill's language usurped his constitutional power to give the final stamp of approval to legislation.

The Rasmussen report was released in October 1975. It found quite small the likelihood of a serious nuclear accident with severe consequences for the public. As a result, the 1975 bill extending the liability limit had no reservation authorizing a repeal, and Ford signed it.

Joint Committee Action

The Joint Committee on Atomic Energy Nov. 10 reported HR 8631 (H Rept 94-648) to the House. An identical measure was reported to the Senate (S 2568 — S Rept 94-454) Nov. 13. The committee report said that early extension of the program was necessary to avoid uncertainty and a slowdown in the long planning process for new nuclear power plants. In 1975 there were 56 such plants in operation in the United States; the Ford administration hoped to quadruple that number — to 200 — by 1985. The report cited the Rasmussen study as support for its earlier findings that a serious nuclear accident was extremely unlikely, and pointed out that the study had concluded that the $560 million coverage provided by Price-Anderson was adequate to cover "any credible accident which might occur."

House Action

The House approved HR 8631 Dec. 8 by a vote of 329-61.

The $560 million liability limit was the target of two unsuccessful floor amendments designed to reduce the amount of protection afforded the industry while increasing that provided for the general public.

The first amendment, proposed by Jonathan B. Bingham, D-N.Y., with the backing of labor, environmental groups and consumer advocate Ralph Nader, would have eliminated the liability limit.

"These are big boys in the industry now," argued Bingham, "and they should be able to stand on their own feet and not say that if the damages from an accident exceed a certain amount, they will only be liable for a set figure so that the people who might be outside the limit would have no remedy."

Opposing the amendment were the Ford administration and the nuclear power and insurance industries. They argued that if an accident did cause more than $560 million in damages, Congress would act to compensate the injured persons.

Melvin Price, D-Ill., playing a key role as he had in 1957, pointed out that the bill did provide for a gradual increase in the liability limit as more plants were built. The most active Republican, John B. Anderson of Illinois, warned that removal of the liability limit would mean "we are not going to get the financing we need to continue this viable industry in this country."

The Bingham amendment was rejected, 176-217.

The second key amendment, proposed by Bob Eckhardt, D-Texas, would have allowed citizens 90 days after HR 8631 became effective to go into federal court and to challenge the liability limitation as unconstitutional. This amendment was also rejected, 161-225.

Senate Action

The Senate approved its version of HR 8631 Dec. 16 by a vote of 76-18. Again, debate on the measure centered on the liability limit.

The Senate rejected an amendment to increase the potential liability of the industry by allowing victims of a nuclear accident who were not sufficiently compensated to sue. The amendment's sponsor, Mike Gravel, D-Alaska, said damages of as much as $15 billion could result from a major accident. Under the $560 million limit, a victim of that accident "could probably get a return of three cents on the dollar for what he has lost," he said.

Opposing the Gravel amendment, John O. Pastore, D-R.I., argued that it effectively meant that "the sky is the limit" on damage suits. "The minute we do that, no insurance company will underwrite it," he continued. "So if one cannot buy insurance we do not build a reactor. If we do not build the reactor, we do not achieve energy independence. We begin to put sections of the country in the dark."

The Senate rejected the Gravel amendment, 34-62.

The Senate subsequently rejected, 46-47, an amendment similar to the Eckhardt amendment rejected by the House, providing for a court test of the constitutionality of the liability limit. By wider margins, it also rejected two other Gravel amendments — one extending the insurance program for only five years and the other accelerating the pace at which the government would phase out its role as insurer of the industry.

Final Action

The House cleared HR 8631 for the president Dec. 17, agreeing by voice vote to the Senate changes.

Provisions

As signed into law, PL 94-197 amended the Atomic Energy Act of 1954 to:

● Extend coverage of the insurance system set up by the Price-Anderson Act to nuclear plants licensed before Aug. 1, 1987. Existing law allowed coverage only for plants licensed before Aug. 1, 1977.

● Phase out the government's role as insurer by requiring all licensed nuclear power plants to pay, in the event of a nuclear accident resulting in damages exceeding the amount of available private insurance, a "deferred premium" between $2 million and $5 million per plant in order to provide funds to pay the damages up to $560 million. The government would continue to pay damages in excess of the combined total of private insurance and deferred premiums until that total reached the $560 million limit.

● Allow the liability limit to increase, once the private insurance/deferred premium total reached $560 million. The limit would increase as the total of private and industry commitments increased.

● Extend Price-Anderson insurance coverage to ocean shipment of fuel between licensed nuclear plants outside the territorial limits of the United States and to nuclear facilities licensed by the government but located outside those territorial limits.

● Require the Nuclear Regulatory Commission to report to the Joint Atomic Energy Committee, senators and representatives from affected states and districts on the causes and extent of any damages resulting from a serious nuclear accident, and to make public such findings except for information damaging to the national defense.

● Extend to 20 years from 10 years the statute of limitations applying to damage suits resulting from nuclear accidents.

Energy Research Authorization

The continuing heavy nuclear emphasis of federal energy research was again confirmed as Congress Dec. 18 approved the first authorization bill for the new Energy Research and Development Administration (ERDA), which formally came into being Jan. 19, 1975.

The bill (HR 3474 — PL 94-187) authorized $5 billion for fiscal 1976 and a proportional amount, $1.27 billion, for the transition quarter (a one-time event when the federal government was changing the dates of its budgetary year). Of the total, approximately $4 billion was for nuclear programs.

In both the House and Senate, advocates of the top-

Congress Rejected Loan Guarantees
To Help Develop Synthetic Fuels

Should U.S. taxpayers guarantee billions of dollars in loans to encourage development of new fuels to substitute for natural gas and oil — "synthetic" fuels made from coal, oil shale, wood and other natural resources?

Congress in 1975 answered "no" to this question, rejecting a Senate-approved and Ford administration-backed provision in the energy research authorization bill (HR 3474) which would have authorized federal guarantees for up to $6 billion in loans to private companies willing to undertake the commercial production of synthetic fuels.

As part of the nation's push for energy independence, President Ford in his 1975 State of the Union message urged Congress to provide new incentives for the commercial production of 1 million barrels per day of synthetic fuel by 1985, a goal requiring construction of at least 20 major synthetic fuel plants.

Synthetic fuels are liquid or gaseous fuels created by treating or processing other natural resources. Most synthetic fuels could be used as substitutes for natural gas, oil or other petroleum products. Among the fuels in this group were:

● Oil extracted from shale.

● Gas of pipeline and lesser quality produced from coal through processes described as gasification.

● Oil produced from coal through liquefaction processes.

● Gas or liquid fuel produced from waste products, often referred to as biomass: this category includes methanol, which can be produced from coal, wood wastes, farm or municipal wastes.

The Ford administration was also urging Congress to approve other economic incentives to convince American industry that production of these fuels was economically feasible. By 1995, administration planners estimated the United States would need to produce at least 5 million barrels per day of synthetic fuels. In order to develop that capability,

the administration proposed a commercialization program for the 1970s and the 1980s to lay to rest industry's doubts about the economic, regulatory, environmental and technological difficulties of producing synthetic fuels.

Although most of the technology for producing synthetic oil and gas already existed, advocates of the loan guarantee program argued that federal action was needed to convince industry to undertake large-scale production of synfuels. Chief among them was Sen. Jennings Randolph, D-W.Va., author of the Senate's loan guarantee language, who described that program as "the single most important action that can be taken by the federal government to expedite the commercial development of a domestic synthetic fuels industry."

On the other hand, Rep. Ken Hechler, D-W.Va., opposed the proposed program as "sort of like attaching a big platinum-plated caboose to the end of the ERDA train. It is very heavy. It is very well-appointed. It is like a private car. It is very difficult for the rest of the taxpayers of this nation to pull it along."

Hechler led the successful effort to delete from the conference report the Senate-approved $6 billion in loan guarantees for synthetic fuel development. First, the House Rules Committee allowed a separate vote on the question. Then Hechler picked up support from both liberal and conservative colleagues who saw the federal aid as a windfall for large oil, gas and coal companies and as unnecessary federal interference in the marketplace.

On the other side were President Ford and members such as J. J. Pickle, D-Texas. "We are simply at the point now where development of synthetic fuels will either go the way of the Roman steam engine — a device for toys only — or will become a valuable addition to our national energy supplies," said Pickle.

The House voted 263-140 to strike the provision for loan guarantees for synthetic fuel development.

priority nuclear demonstration project — the liquid metal fast breeder reactor — defeated efforts to slow work on that program.

In addition to the controversy over the liquid metal fast breeder reactor, the path of the ERDA measure was further complicated by disagreement over Senate language providing up to $6 billion in federal loan guarantees for private industry willing to undertake commercial-scale production of synthetic fuels — oil and gas-like fuels produced from other substances such as coal. In an unusual last-minute maneuver, the House struck this language out of the final version of the bill after the Senate had adopted

the conference report. *(Box, this page)*

Provisions

As signed by the president, PL 94-187 authorized the following amounts for major energy research and development programs in fiscal 1976:

● $498 million for fossil fuel research and development.

● $173 million for solar energy research and development.

● $56 million for geothermal energy research and development.

● $156 million for energy conservation research.

● $158 million for fusion energy research and development operating expenses.

● $506 million for fission energy research and development operating expenses, of which up to $123 million could be spent on the proposed Clinch River demonstration plant in the liquid metal fast breeder reactor program.

● $222 million for the operating expenses of the naval reactor research and development program.

● $1 billion for the operating expenses of the nuclear materials research and development program.

● $985 million for national security programs operating expenses, including $897 million for weapons systems.

In addition, PL 94-187:

● Amended the Federal Non-Nuclear Energy Research and Development Act of 1974 to direct ERDA to set up a central source of information on all non-nuclear energy resources and technology.

● Forbade the air transport of plutonium by ERDA — except as required for medical application, national security, public health and safety or emergency maintenance, or to preserve the chemical, physical or isotopic properties of the material — until ERDA certified to Congress that a safe container had been developed and tested that would not rupture if the airplane crashed and exploded.

Energy Leadership in 1975

Interior Secretary Rogers C. B. Morton, named energy policy coordinator for the Ford administration late in 1974, moved to head the Commerce Department in April 1975, taking with him the hat of energy czar.

However, the most visible energy policymaker in the administration during 1975 was Frank G. Zarb, who continued as head of the Federal Energy Administration (FEA) during the year. Zarb was credited with winning President Ford's signature for the omnibus energy bill (S 622 — PL 94-163) at year's end.

Named to succeed Morton at the Interior Department was former Wyoming Governor Stanley K. Hathaway. Opposed by environmental groups for his conservation actions — or lack thereof — as governor, Hathaway underwent unusually close scrutiny by the Senate Interior Committee during hearings in April and May. The Senate confirmed him June 11 by a vote of 60-36. But after only six weeks in office, Hathaway resigned July 25, citing fatigue and depression as the reasons for his departure.

In September Ford nominated as interior secretary Thomas S. Kleppe, since 1971 head of the Small Business Administration (SBA) and a former member of the House (R-N.D., 1967-1971). Kleppe was quickly confirmed despite a lack of experience with environmental matters and questions raised by charges of undue political influence and loan mismanagement in the SBA during his tenure. The Senate Interior Committee approved his nomination unanimously Oct. 7 after Kleppe told the panel he would, within nine months, divest himself of all stockholdings that might constitute a conflict of interest. The Senate approved his nomination by voice vote Oct. 9.

The membership of the new Nuclear Regulatory Commission remained unchanged through 1975, the first year of its operation, but President Ford named three new members of the five-member Federal Power Commission: Richard L. Dunham, deputy director of the White House Domestic Council, as chairman, confirmed in October; John H. Holloman III, a Mississippi attorney, confirmed in July; and James G. Watt, an Interior Department official, confirmed in November.

Fees on Oil Imports

President Ford revealed his approach to energy conservation in his State of the Union message in January. To discourage oil use, Ford said he would raise by $3 the fee on imported oil, which was then 52.5 cents per 42-gallon barrel.

The increase was to be levied $1 at a time — on Feb. 1, March 1 and April 1, Ford said. He was acting under authority granted by the Trade Expansion Act of 1962, which empowered the president to limit imports of any product affecting national security.

At the same time Ford described the import fee, he announced that, on April 1, he would remove all price controls on domestic oil. Part of the rationale behind these two bold moves was Ford's desire to spur Congress into passing energy policy legislation.

"We've diddled and dawdled long enough," Ford said Jan. 23, as he made official the first scheduled $1 increase in the import fee.

But Congress didn't like Ford's approach. The House Ways and Means Committee Jan. 24 voted, 19-15, for a bill (HR 1767) suspending for 90 days the president's authority to restrict imports — and thus repealing the fee. The report (H Rept 94-1), filed Jan. 30, tacitly acknowledged that the intent was to give Congress time to come up with an alternative solution. The House Feb. 5 passed a measure by a 309-114 vote.

After the Senate Finance Committee reported the House bill without amendment (S Rept 94-11), the Senate cleared the legislation by a 66-28 vote. Ford immediately announced he would veto the bill.

Ford's veto message, sent March 4, agreed to the suggestion by congressional leaders that he postpone until May the second and third $1 increases in the fee. Presumably, that would give Ford and Congress time to work out a compromise. Congress agreed to discuss the matter, delaying any attempt to override the veto. Ford ended up increasing the fee by $2 a barrel, but then rescinded the tariff Dec. 22.

The president March 4 also postponed until at least May 1 his plan to decontrol oil prices. As it turned out, negotiations over price controls took precedence over the issue of import fees.

Court challenges also made less crucial the import fee dispute between Congress and the president. The governors of eight Northeastern states, a group of 10 utilities and Rep. Robert F. Drinan, D-Mass., had filed suit soon after Ford announced the fee increases. They argued that the fee was illegal because it had not been authorized by Congress. The Northeast was expected to feel the first bite of price increases from the fee because of its heavy dependence on imported oil.

In August, the U.S. Court of Appeals, District of Columbia Circuit, rules for the challengers, stating that the fees were an exercise of taxing powers, which were reserved for Congress by the U.S. Constitution. Ford appealed to the U.S. Supreme Court. In 1976, the court upheld the president's power to use fees to control imports.

Energy Taxes

An omnibus energy tax bill (HR 6860), once expected to be a major vehicle for congressional energy policy, languished in the Senate Finance Committee at the end of the 1975 session.

Even before it reached the Senate, it had been severely weakened. First, Ways and Means Committee Democrats, who had initially appeared able to produce a strong bill, were forced to settle for a lot less than they had hoped. Then, when that bill reached the floor, the House voted overwhelmingly to delete the toughest proposal, a 23-cents-a-gallon gasoline tax. The stripped down bill was then passed and sent to the Senate Finance Committee. The committee held a few hearings on the proposal, but took no further action.

Committee Action

The Ways and Means plan was one of several competing Democratic alternatives to President Ford's proposals to curb U.S. dependence on foreign crude oil by raising the cost of energy consumption through import fees. Ford's program, which included other controversial measures such as natural gas price deregulation, called for offsetting the $30 billion energy tax drain on the economy through permanent individual income tax cuts, direct payments to the poor, more revenue sharing with state and local governments and a 6 percent cut in the corporate tax rate.

Democrats' Plan. Working separately from the House and Senate leadership task forces that were preparing energy proposals, the Ways and Means Democrats March 2 outlined a comprehensive energy policy designed to reduce oil imports without undercutting economic recovery.

The plan, drawn up on the basis of initial proposals by Ways and Means Chairman Al Ullman, D-Ore., selected a phased-in approach that would have deferred the full impact of energy use restraints until economic recovery was well under way. Key components included quotas to gradually cut back oil imports, step-by-step gasoline tax increases if gasoline consumption rose, a trust fund to finance energy supply and conservation development, taxes on cars that failed to meet fuel consumption standards, tax incentives for energy-saving investments and a windfall profits tax tied to gradual removal of federal oil and gas price controls.

Although Ways and Means Republicans had been excluded from the drafting, they and administration officials welcomed the Democrats' suggestions as a good start toward compromise with the administration on energy policy. But Republicans thereafter consistently opposed the Demo-

Oil Companies and Taxes

The oil industry's campaign to preserve its 22 percent depletion allowance for oil and gas production ended in failure early in 1975 when Congress repealed that allowance for the major oil companies retroactive to Jan. 1, 1975. This allowance was retained for most natural gas producers and for the first 2,000 barrels of oil or equivalent amount of gas pumped each day by an independent producer who owned no retail outlets or major refineries. The change raised industry taxes an estimated $2 billion a year.

These changes were part of tax cut legislation (HR 2166 — PL 94-12) enacted early in the 1975 session. The oil and gas industry during consideration of that bill did succeed in blocking other proposed revisions that would have increased the tax paid on oil-related foreign income.

crats' key proposals, particularly the gasoline tax and import quotas, and administration officials were not satisfied by concessions that Ullman made during markup.

Nor did the committee Democrats rally behind Ullman's efforts. At the end of a month and a half of markup, the committee majority was badly divided, with oil-state conservatives joining all 12 Republicans in opposition and liberals calling for a tougher auto fuel consumption tax.

In the end, enough Ways and Means Democrats supported the final committee bill (HR 6860), but their votes were evidently cast primarily to keep from embarrassing the panel and its new chairman. The measure was reported by a 19-16 vote on May 12 (H Rept 94-221).

Committee Bill. As sent to the floor, HR 6860 was expected to cut U.S. oil consumption by about 2.1 million barrels a day in 1985, with roughly half of those savings resulting from a 3-cents-per-gallon gasoline tax increase to finance an energy trust fund and an additional 20-cents-a-gallon hike that would be triggered automatically, bit by bit, as consumption rose.

The measure also established yearly quotas that would have cut oil imports to 5.5 million barrels a day by 1979, replaced the president's already imposed $1 per barrel oil import fee with percentage duties, set up a 10-year energy conservation and conversion trust fund, imposed excise taxes on business use of oil and gas for fuel and granted various tax incentives for energy-saving investments by business and homeowners.

HR 6860 also imposed graduated taxes on 1978-80 model automobiles that failed to meet fuel efficiency standards. But the committee, after intense lobbying by auto manufacturers and their employees' union, reduced the standards and curtailed application of the tax.

Floor Disaster

When it reached the floor on June 10, the energy tax bill already was in deep trouble. The Ways and Means

President Ford Proposed 13-Part Energy Independence Act in 1975

Moving quickly to present the 94th Congress with his energy program, President Ford Jan. 31 sent to Capitol Hill a 13-part Energy Independence Act. He urged its quick approval. Without these measures, he warned, "we face a future of shortages and dependency which the nation cannot tolerate and the American people will not accept."

Taken together with other administrative actions — such as his proposed $3-per-barrel increase in the import fee on foreign oil and decontrol of the price of domestic oil — these proposals would reduce oil imports by one million barrels per day by the end of 1975 and by two million barrels per day by the end of 1977, he said.

As proposed, the Energy Independence Act would have:

● Authorized full development and production of oil from the Elk Hills, Buena Vista and Teapot Dome naval reserves (up to 300,000 barrels per day by 1977), and authorized exploration and development of the Alaskan oil reserve.

● Provided for creation of a military strategic petroleum reserve of 300 million barrels and a civilian strategic petroleum reserve of up to one billion barrels of oil.

● Deregulated the price of new natural gas and imposed an excise tax of 37 cents per thousand cubic feet on natural gas.

● Amended the 1974 Energy Supply and Environmental Coordination Act to extend federal authority to require power plants to use coal rather than oil or natural gas.

● Delayed deadlines for compliance with clean air requirements until 1985 for industrial emissions and until 1982 for automobile emissions.

● Deleted from the Clean Air Act the language requiring disapproval of any clean air plan allowing any significant deterioration of air quality, regardless of the original air quality level.

● Allowed utilities to pass through higher costs to their customers and limited the period of time for which proposed rate increases could be delayed.

● Approved development of a national plan for siting and building needed energy facilities and provided $100 million in federal grants to states for implementing this plan.

● Authorized development of mandatory thermal efficiency standards for all new homes and commercial buildings.

● Approved a three-year, $165 million program of federal aid to encourage low-income families to insulate their dwellings.

● Required energy efficiency labeling of all major appliances and automobiles.

● Granted the president standby powers to control supplies, production, allocation and consumption of energy and energy-related materials.

● Authorized the president to impose tariffs, quotas or variable import fees on imported oil when there was a drop in foreign oil prices that threatened to undercut domestic oil prices.

Committee had asked and been granted an open rule for the measure; this was an unusual move because a closed rule, which limits or prevents amendments, normally was sought for tax bills. House leaders had postponed floor debate until after the Memorial Day recess after a deluge of proposed amendments underscored opposition to its provisions.

But the decisive defeats that the House inflicted on the Ways and Means recommendations still were unexpected. In a stunning vote of 345-72 (R 134-5; D 211-67), the House June 11 stripped out the standby 20-cents-per-gallon gasoline tax, then went on to kill the milder 3-cents-per-gallon trust-fund tax. The House also defeated efforts by Ways and Means' liberals to strengthen the auto efficiency tax, finally dropping even the committee's less stringent tax and substituting an Interstate and Foreign Commerce subcommittee's alternative proposal to enforce the standards by fines instead of taxes.

The House upheld the committee's import quota system but raised the limit to 6.5 million barrels a day in 1980 and thereafter. After making several other minor changes, the House passed HR 6860 by a 291-130 vote

divided largely along party lines.

Ullman insisted that the bill still would set "the basic foundation for an energy policy," but he later acknowledged that a much stronger measure would be required to meet the oil import quotas. For its part, the Senate Finance Committee held hearings and conducted a few tentative markup sessions on HR 6860, but took no further action on energy taxes during 1975.

In 1976, the Finance Committee wrote into its version of massive tax revision legislation (HR 10612) several energy conservation tax incentives based on parts of HR 6860. But House-Senate conferees dropped the revenue-losing energy provisions to help meet congressional budget goals for revenue gains by the bill.

Energy Independence Authority

President Ford's proposal that Congress create a $100 billion government corporation to stimulate commercial development of new energy sources met with a resounding lack of enthusiasm on Capitol Hill.

Announcing his plan in San Francisco Sept. 22, Ford said it would help the nation achieve energy independence, stimulate the economy, create jobs and "supplement" the private enterprise system.

But even before the draft bill reached Congress, many doubts had been raised. Liberal Democrats expressed concern that the corporation would not be accountable to Congress and would subsidize one segment of the economy, particularly the major oil companies, at the expense of others. Conservatives were not eager to endorse creation of a new layer of federal bureaucracy, especially one with so much money to dispense.

As outlined in a White House fact sheet, the proposed Energy Independence Authority (EIA) would be a government corporation programmed to self-destruct in 10 years. It was designed to boost commercial development of domestic energy resources by making loans, guaranteeing private loans, investing or otherwise financing operations that "will contribute directly and significantly to energy independence," and "would not be financed without government assistance."

The corporation was to have $25 billion in equity, to be appropriated by Congress gradually, and $75 billion in government-backed borrowing authority, to be raised through the public sale of bonds and other obligations.

The types of projects to be financed, the White House said, would include commercialization of technologies for extracting synthetic fuels such as oil from shale and liquefied coal; other emerging technologies such as production of solar and geothermal energy; and conventional operations such as electric utilities and uranium enrichment plants. "Projects of unusual size or scope could include new energy parks or major new pipelines for transportation of oil and gas."

The authority was to be run by a five-member board of directors to be appointed by the president with Senate confirmation.

The energy corporation idea was developed by the staff of Vice President Nelson A. Rockefeller.

Natural Gas Deregulation

For the first time since 1956, the Senate approved a bill (S 2310) that gradually removed federal price ceilings for new discoveries of natural gas.

Congressional action in 1975 was assisted by increasing public awareness that the nation's reserves of natural gas were dwindling and by predictions of severe shortages in non-producing states during the winters of 1975-76 and 1976-77. Drastic curtailment of gas supplies available to interstate pipelines would result in lost jobs and cold homes.

Advocates of deregulation, including President Ford, argued that higher prices were needed to encourage increased exploration and development of domestic natural gas reserves and to channel more natural gas out of producing states where federal price controls did not apply. In 1975, gas sold in the unregulated "intrastate" system of producing states was priced as high as three or four times the top regulated "interstate" price in non-producing states. The regulated price was 51 cents per thousand cubic feet.

In June, a badly divided Senate Commerce Committee rejected the administration plan and approved a bill of its own (S 692 — S Rept 94-191) that continued price controls while allowing higher prices for new natural gas. Handicapped by a lack of enthusiastic support and blocked by opposition from advocates of deregulation, S 692 never came to the Senate floor.

Alarmed by predictions of a severe natural gas shortage in the coming winter, the Senate late in September took up an emergency natural gas bill (S 2310) that had been introduced earlier in the month and placed directly on the calendar without going to committee. The Senate Democratic leadership planned to consider the short-term measure first and then to move on to consider S 692 and the more controversial long-range issues.

But with administration and industry support, this plan was overridden and the Senate voted, 50-41, to add a gradual deregulation plan to the emergency provisions of S 2310. The deregulation proposal was sponsored by Sens. James B. Pearson, R-Kan., and Lloyd Bentsen, D-Texas. The combination bill was then approved, 58-32, and sent to the House.

The House did not approve a natural gas bill before the end of the year, but at the close of the 1975 session the stage was set for floor consideration of the issue in 1976. Although the impetus for consideration of a natural gas bill had been weakened by the fact that the predicted shortages for the winter of 1975-76 had not materialized, the House Interstate and Foreign Commerce Committee did report an emergency measure (HR 9464). A rule was granted for its consideration by the full House, which would allow consideration of a substitute combining long-term deregulation with the short-term provisions.

1976

Highlights

Energy Policy

Despite criticism of the fledgling agency, Congress extended the life of the Federal Energy Administration (FEA) until Dec. 31, 1977. The Energy Conservation and Production Act (PL 94-385) also gave FEA new responsibilities over reform of utility rate structures, grants for weatherizing low-income homes and state conservation plans. The president was directed to submit a plan for reorganizing the federal energy bureaucracy, and the Department of Housing and Urban Development was required to develop federal performance standards that Congress hoped would force every new building to be energy efficient.

Alaska Gas Pipeline

By setting deadlines for federal decisions related to transportation of natural gas from Alaska, Congress expected to speed delivery of the gas to consumers in the lower 48 states. The Alaska Natural Gas Transportation Act (PL 94-586) also limited court challenges on environmental grounds once Congress had accepted the environmental impact statement.

Aid to Coastal States

Worried about how coastal states would deal with the boom expected in offshore oil and gas development, Congress agreed to provide federal aid of $400 million in grants and $800 million in loan and bond guarantee authority. Supporters of increased drilling on the outer continental shelf hoped the Coastal Zone Management Act Amendments (PL 94-370) would cool congressional efforts to check the traditional independence enjoyed by companies developing energy offshore.

Coal Leasing

Frustrated with the slow pace of coal production from federal lands, Congress revamped coal leasing rules — overriding a veto by President Ford to do so. The Federal Coal Leasing Act Amendments (PL 94-377) required competitive bidding for at least half the leases and said lessees had to attempt to recover the amount of coal that was the maximum economically feasible. The minimum federal royalty per ton was increased, as was the state share of those federal revenues.

Naval Petroleum Reserves

Production from reserves formerly set aside for the Navy was authorized by the Naval Petroleum Reserves Production Act (PL 94-258).

Electric Cars

Congress overrode President Ford's veto to enact legislation to promote development of electric-powered cars (PL 94-413).

Synthetic Fuels Subsidies

By a one-vote margin, the House refused to allow a vote on a plan to provide $4 billion in subsidies to synthetic fuels and a variety of other energy sources. The bill (HR 12112) was defeated by an unusual coalition of fiscal conservatives and liberals sympathetic to environmental issues.

Outer Continental Shelf

By a four-vote margin, the House rejected a conference committee bill (S 521) revising federal rules governing development of oil and gas on the outer continental shelf. The vote was a victory for the oil and gas industry and the Ford administration, who claimed production delays would result from the proposed new rules.

Strip Mining

The House Rules Committee blocked floor consideration of revised strip mining legislation drafted by the Interior Committee.

Energy Research

The energy research authorization for fiscal 1977, providing almost $8 billion, was killed in the Senate by last-minute parliamentary maneuvering unrelated to the bill.

Natural Gas Deregulation

Facing a gas deregulation amendment, the House voted 205-201 for a compromise that ended controls on small producers, but tightened price limits on the 25 to 30 major gas producers. A conference with the Senate was never convened because the 1975 Senate-passed deregulation bill (S 2310) was so different from the House approach (HR 9464).

Uranium Enrichment

After the House reluctantly went along with President Ford's plan to open up the uranium enrichment industry to private enterprise, the legislation (HR 8401) died in the Senate. The fuel for nuclear power plants had been a government monopoly for about 30 years, but the nuclear industry wanted permission to get involved.

Oil Company Divestiture

A Senate committee reported legislation requiring oil companies engaging in production, marketing, refining and transportation to divest themselves of all but one phase of the oil business within five years. The measure did not reach the Senate floor because of the leadership's reluctance to bring up the controversial, time-consuming issue in an election year.

The Year in Review

In the presidential election year of 1976, Congress continued half-heartedly to seek answers to the nation's continuing, but less visible, energy problems. Early in the year, Ford asked Congress to act on 16 energy proposals; by the session's end, only four were enacted.

Congressional ambivalance and unwillingness to make difficult decisions led to oddly unequal treatment for several pairs of measures. A year-and-a-half extension for the Federal Energy Administration, the government's "temporary" energy crisis management agency, was easily approved, but Congress adjourned without completing action on the billion-dollar measure authorizing federal energy research and development programs. Congress approved a billion-dollar program of aid to coastal states affected by development of oil and gas resources on the outer continental shelf, but killed a related bill that would have modernized the procedures for leasing those federally owned resources for development.

Congress overrode one presidential veto to enact a measure authorizing government efforts to promote the development of electric cars, but sustained a veto of a related bill to put federal money behind efforts to develop advanced automobile engines.

After insisting on retaining oil price controls in 1975, Congress acquiesced in Ford administration proposals to lift those controls on a variety of petroleum products.

Congress did enact changes in federal procedures for leasing its coal deposits (over a presidential veto); it approved opening of the naval oil reserves for production; and it set deadlines to spur a decision on transporting Alaskan natural gas to the lower 48 states. It killed, or left dangling, Ford proposals to deregulate the price of natural gas, to allow private industry to get into the uranium enrichment business, to provide federal backing for commercial production of synthetic fuels, and to relax clean air deadlines for auto and industrial emissions.

Energy Act Extends FEA

Congress in 1976 extended the life of the Federal Energy Administration (FEA) for 18 months, until Dec. 31, 1977. The law creating FEA as a temporary agency to cope with the fuel shortages of 1974-75 (PL 93-275) had provided that it would go out of existence June 30, 1976.

The FEA extension measure (HR 12169 — PL 94-385) was transformed by the Senate into a full-fledged energy policy measure, known as the Energy Conservation and Production Act. It authorized the president to submit to Congress late in the year plans for a general reorganization of federal energy policy machinery. PL 94-385 also put new weight behind federal efforts to spur reform of electric rate structures and to encourage energy conservation. The law also made minor changes in the oil pricing system.

The House version of HR 12169 extended the life of FEA for 18 months, half the period recommended by the Interstate and Foreign Commerce Committee (H Rept 94-1113).

But the Senate Government Operations Committee, while recommending a 15-month extension for FEA, laid the groundwork for a complete restructuring of federal energy efforts (S Rept 94-874). Senators also called for expansion of FEA involvement in reform of electric rate structures, a subject also dealt with by the House bill. On the Senate floor, still more policy provisions were added, authorizing new federal financial incentives for energy-efficient buildings, expanding FEA's mandate to collect financial data from oil companies and lifting price controls on certain categories of domestic oil.

Conferees adopted the House's 18-month extension for FEA and most of the House authorization levels for FEA activities. They retained most of both versions after softening some of the more controversial aspects of the Senate building conservation and energy data provisions and dropping House language giving Congress a veto over FEA regulations.

Conferees were unable to work out a final version of the bill between Senate passage June 16 and FEA's June 30 expiration date. The agency was therefore extended for one month by passage of a stopgap extension bill (S 3625 — PL 94-332). When that expired before the conference agreement on HR 12169 was completed, President Ford July 30 signed an executive order creating for the interim a Federal Energy Office to perform the functions of FEA.

Conference Action

House and Senate conferees filed their report on the bill Aug. 4 (H Rept 94-1392). Because few of the provisions of the two versions of the bill collided head-on, conferees were able to adopt most of both measures.

Conferees, however, delayed a final decision on the most controversial aspect of the Senate federal energy efficiency standards for new buildings: the sanctions by which they were to be enforced. HR 12169 provided for Congress to decide, after the performance standards were formulated, whether it was necessary to ensure their application through the sanction of denying all federal financial assistance for construction to an area of a state not adopting these standards.

Final Action

Final action came when the House Aug. 10, by a vote of 293-88, adopted the conference report on the bill. It had earlier adopted the rule for consideration of the conference report, 267-117.

The Senate had adopted the report Aug. 5 by voice vote.

Provisions

The major provisions of PL 94-385:

● Extended the life of the Federal Energy Administration (FEA) for 18 months, to Dec. 31, 1977, from July 1, 1976.

● Authorized appropriations of $189.9 million for existing FEA programs in fiscal 1977, and $41.3 million for the transition quarter between fiscal 1976 and 1977. (The bill set a ceiling of $2.036 million for FEA's controversial communications and public affairs office; it also specifically denied funds for setting up an office of nuclear affairs within FEA.)

● Created an office of energy information and analysis within FEA, to establish and maintain a national energy information system as a basis for the work of FEA, Congress and other energy policy-making officials.

● Directed the president, by Dec. 31, 1976, to submit to Congress a plan for the reorganization of the federal government's activities in energy and natural resources.

● Exempted from federal price controls oil produced from stripper wells, which produce an average of 10 barrels or less per day, but required that its price continue to be factored into the composite price for domestic oil, which the president was required, by the 1975 Energy Policy and Conservation Act, to maintain at a certain gradually rising level.

● Lifted the 3 percent limitation on the overall price increase for domestic oil which the president could allow in order to stimulate domestic production.

● Directed FEA to develop proposals for improving electric utility rate design and to submit them to Congress within six months of enactment.

● Directed FEA to fund demonstration projects to improve electric utility load management procedures and to fund regulatory rate reform initiatives; authorized FEA intervention and participation in state utility regulatory commission proceedings upon the request of a participant.

● Authorized FEA grants to states for setting up offices of consumer services to aid consumer representation in utility regulatory proceedings.

● Directed the Department of Housing and Urban Development (HUD) to develop within three years of enactment federal performance standards for energy efficiency in all new commercial and residential buildings.

● Denied federal financial assistance, including mortgage loans from federally regulated institutions, for construction of any new commercial or residential buildings in a state which did not adopt the performance standards; denied aid to any building not certified by the state as meeting the standards; and conditioned the use of this sanction upon passage, when the regulations were final, of a concurrent resolution by Congress finding this sanction necessary and appropriate to assure application of these standards.

● Authorized FEA grants to states and Indian tribes, and to city governments and community action agencies in a non-participating state, for insulation and other weatherization investments (of up to $400 in materials per unit) in dwellings occupied by low-income persons, providing $55 million for fiscal 1977, $65 million for fiscal 1978 and $80 million for fiscal 1979.

● Directed FEA to develop guidelines for supplemental state energy conservation plans; authorized FEA grants to states for implementing these plans; authorized $25 million for fiscal 1977, $40 million for 1978, $40 million for 1979.

Ford's 1976 Requests Included Gas Deregulation

"We must regain our energy independence," President Ford again asserted to Congress in his 1976 energy message, delivered Feb. 26. "During the past year, we have made some progress toward achieving our energy independence goals, but the fact remains that we have a long way to go.

"Thus far, the Congress has completed action on only one major piece of energy legislation — the Energy Policy and Conservation Act — which I signed into law on Dec. 22, 1975."

Ford then asked Congress to:
● Deregulate the price of new natural gas. This, Ford said, was "the most important action that can be taken by the Congress to improve our future gas supply situation."
● Provide short-term authority needed to deal with severe winter shortages of natural gas.
● Expedite selection of a route and construction of a transportation system to bring Alaskan natural gas to the lower 48 states.
● Streamline licensing procedures for the construction of new power plants.
● Approve the Nuclear Assurance Act to provide the basis for transition from a government monopoly to a private competitive uranium enrichment industry.
● Approve proposed Clean Air Amendments to permit greater use of coal and to delay auto emission standards deadlines.
● Allow production from the Naval Petroleum Reserves.
● Approve creation of an Energy Independence Authority, to assist private sector financing of new energy facilities.
● Authorize loan guarantees to aid in the construction of commercial facilities to produce synthetic fuels.
● Approve energy facilities siting legislation.
● Approve utility rate reform legislation.
● Approve the Federal Energy Impact Assistance Act to set up a $1 billion program of aid to areas affected by new federal energy resources development.
● Set up a $55 million weatherization assistance program for low-income and elderly persons.
● Provide for thermal efficiency standards for new buildings.
● Provide a 15 percent tax credit for conservation improvements in residential buildings.

At the end of the 94th Congress, legislation had been enacted to grant Ford's requests concerning Alaskan natural gas, the naval petroleum reserves, weatherization assistance and thermal building standards, but the other requests had either failed to win final approval or had been ignored by Congress altogether.

● Directed the Department of Housing and Urban Development to undertake a national demonstration program to test the feasibility and effectiveness of aid to encourage energy conservation and adoption of renewable-resource measures in existing dwellings; authorized HUD to use grants, loans, loan subsidies and guarantees to encourage use of these conservation measures; limited the subsidies to $400 or 20 percent of a loan for conventional energy devices and to $2,000 or 25 percent of loans for solar, wind or other renewable resource devices; authorized $200 million for this aid.

● Provided authority for FEA to guarantee loans to corporations, institutions, governments and other eligible borrowers for financing energy conservation or renewable resource measures for industrial goals or otherwise to improve the efficiency of the large-scale use of energy; set a ceiling of $2 billion on aggregate commitments under this program.

Alaskan Gas Pipeline

Hoping to expedite delivery of natural gas from Alaska to the lower 48 states, Congress in 1976 approved a measure (S 3521 — PL 94-586) setting deadlines for federal decisions on how to transport that fuel. President Ford signed it despite administration reservations about certain provisions.

PL 94-586 directed the president to tell Congress by Sept. 1, 1977, whether he recommended construction of a transport system to deliver Alaska's gas, and if so, directed him to specify the delivery system he preferred. For the decision to become effective, Congress would have to approve the choice by joint resolution within 60 days. (The decision was made by President Carter in 1977 and ratified by Congress. *Box, p. 184*)

The measure provided for a streamlined decision process within the executive branch. Once a final decision was approved, the measure authorized federal officials to waive normal procedural restrictions in issuing permits to hasten construction and operation of the transport system.

The legislation also restricted judicial review of its provisions in an effort to avoid lengthy delays in construction of the system due to court challenges.

Congress declared in the legislation that "a natural gas supply shortage exists" and that expediting access to the gas reserves in Alaska could help ease the problem. Proponents of the bill argued that unless it was enacted a pipeline decision could be tied up in litigation for years.

Three proposals were pending before the Federal Power Commission (FPC) when the measure passed. One, submitted by the El Paso Alaska Company, sought permission to build an 800-mile pipeline parallel to the Alaskan oil pipeline from the North Slope to Southern Alaska. Gas would then be liquefied and shipped 1,900 nautical miles to Southern California and distributed from there, primarily through existing pipelines.

A second proposal from the Alaskan Arctic Gas Pipeline Co., a consortium of American and Canadian companies, called for construction of a 3,700-mile-long pipeline from the North Slope to the Mackenzie Delta area of Canada's northwest territories, where other gas reserves lay, then south to Alberta. From there the line would divide into two legs to serve markets in the American West and Midwest. Canadian pipeline customers would be served under that proposal as well as Americans. (In late 1976 the FPC staff recommended this plan.)

A third proposal pending before the FPC was submitted by the Northwest Pipeline Corporation. It called for a new pipeline parallel to the Alaskan oil pipeline to Delta Junction, where the new line would follow the Alcan Highway to the Alaska-Yukon border. Canadian companies would sponsor a pipeline from the Yukon border to Fort Nelson, British Columbia, and Zema Lake, Alberta, to connect with existing systems bringing the gas to the lower 48 states. The proposal would require construction of 1,700 new miles of pipeline.

At least one other proposal pending before Canadian authorities called for an all-Canada pipeline from the Mackenzie Delta. Also, the Westinghouse Oceanic Division and the U.S. Maritime Administration were studying prospects of bringing Alaska's natural gas to the contiguous 48 states in the form of methanol.

There was an estimated 26 trillion cubic feet of proved reserves of natural gas beneath Alaska's Prudhoe Bay, with more at Canada's Mackenzie Delta and Beaufort Sea. Current estimates concluded that the Prudhoe Bay reserves could supply 2 to 6 percent of the United States' total natural gas requirements.

Legislative History

The Senate approved S 3521 by voice vote July 1. The bill was jointly reported (S Rept 94-1020) June 30 by the Senate Commerce and Interior committees.

The House by voice vote approved its version of S 3521 Sept. 30. The House Commerce Committee had reported the bill Sept. 22 (H Rept 94-1658).

The Senate Oct. 1 cleared the measure by voice vote, approving it as amended by the House.

Provisions

As signed into law, the major provisions of PL 94-586:

● Required the FPC to recommend to the president by May 1, 1977, whether to proceed with a natural gas transportation system from Alaska, and if so, what kind.

● Required that the FPC recommendation "include provision for new facilities to the extent necessary to assure direct pipeline delivery of Alaska natural gas contemporaneously to points both east and west of the Rocky Mountains in the lower continental United States."

● Specified information which the FPC report must contain, including estimates of the annual gas volume expected from Alaska for 20 years, environmental and competitive impacts and costs.

● Directed the president to send his recommendation to Congress by Sept. 1, 1977, although he could delay up to 90 days longer.

● Gave Congress 60 days to approve the president's recommendation by joint resolution. If not approved, the president was allowed 30 more days to offer a second and final recommendation.

● Limited judicial review of the legislation to challenges to the act's overall validity or allegations that action under the law denied constitutional rights.

● Required that challenges to the act's constitutionality be filed within 60 days after its enactment.

● Required that challenges to federal actions under the measure be filed within 60 days of the action.

● Declared that congressional and presidential accep-

tance of submitted environmental impact statements would satisfy terms of the National Environmental Policy Act of 1969 and prohibited courts from considering that such accepted statements might be unsatisfactory.

● Required that the president report to Congress within six months on what procedures would be necessary to ensure fair allocation of Alaskan oil to the states of Washington, Oregon, Idaho, Montana, North Dakota, Minnesota, Michigan, Wisconsin, Illinois, Indiana and Ohio.

● Directed the attorney general to study antitrust issues and problems relating to production and transport of Alaskan natural gas and report to Congress within six months.

Coastal States Aid

Congress in 1976 amended the Coastal Zone Management Act of 1972 to authorize $1.2 billion to help coastal states deal with the effects of offshore gas and oil development.

The new aid program (S 586 — PL 94-370) consisted of $800 million in loan and bond guarantee authority to be used over a 10-year period and $400 million authorized for direct grants to coastal states, for use over an eight-year period. Sponsors hoped that the aid would moderate fears in those states of social, environmental and economic disruption resulting from the development of resources on the outer continental shelf (OCS). By relating the amount available to each state to the volume of oil and gas produced off its shores and the level of new energy activity in the state, members of Congress hoped also to speed OCS development.

President Ford signed S 586 July 26 but both the oil industry and his administration doubted the need for new procedures or requirements. In his 1976 energy message, Ford had proposed creation of a $1 billion program of federal aid to both coastal and interior areas affected by energy resource development. Congress did not act on that proposal in 1976.

As it neared enactment, S 586 was criticized by some members who had worked hard for the measure earlier in the process. To escape an administration veto, conferees on the bill inserted new language, which had been in neither the House nor the Senate version, to make federal grants a last resort for states and cities seeking aid for building or expanding public facilities and services made necessary by coastal energy development. By making this use of these funds contingent upon a finding that loans or bond guarantees were unavailable for that purpose, the new provision reduced the probable level of federal spending under the grant program.

Members of Congress from Louisiana, a state already substantially impacted by offshore oil and gas development, protested this change as severely reducing the assistance their state would receive. Proponents of the measure responded with figures estimating that of the $400 million in grant funds, $188 million would go to Gulf states, $112 million to Alaska, $56 million to Atlantic Coast states and $43 million to Pacific Coast states.

At one point, provisions of S 586 were included in a bill (S 521) revising OCS leasing procedures. Enactment of S 586 removed the impetus for action on the more controversial leasing bill, and it died Sept. 28 when the House recommitted the conference report by a four-vote margin.

Senate Action

As approved by the Senate July 16, 1975, by a vote of 73-15, S 586 (S Rept 94-277) authorized automatic grants of up to $100 million a year for fiscal years 1976-78, facility grants or loans of up to $200 million a year for fiscal years 1976-78, and federal guarantees of state or local bond issues needed to finance OCS-related public facilities.

House Floor Action

The House March 11 passed HR 3981 by a 370-14 vote, making only minor changes in the bill drafted by the Merchant Marine and Fisheries Committee (H Rept 94-878). The legislation authorized $1.45 billion in new impact aid to coastal states over five years. The bill also provided federal guarantees for up to $200 million in state and local government bonds for public facilities and services required by offshore energy development.

The complex measure also liberalized federal aid to help 34 states and territories develop coastal management plans.

Conference Action

Conferees filed their report (H Rept 94-1298) June 24. Major differences between the two versions of the bill were resolved by:

● Broadening the Senate formula for calculating a state's share of the automatic grant monies to give more weight to indicators of new energy activity within the state.

● Adopting Senate provisions providing that this aid would be administered through loans, as well as grants and guarantees.

● Providing for an $800 million ceiling on bond and loan guarantees instead of the $200 million ceiling set by the House.

● Authorizing the House amount, $400 million over eight years, for the automatic grants, rather than the Senate amount, $300 million over three years.

In a controversial last-minute change justified by conferees as necessary to avoid a veto of the bill, the conference committee inserted a new provision allowing states to use grant funds for new public services and facilities only if they were not able to obtain the funds for these services and facilities through federal loans or bond guarantees.

Final Action

The Senate adopted the conference report by voice vote June 29.

"The primary assistance offered by the [new aid] program . . . for financing public facilities and services made necessary by any coastal energy activity," explained Ernest F. Hollings, D-S.C., June 29, "are federal loans and bond guarantees, not grants. Initial assistance . . . is in the form of credit rather than grants because in many cases the adverse fiscal impacts experienced by a coastal state or local government will only be temporary and will be offset later on by increased tax revenues from the coastal energy activity involved" which would allow repayment of the loan or retirement of the bonds.

The House June 30 approved the conference report by a 391-14 vote.

Provisions

As signed into law, the major provisions of PL 94-370 amended the 1972 Coastal Zone Management Act to authorize a coastal energy impact program to provide federal aid to help coastal states deal with the impact of offshore oil and gas development. Aid would be provided through:

● Planning grants for up to 80 percent of the cost of studying and planning for any economic, social or environmental consequence of coastal energy development.

● Loans to coastal state and local government units to aid in providing new or improved public facilities or services needed as a result of coastal energy activity.

● Guarantees of bonds issued by coastal states or local governments for the purpose of providing new or improved public facilities or public services required as a result of coastal energy activity.

● Automatic annual grants to states. Each state's share would be calculated on the basis of four factors:

(1) the volume of oil and gas produced from OCS acreage adjacent to the state during the preceding year;

(2) the volume of oil and gas produced from OCS acreage leased by the federal government which was first landed in that state during the preceding year;

(3) the amount of OCS acreage adjacent to the state and newly leased in the preceding year, and

(4) the number of persons residing in that state who obtain new jobs in that year as a result of new or expanded OCS energy activities.

The grant funds could be used for three purposes:

(1) to retire state and local bonds which had been federally guaranteed under this aid program;

(2) to prevent or ameliorate any unavoidable loss, as a result of coastal energy activity, of valuable environmental or recreational resources in the coastal zone;

Location of potential oil and gas fields on the Atlantic Outer Continental Shelf. Shaded areas show onshore regions which would be affected economically by offshore operations.

(3) to provide new or improved public facilities and services required as a direct result of new or expanded OCS energy activity and approved as eligible by the commerce secretary, but funds could be used for this purpose *only if* aid for these programs was unavailable under the loan or bond guarantee provisions.

To finance this aid, the bill set up a Coastal Energy Impact Fund in the Treasury, a revolving fund based on appropriations.

PL 94-370 authorized $50 million for automatic grants for each fiscal year from 1977 through 1984; and $800 million for other forms of aid under the new program through fiscal 1986.

PL 94-370 further amended the 1972 Act to:

● Increase to 80 percent the federal share of costs of completion and initial implementation of state coastal zone management plans, authorizing $20 million per year for development grants and $50 million a year for implementation grants for fiscal years 1977, 1978 and 1979.

● Require every federal lease for exploration, development or production of OCS energy resources that affects the coastal zone of a state to be certified by the state as consistent with its coastal zone management program before any license or permit could be issued for such OCS activity.

Coal Leasing Rules

Congress in 1976 overrode President Ford's veto and coal industry opposition to enact S 391, the Federal Coal Leasing Amendments Act, which revised the procedures for leasing and development of federal coal deposits (PL 94-377).

Ford vetoed the bill July 3, saying it would cause unnecessary delay in coal production from federal lands and increase coal prices.

The Senate Aug. 3 overrode the veto by a 76-17 vote. The House Aug. 4 completed the override by a 316-85 vote. Both votes were well over the required two-thirds majority. Congress contended that the new procedures would force coal production by sometimes reluctant lessees. In addition, states would get additional revenues to cover the cost of services associated with coal development.

Ford's veto was his 24th during the 94th Congress, and his 51st since taking office in August 1974. It was only the sixth Ford veto to be overridden by the 94th Congress.

Background

Coal accounts for almost 75 percent of the fossil fuel reserves of the United States. Federal coal lands are located primarily in Alaska, Colorado, Montana, New Mexico, North Dakota, Oklahoma, Utah and Wyoming. *(See chapter 4, p. 66)*

Only a small amount of the coal located on federal lands has been produced. In 1974 coal production from these lands amounted to only 3 percent of the nation's coal production. The Department of Interior predicted that year that the increasing need for coal should result in production of 17 times as much coal in the year 2000 as in 1972. It noted that much of the federally owned coal was low in sulfur content and could be strip mined.

The Mineral Leasing Act of 1920 authorized the secretary of interior to grant leases on federal coal lands to companies wishing to develop them. This process was left almost entirely to the discretion of the secretary. The leasing company pays the government a royalty plus an annual amount of rent for the lease.

Outstanding coal leases covered over 780,000 acres of federal land.

In 1971 the Interior Department halted issuance of new coal leases to reassess its coal leasing policy. This decision followed a department study in 1970 which showed that the acreage of coal under lease on public lands had increased almost tenfold from 1945 to 1970 but that production of coal from these leases had declined from 10 million tons in 1945 to 7.2 million tons in 1970. Of 533 active federal coal leases in 1974, only 59 leases were currently producing coal.

Floor Action

The Senate approved S 391 (S Rept 94-296) in July 1975, after attaching provisions regulating the strip mining of coal on federal lands. But key members of the House objected to the strip mining section because it dealt only with federal and not private lands. It wasn't until January 1976 that the House passed its version (HR 6721 — H Rept 94-681) without any strip mining provisions. The House vote was 344-51.

For months, the two sides were in a stalemate. The Senate refused to consider the bill without its strip mining provisions. House leaders held out for separate strip mining legislation to cover both public and private lands.

Finally, on June 21, the Senate gave in. Lee Metcalf, D-Mont., chairman of the Senate Interior Committee's Mining Subcommittee, brought the House bill to the floor and recommended that senators accept it without amendment. They did so, sending it to the president.

But Ford July 3 vetoed S 391, objecting that its requirements "would inhibit coal production on federal lands, probably raise prices for consumers and ultimately delay our achievement of energy independence." Following Interior Department objections, he protested provisions setting 12-1/2 percent minimum royalties and requiring production of federal leases within 10 years.

Both chambers easily overrode the veto, enacting the law Aug. 4.

Provisions

As enacted, major provisions of PL 94-377 amended the Mineral Leasing Act of 1920 to:

● Require that coal leases be issued only by competitive bidding and that at least 50 percent of all lands leased in any year be leased on the basis of a deferred bonus bidding system.

● Forbid issuance of new leases to any leaseholder who has not produced any coal on a lease for 15 years, beginning to count only from the date of enactment of PL 94-377.

● Require inclusion of federally owned coal leases in a comprehensive land use plan before any of that land was leased for coal development and allow leasing only if compatible with that plan.

● Require disapproval of any mining plan or lease which will not achieve the maximum economic recovery of coal.

● Eliminate use of coal prospecting permits and preference right leases, replacing them with a system of non-exclusive exploratory licenses; make unlicensed exploration subject to a fine of up to $1,000 per day.

● Authorized the interior secretary to consolidate, or require leaseholders to consolidate, several mining tracts into one logical mining unit (LMU) not to exceed 25,000 acres in order to foster the most economically efficient mining; require all reserves within the unit to be mined within 40 years.

● Provide that coal leases would be for a term of 20 years and so long afterward as coal is being produced in commercial quantities; require termination of any lease not producing in such quantity after 10 years.

● Increase the minimum royalty from $.05 per ton to 12.5 percent of the value of the coal, except for underground coal for which the secretary could set a lower royalty.

● Permit the secretary to waive the requirement that a lease be continuously operated, if the leaseholder paid an advance royalty for each year of non-production no less than that which would have been paid in a producing year.

● Require federal exploration of lands to be offered for leasing, with publication of all resulting data.

● Increase to 50 percent from 37.5 percent the state share in revenues from leases within the state; allow use of the additional 12.5 percent for planning, construction and maintenance of public facilities; provide that all revenues from geothermal leasing be divided between state and federal treasuries in the same manner as those from coal leasing.

● Limit to 100,000 acres the amount of federal coal lands which any corporation, person, association, subsidiary or affiliate could control at one time.

● Give a governor a chance to delay for six months proposed leases for surface mining in national forests within his state. The interior secretary was required to reconsider the proposed lease during that six-month period in light of the governor's objections.

Naval Petroleum Reserves

Congress in 1976 approved the Naval Petroleum Reserves Production Act (HR 49), granting President Ford's request to allow production of oil from reserves heretofore set aside for the exclusive use of the Navy. Ford signed it into law (PL 94-258) April 5.

Without passage of such a measure, petroleum could be produced from these reserves only when Congress and the president agreed it was necessary for the national defense.

HR 49 directed the Navy secretary to begin production of oil from three of the four reserves within 90 days of enactment. Production would continue at the maximum efficient rate for no more than six years, unless the president and Congress approved a three-year extension. The president was given authority to store the oil in a strategic petroleum reserve for use in national emergencies such as another oil embargo. Congress subsequently appropriated $406,116,000 for the production of oil from these reserves. That sum was included in the fiscal 1977 appropriations bill for the Interior Department (HR 14231 — PL 94-355).

HR 49 transferred to the jurisdiction of the Interior Department the fourth reserve, the largest and richest, which was located in Alaska. It designated it a national reserve to be explored and studied. The bill barred production of oil from the Alaskan reserve until Congress explicitly approved it.

Final action came when the House, by a 390-5 vote,

adopted the conference report on the bill. The Senate had adopted the report by voice vote March 24. The original bills had been very different. The final bill, which was completely rewritten, represented a compromise between the two versions.

Debate over the wisdom of tapping these reserves as part of the national effort toward energy self-sufficiency was compounded by several non-energy-related factors. Among them was suspicion of the major oil companies (Standard Oil of California owned 20 percent of one reserve, at Elk Hills, Calif., and the only pipeline out of that reserve) and the extent to which they would benefit from production of these reserves. Other factors included environmental concern about military supervision of the development of the Alaskan reserve, memories of the Teapot Dome scandal and jurisdictional conflicts between those who wished the Navy (and the House and Senate Armed Services committees) to have that supervisory responsibility.

The bill was passed by both chambers in 1975, with the House taking the approach favoring Interior and the Senate taking the approach favored by the military.

Provisions

The major provisions of PL 94-258:

● Directed the transfer by June 1, 1977, of jurisdiction over the Naval Petroleum Reserve #4 to the interior secretary and redesignated that area as the National Petroleum Reserve in Alaska.

● Specified that the interior secretary would assume full responsibility for the protection of environmental, fish and wildlife, and historical or scenic values in this area; excluded these lands from coverage by the Mineral Leasing Act of 1920.

● Prohibited production of petroleum from the reserve, and any development leading to production until such activity was authorized by Congress.

● Provided for continuation of the ongoing petroleum exploration program in the reserve by the Navy secretary until the transfer to Interior; provided for further exploration after the transfer to Interior.

● Directed an executive branch study to determine the best procedure for development, production, transportation and distribution of the petroleum resources in the reserve, giving consideration to the economic and environmental consequences of that production.

● Authorized whatever appropriations were necessary to implement the provisions relating to the Alaskan reserve.

● Directed the Navy secretary to commence production of petroleum from Naval Petroleum Reserves #1 (Elk Hills), #2 (Buena Vista) and #3 (Teapot Dome) within 90 days of enactment of HR 49, and to continue production at the maximum efficient rate for a period of six years.

● Provided that the president could, at the end of the six-year period, extend the period of production for any of the naval reserves by up to three years after an investigation finding such continued production necessary, and after submitting the report of that investigation to Congress and certifying that such production was in the national interest.

● Gave either chamber of Congress 90 days after receiving this report to veto the extension of the production period.

● Conditioned authorization for production from the Elk Hills reserve upon agreement by the private owner of any interest in that reserve to continue operating the reserve

'Energy Actions' Allowed End To Some Controls on Prices

The second session of the 94th Congress passed up opportunities to block Ford administration proposals lifting price and allocation controls on various types of fuel and eliminating an exemption for small oil refiners from the oil entitlements program.

In its omnibus 1975 energy bill (PL 94-163), Congress gave the Federal Energy Administration authority to modify price and allocation controls and the entitlements program, subject to congressional veto. FEA was to send such proposed changes to Congress as "energy actions"; if neither chamber disapproved a change in 15 days, the change could take effect. *(Other energy actions, pp. 177, 196)*

In April the House refused to consider a resolution disapproving the first "energy action": lifting the price and allocation controls on residual fuel oil, the least refined product derived from processing crude oil. In May Congress refused to block a second "energy action" eliminating an exemption from the entitlements program for small refiners.

On June 15, FEA sent to Congress its third and fourth "energy actions," proposing to end the price and allocation controls for the next level of refined products, home heating oil, diesel fuel and all other middle-distillate refined petroleum products. Again, the House and Senate rejected efforts to take up resolutions disapproving those actions.

On Sept. 15, FEA sent Congress proposals to exempt naphtha jet fuel from federal controls. Congress made no effort to disapprove them and they took effect Oct. 1. Aviation gasoline and kerosene fuel remained under controls.

As a result of the "energy actions," more than half of the products of a barrel of crude oil were exempted from controls, but no significant price increases or shortages developed, reported FEA.

Residual Fuel Oil

The House April 13 turned down an effort to block President Ford's plan to end federal controls on residual fuel oil prices on June 1.

By a 109-272 recorded vote, the House defeated an attempt by Commerce Committee Democrats to push to the floor a resolution (H Res 1135) that would have vetoed the administration's initial proposal for phasing out federal price and allocation controls over petroleum products.

In lifting price and allocation controls under authority conferred by 1975 omnibus energy legislation, FEA concluded that the existing system actually was holding residual prices up by restraining competitive market forces. The Senate made no move to disapprove the plan.

Small Refiner Exemption

Congress May 27 turned down efforts to keep the Federal Energy Administration's second "energy action" of 1976 from taking effect.

The second energy action eliminated the 1975 exemption for small oil refiners from the oil entitlements program. The Senate refused to act to discharge a resolution of disapproval from committee on a 28-57 roll-call vote. The House followed suit by a standing vote of 15-34.

Background. The entitlements program was set up in November 1974 to equalize the cost of a barrel of crude oil to refiners, by requiring refiners with sources of cheaper 'old' oil to pay a certain amount to those who had to buy 'new' oil at as much as $8 per barrel more.

Concerned that the program worked to the disadvantage of small refiners because of the high per barrel cost of small-scale operations, Congress in 1975 exempted refiners whose capacity was less than 100,000 barrels per day from having to buy entitlements for the first 50,000 barrels of oil they processed. That law also authorized the Federal Energy Administration (FEA) to modify the exemption if it resulted in further inequities.

The exemption took effect Dec. 31, 1975; FEA moved Feb. 28 to revoke it. On May 12, FEA officially notified Congress of the proposal to eliminate the exemption and to increase the bias in the entitlement regulations favoring small refiners over the major oil companies. FEA explained that the exemption was giving small refiners who would otherwise have had to buy entitlements an unfair advantage over other small refiners who were sellers of entitlements.

Middle Distillate Fuels

Congress June 30 refused to block a Ford administration proposal to end controls on the price and allocation of diesel fuel, home heating oil and other middle distillate refined petroleum products.

The House voted 194-208 to reject a motion to discharge its Commerce Committee from consideration of resolutions disapproving these changes. The Senate voted 52-32 to table a motion to take up similar resolutions.

As a result those controls were lifted July 1.

According to the Senate Interior Committee, these products accounted for 17 percent of the domestic demand for petroleum products: about three million barrels per day of middle distillates. Half of these three million barrels were used for residential and commercial heating, a highly seasonal demand, and another third were used for transportation.

as a unit in a manner adequately protecting the public interest; empowered the secretary, if agreement was not reached in 90 days of enactment of HR 49, to exercise condemnation authority to acquire that interest. (Standard Oil of California owned 20 percent of the Elk Hills reserve.)

● Authorized the use, storage, or sale to the highest bidder, of the petroleum produced from the reserves; stated that no contract could be awarded allowing any person to control more than 20 percent of the estimated annual U.S. share of oil produced from Elk Hills.

● Directed the Navy secretary to consult with the attorney general on matters relating to the development and production of this oil that might affect competition; gave the attorney general veto power over any contract or operating agreement that could create or maintain a situation inconsistent with antitrust laws.

● Redefined the term "national defense" in the law dealing with the naval petroleum reserves to allow production from them to meet economic emergencies such as that resulting from the 1973 Arab oil embargo.

● Stated that any pipeline that carried oil produced from Elk Hills or Teapot Dome should do so without discrimination and at reasonable rates as a common carrier.

● Directed that any new pipeline for the Elk Hills reserve should have the capacity to carry at least 350,000 barrels of oil a day within three years after enactment of PL 94-258.

● Gave the president authority to place any or all of the U.S. share of petroleum produced from the naval petroleum reserves in the national strategic petroleum reserve set up by the Energy Policy and Conservation Act (PL 94-163), or be exchanged for oil of equal value to be placed in that reserve.

● Set up in the Treasury Department a "Naval Petroleum Reserves Special Account" to receive all proceeds from sale of the U.S. share of the oil produced from the reserves, any related royalties or other revenues from the operation of the reserves and any additional sums appropriated for the maintenance, operation or development of the reserves; specified that these funds could be used for 1) further exploration and development of the reserves; 2) production from the reserves; 3) the construction of facilities related to the production and delivery of the petroleum, and their operation; 4) the procurement of oil for and the construction and operation of facilities for the strategic petroleum reserve; and 5) exploration and study of the national petroleum reserve in Alaska.

Electric Car Subsidies

In a notable election-year setback to the president, Congress Sept. 17, 1976, overrode President Ford's veto of a bill (HR 8800) to promote development of electric-powered cars. The bill became PL 94-413.

It was only the 11th override by Congress out of 56 vetoes by Ford during his two years in the White House.

The House voted to override first on Sept. 16, by a 307-101 vote, 35 more than the necessary two-thirds majority.

The Senate followed suit the next day, 53-20, exceeding the two-thirds mark by four votes.

In vetoing the $160 million bill on Sept. 13, Ford had characterized it as an expensive and unnecessary congressional spending scheme. "I am not prepared to commit the federal government to this type of massive spending program which I believe private industry is best able to undertake," he said.

But supporters of the bill contended it was necessary precisely because the automobile industry had failed to meet the need. They said the president had vetoed the bill on "very bad advice," since it had support from Republicans and had been worked out with the administration in advance.

HR 8800 authorized $160 million, plus $60 million in loan guarantees, for a six-year program to develop and demonstrate electric cars suitable for mass production. Over the period, the government would procure some 7,500 such vehicles and distribute them for use by government, business and private motorists. The aim of the program, sponsors said, was at the second-car market that accounts for about 40 percent of the automobiles on the road.

A companion bill (HR 13655) did not fare so well. HR 13655 authorized a five-year federal program to develop propulsion systems, such as the steam engine, that would provide an alternative to the gasoline-dependent internal combustion engine. President Ford vetoed it Sept. 24. The House also overrode that veto, but the Senate voted to sustain it.

Background

Cars powered by electrically charged batteries were popular in the early 1900s, but by the 1930s were almost completely superseded by autos with internal-combustion engines. The need to conserve fuel and reduce tailpipe pollution inspired new interest in electric cars.

Electrically powered cars would not be potential competitors for highway driving in the near future, however, because they could travel an average of only 50 miles before requiring a recharge. But that range was considered more than adequate for use as a second or third car for city driving.

Of all car trips taken nationwide, half are less than five miles in total distance traveled, well within the range of existing electric cars which could go from 30 to 70 miles at speeds of up to 50 mph without recharging.

Electric cars are quieter than gasoline-powered cars and do not emit tailpipe exhaust. The generation of electric power to charge the cars' batteries does cause air pollution, but the House committee report on HR 8800 said it can be "more reliably and effectively controlled at central electric generating plants than at the exhaust pipes of thousands of vehicles in a city."

As for fuel consumption, the report maintained that electric cars use less energy than gasoline-powered cars in heavy traffic and stop-and-go driving because they do not use energy when not in motion. The report also pointed out electric car batteries could be recharged during the "off-peak" hours of generating plants, another energy savings.

Provisions

As enacted into law, PL 94-413:

● Defined electric and hybrid vehicles as those powered by battery or other sources of electric current or by combinations of an electric motor and other engines, including internal combustion engines.

● Established a research, development and demonstration project in ERDA to examine: 1) energy storage systems; 2) vehicle control systems, including regenerative braking; 3) urban design and traffic management to promote energy conservation and protection of the environment; and 4) vehicle design that emphasized durability, ease of repair, and interchangeability of parts.

● Required ERDA, within 12 months of enactment, to develop data on the state of the art of electric car technology.

● Required ERDA, within another three months, to issue performance standards for existing vehicles and, within an additional six months, to purchase or lease 2,500 vehicles or the maximun available up to 2,500 for demonstration by government, business and private entities.

● Required ERDA, within four years of enactment, to issue performance standards for advanced electric and hybrid vehicles and, within another six months, to purchase or lease 5,000 such vehicles, or the maximum available up to 5,000 for demonstration purposes.

● Provided for federal guarantees of up to $60 million in loans for research and development, prototype development, capital construction and initial operating expenses of participants in the program; provided further that a loan could not exceed 90 percent of the cost of a project, and that no loan to a borrower could exceed $3 million, except in specified circumstances.

● Required the U.S. Postal Service, General Services Administration, Defense Department and other federal agencies to study and arrange for use of electrical vehicles; permitted ERDA, if an agency determined vehicles to be uneconomical, to pay an agency for the extra cost of operating electric vehicles.

● Provided that patent provisions of the Federal Non-Nuclear Energy Research and Development Act of 1974 (PL 93-577) apply to contracts under the program.

● Authorized $160 million, spread over fiscal 1977-81, for the program, and directed that $10 million be used for battery research in fiscal 1977.

Synthetic Fuels Development

Legislation (HR 12112) authorizing federal loan guarantees and price supports for development of synthetic fuels was killed by the House late in the 1976 session when it voted 192-193 on Sept. 23 to defeat the rule allowing floor consideration. This was consistent with a 1975 House action that removed synthetic fuels authorizations from a broader bill.

Opponents of the legislation argued that the measure was too new, too complex and too unstudied to be considered responsibly before the scheduled Oct. 2 adjournment. Different versions of HR 12112 had been reported by four committees and a new substitute had been slated for consideration on the House floor.

An unusual coalition of fiscal conservatives and liberals sympathetic to environmental causes formed to reject the measure, which was supported by the Ford administration, the AFL-CIO, the U.S. Chamber of Commerce, the National Association of Manufacturers, the American Gas Association and the oil shale industry. Allied against the bill were the United Auto Workers, the Environmental Policy Center, the Sierra Club, Friends of the Earth and Congress Watch, among others.

House Committee Action

The House Science and Technology Committee May 15 reported HR 12112. The bill (H Rept 94-1170) provided up to $4 billion in federal loan guarantees for programs to demonstrate the feasibility and costs and benefits of synthetic fuel technologies and new methods for conserving energy, converting urban waste to fuel and using solar energy and other renewable sources. It also provided various forms of aid to communities impacted by the development of these new energy technologies, particularly by synthetic fuel plants.

After being reported, HR 12112 was referred to three other House committees. Each reported the bill in June with proposed amendments. The House Banking, Currency and Housing Committee reported the bill June 18, proposing to amend the bill to authorize slightly less, $3.5 billion, in loan guarantees plus $500 million in price supports (H Rept 94-1170, Part 2). The House Ways and Means Committee reported the bill June 21 and suggested allowing ERDA to guarantee municipal or local bonds (H Rept 94-1170, Part 3).

The House Commerce Committee proposed a complete substitute for the Science Committee bill, cutting back the loan guarantee program to a $2 billion program, available only to projects demonstrating synthetic fuel production from biomass (various forms of waste) and oil shale, demonstrating energy-saving techniques or using renewable resources. In new separate programs, the Commerce Committee bill provided regulatory support and up to $500 million in price guarantees for synthetic fuels produced from coal (H Rept 94-1170, Part 4).

The leadership did not move to bring the bill to the floor and new questions about the wisdom of providing such aid to the embryonic synthetic fuels industry were raised by a Government Accounting Office (GAO) study released Aug. 24.

"Synthetic fuels production is not cost effective in that the total cost of output is not price competitive with foreign oil," the report stated.

"In the present circumstances, GAO believes government financial assistance for commercial development of synthetic fuels should not be provided at this time. Full priority should be directed to development of improved synthetic fuels technologies; however, it appears possible to gain adequate information of an environmental and regulatory nature from smaller plants under government control. When commercialization of the technology becomes a prime objective, consideration also should be given to approaches other than loan guarantees for gaining private industry interest."

But Science and Technology Committee Chairman Olin E. Teague, D-Texas, Sept. 1 wrote House Speaker Carl Albert, D-Okla., threatening to tie up the House during its final weeks through parliamentary obstruction unless the Rules Committee acted on the bill. As a result, the panel added HR 12112 to its agenda and Sept. 15 granted a rule by voice vote. The rule allowed for consideration of a Teague substitute not reported from any committee.

Key provisions of the Teague substitute:

● Authorized $3.5 billion in loan guarantees to be administered by the Energy Research and Development Administration (ERDA) over the next nine years for development of synthetic fuel technologies.

● Permitted up to 50 percent of the guarantees to be used for high-Btu coal gasification; up to 30 percent for fossil-based synthetic fuels, including oil shale; and up to 50 percent for such renewable energy sources as solar, geothermal and biomass.

• Authorized $500 million in price supports for synthetic fuels beginning in fiscal 1978.

House Floor Action

The House Sept. 23 rejected, by a vote of 192-193 (R 82-42; D 110-151), the rule (H Res 1545) which would have allowed four hours of debate on the Teague substitute.

Proponents of the measure, led by Teague and John B. Anderson, R-Ill., argued that the legislation's merits had long been studied and that the question deserved to be decided on the House floor. Teague said Senate Interior Committee Chairman Henry M. Jackson, D-Wash., had assured him the Senate would pass the measure this session if it passed the House.

Opponents saw the question differently. "I think it is an absolute outrage that we are asked to consider this important legislation with just five legislative days left," commented Richard L. Ottinger, D-N.Y.

Resentful of Teague's threat of parliamentary obstruction, the chairman of the Rules Committee, Ray J. Madden, D-Ind., said the measure was expected to draw up to 50 amendments and would tie up the House for days. He termed the legislation "too complicated, too controversial and too long delayed" to be considered. "This is not only a turkey, it's a gobbler," he said.

Outer Continental Shelf

The efforts of the 94th Congress to revise the procedures guiding development of federal offshore oil and gas resources ended in failure late in September 1976. The House Sept. 28, by a 198-194 vote, recommitted the Outer Continental Shelf Lands Act Amendments (S 521) to conference.

The chief sponsors of the bill, Rep. John M. Murphy, D-N.Y., and Sen. Henry M. Jackson, D-Wash., decided it would be futile to reconvene the conferees for further action so late in the session.

The vote to recommit the bill was a victory for the oil and gas industry and the Ford administration. They had opposed the measure as creating unnecessary delays in the process of leasing and developing outer continental shelf (OCS) oil and gas. They contended that the existing framework for leasing and development, which left considerable discretion to the interior secretary, was sufficient. If the bill had reached the president, a veto was likely.

The Senate had approved its version of S 521 (S Rept 94-284) in July 1975, by a vote of 67-19. A year later, in July 1976, the House had approved its version (HR 6218 — H Rept 94-1084), 247-140.

Conferees filed their report (H Rept 94-1632) Sept. 20. The final version of the bill was similar to the House measure. Conferees had rejected a list of more than 50 administration-proposed changes in the measure.

The major provisions of S 521 required the interior secretary to develop a five-year leasing plan for frontier OCS areas. All subsequent lease sales would have to be consistent with that plan.

The bill gave the states affected by OCS development a larger voice in federal OCS decisions, requiring the interior secretary to accept the recommendations of governors or regional advisory boards on leasing decisions, unless they were inconsistent with the national interest. It also attempted to open OCS bidding to oil and gas companies other than the majors.

The House recommittal motion directed conferees to reconsider two controversial provisions: Senate language authorizing the federal government to contract for exploratory drilling on the OCS, to obtain an independent evaluation of the resources there before putting them up for bid, and the provisions revamping the existing structure for formulating safety regulations for the OCS operations.

Although S 521 died, the 94th Congress did clear a related bill (S 586 — PL 94-370), some of whose provisions had once been part of S 521, expanding federal aid to coastal states that would feel the economic and environmental impact of offshore energy development.

Natural Gas Deregulation

The continuing effort by the Ford administration and the energy industry to win enactment of legislation deregulating the price of natural gas was again unsuccessful in 1976. The primary reason was a July 27 decision by the Federal Power Commission (FPC) to substantially raise the price ceiling on natural gas sold in interstate commerce. That action reduced the pressure for deregulation.

But even before the FPC move, enactment of a natural gas deregulation bill in the 94th Congress had become unlikely due to a complicated legislative situation. The Senate and House had passed legislation so different that a compromise appeared impossible, and a new "compromise" bill subsequently reported to the Senate became unpopular even among supporters of decontrol.

Early in the 94th Congress, it had appeared that some sort of legislative natural gas deregulation was likely. Advocates of deregulation, including President Ford, argued that the higher prices which would result from deregulation were needed to encourage increased exploration and development of domestic natural gas reserves and to channel more natural gas into interstate sales from the intrastate market where federal price controls did not apply. (When natural gas was sold within the state where it was produced, it sold in 1975 for prices as high as three or four times the top regulated interstate price of 52 cents per thousand cubic feet.)

The Senate Oct. 22, 1975, passed a bill (S 2310) providing for gradual long-term price deregulation. S 2310 would have ended controls on "new" gas from onshore reserves immediately and terminated offshore gas regulation after five years. The House did not pass the bill before adjourning the first session, but the House Commerce Committee did report an emergency short-term bill (HR 9464 — H Rept 94-732) before adjournment.

When the second session convened, HR 9464 was one of the early orders of business. When the bill reached the floor Feb. 3, the prospects for long-term deregulation looked good after the House voted 230-184 to adopt the rule granted by the Rules Committee that provided for consideration of a permanent deregulation alternative offered by Robert Krueger, D-Texas. But then, in a surprise upset, the House voted 205-201 to adopt a substitute ending price controls over small gas producers but enlarging regulation of major companies. The bill was then passed, 205-194.

The House-passed bill was so different from the 1975 Senate-passed measure that Senate supporters of deregulation chose not to take the bills to conference. Instead, they worked out a new bill (S 3422) to retain price controls

Energy Officials in 1976

There was little change in the top energy-related posts in the Ford administration in 1976. Frank G. Zarb, head of the Federal Energy Administration, remained the chief energy spokesman for the administration. Thomas S. Kleppe continued as interior secretary.

At the end of the year vacancies existed on the Nuclear Regulatory Commission (NRC) and the Federal Power Commission (FPC). Marcus Rowden, one of the original members of the NRC, became chairman when William Anders resigned, but the Senate did not confirm Ford's nomination of Joint Atomic Energy Committee executive director George F. Murphy Jr. to fill the fifth commission seat. Confirmation of Murphy's nomination was blocked by a threatened filibuster during the waning hours of the 94th Congress. Also dead at the end of the Congress was Ford's nomination of Barbara Ann Simpson to fill the vacant seat on the FPC; earlier in the year, Ford had re-appointed John H. Holloman to his seat on the FPC.

---

but allow all prices to rise substantially above the existing 52 cents per thousand cubic feet limit set by the FPC. S 3422, which was reported May 19, was first hailed as a major compromise. But as it came under more scrutiny, industry opposed it, calling for a full lifting of controls. Consumer and labor groups objected that it was too costly to consumers. The measure never came up on the Senate floor.

Vertical Divestiture

The explosive oil divestiture issue, long buried in committee, in 1976 was reported to the Senate floor for the first time. But the Senate leadership was reluctant to take the controversial, time-consuming issue to the floor in an election year, especially when the bill faced a certain veto, and it was never brought up for debate.

The proposal approved by the Senate Judiciary Committee June 15 by an 8-7 vote (S 2387) would have forced the breakup of the nation's 18 largest oil companies. It required companies engaged in production, marketing, refining and transportation to divest themselves of all but one phase of the business within five years, a procedure known as vertical divestiture. Under the existing system most major companies operated in all four areas and achieved substantial economies — and, critics said, market domination — by being able to supply their own needs with their own resources. The bill would have forced the companies to compete with each other in buying and selling the resources.

The first signs of growing support for oil company divestiture appeared in October 1975 when the Senate rejected by only nine votes, 45-54, a divestiture measure offered by Philip A. Hart, D-Mich., and James Abourezk, D-S.D., as an amendment to a natural gas deregulation bill (S 2310). Related divestiture amendments to the same bill were rejected by subsequent votes of 40-49 and 39-53.

The oil industry, which had been caught off guard by the 1975 divestiture votes, mobilized a heavy lobbying campaign against the proposal. Birch Bayh, D-Ind., called it "the most sophisticated, elaborate and expensive lobby effort I've ever seen."

Before the 1975 Senate votes, the major congressional action on divestiture had been 10 years of hearings on the issue by the Senate Judiciary Subcommittee on Antitrust and Monopoly. Subcommittee Chairman Hart had nursed the bill through the hearings but avoided a subcommittee vote because he did not have enough support.

That situation changed at the beginning of the 94th Congress when conservative retirees were replaced with more liberal members. The reconstituted subcommittee April 1 approved S 2387, sending it to the full committee by a vote of 4-3.

Provisions

S 2387 was reported (S Rept 94-1005) June 28. Major provisions of the bill:

● Defined a major marketer as one that markets or distributes 100 million barrels of refined petroleum products in a calendar year; a major producer as one that produces 36.5 million barrels of crude oil in a calendar year; a major refiner as one that refines 100 million barrels of oil in a calendar year.

● Made it illegal, five years after enactment, for any major producer to own or control any marketing, refining or transportation asset; for any petroleum transporter, including crude oil and refined product pipelines without regard to size, to own or control any production, refining or marketing asset; for any major refiner or major marketer to own or control any production or transportation asset; for anyone owning a refining, production or marketing asset to transport oil by a transportation asset in which he has an interest.

● Upon enactment, barred major refiners from owning or operating any marketing asset not operated before Jan. 1, 1976.

● Allowed the Federal Trade Commission (FTC) to exempt from the provisions of the act a transportation asset upon finding that the asset is so integral to the operations of the firm that no public purpose would be served by divestiture and that retention of the asset would not injure competition.

● Allowed the FTC to grant exemptions of up to one year from existing laws prohibiting interlocking relationships, in order to facilitate divestiture.

● Required firms affected by divestiture to provide the FTC with information it requests within 120 days.

● Gave the FTC jurisdiction over proxy solicitations by those affected by divestiture until divestiture is completed.

● Empowered the FTC to require submission of divestiture plans within 18 months of enactment; gave the FTC authority to approve, modify and enforce the plans.

● Directed the FTC to sue companies if necessary to assure compliance with the act.

● Provided civil penalties of $100,000 for an individual and $1 million for a corporation for violation of the act.

● Provided civil penalties of $100,000 for persons who violate orders issued by the FTC under the act, or $100,000 per day in cases of continuing non-compliance.

● Established a special Temporary Petroleum Industry Divestiture Court, consisting of at least three judges appointed by the chief justice of the United States from U.S. district court and courts of appeal judges.

● Empowered the U.S. chief justice to designate one of the judges as chief justice of the court.

● Gave the court the powers of a U.S. district court.

● Gave the court exclusive jurisdiction over matters arising from the act.

● Gave the U.S. Supreme Court sole jurisdiction over appeals arising from the temporary court; required any appeal petitions to be made to the Supreme Court within 30 days of an order or judgment by the temporary court; and instructed the Supreme Court to expedite action on matters arising from the act.

1977

Highlights

Energy Department

In a victory for President Carter, Congress approved legislation (PL 95-91) creating a new Cabinet-level Department of Energy, which consolidated a vast array of energy powers and programs.

Emergency Gas Sales

Six days after President Carter asked for extraordinary powers to combat a natural gas shortage, Congress cleared legislation (PL 95-2) granting the president temporary authority to order transfers of interstate natural gas to areas where fuel supplies had been depleted and to approve sales of gas to interstate buyers at unregulated prices.

Alaska Gas Route

Congressional approval was given to President Carter's choice for a natural gas pipeline from Alaska's North Slope through western Canada, where it would link up with existing pipelines going primarily to the Midwestern and Western United States (PL 95-158).

Strategic Oil Reserves

In a move to accelerate the storage of oil in a national reserve, $1.21 billion was authorized for the purchase of that oil (PL 95-70).

Joint Atomic Energy Committee

The once powerful Joint Atomic Energy Committee went out of existence in 1977.

Strip Mining

Passage of the landmark Surface Mining Control and Reclamation Act (PL 95-87) capped a five-year effort, led by environmentalists, to impose federal regulation on the strip mining of coal.

Energy Policy Package

Despite a back-breaking push from May through mid-December, Congress was unable in 1977 to complete action on Carter's national energy plan. The House passed the plan largely intact Aug. 5 as one omnibus bill (HR 8444). The Senate took a different approach, breaking the package into separate bills. The Senate eventually passed five bills, the last on Oct. 31, but they differed drastically from Carter's proposals and the House-passed measure. Two portions of the package, natural gas pricing and energy taxes, were still tied up in conference when Congress adjourned.

Clinch River Reactor/DOE Authorization

Insisting that plutonium production posed a threat to world peace, Carter vetoed a $6.2 billion Energy Department authorization bill which contained $80 million for continued work on the plutonium-producing nuclear breeder reactor at Clinch River, Tenn. Carter had requested $33 million, just enough to terminate the project.

The Year in Review

The first session of the 95th Congress chalked up a record of substantial achievement in the energy field, even though at the year's end, it had not completed work on President Carter's complex package of energy measures.

Early in the session, Congress passed emergency natural gas legislation in response to problems created by severe winter weather. By late summer, Congress had completed action on a measure creating a Cabinet-level Department of Energy.

Both chambers passed their own versions of Carter's proposed energy conservation, coal conversion, oil and gas pricing, energy tax and utility rate measures during 1977. Conferees were still working on the final package as the session ended.

In other action, Congress approved a route to carry natural gas from Alaska to the lower United States and agreed to funding to speed establishment of a national oil reserve. Exercising his veto power for the first time, President Carter rejected an energy research and development authorization because it continued funding for the controversial Clinch River breeder reactor, a program the president wanted killed. No attempt was made to override the veto.

Carter Energy Bill

Jimmy Carter's crusade for a comprehensive national energy policy dominated Congress and public affairs more than any other domestic issue during his first year as president.

Both the new Democratic president and the Democratic congressional leaders made passage of a national energy policy their top legislative priority for 1977.

"I think it's legitimate to measure the success of Congress and my own administration, at least in domestic affairs, on what happens to energy," Carter said as late as Oct. 18, sizing up his first year as president in an interview with the Associated Press.

Yet, when the year ended, there was no comprehensive energy policy signed into law. The House and Senate passed versions of the program, but they differed substantially on two key areas: natural gas regulation and energy tax policy. Conference committees were able to resolve other issues but found themselves mired in gas and tax controversies. Conferees quit work Dec. 22; their next scheduled meeting was Jan. 23, 1978. Final action did not occur until October 1978 when Congress approved a modified version of the president's plan.

The Plan

In April 1977, Carter unveiled his national energy plan. Its primary goal was to cut America's appetite for oil and natural gas and to use available energy more efficiently. Included in the complex package of regulatory and tax measures were recommendations to set mandatory energy efficiency standards for certain home appliances, require certain utilities and other businesses to substitute use of coal and other fuels for the oil and gas they previously burned, encourage property owners to insulate their buildings and place new taxes on gas-guzzling cars and domestically produced oil.

The president acknowledged that his program would not be popular but he insisted that it was necessary. "With the exception of preventing war, this is the greatest challenge our country will face during our lifetimes," Carter said April 18 in a televised address to the nation. "The energy crisis has not yet overwhelmed us, but it will if we do not act quickly. . . ."

Congressional Action

The first session of the 95th Congress could be said to have had two agendas: energy and everything else.

The president's energy plan went to the House first, then to the Senate. In the House, Speaker Thomas P. O'Neill Jr., D-Mass., used all the powers he could muster to strong-arm the Carter program to passage in record time. The proposal was considered by several separate committees and then sent to an ad hoc committee O'Neill created specifically to handle the plan. The various committee versions were merged into one bill (HR 8444) that passed the House Aug. 5, 244-177.

In the Senate, Majority Leader Robert C. Byrd, D-W.Va., cleared all other bills from the Senate agenda to give the energy program undivided attention. It was passed as five separate bills between Sept. 28 and Oct. 31.

The five Senate bills were S 977, intended to encourage utilities and industries to change to the use of coal as their major fuel; S 2057, to encourage conservation of energy; S 2104, to deregulate natural gas; S 2114, to spur reform of electric rates; and HR 5263, to provide tax incentives for more efficient use of energy.

Conference Action

The White House and congressional leaders held out hope following completion of Senate action Oct. 31 that conference agreements on the Carter package could be reached and a final version approved before the year's end.

But that was not to be. The wide gulfs between the Senate and the House on natural gas and tax policy could not be bridged in the time that remained. A secondary

Changing Prices, Supply By 'Energy Actions'

The first session of the 95th Congress acquiesced in two Carter administration proposals concerning energy matters. The first accelerated the schedule for stockpiling 500 million barrels of crude oil as insurance against a future supply crisis. The second extended the government's approval of a 10 percent annual increase in the price of a barrel of domestic crude oil.

Under the 1975 Energy Policy and Conservation Act (PL 94-163), the Federal Energy Administration (FEA) was authorized to modify fuel price and allocation programs through the use of so-called "energy actions." Energy action proposals were to be submitted to Congress and would take effect within set periods of time if neither house disapproved. *(Energy actions, pp. 171, 196)*

Seven energy actions were submitted in 1976. President Ford submitted two early in 1977, providing for decontrol of gasoline prices, but they were rescinded by President Carter.

The two 1977 Carter energy actions that took effect:

● Detailed a program to stockpile 500 million barrels of crude oil in a national petroleum reserve by the end of 1980, rather than by the end of 1982 as the Ford administration had proposed. The stockpile program was authorized by PL 94-163. The change in schedule took effect April 18, 1977. Congress in separate legislation passed in 1977 (S 1468 — PL 95-70) authorized $1.21 billion for purchase of the oil.

● Continued authorization of the 10 percent annual increase in the average price of a barrel of domestic oil first granted under PL 94-163. The price increase was expected to offset inflation and to provide an incentive for production. The proposal took effect March 15, 1977.

reason was that conferees set a fairly relaxed pace in pursuing their negotiations.

Conferees took up the first of the five basic portions of the Carter energy package, general energy conservation, Oct. 18. They reached agreement on it Oct. 31, just under two weeks later. On Oct. 31, they started the second bill, coal conversion, and completed it Nov. 11, again in less than two weeks. On the third bill, utility rates, they reached their key agreement in four days, took a 10-day Thanksgiving recess and returned to finish the conference in five days more.

It was when they reached natural gas regulation that the conference completely bogged down. That conference began Dec. 2. Battle lines on the issue were rigid and there was little middle ground for compromise. Complicating negotiations immensely was the fact that Senate conferees split, 9-9, and could not agree among themselves on much of anything.

Contributing to the conference breakdown was the refusal of conferees to negotiate the complex energy tax proposal until the natural gas bill was resolved.

Because House Speaker O'Neill was insistent that the House not vote on any conference agreement until all could be combined for a single up-or-down vote, none of the Carter energy plan could be sent to the floor for final congressional action until conferees resolved differences on natural gas pricing and tax policy provisions. Consequently, Congress adjourned Dec. 15 with three conference agreements on Carter's energy package on the shelf and two more caught in intense negotiations. *(Details of congressional action, p. 187)*

Energy Department

Succeeding where earlier presidents had failed, President Jimmy Carter Aug. 4, 1977, signed into law a bill (S 826 — PL 95-91) creating a new Cabinet-level Department of Energy. The new department came into existence Oct. 1, 1977.

The first new Cabinet agency since creation of the Department of Transportation in 1966, the Department of Energy assumed the powers and functions of the Federal Power Commission (FPC), the Federal Energy Administration (FEA) and the Energy Research and Development Administration (ERDA). All three of those agencies went out of existence as the new department was born. The new department also absorbed programs formerly administered by the departments of Interior, Defense, Commerce, and Housing and Urban Development, and the Interstate Commerce Commission. In addition, the Energy Department was assigned a consulting role in regard to some of the work of the Department of Transportation and the Rural Electrification Administration.

The first secretary of energy was James R. Schlesinger, who was named to that post after serving as chairman of the Atomic Energy Commission (1971-73), director of the Central Intelligence Agency (1973) and secretary of defense (1973-75). Schlesinger had served as Carter's chief energy adviser during the early months of the Carter administration. The president sent his nomination of Schlesinger as secretary of energy to the Senate on Aug. 4; it was approved that same day by voice vote.

The Department of Energy initially employed almost 20,000 persons transferred with the programs from existing departments and agencies. Its fiscal 1978 budget was $10.6 billion.

Point of Controversy

President Carter formally proposed creation of the new department on March 1, 1977. The bill that arrived on his desk some five months later differed in only one major respect from his original proposal.

Carter and Congress disagreed over who, in the new energy structure, should have the power to set prices for natural gas, oil and electricity. Carter would have authorized the secretary to exercise this power, overseeing the work of an Energy Regulatory Administration within his department.

But majority sentiment in both chambers of Congress ran against that proposal, on the grounds that it was unwise

---

Early ERDA Controversies

Since the creation of the Energy Research and Development Administration in 1974, every one of its authorization measures had found the path through Congress a difficult one.

The first ERDA authorization, passed in 1975, authorized $5 billion. Its passage was marked by controversy over the Clinch River demonstration plant — increasingly more expensive than originally estimated — and over Senate-added language authorizing federal loan guarantees to encourage industry to get into the business of synthesizing oil and gas-like fuels from more plentiful natural resources, such as coal.

The second ERDA authorization bill was never enacted. Reported by conferees late in the 94th Congress, it was blocked from final passage by a senator frustrated in his effort to become a member of the Joint Committee on Atomic Energy. The fiscal 1977 bill, which would have authorized almost $8 billion, died at the end of the 1976 session.

Despite lack of a fiscal 1977 authorization, a fiscal 1977 appropriation bill was passed with provisos forbidding release of the ERDA funds until an authorization was enacted. Congress Feb. 7, 1977, released the fiscal 1977 funds when it repealed the provisos requiring authorization (H J Res 227 — PL 95-3). Congress subsequently enacted a bill (S 36 — PL 95-39) authorizing funds for ERDA's non-nuclear programs in fiscal 1977.

---

to give such power to a single person who served at the pleasure of the president. To shield such sensitive and far-reaching economic decisions from political pressure, Congress included in PL 95-91 language creating an independent Federal Energy Regulatory Commission (FERC) that would set energy prices. However, if the president found that a national emergency required quick action on such matters, the secretary could circumvent the commission on questions of oil prices.

Carter Plan

"Nowhere is the need for reorganization and consolidation greater than in energy policy," Carter said in a March 1 message to Congress unveiling his reorganization plan. "All but two of the executive branch's Cabinet departments now have some responsibility for energy policy, but no agency . . . has the broad authority needed to deal with our energy problems in a comprehensive way."

Carter's proposed Department of Energy called for consolidation of the FEA, the FPC and ERDA in their entireties. Specific energy functions from several other departments and agencies were also marked for transfer to the new department. In addition, the new department would share control over leasing policy for public lands with the Department of the Interior, which had held sole authority over that function.

The Energy Resources Council, which consisted of the heads of several Cabinet departments who coordinated energy policy, would be abolished. Carter said he intended to establish by executive order an interdepartmental body to coordinate energy policy.

The Nuclear Regulatory Commission and the Environmental Protection Agency would remain separate and independent.

Senate Action

The Senate approved creation of the new department May 18 by a vote of 74-10.

Committee Changes. The Senate Committee on Governmental Affairs reported S 826 (S Rept 95-164) May 4. The most important changes that the committee recommended in the president's proposal involved energy pricing and leasing of public lands. The committee located the energy pricing powers in a three-member Energy Regulatory Board, not the secretary of energy. Responding to concern that energy needs might override all other considerations in the leasing of public lands, the committee bill was more explicit than the administration proposal in dividing up duties in that area between the secretaries of energy and the interior.

Floor Consideration. Senate passage was surprisingly easy and quick. As early as April, Capitol Hill rumblings indicated widespread fears that Carter wanted too much power for the department. It appeared the proposal might become entangled with the president's controversial energy policy proposals and face indefinite delay.

But the bill was rushed through the Senate with less than a full day's debate, with Governmental Affairs Chairman Abraham Ribicoff, D-Conn., and Energy Committee Chairman Henry M. Jackson, D-Wash., leading the charge.

Ribicoff may have summed up the main reason for the rush in his introductory remarks. "Mr. President," he said, "there is universal agreement that a consolidation of functions and agencies in the energy area is necessary." But the swift and overwhelming approval also appeared to reflect a determination by Democratic congressional leaders to work with the president in tackling the nation's energy problems.

The debate was not only brief, but was for the most part quite narrowly focused. The Senate made no major changes in the committee version of the bill. Most floor discussion centered on 17 proposed amendments that addressed relatively small issues. Of the amendments, 14 passed by voice vote without significant challenge. Three failed on roll calls. With few and fleeting exceptions, the broad sweep of the measure and its major policy controversies escaped the Senate without examination on the floor.

House Action

The House passed its version of S 826 June 3, just two weeks after Senate passage. The vote on passage, which came after two days of debate, was 310-20.

Committee Changes. The House Government Operations Committee reported the House bill (HR 6804 — H Rept 95-346, Part I) May 16. Part II of the report was filed May 24 by the House Post Office and Civil Service Committee.

The House committees adopted the administration-

suggested approach to energy pricing, leaving price-setting powers with the energy secretary. Like the Senate bill, however, HR 6804 spelled out in considerable detail the division of functions between the new department and the Interior Department with regard to leasing public lands.

The main innovation in the House bill was the addition of an Office of Inspector General within the new department. That office would be responsible for investigating fraud and program abuses.

Floor Consideration. House floor consideration of the Energy Department bill was dominated by concern over one issue: would the head of the new department have an inordinate amount of power over the nation's economic life? As William L. Armstrong, R-Colo., put it: "We're talking about putting in one person authority to say who gets to keep a job and who does not, which regions get fuel in time of shortage, and which do not. . . . We're talking really about the life or death power over every farm, business and industry in the country."

The House considered some 34 proposed amendments, most of which were non-controversial and were adopted by voice votes. The concern over the power of the new secretary of energy climaxed in the adoption June 2 of an amendment curtailing his power over energy prices.

By a vote of 239-116, the House adopted an amendment that placed the power to set the wellhead price of natural gas, and to make other regulations concerning interstate power sales, in a five-member Federal Energy Regulatory Commission. The amendment was proposed by John E. Moss, D-Calif.

Conference, Final Action

Conferees filed their report on S 826 (H Rept 95-539; S Rept 95-367) July 26. The House adopted the report Aug. 2 by a vote of 353-57. A motion to recommit the bill failed earlier, 157-257. The Senate cleared the bill for the White House a few hours later, adopting the report by a vote of 76-14.

Provisions

As signed into law, PL 95-91:

Title I — Findings and Purposes

● Declared that energy problems presented a serious threat to the United States that the government could respond to best through formation of a new Department of Energy.

Title II — Establishment of the Department

● Created a Department of Energy headed by a secretary appointed by the president subject to Senate approval.
● Created within the department the following positions to be filled by presidential appointment subject to Senate confirmation: a deputy secretary, a general counsel, an under secretary and eight assistant secretaries.
● Specified 11 broad areas of functional responsibility over which the assistant secretaries would hold primary management control, including: fuel supply and leasing procedures, research and development, environment, international energy policy, national security, intergovernmental relations, competition and consumer affairs, nuclear waste management, energy conservation, power marketing, and public and congressional relations.
● Specified that upon appointment of each assistant sec-

Joint Atomic Energy Committee Quietly Eliminated in 1977

The Joint Atomic Energy Committee, once described as "the most powerful congressional committee in the history of the nation" quietly died in 1977. The committee's all-inclusive jurisdiction over matters involving atomic energy was divided among standing committees in each chamber.

Background

The Atomic Energy Act of 1946 (PL 79-585) created both the Atomic Energy Commission (AEC) and the joint committee to foster development of the new power of atomic energy.

It was the only permanent joint committee ever created that received continuing authority to report legislation. Granted unique oversight powers in its chartering act, the committee soon dominated policy formation to an extent unprecedented for a legislative panel. Sen. Henry M. Jackson, D-Wash., a longtime committee member, asserted as far back as 1953 that "the committee made the decisions, with the advice and consent of the executive branch," instead of the reverse, as was more usual.

For most of its life, the joint committee functioned almost as a unicameral legislature within the bicameral Congress. It usually reported identical bills simultaneously to each chamber, and when presented with floor amendments, resolved differences between House and Senate versions by functioning as its own conference committee.

Controversy and Challenge

As nuclear power became more and more a matter of public controversy in the 1970s, however, the joint committee drew increasing criticism for its protective attitude toward the subject and the industry.

In 1976 for the first time, opponents of the committee were able to block several major committee initiatives.

The full Senate killed a joint committee bill proposing to allow private investment in the uranium enrichment business, until that time a government monopoly. The committee's bill authorizing fiscal 1977 funds for the Energy Research and Development Administration died on the Senate floor late in the session. And committee opponents also blocked the appointment of a veteran member of the joint committee staff to the Nuclear Regulatory Commission.

Six of the committee's 18 members retired at the end of the 94th Congress or were defeated in the November 1976 elections. With one-third of the seats on the panel vacant, it was clearly a propitious time for its opponents to move.

That move came in early December 1976. Rep. Jonathan B. Bingham, D-N.Y., proposed to the House Democratic Caucus that the House strip the joint committee of virtually all its legislative power, the key factor that had made it so unique among joint committees in the history of Congress. On Dec. 8, the House Democrats agreed to back that proposal.

1977 Action

The full House formally adopted a package of House reforms (H Res 5) on Jan. 4, the opening day of the 95th Congress. Among the changes in House rules made by this package, adopted by a vote of 256-142, was elimination of the legislative authority of the Joint Committee on Atomic Energy. The jurisdiction of the joint committee was then divided among five standing committees, as follows:

• Military nuclear concerns to the Committee on Armed Services;

• General regulation of the nuclear industry to the Committee on Interior and Insular Affairs;

• Nuclear export questions to the Committee on International Relations;

• Research and development questions to the Committee on Science and Technology;

• Facilities regulation and oversight to the Committee on Interstate and Foreign Commerce.

Opponents of nuclear power hailed the reform as providing nuclear power critics with access to policy questions from the subcommittee stage on up for the first time. Also, they welcomed the entry of the Interior Committee, headed by liberal environmentalist Morris K. Udall, D-Ariz., into direct nuclear power policy-making. Finally, the reforms seemed to put nuclear power on an equal footing with other energy technologies.

The Senate concurred in the action of the House Feb. 4, when it approved a major overhaul of the Senate committee structure that included abolition of the Joint Atomic Energy Committee. The Senate resolution (S Res 4) reallocated the joint committee's responsibilities among three standing committees:

• Military nuclear matters to the Senate Armed Services Committee.

• Non-military development of nuclear energy to the new Committee on Energy and Natural Resources.

• Non-military environmental regulation of nuclear energy to the new Committee on Environment and Public Works.

The Senate followed that action with passage March 31 of a bill (S 1153 — PL 95-110) amending the Atomic Energy Act of 1954 (PL 83-703), by abolishing the joint committee. The House passed an amended version of S 1153 by voice vote Aug. 5. The Senate cleared the measure the same day, completing the formal interment of the Joint Atomic Energy Committee.

retary, the president should identify the functions that individual would manage.

• Created within the department a Federal Energy Regulatory Commission.

• Created within the department an Energy Information Administration to be headed by an administrator appointed by the president subject to Senate confirmation.

• Directed the administrator to create a central unified energy data collection and analysis program, and assigned him the energy data gathering functions provided by the Energy Supply and Environmental Coordination Act of 1974 and the Federal Energy Administration Act of 1974.

• Protected the administrator from having to obtain approval from departmental superiors in the collection or analysis of energy data.

• Specified that the administration must provide promptly any information requested by any other office in the department.

• Specified that information held by the administration must be released to the public promptly upon request, except for information exempted by law from disclosure.

• Directed the administrator to identify major energy companies in the United States and to prepare a financial report form for those companies to fill out at least annually.

• Specified that the financial report form should be designed to allow the government to evaluate each company's revenues, profits, cash flow and costs resulting from each phase of its energy-related operations.

• Directed that the form should be in use by the second full calendar year following enactment of the law and that the information gathered should be summarized for inclusion in the department's annual report.

• Created within the department an Economic Regulatory Administration to be headed by an administrator appointed by the president subject to Senate confirmation.

• Created within the department an Office of Inspector General headed by an Inspector General and a deputy appointed by the president subject to Senate approval.

• Provided that the Inspector General and his deputy could be removed from office by the president, but required the president to explain the reasons for the removal to both houses of Congress.

• Charged the Inspector General with responsibility for auditing and investigating department activities in an effort to promote efficiency and economy and to detect and prevent fraud and abuse.

• Required the Inspector General to report on March 31 each year to the secretary, to Congress and to the Federal Energy Regulatory Commission on problems in the department and his recommendations for correcting them.

• Directed the Inspector General to report immediately to the secretary and the Federal Energy Regulatory Commission, and within 30 days thereafter to appropriate congressional committees, upon discovery of any flagrant or serious problems.

• Provided the Inspector General with authority to inspect all documents available to the department, and gave him subpoena power.

• Created within the department an Office of Energy Research to be headed by a director appointed by the president subject to Senate approval.

• Charged the Office of Energy Research with responsibility for monitoring the department's research and development programs and related activities and for advising the secretary on those matters.

• Created a Leasing Liaison Committee composed of an equal number of members appointed by the secretary of energy and the secretary of the interior.

Title III — Transfer of Functions

• Transferred to the secretary of energy all functions held by the Federal Energy Administration (FEA) and the Energy Research and Development Administration (ERDA).

• Transferred to the secretary all functions held by the Federal Power Commission (FPC) except those reserved to the Federal Energy Regulatory Commission (FERC) under Title IV *(see below)*.

• Transferred to the secretary from the Department of the Interior authority over the Southeastern Power Administration, the Southwestern Power Administration, the Alaska Power Administration, the Bonneville Power Administration, and the power marketing functions of the Bureau of Reclamation and of the Falcon Dam and Amistad Dam on the Rio Grande River.

• Provided that the Southeastern, Southwestern, Bonneville and Alaska power administrations would remain separate and distinct entities within the department.

• Created a separate administration within the department to be headed by an administrator appointed by the secretary to oversee functions transferred from the Bureau of Reclamation and the Falcon and Amistad dams.

• Transferred to the secretary from the Department of the Interior's Bureau of Mines authorities to gather data on fuel supplies, and to conduct research on technology for the production of solid fuel minerals and on coal.

• Transferred to the secretary from the Department of the Interior the power to set economic terms of leases for energy development on public lands, including production rates and diligence requirements.

• Reserved to the secretary of the interior all other authority over public lands leasing, including sole power to issue leases and to enforce their regulation.

• Specified that the secretary of energy must consult with the interior secretary before setting down economic regulations for leases and must allow him at least 30 days for comment prior to the issuance of such regulations.

• Specified that the secretary of energy would have 30 days prior to publication of final lease terms to veto any economic terms included in the lease.

• Required that in the event of any veto of a lease term, the secretary must explain his action in a detailed written statement to the interior secretary.

• Transferred to the secretary of energy from the Department of Housing and Urban Development authority to set energy conservation standards for new buildings.

• Provided that in setting automotive fuel efficiency standards, the secretary of transportation must consult with the energy secretary and allow him at least 10 days for comment on standards before they were proposed.

• Transferred to the energy secretary from the Interstate Commerce Commission authority over oil pipelines.

• Transferred to the secretary from the Department of Defense authority over three naval oil reserves and three oil shale reserves.

• Transferred to the secretary from the Department of Commerce authority over industrial energy conservation programs.

• Transferred to the secretary from the Department of Defense authority over the Division of Naval Reactors and the Division of Military Applications.

• Transferred to the Department of Transportation from

Energy Chiefs

Two men served as secretary of energy during the Carter administration — James R. Schlesinger and Charles W. Duncan Jr.

Schlesinger, Carter's top White House adviser on energy during the early months of the administration, was named and confirmed by voice vote as the nation's first secretary of energy on Aug. 4, 1977, the afternoon that President Carter signed the law creating the new department.

Schlesinger had already compiled a long record of government service, including terms as chairman of the Atomic Energy Commission (1971-73), director of the Central Intelligence Agency (1973) and secretary of defense (1973-75). But for all his government experience, Schlesinger drew vigorous criticism of his lack of administrative skill in putting the new department into working order. He resigned in mid-1979.

As his replacement, President Carter chose Duncan, deputy secretary of defense since 1977. President of the Coca-Cola Co. before moving into the government, Duncan was nominated secretary of energy July 20, 1979. He was confirmed July 31 by a 95-1 vote. Duncan served in that post for the remainder of the Carter administration, winning high marks for his management of the new department.

the FEA authority over a van pooling and car pooling program.

Title IV — Federal Energy Regulatory Commission

- Created within the Energy Department an independent regulatory commission of five members appointed by the president subject to Senate approval.
- Provided that the commission's members would serve staggered terms of four years and that not more than three could belong to the same political party.
- Transferred to the commission from the Federal Power Commission power to set rates on the sale of natural gas and wholesale purchases of electricity.
- Transferred to the commission from the Federal Power Commission power to regulate mergers and securities acquisitions under the Federal Power and Natural Gas acts.
- Transferred to the commission from the Interstate Commerce Commission authority to set rates for the transportation of oil by pipelines and for setting the valuation of such pipelines.
- Specified that the commission could claim jurisdiction over any proposal by the energy secretary to alter oil price regulations under the Emergency Petroleum Allocation Act of 1973.
- Provided that if the commission recommended that the proposed oil pricing rule either be changed or killed, the secretary would have to issue the rule as urged by the commission or not issue it at all.

- Provided that the secretary could issue oil pricing decisions without referring them to the commission if the president declared the existence of an emergency of overriding national importance. Oil pricing decisions under those circumstances would be subject to veto by either house of Congress within 15 days of their submission, as provided by the Energy Policy and Conservation Act of 1975 and the Emergency Petroleum Allocation Act of 1973.
- Provided that the commission would hold jurisdiction over any other matter before the department required by law to be settled by on-the-record decision after an opportunity for a hearing.
- Reserved to the secretary jurisdiction over exports and imports of natural gas and electricity.
- Specified that commission decisions on matters under its jurisdiction would be final agency actions.
- Empowered the secretary to propose rules for commission action, to intervene in any commission proceeding and to set reasonable time limits for commission actions.

Title V — Regulations and Review

- Made the Administrative Procedure Act applicable to department rules and orders.
- Provided that any proposed rule had to be posted for comment in the *Federal Register* at least 30 days before it became effective.
- Allowed the secretary to waive notice and comment provisions if he determined that no substantial issue was at stake and that the proposed rule would be unlikely to have a substantial impact on large numbers of people or businesses.
- Provided that when previous law specified which courts held judicial review authority over functions assigned to the new department, review would occur as those laws required; otherwise, federal district courts would hold original jurisdiction for judicial review of the act.
- Provided that a person charged by department administrators with violating the Emergency Petroleum Allocation Act of 1973 had to be issued a written remedial order that would become effective in 30 days unless the person served notice he would contest the order.
- Specified that contested remedial orders would be referred to the FERC for resolution.
- Authorized the secretary to provide adjustments as necessary to any rule to prevent special hardships or inequities.
- Provided that persons believing themselves unfairly denied a special adjustment to a rule could appeal to the FERC.
- Directed the secretary to report to Congress within one year after the act became effective on the department's experience with administrative procedures.

Title VI — Administrative Provisions

- Prohibited departmental supervisory employees from knowingly receiving compensation from or owning any interest in any energy concern.
- Gave personnel transferred to the department six months to comply with the divestiture-of-energy-interests requirement.
- Allowed the secretary to waive the divestiture-of-energy-interests requirement where he determined it would result in exceptional hardship, and provided he published any such waiver in the *Federal Register*.

● Required all employees of the department to disclose the extent of income from energy concerns that they or their dependents received in any year during their service in the department.

● Required employees to disclose within 60 days of taking a supervisory job any payment over $2,500 that they had received from any energy concern within the past five years.

● Prohibited supervisory employees from attempting to influence the department on any matter for one year after leaving the department.

● Prohibited supervisory employees who were formerly with energy concerns from participating for one year in any department proceeding in which their former employers were substantially involved (other than in general rulemaking activities).

● Provided criminal penalties up to one year in jail and fines up to $2,500 for persons who knowingly violated provisions governing disclosure of interests in an energy concern, and fines up to $10,000 for violations of other ethical standards under the title.

● Authorized 689 "supergrade" Civil Service level positions for the department, 200 of which would be exempt from Civil Service laws and regulations.

● Authorized the appointment by the secretary of 14 additional executive level personnel.

● Directed the secretaries of defense, commerce, housing and urban development, transportation, agriculture and interior, and the administrators of the U.S. Postal Service and the General Services Administration to designate one senior official as the agency's energy conservation officer.

● Directed the secretary of energy to submit to the president, for later submission to Congress, an annual report as soon as possible after the end of each fiscal year.

● Specified that such annual reports should include a statement of the secretary's goals and plans and an assessment of progress toward their achievement.

● Directed that the reports include projections on the nation's energy needs, estimates of domestic and foreign energy supplies, estimates on trends in energy pricing and use, a summary of energy research and conservation programs, and to the extent possible, a summary of activities in the United States by companies owned or controlled by foreign interests that owned or controlled domestic energy supplies.

● Directed the secretary of the interior to submit within one year after the measure's enactment a report on the government's leasing operations.

Title VII — Transitional and Other Provisions

● Transferred to the energy secretary all personnel, assets and liabilities that went along with functions transferred under the act.

● Provided that personnel transferred to the department could not be fired or reduced in pay scale for one year.

● Directed the Civil Service Commission to report to Congress within one year on the effect of the department's creation on employees.

Title VIII — Energy Plan

● Required the president to submit to Congress, beginning April 1, 1979, a biennial energy plan outlining the nation's goals for energy production and conservation for the next five years and the next 10 years.

● Required that the plan include estimates of energy supplies needed to meet goals listed.

● Provided that the plan be referred to appropriate congressional committees.

Title IX — Effective Date

● Provided that the act should take effect 120 days after the secretary took office, or sooner if the president so ordered.

● Provided that the president might appoint officers to positions requiring Senate confirmation on an interim basis until the positions could be filled as prescribed.

Title X — Sunset Provisions

● Provided that not later than Jan. 15, 1982, the president should submit to appropriate congressional committees a comprehensive review of each department program, outlining that program's goals, achievements and justification for continued funding.

Emergency Gas Sales

The 95th Congress and the Carter administration worked together to enact the first energy measure of 1977 with stunning speed. President Carter signed the Emergency Natural Gas Act of 1977 (S 474 — PL 95-2) on Feb. 2, barely two weeks after Inauguration Day.

As its title indicated, PL 95-2 was not an energy policy measure, but an emergency bill. It was a partial remedy for a crisis created by a bitterly cold winter that severely depleted fuel supplies in the Eastern United States by January 1977. Industries were shut down, putting millions out of work. Schools were closed, leaving thousands of children at home. Homeowners, usually given top priority in fuel supplies, faced the prospect of lacking the fuel needed to heat their homes.

PL 95-2 gave the president temporary authority to transfer interstate natural gas supplies to areas in need of fuel. It also allowed him to approve sales of gas to interstate buyers at unregulated prices. The price of natural gas sold interstate had been under federal price controls for decades. These extraordinary powers expired within the year.

Bitter Winter

By Inauguration Day 1977, it was clear that the winter of 1976-77 was an unusually cold and bitter one. Frigid arctic air blasted the Eastern half of the nation all the way to Florida; temperatures fell below zero in normally temperate zones. Eight-inch thick ice on major rivers halted delivery of fuel oil transported by barges. Natural gas supplies fell to levels more often seen in April than January.

The depleted supplies of gas required curtailment of delivery to some customers. The first to be cut back were large industrial users with alternative sources of fuel. The last to be curtailed would be residential and small commercial gas users, but the shortage appeared so severe that it seemed likely that some of these top priority customers might find themselves without fuel.

By the beginning of February, 11 states were in emergency status with industries and schools closed because of a lack of natural gas supplies. Hardest hit were Ohio, Pennsylvania, New York, Indiana, Maryland, Idaho and Illinois.

Congress Approved Route For Alaska Gas Pipeline

Congress in 1977 gave its approval to President Carter's choice of a pipeline route through Canada to carry natural gas from Alaska to the continental United States. Congressional approval of the route was required by a 1976 law (PL 94-586) that set deadlines for U.S. decisions on how to transport Alaskan gas to the lower 48 states. *(Story, p. 166)*

Final action on H J Res 621 (PL 95-158) came Nov. 2 when the House and Senate by voice vote approved the route that Carter, acting jointly with Canada's Prime Minister Pierre Elliott Trudeau, had endorsed Sept. 8.

The 3,600-mile pipeline would lead from Alaska's North Slope through western Canada, a path called the Alcan-Foothills route. The gas pipeline would parallel the new oil pipeline from Prudhoe Bay past Fairbanks, then parallel the Alaska Highway through Canada to Calgary, Alberta. At that point the gas pipeline would link with existing pipelines going to Canadian and American markets. Most of the American gas would go to the Midwest and West.

The new pipeline would be built by subsidiaries of Northwest Pipeline Corp. of Salt Lake City, Utah, and Foothills Pipe Lines Ltd. of Calgary. Two other primary routes had been proposed — one following the oil pipeline all the way to Valdez, Alaska, at which point the gas would be liquefied and shipped to California, the so-called El Paso plan, and another through the Mackenzie Delta, the Arctic Gas plan.

The completed pipeline would transport 3.5 billion cubic feet of natural gas a day. It would be the longest natural gas pipeline ever built and the largest single privately financed energy project. Completion was scheduled for 1983. The cost was estimated at from $10 to $15 billion.

Although it was planned that private financing would be available to cover the cost of the new pipeline, a key question in the minds of members of Congress dscussing H J Res 621 was whether or not federal financial aid would eventually be required to complete the project.

The Federal Power Commission, responsible for federal regulation of interstate transportation and sales of natural gas, responded to the crisis by asserting its own power, under the 1938 Natural Gas Act, to permit emergency sales of large volumes of gas to interstate pipelines at prices far above the regulated levels. But such sales only were permitted for up to 60 days.

Legislative Action

On Jan. 26 President Carter requested that Congress grant him temporary authority to move gas, at whatever price necessary, to stricken areas. "Our people are in trouble," he told Congress.

Congress moved with alacrity, although with full awareness that the measure did nothing to increase energy supplies or deal with the nation's long-range energy problems. It was intended to help people live through the current energy crisis. But as House Majority Leader Jim Wright, D-Texas, noted: "When people are drowning, there is time only to throw out a lifeline."

Senate Majority Leader Robert C. Byrd, D-W.Va., introduced S 474 Jan. 26, the same day it was drafted, and took it directly to the Senate floor, bypassing committee review. The Senate approved the measure Jan. 31, after a lengthy debate in which all substantive amendments to the measure were defeated. The vote on passage was 91-2.

After one day of subcommittee hearings Jan. 28, the House Interstate and Foreign Commerce Committee marked up its version Jan. 31 and sent it to the floor without a formal report. The House approved it Feb. 1 by a vote of 367-52.

The major difference between the House bill and that requested by Carter and approved by the Senate was an amendment by Rep. Bob Eckhardt, D-Texas, setting a ceiling price for emergency natural gas sales. The ceiling was set at $2.02 per thousand cubic feet for gas sold to interstate purchasers by intrastate producers, and $2.22 for sales by intrastate pipelines and distributors. The Commerce Committee accepted the amendment, which the House approved.

Conferees filed their report on S 474 (H Rept 95-7) Feb. 2. They agreed to drop the Eckhardt amendment. The Senate adopted the final version of the bill by voice vote the same day; the House sent the measure to the White House shortly thereafter, adopting the report by a vote of 336-82. Carter signed it as soon as it arrived on his desk, shortly before donning a sweater to deliver his first "fireside chat" to the American people via television.

Provisions

As signed into law, PL 95-2:

● Gave the president authority to declare a natural gas emergency if he found a severe shortage endangering the supply for high priority use.

● Defined high-priority use as use in a residence, use in a commercial establishment in amounts of less than 50 thousand cubic feet on a peak day, or use necessary to protect life and health or maintain physical property.

● Empowered the president to require any interstate or intrastate pipeline to transport emergency supplies of interstate gas where directed through April 30, 1977.

● Empowered him to require pipelines to construct or operate facilities necessary for such emergency transportation.

● Authorized through July 31, 1977, emergency purchases of gas from intrastate markets by interstate buyers at unregulated prices as approved by the president.

● Granted the president power to subpoena information to carry out his authority under the act and to require written interrogatories under oath.

● Provided antitrust protections for actions taken to comply with the act.

● Established penalties of $25,000 a day for violations of orders to transport emergency supplies of gas and $50,000 a day for willful violations of such orders.

• Directed the president to require weekly reports on prices and volume of gas transported under the act and to report to Congress Oct. 1, 1977, on the operation of the act.

Strategic Oil Reserves

Responding to an administration plan to accelerate the storage of oil in a national reserve, Congress in 1977 authorized $1.21 billion for the purchase of that oil. The authorization was included in legislation that also extended the life of the Federal Energy Administration (FEA) through fiscal 1978. The measure (S 1468 — PL 95-70) was cleared for the White House June 30. President Carter signed the measure July 21.

The funding level for the strategic oil reserves provided by PL 95-70 was intended to allow the acquisition of 500 million barrels for that reserve by the end of 1980. If that deadline were met, the reserve would be filled two years ahead of the schedule envisioned by the Energy Policy and Conservation Act of 1975 (PL 94-163).

PL 95-70 also extended through Dec. 31, 1978, FEA authority to order utility and industrial facilities to convert to coal. That authority, granted under the Energy Supply and Environmental Coordination Act of 1974 (PL 93-319), was to expire June 30, 1977.

The law's extension of the life of the FEA from Dec. 31, 1977, through fiscal 1978 became superfluous after enactment of legislation creating the new Cabinet-level Department of Energy (PL 95-91). The functions of FEA were merged with those of the new department.

S 1468 (S Rept 95-123) was approved by the Senate May 11. A companion bill (HR 6794 — H Rept 95-323) was approved by the House June 6. The Senate approved the House measure June 8, with an amendment boosting funding for the strategic oil reserves to the final figure. The House accepted the Senate amendment June 30.

Clinch River Reactor

As 1977 ended, a bill authorizing the Department of Energy to devote as much as $6.2 billion to civilian energy research and development in fiscal 1978 was left for dead on Capitol Hill. The bill was a victim of the ongoing dispute between President Carter and Congress over the future of the not-yet-built Clinch River Breeder Reactor Plant, once the nation's No. 1 nuclear power project.

The energy research bill (S 1811 — S Rept 95-328; H Rept 95-349, Parts I, II and III) passed the Senate July 12 and the House Sept. 23. It was cleared for the White House Oct. 20. President Carter vetoed it Nov. 5, casting the first veto of his administration. The veto came primarily because buried deep within the $6,161,445,000 authorization was an $80 million item for continued work on the controversial breeder plant.

No attempt was made during the remaining weeks of the 1977 session to override the veto. In December the House approved a Senate-passed bill (S 1340), which it had amended to be identical to S 1811 except for the Clinch River provisions, which were deleted. The Senate did not act on the revised bill before adjournment of the 1977 session but cleared the measure Feb. 8, 1978.

Nuclear Plant Dispute

Consideration of S 1811 in both chambers was dominated by debate over President Carter's proposal to terminate the nuclear power plant, which was to be built on the Clinch River in Tennessee near Oak Ridge to show that plutonium fueled and plutonium-producing "breeder" reactors were a feasible source of electricity and nuclear fuel.

The original budget request for the plant for fiscal 1978 was $150 million. After Carter decided to terminate the project, because of his concern that increasing the use of plutonium would enlarge the risk of nuclear proliferation, he asked Congress to provide only $33 million in termination costs. Congress eventually decided on $80 million, enough to keep the project going in fiscal 1978 while Congress studied Carter's termination proposal.

Neither the veto of S 1811 nor congressional inaction spelled final doom for the plant. The fiscal 1978 supplemental appropriations bill (HR 9375) left pending at the end of the 1977 session contained $80 million for the re-

FERC Membership

The original five members of the Federal Energy Regulatory Commission, named to their posts by President Carter in 1977, were:

• Chairman Charles B. Curtis, an attorney who had worked on the Carter-Mondale transition team in 1976-77 and who, before that, had spent five years as counsel to the House Interstate and Foreign Commerce Committee.

• Don S. Smith, a member of the Federal Power Commission nominated to that post by President Nixon in 1973 from the Arkansas Public Service Commission.

• George R. Hall, an economist who had worked for the Atomic Energy Commission, the Defense Department and on the energy policy staff in the White House during the first months of the Carter administration.

• Matthew Holden Jr., a professor of political science and a member of the Wisconsin Public Service Commission.

• Georgiana H. Sheldon, a government official who had served in the Defense Department, the Agency for International Development and as vice chairman of the Civil Service Commission.

The membership of the commission remained quite stable throughout its first three years of existence. Commissioner Smith's term expired in 1979. He was succeeded in 1980 by John David Hughes, who came to the commission from six years in the office of the attorney general of the state of Texas, the last of which he had spent as chief of that office's energy division.

Late in 1980, Chairman Curtis announced that although his term would not expire until 1983, he would resign his post in January 1981.

actor, which could be spent even without enactment of the authorizing legislation. The supplemental funding bill containing the $80 million appropriation was signed into law (PL 95-240) early in 1978.

Programs Continued

The total authorized in the vetoed bill included about $3.2 billion for nuclear power projects and $1.8 billion for non-nuclear programs. The projects were to be administered by the research division of the Department of Energy, formerly the Energy Research and Development Administration (ERDA).

Because the regular ERDA appropriations bill (HR 7553 — PL 95-96) had moved through Congress ahead of the authorizing legislation, language allowing expenditure of the appropriated funds, even without authorizing legislation in place, was included in that bill. The presidential veto of S 1811 therefore had no effect on spending for any ongoing ERDA programs, including the Clinch River project. Only programs for which the initial authority was included in or revised by S 1811 were affected by the veto.

New Bill

S 1340 (PL 95-238), the bill that cleared Feb. 8, 1978, was identical to the vetoed measure it replaced except that it omitted authorization for the Clinch River project and language revising uranium pricing agreements to which Carter also had objected.

As signed into law Feb. 25, PL 95-238 provided $6,081,400,000 for energy research programs in fiscal 1978. Of that total, just over half, $3.2 billion, was for nuclear programs, while $1.8 billion was authorized for non-nuclear research and development. The remaining amounts would be used for environmental and safety research, basic research and program management. (Authorization totals include operating expenses and plant and capital equipment costs.)

1978

Highlights

Energy Policy Package

Energy policy legislation cleared by Congress in October 1978, 18 months after it was proposed, contained only remnants of President Carter's original tough measures. Congress had chipped away at the administration plan, preferring generally to encourage conservation, not penalize waste. The plan that finally emerged contained five parts: legislation on natural gas pricing (PL 95-621), coal conversion (PL 95-620), utility rates (PL 95-617), conservation (PL 95-619) and taxes (PL 95-618).

Outer Continental Shelf

After almost four years of reform efforts, Congress approved the first overhaul of offshore oil and gas leasing

laws in 25 years. The legislation (PL 95-372) was designed to foster competition for offshore leases, increase state participation in federal leasing decisions and provide environmental protections.

Solar Energy

Several measures to encourage the development and use of solar energy were enacted. Congress approved a decade-long program, estimated to cost about $1.5 billion, to push the development of solar photovoltaic cells, which convert sunlight directly into electricity (PL 95-590). The measure authorized $125 million in fiscal 1979. Also approved was a $75 million loan program for small businesses involved in the production of solar energy, renewable source and energy conservation equipment (PL 95-315).

Gasoline Marketing

With the passage of the "Dealer Day in Court" bill (PL 95-297), gas station owners were protected from the arbitrary cancellation of their franchises.

Coal Leasing Amendments

Congress authorized the interior secretary to exchange certain leased federal coal lands in Utah and Wyoming for other lands where mining would do less environmental damage (PL 95-554). Congress, however, put off a decision on the larger issue of whether the interior secretary should be authorized to make such exchanges whenever necessary to preserve environmentally valuable land.

Coal Slurry Pipelines

Intense lobbying by the nation's railroads led to the stunning House defeat of legislation to promote development of coal slurry pipelines. The railroads, which did not want competitors in the coal-hauling business, had refused to grant rights-of-way for the pipelines to cross railroad-owned lands. A controversial provision of the defeated measure would have given pipeline developers eminent domain subject to certain restrictions.

Clinch River Reactor/DOE Authorization

The future of the controversial Clinch River breeder reactor plant remained in limbo when Congress failed to clear a Department of Energy bill. Before passing the bill, the House twice voted to refuse to allow the administration to terminate the project. The measure, however, was not taken up by the Senate and funding for the project continued at existing levels.

The Year in Review

The second session of the 95th Congress completed work on six major energy bills — five of which represented the final version of President Carter's multi-part energy program sent to Congress in April 1977.

In October 1978, Congress sent to the White House for the president's signature a natural gas bill providing for an eventual end to federal price controls, a second measure encouraging industries to shift from using oil and gas to using coal, a third imposing new taxes upon the inefficient use of energy, a fourth encouraging reform of utility rate structures and a fifth intended to spur adoption of energy conservation measures at home and at work.

The sixth major energy bill enacted in 1978 was a measure setting out guidelines and procedures for the exploration and development of the nation's energy resources located on the outer continental shelf.

The nation's railroads were successful in their bid to kill a measure that would have eased the way for construction of coal slurry pipelines. Responding to charges that the pipeline competition might sound the death knell for several ailing railroads, the House rejected the measure.

Energy Policy Package

The determined Democratic leadership of the House, stubbornly wearing down opponents in the wee hours of the morning, presented President Carter with a five-part energy package on Sunday, Oct. 15, 1978.

A 15-hour filibuster by Senate opponents held up final action. But at 7:30 a.m. sleepy House members cast the final vote on the package, clearing it for the president, 231-168.

The legislation passed by Congress contained only remnants of the tough plan Carter originally presented in April 1977. That plan was designed to force Americans to use less energy by increasing the cost of that energy. Its purpose was to reduce the use of imported oil on which the United States was dangerously dependent. The United States in 1978 imported about 8 million barrels of oil a day, approximately 45 percent of the nation's consumption of 18.2 million barrels each day. Carter would have raised the cost of energy by increasing gasoline taxes, raising the price of domestic crude oil through taxes and revamping electricity rate-making procedures.

But Congress, worried about the political repercussions of higher prices and buffeted by intense lobbying from industry and other interest groups, chipped away at Carter's plan. The gasoline tax, for example, was dropped early, and the Senate rejected the key element: a tax on domestic crude oil to raise prices to world levels.

Passage of a national energy policy bill through Congress became an 18-month odyssey. The package was the top domestic legislative priority for both Congress and the new president in 1977. Yet when the year ended, Congress had not completed its work. Both the House and Senate had approved versions of the program, but the Senate went far afield from the president's plan in two primary areas: natural gas regulation and energy tax policy.

Conference committees settled other issues but bogged down late in 1977 over gas and taxes. Conferees quit Dec. 22; they did not meet again until February 1978. Then another nine months elapsed before conferees reached a compromise with which the administration and a majority of Congress could agree.

The decision-making required to enact an energy policy bill spawned some of the most bitter congressional fights in years, with members allied or divided by region, by party, by ideology. An example of the depth of the split was the 207-206 House vote Oct. 13, 1978, by which members chose to keep the controversial natural gas pricing bill in a package with the other energy bills. Had the gas bill been separated out, House members might have felt free to reject it while voting for the other, more popular elements of the package.

Although the plan was watered down as it passed through Congress, Carter and Energy Secretary James R. Schlesinger continued to fight for it. When the bill was finally passed a year and a half after it was proposed, Carter said, "We have declared to ourselves and the world our intent to control our use of energy and thereby to control our own destiny as a nation."

Six months later in April 1979, Carter was back before Congress with another package of proposals to make the United States less dependent on foreign oil. Carter's second omnibus energy plan called for deregulation of domestic oil prices and a tax on the windfall profits that oil companies would receive as a result of deregulation. Revenues from the tax were to be set aside to finance development of alternative fuel sources.

Import Savings

Just exactly what effect the 1978 energy bill would have was the subject of some dispute. A primary goal of Carter's original plan was to cut oil imports, which the White House projected would be between 11.5 million and 16 million barrels a day by 1985 if left unchecked. The plan was to use a combination of conservation, increased production and fuel substitution to keep 1985 imports at 4.5 million barrels a day less than projected.

But congressional revision of the original proposal left the amount of imported oil that would be saved in some doubt. The administration estimated that the package would reduce oil imports by between 2.39 million and 2.95 million barrels of oil a day in 1985.

Highlights of Energy Package

Natural Gas (HR 5289 — PL 95-621)

Prices of newly discovered natural gas were allowed to rise about 10 percent a year until 1985, when the price controls would be lifted. Special pricing categories were set up to make industrial users bear the brunt of the higher prices until the cost reached a certain level, when residential users were to begin sharing the burden. For the first time some federal controls were imposed on the price of gas produced and sold within the same state.

Carter originally had proposed that price controls be extended to the gas sold within producing states with the general philosophy that gas, an ideal residential fuel, be saved for that purpose by switching industrial and utility users to other fuels.

Coal Conversion (HR 5146 — PL 95-620)

New industrial and utility plants were required to use coal or a fuel other than oil or gas. Existing utility plants using oil or gas were to switch to other fuels by 1990. The energy secretary could order some industries, on a case-by-case basis, to switch fuels. But he could also exempt utilities and companies from the requirements if certain problems, such as an inadequate supply of coal, existed.

Carter had proposed a stiff tax on industrial use of oil and gas to give gas users an incentive to convert to coal, but Congress dropped that tax.

Utility Rates (HR 4018 — PL 95-617)

State utility commissions and other regulatory agencies were required to consider the use of energy-saving methods, such as pricing electricity at lower levels in off-peak hours to avoid heavy loads in peak periods of use

Smooth, Tough Lobbying Campaign . . .

Faulted in 1977 for poor lobbying on its energy package, the Carter administration apparently learned from its mistakes. In 1978, it mounted a successful effort to win Senate support for a very tenuous conference compromise on gradual deregulation of natural gas.

In 1977, President Carter blamed "special interests" and an irresponsible Senate for failure of his energy package. But the Capitol Hill consensus was that the president and his lobbyists were to blame for the plunder of his energy program in the Senate. Hill observers said Carter waged a poorly timed, politically insensitive and error-plagued lobbying battle on behalf of his energy proposals.

They said he drafted the program in haste, consulted too little with the key committee chairmen, paid inadequate attention to the program during the crucial months prior to the September Senate floor debate and either poorly defended or too easily abandoned major components of the legislation.

Both administration and congressional sources confirmed that various tax proposals were not thoroughly checked out with the administration's own Treasury Department officials or with the Senate Finance Committee. Because the energy package was heavily reliant on tax incentives and disincentives, the failure to sign on members of the tax writing Finance Committee, especially Chairman Russell B. Long, D-La., contributed significantly to that committee's hostility to several crucial pieces of the program, including the crude oil equalization tax and the industrial energy users' tax.

Little Expertise

Some senators and aides were privately contemptuous of the level of expertise the administration group displayed in working the Hill. Aides and lobbyists friendly to the administration program complained that basic work, such as the briefing of staffs on substantive issues and steady checking to reassure dubious legislators, was done either too little or too late. Occasionally, substantive errors by the administration team proved costly.

Examples of such complaints were numerous. In the Senate, the administration was criticized for failing to defend its own "gas guzzler" tax in the Finance Committee. Committee aides were not briefed or even called by the administration up to a week before the committee vote on the proposal.

One document relating to the tax was not given to staffers in time to be useful. The result: On Sept. 20 the committee vote to kill the tax, despite Long's support and widespread belief it would pass. On natural gas, the administration posture appeared, in the opinion of its critics, far too willing to compromise.

But by mid-August 1978, the administration lobbying approach had taken on a new sophistication.

On the afternoon of Aug. 28, two dozen executives from major paper, textile and glass companies crowded into the Roosevelt Room in the White House to hear the hard sell for the unpopular natural gas pricing conference compromise.

No Solid Supporters

Some of the executives were dead set against the bill. Others were ambivalent. Not one could be counted on as a solid supporter.

First, according to the notes taken by one man who was there, Energy Secretary James R. Schlesinger used multicolored charts and new figures on gas production developed by his department to describe the substance of the legislation.

Next, G. William Miller, the ostensibly independent chairman of the Federal Reserve Board, argued that passage of the compromise bill — any bill, really — was essential to the stabilization of the value of the dollar against foreign currencies.

Finally, an hour or so into the meeting, the Carter administration's super salesman took the floor. It was a "time for candor," Robert S. Strauss, the president's all-purpose adviser, told the businessmen, and he was not about to pretend that the compromise bill was first-rate legislation. But, he went on, "it no longer makes a difference whether the bill is a C-minus or an A-plus. Certainly, it is better than a zero, and it must pass."

Then, in the same folksy style he used to raise money for George McGovern in 1972 and to win votes for Jimmy Carter in 1976, in the same Texas drawl with which he spoke to Japanese negotiators on trade policy and labor leaders on inflation, Strauss made his pitch.

"This is close enough," he asserted, "so a half-dozen bankers I had in this morning and the people in this room could pass or defeat the bill."

Some of the executives must have been impressed. Those from glass and paper companies remained opposed, but their opposition seemed muted after the session. Some from the textile industry switched to active support for the administration.

That meeting was one of a dozen held in the White House with key industrial consumers of natural gas in the three weeks before the bill was brought up on the Senate floor Sept. 11.

There were similar sessions, for instance, with representatives of the insurance, steel, automobile, construction and aerospace industries. A group of bankers had lunch with President Carter in the family dining room. One hundred thirty of the most ardent industrial opponents of the bill were called to the East Room on Sept. 6.

. . . Helped Carter Pull Victory from Defeat

The meetings were the cornerstone of the White House effort to win passage of the natural gas bill, the focus of the most extensive administration lobbying on domestic legislation since Carter took office.

By all accounts, the lobbying was effective. In late August, only a handful of important businessmen could be counted on to support the legislation. On Sept. 11, the Department of Energy supplied all senators with a list of 55 major industrial and financial corporations and 20 trade associations that were backing the bill.

Administration Strategy

The administration's basic problem was that the final bill contained so many compromises that it had a wealth of natural opponents and no strong supporters. The strategy, designed primarily by Schlesinger, Strauss and Vice President Walter F. Mondale, was to neutralize the opposition, while pleading for support on the grounds of national prestige and loyalty to the president.

The day-to-day tactics were planned by a group of ranking aides from the White House and the Department of Energy, who met every weekday morning from mid-August on in the White House office of Frank B. Moore, assistant to the president for congressional liaison.

Participants at the meetings said that most of the time was spent deciding which senators should be approached by Strauss, which by Schlesinger, which by Mondale and which by the president. Many uncommitted senators reported receiving repeated calls from each of them.

"It's been Carter, Schlesinger, Strauss, Mondale and then they start all over again," said an aide to Sen. Patrick J. Leahy, D-Vt.

Sen. John C. Culver, D-Iowa, visited Alaska over Labor Day weekend and reportedly received a call from Carter on the natural gas issue at 5 a.m. Alaska time.

All told, a White House spokesman said, the president telephoned 26 senators that weekend. The following weekend, during breaks in the Middle East summit talks, he called several more.

Once the bill was on the Senate floor, Mondale began to spend most of his time in the Capitol, buttonholing senators on the floor and calling them into his private office just off the Senate chamber. Mondale was given much of the credit for swinging Sen. Edmund S. Muskie, D-Maine, the influential chairman of the Budget Committee, to the administration's point of view.

"They don't talk about the merits of the bill," one senator said. "They tell you that the president needs a bill to pass to save face politically and that the country needs it for international prestige."

Primarily, the administration's strategy was to seek support from special interest groups that could put pressure on senators to back the bill. Anne Wexler, special assistant for political matters, was assigned to learn which interest groups were lobbying senators most heavily; it was representatives from those groups who were invited to the White House.

Entire industries, including the oil industry, were split. Some important oil companies, such as the Atlantic-Richfield Corp., agreed to support the bill, and others, such as Exxon, were persuaded to remain neutral. Some oil companies, such as Amoco, continued to oppose the bill.

The divide-and-conquer tactics showed results. A ranking congressional staff member noted, for example, that Sen. Robert P. Griffin, R-Mich., could not support the bill as long as all the major automobile makers were in opposition, but once the Chrysler Corp. announced its support, Griffin, too, felt free to do so.

Opposition Strategy

Opponents of the bill were an unusual coalition of senators and interest groups. Some of them believed that the compromise bill would not lift price regulations on natural gas fast enough while others felt it would allow gas prices to rise too fast.

For example, Sen. Long, one of the most ardent supporters of deregulation of gas prices, met regularly to plot strategy with Sens. James Abourezk, D-S.D., a leader of the 1977 filibuster against deregulation legislation. Other senators who worked to round up votes against the bill included Edward M. Kennedy, D-Mass.; Howard H. Baker Jr., R-Tenn., the minority leader; John Tower, R-Texas; and Clifford P. Hansen, R-Wyo.

Interest groups working against the bill were equally unlikely bedfellows. Amoco officials, for instance, were working hand-in-glove with James Flug, director of Energy Action, an organization representing consumer interests against oil companies.

Lobbyists for the Chamber of Commerce of the United States consulted regularly on tactics with representatives of the AFL-CIO and the United Auto Workers. George Meany, president of the AFL-CIO, and Douglas A. Fraser, president of the UAW, wrote all senators urging defeat of the bill, primarily on the ground that it would be too costly to consumers.

For the most part, those against the bill concentrated on maintaining their strength against administration forays. Republicans were urged not to extricate the president from his political troubles, and Democrats were told that the compromise measure was such bad legislation that they could not afford blind loyalty to the administration.

and discontinuing discounts for large volume users. The energy secretary was authorized to intervene in the regulatory proceedings to argue for energy-saving measures.

Carter had wanted state agencies to be required to follow certain federal guidelines in rate making in order to save energy. But Congress, arguing that the states should continue to oversee the utilities, refused to make the guidelines mandatory.

Conservation (HR 5037 — PL 95-619)

Utilities were required to give customers information about energy conservation devices such as insulation and storm windows. Although the utility could not sell the devices or install them, the utility could arrange for the installation and allow customers to pay for the improvements through utility bills. Direct loans from utilities to consumers of up to $300 were allowed.

Over three years, schools and hospitals were to receive $900 million to install energy-saving equipment. Grants and government-backed loans would be available to low-income families for home conservation investments. Mandatory efficiency standards, effective in the mid-1980s, were authorized for 13 major home appliances, including refrigerators, furnaces and water heaters.

Carter's original proposal had envisioned a more aggressive role for utilities and mandatory conservation standards for new residential and commercial buildings. But, generally, this conservation measure was the least controversial of the five parts of the Carter program and came through Congress relatively intact.

Taxes (HR 5263 — PL 95-618)

Homeowners and businesses would receive tax credits for installing energy-saving devices in their buildings. Homeowners were eligible for a credit of 15 percent on the first $2,000 spent on insulation or other devices, for a maximum credit of $300. Investment in solar, wind or geothermal energy equipment made the homeowner eligible for a tax credit of up to 30 percent on the first $2,000 and 20 percent on the next $8,000, for a total maximum credit of $2,200.

A 10 percent investment credit was made available to businesses that installed specified types of energy conservation equipment. The bill also provided tax incentives for companies that produced synthetic fuels from coal or other resources.

Cars that used fuel inefficiently, known as gas guzzlers, were to be taxed to discourage manufacture and purchase. Starting with 1980 models, new cars getting less than 15 miles per gallon (mpg) would be taxed $200. The tax and mileage standards would increase every year so that by 1986, cars getting less than 12.5 mpg would be taxed $3,850.

Taxes on 1986 models would apply to all cars getting less than 22.5 mpg.

The administration had wanted the gas guzzler tax to start on 1978 models averaging less than 18 mpg, with the first year penalty ranging from $52 to $449. By 1986, Carter wanted to be taxing heavily any car that got less than 27.5 mpg.

Central to Carter's original energy proposal were taxes on industrial use of oil and gas, a wellhead tax on domestically produced crude oil to bring the price to world levels and authority to add a tax of 5 cents per gallon of gasoline each year through 1989 if gasoline consumption exceeded target levels. All of those proposals were dropped by Congress, which emphasized tax credits instead.

Background

It had been painfully evident to policy makers since the Arab oil embargo of 1973-74 that the United States was in need of a national energy plan.

The embargo was imposed Oct. 18, 1973, by the Organization of Arab Petroleum Exporting Countries (OAPEC), which was displeased with the pro-Israeli policy of the United States and certain European countries during the October Middle East war. The embargo remained in effect until March 18, 1974.

During that period a real fear of running out of heating oil led office managers and homeowners to turn down thermostats. Consumers formed long lines at service stations to fill their gas tanks and many stations closed on Sundays. More fundamentally, the cost of foreign oil quadrupled.

When the embargo ended, the high prices remained but public concern about energy availability seemed to fade. Moreover, partisan and regional interests came into play to complicate the efforts of the Republican executive branch and the heavily Democratic 94th Congress to write a national energy policy. Thermostats went back up, gas tanks were full and energy consumption rose.

President Ford in January 1975 offered a plan to cut energy consumption and increase domestic production by allowing prices to rise through a combination of import fees and a lifting of federal price controls.

Sensitive to rising unemployment and seemingly uncontrollable inflation, Democratic leaders were wary of any plan to raise prices or cut back energy use, fearing such moves would slow the already sluggish economy. They advocated a tax-based approach that involved increased gasoline taxes to encourage conservation and tax incentives to encourage production.

Congress rejected both the Ford and Democratic leadership approaches, and came up instead with the "Energy Policy and Conservation Act," whose provisions fell far short of the goals implied by its title. Congressional leaders of both parties ended 1975 with a sense of frustration and weariness born of the long wrangle over energy matters.

"In total candor, I must say ... that what began as a thrilling and dramatic enterprise has degenerated at times into a farcical comedy of frustrations," said Jim Wright, D-Texas, head of the House Democratic task force that developed the Democrats' alternative energy plan early in 1975. "Too often the Congress has been simply unwilling to make the hard decisions and take the difficult steps necessary to achieve energy sufficiency for the United States," he continued.

Strong regional and political differences, compounded by the splintering of energy issues among different committees and the lack of forceful leadership, diluted the leverage the numerically strong Democrats had been expected to have in determining national energy policy.

Congress reorganized the federal energy bureaucracy, but it did not reorganize its own structure to deal with energy matters. As a result, one energy measure might be referred to as many as four different committees in one chamber before reaching the floor, sometimes in four different versions.

With the president and Congress unable to develop a strong national energy policy, consumption continued to rise. At the same time domestic production dropped. By 1976 it was down one million barrels a day from 1973, to 8.2 million barrels, despite the fact that the average wellhead price of domestic oil doubled during this same period, to $7.99 a barrel from $3.89.

By the end of 1976 the United States was not only more dependent on foreign oil than in 1973; it was more dependent on expensive Arab oil. As Canada cut back on its oil exports to ensure fuel for its own future, the percentage of U.S. oil imports coming from Arab countries doubled between 1973 and 1976.

1977 Action

As Jimmy Carter prepared to take the oath of office in January 1977, an unprecedented cold wave caused such rapid depletion of the nation's natural gas supplies that many schools and factories were closed, workers laid off, and several states declared disaster areas. Special legislation was needed to divert supplies to gas-short areas. *(See p. 183)*

This crisis again underscored the need for a comprehensive national energy policy.

Carter's Plan

Upon taking office President Carter ordered a small team of energy planners to construct a national energy program in 90 days.

The deadline was met. The result was an exceedingly complex package of regulatory and tax measures. The Carter plan would have empowered the federal government: to require industries to make products meeting mandated standards of energy efficiency; to tell businesses to burn certain fuels but not others; to sponsor massive programs encouraging property owners to insulate their buildings; to levy stiff taxes against cars that used too much gasoline, against businesses that burned oil or natural gas and against purchasers of domestic oil. The taxes were aimed at conserving energy by driving energy prices higher.

By his own admission, Carter did not expect his program to be popular. But, he said, it was necessary.

Carter and the Democratic leadership pushed hard to complete action on the program in 1977, before the next election year.

Carter spoke to the nation via evening television addresses only three times during his first year in Washington; each time the subject was energy. The only speech Carter made to a joint session of Congress during his first year also concerned energy.

Though his critics at times faulted Carter's tactics, it was clear that no other single domestic issue received so much presidential attention in 1977.

Difficulties

Nonetheless, Carter's energy plan encountered such major difficulties in Congress that it did not finally pass until late 1978. Five basic problems plagued the program from the beginning:

● It was a plan that tackled inherently difficult political problems but was drafted virtually in secret by non-political technicians with no outside consultation. That approach alienated not only Capitol Hill, but also interest groups and even members of the Carter administration who held relevant expertise but were not consulted.

● Its drafting was rushed to meet the 90-day deadline and consequently the plan suffered from technical flaws, which undermined confidence in it.

● It was the object of intense and negative lobbying by a broad range of powerful special interest groups.

● It was poorly sold to Congress by Carter's lobbyists.

● It lacked a ready constituency.

Despite these factors, the new House Speaker, Thomas P. O'Neill Jr., D-Mass., mustered all the powers at his command to strong-arm the Carter program, virtually intact, to passage in record time. The House passed the package as one bill (HR 8444) Aug. 5, 1977, by a 244-177 vote.

In the Senate the plan was butchered. It was passed as five major bills between Sept. 28 and Oct. 31, 1977, but the Senate versions of natural gas regulation and energy taxes were far different from the original administration proposals and there were significant differences on other key aspects as well.

In addition to the basic problems listed above, which continued to dog the Carter plan in the Senate, at least four other problems were thrown on the scales, tilting the balance against the president:

● There was a complete loss of momentum between House passage and Senate consideration, caused principally by two events: an August recess for Congress and the September resignation of Carter's budget director, Bert Lance, who was caught in a scandal stemming from his pre-Washington banking days.

● The two Senate committees handling the Carter energy plan were dominated by a different predisposition toward energy policy than were their counterpart committees in the House. Where the House committees had compiled strong records of support for precisely the kinds of energy programs Carter proposed, conservation through increased costs, the Senate panels either had no records at all or supported opposite kinds of programs: those that eased the shortage by spurring production.

● The Senate was guided by a different style of leadership than was the House, due in part to the nature of the Senate and in part to the nature of Majority Leader Robert C. Byrd, D-W.Va.

In the House, Speaker O'Neill made sure that Carter's program passed, quickly. He made it clear that he saw the program as a test of Congress and of whether the Democratic Party could govern when it controlled both the executive and legislative branches. The House Speaker viewed the Carter energy plan as the Democrats' plan, and he made it the O'Neill plan as well.

Byrd's commitment to the plan was quite different from O'Neill's. The West Virginian's deepest commitment was not to party or president, or to legislative policy, but to the Senate. Though pledged to back the plan and evidently dedicated to working with Carter as smoothly as possible, Byrd stopped short of O'Neill-like efforts.

Byrd's strongest exertions were aimed at getting the energy bill through Congress in 1977, one way or the other. His commitment was, in a phrase he repeated time and again, to "let the Senate work its will" on the program, not necessarily to force the Senate to adopt it.

But even if Byrd had wanted, he could not have manipulated the Senate as O'Neill had the House. Senate rules simply did not allow a leader such power.

● The White House misread the Senate almost to the end, hoping it would come through somehow for the president as had the House.

House Action: 1977

Carter outlined his energy program in an address to a joint session of Congress April 20, 1977. Without fanfare, House Majority Leader Jim Wright, D-Texas, introduced that program as a single bill (HR 6831) May 2.

Various parts of the 283-page bill were referred to

O'Neill Gave Energy Plan an Extra Push . . .

No single figure was more important to congressional approval of President Carter's 1977-1978 energy plan than House Speaker Thomas P. O'Neill Jr., D-Mass.

By the end of Carter's first year in office, it had become evident that he had no better ally in Washington than the new Speaker. O'Neill's captainship of the Carter energy program through the House was a prime illustration of his effectiveness as an ally.

One of O'Neill's most significant steps in moving the multifaceted energy program through the House of Representatives was the creation of a special blue-ribbon select committee to coordinate House action on the program. The impact of the work and support of the Ad Hoc Energy Committee, which was created solely for that purpose and which went out of existence after it had performed its task, was immeasurable.

One of the major difficulties the House had encountered in attempting to deal with energy matters in earlier years was the splintering of jurisdiction over energy issues among a number of standing committees.

Late in 1976, O'Neill had pledged that he would work for creation of a new standing committee on energy. That plan met stubborn resistance from the chairmen of the committees who would lose jurisdiction over energy issues to such a new body.

After months of consultation, however, O'Neill and the affected chairmen reached a compromise, agreeing on the creation of the ad hoc committee — with a limited, but significant, role in House consideration of Carter's energy plan.

Committee Created

O'Neill explained the compromise to House members in a "Dear Colleague" letter April 20, 1977, the day President Carter delivered his energy policy address. Legislation incorporating President Carter's energy proposals first would be sent to appropriate standing committees just as if no ad hoc committee existed. But those committees would have to finish their work within deadlines set by the Speaker. Then their marked-up versions of the legislation would be sent to the ad hoc committee.

"The committee will not have authority to change the recommendations reported by the standing committees," O'Neill's letter said. "It will have authority to recommend amendments for consideration on the floor."

O'Neill promised in the letter that he would recommend to the Rules Committee that the standing committees be allowed to manage those portions of the bill that fell within their jurisdictions when the legislation reached the floor.

Moreover, the Speaker wrote, "when the House finally goes to conference with the Senate on the energy legislation, primary responsibility will rest with representatives of each of the standing committees to settle differences relating to its portion of the bill."

On April 21, one day after release of O'Neill's letter, the House by voice vote approved H Res 508 authorizing the committee's formation.

When Carter's energy plan was introduced and referred to the five standing committees, O'Neill directed the committees to complete their work and report the legislation to the ad hoc committee by July 13, 1977. The timetable was set to ensure House floor action on the bill before the summer recess.

In the meantime, the ad hoc committee members held a few general hearings amid a swirl of publicity, receiving testimony that painted an overview of the nation's energy plight and the Carter energy plan. Once the regular standing committees began hearings and markup on the Carter legislation, the ad hoc panel retreated into the background. Its members kept up with what was happening in the standing committees through regular briefings from congres-

five different committees that were to complete their work on the president's requests by July 13. The bill was then sent to the new House Ad Hoc Select Committee on Energy to be reassembled into one bill. *(Ad hoc committee background, box, this page)*

Standing Committees' Action

The House Ways and Means Committee finished nearly four weeks of work on the crucial tax portions of the energy bill June 30. The administration appeared to win most of the key battles, with only the proposal for a standby gasoline tax rejected outright. But the committee substantially watered down the taxes to force industries and utilities to convert from oil and gas to coal, primarily by exempting numerous categories of industries.

Natural gas regulation was considered by the Interstate and Foreign Commerce Committee and its Energy and Power Subcommittee. Carter suffered an early defeat when the subcommittee voted in favor of deregulation. But the full committee narrowly reversed that decision, replacing deregulation with a modified version of Carter's plan to regulate both interstate and intrastate gas at increased prices. The Commerce Committee gave almost uniform endorsement to the other aspects of the energy plan that came under its purview.

Of the three small parts of the energy plan referred

. . . By Setting Up a Special House Committee

sional and White House aides. Daily packets of updated information were circulated to the panel members as markup progressed.

Membership

Speaker O'Neill chose the new committee's members. He drew almost all of his selections from the standing committees holding jurisdiction over energy affairs.

The ad hoc panel had 40 members, 27 of them Democrats and 13 Republicans, reflecting the partisan alignment in the House. Of those 40, 11 were drawn from the Commerce Committee and 10 from Ways and Means. Five more were selected from the Banking Committee.

Rounding out the 40 members were representatives from Government Operations, Public Works, Interior and Insular Affairs, and Science and Technology. The latter two committees did not have a hand in review of the Carter package, but frequently were involved in energy policy.

The ad hoc committee was allowed to hire a professional staff of only four: a staff director, an office manager, a communications director and a minority staff director. The panel's core professional staff in terms of energy policy knowledge was borrowed from the regular standing committees: two from Commerce, two from Ways and Means, one tax expert from the Joint Committee on Taxation and one representative from the Speaker's office.

In choosing members, O'Neill was careful to balance regional interests; battles over energy policy had sectional overtones. Of the 40 members, 10 were from the East, 11 each were from the South and Midwest, and eight were from the West. Each region's delegation had seven Democrats, except the West, which had six.

Seven members hailed from the oil and gas producing states of Texas, Louisiana and Oklahoma. Six of them habitually sided with the oil and gas industry; the seventh, Bob Eckhardt, was a maverick Texas Democratic liberal who voted on energy questions as if he were from Massachusetts.

Friendly Reception

O'Neill took care to appoint Democrats likely to give the Carter energy program a friendly reception. Robert (Bob) Krueger, D-Texas, the chief gas deregulation proponent, was not among them. Republicans and lobbyists opposed to the administration's program charged that the panel was packed in Carter's favor.

Of the 27 Democrats, a solid majority in the past had supported higher taxes on gasoline, continued regulation of prices of oil and natural gas, stringent controls over strip mining and similar proposals that indicated a philosophical compatibility with Carter's approach to energy policy.

By contrast, the committee's 13 Republicans had a collective record of support for ending government regulation of energy prices and for attacking the problem of energy supply by stimulating domestic production rather than by conservation. But the Republicans were outnumbered better than 2-1. And not more than four or five of the panel's Democrats could be expected to side with them in any clearcut fight with the administration.

To any veteran observer of the House, the most striking thing about the committee's membership was the exceptional amount of leadership and seniority represented. The panel included among its members the chairmen of five full House standing committees and of 11 subcommittees. "These guys are all pros," observed the panel's staff director, Richard Krolik. "That's a lot of august power in one place."

Heading the collection of leaders was Thomas L. Ashley, 54, a well-respected Democrat from Toledo, Ohio, who never before had chaired a full committee despite 22 years in the House.

to other committees, the House Government Operations Committee reported its provisions June 29 (HR 6831 — H Rept 95-496, Part II), the Public Works Committee July 13 (H Rept 95-496, Part I) and the Banking Committee July 11 (HR 7893 — H Rept 95-488, Part I).

The House Ways and Means Committee formally approved its sections of HR 6831 (H Rept 95-496, Part III) July 13. The Commerce Committee finished July 14, a day late (H Rept 95-496, Part IV).

Ad Hoc Energy Committee

When the ad hoc committee received the energy program from the five standing committees, Chairman Thomas L. Ashley, D-Ohio, introduced the compilation July 20 as a clean bill (HR 8444).

The committee hurried through the provisions of the bill in three days, July 20-22. Democratic members of the panel, basically working as an arm of the party leadership that named them, established an unshakable majority to protect President Carter's energy proposals.

They operated principally through private caucuses they held the day before each committee meeting to agree among themselves on specific amendments they would allow the next day.

That pattern prevailed throughout with agreed-upon amendments easily approved and others easily rejected, mostly along party lines. Republicans protested the Democratic domination, claiming they were being frozen out of decisions on national energy policy.

Under the terms by which the ad hoc committee was established, the committee did not add its recommended amendments to HR 8444 but instead offered them on the floor for adoption by the full House. Among the important amendments the committee recommended for floor approval were an additional federal gasoline tax of 4 cents a gallon and an expanded definition of newly discovered natural gas that could be sold at higher prices.

House Floor Action

The House passed HR 8444 Aug. 5, by a vote of 244-177, after a week of debate. The bill gave Carter much of what he wanted. Backers of the package suffered a momentary scare just before passage when Republicans moved to kill the crude oil equalization tax, a major element of the program. The motion almost carried, failing on a close key vote of 203-219 (R 137-3; D 66-216).

Of the key amendments developed by the Ad Hoc Energy Committee, the gasoline tax was overwhelmingly rejected. But the natural gas compromise was accepted, defusing a move to deregulate natural gas.

The carefully drawn compromise, designed to attract enough votes from the deregulation forces to ensure passage for the Carter pricing system, was cosponsored by Texas Democrats Bob Eckhardt and Charles Wilson. Eckhardt traditionally opposed deregulation; Wilson normally supported it.

They proposed to expand the definition of "new" natural gas so that much greater amounts of the fuel could draw the high ceiling price. The Carter plan defined "new" gas as that found in new reservoirs at least two and one-half miles away from or 1,000 feet deeper than existing wells.

The Eckhardt-Wilson amendment changed that language to define as "new" all gas found beyond those limits or in any new reservoirs within those limits. Their proposal gave states the right to determine if a reservoir were new, subject to oversight by the Federal Power Commission.

The Eckhardt-Wilson amendment was adopted by voice vote. The House then rejected an amendment removing all price regulations on gas by a vote of 199-227 (R 127-17; D 72-210).

Senate Action: 1977

The Senate took a very different approach to the Carter energy program, taking up and passing it as five separate bills. Each Senate bill was then added to a minor House-passed bill to facilitate conference action.

The Senate made several major changes in the proposed energy plan, accepting a phased deregulation of natural gas prices and rejecting the crude oil equalization, fuel conversion and "gas-guzzler" taxes.

Natural Gas

Instead of marking up the administration proposal to continue and extend gas regulation while allowing higher prices, a deadlocked Senate Energy Committee sent the proposal to the floor without a recommendation for action. The report on the bill (S 2104 — S Rept 95-436) was filed Sept. 15.

The key committee vote was a 9-9 tie Sept. 12 on a proposal to phase out regulation of new natural gas within five years. Earlier the committee had turned down, 6-12, a proposal to deregulate immediately the price of all natural gas except that under contract.

Floor Action. The Senate passed a substitute version of S 2104 Oct. 6 after 14 days of debate that included a nine-day filibuster led by James Abourezk, D-S.D., and Howard M. Metzenbaum, D-Ohio, who opposed deregulation.

The filibuster was finally broken when Majority Leader Byrd and Vice President Walter F. Mondale decided it was tying up the Senate futilely and joined forces to end it.

The end of the filibuster cleared the way for a Senate vote on a modified deregulation plan offered by James B. Pearson, R-Kan., and Lloyd Bentsen, D-Texas. It was adopted by a vote of 50-46 (R 34-3; D 16-43).

The bill was then passed by voice vote. Its provisions, along with the House-passed natural gas provisions, were attached to a House-passed private bill (HR 5289).

Energy Taxes

The Senate Finance Committee took an entirely different approach to energy tax proposals than the Carter administration and the House. During markups it systematically rejected each of Carter's three key tax proposals — the equalization tax on crude oil, the tax on utility and industrial use of oil and gas and the tax on "gas guzzling" cars.

Together these taxes accounted for roughly half of the revenues that the Carter energy program was expected to produce. Finance Committee Chairman Russell B. Long, D-La., had supported the equalization tax, but only if the revenues were channeled toward production of more energy rather than consumer rebates; the majority of his committee refused to go along even with that. Instead, the committee voted 13-5 Oct. 21 to report out HR 5263 (S Rept 95-529) rolling together a mixture of tax credits for energy production and conservation which, if enacted, would cost the federal Treasury an estimated $40 billion through fiscal 1985 and save an estimated 2.1 million barrels of oil a day.

The only revenue raiser in the Finance Committee bill was an extension of the existing 4-cent-per-gallon tax on gasoline through 1985, estimated by the staff to bring in $20 billion, cutting the bill's negative budget impact in half.

The Senate Oct. 31 passed HR 5263, 52-35.

Passage came after six days of debate, during which 49 amendments were adopted and 15 rejected. Through it all Finance Committee Chairman Long was in firm control.

He bested Energy Committee Chairman Henry A. Jackson, D-Wash., in a direct head-to-head challenge over whether the Senate should allow Long the flexibility he sought to deal in conference. He persuaded Jackson, Budget Committee Chairman Edmund S. Muskie, D-Maine, and Banking Committee Chairman William Proxmire, D-Wis., to drop threatened challenges to his bill as encroaching on the jurisdiction of their committees.

Long also was successful in defeating an attempt to recommit his bill to committee for redrafting. To win, he overcame a coalition broad enough to include conservatives such as Republicans Robert Dole of Kansas and Jesse Helms of North Carolina, and liberals such as Democrats Edward M. Kennedy of Massachusetts and Howard M. Metzenbaum of Ohio.

Only twice was Long forced to accept proposals he opposed, and even then his opposition was qualified.

In the first case, the Senate adopted a greatly scaled-back tax on industrial and utility use of oil and gas, despite Long's argument that adoption might hamper his ability to deal in conference. The tax was offered by Metzenbaum.

In the second, Kennedy succeeded in trimming back the major energy-saving tax break in the committee bill, cutting the credit for business investment in alternate energy equipment from 40 percent to 15 percent. Long agreed to accept that cut only after having failed to table Kennedy's original amendment, which would have cut the credit to 10 percent.

Coal Conversion

The Senate Energy and Natural Resources Committee July 25 reported S 977 (S Rept 95-361). The bill was designed to force electric utilities and major industrial plants to burn coal and other fuels instead of oil and natural gas.

The Senate plan was expected to save less oil and natural gas than the Carter plan and House bill. Unlike those versions, it authorized funds for loans and loan guarantees to cover the costs of coal conversion, authorized grants to companies whose plants could not be easily converted to coal and increased federal aid to "boom towns" created by coal development.

The Senate passed S 977 Sept. 8, 74-8. It then combined the bill's provisions with those of S 701 (S Rept 95-141, S Rept 95-351), passed by voice vote July 20, authorizing $900 million in federal matching grants for approved energy conservation expenses by schools and hospitals. Those provisions, along with the coal conversion provisions of the House bill, were added to a minor House-passed bill (HR 5146).

With three important exceptions, the 29 amendments adopted by the Senate did not change the substance of the measure as reported by the Energy Committee.

The first exception was an amendment by J. Bennett Johnston, D-La., further diminishing the amount of oil the bill would save. The Johnston amendment greatly expanded the number of new major industrial plants that would be allowed to burn oil, but not natural gas, instead of being forced to use coal.

Two related amendments by Jacob K. Javits, R-N.Y., increased the amount of direct and guaranteed loans the Federal Energy Administration could make to help plants cover the costs of converting to coal and an amendment by John A. Durkin, D-N.H., authorized an additional $100 million for the rehabilitation of branch and spur rail lines to transport coal.

Energy Conservation

The Senate Energy Committee's energy conservation bill (S 2057 — S Rept 95-409), reported Aug. 18, 1977, provided $1 billion in authorizations through fiscal 1982 for a broad range of energy conservation programs. Its major change from the Carter proposal was to substitute for the proposed tax on "gas guzzlers" a ban on new cars that did not meet specific standards for fuel efficiency.

The Senate passed S 2057 Sept. 13, 78-4. It then added its provisions and the equivalent provisions of the House energy bill to a House-passed private bill (HR 5037).

Debate on S 2057 lasted three days, during which the Senate adopted 33 largely non-controversial amendments by voice vote. Nine amendments were rejected, including an attempt to kill the "gas guzzler" ban.

Among the rejected amendments were several highly inflammatory proposals, turned down by overwhelming margins.

Included in that category were proposals from Lowell P. Weicker Jr., R-Conn., to require each car to be kept off the road one day a week and to close gasoline stations from Saturday evening until Monday morning.

Equally controversial proposals from Dale Bumpers, D-Ark., to ration gasoline and from Charles H. Percy, R-Ill., to make federal employees pay for parking spaces they used for free were also rejected.

Utility Rates

On Sept. 19, the Senate Energy Committee voted 12-3 to report out a bill (S 2114 — S Rept 95-442) to encourage utilities to conserve energy. But the panel purposely dropped from the measure virtually all of Carter's far-reaching initiatives in this area, including his proposal for national rate-making guidelines. The committee bill provided that the federal government could intervene in state rate-making procedures as an advocate, but gave it no other powers.

Explaining the committee actions to the full Senate Oct. 5, bill manager Johnston of Louisiana said there was no justification for approving such a "radical extension of federal authority into the highly complex matter of the design of retail rates for electricity."

The Senate approved 24 amendments to the bill, most by voice vote, before passing it Oct. 6, 86-7. Most of the amendments were narrow in focus. The most significant required utilities to provide electricity for essential purposes to persons over 62 at the lowest cost available. Two amendments to involve the federal government in state rate-making decisions were spurned.

The Senate attached the provisions of S 2114 to a minor House-passed bill (HR 4018), together with the electric rate provisions of the House energy bill.

1978 Action

All five pieces of the energy package began 1978 in a conference committee where they remained for many months. Three parts of the package — coal conversion, utility rate reform and conservation — had been generally agreed upon by conferees in late 1977, but not formally approved.

Final action on those relatively non-controversial sections of the plan was delayed by long-running disputes over natural gas pricing and energy taxes. The majority of the natural gas conferees refused to finish up the other sections until they resolved the gas controversy. In the tax conference, Senate Finance Committee Chairman Long led senators in their refusal to meet on taxes until an agreement had been reached on natural gas.

For most of the year, it looked as if it would not be possible to reach agreement on the gas pricing section. Nearly every time conferees seemed close to agreement on a plan for gradual deregulation, some new difficulty presented itself. The opposition was a powerful and unusual coalition of consumer advocates who felt prices would go up too fast without federal price controls and industry sympathizers who claimed that price controls would not be lifted fast enough. The deadlock on natural gas threatened the entire energy package, whose passage remained in doubt until the very last day of the session, Oct. 15.

Strategic Oil Reserves

The Senate in 1978 blocked an administration plan to double the nation's strategic oil reserve capacity to one billion barrels. Senate rejection of that plan was not due to disagreement with the planned expansion of the strategic oil reserve but was instead targeted on an administration plan to limit possible sites for storage of some 20 million of those barrels, earmarked for use in New England.

New England senators, led by Sen. Edward M. Kennedy, D-Mass., led the disapproval move, objecting to language in the plan that required storage sites for the New England portion of the reserve to cost no more than the primary storage sites along the Gulf of Mexico, primarily in Louisiana. New England representatives, who wished to store the reserve oil close to home, argued that the limit effectively left no alternative but to store the New England oil in Louisiana.

Under the 1975 Energy Policy and Conservation Act (PL 94-163) either chamber of Congress could disapprove major changes in government fuel price or allocation programs by passing a resolution of disapproval within 15 days of receiving the proposal. The strategic oil reserve expansion and cost limit plan, "Energy Action #1" for 1978, was submitted to Congress April 4. It would have taken effect April 20.

But Kennedy filed a resolution of disapproval (S Res 429) on April 7. The Senate Energy Committee April 11 unanimously backed the Kennedy move (S Rept 95-738), and the full Senate by voice vote April 17 adopted the resolution of disapproval killing the plan. *(Previous energy action proposals, pp. 171, 177; oil reserve, p. 231)*

The Strategies

The Senate chose to handle conference reports on the energy bill as it had in 1977, when it divided the Carter bill into five measures and voted on each separately. The conference report on each measure was voted on as it emerged from conference committee.

In the House, however, Speaker O'Neill insisted on keeping the package together, permitting only one up-or-down vote on energy. That way, he reasoned, members could not approve the popular parts of the package without facing the more politically difficult questions of gas pricing and taxes.

O'Neill's strategy came very close to failing. On Oct. 13, opponents of the natural gas pricing portion came within one vote of splitting that section away from the rest of the package.

Even that crucial House vote did not clear the way for the energy bill. The next day in the Senate, Abourezk began a filibuster against the only part of the energy package still before the Senate — the conference report on energy taxes. A key opponent of the gas bill, Abourezk wanted the Senate to replace the tax report with a Senate-passed version of a bill (HR 112) that gave more generous credits for conservation and solar energy. He vowed to give up his filibuster only if the House passed that Senate bill separately.

O'Neill remained firm, refusing to allow a House vote until the tax conference report was sent over from the Senate. The House had a long wait. Abourezk and a few other senators talked and delayed for about 15 hours — from Saturday morning until 12:30 a.m. Sunday, when they finally gave up. The Senate then easily passed the tax conference report and sent it to the House. There, four hours later, at 7:30 a.m., the House approved the entire package.

Coal Conversion

The first piece of Carter's energy program to emerge from the conference committee was the coal conversion measure, which was reported (HR 5146 — S Rept 95-988) July 13. It was a watered-down version of the president's proposed regulatory scheme to force utilities and major industries to burn coal or other fuels instead of oil and natural gas. Conferees had included multiple grounds for exemptions. Furthermore, the tax conferees voted down the tax penalties for using oil and gas.

Senate and House conferees reached final agreement on basic compromise principles for the coal conversion bill on Nov. 11, 1977. But the hangup over natural gas pricing threw the entire package into a freeze until June.

The conference report on coal conversion was drafted hurriedly, but it was not until July 13 that a majority of conferees from each chamber signed it. Even then, the final language of the bill and report never was discussed in an open meeting of conferees, a fact that so outraged House Republican conferees they refused to sign it.

Final Senate Action. The bill went to the Senate floor July 14. The Democratic leadership wanted quick Senate approval before President Carter attended the economic summit conference July 16 in West Germany. The hope was to allay foreign fears that the United States was doing nothing to curb its massive oil imports, which had been blamed for a number of worldwide economic problems.

But Harrison Schmitt, R-N.M., forced a delay in the vote by insisting upon time to ask extensive questions. The conference report was finally adopted July 18 by a lopsided 92-6 vote.

Energy Conservation

Although generally non-controversial, the energy conservation bill also ran into some snags. It was bogged down along with the other portions in the argument over the gas bill. And also it had the controversial Senate provision the banned production of "gas guzzling" cars. The House preferred Carter's proposal to levy a tax on low-mileage cars.

The tax was conditionally approved in late 1977 by the energy tax conferees. Final agreement depended on whether the non-tax conferees would agree to drop the Senate ban.

After a full day of haggling Sept. 28, Senate conferees agreed to drop their ban in return for an agreement by House conferees to increase penalties under an existing gas-mileage law if certain conditions were met.

The existing law, the Energy Policy and Conservation Act of 1975 (PL 94-163) penalized automakers if their fleets had an average fuel consumption rate that exceeded the national standard. The standard was an average of 18 miles per gallon in 1978. It was to increase to 27.5 miles per gallon in 1985. The compromise raised the penalties as high as $10, up from $5, per car for each tenth of a mile in excess of the standard.

Final Senate Action. The conference report on the conservation bill (HR 5037 — S Rept 95-1294) was not filed immediately. Conferees who opposed the gas bill withheld their signatures from the report, aware that a delay in final Senate action could foul up House plans to cast a single vote on the package.

They eventually relented and the report was filed Oct. 6. The Senate then adopted the conference report Oct. 9, by an 86-3 vote, sending it on to the House for consideration with the rest of the package.

Utility Rate Reform

There was little debate in 1978 over the utility rate reform section of the energy plan because conferees had resolved most of the questions in 1977. All that remained was for staff to put the agreement into legislative language and to draft the conference report.

In November and December 1977, House conferees on the bill gave in to Senate demands that the states retain the power to force electric utilities to reform the way they billed customers.

The House had approved Carter's proposal for a series of minimal federal reforms revising utility pricing practices, which the states would have been required to enforce. The reforms were designed to spread customer demand for electricity more evenly, avoiding the existing pattern of "peak" demand periods. It was hoped the change would result in energy savings and reduce the need for utility expansion.

Although the conference agreement was softer than the House bill, its backers claimed it was much stronger than the original Senate version. They said it would guarantee that each state utility commission would consider thoroughly a wide variety of innovative rate reforms.

Final Senate Action. Once the conference report was drafted, the utility rate bill ran into the same problems as the conservation measure. Some conferees who opposed the natural gas pricing bill refused to sign the conference report, hoping to foil House plans to take a single vote on the entire energy package and possibly defeat the gas bill.

They eventually signed, however, and the report (HR 4018 — S Rept 95-1292) was filed Oct. 6. It passed the Senate Oct. 9 on a 76-13 vote.

Natural Gas

Initial meetings of the conference on natural gas were delayed by the January death of Sen. Lee Metcalf, D-Mont., one of the 18 members of the Senate Energy Committee who served as conferees and who had divided 9-9 on the issue of deregulation during committee consideration.

Metcalf had supported Carter's plan to continue federal controls on gas, and his death apparently tipped the scales in favor of gradual deregulation. On March 7, nine Senate conferees announced that they had formed a tenuous coalition backing a compromise plan to end federal price controls on new natural gas by 1985.

That coalition was badly shaken when House conferees rejected the Senate compromise and insisted on their own counterproposal.

Ironically, the proposed compromises showed that the two sides were closer than ever before.

A majority of the House conferees formally went on record for the first time in favor of phasing out federal price controls over new natural gas. Controls would have ended Dec. 31, 1984, under the Senate plan and six months later under the House plan.

The House version would have accepted the Senate price structure in the interim, with one major change. Instead of adjusting the price annually by an amount equal to the rate of inflation as measured by the Consumer Price Index, plus 3.5 percent through April 20, 1981, and plus 4 percent thereafter, the House version would have tied the inflation adjustor to changes in the gross national product, which was more stable.

The most important difference was the definition of what gas would be "new" and therefore eligible for higher prices and eventual deregulation. The Senate compromise terms were extremely broad, so that almost any newly drilled well — even in already producing reservoirs — could have drawn the high prices. The House version would have redrafted several technical sections to cut back substantially the amount of gas classified as "new."

In another major conflict, the House plan would have required a system of "incremental pricing" whereby industrial gas consumers would bear a disproportionate share of the burden of paying for the new high-priced gas at first, while smaller gas consumers would indefinitely draw lower-priced gas from wells still under controls. The Senate version required only that such pricing plans be drafted and submitted to Congress for separate approval.

Despite personal intervention by President Carter, no headway was made until April 21, when a small group of leading House and Senate conferees announced they had reached an agreement to deregulate most new gas as of Jan. 1, 1985. The new compromise narrowed the Senate definitions of "new" gas so that less was deregulated and accepted a modified version of the House incremental pricing requirement.

The new accommodation was initially accepted by less than a dozen of the 43 conferees, and it took leaders another month to round up enough votes for conference approval. House conferees finally agreed to the compromise in principle, 13-12; Senate conferees approved the plan 10-7.

But the compromise was not yet out of the woods. After formal legislative language was drafted, several conferees refused to sign it, claiming it was not what they had agreed to in principle. Nearly another month elapsed before a majority of the conferees could be persuaded to sign the report (HR 5289 — S Rept 95-1126).

Final Senate Action. On Aug. 23, five days after the report was signed, a coalition composed both of senators opposing and supporting deregulation announced they would move to recommit the bill to conference. When the conference report reached the Senate floor Sept. 11, supporters of the measure averted a threatened filibuster by agreeing not to vote until Sept. 19 on the recommittal motion.

Opponents of the gas deregulation compromise thought the extra time would enable them to win more votes for the motion. But heavy White House lobbying turned the extra days of debate into an advantage for the bill's supporters. The motion to recommit failed on a vote of 39-59 (R 21-15; D 18-44). *(Lobbying, box, p. 188)*

A second try to send the bill back to conference failed Sept. 26, 36-55, and on Sept. 27, the Senate finally approved the natural gas compromise, 57-42.

Energy Taxes

Progress on the energy tax bill was even slower than on the gas bill.

Tax conferees held no meetings between Dec. 7, 1977, and July 14, 1978, largely because of Sen. Long's insistence that the natural gas controversy be resolved first. After meeting in July, conferees did not meet again until Sept. 29.

The major controversy was over the president's proposed tax on crude oil, approved by the House but rejected by the Senate. Senate opposition combined with the negative politics of imposing a new tax in an election year to kill the tax in conference without much fanfare.

But as the summer stretched on with no action on the bill, supporters of its less controversial portions — primarily tax credits for businesses and homeowners that installed solar collectors, insulation and other energy-saving devices — moved to consider them separately. On Aug. 23, the Senate agreed by voice vote to tack them onto a minor House-passed tax bill (HR 112).

Conferees completed work on the energy tax bill (HR 5263 — S Rept 95-1324) Oct. 11, agreeing to tax credits for homeowners and businesses that saved energy and to a tax on cars that used too much gasoline. They dropped the proposed tax on industrial use of oil and natural gas.

Final Senate Action. Senate floor action on the energy tax bill began late in the day Oct. 12, but was quickly cut short by Abourezk's filibuster attempt. Majority Leader Byrd pulled the bill from the floor, filing a cloture petition to be voted on Saturday, Oct. 14, and the Senate went on to other business.

Cloture was voted early Saturday, but Abourezk continued to tie up the bill by using parliamentary procedures to delay a final vote. When it became clear that his effort was to little avail, he quit, and the Senate passed the energy tax bill easily, 60-17.

Final House Action

Even though the Senate had not completed action on the energy tax bill Oct. 12, House Speaker O'Neill went before the House Rules Committee seeking a rule that would prohibit a separate House vote on the fragile natural gas compromise.

After an all-day committee session, neither side had won. A motion to keep the package intact and a motion to split it both failed on 8-8 ties.

But the next day, the Rules Committee voted to keep the package together. Later that afternoon, the House concurred with a dramatic vote of 207-206 (R 8-127; D 199-79). That tally, a major victory for the president, came only after several members voted late or switched their votes.

House action on the package itself, was delayed two more days by Abourezk's filibuster in the Senate on the energy tax bill. He was encouraged by several House members who preferred the separate tax credit bill (HR 112) approved by the Senate in August. They repeatedly told O'Neill that Abourezk would end his stalling tactics as

soon as O'Neill agreed to take up HR 112.

O'Neill refused to give in, and shortly after midnight Oct. 15 Abourezk yielded. The Senate quickly passed the energy tax conference report and sent it to the House, which began debate on the conference reports for all five energy bills at 2:45 a.m. Oct. 15. After four hours of debate, the House voted 231-168 for the energy bill, clearing it for the president.

Major Provisions

Natural Gas Pricing

As cleared by Congress, HR 5289 (PL 95-621):

Title I — Wellhead Pricing

Price Controls. Established a scaled ceiling price for "new" gas starting at $1.75 per million British thermal units (MMBtu's) as of April 20, 1977 — the date Carter proposed his energy program.

● Provided that the initial price would rise monthly to cover inflation as measured by the gross national product (GNP), plus .2 percent, plus another 3.5 percent, until April 1981; and plus 4 percent thereafter, instead of 3.5 percent.

● Defined new natural gas found onshore to include gas from 1) new wells at least 2.5 miles from a "marker" well — one producing commercial quantities of gas between Jan. 1, 1970, and April 20, 1977; 2) a new well with a bottom depth 1,000 feet below the nearest and deepest well bottom within 2.5 miles; 3) a newly drilled onshore reservoir.

● Defined "new" offshore gas to include gas from new leases or from new reservoirs in old leases.

● Excluded from the "new" category 1) gas located "behind the pipe" — in an untapped reservoir adjacent to a well being drilled; 2) gas "withheld" from production; 3) gas from Alaska's Prudhoe Bay.

● Provided that new wells in old onshore reservoirs would draw a new ceiling price of $1.75 per MMBtu, which would then increase at a rate equal to inflation. Some of this gas would be deregulated by 1985.

● Provided that all other interstate gas would draw a ceiling price of $1.45 per MMBtu as of April 20, 1977, and that price would rise by the GNP inflation rate.

● Provided that gas sold under existing intrastate contracts would draw a new price equal to the contract price or the new gas ceiling price, whichever was lower.

● Directed that gas sold under an interstate contract that expired — a "rollover" contract — was eligible to draw the higher price between the applicable "just and reasonable" standard under existing law (the Natural Gas Act — PL 75-690), or $.54 per MMBtu.

● Provided that gas sales under expiring intrastate contracts would get the contract price or $1 per MMBtu, whichever was higher.

● Provided that all gas sold under rollover contracts would draw price increases equal to inflation.

● Specified that certain categories of "high cost" gas would be deregulated about one year after enactment.

● Included in that category gas 1) from wells deeper than 15,000 feet; 2) from geopressurized brine; 3) from coal seams; 4) from Devonian shale; and 5) produced under conditions determined by the Federal Energy Regulatory Commission (FERC) to pose unusual risks or costs.

● Provided that gas produced from "stripper" wells — those producing on average no more than 60 thousand cubic feet (Mcf) per day — would draw an initial ceiling price of $2.09 per MMBtu, which would rise according to a special monthly inflation formula.

● Specified that state severance taxes were not to be considered part of any ceiling prices set by the act.

Decontrol. Eliminated federal price controls as of Jan. 1, 1985, on 1) new natural gas; 2) deep new onshore wells; and 3) existing intrastate contracts over $1 per MMBtu as of Dec. 31, 1984.

● Provided that either the president or Congress could reimpose controls for one 18-month period at any time between July 1, 1985, and June 30, 1987.

● Provided that either the House or Senate could veto the president's decision to reimpose controls, but that both houses would have to act together to reimpose controls.

Title II — Incremental Pricing

● Required FERC to develop within 12 months of enactment an incremental pricing rule for industrial boiler fuel facilities. The rule would define which low priority gas consumers would bear a disproportionately high share of the increased costs of gas to ease the impact on high priority gas users.

● Directed FERC to develop a second incremental pricing rule within 18 months of enactment that would broaden the application to more low priority users.

● Specified that the second incremental pricing rule would be subject to veto by either house of Congress.

● Directed that any costs that could be passed along to low priority users under the incremental pricing rules be placed in a special account. Incrementally priced users would have to pay the higher gas costs until their gas expenses equaled the cost of substitute fuels. Then their costs would be limited to the amount necessary to keep them at the alternative fuel price.

● Exempted from incremental pricing 1) certain small industrial boiler fuel facilities; 2) specific agricultural uses; 3) residences; 4) small commercial uses; 5) schools; 6) hospitals and other institutions, and 7) electric utilities.

Title III — Emergency Authority

● Authorized the president to declare natural gas emergencies.

● Authorized the president to authorize any interstate pipeline or local gas distributor to make emergency purchases of gas under short term contracts.

● Authorized the president in emergencies to allocate supplies to meet high priority needs, but only after the emergency purchase option had been exhausted.

● Barred the president from taking gas from one class of users in one state to give to the same class of users in another state.

Title IV — Curtailment

● Specified that in the event of gas curtailment, the last uses to be curtailed would be residences, small commercial users, schools, hospitals and like institutions, and other users when the energy secretary determined that curtailment to them would endanger life, health or property maintenance.

● Specified that certain agricultural uses would have priority after the uses spelled out above. Certain industrial processes or feedstock uses would hold the next curtailment priority.

Title V — Administration

● Provided FERC with general rule making authority.

● Authorized the state or federal agency with regulatory jurisdiction over gas production to determine the category for which a given well qualified. Authorized FERC to review agency decisions.

● Provided both civil and criminal penalties for violations of the act.

● Gave the energy secretary power to intervene in state proceedings concerning gas production.

● Provided judicial review authority modeled on that under the existing Natural Gas Act.

Title VI — Coordination with Existing Law

● Reserved to states the right to mandate lower price ceilings than provided by the act.

Coal Conversion

As cleared by Congress, HR 5146 (PL 95-620):

Title I — Goals, Definitions

● Established as the bill's goals a cut in oil imports and stimulation of the use of coal and other plentiful substitute fuels to save dwindling supplies of oil and gas.

● Specified that regulatory orders in the measure applied to existing utility plants or major fuel burning installations only if they burned fuel at rates of at least 100 million British thermal units (Btu's) per hour or more. A British thermal unit is the amount of heat required to raise the temperature of one pound of water by one degree Fahrenheit at or near 39.2 degrees Fahrenheit.

● Defined new utility power plants or major fuel burning facilities as those on which construction began or which were acquired after April 20, 1977, the date Carter proposed his energy program. New plants were subject to different terms than existing ones in some sections of the law.

Title II — New Facilities

● Barred new electric power plants and new major fuel burning installations from burning oil or natural gas as their primary energy source.

● Directed that all new power plants be built with the capability to burn coal or another alternate fuel instead of oil or gas.

● Gave the energy secretary power to issue rules prohibiting broad categories of new major fuel burning installations from burning oil or gas in uses other than boilers.

Exemptions. Granted industries permanent or temporary exemptions of up to five years for use of oil or gas if they demonstrated need, such as showing that other fuels would be unreliable or unavailable.

● Required that before granting most exemptions, the energy secretary had to find that use of a mixture of oil and coal or other fuels was not economically or technically feasible.

Title III — Existing Facilities

● Prohibited existing electric power plants from burning natural gas after Jan. 1, 1990, except under rigidly defined circumstances.

● Prohibited power plants that did not use gas as a primary fuel during 1977 from converting to its use.

● Prohibited existing electric power plants that burned gas from consuming more of it than they had burned on average betwen 1974 and 1976.

● Empowered the energy secretary to order oil or gas burning power plants and other major factories, which by design were capable of burning coal or other fuels, to cease burning oil or gas. But the burden of proof that the plants could burn substitute fuels would be on the government.

Exemptions. Established a full range of temporary and permanent exemptions, like those available for new power plants and industrial facilities.

Title IV — Other Prohibitions, Authorities

● Empowered the energy secretary to prohibit the use of natural gas in new or existing boilers used for space heating if the boiler consumed as much as 300,000 cubic feet of gas per day and could run on oil.

Decorative Lighting. Prohibited new outdoor decorative lights fueled by natural gas and empowered the secretary to prohibit gas pipeline and distribution companies from delivering gas to residential, commercial or industrial customers for such purposes. Existing residential and municipal outdoor gas lights had to comply by Jan. 1, 1982.

Emergency Powers. Authorized the president to allocate coal, to order any plant to cease burning oil or gas and to suspend the terms of the law in time of severe energy supply emergencies, as defined in existing law or as he declared. Presidential orders under such emergency powers would last for the extent of the emergency or 90 days, whichever was less.

Title V — System Compliance Option

● Eased the transition from oil and gas dependence for utility systems, such as those in Southwestern states, that were almost entirely dependent upon natural gas to fuel their plants. Gave such utilities the option of submitting compliance plans by Jan. 1, 1980, identifying their gas-dependent plants and outlining how they planned to comply with the mandatory phase-out of natural gas boiler fuel consumption by 1990.

Title VI — Financial Assistance

● Provided that when a governor declared an area of his state to be impacted because of coal or uranium development, the federal government could provide cash grants to ease the impact, subject to conditions.

● Required the governor to demonstrate to the energy secretary's satisfaction that:

1) The development had increased employment directly over the past year by 8 percent or was projected to do so by at least that much annually for the next three years.

2) The increase would require substantial public facilities such as schools and roads.

3) State and local governments could not handle the financial burden.

● Authorized the secretary of agriculture to give 100 percent planning grants to affected states or localities designated as energy impacted areas to help them plan how to cope with the development's impact. Land for public facilities or housing also could be acquired with such funds.

● Authorized $60 million for fiscal 1979 and $120 million for fiscal 1980 to cover program costs.

Pollution Control Loans. Authorized loans for existing power plants to finance the cost of installing pollution control devices required to burn coal under the act.

● Authorized $400 million for such purposes in both fiscal 1979 and 1980.

Titles VII, VIII — Miscellaneous

● Promulgated rules under the act, provided judicial review rights and listed enforcement provisions and penalties for violations. Penalties ranged up to one year in prison and a $50,000 fines for each criminal violation and up to $25,000 for each civil violation.

Utility Rates

As cleared by Congress, HR 4018 (PL 95-617):

● Required that, within three years of enactment, each state utility commission or non-regulated electric company consider, with appropriate public hearings, implementation of the following federal standards for rate making on a utility-by-utility basis:

1) Setting of rates to reflect the actual cost of providing electric service to each class of consumers.

2) Prohibition of the use of "declining block rates" under which the cost of electricity decreased as consumption increased, unless the block rates reflected actual costs.

3) Use of "time-of-day" rates that reflected the cost of providing power at peak hours, when all power plants and backup facilities were in use, versus the cost of power at off hours.

4) Use of "seasonal" rates when different seasons of the year affected the costs of providing electricity.

5) Use of "interruptible" rates when the cost of providing power was less when service could be interrupted.

6) Offering of other "load management techniques" to consumers when they would be practicable, cost effective, reliable and provide useful management advantages to the utility.

● Provided that if a state commission did not comply voluntarily, the Department of Energy or any affected rate payer could request it to consider those standards. If intervention was denied, the department could seek an order from a federal court for compliance.

● Required each commission, within two years of enactment and to the extent deemed appropriate by each commission, to: 1) prohibit or restrict master metering, 2) adopt procedures to review automatic adjustment clauses, 3) adopt procedures to prohibit rate discrimination against solar, wind or other small power systems, 4) adopt procedures to provide consumer information, 5) prohibit charging rate payers for advertising and 6) adopt procedures to protect rate payers from abrupt termination of service.

● Provided that state commission actions on the standards would be subject to review in state courts only, not federal courts, except as existing federal law guaranteed the right to appeal to the U.S. Supreme Court.

● Authorized grants of $58 million each in fiscal 1979 and 1980 for states to use in implementing the rate reforms, with most funds to be spent on additional personnel.

● Authorized the Federal Energy Regulatory Commission (FERC) to order utilities to interconnect their facilities and to exchange energy supplies, subject to tests of reasonableness and judicial review.

● Authorized FERC to order a utility to "wheel" power from one supplier to another, subject to tests of reasonableness.

● Authorized the federal government to provide loans for up to 90 percent of the cost of feasibility studies for small hydroelectric projects on existing dams; authorized government loans of up to 75 percent of the costs of such projects, subject to certain conditions.

Conservation

As cleared by Congress, HR 5037 (PL 95-619):

● Required that gas and electric utilities inform their customers of available energy-saving measures and offer to inspect homes to point out other energy saving steps.

● Required utilities to offer to arrange for financing and installation of home energy conservation improvements, such as insulation and storm windows, and allowed utilities to make direct loans of up to $300 for such improvements unless prohibited from doing so by state law.

● Allowed customer costs for insulation and other home energy conservation measures to be paid through utility bills, regardless of who installed them.

● Authorized the Department of Energy to spend up to $200 million in each of fiscal years 1979 and 1980 for weatherization grants to low-income families, with grants limited to $800 for the costs of materials for each home, except in certain cases. To qualify, a family's income could not exceed 125 percent of the national poverty level.

● Authorized the Government National Mortgage Association (GNMA) to purchase $3 billion in loans from commercial lenders to provide subsidized low interest loans for energy conservation improvements to families whose income was below the median income for their area.

● Authorized GNMA to purchase an additional $2 billion in loans, provided the energy secretary decided the purchase was necessary, to provide loans at market rates for energy conservation improvements by households with incomes above the poverty level.

● Authorized GNMA to purchase up to $100 million in loans to provide loans at market rates to homeowners for purchase and installation of solar energy systems.

● Authorized $295 million in fiscal 1979 and $400 million in fiscal 1980 for grants to schools and hospitals for energy conservation improvements. The grants would be distributed according to population, with consideration also given to such factors as area climate and costs of fuel. No single state could receive more than 10 percent, and each would receive at least 0.5 percent, of the total appropriated.

● Doubled the maximum penalty assessed an automaker whose fleet had an average fuel efficiency below the national standard set in the Energy Policy and Conservation Act of 1975 (PL 94-163). The penalties could be raised as high as $10, up from $5, per car for each tenth of a mile in excess of the average.

● Required the Energy Department to set mandatory energy efficiency standards for 13 major home appliances, effective no later than the mid-1980s. Appliances covered were refrigerators, furnaces, room and central air conditioners, water heaters, freezers, dishwashers, clothes washers and dryers, home space heaters, television sets, kitchen ranges and ovens, humidifiers and dehumidifiers.

● Authorized spending $100 million through fiscal year 1980 for demonstrations in federal buildings of solar heating and cooling technology.

● Authorized spending $98 million through fiscal year 1981 to acquire and operate photovoltaic solar electric systems to meet the energy needs of federal agencies.

Taxes

As cleared by Congress, HR 5263 (PL 95-618):

Title I — Residential Credits

Insulation. Provided a non-refundable income tax credit of 15 percent of the first $2,000 (maximum $300) spent by homeowners to install insulation and other specified energy-conserving improvements at their principal residence between April 20, 1977, and Jan. 1, 1986.

● Provided that the credit would be available for expenditures made for insulation, furnace replacement burners for cutting fuel consumption, flue opening modifications, furnace ignition systems to replace gas pilot lights, storm or thermal windows or doors, automatic energy-saving setback thermostats, caulking or weatherstripping, meters displaying the cost of energy usage, or other items specified in regulations by the energy secretary.

Solar. Provided a non-refundable credit of 30 percent of the first $2,000 and 20 percent of the next $8,000 — for a total maximum of $2,200 — for homeowners who installed solar, wind or geothermal energy equipment in their principal residences between April 20, 1977, and Jan. 1, 1986.

Title II — Transportation

Gas Guzzler Tax. Imposed a "gas guzzler tax" on the sale by the manufacturer of passenger cars — beginning with model year 1980 — that used fuel inefficiently, with certain exceptions for ambulances, police cars and other emergency vehicles.

● For model year 1980, the tax ranged from $550 for cars that got less than 13 miles per gallon (mpg) to $200 for cars that got at least 14 mpg but less than 15 mpg. The tax and the mpg standard increased each year so that for model year 1986, taxes ranged from $3,850 for cars that got less than 12.5 mpg to $500 for cars that got at least 21.5 mpg but less than 22.5 mpg.

Gasohol. Exempted from the federal excise tax on motor fuel, gasohol sold after Dec. 31, 1978, and before Oct. 1, 1984, if the gasohol was at least 10 percent alcohol. The exemption would apply only if the alcohol was made from products — such as grain or solid waste — other than petroleum, natural gas or coal. Gasohol is a blend of gasoline and alcohol.

Excise Taxes. Repealed as of Dec. 31, 1978, the 2-cent-a-gallon reduction of the excise taxes on gasoline and special motor fuels and the refund of the 6-cent-a-gallon tax on lubricating oil for gasoline, special fuels and lubricating oil used for non-business, non-highway purposes (such as lawn mowers and snowmobiles) and for motorboats.

• Specified that there would be no change in the exemptions for commercial fishing vessels.

• Repealed the 10 percent manufacturers' excise tax imposed on the sale of buses over 10,000 pounds, which were sold on or after April 20, 1977.

• Repealed the 8 percent manufacturers' excise tax on the sale of bus parts and accessories.

• Removed the excise taxes on highway tires, inner tubes, tread rubber, gasoline, other motor fuels and lubricating oil for private intercity, local and school bus operations.

Commuter Vehicles. Provided a full 10 percent investment tax credit for "commuter highway vehicles" used in van pooling if the vehicles could carry at least nine adults, were used at least 80 percent of the time for transporting employees to and from work and were acquired after the date of enactment and placed in service before Jan. 1, 1986.

Title III — Business Credits

Provided a special 10 percent investment credit for business that installed:

• Specified equipment for producing synthetic fuels or renewable energy fuels for new buildings.

• Conservation equipment that reduced the amount of heat wasted or energy consumed in existing industrial processes.

• Recycling equipment, shale oil equipment and equipment to produce natural gas from geopressured brine.

• Provided that the credits, which could be applied against 100 percent of tax liability, were available for equipment placed in service after Sept. 30, 1978, and before Jan. 2, 1983.

• *Depreciation.* Provided special treatment for depreciation of a natural gas or oil fueled boiler replaced before it was no longer useful.

• *Geopressured Natural Gas Depletion.* Provided a percentage depletion allowance for gas produced from geopressured brine: 22 percent for production in 1978-1980, 20 percent for 1981, 18 percent for 1982, 16 percent for 1983 and 15 percent for all years thereafter.

Outer Continental Shelf

In mid-September 1978, President Carter signed into law the first changes since 1953 in the laws governing the leasing and development of the oil and gas resources lying off U.S. shores.

The Outer Continental Shelf Lands Act Amendments (S 9 — PL 95-372) were designed to foster increased competition in bidding for oil and gas leases, give states a large role in leasing decisions, and tighten environmental controls on offshore drilling and production.

The outer continental shelf (OCS) was the underwater margin of the North American continent. It began where state jurisdiction ended, three miles from the shoreline, and extended some 150 to 200 miles out to sea. It was estimated that as much as 49 billion barrels of oil and 81 trillion cubic feet of natural gas might be recovered from the offshore lands.

Interest in the offshore resources accelerated in the early 1970s when the Nixon administration advocated stepping up the pace of offshore leasing and exploration. Concern for the environmental and onshore economic impacts

of such development was particularly intense in states adjacent to offshore areas never before developed, off the East Coast and off Alaska.

Congress spent four years trying to reach agreement on changes in the Outer Continental Shelf Lands Act of 1953 (PL 83-212). Most of the proposed changes were bitterly opposed by the oil industry. But the compromise legislation enacted in 1978 as PL 95-372 was generally accepted by the industry, environmentalists and the Carter administration.

White House support for the OCS amendments was a key factor in their adoption by the 95th Congress. In 1975 and 1976 the Ford administration had opposed such legislation, agreeing with the oil industry that existing law was adequate to govern offshore energy development.

Background

Interest in the outer continental shelf and the vast resources thought to lie there accelerated in the early 1970s as the Nixon administration pushed the Interior Department to step up the pace of OCS leasing, moving particularly into frontier OCS areas never before developed.

Until the mid-1970s, the only offshore oil and gas development in the United States was in the Gulf of Mexico, primarily off the shores of Louisiana and Texas, and off the Southern California coast in the Santa Barbara Channel. By 1974 less than 10 million acres had been leased in the entire history of OCS development. The proposed move into frontier OCS areas off New England and other portions of the Atlantic Coast, off the Pacific Coast and the Alaskan coast, suddenly enlarged the constituency of people and governments concerned about OCS development and policy.

In 1974 the Senate passed a bill (S 3221) setting new guidelines for OCS development and creating a grant program to help coastal states cope with the impact of such activity. The House did not act on the measure in the 93rd Congress.

In 1975 the Senate passed two OCS bills, one (S 586) containing primarily the aid provisions, the other (S 521) revising the OCS policy guidelines. The House approved both measures in 1976. The aid measure was enacted as the Coastal Zone Management Act Amendments of 1976, but the policy measure was killed in late September 1976 when the House voted, 198-194, to send it back to conference.

Senate Action

In the 95th Congress, the Senate once again took the lead in acting on OCS legislation. On July 15, 1977, the Senate approved S 9 (S Rept 95-284) by a vote of 60-18.

The measure had been reported June 21 by the Senate Energy and Natural Resources Committee, which had amended the measure to remove some of the provisions that had been most strenuously opposed by the oil industry in 1976. Nevertheless, the changes made by the committee were not sufficient to win industry support for the measure. Industry representatives continued to argue that there was no need for any change in the 1953 law.

Senate passage of S 9 came after two days of debate during which the oil industry lost virtually every battle. The industry's major disappointment came when the Senate added language to S 9 that authorized the interior secretary to contract for exploratory drilling in underdeveloped areas of the OCS, and to authorize such drilling

Plan to Speed Nuclear Power Plant Licensing
Given Little Notice in Congress During 1978

The Carter administration's plan to reform and speed the process of licensing nuclear power plants received only passing attention from Congress in 1978.

The one serious attempt at marking up the measure, led by Morris K. Udall, D-Ariz., chairman of the House Interior Subcommittee on Energy, was blocked by the lack of a quorum.

The Carter proposal, promised in the president's April 1977 energy policy speech to Congress, was finally unveiled 11 months later. Bureaucratic infighting had delayed its introduction.

"We believe at the present time that the nuclear option is barely alive," Energy Secretary James R. Schlesinger told a March 17, 1978, news conference at which the proposal was outlined. The proposed bill, a department release said, "is intended to assure that nuclear power will remain a viable option."

Schlesinger said the proposed legislation would cut from 10 to 12 years to about 6.5 years the period between the decision to build a nuclear power plant and the time it was licensed to operate.

But because it would take several years before the proposal could be implemented, he said, "It will be a decade approximately before we begin to see the effects of these new procedures."

The major provisions of the Carter proposal authorized the Nuclear Regulatory Commission (NRC) to approve sites for nuclear plants and standard designs for nuclear reactors before construction permits were filed. It further authorized the NRC to grant joint construction permits and operating licenses for nuclear power plants, eliminating the need for two separate hearings. The plan also would turn over to the states some functions performed by the NRC.

The proposed legislation was introduced into both chambers of Congress March 21 (S 2775, HR 11704).

The Atomic Industrial Forum, the nuclear industry's trade association, welcomed the bill but said it "needs substantial improvement."

Environmentalists and public interest groups said the bill gave short shrift to environmental concerns, unfairly restricted public access to the licensing process, ignored the real reasons behind nuclear power's development problems, failed to remedy existing problems associated with nuclear plants, such as where to store nuclear wastes, and proposed ineffective reforms.

---

before those areas were offered for leasing. The amendment was adopted by a vote of 52-46.

Adoption of the amendment reflected a general feeling of dissatisfaction with the quality of energy data upon which the federal government based its energy policy. Advocates for the amendment argued that exploratory drilling would give the federal government more reliable data with which to evaluate the worth of areas put up for leasing. Energy Committee Chairman Henry M. Jackson, D-Wash., declared that the Interior Department often undervalued tracts and allowed oil companies to lease them at far too low a price.

House Action

The House Ad Hoc Select Committee on the Outer Continental Shelf reported its OCS amendments bill (HR 1614 — H Rept 95-590) Aug. 29, 1977. But on Oct. 25, the House Rules Committee, responding to intensive lobbying by oil industry representatives, postponed floor action on the measure until 1978.

Early in 1978 the House Rules Committee cleared the bill for floor action. After four days of debate and the addition of a hodgepodge of amendments, the House approved HR 1614 on Feb. 2 by a vote of 291-91.

During debate the House Jan. 26 rejected, 187-211, an industry-backed substitute measure. But later the chief

sponsors of the bill accepted changes in the bill's two most controversial sections, thereby winning the support of key opponents.

The first of the changes was the deletion of provisions calling for dual leasing, that is, leasing of a tract first for exploration, and then leasing of it, perhaps to a different lessee, for production.

The second change modified language giving the government the authority to conduct pre-lease drilling on a tract in order to discover an area's potential value. The amendment removed from HR 1614 language characterized by opponents as authorizing the federal government itself to do such drilling. The effect of the change was to return to the language of the 1953 act, which authorized the government to allow, or contract for, such pre-leasing exploration.

Final Action

Conferees haggled off and on from March until July before filing their report (S Rept 95-1091) on the final version of the bill Aug. 10. On the key issue of exploratory drilling, conferees followed the House approach, rather than the Senate provisions permitting federal government exploration. Although Interior Secretary Cecil D. Andrus claimed the final language gave the federal government authority to conduct its own explorations, it was widely assumed that any federal exploratory drilling would be challenged in court. The conferees did not interpret the law in their report, and the resulting ambiguity was a major reason the compromise was acceptable to some House conferees.

The House adopted the report Aug. 17 by a vote of 338-18. The Senate cleared the measure for the president Aug. 22, approving the report by a vote of 82-7.

Provisions

As enacted, PL 95-372 amended the Outer Continental Shelf Lands Act of 1953 in the following manner:

Exploration and Development

Title I called for more aggressive management of the outer continental shelf, submission of plans by lessees for active exploration and development of OCS tracts and more involvement of coastal states in OCS activities.

New provisions were added to the 1953 law to:

● Require the appropriate Cabinet secretary to develop a comprehensive five-year program for OCS leasing that was to consist of a schedule of proposed sales indicating the size, timing and location of activities. Considerations in developing the program were to include the relative environmental sensitivity and marine productivity of different areas and the return of a "fair market value" for the public lands leased.

● Direct the secretary to solicit recommendations regarding the leasing program from the governors of affected states and from interested federal agencies. If the recommendations were rejected, the secretary was to explain the reasons for doing so.

● Require an environmental study of each general area proposed for leasing.

● Permit "any person having an interest which is or may be adversely affected" to file a suit against any person, including a government agency, for alleged violation of the act or of a lease, or against the secretary for alleged failure to perform a non-discretionary act or duty.

● Set civil penalties of up to $10,000 per day for failure to comply with the act; set criminal penalties of up to $100,000 (per day for some violations) and 10 years in prison or both for deliberate violation of the act or regulations issued under it.

● Require submission of a development and production plan for all future leases and all existing leases where no oil or gas had yet been discovered, except for leases in the Gulf of Mexico.

● Provide that the interior secretary review and approve or disapprove the plan. If a plan were not submitted or complied with, the secretary could cancel the lease.

● Provide that the plan set forth a description of the specific work to be performed; a description of all facilities and operations located on the OCS; the environmental safeguards to be implemented; all safety standards to be met; an expected rate of development and production and a time schedule for performance and any other relevant information required by the secretary.

● Require a lessee to give the secretary access to all data and information relating to OCS activities.

● Provide that the secretary share the information, except for proprietary information, with the affected states.

Existing provisions were amended to:

● Transfer to the energy secretary functions of the interior secretary relating to:

(1) Fostering of competition for federal leases includ-

ing, but not limited to, prohibition on bidding for development rights by certain types of joint ventures.

(2) Implementation of alternative bidding systems authorized for the award of federal leases.

(3) Establishment of diligence requirements for operations conducted on federal leases including, but not limited to, procedures relating to the granting or ordering by the interior secretary of suspension of operations or production as they related to such requirements.

(4) Setting rates of production for federal leases.

(5) Specifying procedures, terms and conditions for acquisition and disposition of federal royalty interests taken in kind.

(The interior secretary retained responsibility for conducting lease sales, for monitoring the effect of exploration and development on the environment and for generally enforcing the OCS law. The interior secretary also retained authority to suspend or cancel a lease.)

● Establish a liaison committee of top energy and interior officials to coordinate administration of the act.

● Provide that a lease be suspended or canceled, after suspension, if there was threat of harm or damage to life (including fish or other aquatic life), to property, to any mineral deposits, to the national security or to the marine, coastal or human environments.

● Provide that a lease be suspended or canceled if the lessee failed to comply with the terms of the lease or act.

● Provide new bidding procedures to be used in addition to cash bonus bids with a royalty of at least 12.5 percent, including variable royalty, variable net profit, fixed net profit and work commitment bidding procedures. The secretary was authorized to use other, unspecified systems if, after 30 days, neither house of Congress had passed a resolution disapproving the alternative system.

● Mandate that new bidding systems be used in at least 20 percent and not more than 60 percent of the tracts offered for leasing in all OCS areas during each of the five years following enactment.

● Allow leases set for five-year terms to have a term of 10 years where the secretary found the longer period to be necessary in areas with "unusually deep water or other unusual adverse conditions."

● Require that lessees offer for purchase to small refiners at least 20 percent of OCS-recovered crude oil or natural gas.

● Permit the attorney general, in consultation with the Federal Trade Commission, to conduct a review of lease sales and make recommendations as to whether the sales indicated a situation inconsistent with antitrust laws. If the secretary rejected the attorney general's recommendations, the secretary would have to notify the lessee and the attorney general of the reasons for his decision.

● Retain language in the 1953 law that provided that: "Any agency of the United States and any person authorized by the [interior] secretary may conduct geological and geophysical explorations in the outer continental shelf, which do not interfere with or endanger actual operations under any lease maintained or granted pursuant to this act, and which are not unduly harmful to aquatic life in such area."

● Require that a lessee submit to the secretary a plan for exploring a leased OCS tract that included a schedule of anticipated exploration activities; a description of equipment to be used; the general location of each well to be drilled and other information deemed pertinent by the secretary.

Offshore Oil Pollution Funds

To deal with spills from offshore production and transportation of oil, Title III:

● Established an Offshore Oil Pollution Compensation Fund of up to $200 million, funded by a 3-cent-per-barrel fee on oil produced on the OCS.

● Provided that owners and operators of offshore facilities and vessels had unlimited liability for cleanup of oil spills and a liability for damages of up to $35 million for offshore facilities and of $300 per gross ton, up to $25,000, for vessels.

● Authorized the president to clean up an oil spill, using money from the fund, if the owner or operator responsible would not clean up or had not been identified.

● Provided that damaged parties could make claims on the fund and be paid by the fund, with the fund subsequently acquiring the claimant's rights to sue the spiller.

Fishermen's Contingency Fund

To aid commercial fishermen whose livelihoods were jeopardized because of OCS activity, primarily damage to equipment, Title IV:

● Established a Fishermen's Contingency Fund of up to $1 million, with area accounts established therein of up to $100,000.

● Required each lessee to pay into the fund up to $5,000 per calendar year per lease, permit, easement or right of way.

Coastal Zone Management Act Amendments

Contained in Title V were amendments to the Coastal Zone Management Act Amendments of 1976 (PL 94-370) to:

● Modify the formula used to distribute OCS formula grants to coastal states affected by offshore development. The measure based allocation of funds on new acreage leased adjacent to a coastal state (50 percent); oil and gas produced adjacent to a coastal state (25 percent); and oil and gas first landed in the coastal state (25 percent).

● Ensure that no state eligible under the existing formula would receive less than 2 percent of the total appropriation. States not eligible under the formula, but that were in the region of affected coastal states, would be entitled to receive 2 percent of the total if the secretary of commerce determined that the state was affected by OCS activity and could use the money as required by the coastal zone act.

● Provide that no state could receive more than 37.5 percent of the total.

● Authorize appropriation of $130 million annually for the OCS formula grants.

● Authorize appropriations of $5 million annually to help states carry out their responsibilities under the OCS act.

Gasoline Marketing

After five years of debate, Congress in 1978 approved legislation (HR 130 — PL 95-297) protecting gas station owners from the arbitrary cancellation of their franchises.

In addition to that major purpose, PL 95-297, often called the "Dealer Day In Court" bill, required that gasoline octane ratings be posted on gas pumps and directed that there be a federal study of the extent to which fuel sales were subsidized by fuel suppliers.

The House approved HR 130 (H Rept 95-161) April 5, 1977. The Senate approved its version of the measure (S Rept 95-731) May 9. The House accepted the Senate version by voice vote June 6, clearing the bill for the White House.

Provisions

Title I of the bill prohibited a franchisor from terminating or failing to renew a franchise agreement with a gasoline distributor or retailer unless he could meet certain standards of reasonableness for his action. At least 90 days notice of termination or non-renewal was required in most cases. PL 95-297 gave retailers or distributors the right to contest cancellation of their franchise in federal court.

Title II required refiners to determine and certify the octane rating of their gasoline and require the retailer to post those ratings on the pumps.

Title III required the Department of Energy to study the extent to which producers, refiners and other fuel suppliers subsidized company-owned gasoline stations with funds or services derived from other operations of the parent company.

Coal Slurry

An intense lobbying campaign by the nation's railroads culminated in mid-1978 with the stunning defeat on the House floor of a long-sought bill (HR 1609) to facilitate the building of coal slurry pipelines. Coal slurry pipelines would carry coal from mines to consumers, a task performed in the 1970s almost exclusively by railroads.

A mixture of pulverized coal and water would be piped through the pipelines from mine to market. Five major pipelines had been on the drawing board for a number of years, but they would need to cross lands owned by railroads, which refused to grant the necessary rights of way.

Pipeline advocates pushed for legislation — such as HR 1609 (H Rept 95-924, Parts I and II) — which would authorize the Interior Department to grant pipeline developers the federal power of eminent domain. Developers would then exercise this power, defined as the authority to take private land in the public interest, to acquire the necessary rights of way over the opposition of railroads and other landowners. The Senate had approved a coal slurry measure in 1974, but the House had not acted before on such a bill.

House Rejection

On July 19, the full House rejected the recommendation of two of its standing committees and voted, 161-246, to kill such a measure.

Passage of HR 1609 had been urged by the House Interior Committee, which had reported the bill in March, and the House Public Works and Transportation Committee in May. The week before the crucial House vote, however, the House Interstate and Foreign Commerce Committee had urged the House to reject the bill, arguing that the loss of the coal traffic could kill a number of barely surviving railroads.

Proponents of the bill — led by Bob Eckhardt, D-Texas, the measure's sponsor, and Morris K. Udall, D-

Ariz., chairman of the Interior Committee — argued it was necessary to provide another means of moving the increased loads of needed coal and would benefit consumers by providing competition to the railroads. Bringing coal to gas- and oil-producing states such as Texas would free those fuels for other uses elsewhere. Lastly, they argued the pipelines were less harmful to the environment than trains.

Opponents of the measure — led by Fred B. Rooney, D-Pa., chairman of the Commerce Subcommittee on Surface Transportation, and Joe Skubitz, R-Kan., ranking minority member of the Interior Committee and of Rooney's subcommittee — argued it would deprive railroads of vitally needed future income, drain scarce Western water and give an unwarranted grant of federal power to private developers.

Railroad Opposition

The railroad industry, led by the Association of American Railroads and rail-affiliated unions, spearheaded opposition to the bill. As the measure neared a floor vote, the group called in members from all over the country to press their regional congressmen to defeat it.

The railroads were aided by some farmers and landowners concerned about the impact of slurry pipelines on their property and by some environmentalists and Western state House members fearful that the pipelines would deplete scarce Western water supplies.

But only one environmental group, the Environmental Policy Center, ever testified against the bill. And Western state members voted for the measure by a nearly 2-1 margin.

Although the Carter administration had announced in January that it would back HR 1609, with amendments, it ultimately took no position on the bill as reported.

The Senate Energy Subcommittee on Public Lands and Resources, chaired by Dale Bumpers, D-Ark., completed three days of hearings June 19 on two coal slurry pipeline measures (S 707, S 3046) but took no further action.

Clinch River Reactor

Congress adjourned in 1978 without completing action on legislation authorizing the non-military programs administered by the new Department of Energy in fiscal 1979.

Failure of Congress to complete action left in limbo the future of the controversial breeder reactor plant planned for construction on the Clinch River in Tennessee.

Three authorization bills (S 2692, HR 12163, HR 11392) were reported by committees. Two of them, S 2692 (S Rept 95-967) and HR 11392 (H Rept 95-1166), never reached a floor vote. The third measure, HR 12163 (H Rept 95-1078), was passed by the House July 17 but was not taken up by the Senate.

The legislation languished when the Democratic leadership in both houses refused to bring it up for fear it would become the vehicle for several controversial attempts to remove or modify price controls on oil.

The leaders wanted to avoid a major floor flight on energy until after Congress had completed action on President Carter's energy policy package. But the energy bill did not clear until the final day of the session, which did not leave enough time before adjournment for action on the Energy Department authorization.

Authorization of $2.97 billion for military energy programs administered by the Energy Department was contained in separate legislation (HR 11686 — PL 95-509).

Spending Continued

Because Congress failed to act, spending for the Clinch River reactor project, which was opposed by the administration, continued at the rate of about $15 million a month.

Without a new bill providing authority to modify or terminate the plutonium breeder, the Energy Department had to continue to operate under existing authority, which required construction. The $172 million appropriated for the project in fiscal 1979 in the public works appropriations bill (HR 12928 — H J Res 1139) had to be spent on new parts, engineering, design and other scheduled work on the $2.56 billion reactor.

Carter wanted the project killed because he said it was too expensive, its design was obsolete and it would lead to the spread of nuclear weapons.

Throughout the year, the administration attempted to work out some sort of compromise that would end the project. But in July, the House voted twice to refuse to allow the administration to terminate the breeder. The two votes were on amendments to HR 12163.

The Senate Energy Committee, on the other hand, in its bill (S 2692) gave Carter authority to end the Clinch River project. But the full Senate did not vote on that bill during the session.

1979

Highlights

Windfall Profits Tax

When President Carter announced in April that he would gradually end price controls on domestic oil, he also asked Congress for a tax to capture some of the "windfall" profits oil companies would enjoy from decontrol. The House passed a windfall tax bill that was expected to bring in $277 billion in revenues by 1990, while the Senate approved a version expected to cost the oil industry an estimated $178 billion in the next decade. The bill was in conference at the end of 1979.

Synthetic Fuels

Also in conference at the end of 1979 was a multi-billion-dollar measure to spur development of alternative fuels such as gas from coal and oil from shale. First, the House approved more than $3 billion for the development of the fuels. Carter followed with a proposal for $88 billion for their development, with the revenue to be raised through the windfall profits tax. The Senate slashed the price tag to an initial $20 billion investment.

Energy Mobilization Board

The third part of Carter's 1979 energy package — creation of an energy mobilization board — was also in conference at the end of the year. The board's job would be to put energy projects on a "fast track" through the bureaucracy.

Oil Price Decontrol

Carter's decision to end price controls on domestic oil by Oct. 1, 1981, went unchallenged by the 96th Congress, despite some initial — largely symbolic — opposition.

Nuclear Energy

The March accident at the Three Mile Island reactor in Pennsylvania jolted Congress into renewed concern about nuclear safety, but little progress was made on new legislation. Attempts to halt new reactor construction for six months were rejected in both houses of Congress.

Gasoline Rationing

With the nation feeling the effects of cutbacks in Iranian oil exports, the administration proposed a standby plan that would use coupons to ration gasoline. After the House rejected the Carter plan, Congress approved legislation designed to limit the role of politics in emergency energy planning (PL 96-102). But, while the measure made it more difficult to reject a plan, Congress still retained a veto.

Naval Oil Reserve

Up to $85.2 million was authorized in fiscal 1980 for exploring, developing and conserving U.S. naval oil reserves (PL 96-137).

Oil Import Quotas, Fees

The 96th Congress failed in its attempt to claim a role for itself in Carter's 1979 decision to re-impose quotas on oil imports but it did add language to the windfall profits tax bill assuring itself a say in future decisions. Congress was more successful the next year in claiming a role in decisions to use import fees to restrict foreign oil imports. In a major setback for the administration, Congress in 1980 overrode a presidential veto of a resolution blocking an import fee imposed by Carter as part of his anti-inflation program.

Temperature Restrictions

Congress gave routine approval to a standby plan allowing the president to limit the temperatures in public buildings.

Oil Antitrust Exemption

Congress approved legislation extending a special antitrust exemption for the major oil companies that permitted them to participate in oil-sharing agreements the United States made with other countries (PL 96-133).

Energy Authorization

For the fourth consecutive year, Congress ended its annual session without enacting legislation to authorize energy research and development programs. The House — after debating the perennial issues of the Clinch River reactor and price controls — passed the measure but the bill did not reach the Senate floor.

Oil Company Mergers

A controversial measure designed to block the major U.S. oil companies from acquiring other large corporations was reported by a Senate committee but there was no further action in the 96th Congress.

The Year in Review

Although the only major energy legislation cleared by the first session of the 96th Congress was a bill revising the system for developing a standby plan for gas rationing, Congress in 1979 made large strides toward approval of a national energy development policy.

Both chambers approved all three parts of Carter's second energy plan — a windfall profits tax on oil company revenues, a massive federal push to develop a synthetic fuels industry, and creation of an energy mobilization board to speed high-priority energy projects through the red tape to completion. All three measures were still in conference as the year ended.

Energy Development Package

Convinced that a realistic national energy policy required Americans to pay as much for domestic oil as for imported, President Carter began in 1979 to lift the oil price controls that had kept American fuel bills unrealistically low since the early 1970s.

The decontrol plan was part of a larger 1979 energy program that Carter proposed in two parts. In the first, announced in April, the president presented his decontrol plan and asked Congress for a tax on the windfall profits the oil companies would reap as domestic prices rose to world levels.

The second, announced in July, mirrored legislation already moving through Congress. Carter proposed that a special government corporation be set up to handle an $88 billion federal program to encourage production of synthetic fuels, such as liquids from coal. He also asked Congress to establish an energy mobilization board to cut red tape and speed up government decisions related to priority energy projects such as refineries, pipelines and synthetic fuel plants.

Both packages also contained other less dramatic steps to reduce oil imports, such as increasing fuel production from federal lands, delaying a scheduled reduction in the lead content of gasoline and turning down thermostats in non-residential buildings.

By the end of the year, both chambers had passed windfall profits tax, mobilization board and synthetic fuels production legislation. But House-Senate conferees were still working out the final details. The tax and fuel measures were given final approval in 1980. The mobilization board measure died at the end of the 96th Congress.

April Announcement

Carter went on television April 5, 1979, to announce his decision to use his authority to end price controls on domestic oil. Decontrol would begin on June 1, 1979. All controls would end by Oct. 1, 1981, when the price control

Quotas and Fees on Oil from Abroad . . .

When President Carter in mid-1979 imposed a quota on the amount of foreign oil the United States could import each year, he returned the nation to a system that had been the dominant element in its oil import policy during the 1960s and early 1970s. Such a quota system was in effect, for a different reason, from 1959 until 1973.

While Carter imposed quotas as part of his effort to reduce the nation's heavy dependence on foreign oil, the earlier quotas were designed primarily to protect domestic oil producers from competition from foreign oil supplies. Some petroleum analysts later viewed that use of the quota system as a misguided "drain America first" policy that rapidly depleted domestic reserves instead of using cheaper foreign oil.

Carter Quotas

President Carter announced July 15, 1979, that he would limit 1979 oil imports to an average of 8.2 million barrels a day, and hold all future oil imports to below the 1977 average net import level of 8.6 million barrels.

Gross imports, an Energy Department measure that counted refined products from Puerto Rico but did not consider North American oil swaps, were 8.8 million barrels a day in 1977.

Two weeks before Carter's announcement, the Organization of Petroleum Exporting Countries (OPEC) had voted to increase the price of a barrel of crude oil from $14.55 to anywhere between $18 and $23.50. The 24 percent increase announced June 28 was the largest since 1974, when prices quadrupled during the Arab oil embargo. In March 1979 OPEC prices had risen 9 percent.

The day after the OPEC announcement, the United States and six other major industrial nations — France, Britain, Canada, Japan, West Germany and Italy — agreed at a meeting in Tokyo that they would reduce their future oil imports. The United States pledged to hold its imports to 8.5 million barrels a day through 1985.

By decreasing the demand for oil, these industralized countries hoped to curb OPEC's power to increase prices. Without restraints the demand in the United States for imported oil had been expected to rise to between 9.5 million and 10 million barrels a day by 1985.

Carter's July 15 goal of reducing imports to 8.2 million barrels per day went beyond the Tokyo pledge.

Import Quota Authority

In 1955 Congress gave the president virtually unlimited authority to curb imports that threatened the national security. That authority was provided in a set of amendments to the 1953 Trade Expansion Act.

When the quotas were first imposed, there was a surplus of oil. Worried about declining profits caused by the influx of foreign oil, some oil companies tried voluntarily to limit imports. But because not all companies complied, President Eisenhower in 1959 used his authority to impose mandatory import quotas. They remained until 1973, when President Nixon removed them.

Unlike Carter's action, which set an absolute limit on the number of barrels imported, the earlier quotas were tied to the level of domestic production and consumption. For most of the program, imports were limited to about one-eighth of domestic production. During the early 1970s, the quota allowed importation of enough oil to fill the gap between domestic production and consumption.

Quota System Criticism

Criticism of the quota system grew during the 1960s. Analysts argued that the quotas helped to deplete domestic energy reserves and added several billion dollars a year to consumer energy costs, because domestic oil averaged about $1.25 more a barrel than foreign oil.

In 1973, however, with energy supplies growing short, Nixon did away with the quotas. In their place he ordered fees on imports of 10.5 cents for every barrel of crude oil and 52 cents for each barrel of gasoline. The fees were set much higher for refined products, such as gasoline, in an effort to encourage domestic refining.

An attempt to reimpose the quotas came in 1975, when the House passed a bill that would have held imports below 6.5 million barrels a day after 1980. But the bill was not acted on by the Senate, and the proposal was not included in the energy policy act (PL 94-163) that passed that year.

Import Trends

Total oil imports almost doubled in the seven years after quotas were removed in 1973. In 1972, the last full year of the quota system, the United States imported an average of 4.7 million barrels a day — 29 percent of domestic demand.

By contrast, figures for the first six months of 1979 indicated that imports were averaging about 7.7 million barrels daily — about 43 percent of domestic demand.

Moreover, imports had risen sharply during the last few years of the quotas. Because of the change in quota rules allowing importation of enough oil to fill the gap between domestic demand and production, imports had grown from a 3.4-million-barrel-per-day average in 1970 to 4.7 million in 1972.

. . .Were Major Elements in U.S. Import Policies

The Arab oil embargo and the recession of the mid-1970s kept imports from growing during the first few years after quotas were removed. Imports in 1975 were well below the 1973 level.

With economic improvement, however, imports soared dramatically. They grew by about 45 percent from 1975 to 1977, bringing total net imports to their highest level in history, an 8.6 million barrel daily average in 1977.

Oil analysts saw hopeful signs in 1978, when imports fell from their 1977 high to an average of 8.2 million barrels daily. With the addition of new oil from Alaska and intensified exploitation of old domestic sources, production rose and imports fell.

But the decline seemed temporary. Imports fell during the first half of 1978, but rose after that until a cutback in Iranian production reduced imports in early 1979.

By 1980 it appeared that conservation efforts, encouraged by higher and higher fuel prices, were beginning to have an impact on U.S. oil imports. For the first six months of 1980, imports were down 13 percent from the same period in 1979 — a drop of more than one million barrels a day.

The Role of Congress

The 96th Congress failed in its attempt to claim a role for itself in Carter's decision to re-impose quotas on oil imports, but it did succeed in claiming the right to veto future decisions of that sort.

In 1979, the Senate added language to two bills allowing Congress to block imposition of oil import quotas by a joint resolution of disapproval. The president could veto such a resolution, but Congress could override that veto.

Late in October, the Senate added this language to legislation (S 1871) exempting oil companies from federal antitrust laws to the degree necessary for the United States to take part in an international oil-sharing agreement. But the House objected to that amendment and the Senate agreed to drop it. S 1871 was enacted without it. *(Story, p. 218)*

In November, however, the Senate again added the language to the windfall profits tax bill (HR 3919), a key element in President Carter's energy plan. The provision remained in HR 3919 as enacted in 1980, giving Congress the power to block future presidential decisions to impose import quotas on oil. *(Story, p. 220)*

Import Fees

Congress was more successful in claiming a role in presidential decisions to use import fees to restrict imports of foreign oil.

In 1975, President Ford proposed to reduce imports of oil by raising the import fee on each barrel by $3. But the attempt ran into strong opposition from members of Congress. Although President Ford successfully vetoed a bill that was intended to delay the increases, he later agreed to rescind the additional fees.

In 1978, in an effort to pressure Congress to finish his energy bill, President Carter hinted that he was considering new import fees of up to $5 a barrel. That produced strong opposition from the Senate, particularly from members representing northeastern states heavily dependent on imported oil.

The Senate approved an amendment, that was added to the Treasury appropriations bill, to prevent Carter from imposing new fees. The House narrowly rejected the provision, which was dropped in conference.

Carter Fee

In 1980, as part of his anti-inflation program, Carter imposed a fee of $4.62 on each barrel of foreign oil. The fee, which was expected to raise $126 million in revenues, was to be passed through to consumers as a 10-cent surcharge on gasoline.

The proposal was anything but politically popular. In May, just before that pass-through was to take effect, a federal judge held the levy improper, saying it exceeded the authority granted to the president by the Trade Expansion Act.

In June, Congress attached a resolution killing the oil import fee (H J Res 531) to essential legislation extending the ceiling on the federal debt (HR 7428). The House approved the resolution by a vote of 376-30; the Senate vote was equally clear, 73-16.

President Carter immediately vetoed the measure, casting his 22nd veto of a public bill June 5. The following day, Congress overrode his veto, by votes of 335-34 (R 142-0; D 193-34) in the House and 68-10 (R 33-0; D 35-10) in the Senate.

It was one of the worst setbacks of Carter's four-year presidency — and the first time Congress had overridden a Democratic president's veto since 1952. The action did, however, accurately reflect the resistance in the nation to limitations on the use of gasoline.

Although the earlier votes left no doubt the veto would be overridden, Carter appealed to the legislators to "stand up and take the political heat by making tough decisions."

He said blocking the fee would "send a clear signal . . . that we do not mean business."

But opponents of the fee charged that it was inflationary and would save little gasoline. They said Americans had already cut gasoline consumption by 8 percent to 10 percent in the last year.

provisions of the 1975 Energy Policy and Conservation Act were scheduled to expire.

Decontrol meant that domestically produced oil selling for $6 and $13 a barrel would suddenly bring a producer the world oil price, which by the end of 1979 was about $30 a barrel. Carter called that additional money for the oil companies "huge and undeserved windfall profits," and he asked Congress to pass a tax that would capture some of it for public use, including development of synthetic fuels.

The president's program extended only through fiscal 1982, and estimates of anticipated revenues from decontrol and the tax covered only the first few years. Later, Congress and Carter began to talk in terms of revenues expected over a five-year period and finally over a 10-year period. The revenue estimates were also revised to reflect further increases in world oil prices.

July Proposals

By mid-summer, U.S. energy problems were visible in the waiting lines at gasoline pumps in many cities. Carter's standing in public opinion polls dropped to its lowest level yet in late June.

The president scheduled a major televised address on energy for July 5. But then he abruptly cancelled it and called a 10-day "domestic summit" at Camp David, the Maryland presidential retreat, where he conferred with Americans from all segments of life.

On July 15, in a televised speech, Carter assessed for the nation what he had learned at the summit. Describing the United States as suffering from "a crisis of confidence," Carter said the energy crisis could be the issue through which the nation could generate "a rebirth of the American spirit."

"On the battlefield of energy, we can win for our nation a new confidence, and we can seize control again of our common destiny," Carter said.

The president announced he was setting import quotas that would limit oil imports to 1977 levels, which were an all-time high. *(Import quotas, box, p. 208)*

He also asked Congress to authorize "the most massive peacetime commitment of funds and resources in our nation's history to develop America's own alternative sources of fuel." He proposed that a special Energy Security Corporation spearhead this effort. In addition, he asked Congress to establish an energy mobilization board with the authority to place energy projects on a "fast track" through the bureaucracy in order to speed construction.

Windfall Profits Tax

One measure of the changing national mood was the joint decision in 1979 by the president and Congress that for the first time a new tax should be used to capture for public benefit some of the record-high profits that oil companies would reap as decontrolled domestic oil rose to the rapidly escalating world price.

The Windfall Tax Plan

Carter's windfall profits tax plan had two parts. Under the first part, in effect until 1981, 50 percent of the price increase the oil industry would get for most already-flowing oil as a result of decontrol would go to the government. Oil that was expensive to produce or that was discovered in the future would not be taxed.

The second part of the plan called for an "OPEC tax" that would apply indefinitely to all oil once it was decontrolled. If OPEC raised prices again, thus boosting the market price of all oil, the tax would take 50 percent of the increased revenues of U.S. companies.

The revenue that the federal government would receive from the oil tax, Carter proposed, should be deposited into an Energy Security Trust Fund, used to help low-income persons pay their fuel bills, to improve mass transit and to reduce U.S. dependence on foreign oil by developing new sources of energy.

House Action

Congress went immediately to work on the tax proposal, despite strong opposition from the oil industry. The House Ways and Means Committee reported a bill June 22 (HR 3919 — H Rept 96-304), after shifting the burden of the tax bite to place more of it on oil already being produced and less on newly discovered oil.

The full House, however, rejected the committee version of the bill, approving a substantially weaker measure June 28. As approved by the House, the tax would not be permanent, but would end in 1990. The House measure made no mention of how the revenue raised by the tax should be used.

Senate Action

After long consideration, the Senate Finance Committee Nov. 1 filed its report on HR 3919 (S Rept 96-394). Its bill also was much weaker than Carter had proposed, primarily because the committee exempted from the tax income on several types of oil, including oil discovered after 1978 and hard-to-produce oil.

The full Senate considered the bill for a month, approving it Dec. 17. During debate, the Senate added a number of amendments tightening the committee bill. However, in a further blow to the Carter plan, the Senate all but eliminated any link between revenues generated by the new tax and any energy spending programs.

Conference Action

Conferees went right to work on the bill, but only one key point was decided before they left for the Christmas recess. Conferees split the difference between the amount of revenue that the House and Senate versions of the bill were expected to produce and agreed that at least $227.3 billion should be generated by the new tax by 1990.

Conferees were scheduled to resume work in early 1980. *(Details, 1979-80 action, p. 220)*

Synthetic Fuels Programs

Congress and President Carter agreed in 1979 to commit billions of federal dollars to encourage private industry to create new synthetic fuels from coal, farm wastes, grain and oil shale.

The goal of the program was the production, by the mid-1990s, of 1.5 million to 2.5 million barrels a day in substitute fuels to replace that amount of oil.

President Carter in July proposed a decade-long $88 billion synfuels program to be managed by an Energy Security Corporation.

Democrats and Decontrol:
A Long and Losing Battle

President Carter's decision in April 1979 to end federal controls on the price of domestic oil put his former teammates, the liberal Democrats in Congress, on the losing side of the price control issue without a quarterback.

Thus, despite vigorous protest and some symbolic votes opposing decontrol, the president's plan went unchallenged by the 96th Congress. The only vote by either chamber on the measure came in October, when the House — by a vote of 135-257 — rejected a proposal to retain controls. Only seven Republicans voted for retaining controls; the voting Democrats divided almost evenly on the issue.

A Decade of Controls

Oil price controls, which were to expire Oct. 1, 1981, would have been a fact of American life for a decade. They were imposed by President Nixon in 1971 as part of his general wage and price controls intended to combat inflation. In 1973, Congress approved continuation of controls as part of the Emergency Petroleum Allocation Act, enacted during the Arab oil embargo of 1973-74.

Endorsing "conservation by price," President Ford in 1975 moved to lift price controls. The Democratic-dominated Congress protested, arguing that decontrol would benefit the oil companies at the expense of the already pressed consumer. The result was the extension, in the 1975 Energy Policy and Conservation Act, of mandatory price controls on oil until June 1, 1979. After that date, the act gave the president power to continue, modify or remove the controls.

In the four years between 1975 and 1979, advocates of price controls steadily lost strength as energy prices rose despite controls, inflation continued unabated and energy supplies diminished.

But the intensity of the opposition decreased slowly. In 1978, the threat of an amendment decontrolling the price of about half the oil produced in the United States — that from so-called "stripper" wells — was sufficient to block congressional approval of the $6.2 billion energy authorization bill (HR 11392, S 2692) for that year.

After Congress rejected his earlier proposal to use a tax on domestic oil to bring its price up to world levels, Carter in 1979 proposed an end to price controls.

His proposal encountered some initial opposition in the House, but it was largely symbolic. Early in May, the House Commerce Committee rejected, by a tie vote of 21-21, an extension of price controls. The tie vote demonstrated considerably more pro-control strength than had been expected. The proposal came as an amendment to the Energy Department authorization bill for fiscal 1980 (HR 3000).

The Votes Weren't There

The pro-control members of the House Commerce Committee were operating without the support of the panel's Energy Subcommittee chairman, Rep. John D. Dingell, D-Mich., who saw the effort to extend controls as a lost cause. "Politically, it is totally impossible for this Congress to succeed in this amendment," he said. "There are not the votes in the Senate."

Late in May the House Democratic Caucus voted overwhelmingly to retain old price controls. The 138-69 vote in the caucus on May 24 placed House Democrats clearly on record in opposition to their Democratic president's plan to begin to phase out those controls a week later.

But House Speaker Thomas P. O'Neill Jr., D-Mass., made clear his view that the pro-control effort was doomed. "We are going through a bit of a charade," he said, predicting that any House-approved measure extending controls would be blocked by a Senate filibuster.

And in October, the full House gave a strong endorsement to Carter's plan to phase out oil price controls. On Oct. 11 the House rejected a price-control extension amendment to the Energy Department authorization bill, by a vote of 135-257.

The following day, the House in a surprise for the White House and the Democratic leadership also voted to end price controls on gasoline, a move not endorsed by Carter. By a three-vote margin the House approved gasoline decontrol, 191-188.

Three weeks later, as the oil industry again reported sharply higher profits for the preceding quarter, the House reversed the gasoline decontrol vote.

In the Senate, the fight against oil decontrol was led by Henry M. Jackson, D-Wash., chairman of the Energy Committee. Most members of Jackson's committee, however, supported decontrol, and the Senate never voted on the issue.

Several weeks earlier on June 26 the House had acted to encourage synthetic fuel development by adding to a measure extending the Defense Production Act (HR 3930 — H Rept 96-165) provisions requiring the federal government to buy the equivalent of 500,000 barrels a day of synthetic fuels by 1984. The measure also provided price supports, loans and loan guarantees for synthetic fuels producers.

Temperature Restrictions

Three other "standby" plans for dealing with energy emergencies came to Capitol Hill from the Energy Department along with the doomed gasoline rationing proposal.

Of the three, only one — equipping the president with the authority to limit the temperatures in public buildings — was approved.

The other two plans proposed to give the president the authority to curtail weekend sales of gasoline and to restrict lighted outdoor advertising.

Neither chamber acted on the weekend gas sales plan by the May 11 deadline, allowing it to die quietly. The Senate rejected the advertising lighting plan (S Res 123 — S Rept 96-98) May 2 by a vote of 24-70. The House Commerce Committee reported it unfavorably (H Res 210 — H Rept 96-122), but the full House did not act on it.

Building Restrictions

In contrast, Congress gave routine approval to the standby plan allowing the president to require that thermostats in public buildings be set no lower than 80 degrees in summer and no higher than 65 degrees in winter.

The Senate approved the plan May 2, by a vote of 89-3 (S Res 122 — S Rept 96-97). The House approved it May 10 by voice vote (H Res 209 — H Rept 96-105).

President Carter immediately exercised his new authority, putting the temperature limiting rules into effect as of July 16, 1979. He did modify the cooling limit in the summer to allow thermostats to be set as low as 78 degrees. On April 15, 1980, the president extended the temperature restrictions for nine months to Jan. 16, 1981. The administration hoped that such rules would save the equivalent of 200,000 to 400,000 barrels of oil a day, about 2 percent of U.S. oil consumption.

Late in the year, the Senate Nov. 8 approved Carter's proposal (S 932 — S Rept 96-387) after dividing it into a two-step program. The Senate approved a five-year $20 billion program under the direction of a new Synthetic Fuels Corp. If Congress approved the progress made in the first five years, the corporation would then be authorized to spend an additional $68 billion.

As the year ended, conferees were still working on the final version of the bill. They had already agreed to authorize $20 billion for the first years of the program and to create the new corporation to administer the program. A final compromise was approved in 1980. *(Details, 1979-80 action, p. 226)*

Carter had proposed that funding for the synthetic fuels program be provided by a trust fund set up to receive the revenues generated by the windfall profits tax he proposed to impose upon the oil industry.

Although neither the House nor the Senate provided that link between the new tax and the synfuels program, initial funding for the synfuels program appeared assured. Congress included $19 billion for alternative and synthetic fuels development in the interior and energy development appropriations bill for fiscal 1980 (HR 4930 — PL 96-126). Of that amount $2.2 billion was immediately available while the remainder would be available after the enactment of authorizing legislation, such as S 932.

Energy Mobilization Board

Work was already under way to create a new agency empowered to put priority energy projects on a "fast track" to completion when President Carter in July 1979 asked Congress to approve creation of an energy mobilization board.

Carter described the board as similar to the "War Production Board in World War II," an agency that "will have the responsibility and authority to cut through the red tape, the delays and the endless road blocks to completing key energy projects."

Early in July, both House and Senate committees had held hearings on similar proposals. The House measure (HR 4573) had been introduced by Interior Committee Chairman Morris K. Udall, D-Ariz.; the Senate version was included in an omnibus energy bill (S 1308) co-sponsored by many members of the Senate Energy Committee.

Despite the fast start, it was October before the Senate approved its version of the board, and November when the House acted. Conferees began work early in December but did not complete their task before the Christmas recess.

The major difference between the House and Senate versions of S 1308 — and the major point of controversy during consideration of the bill — was whether the board would have the power to waive or override substantive requirements of federal laws that threatened to delay priority energy projects. The Senate approved an agency without such power; the House granted that power to the agency it endorsed.

Conferees in 1980 settled on a compromise that would give Congress the final decision in some cases. But a coalition of House Republicans and liberal Democrats were still not satisfied with the measure and sent it back to conference in June 1980. The bill never re-emerged. *(Details, 1979-80 action, p. 230)*

Nuclear Power

When the 96th Congress convened, both the nuclear industry and its critics were hoping that the legislators would move to resolve some of the long-standing, fundamental controversies over nuclear power. Facing the legislators were such issues as the licensing process for new plants, the storage of spent fuel and nuclear waste and the future of the fast breeder reactor.

On March 28, 1979, these priorities were dramatically disarranged by the accident at the Three Mile Island nuclear plant near Harrisburg. *(Details, box, p. 89)*

The issues raised by the accident — plant compliance with safety regulations, the lack of an effective emergency plan for the surrounding area, the uncoordinated response of the Nuclear Regulatory Commission (NRC) — suddenly took precedence over matters of licensing and waste storage. Three Mile Island and its legacy dominated congressional discussion of nuclear power in 1979.

Continuing Support

Despite the accident and the deficiencies it revealed in the nation's existing system for operating and regulating nuclear power plants, Congress and the Carter administration reaffirmed their support for nuclear power in 1979.

Both chambers of Congress refused to impose a six-month moratorium on the issuance of construction permits for new reactors. The Senate, however, did endorse a shutdown of all plants in states without approved emergency plans for dealing with a nuclear accident.

President Carter named a special commission to study the accident. After the Kemeny Commission issued its report and recommendations — chief among them abolition of the NRC — late in October, President Carter responded by endorsing some of the suggestions, countering others with his own proposals, replacing the chairman of the NRC and reminding the nation that nuclear power was still an important factor in its energy future. Some of those recommendations were acted on in 1980. *(Kemeny Commission, box, p. 89; 1980 action, p. 230)*

NRC Authorization

Notwithstanding the national alarm over nuclear safety that followed the Three Mile Island accident, both chambers of Congress in 1979 decisively rejected proposals to impose a six-month moratorium on permits for constructing new nuclear power plants.

Those permits were issued by the Nuclear Regulatory Commission (NRC), which blunted the force of the moratorium proposal by voluntarily halting issuance of new permits and licenses. The commission said it would resume licensing after the accident had been fully studied, probably early in 1980.

The moratorium requirement was proposed as an amendment to the NRC authorization bill for fiscal 1980 (HR 2608, S 562). At year's end that measure was still in conference. Congress completed action on the measure in mid-1980.

The major point of difference between the House and Senate bills was a Senate provision requiring a shutdown of all nuclear power plants in states that lacked an approved plan for dealing with a nuclear emergency such as Three Mile Island. This provision faced stiff House opposition. *(Details, 1979-80 action, p. 233)*

NRC Moratorium. The senior staff of the NRC decided May 21 not to issue new construction permits or operating licenses for plants until August. This delay would allow the commission to evaluate the results of investigations of the Three Mile Island accident. The commission subsequently approved this decision. In November the commission extended its self-imposed moratorium into 1980.

Nuclear Waste Disposal

Late in 1979, the Senate Energy Committee approved legislation (S 2189) requiring the Energy Department to come up with a design and site for a long-term nuclear waste storage facility within one year. The panel admitted

NRC Membership

The Nuclear Regulatory Commission (NRC), which came under sharp criticism during the Carter administration, underwent a number of changes in its membership during the 1977-80 period.

President Carter had the opportunity to name three of the commission's five members in his first year in office, but only two of his choices won confirmation. Those two were Joseph M. Hendrie, chairman of the department of applied science at the Brookhaven (N.Y.) National Laboratory, whom Carter named as chairman of the NRC; and Peter A. Bradford, a member of the Maine Public Service Commission.

Carter also named Kent F. Hansen, a professor of nuclear engineering at the Massachusetts Institute of Technology, to a seat on the commission, but his nomination was rejected by the Senate Environment and Public Works Committee. Lack of experience in policy matters and a possible conflict of interest were cited as the reasons for the committee's action.

In 1978 Carter filled the vacant seat on the commission, naming John F. Ahearne, who had served on the White House energy policy staff and in the Department of Energy before moving to the commission. In December 1979, after the Three Mile Island incident, Carter removed Hendrie as chairman (although he remained a commissioner) and named Ahearne acting chairman, a post he retained for the remainder of the Carter administration, due in part to the refusal of the Senate to confirm Carter's choice of a new chairman.

Two of the original members of the NRC, Victor Gilinsky and Richard T. Kennedy, served in those posts during the Carter administration. Gilinsky was nominated by Carter to a second term in 1979, and was confirmed. His new term expired in June 1984. Kennedy's term expired in June 1980, at which time he left his post.

In July 1980, Carter named Albert Carnesale as Kennedy's successor, indicating his intention to designate Carnesale as chairman of the commission, once he was confirmed. Carnesale, a nuclear engineer and professor of public policy at Harvard's John F. Kennedy School of Government, served from 1969 until 1972 as chief of defense weapons at the Arms Control and Disarmament Agency.

After Carter lost his bid for re-election and after several key Republican senators voiced reservations about Carnesale's position on the controversial issues of nuclear reprocessing and breeder reactors, the Senate Environment Committee shelved the nomination, letting it die with the end of the 96th Congress.

Clinch River Breeder Reactor Project. . .

The Clinch River Breeder Reactor — once the nation's number-one energy demonstration project — found itself demoted to the Carter administration's "hit list" in 1977. But with tenacious backing from certain members of Congress, the project, first authorized in 1970, managed to survive the Carter years slowed but otherwise unscathed.

As of early 1981, almost $1 billion had been spent on the project, whose design was 80 percent complete. More than $500 million of equipment was on order and another $105 million in equipment was on hand.

The site for the plant on the Clinch River near Oak Ridge, Tenn., was untouched. Without initial permission from the Nuclear Regulatory Commission (NRC), not even initial site clearing could be undertaken. The licensing process that would provide such permission had been suspended in 1977 and was not resumed before the end of Carter's term.

During the decade, the cost estimate of the project quadrupled to $2.886 billion — and its operational (criticality) date had slipped eight years to late 1988. Even those figures, although the latest available, were outdated, according to an official at the Department of Energy, who pointed out that they were both based upon the assumption that NRC would resume licensing procedures for the plant by Dec. 1, 1980. The licensing process did not resume by that date and was not expected to resume under any circumstances before mid-1981.

Background: Showing Feasibility

The Clinch River plant was intended to demonstrate to the electric power industry that "breeder" reactors, which produced fuel even as they consumed it to produce energy, were feasible means for the commercial generation of electric power. The construction of the plant with government backing was also intended to spur the development of the industrial base necessary for building additional plants.

The technology of breeder reactors was developed during the 1950s and 1960s. By 1970 there were several liquid metal cooled fast breeder reactors already built and in operation.

Congress in 1970 authorized a project, administered jointly by government and the electric power industry, to show that those reactors were useful and economical sources of electric power and of new nuclear fuel. The demonstration plant would use a fuel consisting of uranium and plutonium and it would produce plutonium — fuel for subsequent plant operations.

At the time of its initial authorization (PL 91-273), the cost of the project was estimated at $700 million. Participating utilities would pay $250 million while the government paid the rest.

In 1973, the Atomic Energy Commission (AEC), then administering the project for the government, signed a contract with the Tennessee Valley Authority and Commonwealth Edison to build the plant near the Clinch River.

By 1976 the cost of the plant had soared to nearly $2 billion. The industry share remained around $250 million despite repeated efforts to legislate a requirement that the industry bear more of the cost overruns. The Energy Research and Development Administration, successor to the AEC, took over complete responsibility for direct management of the project in 1976. The start-up date for the plant, originally 1980, was pushed forward to 1984. Despite its escalating costs, however, the project was still heartily endorsed by the Ford administration as it had been by the Nixon White House. And by fiscal 1978, almost $500 million had been authorized and appropriated for the project.

Carter's Opposition

Criticism of the project began building in the mid-1970s, focusing less on the rising cost and more on the environmental, safety and policy questions raised by going ahead with a project that would increase the world's supply of plutonium — a key ingredient in nuclear weapons.

With the arrival of Jimmy Carter in the White House, critics of the project found themselves a powerful ally. In April 1977, Carter renounced plans to use plutonium as nuclear fuel in the United States. He first indicated he would defer the operational data for the Clinch River plan and then toughened his stance and asked Congress simply to provide termination funds for the project. Instead of the $150 million requested in the Ford budget for fiscal 1978, Carter asked for $33 million.

Carter's opposition to the project was founded primarily upon his concern over nuclear proliferation and the risk that plutonium produced by nuclear breeder reactors might be diverted illegally from its intended use of power generation to the deadly objective of producing atomic weapons.

Plutonium, a radioactive and highly toxic element, is derived from nuclear fission. Conventional nuclear reactors used in the 1970s to generate electricity were fueled by uranium, of which there were finite supplies. To serve as nuclear fuel, uranium had to be "enriched." Once it was "burned," the uranium could be processed to separate out the plutonium.

Breeder reactors had long been considered the logical next step in the development of nuclear power capability. Because they produced fuel they appeared to be an answer to the energy supply problems that were bedeviling national policy planners.

. . .Remained Alive but Future Was Uncertain

The sticking point to the happy equation of breeder reactor technology, however, was plutonium's use in nuclear weapons. All atomic reactors produced plutonium, but the breeder reactor produced much more than the existing conventional reactors.

The 95th Congress, and later the 96th Congress, refused to go along with Carter's plan to kill the project. This controversy was one reason that no authorization bill for civilian Department of Energy programs was passed. In the absence of any congressional direction in such an authorization bill, planning for the project continued.

95th Congress

In 1977, Congress approved an $80 million authorization level for the plant. It was included in a measure (S 1811) authorizing funds for the civilian nuclear programs administered by the Energy Research and Development Administration and later the Department of Energy.

Both chambers in 1977 rejected Carter's plan to terminate work on the project. The Senate's vote on that point was 38-49; the House margin was even wider, 162-246. The Senate approved $75 million in its version of S 1811 in July. In its bill (HR 6796) passed in September, the House insisted upon the full original funding request of $150 million. Conferees settled on the figure of $80 million.

Veto. Carter cast the first veto of his administration to kill the bill containing those funds. In addition to his concern for nuclear proliferation, Carter vetoed the bill because he said the Clinch River project was "unnecessarily expensive . . . technically obsolete . . . and economically unsound."

Congress did not attempt to override the veto. Instead, it included $80 million for the project in the fiscal 1978 supplemental appropriations bill enacted in March 1978. To make clear its determination that the project should proceed, Congress struck out of that bill language that barred spending of the funds without passage of authorizing legislation.

1978 Action. In March 1978, Carter signed the supplemental funding bill containing the money for the Clinch River project (HR 9375 — PL 95-240), but said he would use that money to wind up the project. That plan was dropped after Comptroller General Elmer B. Staats informed Carter that such use of the money would be illegal.

Carter's fiscal 1979 budget request for the project was only $13 million in termination funds. By 1978 the cost estimate for the project had escalated to $2.5 billion.

Ignoring the Carter request, Congress approved appropriations of $172.4 million for the plant in fiscal 1979 (H J Res 1139 — PL 95-482).

In the spring of 1978, the administration offered Congress a compromise. In exchange for congressional approval of an end to the Clinch River project, the administration would set in motion a study of alternate breeder technologies, looking toward possible construction of a plant that would produce 900 megawatts of power — almost three times the planned capacity of the Clinch River plant.

Carter won a small victory when the Senate Energy Committee approved the compromise. But its bill (S 2692) did not come before the full Senate for a vote because of the threat that it would become a vehicle for language ending federal controls on oil prices. *(Stories, pp. 206, 211)*

The House firmly rejected the compromise proposal. In July the House voted twice — 142-187 and 157-238 — to turn down such a plan. As approved by the House, the energy authorization bill for fiscal 1979 (HR 12163) provided the full $172.4 million for the demonstration project. Because of the Senate's inaction, the energy authorization for fiscal 1979 was never enacted.

96th Congress

Controversy over the Clinch River plant continued throughout the 96th Congress, muted by weariness with the issue and concern with more pressing energy matters.

Neither in 1979 or in 1980 did Congress complete work on the energy authorization measure, thus leaving in place the original language authorizing work on the project. Funding for the plant continued at the fiscal 1979 level.

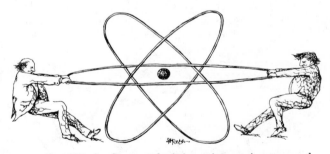

In 1979 the Carter administration again proposed a compromise, promising to study alternate plans for a breeder project if Congress would terminate the Clinch River plan.

As it had a year earlier, the Senate Energy Committee agreed to that proposal. But the full House again rejected it, 182-237. That vote came during consideration of the energy authorization bill for fiscal 1980, which included $183.8 million for the project. That bill (HR 3000) was never enacted.

that its action was intended to force Congress to solve the longstanding problem of what to do with nuclear waste.

Congress in 1980 approved a weakened version of S 2189 (PL 96-573) giving the states responsibility for disposing of nuclear wastes generated by nuclear power plants, hospitals and industry. But it could not agree on what should be done about disposal of spent nuclear fuel and wastes created from reprocessing nuclear reactor fuels.

The intent of S 2189 as approved by the Senate committee was to force the government to design a giant, concrete vault-like facility from which nuclear waste could eventually be retrieved and placed in permanent storage. The waste would be monitored and could be stored there for decades or longer.

In the meantime, the government would continue its studies of and planning for permanent storage, probably in an underground site that could isolate the waste for the centuries during which it would be radioactive.

Gasoline Rationing

Congress in 1979 worked to revise the system it had set up in 1975 for drafting a national gasoline rationing plan. But the measure it approved late in the year (S 1030 — PL 96-102) made far less change than expected.

Proving the political difficulty inherent in any effort to limit the amount of gasoline Americans could buy, Congress failed in the major objective of its reform effort — to reduce the role of politics, and Congress, in drafting and imposing a rationing plan. Under PL 96-102 Congress retained the power to veto a proposed plan as well as a presidential decision to implement such a plan.

The major change effected by PL 96-102 was to give the states, not the federal government, the primary responsibility for developing conservation plans. Unless a state failed to develop a plan that effectively encouraged its citizens to save energy, the federal government would not step in to impose a federal plan.

In 1980, both the House and Senate July 30 overrode gas rationing opponents to approve a rationing plan that could be put into effect in the event of a serious shortage. *(Details, p. 237)*

The push to reform the system for drafting a gas rationing plan came after the House in May rejected President Carter's proposed "standby" plan for rationing gasoline in an energy emergency. The executive had been directed to submit such a plan by the Energy Policy and Conservation Act of 1975 (PL 94-163). Under that 1975 law, such "standby" plans for conservation of energy in an emergency had to be approved by both chambers of Congress before they could be imposed.

PL 94-163 required submission of gas rationing and other "standby" plans by June 1976. But it was January 1977 before the outgoing Ford administration sent such plans to Capitol Hill. A few days later the incoming Carter administration withdrew the Ford plans, setting to work instead on its own proposals.

Not until June 1978 did the Carter administration publish its draft version of a standby gas rationing plan, and not until February 1979 did the plan reach Capitol Hill. By that time the disruption of the world oil market caused by the revolution in Iran again made the possibility of gasoline shortages a real one.

Carter submitted three other "standby" energy conservation plans to Congress at the time he sent up the gas rationing proposal. Only one was approved.

Under the Carter proposal, each owner of a car or other registered motor vehicle would receive a set number of government ration checks in the mail from the Department of Energy. In order to buy gas, motorists would have to present the coupons and the money for the gas at the service station. The service station would have to turn in the coupons in order to obtain additional supplies of gasoline.

Priority activities such as police and fire protection would receive additional coupon allotments. Persons willing to pay for extra gas coupons could legally buy them from others willing to sell.

Under the 1975 energy law, Congress had to approve Carter's rationing plan within 60 days — by May 11, 1979.

Senate Action. The Senate approved the plan (S Res 120 — S Rept 96-115) May 9 by a vote of 58-39. Senate approval, however, was achieved only after the Senate Energy Committee persuaded the administration to make a major change in its proposal. Concerned that rural states, where residents were more dependent upon their auto-

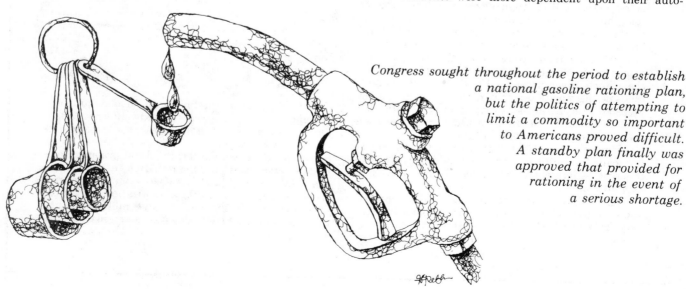

Congress sought throughout the period to establish a national gasoline rationing plan, but the politics of attempting to limit a commodity so important to Americans proved difficult. A standby plan finally was approved that provided for rationing in the event of a serious shortage.

mobiles, would be shortchanged under the original allocation formula proposed by the administration, the committee convinced the Carter administration that gasoline, during rationing, should be allocated among the states based entirely on historic gasoline consumption patterns.

The margin of Senate approval, however, was still narrow until the Senate adopted another resolution (S Res 151) expressing the sense of the Senate that rationing should not be imposed until such time as gasoline supplies were cut by 20 percent over a 30-day period, and all other efforts to cope with that shortage had failed. That resolution was not legally binding on the president, but did carry some weight because the Senate retained the power to veto a presidential decision to impose the rationing plan.

House Action. In the House, the rationing plan was doomed from the beginning. On May 10, the House rejected it by a wide margin, 159-246.

The House Commerce Committee rejected the plan twice (H Res 212), voting the second time to send it to the floor without any recommendation for action (H Rept 96-123).

Carter responded to the House action with an angry blast at members for letting "political timidity prevent their taking action in the interest of our nation." Only seven Republicans voted for the plan. One hundred and six Democrats opposed it. Opposition came from representatives of all geographic regions, most heavily from the West, where members voted 2-1 to kill the plan.

Revising the System

Congress' rejection of the standby gas rationing plan and two of the three other emergency energy conservation plans demonstrated the difficulty of persuading politicians to approve laws that would force voters to change their energy consumption habits.

Sen. J. Bennett Johnston, D-La., the leading critic of the rationing plan, and other members of the Senate Energy Committee were among the first to acknowledge that the procedure established in 1975 for congressional approval of emergency energy plans was not working.

And concerned by the apparent inability of Congress to deal with an energy emergency, they fashioned a bill (S 1030) that would give the president broad authority during energy shortages to force conservation in states that had not devised adequate plans of their own. The steps could include use of automobiles only every other day and other measures worked out by the president and the governors without express congressional approval.

As introduced and passed by the Senate, S 1030 made no mention of gasoline rationing.

Senate Action. The Senate approved and passed S 1030 (S Rept 96-117) June 5 by a vote of 77-13.

As passed, S 1030 authorized the president to create an emergency energy conservation program and permitted governors to identify the most appropriate methods of conserving energy in their states.

The president would be permitted to carry out the emergency program only after a presidential finding that a severe energy supply interruption existed or was imminent or that restraint of domestic energy consumption was required to meet U.S. obligations under international energy agreements.

House Action. Spurred by lengthening gasoline lines across the nation, the House injected the gasoline rationing issue into consideration of S 1030.

The House Commerce Subcommittee on Energy and Power in mid-July gave the president limited authority to impose gas rationing when there was a 20 percent shortage of gasoline. The full Commerce Committee refused to change the rationing provisions before sending the bill (H Rept 96-373) to the full House 10 days later.

The House approved S 1030 by a vote of 263-159 on Aug. 1. The breadth of the margin, however, belied the difficulty the bill encountered, as House members disagreed over the proper role for Congress in a decision to ration gasoline.

The House first adopted, and then rejected, an amendment putting into S 1030 exactly what its sponsors and President Carter had hoped to take out of existing law — a provision allowing Congress to veto a "standby" rationing plan as well as the decision to put such a plan into effect.

The House adopted that amendment July 25 by a vote of 232-187. Under its language either chamber had 30 days within which to veto such a "standby" plan. Surprised by this turn of events, the House Democratic leaders pulled the bill off the floor.

When they brought it back to the floor, they had rounded up the votes to reverse the earlier action. On July 31, the House voted 234-189 to drop the one-house veto provision adopted July 25. Under the provision approved in its place, Congress did not have to approve any "standby" rationing plan, but either chamber could veto a president's decision to put such a plan into effect. Only three Republicans voted for this new language.

After dealing with a long string of Republican amendments intended to curb the president's power under S 1030 and exempt certain industries and groups from mandatory conservation plans, the House approved S 1030 Aug. 1.

Congressional leaders had hoped that the bill could be sent to the White House before the traditional August recess, which began Aug. 3, but hopes for that were dashed when the Senate Aug. 2 voted to reject the House changes in S 1030, making a conference necessary.

Conference Action. After meeting for five weeks, House and Senate conferees filed their report on S 1030 (S Rept 96-366, H Rept 96-516) Oct. 12. They compromised on the gas rationing review issue by giving Congress an opportunity to review a "standby" plan but making it difficult for Congress to reject such a proposal. S 1030, as finally approved, required that rejection of such a plan come by joint resolution of both houses within 30 days of its submission.

Final Action. The Senate adopted the conference report Oct. 17 by a vote of 77-18. The House cleared the bill Oct. 23 by a vote of 301-112.

Provisions

As signed into law Nov. 5, 1979, PL 96-102:

● Required the president to draft a standby gasoline rationing plan and submit it to Congress for review. The plan would be considered approved unless Congress, within 30 legislative days, adopted a joint resolution of disapproval. If the two chambers passed opposing resolutions, the plan was approved. The president could veto a joint resolution of disapproval; a two-thirds majority of both houses would be necessary to override that veto.

● Specified that rationing could not be imposed unless there was a "severe energy supply interruption" or unless rationing was necessary to comply with the obligations of the United States under the international energy program, which required participating nations to share energy shortages.

● Defined a severe supply interruption as a daily shortage of 20 percent for more than 30 days of gasoline, diesel fuel or home heating oil.

● Waived the 20 percent threshold requirement and allowed the president to impose rationing without such a finding if both houses of Congress passed a resolution of approval within 30 days of his requesting it. Once such a resolution was approved, the president could impose rationing at any time within the next 60 days. Waiver of the 20 percent requirement was limited to nine months.

● Gave either house of Congress 30 days within which to veto a presidential decision to impose rationing.

● Specified that rationing coupons be distributed so that motorists in each state had the same percentage reduction in gasoline and that any rationing plan recognize the relative needs of users.

● *Conservation.* Authorized the president, upon finding an actual or potential severe interruption of energy supplies, to set monthly conservation targets for the nation and each state for specific energy sources or fuels. In connection with setting such a national target, the president was required to put into effect an emergency energy conservation plan for federal government activities.

● Directed each state, in anticipation of such conservation goals, to develop its own energy conservation plan. Such plan would not be required until a president actually set the conservation targets. Once a target had been set, a state would have 45 days to submit to the energy secretary a plan spelling out how the state would meet the target. The secretary could approve or reject the plan.

● Directed the secretary of energy to develop a standby federal emergency conservation plan within 90 days of enactment of PL 96-102. That plan could not impose unduly on any class of industry or business, and could not include a tax or user fee or weekend closings of gas stations, unless the last was part of a plan to restrict gas sales each day on a rotating basis.

● Authorized the federal government, during an energy emergency, to impose conservation restrictions on a state without an approved conservation plan, if it appeared that otherwise an energy conservation target would not be met. In a state with a plan, but still not meeting the target, the president could impose the federal restrictions when energy supplies fell, or were expected to fall, at least 8 percent short of normal demand over a 60-day period.

● Authorized the president in an emergency to require that motorists purchase at least a minimum amount of gasoline at a station stop.

● Specified that under an odd-even plan for gasoline purchases, the odd-even requirement would not apply to out-of-state cars unless they were from a state adjoining that in which they were trying to buy gas. (Odd-even plans allowed cars with license plate numbers ending in an odd number to buy gas on odd-numbered days, while cars with even-numbered plates could buy gas on even-numbered days.)

● Authorized state and local governments to offer local building operators an exemption from the temperature limits put into effect in July 1979 so long as the building operator complied with an alternate method of saving a comparable amount of energy.

Naval Oil Reserves

Congress in 1979 authorized spending of up to $85.2 million in fiscal 1980 for exploring, developing and conserving the nation's naval oil reserves. The amount authorized by HR 3354 (PL 96-137) was $10.3 million more than requested by the Carter administration.

Background

Between 1912 and 1924, the federal government set aside six parcels of land believed to contain petroleum deposits — three for oil shale and three for petroleum — to provide fuel supplies for the military in the event of war.

In 1976, prompted by energy crunches and a fear that the dormant reserve fields would not be immediately usable when needed, Congress voted to change the strict conservation status the petroleum reserves had been given. The Naval Petroleum Reserves Production Act of 1976 (PL 94-258) permitted production at the "maximum efficient rate" until 1982.

Between 1976 and 1979, production from two petroleum reserves averaged 121,000 barrels a day and brought in more than $481 million in revenues. The oil shale reserves, estimated to contain 26 billion barrels of shale oil, were not in production.

Legislative Action

The House April 25 approved HR 3354 (H Rept 96-91) by a vote of 394-12. The additional $10 million above the administration request was intended to ensure continued exploration of the reserves. The House bill also required that at least 16 Navy officers continue to be assigned to the Department of Energy to oversee management of the reserves and to preserve their national defense character.

The Senate Sept. 27 approved its version of HR 3354 (S Rept 96-325) by voice vote, after deleting the requirement that Navy officers be detailed to manage the reserve program.

Conferees filed their report (H Rept 96-596, S Rept 96-410) Nov. 8. They modified House language to require that an unspecified number of Navy officers be assigned to oversee development of the reserves.

The Senate adopted the conference report Nov. 9, and the House cleared the bill Nov. 28. President Carter signed the measure Dec. 12.

Oil Antitrust Exemption

Congress in late 1979 cleared legislation (S 1871 — PL 96-133) to extend a special antitrust exemption for the major oil companies that permitted them to participate in oil-sharing agreements the United States made with other countries.

Without the extension, the companies said, they could not continue to provide information to the International Energy Agency. The agency implemented an agreement among 20 Western countries and Japan that called for equitable distribution of available oil supplies. The agreement meant, for example, that other countries would share their supplies with a country hit by an embargo.

It also meant that the international oil companies were asked to allocate their supplies in an equitable fashion among nations. That was the function that most clearly violated U.S. antitrust laws.

Passage of the legislation had been threatened by a controversial provision relating to oil import quotas that was added by the Senate Oct. 30. The amendment, offered by J. Bennett Johnston, D-La., would have given Congress a say in a presidential decision to impose quotas on oil imports. Existing law gave that authority solely to the president. *(Oil import quotas, 208)*

The House Nov. 8 formally objected to the amendment, claiming that it was tax-related and thus, under the Constitution, had to originate in the House. The Senate dropped the provision Nov. 16.

The major remaining difference between the two bills was the length of the extension of the antitrust exemption. The House bill set Oct. 31, 1981, as the termination date, while the Senate bill extended the exemption only until June 30, 1980. The conferees split the difference, ending up with an extension until March 15, 1981. The Senate adopted the conference report (H Rept 96-669) Nov. 28, and the House agreed Nov. 29.

1980 Energy Authorization

For the fourth consecutive year, Congress in 1979 ended its annual session without enacting legislation to authorize the nation's federal energy research and development program.

A $7 billion Energy Department authorization bill for fiscal 1980 did not make it to the Senate floor by the end of 1979 although the Senate Energy Committee had reported a bill (S 688 — S Rept 96-232) in June. The House had approved its version of the measure (HR 3000 — H Rept 96-196, Parts I-V) Oct. 24. There was no further action on the bill in the 96th Congress.

Not since 1975 had Congress successfully completed action on a full-fledged energy authorization bill. Congress failed to finish work on the fiscal 1977 and 1979 measures, and President Carter killed the fiscal 1978 bill with his first veto. Congress also failed in 1980 to approve the fiscal 1981 energy authorization.

Congress in 1979 did approve, and President Carter signed into law, a measure (HR 4930 — PL 96-126) appropriating $22 billion in funds for the Energy Department in fiscal 1980. A large portion of those funds, however, was not to be made available for disbursement until authorizing legislation was enacted.

Passage of the energy authorization bill was again complicated by controversy over the future of the "fast breeder" nuclear reactor program. Carter wished to terminate funding for construction of a demonstration fast breeder plant on the Clinch River in Tennessee. The Senate committee agreed, but the full House voted to continue funding. *(Clinch River controversy, p. 214)*

The perennial issue of price controls on fuel sparked several amendments to HR 3000, as the House first adopted — and later rejected — an amendment decontrolling gasoline prices. Decontrol advocates had succeeded earlier in defeating amendments calling for a restoration of price controls on crude oil, heating oil and diesel fuel.

Oil Company Mergers

Late in 1979, the Senate Judiciary Committee reported a measure (S 1246 — S Rept 96-444) designed to block the major U.S. oil companies from acquiring other large corporations.

No further action was taken on the highly controversial bill during the 96th Congress.

The bill was intended to encourage the major oil companies to invest the profits they reaped from the sale of decontrolled oil back into exploration and development of oil and gas wells. But the target companies argued that the measure was just another effort by Congress to make "big oil" the scapegoat for the energy crisis. Also opposing the measure were the national business associations — the U.S. Chamber of Commerce, Business Roundtable and National Association of Manufacturers. They saw S 1246 as a harbinger of a broad assault on conglomerate mergers.

Provisions

As approved by the committee, S 1246 would prohibit 18 major U.S. oil producers and their affiliates from acquiring or merging with another corporation in the energy industry if the other firm had total assets of $100 million or more. An acquisition of or merger with a non-energy business would be prohibited if the business had total assets of at least $50 million.

Exceptions would be allowed for acquisitions or mergers that would "substantially enhance competition" or whose effect "would be materially to increase or substantially to promote" energy exploration and production.

The companies covered would be Amerada Hess, Atlantic Richfield, Cities Service, Continental, Exxon, Getty Oil, Gulf, Marathon Oil, Mobil, Occidental Petroleum, Phillips Petroleum, Shell Oil, Standard Oil of California, Standard Oil of Ohio, Standard Oil of Indiana, Sun Oil, Texaco and Union Oil of California.

Foreign subsidiaries of U.S. firms would be covered by the bill, but foreign parent corporations such as British Petroleum and Royal Dutch Shell would be excluded.

1980

Highlights

Windfall Profits Tax

Congress gave final approval to a major element of President Carter's energy program — a tax on the windfall profits of oil companies (PL 96-223). The tax, the largest ever levied on an American industry, was expected to provide revenues of more than $227 billion over the next decade.

Synthetic Fuels

Another major part of Carter's energy program — subsidies for the commercial development of synthetic fuels

— also cleared in 1980 (PL 96-294). Congress approved an initial authorization of $20 billion to be allocated to private industry. As much as $88 billion in federal funds could be spent on the program in the 1980s.

Energy Mobilization Board

The third major element of Carter's energy package — creation of an energy mobilization board to cut federal red tape on energy projects — was rejected. Although approved by both chambers in 1979 and reported from conference after seven months of negotiations, the measure was killed when the House voted to send it back to conference.

Nuclear Power

Congress gave Carter the go-ahead to reorganize the Nuclear Regulatory Commission and it approved the first statutory reforms concerning nuclear power plant safety since the March 1979 accident at the Three Mile Island nuclear plant (PL 96-295). But Congress left unresolved the issue of nuclear waste disposal. Unable to reach a compromise on a comprehensive nuclear waste policy bill, Congress cleared legislation giving the states responsibility for burying low-level radioactive waste (PL 96-573).

Gasoline Rationing

A standby gasoline rationing plan to be used in an emergency was in place in August 1980 after both houses of Congress declined to block it.

Temperature Restrictions

Carter signed an executive order extending temperature limits in public buildings through Jan. 16, 1981.

Pacific Northwest Power

A four-state regional council was created in the Pacific Northwest to allocate power from federal hydroelectric projects, to promote energy conservation and to acquire new energy sources (PL 96-501).

Ocean, Wind Energy

Two measures to encourage the commercial use of ocean thermal energy were approved. One measure provided $75 million for an accelerated federal research and development program on ocean thermal energy (PL 96-310). The other set up a legal framework to govern the operation of ocean thermal energy conversion plants on the high seas (PL 96-320). Also approved in 1980 was a bill to authorize up to $100 million in fiscal 1981 to encourage the development of wind energy systems (PL 96-345).

Energy Authorization

Controversy over nuclear waste disposal blocked House floor action on the fiscal 1981 authorization for energy research and development programs.

Coal Conversion

Legislation to provide as much as $4.2 billion to help convert 80 oil-fired power plants to coal was approved overwhelmingly by the Senate but was not reported out of committee in the House. Supporters argued that the switches would save from 250,000 to 300,000 barrels of oil a day.

Energy Planning Grants

The House rejected a Carter proposal to provide grants to state and local governments for energy planning and conservation. The measure would have authorized $720 million over three years. The version approved by the Senate would have authorized half that amount — $360 million — over two years.

The Year in Review

Before election-year schedules and pressures slowed the pace of action on Capitol Hill, Congress sent to the White House two landmark energy bills — the Crude Oil Windfall Profits Tax Act of 1980 and the Energy Security Act, the synthetic fuels measure.

The third element of Carter's energy package — the energy mobilization board — was killed when the House rejected the conference version of the bill. Congress was unsuccessful in approving comprehensive nuclear waste legislation in 1980, although it did pass a bill setting out federal policy on the disposal of low-level radioactive wastes.

Energy Development Package

Two new elements of the nation's energy policy were set in place by the 96th Congress in 1980 — a stiff tax on the windfall profits of the nation's oil industry and a multi-billion dollar federal push for the development of a synthetic fuels industry. Both measures were requested in 1979 by President Carter, who designated them as two of the key parts of his three-part energy plan.

The third element — creation of a special government board to speed high-priority energy projects through government red tape — was killed by Congress in June 1980, despite the fact that both chambers had approved such a board in 1979.

Windfall Profits Tax

Congress in 1980 responded to public unhappiness with recurring energy shortages, rising energy prices and reports of record profits for the major oil companies by imposing a tax on the windfall profits of the domestic oil industry.

The tax, intended to produce more than $227 billion in revenue for the federal government over the decade of the 1980s, was the largest tax ever levied on a single U.S. industry.

It was the crucial element in President Carter's energy plan, a necessary counterpoint to his decision to lift the federal price controls that had held down the price of domestic oil during the 1970s while the price of foreign oil skyrocketed. The purpose of the windfall tax was to recapture for general use some of the profits the oil companies were expected to receive as a result of price decontrol. The new tax was not levied on all income from domestic oil production, but only that portion attributable to the difference between a certain base price for each barrel of domestic oil and the actual sale price of that oil.

Congress completed action on the measure late in March 1980, just less than a year from the time that President Carter had formally requested passage of such a measure. The Senate gave its final approval to the measure (HR 3919 — PL 96-223) March 27 by a vote of 66-31. House approval came March 13 by a vote of 302-107. But the breadth of those margins masked the difficulty of the bill's passage through the legislative process.

Background

President Carter requested the tax in April 1979, as he announced his plan to lift controls on domestic oil prices. The windfall profits tax was the first element in his three-part energy package to clear Congress. The second element, subsidies for synthetic fuels production, was enacted later in 1980. The third, creation of an energy mobilization board, died.

The idea of a windfall profits tax coupled with an end to price controls was not original with Carter. President Ford had proposed such a move in 1975, but Congress chose to retain price controls and gave scant attention to the tax proposal.

In 1979, Carter's move to decontrol domestic oil prices drew little more than rhetorical opposition in Congress. And as world oil prices soared and, along with them, the profits of domestic oil producers, even the oil industry and other staunch opponents of the windfall tax realized they were fighting a losing battle. Recognizing that Congress would enact some sort of tax, the industry and other opponents of such a measure concentrated their efforts on weakening it.

The final version of the tax differed in three major respects from that proposed by Carter.

Carter proposed a permanent tax, which, in the view of the industry, was the most onerous aspect of his proposal. Congress decided to phase out the tax over a 33-month period. The earliest the tax would end was the beginning of October 1990; the latest would be the beginning of October 1993. When the phase-out would begin depended on how long it took the tax to generate the agreed-upon total of $227.3 billion. (Future Congresses, however, could vote to extend the life of the oil tax.)

Carter proposed that revenue from the tax be channeled into a special energy security trust fund. From there it would be allocated for aid to low-income families hit with high fuel bills, for development of synthetic fuels, and for mass transportation. Congress, however, decided to allow the additional revenue to go directly into the general revenue fund. From there Congress could allocate the money as it wished. Congress did make some suggestions in PL 96-223 about how the money from the tax might be used, but without future legislation, those suggestions carried little weight.

The third difference between Carter's proposal and the final version of the tax measure was the tax rate. Carter had proposed a flat tax rate of 50 percent. Congress decided to vary the rate, depending upon the type of production and the time at which the well began producing.

House Action

The House Ways and Means Committee gave its approval to a windfall tax measure (HR 3919 — H Rept 96-304) June 22, 1979. It modified the Carter plan to tighten the tax on oil already in production and to ease the tax bite on future discoveries of oil. The effect of

that shift was to increase the amount of revenue generated by the tax in its first three or four years, but to reduce the long-run cost to the industry by lowering the tax on future production. The Carter administration did not object to the changes.

The committee requested a rule that would allow no changes in HR 3919 on the House floor. The Rules Committee refused the request and instead provided that the House could vote on three items other than the bill as reported. One was a substitute proposed by James R. Jones, D-Okla., and W. Henson Moore, R-La., which the industry found far more palatable than the committee bill.

On June 28, the House tossed out the Ways and Means version of the bill and adopted the Jones-Moore substitute in its place. The vote to adopt the substitute was 236-

Timing of the Tax Bill

Rarely do events outside official Washington coincide so well with a president's push for legislation as they did during congressional consideration in 1979 of President Carter's windfall tax proposal.

President Carter sent his proposal to Congress in April, as the major oil companies announced their first quarter profits — figures that in some cases were as much as 80 percent above the comparable profit totals for 1978.

Just before the House began consideration of the windfall profits tax bill late in June, the Organization of Petroleum Exporting Countries (OPEC) announced the largest increase in world oil prices since 1973. The increase — to an official price of $23.50 a barrel — would boost the world price from $16 to $30 a barrel during the year.

As the Senate Finance Committee began work on its version of the bill in July, President Carter's urging that citizens let the Senate know they wanted a stiff windfall profits tax was underscored by second quarter profit reports from the major oil companies. Those profits increased over the 1978 figures by a range of 20 to 132 percent, increases that did nothing to dispel the belief of many consumers that they were being victimized for the benefit of the oil industry.

And by the time the Senate committee finished work and the full Senate prepared to consider the bill, the third quarter profit figures were announced. Exxon Corp. reported profits up 118 percent over the third quarter of 1978. Mobil Corp. topped that with profits that had increased 130 percent over the previous year.

President Carter pointed to such totals as demonstrating vividly "the need for a major portion of unearned profits from the oil companies to go into the general service of the American people."

183. The amended version of HR 3919 then passed the House by voice vote.

Adoption of the substitute version of HR 3919 was a major victory for the oil industry, primarily because in adopting it, the House rejected the idea of a permanent windfall tax. The version of the bill approved by the House provided that the tax would end in 1990. It also reduced the tax rate from the level approved by the committee and gave a further tax break to oil produced from marginal wells.

The House, however, did reject another major amendment backed by the industry. By a vote of 186-229, the House refused to send the bill back to committee with instructions to add a provision giving oil companies a tax credit for 75 cents of each dollar they "plowed back" into energy production.

Senate Action

The Carter administration appealed to the Senate to approve a tougher tax bill than the House version. The administration particularly urged the Senate to reinstate the permanent tax, warning that without it, a return to price controls might be necessary.

Committee Bill. The Senate Finance Committee began marking up HR 3919 Sept. 6 and worked until Oct. 25, 1979. The committee filed its report (S Rept 96-394) on Nov. 1, 1979.

As reported, the Finance Committee bill was substantially weaker than either the House bill or the administration proposal, producing roughly half the total revenues the other versions were expected to generate during the 1980s. The chief reason for the reduction was that the Senate committee exempted several types of oil from the tax altogether, including oil discovered after 1978 and most hard-to-extract oil. The revenue total of the Senate bill was also reduced by an earlier phase-out date.

The Senate bill was more like Carter's original proposal than the House bill, however, in earmarking portions of the expected revenue for mass transit and fuel assistance for low-income families. In addition, the committee provided for numerous tax credits to encourage individuals and businesses to conserve or produce energy.

Floor Action. The Senate spent a month debating HR 3919 before approving its version Dec. 17, 1979, by a vote of 74-24.

The Senate approved a number of amendments stiffening the Finance Committee bill — increasing the tax rate, extending the life of the tax, and imposing it upon oil that the committee had chosen to exempt entirely from its bite.

Notwithstanding those changes, the Senate bill was still expected to raise far less in revenue than the House bill, only about $178 billion by 1990 compared to $277 billion.

The Senate rebuffed other efforts to weaken the tax, but did agree to grant independent producers a further break, exempting entirely the first 1,000 barrels they produced each day.

In addition, the Senate eliminated any link between revenues from the windfall tax and energy spending, deleting the provisions earmarking some of those revenues for mass transit and fuel assistance. The Senate did, however, add to HR 3919 authorization for a $7 billion program to help low-income households pay their fuel bills during the winters of 1980-81 and 1981-82.

Oil state Democrats and Republicans mounted a filibuster effort in mid-December in an effort to block Senate approval of an amendment extending the tax to newly discovered oil and the other types of oil that the committee had left exempt. Three efforts to cut off debate failed, but a compromise was finally reached and adopted on the afternoon of Dec. 14. The Senate agreed to impose the tax on new oil, but minimized its bite initially by setting the tax rate low — 10 percent — and the base price high — $20. The compromise was approved by a vote of 52-38.

In addition, the Senate approved several amendments that were unrelated to the windfall tax. Among them were provisions repealing a 1976 change in the capital gains tax that persons paid on inherited property, allowing Congress to block a presidential decision to impose oil import quotas, and enlarging the personal income tax exemption for interest and dividends earned.

The Senate version of HR 3919 would cost the Treasury some $60 billion in lost revenues over the 1980s — a loss offsetting a substantial part of the revenue expected from the new tax.

The change in capital gains laws was expected to cost $4.3 billion, and the larger interest and dividend exemption, $27 billion. In addition, the energy tax credits and incentives provided by the Senate in HR 3919 were expected to result in revenue losses of about $30 billion.

Conference Action

Before leaving Washington in December 1979 for the holidays, conferees on HR 3919 reached one key decision. In accord with the wishes of the Carter administration, they agreed that the final version of the tax bill would generate a total of $227.3 billion by 1990. That figure was halfway between the estimated revenues for the House and the Senate bills.

Three major differences remained when conferees resumed work in 1980:

• The taxation of newly discovered oil — the Senate took only 10 percent of the "windfall profits" on that oil, while the House taxed about 50 percent.

• Production by independent producers — the Senate exempted a large portion of independents' production; the House gave them no special treatment.

• The termination point for the tax — the House ended the tax on new discoveries by 1990, while continuing the tax on oil found before 1979 until those wells ran dry; the Senate did not set a date for the end of the tax, but simply provided that it would end when it had produced a certain amount of revenue.

To reach the goal of $227.3 billion, conferees had to increase the tax bite on new oil above the Senate bill, or place more of the tax burden on independent producers.

In late January, conferees resolved that problem with a compromise. New oil discoveries would be taxed at a 30 percent rate — substantially higher than the Senate had provided — but independent producers would be given a lower tax rate than the major oil companies on the first 1,000 barrels per day of stripper oil they produced and on the first 1,000 barrels per day of "old" oil they produced from pre-1979 wells. (Stripper wells were those with an average annual yield of 10 or fewer barrels a day.)

Early in February, the conferees settled the question of how to end the tax. They agreed that the tax would

Synthetic Fuels Given Billion-Dollar Nudge

The new United States Synthetic Fuels Corporation was designed to nudge private industry into the synthetic fuels business.

That nudge could cost U.S. taxpayers as much as $88 billion during the 1980s.

But supporters of the corporation said it was unlikely the tab would be that high. Some contended that the synfuels industry would be so successful that it would cost the government very little.

The legislation setting up the corporation (S 932) directed its seven-member board to provide loans, loan guarantees, purchase agreements or price guarantees to companies producing synfuels.

If a type of synthetic fuel ended up selling for less than the prevailing price of oil, then demand would soar and government expense would be minimal.

But if cost overruns, higher coal prices or other factors made liquids from coal or other synfuels too high-priced to compete on the open market, then the government could be forced to buy the costly fuel.

If necessary to the development of a synthetic fuels industry, the government could, as a last resort, contract with industry to build and operate a government-owned commercial facility. That would be the most expensive route because a full-scale plant could cost from $2 billion to $5 billion.

Wide Interest Expected

Interest in synfuels projects among private companies was expected to be high. The Energy Department in mid-1980 already had received 951 applications for just $200 million in grants that companies could use to study the feasibility of commercial synfuels facilities or to push planned projects into final stages. If the projects were successful, the agency would have to be repaid for the grants, but the energy secretary could waive the repayment.

The grant money was provided in the fiscal 1980 Interior appropriations bill, which made available to the Energy Department $2.2 billion of a special $19 billion reserve for synthetic and alcohol fuels. The reserve was set up in the same legislation (PL 96-126).

Production Goals Set

The corporation was expected to operate as if it were a private enterprise, even though it would be federally owned. Congress asked for a comprehensive plan within four years that would spell out how the corporation would achieve the synfuels production goals.

At that point, under the new synfuels legislation, Congress, using expedited procedures, could authorize $68 billion in addition to the $20 billion already provided. However, the legislators still would have to appropriate the funds annually.

The legislation directed the corporation, which was given a life of 12 years, to work toward production by 1987 of the equivalent of at least 500,000 barrels a day of crude oil, increasing to 2 million barrels a day by 1992.

The nation in 1980 was using about 18 million barrels of oil a day, of which about 7.5 million barrels were imported.

---

begin phasing out when the revenue goal of $227.3 billion had been reached or in 1988, whichever was later.

Conferees filed their report (H Rept 96-817) March 7.

Final Action

During consideration of the conference report, the House March 13 rejected an attempt by opponents of the measure to send it back to conference. The recommittal move was led by those who wished to exempt small oil companies from the tax altogether. It was rejected by a vote of 185-227.

On March 12, the House rejected a separate resolution (H Res 602) that suggested to future Congresses that half of the tax revenues be used for energy, rather than the 15 percent stipulated in the conference report. The resolution, which would not have affected the conference report and which was labeled symbolic by both sides, was rejected by a vote of 201-215.

The House adopted the conference report March 13 by a vote of 302-107.

After a move to recommit the conference report in the Senate was defeated by a vote of 35-61, the Senate approved the report March 27 by a vote of 66-31, sending the bill to the White House.

President Carter signed the measure April 2, 1980.

Provisions

As signed into law April 2, 1980, PL 96-223 — The Crude Oil Windfall Profits Tax Act — established a new federal tax to be imposed solely upon the income from domestically produced oil.

In addition the law provided various incentives for individuals and businesses to cut back on their use of oil and natural gas and set up a program to aid poor families with rising energy bills.

The Tax

PL 96-223 provided for a new tax to be imposed upon a portion of the income that oil producers received from the sale of domestic oil. The tax would be imposed upon the portion of that income that could be attributed to the difference between a base price and the actual selling price for each barrel. The tax was designed to recapture for general use a portion of the "windfall profits" oil producers would receive as a result of the end of federal controls on the price of domestic oil.

The tax was imposed at a different rate — and the base price varied — depending upon the type of oil, the date upon which the well from which it came was first tapped, the method of its production and its producer. The tax rate varied from 30 percent to 70 percent and the base ranged between $12.81 and $16.55. (The base price was to be adjusted each year for inflation.)

The tax applied to income from all oil produced from wells after 1 a.m. on March 1, 1980.

Under the structure set up by PL 96-223:

● The income from most domestic oil from wells in production before 1979 was to be taxed at a rate of 70 percent of the difference between the actual per-barrel sale price and a base of $12.81.

● An exception to that 70 percent rate for pre-1979 oil was provided for the first 1,000 barrels per day produced from pre-1979 wells by independent producers (those who did not refine the oil or engage in retail sales). That income would be taxed at a special 50 percent rate.

● The income from stripper oil (so-called because expensive techniques "stripped" the oil remaining in a well) would be taxed at a 60 percent rate, with a base price of $15.20.

● The income from the first 1,000 barrels a day of stripper oil produced by independents would be taxed at a 30 percent rate. The same rate and base price would apply to income from production from a National Petroleum Reserve.

● The income from oil discovered after 1978, certain heavy oil, and production by tertiary techniques that exceeded the average production level from a well would be taxed at a 30 percent rate on revenues generated by sales of that oil at a price above the base of $16.55 per barrel. The base price would be adjusted 2 percent annually in addition to the inflation adjustment made each year in the base price of all oil categories.

● Alaskan oil was exempt from the tax except that from the Sadlerochit reservoir on the Alaskan North Slope, which was taxed as pre-1979 oil.

● Oil production from property owned by Indians and by state and local governments was also exempt, as were properties that, as of Jan. 21, 1980, were owned by nonprofit medical or educational institutions or by churches that had dedicated the proceeds to a medical or educational institution.

In addition, PL 96-223:

● Limited the tax to a maximum of 90 percent of the net income from a property.

● Defined the tax as a deductible business expense for income tax purposes.

● Provided that the windfall profit subject to the tax could be reduced by the amount of state severance taxes on the windfall profit. Specified that if a state increased its severance tax after March 31, 1979, the deduction would still be allowed only if the state increase applied equally to the entire price of the barrel and only if the state severance tax did not exceed 15 percent.

● Provided a 33-month gradual phase-out of the tax that would begin in January 1988, if $227.3 billion in revenues had been raised by the tax. Specified that if that

revenue target were not reached, the phase-out was to begin one month after the Treasury secretary estimated that $227.3 billion had been raised. Provided that even if the $227.3 billion had not been raised by Jan. 1, 1991, the phase-out was to start on that date.

Residential Energy Tax Credits

PL 96-223 sought to encourage homeowners to reduce their use of oil and natural gas and to switch to renewable energy sources. To that end, the law:

● Increased the tax credit available for residential solar, wind and geothermal equipment to 40 percent of the first $10,000 in expenditures, or a maximum of $4,000. Existing law, the Energy Tax Act of 1978 — PL 95-618, provided a credit for 30 percent of the first $2,000 and 20 percent of the next $8,000 in expenditures, for a maximum credit of $2,200. *(Story, pp. 187, 201)*

● Authorized the Treasury secretary to add items to the list of property already eligible for residential and business energy credits. Required that the added item reduce the nation's use of oil by an amount large enough to justify the associated loss of federal revenues.

Business Tax Incentives

To encourage businesses to conserve oil and natural gas, to switch to other energy sources, and to recapture and reuse waste energy, PL 96-223:

● Increased the tax credit available to businesses that installed solar, wind or geothermal equipment to 15 percent from 10 percent, and extended the credit from 1982 through 1985. Changed the credit from refundable, as it was in existing law, to non-refundable. (A refundable credit meant the government paid the taxpayer if he did not have enough tax liability to claim the full credit through tax deductions.)

● Provided a tax credit equal to 11 percent of the cost of equipment to produce up to 125 megawatts of electricity that was installed at an existing dam or at a site that did not involve the use of a dam.

● Provided a tax credit equal to 10 percent of the cost of cogeneration equipment, which tapped waste steam or heat and reused that energy. Specified that a system, to be eligible, had to depend on oil or natural gas for less than 20 percent of all fuel used annually.

● Extended a 10 percent tax credit to equipment that used or produced fuel from biomass — organic material such as sewage and crop residues.

● Also extended the 10 percent energy credit to bus companies for investment that expanded bus seating capacity.

● Made petroleum coke and pitch eligible for the regular 10 percent investment credit and accelerated depreciation. Made equipment to produce coke and coke gas eligible for a 10 percent energy credit through 1982.

● Established a rule to make energy credits that would have expired in 1982 available until 1991 if commitments for long-term projects had been made before that date.

● Made available a tax credit of $3 a barrel, adjusted annually for inflation, to producers of synthetic fuels, such as oil from shale or liquids from coal, if the average uncontrolled price of domestic oil fell below $29.50 a barrel.

● Specified that a solid waste disposal facility that converted waste to fuel was eligible for a tax exemption on the interest paid on industrial development bonds used to finance the facility. (Existing law did not allow the exemption for facilities that converted waste to fuel.)

● Made the tax exemption for industrial development bonds available for bonds used to finance the addition to existing dams or water sites of hydroelectric equipment capable of generating up to 125 megawatts of electricity.

● Extended the tax exemption for industrial development bonds to bonds used to finance facilities that produced energy from renewable energy sources, such as wind or solar, as long as the facility was state owned, backed by sufficient taxation authority and, under state law, eligible for financing by general obligation bonds.

● Extended through 1992 the existing exemption from the 4-cent-a-gallon federal excise tax for fuels that were at least 10 percent alcohol. (The exemption was to expire in 1984, under existing law.) Specified that the exemption did not apply to any future increases in the excise tax.

● Provided users of alcohol fuels who did not buy fuel at a public pump, and thus did not pay the excise tax, a tax credit of from 30 cents to 40 cents a gallon, depending on the proof of the alcohol.

● Authorized the Treasury secretary to waive or reduce existing regulatory requirements for distilleries if they produced alcohol used as a fuel.

Low-Income Energy Assistance

To cushion the effect of rising energy costs on poor families, PL 96-223 set up a program of aid to low-income families. The law provided an initial authorization of $3.1 billion in block grants to states in fiscal 1981; the funds then were to be distributed by state agencies. PL 96-223 went on to:

● Define eligible families as those with incomes less than the Bureau of Labor Statistics lower living standard. (For 1979, the national average in that category for a family of four was $11,000.)

● Authorize states to give assistance, regardless of income, to households receiving food stamps, aid to families with dependent children (AFDC), veterans' pensions based on need or, with some exceptions, supplemental security income (SSI) benefits.

● Specify that in determining a state's share of the appropriation, half of the funds would be allotted according to the state's total residential energy expenditures, such as utility bills, and half according to heating degree days, which measured cold weather. Specified also that a state's share would be increased by the amount necessary to provide at least $120 to each AFDC, SSI and food stamp household.

● Reserve 5 percent of the total appropriation for U.S. territories, the Community Service Administration's crisis intervention program and matching incentive grants for states.

● Require each state to submit an energy assistance plan to the secretary of health, education and welfare (subsequently the secretary of health and human services) for approval.

Spending Guidelines

PL 96-223 set out general standards for the use of revenues from the tax. They included provisions that:

● For accounting purposes only, allocated revenues from the windfall profits tax to a separate account of the Treasury. Allocated net revenues under the price assumption as follows: 25 percent for aid to low-income families; 60 percent for income tax reductions and 15 percent for energy and transportation programs.

● Allocated revenues in excess of $227 billion one-third

Temperature Limits Extended

President Carter in April 1980 extended through Jan. 16, 1981, federal restrictions on heating and cooling in offices, factories and other non-residential buildings. The extension came by executive order, signed April 15.

Carter had initially ordered the temperature restrictions into effect in July 1979, soon after Congress gave him the authority to take such action. Under the federal rules, buildings could not be cooled to a temperature lower than 78 degrees in the summertime, and could not be heated to a temperature higher than 65 degrees in winter.

The controls were mandatory, but little enforcement was necessary during the first nine months of the program. Deputy Energy Secretary John C. Sawhill reported in March 1980 that the limits seemed to be largely self-enforcing. He claimed that the temperature controls had resulted in savings of 200,000 to 400,000 barrels of oil a day.

---

to the poor and two-thirds for income tax reductions.

● Specified that the energy tax incentives provided in the windfall tax legislation and any synthetic fuels programs were to be funded by general revenues. (The actual distribution of revenues from the tax was dependent on future legislation.)

Other Tax Provisions

PL 96-223 also made some changes in the general income tax law. They included provisions that:

● Repealed the provision of existing law, scheduled to take effect after Dec. 31, 1979, that would have required persons who inherited property to pay capital gains tax on the difference between the original purchase price and the price when it was sold by the heir. The repeal left in effect existing law that required payment of capital gains tax only on the difference between the value of the property when it was inherited and when it was sold.

● Increased to $200 from $100 (to $400 from $200 for married couples) the existing exclusion from taxable income of dividends, and broadened the exclusion to include interest earned from domestic sources. Eligible interest included that from a bank, savings and loan or other thrift institution, certain types of corporate debt, government, and a share in a trust established and maintained by a corporation. Thus, qualifying obligations included interest-bearing bank deposits, certificates or notes of deposit, commercial paper, bills, notes and bonds.

● Authorized a tax break for companies that involuntarily liquidated inventories in response to a government regulation or request. (For example, oil companies could be asked to sell from stocks to meet demand. The Treasury secretary was to designate in advance those situations to which this provision would apply.)

● Tightened the method for taxing the inventory of a liquidating corporation.

Oil Imports

PL 96-223 also amended the Trade Expansion Act of 1962 to limit the president's unilateral authority to impose oil import quotas. Specified that the president could be blocked from imposing quotas if each house of Congress approved an identical resolution disapproving his action. The joint resolution could be vetoed by the president, but then Congress, by a two-thirds vote in both houses, could override the veto.

Synthetic Fuels

Congress in mid-1980 cleared for the White House a bill (S 932 — PL 96-294) authorizing a $20 billion program to spur commercial development of synthetic fuels.

The $20 billion was to be allocated to private industry by a Synthetic Fuels Corporation, to be governed by a seven-member board. The corporation, which eventually could be responsible for $88 billion, was directed to stimulate the production of 2 million barrels a day of synfuels by 1992 by investing federal funds through loans, loan guarantees and price guarantees.

The corporation also would be able to enter into joint ventures with private companies, with the corporation financing up to 60 percent of a synthetic fuels plant. In addition, the corporation could help finance coal mines or transportation facilities when developed as part of a synthetic fuels project.

The $20 billion authorization included $1.45 billion for alcohol fuels and $3.025 billion for a solar and conservation bank and required the president to resume filling the Strategic Petroleum Reserve. By 1984, up to $68 billion in additional funds could be authorized by Congress after the corporation issued a progress report on its production strategy. Carter in July 1979 had included subsidies for synthetic fuels as one of three major elements in his energy program; the others were an oil windfall profits tax, which was approved, and an Energy Mobilization Board, which was not.

Both chambers had approved versions of a synfuels bill in 1979, but conferees did not complete work on the final measure until mid-June 1980. Congress sent the bill to the White House June 26; President Carter signed it into law June 30.

Background

The idea of creating oil- and gas-like fuels from coal, oil shale and other natural resources was not new. The technology for synthesizing such fuels had existed for decades. But the high cost of producing synthetic fuel discouraged entrepreneurs from undertaking such an enterprise on a commercial scale.

President Gerald R. Ford in 1975 and 1976 backed proposals for federal programs to encourage commercialization of synthetic fuels.

In 1975 Congress rejected a provision authorizing federal guarantees of up to $6 billion in loans to private companies willing to undertake commercial production of these fuels. In 1976 the House refused, by a one-vote margin, to consider legislation authorizing federal loan guarantees and price supports for the development of a synthetic fuels industry.

By 1979, however, the plain reality of the nation's need to develop alternatives to imported oil — and the steadily rising price of oil and natural gas — convinced Congress that it was time to move ahead to foster the development of this new industry.

In June 1979 the House approved legislation (HR 3930) designed to spur development of a synthetic fuels industry in the United States by assuring producers of those fuels a government market for their product. HR 3930 required the Defense Department to become that market, purchasing the equivalent of 500,000 barrels of synthetic fuel a day by 1984. In addition, HR 3930 authorized federal aid to companies willing to undertake production of those fuels.

The Carter Proposal

A month later, President Carter announced the second part of his 1979 energy plan. At its heart was a proposal to launch an $88 billion, decade-long effort to boost production of synthetic fuels.

Carter proposed that Congress create a special Energy Security Corporation, run by a board of seven members, to manage investment of the funds — which would be provided by the windfall profits tax he earlier proposed to levy on the oil companies.

The corporation's goal would be the production of 2.5 million barrels a day in substitute fuels by 1990. Those fuels were to include liquids and gases produced from coal, biomass (agricultural wastes, urban garbage, or other organic matter) and peat; oil shale (rock permeated with oil) and "unconventional" natural gas (located in rock crevices and other hard-to-get areas that could not be tapped by conventional methods).

The corporation would be an independent, government-sponsored entity managed by its board. The board would consist of the energy secretary, the Treasury secretary, and the secretary of another Cabinet department. The four other directors, including the chairman, would be appointed by the president and confirmed by the Senate.

The board of directors would decide how to invest the $88 billion and could even set up synfuels plants owned and operated by the government. It could offer price guarantees, which would amount to subsidies; contracts for federal purchase of synfuels; direct loans and loan guarantees.

The bulk of funding for the corporation — $83 billion — would come from receipts from the proposed windfall profits tax. The corporation would get another $5 billion from the sale of special energy bonds.

House Action

The measure already approved by the House (HR 3930 — H Rept 96-165) provided for a much smaller federal commitment than Carter wanted. As approved by the House on June 26 by a vote of 368-25, HR 3930 amended the Defense Production Act of 1950 (PL 81-774) to require the Defense Department to purchase the equivalent of 500,000 barrels a day of synthetic fuels by 1984.

HR 3930 directed the government to spur production of that much synthetic fuel by then — and as much as two million barrels a day by 1990 — through the use of price supports and loan guarantees. The House measure authorized $3 billion for price supports and placed no ceiling on other expenditures, such as loans and loan guarantees. Congress retained the power to review large loan and purchase contracts.

HR 3930 also extended the Defense Production Act for one year, to Sept. 30, 1980. That law gave the president broad authority to purchase and sell critical materials and encourage their location and production.

The House then substituted HR 3930 for the text of S 932, a bill simply extending the Defense Production Act for two years. The Senate had routinely passed S 932 (S Rept 96-166) June 20.

Senate Action

Because the Senate had never considered the synthetic fuel issue, it decided to refer S 932 as amended by the House to committee. Two Senate committees — Banking and Energy — had jurisdiction over synthetic fuels. On Oct. 30, 1979, they jointly reported two very different versions of the synthetic fuels bill (S 932 — S Rept 96-387).

The Energy Committee basically embraced the Carter administration's idea of a crash program with heavy government involvement. But the Banking Committee soundly rejected it, preferring to use only limited government funds to spur development of synfuels by private industry.

Energy agreed to establish a synthetic fuels corporation, similar to the one Carter proposed, that could own or operate plants if the corporation decided that was necessary to promote synfuels. But of the $88 billion requested by Carter, only $20 billion was authorized in the first phase. After three years, if Congress did not object, the other $68 billion would be provided.

The Banking Committee decided the special corporation was not needed and instead gave the president authority to decide how to distribute the financial assistance. Only $3 billion to $9 billion in government funds would be available, primarily for loans, loan guarantees and price supports. The Banking version did not permit the government to own or operate synfuels plants.

Neither committee tied the synfuels program to the windfall profits tax, providing that other sources of funds would be used to spur synfuels production.

The full Senate adopted the Energy Committee's version of S 932, approving it Nov. 8, 1979, by a vote of 65-19. The Senate rejected the Banking Committee's bill Nov. 7 by a vote of 37-57. Before passing S 932, the Senate converted it into a $39 billion, multi-purpose measure, adding provisions to spur energy conservation, the use of solar energy and the production of gasohol.

In addition to authorizing the $20 billion synthetic fuels program, the Senate bill provided $6.2 billion for gasohol, $5.75 billion for conservation and $2 billion for solar, wind and geothermal energy development.

Conference, Final Action

House and Senate conferees began work on the synthetic fuels bill before Christmas 1979, but did not complete their task before the recess. They did reach general agreement, however, on the outlines of the final legislation, agreeing to provide an initial $20 billion for synthetic fuels development and to set up the special corporation to manage the program.

Because the House had approved its synfuels bill before Carter announced his proposal — and because the House had never passed solar and conservation bank measures like those included in S 932 — House conferees did a lot of original work during the House-Senate conference. (A House committee had reported a solar and conservation bank bill (HR 605 — H Rept 96-625) but that measure had not come before the full House.)

Conferees completed action June 16, 1980, and filed their report (H Rept 96-1104, S Rept 96-824) June 19. The Senate immediately approved the report June 19 by a vote of 78-12. The House cleared the measure a week later, on June 26, adopting it by a vote of 317-93.

Provisions

PL 96-294, the Energy Security Act, contained eight titles.

Title I — Synthetic Fuels

PL 96-294 authorized creation of the United States Synthetic Fuels Corporation.

The corporation would be funded at the $20 billion level through federal purchases of its notes and obligations. It would be run by a seven-member board of directors, nominated by the president and confirmed by the Senate. The chairman would serve full-time, but the other directors could work only part-time for the corporation. The president could remove a board member, but only for neglect of duty or malfeasance. The normal term would be seven years.

The board would be required to have open meetings, though meetings could be closed to negotiate contracts or if information disclosed would affect financial markets adversely. Board members and top officials would have to comply with financial disclosure provisions of the Ethics in Government Act of 1978 (PL 95-521).

Up to 300 employees could be hired by the corporation. The usual Civil Service rules about government personnel would not apply. The corporation was authorized to spend $35 million a year on administrative expenses and $10 million on contracts. An inspector general, who would oversee the corporation, was authorized to spend $2 million a year.

The corporation would be advised by a committee composed of the secretaries of defense, Treasury, interior and energy; the administrator of the Environmental Protection Agency and the chairman of the proposed energy mobilization board. (The board was not authorized.)

The corporation's major purpose was to use price guarantees, purchase agreements and loan guarantees to encourage private industry to produce the equivalent of at least 500,000 barrels a day of crude oil by 1987, increasing to 2 million barrels a day by 1992.

The corporation was required to submit to Congress, for its approval by joint resolution, its comprehensive strategy for attaining that goal. The plan was due four years after the corporation was established.

Synthetic fuels were defined as substitutes for natural gas or petroleum made from coal (including lignite and peat), shale, tar sands (including heavy oil) and hydrogen from water. Also eligible for subsidies would be facilities mixing coal and oil.

Financial assistance would be available for:
- Construction of production facilities.
- Land and mineral rights required for use in connection with a plant.
- Equipment used to extract minerals for conversion to synthetic fuels from either a mine located next to a plant or located elsewhere if no other source of the mineral for the plant were available.
- Transportation facilities, electric power plants, transmission lines or other equipment necessary to the project.

To encourage synfuels production, the corporation could offer price guarantees, purchase agreements and loan guarantees covering up to 75 percent of estimated cost.

If those financial incentives were not adequate, the board could agree to contribute up to 60 percent of the cost of joint industry-government ventures or provide loans, which normally could cover up to 49 percent of the estimated project cost. But if necessary to insure financial viability, loans for up to 75 percent of estimated costs could be provided.

If the corporation were unable to spur private industry to produce synfuels, the board could hire contractors to build and operate as many as three government-owned synfuels plants.

The corporation also could provide financial assistance for two synfuels projects located outside the United States but in the Western Hemisphere. The resource used in the plant would have to be available in the United States, but could not be close to commercial production in the United States as a synthetic fuel. That requirement was designed to ensure that the technology developed at the plant could eventually be used in the United States. The host country would have to contribute financial aid and the fuel produced by the plant would have to be available on equitable terms to the United States.

After Sept. 30, 1992, the corporation could no longer obligate funds. Its operations would end by Sept. 30, 1997.

Defense Production Act

Until the corporation was operational, the authority to encourage production of synthetic fuels would rest with the president. Under an amendment to the Defense Production Act of 1950 (PL 81-774) included in PL 96-294, he could delegate to the Department of Defense and other agencies authority to stimulate synfuels production to meet national defense needs.

After the corporation was in operation, this presidential authority would revert to standby status. It could be invoked in an energy shortage that threatened supplies needed for national defense.

Title II — Biomass, Alcohol Fuels, Urban Waste

PL 96-294 authorized a new $1.2 billion program to promote production of alcohol and other fuels from biomass, which included crops and crop residues, timber and timber waste and animal waste. The program was to be jointly administered by the departments of Agriculture and Energy.

The energy and agriculture secretaries would have to submit by Jan. 1, 1982, a plan for achieving a production level of at least 60,000 barrels a day of alcohol by the end of 1982. The goal for 1990 was that alcohol fuel production equal at least 10 percent of domestic gasoline consumption.

The agriculture and energy secretaries each were authorized to distribute $600 million in loans, loan guarantees, price guarantees and purchase agreements.

Facilities that used agriculture and forestry resources and were expected to produce less than 15 million gallons of alcohol fuels per year would receive their aid from the Agriculture Department.

Projects producing more than 15 million gallons a year using forestry resources, or using agricultural resources and owned and operated by cooperatives, could be funded by either agency, subject to approval by the other agency. All other plants producing more than 15 million gallons a year would be the responsibility of the Energy Department.

Urban Waste

The bill required that a new Office of Energy from Municipal Waste be established within the Energy Department to continue and expand existing programs to produce energy from urban waste. Financial assistance of $250 million was authorized for those projects. The aid would be provided in the form of price supports or loans and loan guarantees for up to 75 percent of the cost of a project.

Title III — Energy Targets

PL 96-294 directed the president to submit annually a set of targets for the nation's consumption and production of energy for the years 1985, 1990, 1995 and 2000. The House and Senate would be required to vote on the nonbinding targets during consideration of the annual Energy Department authorization bill.

Title IV — Renewable Energy

PL 96-294 directed the energy secretary to prepare a plan within one year for demonstrating energy self-sufficiency in one or more states through the use of renewable energy resources. An authorization of $10 million was provided.

The Public Utility Regulatory Policies Act of 1978 (PL 95-617) was amended to increase the size of small-scale hydropower plants eligible for federal loans from 15 megawatts to 30 megawatts. In addition, the energy secretary was required to promulgate regulations to carry out the 1978 act within six months of enactment of the 1980 law. The existing authorization of $110 million was extended for each of fiscal years 1981 and 1982.

Title V — Solar Energy and Energy Conservation

PL 96-294 established a Solar Energy and Conservation Bank within the Department of Housing and Urban Development (HUD) to provide subsidized loans to persons or companies making energy conservation improvements or installing solar equipment in residential or commercial buildings.

The bank, authorized through Sept. 30, 1987, would have the same corporate powers as the Government National Mortgage Association. The bank was authorized to spend $2.5 billion in fiscal years 1981 through 1984 for conservation and $525 million in fiscal years 1981 through 1983 for solar energy.

The bank would have a president, an executive vice president for energy conservation and an executive vice president for solar energy. It would be governed by a board of directors chaired by the HUD secretary and composed of the secretaries of energy, Treasury, agriculture and commerce.

Local financial institutions that agreed to provide loans at interest rates below the market level or who agreed to reduce the principal on the loans would receive payments from the bank.

Eligibility for the subsidy and the level of subsidy would depend on the type of structure and the income level of the applicant.

Conservation

The subsidy for conservation improvement loans would be limited to owners or tenants of existing residences with one to four units whose household income did not exceed 150 percent of the area's median income level.

The maximum subsidy for a borrower whose income was 80 percent or less of the median would be 50 percent of the cost of the improvements — up to $1,250 for a single family dwelling and up to $3,500 for a four-unit building. A borrower whose income was 120 percent to 150 percent of the median could be subsidized for only 20 percent of his costs, up to $500 for a single family house or up to $1,440 for a four-family building.

Owners of larger multi-family or commercial buildings could receive up to 20 percent of their conservation improvement costs, with a cap on the subsidy of $400 per unit of multi-family dwellings and $5,000 for a commercial building.

The bill specified that at least 15 percent of the funds authorized for conservation ($375 million) be used to assist owners or tenants in existing buildings whose income did not exceed 80 percent of the area median income. In addition to qualifying for loans, those persons would be eligible for direct grants. No grant, however, would be available unless the total conservation expenditure exceeded $250.

Solar Energy

Aid for solar energy equipment was made available to all income levels, though a larger subsidy was provided for lower-income households.

For residences with one to four units, the maximum subsidy would be 60 percent of cost for owners with income less than 80 percent of their area's median income; 50 percent for those with an income between 80 and 160 percent of the median and 40 percent of the cost for owners whose income exceeded 160 percent of the median.

For a single-family dwelling, the maximum subsidy would be $5,000; for two-unit buildings, $7,500; for three- to four-unit buildings, $10,000; and for buildings with more than four units, $2,500 per unit or 40 percent of costs, whichever was less.

Synfuels Directors Given Recess Appointments After Republican Senators Block Confirmation

Late in 1980 President Carter gave recess appointments to his nominees for chairman and members of the board of directors of the multi-million-dollar Synthetic Fuels Corp. after Senate Republicans blocked their confirmation by threat of filibuster.

Although they could legally hold the positions through 1981 under the recess appointments, the Carter appointees indicated they would submit their resignations if and when the new Republican president, Ronald Reagan, chose to replace them.

After a long search, and after several candidates reportedly turned down the post, Carter Sept. 10 nominated Deputy Energy Secretary John C. Sawhill to be the corporation's chief executive officer and chairman of the board.

Sawhill, who had served as president of New York University before accepting the Energy Department post, was head of the Federal Energy Administration under Presidents Nixon and Ford.

On Sept. 13 Carter named six directors: AFL-CIO President Lane Kirkland; Interior Secretary Cecil D. Andrus; Frank Savage, Equitable Life Assurance Society vice president; Frank T. Cary, chairman of International Business Machines Corp. (IBM); Catherine Cleary, professor of business administration at the University of Wisconsin and former chairman of First Wisconsin Trust Co. of Milwaukee, and John D. deButts, retired chairman of American Telephone & Telegraph Co. (Cary subsequently withdrew rather than disclose his finances, as required of executive branch nominees.)

The Senate Energy Committee approved the nominations Sept. 25 by a 12-6 vote. The vote came after the White House had rejected a Republican proposal to confirm only Sawhill and three other directors. That would give the corporation a quorum to start work but would preserve three nominations for Reagan, if he were elected president, argued the Republicans, led by Sen. Mark O. Hatfield, Ore. If Carter rejected the proposal, the Republicans said, they would filibuster to block his nominations.

Although the White House reportedly was preparing to accept the proposal, before the nominations were called up Oct. 1 the compromise fell apart when Sen. Gary Hart, D-Colo., said he also would filibuster the nominations unless Carter agreed to name a Westerner to replace Cary. Of the original seven appointments, only Andrus, a former Idaho governor, was from the West, the region where most synthetic fuels development was expected to occur.

With the president out of town campaigning, the White House was unable to make a commitment in time to prevent the collapse of the compromise, and the nominations were pulled from the calendar.

On Oct. 5 Carter gave recess appointments to Sawhill and the five directors. All except Andrus assumed office immediately, and the board held its first meeting Oct. 8.

The Energy Department had said quick board action was necessary in order to solicit contracts by Nov. 30, the date set by the synfuels law, and to let contracts for synthetic fuels projects before the end of the year.

As required by law, Carter resubmitted the nominations after Congress returned from its election recess Nov. 12, but the Senate never considered them during the lame-duck session.

Commercial buildings, including some agricultural buildings, could receive subsidies of up to 40 percent of costs or $100,000, whichever was less.

Builders could receive subsidies of up to 40 percent of costs or the limits per unit specified by owners.

Residential Energy Efficiency

The energy secretary was authorized to set up four demonstration programs of new approaches to energy conservation.

Interested state or local governments and utilities could contract with one or more independent energy conservation companies, which would be paid an amount equal to the value of energy saved because of residential conservation improvements. The conservation companies would do house-by-house, block-by-block inspections and prescribe improvements designed to save energy.

Utilities would then pay for the recommended energy-saving equipment based on energy saved by the improvements. Utilities would be expected to participate because the conservation efforts would reduce the amount of electrical generating capacity required by the utility's customers, thus theoretically reducing the utility's operating and capital costs. Paying for the conservation equipment was expected to be cheaper than building new power plants.

In case the program did not work as planned, state and local governments would back up the utility with a total of $10 million in federal funds authorized for fiscal 1981 and 1982.

Utility Residential Conservation

The National Energy Conservation Policy Act (PL 95-619) was amended to remove a prohibition on utility financing of residential energy conservation improvements.

The utilities also could provide and install the conservation equipment as long as they subcontracted the work to qualified independent firms.

Auditor Training

The energy secretary was authorized to make grants to states to support programs to train and certify energy auditors, who would inspect residential and commercial buildings and evaluate energy use. Authorizations of $10 million for fiscal 1981 and $15 million for fiscal 1982 were provided.

Industrial Conservation

The energy secretary was authorized to provide financial aid to industry for research, development and demonstration of energy productivity in industry. Authorization of $40 million in each of fiscal years 1981 and 1982 was provided.

Title VI — Geothermal Energy

PL 96-294 authorized the energy secretary to provide financial assistance for exploration and confirmation of geothermal reservoirs and for construction of specific geothermal projects that would tap the energy from heat trapped underground. For fiscal 1981 through 1985, $85 million in loans and loan guarantees was authorized for geothermal reservoir confirmation. For fiscal 1981, $5 million was authorized to finance feasibility studies.

Title VII — Studies

Acid Rain

PL 96-294 required the creation of a task force to plan a 10-year program to identify the causes and effects of acid precipitation. The task force would be headed by the administrators of the National Oceanic and Atmospheric Administration (NOAA) and the agriculture secretary. Funding of $5 million for the initial task force activities was provided to NOAA. Subsequent authorizations would be required to carry out the study.

Carbon Dioxide

The Office of Science and Technology Policy was directed to collaborate with the National Academy of Sciences on a study of the impact of fossil fuel combustion, coal conversion, synthetic fuels production and other sources on the level of carbon dioxide in the atmosphere. The study also would consider the effect of any increase in the carbon dioxide level. The report would be due to Congress in three years. An authorization of $3 million was provided.

Title VIII — Strategic Petroleum Reserve

PL 96-294 directed the president to begin by Oct. 1, 1980, filling the Strategic Petroleum Reserve at a rate that would average 100,000 barrels a day. If the president did not comply with the directive, the government could not sell oil produced from the federally owned fields at Elk Hills, Calif., and Teapot Dome, Wyo., and instead would have to put it into the reserve. Stopping the sale of that oil would result in a loss of federal revenues of $2 billion a year.

The Energy Policy and Conservation Act of 1975 (PL 94-163) was amended to allow the government to buy oil at a cheaper price. Oil bought for the reserve was exempted from the federal "entitlements" program set up by the 1975 law. The effect would be that instead of paying up to $35 per barrel the government could pay as little as $7 a barrel. The entitlements program required refineries with access to lower priced oil still under domestic controls to pay into a fund that was distributed to refiners whose supplies were more expensive. The special treatment for the reserve would be valid only until Oct. 1, 1981, the expiration date of the entitlements program and all domestic price controls on oil.

Energy Mobilization Board

The 96th Congress rejected the third major prong of President Carter's three-part energy package — creation of a special energy mobilization board to speed high-priority energy projects through legal and bureaucratic red tape.

Legislation creating the board (S 1308) was approved by both chambers in 1979, and the final version of the Priority Energy Project Act was reported by conferees in June 1980.

But on June 27, an unusual coalition of House Republicans and liberal Democrats killed the bill, voting 232-131 to return it to conference.

S 1308 would set up a board to speed government decisions related to energy projects. If a government agency dawdled and missed a deadline set by the board, the board could act in its place. Judicial review of decisions sanctioned by the board was limited. And laws passed after

A Slow Start on a Strategic Oil Reserve

A freshman senator's persistence and a veteran representative's strategic skill helped in 1980 to renew the life of the nation's faltering plan to stockpile oil for use in an emergency.

In 1975, Congress approved creation of a strategic petroleum reserve, a stockpile of one billion barrels of oil for use in a national energy emergency, such as the Arab oil embargo of 1973-74. Authority for the reserve was contained in the 1975 Energy Policy and Conservation Act (PL 94-163).

In the first year of the Carter administration, plans for the reserve were reflected in the administration's request of $3 billion in appropriations for purchase of the oil. Congress responded by providing $2.8 billion. The administration also indicated to Congress that it planned to speed the pace of acquisition of oil for the stockpile, planning to have 500 million barrels in place by the end of 1980, instead of by late 1982, as the Ford administration had planned.

In 1978 those plans were frustrated. Although Congress appropriated an additional $3 billion for the reserve, purchases of oil for the stockpile were halted altogether late in the year. The generally tight oil market, stretched even further by the Iranian revolution and the disruption of oil supplies from Iran, pushed prices up and the government found it difficult to locate oil to purchase.

In 1979, work on the reserve remained at a standstill. Concerned about the situation, two senators, Republican Robert Dole, Kan., and freshman Democrat Bill Bradley, N.J., proposed an amendment to S 932, the synthetic fuels measure working its way through the Senate. The amendment, which the Senate approved despite opposition from the Carter administration, required the government to resume putting oil into the reserve at a rate of 100,000 barrels a day.

Despite the Senate directives, Carter early in 1980 cut $600 million in outlays earmarked for buying oil for the strategic reserve. The administration cut was indicated in its revised budget requests submitted to Congress in March. Budget documents stated that more than $2.2 billion in budget authority for the reserve was left over from previous years.

Saudi Opposition

Saudi opposition to U.S. government purchases for the reserve played a part in the administration's decision to delay the resumption of oil purchases. Saudi officials worried that additional U.S. purchases for the reserve would increase demand for oil. Then it would be more difficult for the Saudis to resist price hikes sought by others within the Organization of Petroleum Exporting Countries.

Saudi officials also were concerned that U.S. conservation efforts might lag if the reserve were available.

Energy Secretary Charles W. Duncan Jr. went to Saudi Arabia in March to discuss the reserve and other issues with Sheik Ahmed Zaki Yamani, the Saudi oil minister. But Yamani reiterated his country's earlier-stated intention to cut production by as much as one billion barrels a day if the reserve were filled.

Bradley went to the Middle East in April and returned convinced that the advantages of the reserve far outweighed any disadvantages. The probability of an interruption in oil supplies in the next few years, Bradley said, made the reserve essential to the nation's energy security.

Even if the Saudis did cut back, Bradley said, filling the reserve would help the Saudis "understand that we know what our national security interest is, articulate it and accept the consequences. And in future dealings, I think it might strengthen the relationship."

Directive Issued

While the synfuels measure was being put into final form by conferees, veteran House legislator John D. Dingell, D-Mich., suggested a device to make it costly for the executive to ignore the directive that it resume filling the national reserve.

Conferees approved language contained in PL 96-294, the final version of the measure, which informed the government that if it did not resume filling the national petroleum reserve at a rate of 100,000 barrels per day after Oct. 1, 1980, it would have to stop producing oil from naval petroleum reserves at Elk Hills, Calif., and Teapot Dome, Wyo. To halt that production — and the sale of that oil — would cost the government more than $2 billion a year.

Any lapse in filling the reserve would trigger the halt of production from the government fields, at least until 500 million barrels had been placed in the reserves.

As of September 1980, only 92 million barrels of oil — two weeks worth of oil imports — were stored in the deep caverns in Louisiana used for the stockpile.

In August the federal government asked the oil industry to bid on an oil-swapping scheme to fill the reserves. In return for oil that the companies would place in the reserves, they could get oil from the Elk Hills field. Energy Department officials even indicated that it might be possible, depending upon market conditions, to fill the reserve even more quickly than Congress directed, at rates as high as 250,000 barrels per day.

a project was under way could not be used to block the project.

The major objection raised to the conference version by Republicans was the fear that the board would override state's rights and prerogatives. Liberal Democrats, on the other hand, objected to the board as having too much power to override environmental laws.

The action sent the measure back to a House-Senate conference committee to be rewritten with the threats to state and local laws deleted. That was its last gasp in the 96th Congress.

Senate Action

The Senate approved creation of an energy mobilization board Oct. 4, 1979. The wide margin in favor of S 1308 (S Rept 96-331) reflected the consensus of the Senate that the nation's need to develop new sources of energy was sufficiently compelling to merit special treatment outside the regular system of laws and procedures.

The Senate bill was quite similar to Carter's original proposal, and the vote approving the energy mobilization board was a major victory for President Carter. "That vote represents a major step forward in the joint effort of the Congress and my administration to achieve energy security for our nation," he said.

Opponents of the board — an unusual coalition of liberals and conservatives — warned that it would ignore environmental dangers and trample states' rights. Edmund S. Muskie, D-Maine, called it an "unprecedented intrusion into state and local prerogatives to protect the health and safety of citizens."

But the opponents failed in several efforts to curb the board's powers, which included authority to act in place of federal, state and local agencies in certain instances and to modify procedures in federal, state and local laws.

Members of the Senate Energy Committee, deeply split in the past on many energy issues, were strongly united in support of their bill. Their votes were a key reason for the roughly 20-vote margin by which repeated attempts to weaken the board were defeated.

Committee solidarity was also important in defeating a proposal to authorize the president, upon recommendation from the board, to override any substantive federal law. That amendment was rejected by a vote of 37-56.

The Senate Board

Under the Senate bill, sponsors of energy projects could apply to the four-member energy mobilization board for special status. The board could choose projects that would "reduce U.S. dependence on insecure foreign oil or petroleum products." But there were no other limits placed on which projects could be given priority status.

The board would have the power to set deadlines for federal, state and local agencies faced with priority project decisions, such as whether to grant a zoning variance or an air pollution permit. The board also could alter procedural aspects of federal, state and local laws, such as the amount of time set aside for public hearings, but not substantive provisions, such as air quality standards. The board chairman would have the power to act alone, except in designating priority projects.

If an agency missed a deadline, the federal board could step in and make the decision for the agency, applying the relevant federal, state or local law. However, an agency

decision not to allow a project to proceed could not be overruled by the board.

House Action

After two days of dickering, the House Nov. 1, 1979, approved a measure (HR 4985) creating an energy mobilization board similar to that sought by President Carter.

By a 299-107 vote, the House agreed to set up the powerful new agency to speed construction of pipelines, refineries, synthetic fuels plants and other energy projects.

The House action was a victory for the president. But the "fast track" board created by the House was even more powerful than the panel sought by Carter.

Majority Leader Jim Wright, D-Texas, said the strong board would help Congress get rid of unnecessary regulations written by bureaucrats who had "a thirst to write laws without the inconvenience of running for Congress."

But Interior Committee Chairman Morris K. Udall, D-Ariz., criticized the measure. "This bill is a formula for dismantling the environmental, health and safety laws put together in the appropriate committees in this Congress in the past 20 years," he said.

Strong vs. Weak Board

The House had originally faced two dramatically different versions of the energy mobilization board. One, reported Sept. 21 by the House Commerce Committee (H Rept 96-410, Part 2), provided for an extremely powerful board. The other, reported Aug. 2 by the House Interior Committee (H Rept 96-410, Part 1), created a far weaker board.

Commerce's original, powerful board would have been authorized to recommend to the president waiver of substantive and procedural federal, state and local laws. The president could waive almost any law as long as either house of Congress did not object.

The Commerce version was strongly opposed by the National Governors' Association and other local government organizations and by the major environmental groups.

The Interior Committee, however, had taken a different approach, allowing no waiver of substantive laws. Only time requirements could be waived and that would require concurrence from both houses of Congress. The president could act in place of tardy federal agencies, but not for state and local agencies. The Carter administration opposed this measure as too weak.

Both bills were modified when their sponsors realized the majority of the House preferred a board weaker than the Commerce version, but stronger than the one set up by Interior.

The House rejected the modified Interior department bill Nov. 1 by a vote of 192-215. The same day, the House also rejected an amendment to the Commerce bill that would have barred waiver of substantive federal law. That amendment was rejected by a key vote of 153-250.

House Board's Powers

The five-member board approved by the House could give priority status to an unlimited number of energy projects seeking expedited treatment. The board would have authority to act in place of federal, state and local agencies that did not meet deadlines for making decisions related to priority projects.

The board would also have sweeping power over federal law. If a federal law were blocking a priority project, the board could recommend that it be waived. If the president agreed and both the House and Senate voted for the waiver, the federal law simply would not be applied to that project.

The waiver was directed primarily at environmental laws, such as those governing air, water and toxic substances. The bill specified that certain other laws, such as those covering labor, water rights and civil rights, could not be waived.

The Carter administration did not ask for a waiver of substantive law, but it did not mount a major lobbying offensive against that provision in the House. Bert Carp, a top White House aide, said the administration would ask House-Senate conferees to strike the federal substantive waiver.

Conference Action

Conferees began work on the bill Nov. 13, 1979, and filed their report June 21, 1980 (H Rept 96-1119).

In between, the conference was stalemated for months over the issue of whether the board could waive the substantive provisions of existing laws that would hinder construction of a priority energy project.

Industry associations and company officials made a strong lobbying push for a powerful energy mobilization board with authority to waive existing laws. Environmental and citizens' groups were just as determined to defeat or weaken the waiver provision, and the conflict was reflected in the conference's indecision.

That deadlock was broken when the conferees agreed April 23 by a 9-8 vote to accept a compromise proposed by the House.

Under the final plan, the three-member board and the president could ask Congress to exempt a project from laws blocking energy construction projects. If the committees with jurisdiction over the law to be waived agreed, then both houses would have a chance to vote on the waiver.

If both chambers agreed within 60 days and the president signed the measure, the exception would become law. In a two-year congressional session, only 12 projects would be eligible for waivers.

Laws passed after construction of a project began could be waived by the board without congressional involvement. The board also could force federal, state and local agencies to make timely decisions and streamline procedures.

Final Action

The House rejected the conference report on a vote of 232-131.

Although some objected to the bill because of its potential impact on states' rights and the environment, many of the 125 Republican votes against the conference version reportedly were cast to embarrass Carter and boost the presidential campaign of Ronald Reagan, who had announced his opposition to the board.

The adverse House vote sent the report back to a conference committee with instructions to revise the bill to prohibit any waiver, by the board or Congress, of existing state or local laws, even those derived from federal laws. And it instructed conferees to require that Congress approve any waiver of future laws, as well as of existing laws.

No further action was taken on the bill and it died at the end of the 96th Congress.

Nuclear Power

Congress in 1980 gave President Carter the go-ahead to reorganize the Nuclear Regulatory Commission. And it approved the first changes in federal law reflecting increased national concern over nuclear safety after the 1979 accident at Three Mile Island. In addition, Congress approved a new federal push to develop nuclear fusion as a source of energy.

But it was unable to resolve conclusively the increasingly serious issue of nuclear waste disposal. Congress gave to the states responsibility for taking care of nuclear waste from power plants and industry but was unable to reach agreement on the more difficult issue of how to dispose of spent nuclear fuel and the wastes generated from reprocessing nuclear fuel.

Nuclear Regulatory Funds 1980

Almost a year late, Congress in June 1980 sent to the White House a bill (S 562 — PL 96-295) authorizing $426.8 million for the Nuclear Regulatory Commission (NRC) in fiscal 1980. PL 96-295 also contained the first statutory reforms concerning nuclear power plant safety since the March 1979 accident at the Three Mile Island nuclear plant.

PL 96-295 made plain the feeling of Congress that all states should have federally approved plans for responding to emergencies such as the Three Mile Island incident. The law forbade the NRC to issue any new operating licenses to power plants in any state that lacked such a plan.

The law also required the NRC to develop a plan for a federal response to such a crisis and standards requiring that all new power plants be located a certain distance from large population centers. In addition, the measure substantially increased the penalties that could be imposed upon plant operators who violated safety regulations, removing the existing ceiling of $25,000 per month in fines for such violations.

S 562 was approved by the Senate in mid-1979 and the House in December 1979. Final action was delayed for six more months, however, as conferees wrangled over a Senate provision requiring the shut-down of all nuclear power plants in states lacking approved plans for dealing with a nuclear plant emergency.

Senate Action

The Senate July 17, 1979, approved the NRC authorization bill (S 562 — S Rept 96-176), allowing appropriation of up to $398.3 million for the commission in fiscal 1980.

As approved by the Senate, S 562 included language requiring the NRC, by June 1, 1980, to shut down nuclear plants in states without approved emergency evacuation plans for use in case of a nuclear accident.

Senate critics of the measure, working with the nuclear industry, tried three times to defeat the shut-down requirement. But each time they narrowly lost to a bipartisan majority that wanted to force states to devise emergency plans.

However, supporters of nuclear power did succeed in defeating, by a vote of 35-57, the proposal for a six-month moratorium on construction of new nuclear plants. And, by a vote of 55-37, the Senate agreed to table a proposal

Reorganizing the NRC

With congressional approval, President Carter in 1980 reorganized the Nuclear Regulatory Commission to place more authority in the hands of its chairman. This restructuring was Carter's solution to the problems that had impeded the NRC from responding effectively to the Three Mile Island accident in 1979.

In October 1979, the Kemeny Commission, which Carter had appointed to investigate the accident, called for the abolition of the NRC. Carter answered in December 1979 with some less drastic proposals, which were set out in detail in Reorganization Plan No. 1 for 1980, sent to Congress in March 1980.

Even before proposing the reorganization at the NRC, Carter had removed Joseph H. Hendrie as chairman. Hendrie, whom Carter had placed on the commission as chairman in 1977, remained a member. As acting chairman, Carter chose John Ahearne, a former Energy Department official whom Carter had appointed to the NRC in 1978.

Carter in 1980 nominated Harvard professor Albert Carnesale to a vacant seat on the NRC, indicating that he would name him its chairman once he was confirmed. But political considerations in an election year worked against Carnesale's confirmation, and the seat remained vacant for most of 1980. Ahearne continued to act as chairman through the last months of the Carter administration.

Reorganization Approved

Reorganization Plan No. 1 substantially upgraded the authority of the NRC chairman, making clear that he was the principal executive officer and spokesman for the commission. The plan further authorized the chairman to act for the commission in an emergency.

Carter modified his initial proposals, sending amendments to the plan to Congress in May. Those amendments were in response to criticism that the chairman would wield too much power, leaving little for the other members of the commission to do. The amendments clarified the roles that the other commissioners would have.

Had Congress wished to block the proposed changes, it would have had to demonstrate its disapproval by June 11.

On May 22, the Senate tacitly gave its approval to the plan when the Senate Governmental Affairs Committee recommended against passage of a resolution of disapproval (S Res 397 — S Rept 96-790).

A week later, on May 30, the House by voice vote rejected a resolution (H Res 624 — H Rept 96-1043) disapproving the plan.

to give each state a veto over storage of nuclear waste within its boundaries.

House Action

The House Dec. 4, 1979, approved its version of the 1980 NRC authorization bill after rejecting a proposed six-month halt in the construction of new reactors. As approved by the House, S 562 (HR 2608 — H Rept 96-194, Parts I, II) authorized $426.8 million in appropriations, $28.5 million more than the Senate version.

The House rejected the moratorium amendment Nov. 29 by a vote of 135-254, a wide enough margin to discourage James Weaver, D-Ore., from offering an amendment, as he had planned, to prohibit the NRC from issuing operating licenses to new reactors in states without approved emergency plans. The House did add language to the bill requiring the NRC to report which of the nation's 70 operating nuclear power plants were not in compliance with existing safety rules and standards.

Final Action

Conferees finally dropped the plant shut-down requirement but adopted in its place the prohibition on operating licenses for new plants located in states lacking emergency plans. That compromise was then further watered down by the addition of language allowing a local government or utility to submit an emergency plan for federal approval if a state government refused to do so. If that plan was approved, operating licenses could be issued for new plants in that state.

Conferees filed their report (H Rept 96-1070) June 4, 1980. The House adopted it June 10 and the Senate approved it June 16, clearing the bill for the president.

Provisions

As signed into law, PL 96-295 authorized a total of $426,821,000 in fiscal 1980 for the NRC. Within that grand total, $213 million was allocated to nuclear regulatory research, $66.5 million to nuclear reactor regulation, $15.9 million to standards development, $42.4 million to inspection and enforcement, $32.4 million to nuclear materials safety and safeguards, $18.1 million to program technical support, and $38.4 million to program administration and direction.

In addition, PL 96-295 contained provisions that:

● Required that no new operating licenses be issued in a state unless the state had an NRC-approved plan for evacuations and other steps in case of a nuclear emergency. If a state were uncooperative, then a utility could draft an emergency response plan and submit it to the NRC for approval. The NRC was directed to write standards that states and utilities would follow in drafting their plans.

● Required the NRC to develop by Sept. 30, 1980, a plan for federal government response to nuclear accidents.

● Required that a proposed reactor meet new federal standards for siting away from population centers before it could be issued a construction permit. The NRC was directed to write the standards, which would have to specify allowable population density and other criteria.

● Directed the NRC to list for Congress all safety-related rules and regulations that were not being met by individual nuclear reactors.

● Made it a federal crime to sabotage nuclear facilities or murder, assault, intimidate or otherwise interfere with NRC personnel on a project licensed by the NRC.

● Set criminal penalties of $25,000 a day or two years in jail for any director, officer or employee of a firm constructing or supplying components of a nuclear facility who knowingly and willfully violated the Atomic Energy Act. On a second conviction, the fine would increase to $50,000 a day.

● Authorized the NRC to assume control of emergency response actions, thus pre-empting state responsibility, if the NRC determined that a state had failed to protect the public health and safety. However, conferees stated in the report that they intended the NRC to exercise that authority "only as a last resort."

● Increased civil penalties for safety violations at nuclear plants from $5,000 to $100,000 per violation. The cap in existing law of $25,000 in fines per month was removed.

● Exempted from the Freedom of Information Act any nuclear data whose release "could reasonably be expected to have a significant adverse effect on health and safety of the public."

● Required the NRC to notify governors in advance of shipments of nuclear wastes through their states except when shipments would not pose a hazard to public health and safety because of the type of waste or quantity.

● Prohibited the storage of any nuclear wastes in oceans.

● Required the NRC to develop within six months a plan for improving operator training.

1981 NRC Funds

Congress adjourned in 1980 without completing action on the fiscal 1981 authorization bill for the Nuclear Regulatory Commission (NRC).

The Senate easily approved its version (S 2358 — S Rept 96-767) of the $445 million measure July 31. But the House never considered its version (HR 6628). That bill had been reported by both the House Interior Committee and the House Interstate and Foreign Commerce Committee (H Rept 96-990, Parts I and II).

A main point of contention appeared to be whether the NRC should provide funding to public interest groups, individuals and others who wished to intervene in NRC licensing and rule-making procedures. The Senate and the House Interior Committee rejected the administration's request for a demonstration intervenor program; the House Commerce Committee supported the proposal.

Nuclear Waste Disposal

Unable to reach agreement upon a national policy for disposing of nuclear waste, the 96th Congress late in 1980 passed the task of finding a solution to the 97th Congress. As a step in that direction, Congress in December 1980 approved legislation (S 2189 — PL 96-573) giving the states the primary responsibility for disposing of low-level radioactive wastes.

Low-level wastes were produced by power plants, hospitals and industrial plants in every state. They could be paper, plastics, construction materials, tools, clothing, vials or other items contaminated by radioactivity. The term "low-level" was in some sense misleading, for it referred to the source of the radioactivity, not the degree of radioactivity of the waste. Low-level waste was the phrase used to describe all radioactive waste except that produced in nuclear reactors or in the reprocessing of nuclear fuels.

Background

When the 96th Congress convened, both the nuclear industry and its critics were hoping that the legislators would act to resolve some of the long-standing questions regarding the future of nuclear power. One of those key issues was nuclear waste. Despite decade-old accumulations of nuclear waste materials, the nation was still without any comprehensive policy to guide the management or long-term storage of those hazardous substances. Most of those wastes were stored in 1980 in pools of water at the reactor sites where they were produced.

The Three Mile Island nuclear accident in March 1979 rearranged any plans the 1979 session had for considering nuclear waste disposal, but late in that year the Senate Energy Committee ordered reported legislation (S 2189 — S Rept 96-548) calculated to force action on the matter. As reported, S 2189 required the Energy Department to find a site and produce a design for a long-term nuclear waste storage facility within one year of the bill's enactment. *(1979 action, p. 213)*

High-Level Waste: 1980 Stalemate

In mid-summer 1980, the Senate approved S 2189, which directed the federal government to build aboveground vaults in which high-level radioactive waste could be stored for as long as a century. The Senate bill, approved July 30 by a vote of 88-7, was backed by the nuclear industry and utilities. It was clearly a temporary solution to the problem of containing those wastes, most of which would remain active for hundreds of years.

S 2189 provided for federal storage of spent nuclear fuel produced by commercial reactors at sites away from those reactors. It also gave the states the power to veto a federal decision to deposit such waste within the state's boundaries, so long as one chamber of Congress agreed with the state's opposition. If the waste involved was generated by military nuclear activities, however, and the president decided that storage in a particular state was essential to the national security, a state's veto of that decision would hold only if it was supported by both chambers of Congress.

S 2189 stated that federal policy was to require each state to be responsible for the low-level waste generated by non-federal activities within its borders. The bill suggested that states might enter into compacts or other regional agreements for developing multi-state plans and facilities for disposing of such waste.

House Action

Three House committees — Science, Commerce and Interior — reported five versions of two bills dealing with nuclear waste disposal in 1980 (HR 7418 — H Rept 96-1156, Parts I-III; HR 6390 — H Rept 96-1382, Parts I-II).

In mid-November, key members of the Commerce and Interior committees agreed on a compromise bill (HR 8378) that the House considered and passed by voice vote on Dec. 3.

The House bill, substituted for the Senate-approved text of S 2189, was radically different from the Senate measure. The House bill set out a timetable for federal decisions on siting and building permanent repositories in natural rock and other geologic formations for high-level nuclear waste by the mid 1990s. A site would have to be chosen by 1987.

New York Nuclear Waste

To show that it could be done, Congress agreed in 1980 that the federal government would undertake, with the state of New York, to remove high-level radioactive liquid wastes from the site of a defunct nuclear reprocessing plant.

S 2443 (PL 96-368) obligated the U.S. government to demonstrate how large quantities of such wastes can be solidified and moved to a permanent storage site. The total cost of the project was estimated at $300 million, of which the United States would pay 90 percent and the state the remainder. The cleanup was expected to take a decade or longer to complete. PL 96-368 provided an initial authorization of $5 million for work in fiscal 1981.

Background

The plant that generated this waste — the Western New York Nuclear Service Center — was a private venture, established with federal encouragement in the 1950s to turn spent fuel from nuclear reactors into additional fuel. It began operating in 1966; it was the only commercial reprocessing plant ever operated in the United States. Owned by the state of New York, the site was located 30 miles from Buffalo.

In the early 1970s the federal government changed the rules for such reprocessing, amending the standards concerning storage of liquid nuclear wastes. As a result of those changes, the operators of the Western New York plant found it impossible to operate profitably and shut down the plant in 1972.

About 580,000 gallons of high-level radioactive liquids remained at the site in 1980, contained in two carbon tanks. The liquids were corrosive and leaks were possible. Under PL 96-368, the liquids would be solidified and taken to a federal repository.

Legislative History

S 2443 (S Rept 96-787) was approved by the Senate June 12. The House approved its version of the bill (HR 6865 — H Rept 96-1100, Parts I and II) Sept. 15. The Senate insisted upon two of its provisions Sept. 17, and the House concurred with those provisions the same day, clearing the bill for the White House.

Unlike the Senate bill, the measure did not give the federal government responsibility for away-from-reactor storage of spent nuclear fuel used by utilities. Nor did the House measure make any provision for above-ground storage of nuclear wastes.

The House bill, however, did contain language allowing a state to veto the storage of nuclear waste within its boundaries so long as one chamber of Congress passed a resolution supporting that veto. By a vote of 161-218, the House rejected an amendment that would have allowed a state veto to stand unless both chambers voted to override it. The House version of the bill also contained language giving states the primary responsibility for disposing of their own low-level wastes.

Compromise Negotiations

As soon as the House approved its version of S 2189 Dec. 3, key members sought to work out a compromise with the Senate, meeting in the back room of the Capitol beyond public view. But by Dec. 12, it was clear that a compromise would not be reached before adjournment. The critical issue was the power of states to veto the storage within their boundaries of nuclear waste generated by federal military activities, such as the production of nuclear weapons.

Senate Energy Committee Chairman Henry M. Jackson, D-Wash., insisted that the states should not be permitted to veto storage of military nuclear waste. But other key senators, led by John Glenn, D-Ohio, and backed by members of the House committees dealing with the issue, argued that the states should have some voice in such decisions. Faced with that impasse, Jackson and Glenn agreed to defer further consideration of the matter until the 97th Congress.

Low-Level Waste: 1980 Action

Only three states had dumps in which commercial low-level wastes could be buried in 1980 — Washington, Nevada and South Carolina. But the first two had already moved to close their dumps to out-of-state nuclear waste, and the third had indicated it would curtail the amount it would accept from out-of-state sources in the future.

When the comprehensive nuclear waste bill appeared dead for the 96th Congress, South Carolina Gov. Richard W. Riley let it be known that the state's dump could be closed to all out-of-state waste if Congress did not pass at least some measure dealing with low-level wastes.

Rep. Butler Derrick, D-S.C., then began a forceful effort to win enactment of the provisions of the House and Senate measures concerning low-level waste. He camped on or just off the Senate floor for more than nine hours Dec. 13, working persistently to convince senators to approve that portion of S 2189. He was successful, and the Senate approved the low-level provisions on Saturday, Dec. 13. The House cleared the bill a few hours later, approving the Senate amendments.

As enacted, S 2189 made the disposal of commercial low-level waste a state responsibility. States could decide whether to build dump sites or form regional compacts with other states to establish a mutual dump site. Waste generated by the federal government would not be a state responsibility, and the compacts could not make policies affecting federal waste.

Nuclear Fusion

Hoping to have a commercial demonstration plant using nuclear fusion to generate an infinite supply of clean, safe energy by the year 2000, Congress in 1980 accelerated the federal nuclear fusion development program.

HR 6308 (PL 96-386) was intended to speed up current Energy Department fusion work by 15 to 20 years; it envisioned the spending of as much as $20 billion by the year 2000.

Existing nuclear reactors produced heat to make electricity by a process called fission, which involved splitting atoms of uranium. Nuclear fusion involved combining hydrogen atoms, which could be extracted from water, to form helium. That process released vast amounts of energy. To make it occur, it was necessary to heat the hydrogen gas to more than 100 million degrees centigrade while confining it within a very strong magnetic field; thus the process was known as magnetic fusion.

The House passed HR 6308 (H Rept 96-1096) Aug. 25. The Senate passed a slightly different version (S 2926 — S Rept 96-942) Sept. 23. The House agreed to the Senate changes the following day, clearing the bill for the president. The administration supported the legislation.

Provisions

PL 96-386 declared that it was U.S. policy to "accelerate the national effort" on fusion. The bill did not authorize specific funding, but called for a doubling of present funding within seven years, increasing spending by 25 percent in fiscal 1982 and again in fiscal 1983.

The fiscal 1981 appropriations bill for energy and water resources (PL 96-367 — HR 7590) provided $393 million for fusion research.

The bill also required the secretary of energy to:
● Maintain a broadly based fusion research program.
● Establish a national magnetic fusion center.
● Initiate design of a fusion engineering test device, to be operational no later than 1990.
● Initiate as soon as practicable all activities required to meet the national goal of operating a nuclear fusion demonstration plant by 2000.
● Establish a comprehensive fusion development program by Jan. 1, 1982.

Rationing Plan in Place

In August 1980, the United States for the first time had in place a standby plan for rationing gasoline — a plan that could be put into effect in the event that gasoline supplies fell short of the national needs by at least 20 percent.

The political sensitivity of the issue of gas rationing had been amply demonstrated in 1979, when the House rejected the first plan submitted by the Carter administration.

Congress then revised the procedure for congressional approval of such a standby plan.

In 1980 the Carter administration sent to Congress a revised plan, which followed the general outline of that rejected in 1979. Under the revised plan, car owners and businesses would receive special "checks" through the mail that could be cashed for ration coupons at banks and other outlets. The ration coupons would have to be turned in, with the appropriate amount of cash, at gasoline stations in order to buy fuel.

The plan could be put into effect only if there were a 20 percent shortage of gasoline for 30 days. Either house of Congress could veto the president's decision to put the plan into effect.

Unlike the 1979 plan, the 1980 plan took into account historical patterns of gasoline consumption by various states, provided special coupon allotments for businesses, and gave the states more responsibility to distribute extra coupons.

On July 30, the last day of the period provided by law for congressional action to block such a plan, opponents of the proposal failed in both chambers to win rejection of the plan. In the Senate, the margin of failure was 2-to-1; in the House, however, it was only four votes.

Pacific Northwest Power

To prevent a threatened regional war in the Pacific Northwest over the allocation of available electric power, Congress in 1980 approved creation of a four-state regional council to allocate power from federal hydroelectric projects, to promote energy conservation and to acquire new energy sources to meet the energy needs of the area.

The Pacific Northwest power bill (S 885 — PL 96-501) was cleared by Congress late in the session, after the House finally overrode a one-man "filibuster" against the measure mounted by James Weaver, D-Ore.

Background

Since late in the 1930s, the Pacific Northwest (Washington, Oregon and western Idaho and Montana) had been supplied with relatively inexpensive hydroelectric power generated from federal dams, administered by the Bonneville Power Administration (BPA). That power accounted for about half the electricity used by the region.

Beginning in the early 1970s, the demand for BPA's electricity exceeded the available supply, and customers began battling over the low-cost power. BPA was required to give preference to the 116 public utilities it served. The first customers terminated in 1973 were investor-owned utilities. Soon thereafter, the public utilities were informed that their needs for additional power could not be met after mid-1983.

Provisions

To head off the litigation and other battles that were expected to erupt over BPA power, PL 96-501:
● Required BPA to sign new contracts agreeing to provide all the power requested by its customers, including industrial customers and investor-owned utilities.
● Established a regional, eight-member planning council, with two members from each state, to develop the additional power needed by BPA.
● Required the council to issue within two years a comprehensive regional energy plan emphasizing conservation first, renewable energy, such as solar, second, and finally, the acquisition of additional coal or nuclear power plants.
● Required BPA to promise to buy the electric capacity produced by new plants, thus ensuring financing for those plants.
● Based electric rates in the region on a melding of cheap, hydroelectric power and the much more expensive power from coal or nuclear plants. Customers who refused to implement conservation measures could be charged higher rates. The industries directly served by BPA would pay higher rates but would be assured of receiving power.
● Directed the council to establish a comprehensive fish and wildlife protection program for the region.

Legislative History

The Senate approved S 885 (S Rept 96-272) by voice vote Aug. 3, 1979.

The House began consideration of the measure more than a year later, on Sept. 29, 1980, after the bill had been reported by the House Commerce and Interior committees (H Rept 96-976, Parts I and II).

Although a majority of the members of the House from the affected area supported the bill, Weaver's opposition was sufficient to delay House action.

Weaver insisted that S 885 would be a disaster for the area and that it represented an unwarranted government intrusion into the private sector, a step toward nationalization of the area's utilities. Armed with more than 70 amendments he intended to propose to the measure — just one of which was 56 pages in length — Weaver effectively "filibustered" the bill, although an actual filibuster was not permitted under House rules. After Weaver began his dilatory tactics, the leadership Sept. 29 withdrew the bill temporarily from the floor.

The House resumed consideration of S 885 after the election recess, debating it for more than 13 hours over six days before the leadership cut off Weaver's continuing filibuster-by-amendment by placing the bill on the suspension calendar. The House then passed the bill Nov. 17 under suspension of the rules — a procedure under which amendments were prohibited and a two-thirds majority vote was required to approve a measure. The House approved S 885 by a vote of 284-77.

The Senate agreed to the House version Nov. 19 by voice vote, clearing the bill for the White House.

1981 Energy Authorization

Reversing roles with no change in result, the Senate, but not the House in 1980, approved a measure authorizing funds for the programs administered by the Energy Department in fiscal 1981.

The measure approved by the Senate July 31 (S 2332 — S Rept 96-687) was the first Energy authorization bill passed by that chamber since the new department was created in 1978. Bills authorizing fiscal 1979 and 1980 funds

never reached the Senate floor because of the leadership's desire to avoid floor fights over controversial amendments.

Senate Measure

As approved by the Senate July 31, S 2332 authorized a total of $9.6 billion for the Energy Department.

In contrast to its earlier years, when it had approved line-by-line authorizations for programs, the Senate Energy Committee simply authorized ongoing programs for fiscal 1981 authorization bill (HR 6627 — H Rept 96-967, Parts percent. New programs and construction projects and special directives were described in the legislation. A new demonstration project, for example, was authorized at the amount expected to cover the full cost of the project, with decisions about the allocation of those funds, year to year, left to the Appropriations Committee.

S 2332 also authorized a total of $1.6 billion in fiscal 1982-1985 for aid to energy boom towns, communities where substantial new growth was triggered by energy development.

The measure restricted the use of funds authorized for nuclear waste disposal until a national policy on that issue had been adopted. Until that time, those funds could be used only for research.

House Action

The controversy over nuclear waste disposal blocked House action on S 2332 in 1980. In the House three committees — Science, Interior and Commerce — shared jurisdiction over the programs administered by the Energy Department. All three reported their versions of a fiscal 1981 authorization bill (HR 6627 — S Rept 96-967, Parts I-IV) by mid-year, but no further action occurred on the measure in the 96th Congress.

The three House committees disagreed over the proper manner of considering nuclear waste legislation. The Science Committee added several provisions on nuclear waste to its version of HR 6627, but the other two committees wanted the House to consider the issue separately. Furthermore, the Science Committee sought to limit federal authority over nuclear waste disposal, while the Interior and Commerce committees endorsed heightened federal responsibility.

The Presidents on Energy

Three American presidents — Richard M. Nixon, Gerald R. Ford and Jimmy Carter — were confronted, and in many respects confounded, by the fundamental changes in energy since the Arab oil embargo in 1973. The three presidents addressed the nation several times on the issue and sent Congress a multitude of proposals to reduce American energy consumption and dependence on foreign oil. These messages contained many similar or related proposals, but underlying them all was the stark warning to Americans that for at least the remainder of the 20th century energy supplies will be more scarce than in the past and energy costs will be much higher. On the following pages are the texts of the major energy speeches of the three presidents.

Nixon's 1973 Energy Speech

President Nixon outlined for the public Nov. 7, 1973, a far-reaching program to curb the country's fuel consumption in the face of growing shortages. In a televised address to the nation, Nixon announced six steps that he would take immediately which did not require congressional approval. Beyond those, he proposed new emergency legislation, urged quick action on four long-range measures already pending in Congress and unveiled a crash program to achieve energy self-sufficiency in the United States by 1980.

I want to talk to you tonight about a serious national problem, a problem we must all face together in the months and years ahead.

As America has grown and prospered in recent years, our energy demands have begun to exceed available supplies. In recent months, we have taken many actions to increase supplies and to reduce consumption. But even with our best efforts, we knew that a period of temporary shortages was inevitable.

Unfortunately, our expectations for this winter have now been sharply altered by the recent conflict in the Middle East. Because of that war, most of the Middle Eastern oil producers have reduced overall production and cut off their shipments of oil to the United States. By the end of this month, more than 2 million barrels a day of oil we expected to import into the United States will no longer be available.

We must, therefore, face up to a very stark fact: We are heading toward the most acute shortages of energy since World War II. Our supply of petroleum this winter will be at least 10 percent short of our anticipated demands, and it could fall short by as much as 17 percent.

Now, even before war broke out in the Middle East, these prospective shortages were the subject of intensive discussions among members of my Administration, leaders of the Congress, Governors, mayors, and other groups. From these discussions has emerged a broad agreement that we, as a Nation, must now set upon a new course.

Less Energy, New Resources

In the short run, this course means that we must use less energy — that means less heat, less electricity, less gasoline. In the long run, it means that we must develop new sources of energy which will give us the capacity to meet our needs without relying on any foreign nation.

The immediate shortage will affect the lives of each and every one of us. In our factories, our cars, our homes, our offices, we will have to use less fuel than we are accustomed to using. Some school and factory schedules may be realigned, and some jet airplane flights will be canceled.

This does not mean that we are going to run out of gasoline or that air travel will stop or that we will freeze in our homes or offices anyplace in America. The fuel crisis need not mean genuine suffering for any American. But it will require some sacrifice by all Americans.

We must be sure that our most vital needs are met first — and that our least important activities are the first to be cut back. And we must be sure that while the fat from our economy is being trimmed, the muscle is not seriously damaged.

To help us carry out that responsibility, I am tonight announcing the following steps:

First, I am directing that industries and utilities which use coal — which is our most abundant resource — be prevented from converting from coal to oil. Efforts will also be made to convert powerplants from the use of oil to the use of coal.

Second, we are allocating reduced quantities of fuel for aircraft. Now, this is going to lead to a cutback of more than 10 percent of the number of flights and some rescheduling of arrival and departure times.

Third, there will be reductions of approximately 15 percent in the supply of heating oil for homes and offices and other establishments. To be sure that there is enough oil to go around for the entire winter, all over the country, it will be essential for all of us to live and work in lower temperatures. We must ask everyone to lower the thermostat in your home by at least 6 degrees, so that we can achieve a national daytime average of 68 degrees. Incidentally, my doctor tells me that in a temperature of 66 to 68 degrees, you are really more healthy than when it is 75 to 78, if that is any comfort. In offices, factories, and commercial establishments, we must ask that you achieve the equivalent of a 10-degree reduction by either lowering the thermostat or curtailing working hours.

Fourth, I am ordering additional reductions in the consumption of energy by the Federal Government. We have already taken steps to reduce the Government's consumption by 7 percent. The cuts must now go deeper and must be made by every agency and every department in the Government. I am directing that the daytime temperatues in Fedral offices be reduced immediately to a level of between 65 and 68 degrees, and that means in this room, too, as well as in every other room in the White House. In addition, I am ordering that all vehicles owned by the Federal Government — and there are over a half-million of them — travel no faster than 50 miles per hour except in emergencies. This is a step which I have also asked Governors, mayors, and local officials to take immediately with regard to vehicles under their authority.

Fifth, I am asking the Atomic Energy Commission to speed up the licensing and construction of nuclear plants. We must seek to reduce the time required to bring nuclear plants on line — nuclear plants that can produce power — to bring them on line from 10 years to 6 years, reduce that time lag.

Sixth, I am asking that Governors and mayors reinforce these actions by taking appropriate steps at the State and local level. We have already learned, for example, from the State of Oregon, that considerable amounts of energy can be saved simply by curbing unnecessary lighting and slightly altering the school year. I am recommending that other communities follow this example and also seek ways to stagger working hours, to encourage greater use of mass transit and car pooling.

How many times have you gone along the highway or the freeway, wherever the case may be, and seen hundreds and hundreds of cars with only one individual in the car. This we must all cooperate to change.

Consistent with safety and economic considerations, I am also asking Governors to take steps to reduce highway speed limits to 50 miles per hour. This action alone, if it is adopted on a nationwide basis, could save over 200,000 barrels of oil a day — just reducing the speed limit to 50 miles per hour.

Now, all of these actions will result in substantial savings of energy. More than that, most of these are actions that we can take right now — without further delay.

The key to their success lies, however, not just here in Washington, but in every home, in every community across this country. If each of us joins in this effort, joins with the spirit and the determination that have always graced the American character, then half the battle will already be won.

Actions by Congress

But we should recognize that even these steps, as essential as they are, may not be enough. We must be prepared to take additional steps, and for that purpose, additional authorities must be provided by the Congress.

I have therefore directed my chief adviser for energy policy, Governor Love, and other Administration officials, to work closely with the Congress in developing an emergency energy act.

I met with the leaders of the Congress this morning, and I asked that they act on this legislation on a priority, urgent basis. It is imperative that this legislation be on my desk for signature before the Congress recesses this December.

Because of the hard work that has already been done on this bill by Senators Jackson and Fannin and others, I am confident that we can meet that goal and that I will have the bill on this desk and will be able to sign it.

This proposed legislation would enable the executive branch to meet the energy emergency in several important ways:

First, it would authorize an immediate return to Daylight Saving Time on a year-round basis.

Second, it would provide the necessary authority to relax environmental regulations on a temporary, case-by-case basis, thus permitting an appropriate balancing of our environmental interests, which all of us share, with our energy rquirements, which, of course, are indispensable.

Third, it would grant authority to impose special energy conservation measures, such as restrictions on the working hours for shopping centers and other commercial establishments.

And fourth, it would approve and fund increased exploration, development, and production from our Naval Petroleum Reserves. Now, these reserves are rich sources of oil. From one of them alone — Elk Hills in California — we could produce more than 160,000 barrels of oil a day within 2 months.

Fifth, it would provide the Federal Government with authority to reduce highway speed limits throughout the Nation.

And finally, it would expand the power of the Government's regulatory agencies to adjust the schedules of planes, ships, and other carriers.

Stronger Measures Possible

If shortages persist despite all of these actions and despite inevitable increases in the price of energy products, it may then become necessary — may become necessary — to take even stronger measures.

It is only prudent that we be ready to cut the consumption of oil products, such as gasoline, by rationing, or by a fair system of taxation, and consequently, I have directed that contingency plans, if this becomes necessary, be prepared for that purpose.

Now, some of you may wonder whether we are turning back the clock to another age. Gas rationing, oil shortages, reduced speed limits — they all sound like a way of life we left behind with Glenn Miller and the war of the forties. Well, in fact, part of our current problem also stems from war — the war in the Middle East. But our deeper energy problems come not from war, but from peace and from abundance. We are running out of energy today because our economy has grown enormously and because in prosperity what were once considered luxuries are now considered necessities.

How many of you can remember when it was very unusual to have a home air-conditioned? And yet, this is very common in almost all parts of the Nation.

As a result, the average American will consume as much energy in the next 7 days as most other people in the world will consume in an entire year. We have only 6 percent of the world's people in America, but we consume over 30 percent of all the energy in the world.

Now, our growing demands have bumped up against the limits of available supply, and until we provide new sources of energy for tomorrow, we msut be prepared to tighten our belts today.

Long-Range Plans

Let me turn now to our long-range plans.

While a resolution of the immediate crisis is our highest priority, we must also act now to prevent a recurrence of such a crisis in the future. This is a matter of bipartisan concern. It is going to require a bipartisan response.

Two years ago, in the first energy message any President has ever sent to the Congress, I called attention to our urgent energy problem. Last April, this year, I reaffirmed to the Congress the magnitude of that problem, and I called for action on seven major legislative initiatives. Again in June, I called for action. I have done so frequently since then.

But thus far, not one major energy bill that I have asked for has been enacted. I realize that the Congress has been distracted in this period by other matters. But the time has now come for the Congress to get on with this urgent business — providing the legislation that will meet not only the current crisis but also the long-range challenge that we face.

Our failure to act now on our long-term energy problems could seriously endanger the capacity of our farms and of our factories to employ Americans at record-breaking rates — nearly 86 million people are now at work in this country — and to provide the highest standard of living we, or any other nation, has ever known in history.

It could reduce the capacity of our farmers to provide the food we need. It could jeopardize our entire transportation system. It could seriously weaken the ability of America to continue to give the leadership which only we can provide to keep the peace that we have won at such great cost, for thousands of our finest young Americans.

That is why it is time to act now on vital energy legislation that will affect our daily lives, not just this year, but for years to come.

Coal, Gas and Pipelines

We must have the legislation now which will authorize construction of the Alaska pipeline — legislation which is not burdened with irrelevant and unnecessary provisions.

We must have legislative authority to encourage production of our vast quantities of natural gas, one of the cleanest and best sources of energy.

We must have the legal ability to set reasonable standards for the surface mining of coal.

And we must have the organizational structures to meet and administer our energy programs.

And therefore, tonight, as I did this morning in meeting with the congressional leaders, I again urge the Congress to give its attention to the initiatives I recommended 6 months ago to meet these needs that I have described.

Finally, I have stressed repeatedly the necessity of increasing our energy research and development efforts. Last June, I announced a 5-year, $10 billion program to develop better ways of using energy and to explore and develop new energy sources. Last month I announced plans for an immediate acceleration of that program.

We can take heart from the fact that we in the United States have half the world's known coal reserves. We have huge, untapped sources of natural gas. We have the most advanced nuclear technology known to man. We have oil in our continental shelves. We have oil shale out in the Western part of the United States, and we have some of the finest technical and scientific minds in the world. In short, we have all the resources we need to meet the great challenge before us. Now we must demonstrate the will to meet that challenge.

The Atom and the Moon

In World War II, America was faced with the necessity of rapidly developing an atomic capability. The circumstances were grave. Responding to that challenge, this Nation brought together its finest scientific skills and its finest administrative skills in what was known as the Manhattan Project. With all the needed resources at its command, with the highest priority assigned to its efforts, the Manhattan Project gave us the atomic capacity that helped to end the war in the Pacific and to bring peace to the world.

Twenty years later, responding to a different challenge, we focused our scientific and technological genius on the frontiers of space. We pledged to put a man on the moon before 1970, and on July 20, 1969, Neil Armstrong made that historic "giant leap for mankind" when he stepped on the moon.

The lessons of the Apollo project and of the earlier Manhattan Project are the same lessons that are taught by the whole of American history: Whenever the American people are faced with a clear goal and they are challenged to meet it, we can do extraordinary things.

Today the challenge is to regain the strength that we had earlier in this century, the strength of self-sufficiency. Our ability to meet our own energy needs is directly limited to our continued ability to act decisively and independently at home and abroad in the service of peace, not only for America, but for all nations in the world.

I have ordered funding of this effort to achieve self-sufficiency far in excess of the funds that were expended on the Manhattan Project. But money is only one of the ingredients essential to the success of such a project. We must also have a unified commitment to that goal. We must have unified direction of the effort to accomplish it.

Project Independence

Because of the urgent need for an organization that would provide focused leadership for this effort, I am asking the Congress to consider my proposal for an Energy Research and Development Administration separate from any other organizational initiatives, and to enact this legislation in the present session of the Congress.

Let us unite in committing the resources of this Nation to a major new endeavor, an endeavor that in this Bicentennial Era we can appropriately call "Project Independence."

Let us set as our national goal, in the spirit of Apollo, with the determination of the Manhattan Project, that by the end of this decade we will have developed the potential to meet our own energy needs without depending on any foreign energy sources.

Let us pledge that by 1980, under Project Independence, we shall be able to meet America's energy needs from America's own energy resources.

In speaking to you tonight in terms as direct as these, my concern has been to lay before you the full facts of the Nation's energy shortage. It is important that each of us understands what the situation is and how the efforts we together can take to help to meet it are essential to our total effort.

No people in the world perform more nobly than the American people when called upon to unite in the service of their country. I am supremely confident that while the days and weeks ahead may be a time of some hardship for many of us, they will also be a time of renewed commitment and concentration to the national interest.

We have an energy crisis, but there is no crisis of the Aemrican spirit. Let us go forward, then, doing what needs to be done, proud of what we have accomplished together in the future.

Let us find in this time of national necessity a renewed awareness of our capacities as a people, a deeper sense of our responsibilities as a Nation, and an increased understanding that the measure and the meaning of America has always been determined by the devotion which each of us brings to our duty as citizens of America.

I should like to close with a personal note.

It was just one year ago that I was reelected as President of the United States of America. During this past year we have made great progress in achieving the goals that I set forth in my reelection campaign.

We have ended the longest war in America's history. All our prisoners of war have been returned home. And for the first time in 25 years, no young Americans are being drafted into the Armed Services. We have made progress toward our goal of a real prosperity, a prosperity without war. The rate of unemployment is down to 4-1/4 percent, which is the lowest unemployment in peacetime that we have had in 16 years, and we are finally beginning to make progress in our fight against the rise in the cost of living.

These are substantial achievements in this year 1973. But I would be less than candid if I were not to admit that this has not been an easy year in some other respects, as all of you are quite aware.

As a result of the deplorable Watergate matter, great numbers of Americans have had doubts raised as to the integrity of the President of the United States. I have even noted that some publications have called on me to resign the Office of President of the United States.

Tonight I would like to give my answer to those who have suggested that I resign.

I have no intention whatever of walking away from the job I was elected to do. As long as I am physically able, I am going to continue to work 16 to 18 hours a day for the cause of a real peace abroad, and for the cause of prosperity without inflation and without war at home. And in the months ahead, I shall do everything that I can to see that any doubts as to the integrity of the man who occupies the highest office in this land — to remove those doubts where they exist.

And I am confident that in those months ahead, the American people will come to realize that I have not violated the trust that they placed in me when they elected me as President of the United States in the past, and I pledge to you tonight that I shall always do everything that I can to be worthy of that trust in the future.

Nixon's 1974 Energy Speech

Following is the text of President Nixon's Jan. 23, 1974, special energy message to Congress.

As the 93rd Congress reconvenes this week, it returns to an agenda that is piled high with vital legislative questions.

America is undergoing a period of rapid change and growth when decisions made in Washington could affect the patterns of our national life for the rest of this century. These decisions demand not only the collective wisdom of our national leadership but also a continuing spirit of cooperation between the executive and legislative branches of our Government. In this first legislative message of 1974, I want to renew my pledge that I stand ready and eager to work with the Members of the Congress in shaping the solutions that are best for America.

In the next few weeks, I will send to the Congress a series of messages requesting swift legislative action in the areas where I feel that progress is most keenly needed. In each of these areas — health, education, transportation, natural resources, and others — these proposals reflect the best efforts of my Administration to solve a wide range of difficult domestic problems.

No single legislative area is more critical or more challenging to us as a people, however, than the subject of this first message to the Congress: The energy crisis. It is because of its importance and because of the urgent need for action that I have chosen to break tradition, outlining to the Congress my legislative requests in energy before delivering my State of the Union Address.

I first warned of approaching energy shortages in a message to the Congress in 1971 — the first energy message ever presented by an American President. In 1973, an embargo was suddenly imposed upon many of our foreign supplies of oil, the crisis broke upon us, and the entire country took the first steps toward coping with the emergency. We have made solid progress since then, but it is clear that our efforts in 1973 were just the beginning. As our first order of business in the new year, therefore, let us resolve that 1974 shall be the year that we build a permanent framework for overcoming the energy crisis.

In the initial portion of this message, I want to report to the Congress on our progress over the last three months. The remainder of the message addresses the legislative program on which I am urging Congressional action in 1974:

—First, the proposals that I believe are essential to meet the short-term emergency, including:

● A special energy act that would permit restrictions on the private and public consumption of energy and would temporarily relax certain Clean Air Act requirements for power plants and automotive emissions;

● A windfall profits tax that would prevent private profiteering at the expense of public sacrifice;

● Unemployment insurance to help those who lose their jobs because of the energy crisis;

● And establishment of a Federal Energy Administration.

—Second, the legislative proposals that I have previously submitted in order to meet our long-range goal of achieving self-sufficiency in energy, including proposals that would:

● Allow market pricing of new natural gas;

● Allow temporary oil production from the Elk Hills Naval Petroleum Reserve in California;

● Permit surface mining of coal in a manner that is environmentally safe;

● Permit the development of new deep-water port facilities offshore;

● Amend the tax laws regarding drilling investments;

● Modernize the laws regarding mineral leasing on Federal lands;

● And reorganize the executive branch so that it may deal more effectively with energy and natural resource problems.

—Third, proposals which are designed to help us achieve self-sufficiency in energy and which I am submitting to the Congress this year for the first time, including proposals that would:

● Eliminate depletion allowances for foreign oil and gas production;

● Accelerate the licensing and construction of nuclear facilities;

● Require labeling of products for energy efficiency;

● And streamline the site selection process for energy facilities.

In addition to these legislative proposals, the Administration is moving forward this year with a series of executive actions and studies relating to our long-term energy needs. The latter are addressed in the last section of the message.

I. Report on the Current Emergency

Last year the United States consumed roughly 18 million barrels of petroleum, in one form or another, every day. This represented about one-half of our total energy consumption. The level of petroleum consumption was also rising, so that we expected demands to reach about 20 million barrels a day in 1974.

While the country is rich in natural resources, our production of petroleum resources is far less than our demands. Last year we were producing approximately 11 million barrels of petroleum a day, and the level of production was declining.

The difference between our demands and our domestic consumption must be made up, of course, by imports from abroad, reductions in demand, or increased domestic production. Even before the embargo on oil in the Middle East, our foreign supplies were barely adequate. Since the embargo, the shortage has become a good deal more serious. The Federal Energy Office has estimated that during the first three months of 1974, our imports will fall short of our normal demands by 2.7 million barrels a day. If the embargo continues, shortages could exceed three million barrels a day during the rest of the year. That shortfall is the major factor in our current emergency.

Encouraging Progress

With the Nation confronting a severe energy shortage, I appealed to the public eleven weeks ago to undertake a major conservation effort on a personal, voluntary basis. My appeal was repeated by public servants across the land. The Congress acted quickly to pass laws putting the Nation on year-round daylight savings time and reducing the national highway speed limits to no more than 55 miles per hour. The Federal Government began moving swiftly to ensure that fuel supplies were allocated fairly and that conservation measures were undertaken within the Government. Most importantly, the people themselves responded positively, lowering the thermostats in their homes and offices, reducing their consumption of gasoline, cutting back on unnecessary lighting, and taking a number of other steps to save fuel.

Largely because of the favorable public response, I can report to the Congress today that we are making significant progress in conserving energy:

—Total consumption of gasoline in the United States during the month of December was nearly nine percent below expectations.

—Consumption of home heating oil has been reduced. A recent survey of 19,000 homes in New England showed they had reduced heating oil consumption by more than 16 percent under last year, after making adjustments for warmer weather.

—Utilities report that consumption of natural gas across the country has been reduced by approximately 6 percent over last year, while the consumption of electricity is down about 10 percent.

Beyond the progress we have made because of voluntary conservation, we have also been fortunate in two other respects. The weather in the last quarter of 1973 was warmer than usual, so that we did not consume as much fuel for heating as we expected. In addition, the oil embargo in the Middle East has not yet been totally effective, allowing us to import more oil than we first anticipated.

Action at the Federal Level

The Federal Government clearly has a major responsibility in helping to overcome the energy crisis. To fulfill that responsibility, several steps have been taken in the last three months:

—A major conservation program has been established and has cut consumption of energy by Federal agencies by more than 20 percent below anticipated demands in the third quarter of 1973.

—A sweeping investigation of fuel prices charged at gasoline stations and truck stops has been launched, putting an end to price gouging wherever it is found.

—A Federal Energy Office has been created to serve as a focal point for energy actions taken by the Government.

—Finally, a fuel allocation program has been set up to assure that no area of the Nation is subjected to undue hardships and to assure that in allocating fuel, the protection of jobs comes ahead of the satisfaction of comforts. As part of this allocation effort, refiners are being encouraged to produce less gasoline and more of the products that are needed in homes and industry, such as heating oil, diesel oil, residual fuel oil, and petrochemical feed-stocks. The Cost of Living Council has issued regulations to encourage the shift away from gasoline production. If necessary, additional steps will be taken to encourage shifts in refinery production.

The allocation program now underway will mean some cutbacks in travel, heating and other end uses of fuel, while uses which keep our economy operating at a high level will be permitted to remain at or above last year's levels.

Market forces are also at work allocating fuel. Due primarily to huge increases in prices for foreign oil, the price of gasoline has risen by 12 to 15 cents per gallon over last year. This obviously discourages the consumption of gasoline. Heating oil has also shown a comparable rise with similar effect.

There is a limit, however, to the amount of market allocation through higher prices which we will allow. We will not have consumers paying a dollar a gallon for gasoline. We must therefore seek to maximize the production of domestic oil at a price lower than the price of foreign oil. We will also carefully review requests for energy price increases, to ensure that they are genuinely needed.

All of the measures of conservation and allocation have greatly improved the Nation's chances of avoiding hardships this winter and gas rationing this spring. *Gas rationing, with its attendant bureaucracy and cost to the taxpayer, should be only a last resort.* Nevertheless, we are attempting to be prudent and therefore have developed a system of coupon rationing. The system is now on the record for public comment, and will be ready for use this spring should it prove necessary.

The system would provide for transferable coupons for all licensed drivers over 18 years old. The coupons, unlike the World War II coupons, would be freely transferable. Thus those who can economize and use less than their allotment would be given tangible incentive to do so, while those who seriously need larger amounts would be able to buy coupons legally.

The measures of allocation and conservation are, in the very short-run, the only actions which will have an effect in lessening the crisis. However, in the slightly longer term, we can and we are making efforts to increase domestic supplies of petroleum very rapidly.

Increases in supplies of domestic crude oil are necessary not only to assure supplies, but to keep the prices for consumers at a reasonable level. The prices charged by a foreign cartel for crude oil have risen so dramatically that U.S. oil prices are now greatly below the world market price.

To ensure that domestic oil exploration continues and grows, the price of oil from new exploration and development has been removed from Economic Stabilization Act controls. Also, to compensate for increased production costs and to stimulate advanced techniques for recovering oil, we have permitted a $1 per barrel increase in the cost of petroleum under existing oil contracts.

As a result, domestic oil wells that had been abandoned because they were no longer profitable are being put back into production, and new American oil is now beginning to come into the market. We anticipate additional increases in the oil in the future.

As a greater domestic production fills more of our oil needs, we will be demanding less foreign oil, and the price for foreign oil will not be driven upwards by our demands. Our own domestic production will tend to put a cap on the prices foreign suppliers may charge.

To deal further with the world shortage of oil and its increasingly unrealistic price levels, I have invited major consuming nations to a conference in Washington on February 11. The conference will, I hope, eventually lead to greater international cooperation in the areas of energy conservation, research, pricing policy, oil exploration, and monetary policy.

II. Legislation To Meet the Current Emergency

Although we have made significant progress over the last three months in reducing consumer demands for energy and in allocating fuel supplies, additional legislative measures must be enacted if we are to maintain our momentum. I am therefore asking that the Congress give its highest priority to five proposals which I have previously recommended for dealing with the short-term emergency:

1. Special Energy Act

The principal purposes of this legislation are to grant the executive branch authority to restrict the public and private consumption of energy and to modify certain Clean Air Act requirements.

During the closing weeks of December, both Houses of Congress labored long and hard on this emergency bill. As presently drafted in the House-Senate conference, the bill is laden with so many extraneous provisions that I would have difficulty signing it. I urge the Congress to pass a basic bill dealing with mandatory conservation, fuel conversion, rationing, and changes to the Clean Air Act. I would also urge that the extraneous provisions be placed in separate legislation where they belong.

2. Windfall Profits Tax

The solution to the energy crisis must ultimately depend in large measure upon the response of the public, and their actions will in turn be based upon their recognition that an energy crisis actually exists and that it has not been contrived for the benefit of big business. For weeks, believing that the crisis is genuine, millions of Americans have made sacrifices in their comfort and convenience so that no Americans would have to suffer personal hardships. Those sacrifices are continuing today, and they will be needed in the future. It is up to the leaders of the Nation to ensure that the public trust is not abused.

As President, I am deeply committed to a firm policy: *We must not permit private profiteering at the expense of public sacrifice.* The sacrifices made by the American people must be for the benefit of all the people, not just for the benefit of big business. *In equal measure, we must not permit the big oil companies or any other major domestic energy producers to manipulate the public by withholding information on their energy supplies.* That information must be made available to the public, and it must be accurate and complete.

The windfall profits tax that I outlined last December and am again asking the Congress to pass would serve this policy by preventing major domestic energy producers from making unconscionable profits as a result of the energy crisis. It would exact a tax of up to 85 percent on receipts from sales of crude oil above the ceiling set by the Cost of Living Council in December of 1973.

3. Energy-Related Unemployment Insurance

The energy emergency will undoubtedly result in some dislocation within the economy. Selected labor market areas may experience unusually large rises in unemployment despite our best efforts to minimize economic disruption. Jobs in those areas may become harder than usual to find. Therefore, as an integral part of the same philosophy which had led me to seek a windfall profits tax that prevents a few people from benefitting unduly from the energy emergency. I will also recommend new unemployment insurance measures to cushion American workers against the shocks of economic adjustment. Last April, I submitted legislation to improve the unemployment insurance program by increasing benefit levels and expanding coverage. I call again for the enactment of those measures. In addition, I will submit unemployment insurance amendments that would, on enactment, extend the duration of benefit entitlement and expand coverage in those labor market areas that experience significant increases in the level of unemployment. These provisions, coupled with the recently enacted Comprehensive Employment and Training Act will provide a solid foundation for the more rapid re-absorption of workers into the Nation's economy.

4. Mandatory Reporting of Information by Private Industry

The information now provided to the public and to the Government by the energy industry is insufficient for public planning purposes. This is a serious deficiency which has understandably become a matter of intense public interest. To correct it, I will shortly submit legislation requiring major energy producers to provide to the Government a full and constant accounting of their inventories, their production and their reserves. Where required for national security or competitive purposes, confidentiality of the information will be protected. Most of this data, however, can and will be made available to the public.

To provide a focus for the collection and analysis of this data, I have directed the Federal Energy Office to establish an Energy Information Center. This center will coordinate energy data within the Government and provide the information to the public, the Congress and other Federal agencies.

5. Federal Energy Administration

FEA would bring together and significantly expand programs to deal with the current energy emergency. It would also carry out major new activities in energy resource development, energy information and energy conservation. Included within this agency would be the functions of the Office of Petroleum Allocation, Energy Data and Analysis, Oil and Gas, and Energy Conservation from the Department of the Interior and the Energy Division of the Cost of Living Council.

III. Our Program for the Future: Project Independence

Energy demand in the United States will certainly continue to rise. Were domestic oil production to continue to decline and demand continue to grow at over 4 percent annually, as it did before the embargo, imports would increase from 35 percent of U.S. consumption in 1973 to roughly half of U.S. consumption by 1980.

We must also face the fact that when and if the oil embargo ends, the United States will be faced with a different but no less difficult problem. Foreign oil prices have risen dramatically in recent months. If we were to continue to increase our purchase of foreign oil, there would be a chronic balance of payments outflow which, over time, would create a severe problem in international monetary relations.

Without alternative and competitive sources of energy here at home, we would thus continue to be vulnerable to interruptions of foreign imports and prices could remain at these cripplingly high levels. Clearly, these conditions are unacceptable.

To overcome this challenge, I announced last November 7 that the United States must embark upon a major effort to achieve self-sufficiency in energy, an effort I called Project Independence. If successful, Project Independence would by 1980 take us to a point where we are no longer dependent to any significant extent upon potentially insecure foreign supplies of energy.

Project Independence entails three essential concurrent tasks.

The first task is to rapidly increase energy supplies — maximizing the production of our oil, gas, coal and shale reserves by using existing technologies and accelerating the introduction of nuclear power. These important efforts should begin to pay off in the next 2 to 3 years. They will provide the major fraction of the increased supplies needed to achieve energy self-sufficiency.

The second task is to conserve energy. We must reduce demand by eliminating non-essential energy use and improving the efficiency of energy utilization. This must be a continuing commitment in the years ahead.

The third task is to develop new technologies through a massive new energy research and development program that will enable us to remain self-sufficient for years to come.

We cannot accept part of the overall program and ignore the others. Within the Federal sector, success will depend on a wide range of actions by many agencies. As an important part of that effort, the head of the Federal Energy Office, William Simon, will mount a major effort this year to accelerate the development of new energy supplies for the future.

Our strategy for Project Independence is reflected in urgent measures now pending in the Congress as well as many new legislative proposals and administrative actions I now plan to take.

A. Legislation Still Awaiting Congressional Action

Over the past three years, I have submitted a number of legislative proposals that are essential to our pursuit of energy self-sufficiency but are still awaiting final Congressional action. I ask that the 93rd Congress move ahead with these proposals, and I pledge the cooperation of this Administration in working out any differences. These proposals include the following:

Natural Gas Supply Act

The artificially low prices for natural gas created by Government regulations continue to create a double problem: consumers wish to purchase more of this cheap, clean fuel than is available, while suppliers have little incentive to develop it. I again ask the Congress to provide for competitive pricing of newly developed gas supplies in order to encourage new drilling and to direct available gas into the premium uses.

Although my deregulation proposal should not cause a significant rise in consumer prices for natural gas for some years, I recognize that there is a strong desire to provide added insurance that unreasonable price increases do not occur. This insurance can be provided by adding to the Administration's legislative proposal a provision authorizing the Federal Power Commission to establish limits on absolute price increases. We are prepared to work with the Congress on these changes.

Naval Petroleum Reserves

The Nation has vast oil and oil shale reserves which years ago were set aside for national defense purposes by placing them under the control of the Secretary of the Navy. That action was taken at a time when naval petroleum requirements were an especially important share of total national petroleum consumption. Some of these oil reserves, principally those located in Wyoming and California, have been explored and developed to the point where limited production is possible. The largest reserve, located in Alaska, has not been significantly explored or developed and could not be available for production for several years, even in a grave national emergency. I have proposed legislation that would greatly improve the availability of the reserves for future needs and would permit limited production from the Elk Hills

Reserve in California to assist in meeting our short-term energy problems.

In accordance with law, the Secretary of the Navy has issued and I have approved a finding that production of oil from Naval Petroleum Reserve #1 (Elk Hills) is necessary for national defense purposes. Approval of the Congress is also necessary and I have proposed legislation that would give such Congressional approval. It would also provide that funds from the sale or exchange of the oil could be used for further exploration and development of Elk Hills and for exploration of Naval Petroleum Reserve #4 in Alaska. I am pleased that the Senate has already passed this legislation, and I am hopeful that immediate action will now be taken by the House of Representatives.

Mined Area Protection

A Mined Area Protection Act is needed to encourage the development of State programs which permit the mining of coal and other minerals to go forward in a way that is environmentally safe. The absence of clear legislation in this area is inhibiting the development of our coal reserves. The Senate has passed a bill, but it deals only with surface mining of coal rather than all mining and it contains provisions which would actually impede production of coal.

The House Committee on Interior and Insular Affairs is scheduled to take up the matter soon and I am hopeful that it will act favorably on the Administration's proposal.

Deepwater Port Facilities

Even though our policy is to achieve self-sufficiency, we will clearly continue to import oil as long as it is available at reasonable prices. To enable us to import fuel more economically, I have proposed Federal Government licensing of the construction and operation of deepwater port facilities three miles or more at sea on the Outer Continental Shelf. The main use of these facilities would be to import crude oil in ships that are economically and environmentally desirable, but are too deep of draft to permit their entry into our port facilities on the East and Gulf Coasts.

This legislation would also eliminate many of the legal uncertainties which now drive private investors away from American waters and to other nations of the Western Hemisphere. The present system only serves to create investments and jobs abroad and raises our costs of imported oil, already high, even further.

Drilling Investment Credit

Last April I proposed that the investment credit provisions of present tax laws be extended to provide a credit for all exploratory drilling for new oil and gas fields. Approval of this provision would provide an essential incentive for new oil and gas exploration. At the same time, I am asking the Congress to eliminate the tax shelter that now exists for wealthy taxpayers who reduce their taxes by taking deductions for investments in oil drilling.

Mineral Leasing Act

The Mineral Leasing Act of 1920 governs the exploration and production of oil, gas, coal, and other minerals on Federal lands while the Mining Act of 1872, governs the exploration and mining for "hard-rock" (gold, silver, copper, etc.) minerals. Both acts have become obsolete. Last February, I proposed a bill that would assure that the persons who obtain the leases are those who have an interest in early exploration for oil, gas, and other minerals. It would also require that exploration meet the environmental standards of the Administration's proposed Mined Area Protection Act.

Organizing the Federal Energy Effort

If the Federal Government is to achieve prompt and productive results in the energy field, its many energy programs and resources must be organized in the best possible manner. Toward this end, I have submitted several organizational proposals to the Congress and urged their prompt adoption. One calls for establishment of the Federal Energy Administration as discussed above. The others call for statutory establishment of the following:

(1) Energy Research and Development Administration: This new organization would provide unified leadership and direction for energy technology programs at the Federal level. ERDA would include the research and development as well as the production functions of the Atomic Energy Commission, along with selected energy research and development functions of the Department of the Interior, the National Science Foundation, and the Environmental Protection Agency. Under this proposal, the five-member Atomic Energy Commission would be renamed the Nuclear Energy Commission and would carry out the vital task of licensing and regulating the rapidly growing use of nuclear power.

(2) Department of Energy and Natural Resources: As the longer-run solution to the many interrelated problems in the energy and natural resources area, I have proposed the establishment of this new department. DENR would incorporate most of the responsibilities of the Department of the Interior; the activities of the Forest Service and certain water resource functions of the Department of Agriculture; the activities of the National Oceanic and Atmospheric Administration of the Department of Commerce; the water resource planning functions of the Corps of Engineers; the gas pipeline safety functions of the Department of Transportation, and the Water Resources Council. Drawn together, these responsibilities would form the basis of a modern department truly capable of providing a much needed balance between the wise utilization and careful conservation of our Nation's precious natural resources.

Because of the energy crisis, I urge that the Congress give priority attention to the creation of FEA and ERDA. Because of its comprehensive scope, DENR may require additional examination by the Congress, but I reaffirm the need for this modern Cabinet department. Once DENR is established, it should incorporate the functions of ERDA and FEA.

B. New Legislative Initiatives

In addition to the legislation now pending before the Congress still further steps must be taken if we are to progress at a proper pace toward self-sufficiency. Within the next several weeks, I will be sending to the Congress a number of legislative proposals to help us take those steps, including:

Changes in Foreign Tax Treatment

U.S. companies that produce oil overseas have been granted the same 22 percent depletion allowance abroad that is granted to U.S. companies producing oil in the United States. Both allowances provide an incentive for oil production.

As we move toward U.S. self-sufficiency in energy, however, we want to encourage greater development of U.S. energy resources rather than foreign resources. I am therefore asking the Congress to eliminate these foreign depletion allowances, while retaining the depletion allowance for domestic oil production.

Taxes paid to foreign governments by U.S. oil companies drilling abroad have increased dramatically. There is growing concern about the degree to which such increases should be allowed as credits against U.S. tax on other income. Under these circumstances, it is no longer realistic to treat these payments to foreign governments entirely as income taxes creditable against the U.S. tax. Obviously, however, the oil producing countries, like any other country, have the right to impose taxes and some reasonable portion of those taxes should be creditable. I have asked the Treasury Department to prepare proposals which would cause part of these amounts to be designated as a creditable tax and the balance to be allowed solely as a deduction.

Accelerating the Licensing and Construction of Nuclear Facilities

Nuclear power, which lessens our dependence on foreign fuel, is an essential part of our program of achieving energy self-sufficiency. At present, however, it takes 9-10 years to complete the planning, licensing, and construction of nuclear power plants. In order to get vitally needed nuclear power on-line more rapidly, I have directed that steps be taken to reduce the licensing and construction cycle to 5-6 years, without compromising safety and environmental standards.

I will soon transmit a legislative proposal to expedite the completion of nuclear power plants by separating the approval process for plant sites from the reactor licensing process and by encouraging the use of standardized plant designs. These designs, once approved, would reduce the required licensing review time and would enhance safety. This legislation would also permit the establishment of an inventory of approved sites for nuclear plants.

Efficiency Labels

Energy conservation must play a major role in achieving self-sufficiency, but few of the products we now purchase clearly indicate how much energy they require to operate. To assure that such information is available, I will shortly submit to the Congress legislation requiring that all major appliances and automobiles produced or imported into the United States be clearly labeled to indicate their energy use and energy efficiency.

Energy Facilities Siting

The present multitude of Federal, State, and local approvals require for the construction of energy facilities has caused serious delays in their availability. There is also no provision for advanced approval of sites which will be needed in the future. In addition, the public has often been frustrated because public participation in the site approval process seldom occurs early enough to affect the basic siting decision.

In 1971 I requested legislation to overcome these problems for electrical power plants and transmission lines. I resubmitted similar legislation in February 1973, but the Congress has not acted on my proposal. I have now directed that new legislation be prepared, building upon my earlier proposals but covering additional critical energy facilities. This legislation will be directed toward:

—advanced approval of adequate sites for energy facilities on a regional basis;

—better coordination of the various approvals now required by all levels of Government;

—and improved long range planning of energy facility requirements.

Changes in the Clean Air Act

The Clean Air Act has provided the basis for major improvements in air quality and we must continue our progress toward even greater improvement. However, during the current energy shortage, it has become clear that some changes in the act are needed to provide greater flexibility in deadlines and other requirements. The special energy legislation now before the Congress would permit temporary relaxation in some requirements applicable to power plants when an adequate supply of clean energy is not available. It would also extend the deadlines for the reduction of emissions from automobiles. I hope the Congress will move quickly to grant authority for temporary relaxation of requirements and freezing the standards for auto emissions — now applicable to 1975 model cars — for two additional years. This latter action will permit auto manufacturers to concentrate greater attention on improving fuel economy while retaining a fixed target for lower emissions. These changes can be made without significantly adverse effect on our progress in improving air quality.

The Congress has also been advised by the Environmental Protection Agency of evidence demonstrating that the reductions of nitrogen oxides from automobiles as required by the Clean Air Act are unnecessarily stringent and that technology to achieve the reductions is not yet practicable. In addition, the Congress

has been advised by the Environmental Protection Agency that deadlines cannot be met for meeting air quality standards in some metropolitan areas without drastically curtailing the use of motor vehicles. For instance, these deadlines would require that motor vehicle usage in Los Angeles be reduced by as much as 87 percent.

An extensive review is now underway within the executive branch of the implications of court decisions which require that EPA act to prevent "significant deterioration" of air quality — a requirement that is not defined in either the law or court decisions. This matter has far-reaching implications for public policy regarding land use as well as air quality. Changes in the law may thus be required to deal with this problem, and we will consult with the Congress as appropriate.

We must continue to assess the impact of actions required by the Clean Air Act so that there will be a basis for sound decisions that provide an appropriate balance among our objectives for environmental quality, economic and social growth, energy supply and national security.

IV. New Administrative Actions and Studies

In addition to preparing the legislative proposals above, I have directed that a number of executive actions be taken and additional legislative studies be made which could help us to succeed with Project Independence. Among these actions are the following:

Outer Continental Shelf Development

The undiscovered oil and gas beneath our Outer Continental Shelf can provide a significant portion of the energy necessary to make us self-sufficient. I have already ordered leasing in that area to be stepped up. Today I am directing the Secretary of the Interior to increase the acreage leased on the Outer Continental Shelf to 10 million acres beginning in 1975, more than tripling what had originally been planned. In later years, the amount of acreage to be leased will be based on market needs and on industry's record of performance in exploring and developing leases. In contracting for leases, the Secretary of the Interior is also to ensure that the proper competitive bidding procedures are followed and that environmental safeguards are observed. He will, in addition, set up an interagency program for monitoring the environmental aspects of the new leasing program. There will be no decision on leasing on the Outer Continental Shelf in the Atlantic and in the Gulf of Alaska until the Council on Environmental Quality completes its current environmental study of those areas.

Alaska Pipelines

In 1973, the Congress passed the Alaskan pipeline bill, allowing the construction of a vitally needed oil pipeline. The Secretary of the Interior plans to issue the construction permit for that pipeline this afternoon, and construction should begin this year.

It has long been clear that while an oil pipeline was needed, it alone would not be enough. In addition to the huge oil reserves in the North Slope of Alaska, there are also gas reserves there of at least 26 trillion cubic feet — enough to heat 10 million homes for 20 years. Construction of a gas pipeline should thus accompany the construction of the oil pipeline. What is now needed, and what I am directing, is prompt action by the Administration. Interior Secretary Morton expects to receive two competing applications for the gas pipeline in the near future, one proposing construction across Alaska and the other proposing construction across Canada. I have asked the Secretary to consider these proposals carefully but promptly and to deliver a recommendation to me as soon as possible. I have also asked the Secretary to undertake a further study of the need for future oil and gas pipeline capacity and the best routes for new pipelines should they prove necessary.

Stimulation of Synthetic Fuel Production

At current rates of consumption, our coal reserves could supply our needs for 300 years while shale oil could satisfy an additional 150 years of demand. However, these resources are not easily recoverable, or usable in a manner that is environmentally acceptable. Therefore, the development of a domestic synthetic fuels industry — the production of oil from shale and the production of gas or oil from coal — can be an important element of our program for reducing our future dependence on energy imports.

The recent bidding for the first commercial oil shale lease indicates strong commercial interest in shale oil development. Five other lease offerings of Federal oil shale lands will be made this year. Several companies have also announced plans to construct plants for the production of commercially usable gas from coal. Nevertheless, a variety of factors including environmental, economic, technical, and regulatory problems impose constraints on any major increase in the commercial production and industrial use of synthetic fuels. I have therefore asked the Administrator of the Federal Energy Office to head up an interagency evaluation of financial or economic incentives or regulatory changes that may be needed to stimulate domestic production.

Evaluating Energy Efficient Products

There are now several products on the market which, if given wider use, might help us to use energy more efficiently and could conceivably reduce air pollution. Among them are chemical catalysts and additives, attachments for automobile engines and more efficient heat transfer devices for industrial and home furnaces. Previously, these products have not been commercially profitable because of the low price of fuel. With an increase in fuel prices, however, they have become more attractive. I have therefore directed the Federal Energy Office to collect information on these products and on their energy efficiency. As results are available, we will publicize them and, where appropriate, will purchase the products for use by the Government.

Improving Urban Transportation

It is widely recognized now that the development of better mass transit systems may be one of the key solutions to both our energy and environmental problems. My budget for fiscal year 1975, which will be sent to the Congress in the next two weeks, gives special priority to the improvement of urban transportation, especially transit bus fleets. In addition, I will soon propose legislation to increase the amount and flexibility of Federal transportation aid which is available to local communities.

Energy Research and Development

Nowhere will the need for the combined efforts of industry and Government be greater than in energy research and development. If we are to see the successful culmination of Project Independence, the Federal Government must work in partnership with American industry.

For the last five years, I have provided for a continual expansion of our efforts in energy research and development. Federal funding increased almost 75 percent from $382 million in fiscal year 1970 to $672 million in fiscal year 1973 and was then raised to $1 billion for fiscal year 1974. Last June I announced my commitment to an even more rapid acceleration of this effort through a $10 billion Federal program over the next five years, and I asked the Chairman of the Atomic Energy Commission to develop recommendations for the expanded program.

Today I am announcing that in fiscal year 1975 — the first year of my proposed five year, energy R&D program — total Federal commitment for direct energy research and development will be increased to $1.8 billion, almost double the level of a year ago. In addition, I will be requesting an increase of $216 million for essential supporting programs in basic and environmental effects research.

Regardless of short-term fluctuations in the energy supplies, our Nation must move swiftly and steadily on a course to self-sufficiency. The private sector clearly must provide most of the money and the work for this effort. We must also guard against Government expenditures which merely replace private sector investments. But the Federal Government does have a role to play in supplementing and accelerating private development and in filling major technological gaps where market incentives are lacking. The Federal expenditures which I am announcing today are designed to serve those purposes.

In pursuing our energy R&D program, we must maintain balance. We cannot afford to direct all our efforts to finding long-term solutions while ignoring our immediate problems, nor can we concentrate too strongly on finding short-range solutions. Our program must be structured to provide us with payoffs in the near, middle, and far term.

For the near term — the period before 1985 — we must develop advanced technologies in mining and environmental control that will permit greater direct use of our coal reserves. We must speed the widespread introduction of nuclear power. And we must direct work to develop more efficient, energy-consuming devices, for use in both home and industry.

Beyond 1985, we can expect considerable payoffs from our programs in nuclear breeder reactors and in advanced technologies for the production of clean synthetic fuels from coal. By this time, we should also have explored the potential of other resources such as solar and geothermal energy.

For the far term, our programs in nuclear fusion, advanced breeder reactors, hydrogen generation and solar electric power appear to be the ultimate keys to our energy future.

V. Conclusion

Although shortages were long in appearing, the energy crisis itself came suddenly, borne by a tragic war in the Middle East. It was a blow to American pride and prosperity, but it may well turn out to be a fortunate turning point in our history.

We learned, at a stage short of the truly critical, that we had allowed ourselves to become overly dependent upon foreign supplies of a vital good. We saw that the acts of foreign rulers, even far short of military action, could plunge us into an authentic crisis. The Arab oil embargo will temporarily close some gasoline stations, but it has opened our eyes to the short-sighted policy we had been pursuing.

The energy emergency has shown us that we must never again be caught so dependent upon uncertain supplies. It is a lesson the American people must and will take to heart. By 1980, if we move forward with the proposals I have outlined today, I believe we can place ourselves in a position where we can be essentially independent of foreign energy producers.

America has half the world's reserves of coal. It has billions of barrels of oil in the ground, as well as convertible oil shale. It has vast natural gas reserves. We have the world's largest installed nuclear capacity and half the world's hydroelectric plants. This represents a truly enormous store of energy.

The United States also has the largest pool of highly trained scientific talent in the world. Our managerial skills in the private sector are enormous. And our organized facilities for solving technical problems in universities, businesses, and government are unparalleled.

I have no doubt that the bringing together of these natural and human resources can propel us toward an era of energy independence.

It will take time. But along the way we will assure that no groups of Americans are better off because other groups are suffering. We will assure that the genius of the free enterprise system is maintained and not destroyed by its response to this crisis.

Years from now, let us look back upon the energy crisis of the 1970s as a time when the American spirit reasserted itself for the lasting benefit of America and the world.

Ford's 1975 Energy Proposals

President Ford's first energy proposals were presented to Congress as part of his Jan. 13, 1975, State of the Union address. Following is the text of the energy portion of Ford's address.

The economic disruption we and others are experiencing stems in part from the fact that the world price of petroleum has quadrupled in the last year. But in all honesty, we cannot put all of the blame on the oil exporting nations. We, the United States, are not blameless. Our growing dependence upon foreign sources has been adding to our vulnerability for years and years, and we did nothing to prepare ourselves for an event such as the embargo of 1973.

During the 1960s, this country had a surplus capacity of crude oil, which we were able to make available to our trading partners whenever there was a disruption of supply. This surplus capacity enabled us to influence both supplies and prices of crude oil throughout the world. Our excess capacity neutralized any effort at establishing an effective cartel, and thus the rest of the world was assured of adequate supplies of oil at reasonable prices.

By 1970 our surplus capacity had vanished and, as a consequence, the latent power of the oil cartel could emerge in full force. Europe and Japan, both heavily dependent on imported oil, now struggle to keep their economies in balance. Even the United States, our country, which is far more self-sufficient than most other industrial countries, has been put under serious pressure.

I am proposing a program which will begin to restore our country's surplus capacity in total energy. In this way, we will be able to assure ourselves reliable and adequate energy and help foster a new world energy stability for other major consuming nations.

But this nation and, in fact, the world must face the prospect of energy difficulties between now and 1985. This program will impose burdens on all of us with the aim of reducing our consumption of energy and increasing our production. Great attention has been paid to considerations of fairness and I can assure you that the burdens will not fall more harshly on those less able to bear them.

I am recommending a plan to make us invulnerable to cutoffs of foreign oil. It will require sacrifices. But it — and this is most important — will work.

Proposals

I have set the following national energy goals to assure that our future is as secure and as productive as our past:

● First, we must reduce oil imports by 1 million barrels per day by the end of this year and by 2 million barrels per day by the end of 1977.

● Second, we must end vulnerability to economic disruption by foreign suppliers by 1985.

● Third, we must develop our energy technology and resources so that the United States has the ability to supply a significant share of the energy needs of the free world by the end of this century.

To attain these objectives, we need immediate action to cut imports. Unfortunately, in the short term there are only a limited number of actions which can increase domestic supply. I will press for all of them.

I urge quick action on the necessary legislation to allow commercial production at the Elk Hills, California, Naval Petroleum Reserve. In order that we make greater use of domestic coal resources, I am submitting amendments to the Energy Supply and Environmental Coordination Act which will greatly increase the number of power plants that can be promptly converted to coal.

Obviously voluntary conservation continues to be essential, but tougher programs are also needed — and needed now. Therefore, I am using presidential powers to raise the fee on all imported crude oil and petroleum products. Crude oil fee levels will be increased $1 per barrel on February 1, by $2 per barrel on March

1 and by $3 per barrel on April 1. I will take action to reduce undue hardships on any geographic region. The foregoing are interim administrative actions. They will be rescinded when the broader but necessary legislation is enacted.

New Taxes

To that end, I am requesting the Congress to act within 90 days on a more comprehensive energy tax program. It includes:

● Excise taxes and import fees totalling $2 per barrel on product imports and on all crude oil.

● Deregulation of new natural gas and enactment of a natural gas excise tax.

I plan to take presidential initiative to decontrol the price of domestic crude oil on April 1. I urge the Congress to enact a windfall profits tax by that date to insure that oil producers do not profit unduly.

The sooner Congress acts, the more effective the oil conservation program will be and the quicker the federal revenues can be returned to our people.

I am prepared to use presidential authority to limit imports, as necessary, to guarantee success.

I want you to know that before deciding on my energy conservation program, I considered rationing and higher gasoline taxes as alternatives. In my judgment, neither would achieve the desired results and both would produce unacceptable inequities.

Increasing Supply

A massive program must be initiated to increase energy supply, to cut demand and provide new standby emergency programs to achieve the independence we want by 1985. The largest part of increased oil production must come from new frontier areas on the Outer Continental Shelf and from the Naval Petroleum Reserve No. 4 in Alaska. It is the intent of this administration to move ahead with exploration, leasing and production on those frontier areas of the Outer Continental Shelf where the environmental risks are acceptable.

Use of our most abundant domestic resource — coal — is severely limited. We must strike a reasonable compromise on environmental concerns with coal. I am submitting Clean Air amendments which will allow greater coal use without sacrificing clean air goals.

I vetoed the strip mining legislation passed by the last Congress. With appropriate changes, I will sign a revised version when it comes to the White House.

I am proposing a number of actions to energize our nuclear power program. I will submit legislation to expedite nuclear licensing and the rapid selection of sites.

In recent months, utilities have cancelled or postponed over 60 percent of planned nuclear expansion and 30 percent of planned additions to non-nuclear capacity. Financing problems for the industry are worsening. I am therefore recommending that the one year investment tax credit of 12 percent be extended an additional two years to specifically speed the construction of power plants that do not use natural gas or oil. I am also submitting proposals for selective reform of state utility commission regulation.

To provide the critical stability for our domestic energy production in the face of world price uncertainty, I will request legislation to authorize and require tariffs, import quotas or price floors to protect our energy prices at levels which will achieve energy independence.

Conservation

Increasing energy supplies is not enough. We must take additional steps to cut long-term consumption. I therefore propose to the Congress:

● Legislation to make thermal efficiency standards mandatory for all new buildings in the United States.

● A new tax credit of up to $150 for those homeowners who install insulation equipment.

● The establishment of an energy conservation program to help low income families purchase insulation supplies.

● Legislation to modify and defer automotive pollution standards for 5 years which will enable us to improve new automobile gas mileage by 40 percent by 1980.

These proposals and actions, cumulatively, can reduce our dependence on foreign energy supplies to 3-5 million barrels per day by 1985. To make the United States invulnerable to foreign disruption, I propose standby energy legislation and a strategic storage program of 1 billion barrels of oil for domestic needs and 300 million barrels for national defense purposes.

I will ask for the funds needed for energy research and development activity. I have established a goal of 1 million barrels of synthetic fuels and shale oil production per day by 1985 together with an incentive program to achieve it.

I have a very deep belief in America's capabilities. Within the next ten years, my program envisions:

● 200 major nuclear power plants,
● 250 major new coal mines,
● 150 major coal-fired power plants,
● 30 major new refineries,
● 20 major new synthetic fuel plants,
● the drilling of many thousands of new oil wells,
● the insulation of 18 million homes,
● and the manufacturing and sale of millions of new automobiles, trucks and buses that use much less fuel.

I happen to believe that we can do it. In another crisis — the one in 1942 — President Franklin D. Roosevelt said this country would build 60,000 [50,000] military aircraft. By 1943, production in that program had reached 125,000 airplanes annually.

They did it then; we can do it now.

If the Congress and the American people will work with me to attain these targets, they will be achieved and will be surpassed.

From adversity, let us seize opportunity. Revenues of some $30 billion from higher energy taxes designed to encourage conservation must be refunded to the American people in a manner which corrects distortions in our tax system wrought by inflation.

Ford's 1976 Energy Proposals

Following is the White House text of President Ford's Feb. 26, 1976, legislative proposals for achieving U.S. energy independence, delivered in an address to Congress.

A little over two years ago, the Arab embargo proved that our Nation had become excessively dependent upon others for our oil supplies. We now realize how critical energy is to the defense of our country, to the strength of our economy, and to the quality of our lives.

We must reduce our vulnerability to the economic disruption which a few foreign countries can cause by cutting off our energy supplies or by arbitrarily raising prices. We must regain our energy independence.

During the past year, we have made some progress toward achieving our energy independence goals, but the fact remains that we have a long way to go. However, we cannot take the steps required to solve our energy problems until the Congress provides the necessary additional authority that I have requested. If we do not take these steps, our vulnerability will increase dramatically.

In my first State of the Union Address last year, I pointed out that our vulnerability would continue to grow unless a comprehensive energy policy and program were implemented. I outlined these goals for regaining our energy independence:

—First, to halt our growing dependence on imported oil during the next few critical years.

—Second, to attain energy independence by 1985 by achieving invulnerability to disruption caused by oil import embargoes. Specifically, we must reduce oil imports to between 3 and 5 million barrels a day, with an accompanying ability to offset any future

embargo with stored petroleum reserves and emergency standby measures.

—Third, to mobilize our technology and resources to supply a significant share of the free world's energy needs beyond 1985.

In pursuing these goals, we have sought to provide energy at the lowest cost consistent with our need for adequate and secure supplies. We should rely upon the private sector and market forces since it is the most efficient means of achieving these goals. We must also achieve a balance between our environmental and energy objectives.

These goals were reasonable and sound a year ago and they remain so today.

Since January of 1975, this Administration has initiated the most comprehensive set of energy programs possible under current authority. This includes actions to conserve energy, to increase the production of domestic energy resources, and to develop technology necessary to produce energy from newer sources.

During this time, I have also placed before the Congress a major set of legislative proposals that would provide the additional authority that is needed to achieve our energy independence goals.

Thus far, the Congress has completed action on only one major piece of energy legislation — the Energy Policy and Conservation Act — which I signed into law on December 22, 1975. That law includes four of the original proposals I submitted to the Congress over a year ago. Eighteen other major legislative proposals still await final action by the Congress.

Natural Gas

The need for Congressional action is most critical in the area of natural gas. We must reverse the decline in natural gas production and deal effectively with the growing shortages that face us each winter.

Deregulating the price of new natural gas remains the most important action that can be taken by the Congress to improve our future gas supply situation. If the price of natural gas remains under current regulation, total domestic production will decline to less than 18 trillion cubic feet in 1985. However, if deregulation is enacted, production would be about 25 percent higher by 1985. Natural gas shortages mean higher costs for consumers who are forced to switch to more expensive alternative fuels and mean, inevitably, an increasing dependence on imported oil. Curtailment of natural gas to industrial users in the winters ahead means more unemployment and further economic hardships.

Therefore, I again urge the Congress to approve legislation that will remove Federal price regulation from new natural gas supplies and will provide the added short-term authorities needed to deal with any severe shortages forecast for next winter.

I also urge prompt action by the Congress on a bill I will be submitting shortly which is designed to expedite the selection of a route and the construction of supplies of natural gas from the North Slope of Alasa to the "lower 48" markets. This legislation would make possible production of about 1 trillion cubic feet of additional natural gas each year by the early 1980s.

We expect imports of liquefied natural gas (LNG) to grow in the next several years to supplement our declining domestic supply of natural gas. We must balance these supply needs against the risk of becoming overly dependent on any particular source of supply.

Recognizing these concerns, I have directed the Energy Resources Council to establish procedures for reviewing proposed contracts within the Executive Branch, balancing the need for supplies with the need to avoid excessive dependence, and encouraging new imports where this is appropriate. By 1985, we should be able to import 1 trillion cubic feet of LNG to help meet our needs without becoming overly dependent upon foreign sources.

Nuclear Power

Greater utilization must be made of nuclear energy in order to achieve energy independence and maintain a strong economy. It is likewise vital that we continue our world leadership as a reliable supplier of nuclear technology in order to assure that worldwide growth in nuclear power is achieved with responsible and effective controls.

At present 57 commercial nuclear power plants are on line, providing more than 9 percent of our electrical requirements, and a total of 179 additional plants are planned or committed. If the electrical power supplied by the 57 existing nuclear power plants were supplied by oil-fired plants an additional one million barrels of oil would be consumed each day.

On January 19, 1975, I activated the independent Nuclear Regulatory Commission (NRC) which has the responsibility for assuring the safety, reliability, and environmental acceptability of commercial nuclear power. The safety record for nuclear power plants is outstanding. Nevertheless, we must continue our efforts to assure that it will remain so in the years ahead. The NRC has taken a number of steps to reduce unnecessary regulatory delays and is continually alert to the need to review its policies and procedures for carrying out its assigned responsibilities.

I have requested greatly increased funding in my 1977 budget to accelerate research and development efforts that will meet our short-term needs to:

—make the safety of commercial nuclear power plants even more certain;

—develop further domestic safeguards technologies to assure against the theft and misuse of nuclear materials as the use of nuclear-generated electric power grows;

—provide for safe and secure long-term storage of radioactive wastes;

—and encourage industry to improve the reliability and reduce the construction time of commercial nuclear power plants.

I have also requested additional funds to identify new uranium resources and have directed ERDA to work with private industry to determine what additional actions are needed to bring capacity online to reprocess and recycle nuclear fuels.

Internationally, the United States in consultation with other nations which supply nuclear technology has decided to follow stringent export principles to ensure that international sharing of the benefits of nuclear energy does not lead to the proliferation of nuclear weapons. I have also decided that the U.S. should make a special contribution of up to $5-million in the next 5 years to strengthen the safeguards program of the International Atomic Energy Agency.

It is essential that the Congress act if we are to take timely advantage of our nuclear energy potential. I urge enactment of the Nuclear Licensing Act to streamline the licensing procedures for the construction of new powerplants.

I again strongly urge the Congress to give high priority to my Nuclear Assurance Act to provide enriched uranium needed for commercial nuclear powerplants here and abroad. This proposed legislation, which I submitted in June 1975, would provide the basis for transition to a private competitive uranium enrichment industry and prevent the heavy drain on the Federal budget. If the Federal Government were required to finance the necessary additional uranium enrichment capacity, it would have to commit more than $8 billion over the next 2 to 3 years and $2 billion annually thereafter. The taxpayers would eventually be repaid for these expenditures but not until sometime in the 1990s. Federal expenditures are not necessary under the provisions of this act since industry is prepared to assume this responsibility with limited Government cooperation and some temporary assurances. Furthermore, a commitment to new Federal expenditures for uranium enrichment could interfere with efforts to increase funding for other critical energy programs.

Coal

Coal is the most abundant energy resource available in the United States, yet production is at the same level as in the 1920s and accounts for only about 17 percent of the Nation's energy consumption. Coal must be used increasingly as an alternative to scarce, expensive or insecure oil and natural gas supplies. We must act to remove unnecessary constraints on coal so that production can grow from the 1975 level of 640 million

tons to over 1 billion tons by 1985 in order to help achieve energy independence.

We are moving ahead where legislative authority is available.

The Secretary of the Interior has recently adopted a new coal leasing policy for the leasing and development of more coal on Federal lands. To implement this policy, regulations will be issued governing coal mining operations on Federal lands, providing for timely development, and requiring effective surface mining controls which will minimize adverse environmental impacts and require that mined lands be reclaimed. As a reflection of the States' interests, the Department proposes to allow application on Federal lands of State coal mine reclamation standards which are more stringent than Federal standards, unless overriding National interests are involved.

I have directed the Federal Energy Administration and the Environmental Protection Agency to work toward the conversion of the maximum number of utilities and major industrial facilities from gas or oil to coal as permitted under recently extended authorities.

We are also stepping up research and development efforts to find better ways of extracting, producing and using coal.

Again, however, the actions we can take are not enough to meet our goals. Action by the Congress is essential.

I urge the Congress to enact the Clean Air Act amendments I proposed which will provide the balance we need between air quality and energy goals. These amendments would permit greater use of coal without sacrificing the air quality standards necessary to protect public health.

Oil

We must reverse the decline in the Nation's oil production. I intend to implement the maximum production incentives that can be justified under the new Energy Policy and Conservation Act. In addition, the Department of the Interior will continue its aggressive Outer Continental Shelf development program while giving careful attention to environmental considerations.

But these actions are not enough. We need prompt action by the Congress on my proposals to allow production from the Naval Petroleum Reserves. This legislation is now awaiting action by a House-Senate Conference Committee.

Production from the reserves could provide almost 1 million barrels of oil per day by 1985 and will provide both the funding and the oil for our strategic oil reserves.

I also urge the Congress to act quickly on amending the Clean Air Act auto emission standards that I proposed last June to achieve a balance between objectives for improving air quality, increasing gasoline mileage, and avoiding unnecessary increases in costs to consumers.

Building Energy Facilities

In order to attain energy independence for the United States, the construction of numerous nuclear power plants, coal-fired power plants, oil refineries, synthetic fuel plants, and other facilities will be required over the next two decades.

Again, action by the Congress is needed.

I urge Congress to approve my October 1975 proposal to create an Energy Independence Authority, a new Government corporation to assist private sector financing of new energy facilities.

This legislation will help assure that capital is available for the massive investment that must be made over the next few years in energy facilities, but will not be forthcoming otherwise. The legislation also provides for expediting the regulatory process at the Federal level for critical energy projects.

I also urge Congressional action on legislation needed to authorize loan guarantees to aid in the construction of commercial facilities to produce synthetic fuels so that they may make a significant contribution by 1985.

Commercial facilities eligible for funding under this program include those for synthetic gas, coal liquefaction and oil shale, which are not now economically competitive. Management of this program would initially reside with the Energy Research and Development Administration but would be transferred to the proposed Energy Independence Authority.

My proposed energy facilities siting legislation and utility rate reform legislation, as well as the Electric Utilities Construction Incentives Act complete the legislation which would provide the incentives, assistance and new procedures needed to assure that facilities are available to provide additional domestic energy supplies.

Energy Development Impact Assistance

Some areas of the country will experience rapid growth and change because of the development of Federally-owned energy resources. We must provide special help to heavily impacted areas where this development will occur.

I urge the Congress to act quickly on my proposed new, comprehensive, Federal Energy Impact Assistance Act which was submitted to the Congress on February 4, 1976.

This legislation would establish a $1 billion program of financial assistance to areas affected by new Federal energy resource development over the next 15 years. It would provide loans, loan guarantees and planning grants for energy-related public facilities. Funds would be repaid from future energy development. Repayment of loans could be forgiven if development did not occur as expected.

This legislation is the only approach which assures that communities that need assistance will get it where it is needed, when it is needed.

Energy Conservation

The Nation has made major progress in reducing energy consumption in the last two years but greatly increased savings can yet be realized in all sectors.

I have directed that the Executive Branch continue a strong energy management program. This program has already reduced energy consumption by 24 percent in the past two years, saving the equivalent of over 250,000 barrels of oil per day.

We are moving to implement the conservation authorities of the new Energy Policy and Conservation Act, including those calling for State energy conservation programs, and labeling of appliances to provide consumers with energy efficiency information.

I have asked for a 63 percent increase in funding for energy conservation research and development in my 1977 budget.

If the Congress will provide needed legislation, we will make more progress. I urge the Congress to pass legislation to provide for thermal efficiency standards for new buildings, to enact my proposed $55 million weatherization assistance program for low-income and elderly persons, and to provide a 15 percent tax credit for energy conservation improvements in existing residential buildings. Together, these conservation proposals can save 450,000 barrels of oil per day by 1985.

International Energy Activities

We have also made significant progress in establishing an international energy policy. The U.S. and other major oil consuming nations have established a comprehensive long-term energy program through the International Energy Agency (IEA), committing ourselves to continuing cooperation to reduce dependence on imported oil. By reducing demand for imported oil, consuming nations can, over time, regain their influence over oil prices and end vulnerability to abrupt supply cutoffs and unilateral price increases.

The International Energy Agency has established a framework for cooperative efforts to accelerate the development of alternative energy sources. The Department of State, in cooperation with FEA, ERDA, and other Federal agencies, will continue to work closely with the IEA.

While domestic energy independence is an essential and attainable goal, we must recognize that this is an interdependent world. There is a link between economic growth and the availability of energy at reasonable prices. The United States will need some energy imports in the years ahead. Many of the other consuming nations will not be energy independent. Therefore, we must continue to search for solutions to the problems of both the world's energy producers and consumers.

The U.S. delegation to the new Energy Commission will pursue these solutions, including the U.S. proposal to create an International Energy Institute. This Institute will mobilize the technical and financial resources of the industrialized and oil producing countries to assist developing countries in meeting their energy problems.

1985 and Beyond

As our easily recoverable domestic fuel reserves are depleted, the need for advancing the technologies of nuclear energy, synthetic fuels, solar energy, and geothermal energy will become paramount to sustaining our energy achievements beyond 1985. I have therefore proposed an increase in the Federal budget for energy research and development from $2.2 billion in 1976 to $2.9 billion in the proposed 1977 budget. This 30 percent increase represents a major expansion of activities directed at accelerating programs for achieving long-term energy independence.

These funds are slated for increased work on nuclear fusion and fission power development, particularly for demonstrating the commercial viability of breeder reactors; new technology development for coal mining and coal use; enhanced recovery of oil from current reserves; advanced power conversion systems; solar and geothermal energy development; and conservation research and development.

It is only through greater research and development efforts today that we will be in a position beyond 1985 to supply a significant share of the free world's energy needs and technology.

Summary

I envision an energy future for the United States free of the threat of embargoes and arbitrary price increases by foreign governments. I see a world in which all nations strengthen their cooperative efforts to solve critical energy problems. I envision a major expansion in the production and use of coal, aggressive exploration for domestic oil and gas, a strong commitment to nuclear power, significant technological breakthroughs in harnessing the unlimited potential of solar energy and fusion power, and a strengthened conservation ethic in our use of energy.

I am convinced that the United States has the ability to achieve energy independence.

I urge the Congress to provide the needed legislative authority without further delay.

Carter's 1977 Energy Messages

Following is the text, as delivered, of President Carter's televised address to the nation April 18, 1977, on the energy problem:

Tonight I want to have an unpleasant talk with you about a problem unprecedented in our history. With the exception of preventing war, this is the greatest challenge our country will face during our lifetime. The energy crisis has not yet overwhelmed us, but it will if we do not act quickly.

It's a problem we will not solve in the next few years, and it is likely to get progressively worse through the rest of this century.

We must not be selfish or timid if we hope to have a decent world for our children and grandchildren. We simply must balance our demand for energy with our rapidly shrinking resources. By acting now we can control our future instead of letting the future control us.

Two days from now, I will present to the Congress my energy proposals. Its members will be my partners and they have already given me a great deal of valuable advice.

Many of these proposals will be unpopular. Some will cause you to put up with inconveniences and to make sacrifices. The most important thing about these proposals is that the alternative may be a national catastrophe. Further delay can affect our strength and our power as a nation.

Our decision about energy will test the character of the American people and the ability of the President and the Congress to govern this nation. This difficult effort will be the "moral equivalent of war" — except that we will be uniting our efforts to build and not to destroy.

Public Skepticism

I know that some of you may doubt that we face real energy shortages. The 1973 gas lines are gone, and with the springtime weather our homes are warm again.

But our energy problem is worse tonight than it was in 1973 or a few weeks ago in the dead of winter. It is worse because more waste has occurred, and more time has passed by without our planning for the future. And it will get worse every day until we act.

The oil and natural gas we rely on for 75 percent of our energy are simply running out. In spite of increased effort, domestic production has been dropping steadily at about 6 percent a year. Imports have doubled in the last five years. And our nation's independence of economic and political action is becoming increasingly constrained. Unless profound changes are made to lower oil consumption, we now believe that early in the 1980s the world will be demanding more oil than it can produce.

The world now uses about 60 million barrels of oil a day, and demand increases each year about 5 percent. This means that just to stay even we need the production of a new Texas every year, an Alaskan North Slope every nine months, or a new Saudi Arabia every three years. Obviously this cannot continue.

We must look back into history to understand our energy problem. Twice in the last several hundred years there has been a transition in the way people use energy. The first was about 200 years ago, when we changed away from wood — which had provided about 90 percent of all fuel — to coal, which was more efficient. This change became the basis of the Industrial Revolution.

The second change took place in this century, with the growing use of oil and natural gas. They were more convenient and cheaper than coal, and the supply seemed to be almost without limit. They made possible the age of automobile and airplane travel. Nearly everyone who is alive today grew up during this age and we have never known anything different.

Because we are now running out of gas and oil, we must prepare quickly for a third change, to strict conservation and to the renewed use of coal and permanent renewable energy sources, like solar power.

The world has not prepared for the future. During the 1950s, people used twice as much oil as during the 1940s. During the 1960s, we used twice as much as during the 1950s. And in each of those decades, more oil was consumed than in all of mankind's previous history combined.

World consumption of oil is still going up. If it were possible to keep it rising during the 1970s and 1980s by 5 percent a year as it has in the past, we could use up all the proven reserves of oil in the entire world by the end of the next decade.

I know that many of you have suspected that some supplies of oil and gas are being withheld. You may be right, but suspicions about the oil companies cannot change the fact that we are running out of petroleum. All of us have heard about the large oil fields on Alaska's North Slope. In a few years when the North Slope is producing fully, its total output will be just about equal to two years' increase in our own nation's energy demand.

Each new inventory of world oil reserves has been more disturbing than the last. World oil production can probably keep going up for another six or eight years. But sometime in the 1980s it can't go up any more.

Demand will overtake production. We have no choice about that. But we do have a choice about how we will spend the next few years. Each American uses the energy equivalent of 60 barrels of oil per person each year. Ours is the most wasteful nation on earth. We waste more energy than we import. With about the same standard of living, we use twice as much energy per person as do other countries like Germany, Japan and Sweden.

Consequences of Drift

One choice is to continue doing what we have been doing before. We can drift along for a few more years. Our consumption of oil would keep going up every year. Our cars would continue to be too large and inefficient. Three-quarters of them would carry only one person — the driver — while our public transportation system continues to decline. We can delay insulating our houses, and they will continue to lose about 50 percent of their heat in waste.

We can continue using scarce oil and natural gas to generate electricity, and continue wasting two-thirds of their fuel value in the process. If we do not act, then by 1985 we will be using 33 percent more energy than we do use today.

We can't substantially increase our domestic production, so we would need to import twice as much oil as we do now. Supplies will be uncertain. The cost will keep going up. Six years ago, we paid $3.7-billion for imported oil. Last year we spent $36 billion — nearly ten times as much — and this year we may spend $45 billion.

Unless we act, we will spend more than $550 billion for imported oil by 1985 — more than $2,500 for every man, woman, and child in America. Along with that money — that we transport overseas — we will continue losing American jobs and becoming increasingly vulnerable to supply interruptions.

Now we have a choice. But if we wait, we will live in fear of embargoes. We could endanger our freedom as a sovereign nation to act in foreign affairs. Within ten years we would not be able to import enough oil — from any country, at any acceptable price.

If we wait, and do not act, then our factories will not be able to keep our people on the job with reduced supplies of fuel. Too few of our utilities will have switched to coal, which is our most abundant energy source. We will not be ready to keep our transportation system running with smaller, more efficient cars and a better network of buses, trains, and public transportation.

We will feel mounting pressure to plunder the environment. We would have a crash program to build more nuclear plants, strip-mine and burn more coal, and drill more off-shore wells than if we begin to conserve now. Inflation will soar, production will go down, people will lose their jobs. Intense competition for oil will build up among nations, and among the different regions within our own country. If we fail to act soon, we will face an economic, social and political crisis that will threaten our free institutions.

But we still have another choice. We can begin to prepare right now. We can decide to act while there is still time. That is the concept of the energy policy we will present on Wednesday.

Ten Principles

Our national energy plan is based on ten fundamental principles.

The first principle is that we can have an effective and comprehensive energy policy only if the government takes responsibility for it and if the people understand the seriousness of the challenge and are willing to make sacrifices.

The second principle is that healthy economic growth must continue. Only by saving energy can we maintain our standard of living and keep our people at work. An effective conservation program will create hundreds of thousands of new jobs.

The third principle is that we must protect the environment. Our energy problems have the same cause as our environmental problems — wasteful use of resources. Conservation helps us solve both problems at once.

The fourth principle is that we must reduce our vulnerability to potentially devastating embargoes. We can protect ourselves from uncertain supplies by reducing our demand for oil, making the most of our abundant resources such as coal, and by developing a strategic petroleum reserve.

The fifth principle is that we must be fair. Our solutions must ask equal sacrifices from every region, every class of people, and every interest group. Industry will have to do its part to conserve, just as consumers will. The energy producers deserve fair treatment, but we will not let the oil companies profiteer.

The sixth principle, and the cornerstone of our policy, is to reduce demand through conservation. Our emphasis on conservation is a clear difference between this plan and others which merely encouraged crash production efforts. Conservation is the quickest, cheapest, most practical source of energy. Conservation is the only way we can buy a barrel of oil for a few dollars, for about $2. It costs about $13 to waste it.

The seventh principle is that prices should generally reflect the true replacement cost of energy. We are only cheating ourselves if we make energy artificially cheap and use more than we can really afford.

The eighth principle is that government policies must be predictable and certain. Both consumers and producers need policies they can count on so they can plan ahead. This is one reason I am working with the Congress to create a new Department of Energy, to replace more than 50 different agencies that now have some control over energy.

The ninth principle is that we must conserve the fuels that are scarcest and make the most of those that are plentiful. We can't continue to use oil and gas for 75 percent of our consumption as we do now when they make up only 7 percent of our domestic reserves. We need to shift to plentiful coal while taking care to protect the environment, and to apply stricter safety standards to nuclear energy.

The tenth and last principle is that we must start now to develop the new, unconventional sources of energy that we will rely on in the next century.

Now, these ten principles have guided the development of the policy I will describe to you and the Congress on Wednesday night.

Goals for 1985

Our energy plan will also include a number of specific goals, to measure our progress toward a stable energy system. These are the goals that we set for 1985:

● To reduce the annual growth rate in our energy demand to less than 2 percent.
● To reduce gasoline consumption by 10 percent below its current level.
● To cut in half the portion of U.S. oil which is imported — from a potential level of 16 million barrels to 6 million barrels a day.
● To establish a strategic petroleum reserve of one billion barrels, more than a six-month supply.
● To increase our coal production by about two-thirds to more than 1 billion tons a year.
● To insulate 90 percent of American homes and all new buildings.
● To use solar energy in more than two and one-half million houses.

We will monitor our progress toward these goals year by year. Our plan will call for strict conservation measures if we fall behind.

I can't tell you that these measures will be easy, nor will they be popular. But I think most of you realize that a policy which does not ask for changes or sacrifices would not be an effective policy at this late date. This plan is essential to protect our jobs, our environment, our standard of living, and our future.

Whether this plan truly makes a difference will not be decided now here in Washington, but in every town and every factory, in every home and on every highway and every farm.

I believe this can be a positive challenge. There is something especially American in the kinds of changes that we have to make. We have been proud, through our history, of being efficient people.

We have been proud of our ingenuity, our skill at answering questions. We need efficiency and ingenuity more than ever. We have been proud of our leadership in the world. And now we have a chance again to give the world a positive example.

And we've always been proud of our vision of the future. We have always wanted to give our children and grandchildren a world richer in possibilities than we've had. They are the ones

we must provide for now. They are the ones who will suffer most if we don't act.

I've given you some of the principles of the plan.

I am sure each of you will find something you don't like about the specifics of our proposal. It will demand that we make sacrifices and changes in every life. To some degree the sacrifices will be painful — but so is any meaningful sacrifice. It will lead to some higher costs, and to some greater inconveniences for everyone.

But the sacrifices can be gradual, realistic, and they are necessary. Above all, they will be fair. No one will gain an unfair advantage through this plan. No one will be asked to bear an unfair burden. We will monitor the accuracy of data from the oil and natural gas companies for the first time, so that we will know their true production, supplies, reserves, and profits.

Those citizens who insist on driving large, unnecessarily powerful cars must expect to pay more for that luxury.

We can be sure that all the special interest groups in the country will attack the part of this plan that affects them directly. They will say that sacrifice is fine, as long as other people do it, but that their sacrifice is unreasonable, or unfair, or harmful to the country. If they succeed with this approach, then the burden on the ordinary citizen, who is not organized into an interest group, would be crushing.

There should be only one test for this program — whether it will help our country. Other generations of Americans have faced and mastered great challenges. I have faith that meeting this challenge will make our own lives even richer. If you will join me so that we can work together with patriotism and courage, we will again prove that our great nation can lead the world into an age of peace, independence, and freedom. Thank you very much and good night.

Carter's Message to Congress

Following is the prepared text of President Carter's address on energy April 20, 1977, to a joint session of Congress.

The last time we met as a group was exactly three months ago on Inauguration day. We've had a good beginning as partners in addressing our nation's problems.

But in the months ahead, we must work together even more closely, for we have to deal with the greatest domestic challenge our nation will face in our lifetime. We must act now — together — to devise and to implement a comprehensive national energy plan to cope with a crisis that otherwise could overwhelm us.

This cannot be an inspirational speech tonight. It is a sober and difficult presentation. During the last three months, I have come to realize very clearly why a comprehensive energy policy has not already been evolved. It is a thankless job, but it is our job, and I believe we have a fair, well balanced and effective plan to present to you. It can lead to an even better life for the people of America.

The heart of our energy problem is that our demand for fuel keeps rising more quickly than our production, and our primary means of solving this problem is to reduce waste and inefficiency.

Oil and natural gas make up 75 percent of our consumption in this country, but they represent only about 7 percent of our reserves. Our demand for oil has been rising by more than 5 percent each year, but domestic oil production has been falling lately by more than 6 percent. Our imports of oil have risen sharply — making us more vulnerable if supplies are interrupted — but early in the 1980s even foreign oil will become increasingly scarce. If it were possible for world demand to continue rising during the 1980s at the present rate of 5 percent a year, we could use up all the proven reserves of oil in the entire world by the end of the next decade.

Our trade deficits are growing. We imported more than $35 billion worth of oil last year, and we will spend much more than that this year. The time has come to draw the line.

We could continue to ignore this problem — but to do so would subject our people to an impending catastrophe.

That is why we need a comprehensive national energy policy. Your advice has been an important influence as this plan has taken shape. Many of its proposals will build on your own legislative initiatives.

Two nights ago, I spoke to the American people about the principles behind our plan and our goals for 1985:

- to reduce the annual growth rate in our energy demand to less than 3 percent;
- to reduce gasoline consumption by 10 percent;
- to cut imports of foreign oil to 6 million barrels a day, less than half the level it would be if we did not conserve;
- to establish a strategic petroleum reserve of one billion barrels, about a ten months' supply;
- to increase our coal production by more than two-thirds, to over one billion tons a year;
- to insulate 90 percent of American homes and all new buildings; and
- to use solar energy in more than two and a half million homes.

I hope that the Congress will adopt these goals by joint resolution as a demonstration of our mutual commitment to achieve them.

Tonight I want to outline the specific steps by which we can reach those goals. The proposals fall into these central categories:

- conservation
- production
- conversion
- development, and
- fairness, which is a primary consideration in all our proposals.

We prefer to reach these goals through voluntary cooperation with a minimum of coercion. In many cases, we propose financial incentives, which will encourage people to save energy and will harness the power of our free economy to meet our needs.

But I must say to you that voluntary compliance will not be enough — the problem is too large and the time is too short.

In a few cases, penalties and restrictions to reduce waste are essential.

Conservation

Our first goal is conservation. It is the cheapest, most practical way to meet our energy needs and to reduce our growing dependence on foreign supplies of oil.

With proper planning, economic growth, enhanced job opportunities and higher quality of life can result even while we eliminate the waste of energy.

The two areas where we waste most of our energy are transportation and our heating and cooling systems.

Transportation consumes 26 percent of our energy — and as much as half of that is waste. In Europe the average automobile weighs 2,700 pounds; in our country 4,100 pounds.

The Congress has already adopted fuel efficiency standards, which will require new cars to average 27.5 miles per gallon by 1985 instead of the 18 they average today.

To insure that this existing Congressional mandate is met, I am proposing a graduated excise tax on new gas guzzlers that do not meet federal average mileage standards. The tax will start low and then rise each year until 1985. In 1978, a tax of $180 will be levied on a car getting 15 miles per gallon, and for an 11 mile-per-gallon car the tax will be $450. By 1985, on wasteful new cars with the same low mileage, the taxes will have risen to $1,600 and $2,500.

All of the money collected by this tax on wasteful automobiles will be returned to consumers, through rebates on cars that are more efficient than the mileage standard. We expect that both efficiency and total automobile production and sales will increase under this proposal. We will insure that American automobile workers and their families do not bear an unfair share of the burden.

Gasoline Tax. Now I want to discuss one of the most controversial and misunderstood parts of the energy proposal — a standby tax on gasoline. Gasoline consumption represents half of our total oil usage.

We simply must save gasoline, and I believe that the American people can meet this challenge. It is a matter of patriotism and commitment.

Between now and 1980 we expect gasoline consumption to rise slightly above the present level. For the following five years, when we have more efficient automobiles we need to reduce consumption each year to reach our targets for 1985.

I propose that we commit ourselves to these fair, reasonable and necessary goals and at the same time write into law a gasoline tax of an additional 5 cents per gallon that will automatically take effect every year that we fail to meet our annual targets. As an added incentive, if we miss one year but are back on track the next, the additional tax would come off. If the American people respond to our challenge, we can meet these targets, and this gasoline tax will never be imposed. I know and you know it can be done.

As with other taxes, we must minimize the adverse effects of our economy — reward those who conserve — and penalize those who waste. Therefore, any proceeds from the tax — if it is triggered — should be returned to the general public in an equitable manner.

I will also propose a variety of other measures to make our transportation system more efficient.

One of the side effects of conserving gasoline is that state governments collect less money through gasoline taxes. To reduce their hardships and to insure adequate highway maintenance, we should compensate states for this loss through the highway trust fund.

Homes and Buildings. The second major area where we can reduce waste is in our homes and buildings. Some buildings waste half the energy used for heating and cooling. From now on, we must make sure that new buildings are as efficient as possible, and that old buildings are equipped — or "retrofitted" — with insulation and heating systems that dramatically reduce the use of fuel.

The federal government should set an example. I will issue an executive order establishing strict conservation goals for both new and old federal buildings — a 45 percent increase in energy efficiency for new buildings, and a 20 percent increase for existing buildings by 1985.

We also need incentives to help those who own homes and businesses to conserve.

Those who weatherize buildings would be eligible for a tax credit of 25 percent of the first $800 invested in conservation, and 15 percent of the next $1,400.

If homeowners prefer, they may take advantage of a weatherization service which all regulated utility companies will be required to offer. The utilities would arrange for the contractors and provide reasonable financing. The customer would pay for the improvements through small, regular additions to monthly utility bills. In many cases, these additional charges would be almost entirely offset by lower energy consumption brought about by energy savings.

Other proposals for conservation in home and buildings include:

- direct federal help for low-income residents;
- an additional 10 percent tax credit for business investments;
- federal matching grants to non-profit schools and hospitals; and
- public works money for weatherizing state and local government buildings.

While improving the efficiency of our businesses and homes, we must also make electrical home appliances more efficient. I propose legislation that would, for the first time, impose stringent efficiency standards for household appliances by 1980.

We must also reform our utility rate structure. For many years we have rewarded waste by offering the cheapest rates to the largest users. It is difficult for individual states to make such reforms because of the competition for new industry. The only fair way is to adopt a set of principles to be applied nationwide.

I am therefore proposing legislation which would require the following steps over the next two years:

• phasing out promotional rates and other pricing systems that make natural gas and electricity artificially cheap for high-volume users and which do not accurately reflect costs;

• offering users peak-load pricing techniques which set higher charges during the day when demand is great and lower charges when demand is small; and

• individual meters for each apartment in new buildings instead of one master meter.

Plans are already being discussed for the TVA System to act as a model for implementing such new programs to conserve energy.

One final step toward conservation is to encourage industries and utilities to expand "cogeneration" projects, which capture much of the steam that is now wasted in generating electricity. In Germany, 29 percent of total energy comes from cogeneration, but only 4 percent in the United States.

I propose a special 10 percent tax credit for investments in cogeneration.

Production and Pricing

Along with conservation, our second major strategy is production and rational pricing.

We can never increase our production of oil and natural gas by enough to meet our demand, but we must be sure that our pricing system is sensible, discourages waste and encourages exploration and new production.

One of the principles of our energy policy is that the price of energy should reflect its true replacement cost, as a means of bringing supply and demand into balance over the long-run. Realistic pricing is especially important for our scarcest fuels, oil and natural gas. However, proposals for immediate and total decontrol of domestic oil and natural gas prices would be disastrous for our economy and for working Americans, and would not solve long range problems of dwindling supplies.

The price of newly discovered oil will be allowed to rise, over a three-year period, to the 1977 world market price, with allowances for inflation. The current return to producers for previously discovered oil would remain the same, except for adjustments because of inflation.

Because fairness is an essential strategy of our energy program, we do not want to give producers windfall profits, beyond the incentives they need for exploration and production. But we are misleading ourselves if we do not recognize the replacement costs of energy in our pricing system.

Therefore, I propose that we phase in a wellhead tax on existing supplies of domestic oil, equal to the difference between the present controlled price of oil and the world price, and return the money collected by this tax to the consumers and workers of America.

We should also end the artificial distortions in natural gas prices in different parts of the country which have caused people in the producing states to pay exorbitant prices, while creating shortages, unemployment and economic stagnation, particularly in the Northeast. We must not permit energy shortages to balkanize our nation.

I want to work with the Congress to give gas producers an adequate incentive for exploration, working carefully toward deregulation of newly discovered natural gas as market conditions permit.

I propose now that the price limit for all new gas sold anywhere in the country be set at the price of the equivalent energy value of domestic crude oil, beginning in 1978. This proposal will apply both to new gas and to expiring intrastate contracts. It would not affect existing contracts.

Conversion

We must be sure that oil and natural gas are not wasted by industries and utilities that could use coal instead. Our third strategy will be conversion from scarce fuels to coal wherever possible.

Although coal now provides only 18 percent of our energy needs, it makes up 90 percent of our energy reserves. Its production and use create environmental difficulties, but we can cope with them through strict strip-mining and clean air standards.

To increase the use of coal by 400 million tons, or 65 percent, in industry and utilities by 1985, I propose a sliding scale tax, starting in 1979, on large industrial users of oil and natural gas. Fertilizer manufacturers and crop dryers which must use gas would be exempt from the tax. Utilities would not be subject to these taxes until 1983, because it will take them longer to convert to coal.

I will also submit proposals for expanded research and development in coal. We need to find better ways to mine it safely and burn it cleanly, and to use it to produce other clean energy sources. We have spent billions on research and development of nuclear power, but very little on coal. Investments here can pay rich dividends.

Even with this conversion effort, we will still face a gap — between the energy we need and the energy we can produce and import. Therefore, as a last resort we must continue to use increasing amounts of nuclear energy.

We now have 63 nuclear power plants, producing about 3 percent of our total energy and about 70 more are licensed for construction. Domestic uranium supplies can support this number of plants for another 75 years. Effective conservation efforts can minimize the shift toward nuclear power. There is no need to enter the plutonium age by licensing or building a fast breeder reactor such as the proposed demonstration plant at Clinch River.

We must, however, increase our capacity to produce enriched uranium for light water nuclear power plants, using the new centrifuge technology, which consumes only about 1/10th the energy of existing gaseous diffusion plants.

We must also reform the nuclear licensing procedures. New plants should not be located near earthquake fault zones or near population centers, safety standards should be strengthened and enforced, designs standardized as much as possible, and more adequate storage for spent fuel assured.

However, even with the most thorough safeguards, it should not take ten years to license a plant. I propose that we establish reasonable, objective criteria for licensing, and that plants which are based on a standard design not require extensive individual design studies for licensing.

Development

Our fourth strategy is to develop permanent and reliable new energy sources.

The most promising is solar energy, for which much of the technology is already available. Solar water heaters and space heaters are ready for commercialization. All they need is some incentive to initiate the growth of a large market.

Therefore, I am proposing a gradually decreasing tax credit, to run from now through 1984, for those who purchase approved solar heating equipment. Initially, it would be 40 percent of the first $1,000 and 25 percent of the next $6,400 invested.

Increased production of geothermal energy can be insured by providing the same tax incentives as for gas and oil drilling operations.

Fairness

Our guiding principle, as we developed this plan, was that above all it must be fair.

None of our people must make an unfair sacrifice.

None should reap an unfair benefit.

The desire for equity is reflected throughout our plan:

• in the wellhead tax, which encourages conservation but is returned to the public;

• in a dollar-for-dollar refund of the wellhead tax as it affects home heating oil;

• in reducing the unfairness of natural gas pricing;

• in ensuring that homes will have the oil and natural gas they need, while industry turns toward the more abundant coal that can also suit its needs;

• in basing utility prices on true cost, so every user pays a fair share;

• in the automobile tax and rebate system, which rewards those who save our energy and penalizes those who waste it.

I propose one other step to insure proper balance in our plan. We need more accurate information about our supplies of energy, and about the companies that produce it.

If we are asking sacrifices of ourselves, we need facts we can count on. We need an independent information system that will give us reliable data about energy reserves and production, emergency capabilities and financial data from the energy producers.

I happen to believe in competition, and we don't have enough of it.

During this time of increasing scarcity, competition among energy producers and distributors must be guaranteed. I recommend that individual accounting be required from energy companies for production, refining, distribution and marketing — separately for domestic and foreign operations. Strict enforcement of the anti-trust laws can be based on this data, and may prevent the need for divestiture.

Profiteering through tax shelters should be prevented, and independent drillers should have the same intangible tax credits as the major corporations.

The energy industry should not reap large unearned profits. Increasing prices on existing inventories of oil should not result in windfall gains but should be captured for the people of our country.

We must make it clear to everyone that our people, through their government, will now be setting our energy policy.

The new Department of Energy should be established without delay. Continued fragmentation of government authority and responsibility for our nation's energy program is dangerous and unnecessary.

Two nights ago, I said that this difficult effort would be the moral equivalent of war. If successful, this effort will protect our jobs, our environment, our national independence, our standard of living, and our future. Our energy policy will be innovative, but fair and predictable. It will not be easy. It will demand the best of us — our vision, our dedication, our courage, and our sense of common purpose.

This is a carefully balanced program, depending for its fairness on all its major component parts. It will be a test of our basic political strength and ability.

But we have met challenges before, and our nation has been the stronger for it. That is the responsibility that we face — you in the Congress, the members of my administration, and all the people of our country. I am confident that together we will succeed.

Carter's 1979 Energy Message

Following is the prepared text of President Carter's energy address to the nation April 5, 1979.

Our nation's energy problem is serious — and it's getting worse. We are wasting too much energy, we are buying far too much oil from foreign countries, and we are not producing enough oil, gas or coal in the United States. To control energy price, production and distribution, the federal bureaucracy and red tape have become so complicated, it's almost unbelievable. Energy prices are high and going higher, no matter what we do. The use of coal and solar energy, which are in plentiful supply, is lagging far behind their great potential. The recent accident at the Three Mile Island nuclear power plant in Pennsylvania has demonstrated dramatically that we have other energy problems.

What can we do? We can solve these problems together.

Federal government price controls now hold down our own production and encourage waste and increasing dependence on foreign oil.

Present law requires that these federal government controls on oil be removed by September 1981, and the law gives me the authority at the end of next month to carry out this decontrol process. In order to minimize sudden economic shock, I have decided that phased decontrol of oil prices will begin on June 1st and continue at a fairly uniform rate over the next 28 months. The immediate effect of this action will be to increase production of oil and gas in our own country.

As government controls end, prices will go up on oil already discovered, and unless we tax the oil companies, they will reap huge and undeserved windfall profits. We must impose a windfall profits tax on the oil companies to capture part of this money for the American people. This tax money will go into an Energy Security Fund, and will be used to protect low-income families from energy price increases, to build a more efficient mass transportation system, and to put American genius to work solving our long-range energy problems.

Let me explain all of this in more detail. This is very important, and I hope all of you will listen carefully and give me your cooperation and support.

Crisis Real

The energy crisis is real. I said so in 1977, and I say it again tonight, almost exactly two years later. Time is running short.

While the situation at Three Mile Island is improving and we have taken every precaution to protect the people of the area, this nuclear accident obviously causes all of us concern.

I have directed the establishment of an independent Presidential Commission of experts to investigate the causes of this accident and to make recommendations on how we can improve the safety of nuclear power plants. You deserve a full accounting, and you will get it.

Although this accident is of immediate concern, the fundamental cause of our nation's energy crisis is petroleum. We are dangerously dependent on uncertain and expensive sources of foreign oil.

Since the 1973 embargo, oil production in the United States has actually dropped. Our imports have been growing. Just a few foreign countries control the amount of oil that is produced and the price we must pay.

Just ten years ago, we imported hardly any oil. Today, we buy about half the oil we use from foreign countries. We are by far the largest customer for OPEC oil, buying one-fourth of that foreign cartel's total production. This year, we will pay out $50 billion for imported oil — about $650 for every household in the United States.

This growing dependence has left us dangerously exposed to sudden price rises and interruptions in supply. In 1973 and 1974, shipment of oil was embargoed and the price quadrupled almost overnight. In the last few months, the upheaval in Iran again cut world supplies of oil, and the OPEC cartel prices leaped up again.

These shocks have sent us stern warnings about energy, but our nation has not yet responded to these warnings. Our national strength is dangerously dependent on a thin line of oil tankers stretching halfway around the earth, originating in the Middle East and around the Persian Gulf — one of the most unstable regions in the world.

The National Energy Plan which I proposed in April 1977 was the first major effort to deal with these problems. Then, for 18 long months, Congress debated and special interests struggled for advantage. Some of my original proposals were enacted and benefits are already obvious, but proposals dealing with oil were not adopted, and we have now lost time we could not afford.

With new legal authority, I am now able to act without delay.

No Single Answer

There is no single answer. We must produce more. We must conserve more. And now we must join together in a great national effort to use American technology to give us energy security in the years ahead.

The most effective action we can take to encourage both conservation and production here at home is to stop rewarding those who import foreign oil and to stop encouraging waste by holding the price of American oil down far below its replacement or true value.

This is a painful step, and I'll give it to you straight: Each one of us will have to use less oil and pay more for it.

But this is a necessary step, and I want you to understand it fully.

Excessive federal government controls must end.

Phased decontrol will gradually increase the price of petroleum products. In the short run it will add a small amount to our rate of inflation, but that is the cost we must pay to reduce our dependence on the foreign oil cartel.

In the longer run the actions I'm announcing tonight will help us to fight inflation. Other nations will join and support us as we cut down our use of oil and increase our own production of energy. The foreign oil cartel will then find it harder to raise prices. The dollar will grow stronger and the prices we pay for many imported goods will be less. This will strengthen our economy and reduce inflation in future years.

But decontrol could also further inflate the already large profits of oil companies. As I have said, part of this excessive new profit will be totally unearned — what is called a "windfall" profit.

Windfall Profits

That is why we must have a new windfall profits tax to recover the unearned billions of dollars, and to ensure that you — the American people — are treated fairly.

I want to emphasize that this windfall profits tax is not a tax on the American people. It is purely and simply a tax on the new profits of the oil producers which they will receive but not earn.

Even with the windfall profits tax in place, our oil producers will get substantial new income — enough to provide plenty of incentive for increased domestic production. I will demand that they use their new income to develop energy for America, and not to buy department stores and hotels, as some have done in the past.

Congressional leaders, who share my belief that a windfall profits tax is necessary, warn me that we face two very real threats to these proposals.

First, as surely as the sun will rise, the oil companies can be expected to fight to keep the profits which they have not earned. Unless you speak out, they will have more influence on the Congress than you do.

Second, the inevitable scrambling by interest groups for a larger share of these revenues can leave the Congress divided, bogged down, and unable to act. Unless your voice is heard, once again the selfishness of a few will block action which is badly needed to help our entire nation.

Let Congress Know

I will fight to get this tax passed, to establish the Energy Security Fund, and to meet our future energy needs, and tonight I appeal for your support. Please let your Senators and Representatives in Congress know that you support the windfall profits tax — and that you do not want the need to produce more energy to be turned into an excuse to cheat the public and to damage our nation.

We can meet our energy challenge, but I am not going to put an undue burden on people who can hardly make ends meet as it is.

Part of the proceeds of the windfall profits tax will go to help those among us who will be hurt most by rising energy prices.

I will also ask every State to pass laws protecting Americans from arbitrary cutoffs of heat for their homes.

We will channel the tens of millions of dollars we are already winning in lawsuits against oil companies for price gouging into further energy assistance for lower-income citizens.

For the sake of fairness, I will ask Congress to close foreign tax credit loopholes that now give unnecessary benefits to the major oil companies.

And, to ease short run inflationary pressures, I will propose that existing fees and duties now applicable to imported crude oil and products be lifted temporarily.

Other Actions

Besides removing government controls on oil to encourage production, we must take other actions to increase supply and to make the most of our own domestic fuel reserves.

- I have today signed an executive order that will set strict deadlines for cutting through federal red tape on important new energy projects such as pipelines, seaports, and refineries.
- We will move to eliminate bureaucratic barriers to construction of the pending pipeline from California to Texas, which has been stuck in a quagmire of more than 700 State and local permit applications for the last 14 months.
- We will step up exploration and production of oil and gas on federal lands.
- This week my personal representatives began negotiations in Mexico City which we hope will lead to an agreement on sales of Mexican natural gas to the United States, at a price that is fair to both countries.
- The three federal agencies which regulate the coal industry will report to me within 60 days on ways to encourage greater use of coal — our most abundant fuel resource.
- And I will soon announce significant measures to increase and to accelerate the use of solar energy.

Conservation Efforts

In addition to producing more energy, we must conserve more energy. Conservation is our cheapest and cleanest energy source. It helps to control inflation, and every barrel of oil we save is a barrel we don't have to import.

We have recruited 19 other consuming nations to join us in pledging to reduce expected oil consumption by 5 percent.

To help accomplish this conservation goal:

- I have asked Congress to grant me standby authority in four areas, one of which is to require that thermostats in all commercial buildings be set no higher than 65 degrees in winter and no lower than 80 degrees in summer. As soon as I get that authority, I will use it.
- Steps will be taken to eliminate free parking for government employees in order to reduce the waste of gasoline in commuting to work. I call on all employers to follow suit.
- Tax credits will encourage the use of wood-burning stoves.
- I am asking all citizens to honor, and all States to enforce, the 55-mile-per-hour speed limit. This is one of the most effective ways to save fuel.
- I will set targets for our 50 States to reduce gasoline consumption, and ask each State to meet its target. The timetable will be strict. If States fail to meet their targets when gasoline shortages exist, then I will order mandatory steps to achieve the needed savings, including the weekend closing of service stations. If these savings are not made, we will almost certainly have gasoline shortages as early as this summer.

Drive Less

In addition, I ask each of you to take an important action on behalf of our nation. I ask you to drive 15 miles a week fewer than you do now. One way to do this is not to drive your own car to work every day. At least once a week take the bus, go by carpool — or, if you work close to home, walk.

This action can make a difference for our country. For each day that we do this, we can save hundreds of thousands of barrels of oil. This will help to hold down prices of fuel, and you obviously will save money you would otherwise have spent on gasoline.

As needed on a temporary basis:

- I may extend certain environmental deadlines and make regulatory changes to help avoid serious shortages of gasoline.
- Unless utilities do so voluntarily, they may be ordered to run non-oil-burning generating plants at full capacity and to trans-

mit the extra power to areas where oil burners can be phased out.

So far I have spoken about producing more energy and conserving more energy.

Now in the next few minutes, I would like to talk about the third — and most promising — part of our battle for energy security: shifting to more abundant sources of energy by the development and use of American technology.

We are already investing some $3.5 billion each year to develop the new energy supplies we will need for the future.

But we must step up this effort. Just as we harnessed American dedication and brainpower to put men on the moon, we will make the same kind of massive, purposeful effort to achieve the goal of national energy security through technology. We must begin now so that we can regain control over our energy future.

Energy Security Fund

That is why the Energy Security Fund — with the tax on windfall oil profits that will pay for it — is so vitally important. That is why every vote in Congress for this Fund will be a vote for America's future — and every vote against it will be a vote for excessive oil company profits and for reliance on the whims of the foreign oil cartel.

The Energy Security Fund will let us pursue a sound strategy of energy research and development.

In years to come, we can design automobiles, buildings, appliances and engines that serve us better and use less energy.

We can improve mass transit and make our entire transportation system cleaner, faster, and more efficient.

We can broaden the use of our huge coal deposits by turning coal into clean gas, liquid, and solid fuels.

We can learn how to use our immense reserves of oil shale.

From the products of our forests and croplands, we can produce more gasohol — already being used to replace gasoline in several Midwestern states.

We can promote the use of small-scale hydroelectric plants, powered by the flow of ordinary streams without the need for big dams.

Solar Power

And we can turn increasingly toward the ultimate source of all our energy — the sun.

There are solar techniques that are economical right now. With existing tax credits and with our new Energy Security Fund, we can encourage even more rapid development and use of solar power. In the future, we will use solar energy in many other ways, including the direct conversion of sunlight into electricity. We already use this method for limited purposes such as in our space program, but scientific discoveries will be needed to make it more useful in our homes and factories.

The Energy Security Fund derived from the windfall profits tax will pay for these exciting new energy programs.

All of these steps can be part of a wider international effort. Other nations are eager to cooperate.

The actions and plans I have announced tonight will move us away from imported oil and toward a future of real energy security. These actions will give us a better life. These are necessary steps, because our country faces a serious petroleum problem and a broader energy challenge. The future of the country we love is at stake.

We Americans have met equal challenges in the past. Our nation has endured and prospered. Ours is a great country, and we have bountiful resources and technological genius.

We must recognize the urgency of this challenge — and we must work together to meet it. Then we too will endure. We too will prosper. We too will triumph.

Thank you, and good night.

Glossary

The glossary below defines basic legislative and energy terms used in this book.

Act

The term for legislation which has passed both houses of Congress and has been signed by the president or passed over his veto, thus becoming law.

Amendment

Proposal of a member of Congress to alter the language or stipulations in a pending bill or an existing law. It is usually printed, debated and voted upon in the same manner as a bill.

Appropriations bill

Grants the actual monies approved by authorization bills, but not necessarily in the total amount permissible under the authorization bill. An appropriations bill originates in the House and normally is not acted on until the related authorization measure has been enacted. General appropriations bills are supposed to be enacted by the seventh day after Labor Day before the start of the fiscal year to which they apply, but in recent years this has rarely happened.

Atomic Energy Commission

Five-member panel that from 1946 to 1974 was responsible for development and regulation of civilian uses of nuclear power, particularly commercial generation of electricity from nuclear reactors. *(See ERDA, below)*

Authorization bill

Authorizes a program, specifies its general aim and conduct and, unless "open-ended," puts a ceiling on monies that can be used to finance it. Usually enacted before the related appropriations bill is passed.

Barrel

Equal to 42 gallons.

Bill

Most legislative proposals before Congress are in the form of bills which are designated as HR (House of Representatives) or S (Senate), according to the house in which they originated. A number is assigned in the order in which the bills are introduced, from the beginning of each two-year congressional term.

British Thermal Unit

Traditional unit of measure, known as a Btu, which refers to the amount of heat required to raise the temperature of one pound of water by one Fahrenheit degree.

Building Energy Performance Standards

Known as BEPS, these standards of the energy efficiency of new buildings were required by Congress in 1976 but regulations to implement the law were not completed as of early 1981 because of controversies. Each building would have a Btu "budget" according to square footage, which would be allocatged among energy uses, such as heating or lighting.

Cartel

Association of countries or companies established to create an international monopoly of a commodity by controlling supplies and prices; the Organization of Petroleum Exporting Countries (OPEC) is a cartel.

Coal Conversion

The process of switching to coal as a fuel for existing oil- or gas-burning powerplants or industrial boilers.

Crude Oil Equalization Tax

Tax on oil at the wellhead sought unsuccessfully by President Carter in 1977 to bring the price of oil to 1977 world levels while retaining controls on the price charged by producers.

Decontrol

Removal of restrictions on the price and/or allocation of oil and natural gas.

Deregulation

Similar to decontrol; usually refers to the lifting of controls on price and distribution of natural gas.

Embargo

Prohibition on sale of a particular commodity to a certain country or countries.

Economic Regulatory Administration

Branch of the Energy Department responsible for regulations, such as oil pricing controls and plans for rationing gasoline in emergencies.

Energy Department

Cabinet-level agency established in 1977 to consolidate energy activities previously spread among various agencies, and to give new visibility to energy.

Energy Information Administration

Branch of the Energy Department responsible for statistics on energy production and consumption, and for forecasts of future energy needs.

Energy Mobilization Board

Panel sought by President Carter to speed bureaucratic decisionmaking related to top priority energy projects; proposal died in 96th Congress amid controversy over how much power the board should have to waive to revise laws.

Energy Research and Development Administration

Established in 1974 to handle energy research and development, including those responsibilities for nuclear power R&D previously handled by the dismantled Atomic Energy Commission; absorbed by the Energy Department in 1977.

Federal Energy Administration

Established in 1974 to handle regulation of pricing, production and consumption of energy; absorbed by the Energy Department in 1977.

Federal Energy Regulation Commission

Revamped Federal Power Commission set up in 1977 as an independent regulatory agency within the Energy Department; oversees interstate sales of natural gas and interstate sales of electricity at wholesale.

Federal Power Commission

Predecessor of FERC, with similar responsibilities.

Filibuster

A delaying tactic used in the Senate by a minority in an effort to prevent a vote on a bill which probably would pass if brought to a vote.

Floor Manager

A member of Congress, usually representing sponsors of a bill, who attempts to steer it through debate and amendment to a final vote in the chamber. Floor managers are frequently chairmen or ranking members of the committee that reported the bill.

Fusion

Combination of light nuclei into a heavier mass which releases energy; the energy of the sun and stars results from fusion.

Gas Guzzler

Automobile that gets poor gasoline mileage.

Gasohol

Mixture of 90 percent gasoline and 10 percent alcohol that can be used in most automobiles.

Import Fees

Fees assessed on imported products, such as oil, which are designed to discourage imports of the product.

Import Quotas

Legal limits on the amount of certain imported products allowed into the country.

Independents

Producers of oil or natural gas that do not also process, distribute or sell at retail oil or gas products.

Interstate

Sales of natural gas outside of the state in which it was produced.

Intrastate

Sales of natural gas within the producing state.

Lobby

A group seeking to influence the passage or defeat of legislation. Originally the term referred to persons frequenting the lobbies or corridors of legislative chambers in order to speak to lawmakers.

Majors

Petroleum companies that produce, refine, distribute and sell at retail oil and oil products.

Natural Gas Liquids

Natural gas liquified at field facilities or processing plants; yields a variety of liquid petroleum products.

Nuclear Fission

The splitting apart of a heavy atomic nucleus as a neutron strikes the nucleus. The splitting releases energy, which in a nuclear powerplant is used to heat water and create steam, which powers generators to create electricity.

Nuclear Regulatory Commission

Five-member panel responsible since 1974 for regulation of the commercial use of nuclear power.

Organization of Petroleum Exporting Countries

(OPEC) Cartel of 13 oil-producing countries which won control of the world oil market in late 1973. The member countries are Algeria, Iraq, Kuwait, Libya, Qatar, Saudi Arabia, United Arab Emirates, Indonesia, Iran, Nigeria, Venezuela, Ecuador and Gabon.

Outer Continental Shelf

Federally controlled offshore land, beginning three miles from the shoreline.

Radioactive

Material that emits energy known as ionizing radiation, which when absorbed by biological tissue can damage cell or genetic material.

Spot Market

Sales of oil not under contract.

Strategic Petroleum Reserve

Stockpile of federally owned oil in Louisiana and Texas designed to be used in case of emergency energy shortages.

Strip Mining

Removal of coal deposited near the surface by stripping away the surface soil layer to expose coal.

Stripper Wells

Wells producing 10 or fewer barrels of oil a day.

Synthetic Fuels

Liquids or gases from coal, oil from shale, alcohol from plant matter and other energy sources similar to naturally formed oil and natural gas.

Tax Credit

Amount subtracted from taxes owed; often offered by the government as an incentive for investment, such as in insulation or other conservation equipment.

Three Mile Island

Name of nuclear reactor for producing electricity, located near Harrisburg, Pa., and operated by Metropolitan Edison Company, where on March 28, 1979, occurred the worst accident in the history of nuclear power.

Energy Policy Bibliography

Books and Reports

Abrahamsson, Bernhard, ed. *The Changing Economics of World Energy.* Boulder, Colo.: Westview Press, 1976.

Ahmed, S. Basheer. *Nuclear Fuel and Energy Policy.* Lexington, Mass.: D. C. Heath, 1979.

Allen, Loring. *OPEC Oil.* Cambridge, Mass. Oelgeschlager, Gunn & Hain, 1979.

Arrow, Kenneth J. et al. *Energy: The Next Twenty Years: Report by a Study Group Sponsored by the Ford Foundation and Administered by Resources for the Future.* Cambridge, Mass.: Ballinger, 1979.

Barzel, Yoram and Hall, Christopher D. *The Political Economy of the Oil Import Quota.* Stanford, Calif.: Hoover Institution Press, 1977.

Blair, John M. *The Control of Oil.* New York: Pantheon Books, 1977.

Bohi, Doughlas R. *U.S. Energy Policy: Alternatives for Security.* Baltimore: The Johns Hopkins University Press, 1975.

—, and Russell, Milton. *Limiting Oil Imports.* Baltimore: Johns Hopkins University Press, 1978.

Brannon, Gerard M. *Energy Taxes and Subsidies: A Report to the Energy Policy Project of the Ford Foundation.* Cambridge, Mass.: Ballinger, 1974.

Burton, Dudley J. *The Governance of Energy: Problems, Prospects and Underlying Issues.* New York: Praeger, 1980.

Carnesale, Albert et al. *Options for U.S. Energy Policy.* San Francisco: Institute for Contemporary Studies, 1977.

Commission on Critical Choices for Americans. *Vital Resources.* Lexington, Mass.: D. C. Heath, 1977.

Commoner, Barry, ed. *Energy and Human Welfare: A Critical Analysis.* 3 vols. New York: Macmillan, 1975.

—, *The Poverty of Power: Energy and the Economic Crisis.* New York: Knopf; distributed by Random House, 1976.

Congressional Quarterly. *Continuing Energy Crisis in America.* Washington: Congressional Quarterly Inc., 1975.

Coyne, John R. and Coyne, Patricia. *The Big Breakup: Energy in Crisis.* Mission, Kan.: Sheed Andrews & McMeel Inc., 1977.

Davis, Howard David. *Energy Politics.* New York: St. Martin's Press, 1978.

Deese, David and Nye, Joseph S. Jr., eds. *Energy and Security.* Cambridge, Mass.: Ballinger, 1980.

Doran, Charles F. *Myth, Oil, and Politics: Introduction to the Political Economy of Petroleum.* New York: The Free Press, 1977.

Editorial Research Reports. *Earth, Energy and Environment.* Washington: Congressional Quarterly Inc., 1977.

Engler, Robert. *The Brotherhood of Oil: Energy Policy and the Public Interest.* Chicago: University of Chicago Press, 1977.

—. *The Politics of Oil: A Study of Private Power and Democratic Directions.* Chicago: University of Chicago Press, 1961.

—, ed. *America's Energy: Reports from "The Nation" On 100 Years of Struggles for the Democratic Control of Our Resources.* New York: Pantheon Books, 1980.

Eppen, Gary D., ed. *Energy: The Policy Issues.* Chicago: University of Chicago Press, 1977.

Gordon, Richard L. *Coal and the Electric Power Industry.* Baltimore: Johns Hopkins University Press, 1975.

Hagel, John. *Alternative Energy Strategies: Constraints and Opportunities.* New York: Praeger, 1976.

Herman, Stewart H. et al. *Energy Futures: Industry and New Technologies.* Cambridge, Mass.: Ballinger, 1977.

Johnson, William et al. *Competition in the Oil Industry.* Washington: George Washington University Energy Policy Research Project, 1976.

Kalter, Robert J. and Vogely, William, eds. *Energy Supply and Government Policy.* Ithaca, N.Y.: Cornell University Press, 1976.

Kannan, Narasimhan P. *Energy, Economic Growth and Equity in the United States.* New York: Praeger, 1979.

Krueger, Robert B., ed. *The United States and International Oil: A Report for the Federal Energy Administration on U.S. Firms and Government Policy.* New York: Praeger, 1975.

MacAvoy, Paul W. *Federal Energy Administration Regulation: Report of the Presidential Task Force.* Washington: American Enterprise Institute for Public Policy Research, 1977.

—, and Pindyck, Robert S. *Price Controls and the Natural Gas Shortage.* Washington: American Enterprise Institute for Public Policy Research, 1975.

Mancke, Richard. *The Failure of U.S. Energy Policy.* New York: Columbia University Press, 1974.

—. *Squeaking By: U.S. Energy Policy Since the Embargo.* New York: Columbia University Press, 1976.

Markham, Jesse et al. *Horizontal Divestiture and the Petroleum Industry.* Cambridge, Mass.: Ballinger, 1977.

Mitchell, Edward J. *Perspective on U.S. Energy Policy: A Critique of Regulation.* New York: Praeger, 1976.

—, ed. *The Question of Offshore Oil.* Washington: American Enterprise Institute for Public Policy Research, 1976.

Myers, Desaix B., III. *The Nuclear Power Debate: Moral, Technical, and Political Issues.* New York: Praeger, 1977.

Nash, Gerald D. *United States Oil Policy, 1890-1964.* Pittsburgh: University of Pittsburgh Press, 1968.

Noreng, Oystein. *Oil Politics in the 1980s: Patterns of International Cooperation.* New York: McGraw-Hill, 1978.

Organization for Economic Cooperation and Development. *World Energy Outlook.* Paris: Organization for Economic Cooperation and Development, 1979.

Phelps, Charles and Smith, Rodney T. *Petroleum Regulation: The False Dilemma of Decontrol.* Santa Monica, Calif.: Rand Corporation, 1977.

Phillips, Owen. *The Last Chance Energy Book.* Baltimore: The Johns Hopkins University Press, 1978.

Richardson, Harry W. *Economic Aspects of the Energy Crisis.* Lexington, Mass.: Lexington Books, 1975.

Rosenbaum, Walter A. *Energy, Politics and Public Policy.* Washington: Congressional Quarterly Inc., 1981.

Sampson, Anthony. *The Seven Sisters: The Great Oil Companies and the World They Made.* New York: Viking Press, 1975.

Sawhill, John C., ed. *Energy Conservation and Public Policy.* Englewood Cliffs, N.J.: Prentice-Hall, 1979.

Scheffer, Walter F., ed. *Energy Impacts on Public Policy and Administration.* Norman, Okla.: University of Oklahoma Press, 1976.

Schelling, Thomas C. *Thinking Through the Energy Problem.* New York: Committee for Economic Development, 1979.

Schurr, Sam H. *Energy in the American Economy 1850-1975.* Baltimore: Johns Hopkins University Press, 1972.

—, et al. *Energy In America's Future: A Study Prepared for Resources for the Future.* Baltimore, Md.: Johns Hopkins University Press, 1979.

Scott, David L. *Financing the Growth of Electric Utilities.* New York: Praeger, 1976.

Slesser, Malcolm. *Energy In the Economy.* New York: St. Martin's Press, 1978.

Stobaugh, Robert and Yergin, Daniel, eds. *Energy Future: Report of the Energy Project at the Harvard Business School.* New York: Random House, 1979.

Sunder, William. *Oil Industry Profits.* Washington: American Enterprise Institute for Public Policy Research, 1977.

Tietenberg, Thomas H. and Toureille, Pierre. *Energy Planning and Policy: The Political Economy of Project Independence.* Lexington, Mass.: Lexington Books, 1976.

Trager, Frank N., ed. *Oil, Divestiture and National Security.* New York: Crane, Russak & Company Inc., 1977.

Turner, Louis. *Oil Companies in the International System.* London: Institute of International Affairs. Boston: Allen & Unwin, 1978.

Twentieth Century Fund, Task Force on United States Energy Policy. *Providing for Energy.* New York: McGraw-Hill, 1977.

Vernon, Raymond. *The Oil Crisis.* New York: Norton, 1976.

Wildhorn, Sorrel. *How to Save Gasoline: Public Policy Alternatives for the Automobile.* Cambridge, Mass.: Ballinger, 1976.

Wilson, Carroll L., et al. *Energy: Global Prospects 1985-2000: A Report of the Workshop on Alternative Energy Strategies.* New York: McGraw-Hill, 1977.

Articles

"America's Energy Resources: An Overview." *Current History,* May/June 1978.

Beorse, B. "Ocean Thermal Energy Conservation." *Humanist,* July 1979, pp. 12-19.

Bethe, H. "The Case for Coal and Nuclear Energy." *Center Magazine,* May/June 1980, pp. 14-27.

Boulding, Kenneth E. "Anxiety, Uncertainty, and Energy." *Society,* January 1978, pp. 28-33.

Brannon, Gerald M. "Taxation and the Political Economy of the Energy Crisis," *Natural Resources Journal,* October 1978, pp. 825-843.

Bruner, Ronald D. "Decentralized Energy Policies." *Public Policy,* winter 1980, pp. 71-91.

Cambel, A. B. "Alternatives to the Energy Crisis." *Current History,* July 1978, pp. 16-18.

"Can the U.S. Become Energy Self-Sufficient? - The Outlook for Coal: Report and Recommendations by Members of the Study Section on Environment and Energy." *Commonwealth Club of California Transactions,* March 19, 1979, pp. 3-30.

Chambers, R. S., et al. "Gasohol: Does It or Doesn't It Produce Positive Net Energy?" *Science,* November 16, 1979, pp. 789-795.

Church, Frank. "The Impotence of Oil Companies," *Foreign Policy,* summer 1977, pp. 27-51.

Commoner, Barry. "For A New Energy Policy." *Current,* March 1977, pp. 17-22.

"Controversy Over U.S. Energy Policy: Pros and Cons." *Congressional Digest,* August/September 1978, pp. 193-224.

Davidson, P. "U.S. Internal Revenue Service: Fourteenth Member of OPEC?" *Journal of Post-Keynesian Economics,* winter 1978/79, pp. 47-58.

"The Energy Crisis: Reality or Myth." *Annals of the American Academy of Political and Social Science,* November 1973.

England, Glyn. "Renewable Sources of Energy: The Prospects for Electricity." *Atom,* October 1978, pp. 270-272.

Engler, Robert. "Letting Big Oil Do It." *Nation,* October 25, 1980, pp. 393, 407-412.

Gibbons, John H. and Chandler, William U. "A National Energy Conservation Policy." *Current History,* July/August 1978, pp. 13-15.

Goldstein, Walter. "The Political Failure of U.S. Energy Policy." *Bulletin of the Atomic Scientists,* November 1978, pp. 17-19.

Greening, Timothy S. "Increasing Competition in the Oil Industry: Government Standards for Gasoline." *Harvard Journal on Legislation,* February 1977, pp. 193-224.

Hall, Robert E., and Pindyck, Robert S. "The Conflicting Goals of National Energy Policy." *Public Interest,* spring 1977. pp. 3-15.

Heiman, Grover. "Energy: Searching for Substitutes." *Nation's Business,* September 1978, pp. 78-84.

Hohenemser, K. H. "Energy Efficiency vs. Energy Growth." *Environment,* June 1978, pp. 4-5.

Hudson, Edward A. and Jorgenson, Dale W. "Energy Policy and U.S. Economic Growth." *American Economic Review,* May 1978, pp. 118-130.

Hyatt, Sherry V. "Thermal Efficiency and Taxes: The Residential Energy Conservation Tax Credit." *Harvard Journal on Legislation,* February 1977, pp. 281-326.

Jackson, Henry M. "World Oil Supply: Its Significance for the U.S. Economy." *Public Utilities Fortnightly,* April 26, 1979, pp. 17-21.

Jeffress, Philip W. "The Political Economy of United States Energy Policy." *Journal of Social and Political Studies,* spring 1979, pp. 53-66.

Khalilzad, Zalmay and Benard, Cheryl. "Energy: No Quick Fix for a Permanent Crisis." *The Bulletin of the Atomic Scientist,* December 1980, pp. 15-20.

Leepson, Marc. "Synthetic Fuels." *Editorial Research Reports,* August 31, 1979, pp. 623-640.

Levy, Walter. "Oil and the Decline of the West." *Foreign Affairs,* summer 1980, p. 1014.

Levy, Walter J. "The Years That the Locust Hath Eaten: Oil Policy and OPEC Development Prospects." *Foreign Affairs,* winter 1978/79, pp. 287-305.

Lovins, A. B. "Energy Strategy: The Road Not Taken?" *Foreign Affairs,* October 1976, pp. 65-96.

Manne, Alan S. "What Happens When Our Oil and Gas Runs Out?" *Harvard Business Review,* July/August 1975, pp. 123-137.

Moran, Theodore H. "Why Oil Prices Go Up — The Future: OPEC Wants Them." *Foreign Policy,* winter 1976, pp. 58-77.

Nye, Joseph S. Jr. "Energy Nightmares." *Foreign Policy,* fall 1980, pp. 132-154.

Oppenheim, V. H. "Why Oil Prices Go Up — The Past: We Pushed Them." *Foreign Policy,* winter 1976, pp. 24-57.

Pindyck, Robert S. "OPEC's Threat to the West." *Foreign Policy,* spring 1978, pp. 36-52.

Quiros Corrado, Alberto. "Energy and the Exercise of Power." *Foreign Affairs,* summer 1979, pp. 1144-1166.

Rosen, G. R. "Coal: Carter and Congress Hold the Key." *Dun's Review,* February 1977, pp. 56-60.

Rustow, Dankwart A. "U.S.-Saudi Relations and the Oil Crises of the 1980s." *Foreign Affairs,* April 1977, pp. 494-516.

Rycroft, Robert W. "U.S. Energy Demand and Supply." *Current History,* March 1978, pp. 100-103.

Sawhill, John C. "A Gasoline Tax-Rebate: Needed Now." *The Journal of the Institute for Socioeconomic Studies,* spring 1977, pp. 71-79.

Scandalls, Helen. "Coal — and Consequences." *Environmental Action.* Nov. 5, 1977, pp. 3-5.

Sillin, John O. "Synthetic Versus Conventional Fuel: A Total System Comparison." *Public Utilities Fortnightly,* April 24, 1980, pp. 32-38.

Singer, S. Fred. "Limits to Arab Oil Power." *Foreign Policy,* spring 1978, pp. 53-67.

Sweet, William. "Nuclear Fusion Development." *Editorial Research Reports,* September 12, 1980, pp. 659-676.

Weinberg, Alvin M. "Reflections on the Energy Wars." *American Scientist,* March/April 1978, pp. 153-158.

Wirth, Timothy E. "Congressional Policy Making and the Politics of Energy." *Journal of Energy and Development,* autumn 1975, pp. 93-104.

Yergin, Daniel. "The Real Meaning of the Energy Crunch." *New York Times Magazine,* June 4, 1978, pp. 32; 92-98.

Government Publications

Solar Energy and America's Future. Prepared by Stanford Research Institute for the Energy Research and Development Administration. Springfield, Va.: National Technical Information Service, 1977.

The President's Commission on the Accident at Three Mile Island. *Report.* Washington, D.C.: Government Printing Office, 1979.

U.S. Congress. Congressional Budget Office. *Energy Policy Alternatives.* Washington: Government Printing Office, 1977.

U.S. Congress. Congressional Budget Office. *World Oil Markets in the 1980s: Implications for the United States.* 96th Cong., 2nd Sess. Washington, D.C.: Government Printing Office, 1980.

U.S. Congress. Congressional Budget Office. *President Carter's Energy Proposals: A Perspective.* Washington: Government Printing Office, 1977.

U.S. Congress. House. Committee on Energy and Natural Resources. *Energy In Transition: 1985-2010, Hearings, April 18, 1980.* 96th Cong., 2nd sess. Washington, D.C.: Government Printing Office, 1980.

U.S. Congress. House. Committee on Government Operations. Subcommittee on Environment, Energy, and Natural Resources. *Clean Air Act and Increased Coal Use; Environmental Protection Agency Oversight, Hearings, September 11, 13, 1979.* 96th Cong., 1st sess. Washington, D.C.: Government Printing Office, 1980.

U.S. Congress. House. Committee on Interstate and Foreign Commerce. Subcommittee on Energy and Power. *Domestic Crude Oil Decontrol, Hearings, April 24; May 16, 17, 31, 1979.* 96th Cong., 1st sess. Washington, D.C.: Government Printing Office, 1980.

U.S. Congress. House. Committee on Interstate and Foreign Commerce. Subcommittee on Energy and Power. *Will the Lights Go On In 1990: CRS Study Prepared by Alvin Kaufman.* 96th Cong., 2nd sess. Washington, D.C.: Government Printing Office, 1980.

U.S. Congress. House. Committee on Interstate and Foreign Commerce. Subcommittee on Oversight and Investigations. *Energy: Is There a Policy To Fit the Crisis?: CRS Study Prepared by John W. Jimison.* 96th Cong., 2nd sess. Washington, D.C.: Government Printing Office, 1980.

U.S. Congress. House. Committee on Science and Technology. Subcommittee on Energy Development and Application. *National Solar Energy Policy, Hearings, June 14, 21, 1979.* 96th Cong., 1st sess. Washington, D.C.: Government Printing Office, 1980.

U.S. Congress. House. Committee on Science and Technology. Subcommittee on Energy Research and Production. *Nuclear Energy Production in the Coming Decade, Hearings, September 20, 1979.* 96th Cong., 1st sess. Washington, D.C.: Government Printing Office, 1980.

U.S. Congress. House. Committee on Science and Technology. Subcommittee on Energy Research and Development. *Nuclear Powerplant Safety Systems, Hearings, May 22-24, 1979.* 96th Cong., 1st sess. Washington, D.C.: Government Printing Office, 1980.

U.S. Congress. House. Committee on Science and Technology. Subcommittee on Energy Development and Applications. *Pros and Cons of a Crash Program to Commercialize Synfuels.* Committee Print. 96th Cong., 2nd sess. Washington, D.C.: Government Printing Office, 1980.

U.S. Congress. House. Committee on Ways and Means. *Windfall Profits Tax and Energy Trust Fund, Hearings, May 9-11, 16-18, 1979.* 96th Cong., 1st sess. Washington, D.C.: Government Printing Office, 1980.

U.S. Congress. House. Select Committee on Intelligence. Subcommittee on Oversight. *Intelligence on World Energy Outlook and Policy Implications, Hearings, October 17, 18, 1979.* 96th Cong., 1st sess. Washington, D.C.: Government Printing Office, 1980.

U.S. Congress. House. Committee on Interstate and Foreign Commerce, Subcommittee on Energy and Power. *Energy Information Digest: Basic Data on Energy Resources, Reserves, Production, Consumption and Prices.* 95th Cong., 1st sess. Washington: Government Printing Office, 1977.

U.S. Congress. House. Committee on Interstate and Foreign Commerce. Subcommittee on Energy and Power. *U.S. Energy Demand and Supply, 1976-1985: Limited Options, Unlimited Constraints; Final Report, March 1978.* 95th Cong., 2nd sess. Washington: Government Printing Office, 1978.

U.S. Congress. House Committee on Interstate and Foreign Commerce. Subcommittee on Oversight and Investigations. *Proposed National Energy Plan, Hearings, June 14, 1977.* 95th Cong., 1st sess. Washington: Government Printing Office, 1977.

U.S. Congress. Joint Economic Committee. *The Economics of the President's Proposed Energy Policies, Hearings May 20, 25, 1977.* 95th Cong., 1st sess. Washington: Government Printing Office, 1978.

U.S. Congress. Joint Economic Committee. *JEC Staff Analysis: Projected Taxes and Revenues Under President Carter's Energy Package.* 95th Cong., 1st sess. Washington: Government Printing Office, 1977.

U.S. Congress. Joint Economic Committee. *Economics of Solar Home Heating.* 95th Cong., 1st sess. Washington: Government Printing Office, 1977.

U.S. Congress. Joint Economic Committee. Subcommittee on Energy. *Energy In the Eighties: Can We Avoid Scarcity and Inflation? Hearings, March 8-21, 1978.* 95th Cong., 2nd sess. Washington: Government Printing Office, 1978.

U.S. Congress. Office of Technology Assessment. *Analysis of the Proposed National Energy Plan.* 95th Cong., 1st sess. Washington: Government Printing Office, 1977.

U.S. Congress. Senate. Committe on the Budget. Subcommittee on Synthetic Fuels. *Synthetic Fuels,* September, 27, 1979. 96th Cong., 1st sess. Washington, D.C.: Government Printing Office, 1979.

U.S. Congress. Senate. Committee on Energy and Natural Resources. *Energy Impact Assistance Legislation, Hearings October 18, 19, 1979.* 96th Cong., 1st sess. Washington, D.C.: Government Printing Office, 1980.

U.S. Congress. Senate. Committee on Energy and Natural Resources. *Six-Year Review of Energy by the Harvard School of Business, Hearings July 27, 1979.* 96th Cong., 1st sess. Washington, D.C.: Government Printing Office, 1980.

U.S. Congress. Senate. Committee on Energy and Natural Resources. *Synthetic Fuels from Coal: Status and Outlook of Coal Gasification and Liquefaction.* 96th Cong., 1st sess. Washington, D.C.: Government Printing Office, 1979.

U.S. Congress. Senate. Committee on Energy and Natural Resources. *Energy: An Uncertain Future: Analysis of the U.S. and World Energy Projections Through 1990.* 95th Cong., 2nd sess. Washington, D.C.: Government Printing Office, 1978.

U.S. Congress. Senate. Committee on Energy and Natural Resources. *Economic Impact of President Carter's Energy Program, Hearings, May 3, 1977.* 95th Cong., 1st sess. Washington: Government Printing Office, 1977.

U.S. Congress. Senate. Committee on Energy and Natural Resources. *Project Independence: U.S. and World Energy Outlook Through 1990.* 95th Cong., 1st sess. Washington: Government Printing Office, 1977.

U.S. Congress. Senate. Committee on Finance. *Energy Tax Provisions: Summary and Section-by-Section Explanation of Title II of H.R. 8444 as Passed by the House.* 95th Cong., 1st sess. Washington: Government Printing Office, 1977.

Index